SURVIVING THROUGH THE DAYS

SURVIVING THROUGH THE DAYS

Translations of Native California Stories and Songs

A CALIFORNIA INDIAN READER

EDITED BY

Herbert W. Luthin

University of California Press

BERKELEY / LOS ANGELES / LONDON

University of California Press
Berkeley and Los Angeles, California

University of California Press, Ltd.
London, England

© 2002 by the Regents of the University of California

For permissions, see acknowledgments of permissions
at back of book.

Library of Congress Cataloging-in-Publication Data

Surviving through the days : translations of Native California
    stories and songs : a California Indian reader / Herbert W.
    Luthin, editor.
        p.   cm.
    Includes bibliographical references and index.
    ISBN 0-520-22269-5 (alk. paper) —ISBN 0-520-22270-9
(pbk. : alk. paper)
        1. Indians of North America—California—Folklore.
    2. Indians of North America—California—Music.
    3. Indian mythology—California.
    I. Luthin, Herbert W., 1954–
    E78.C15.S94   2002
    398'.089'97—dc21   00-031630
    MN   CIP

Manufactured in the United States of America

12   11   10   09   08   07   06   05   04   03   02
10   9   8   7   6   5   4   3   2   1

The paper used in this publication meets the minimum
requirements of ANSI / NISO Z39 0.48-1992(R 1997)
(Permanence of Paper).♾

For Kay—
    my own true Shady Grove . . .

Tásmomaytal nevétiqankwa,
táásutal chulúpiqankwa.
'áá, temét nóó nevétqankwa,
temét nóó chulúpiqankwa.

I suppose I've survived the first little month,
I suppose I've survived the first big month.
Oh, I am surviving through the days,
I am surviving through the days.

"Chalááwaat Song"
Luiseño, Villiana Calac Hyde

CONTENTS

ILLUSTRATIONS

FIGURES

MAPS

TABLES

ACKNOWLEDGMENTS

I've been at work on this project, off and on, for more than seven years—a long enough stretch of time that I fear those who lent a hand back at the beginning will no longer remember the occasion. Yet I benefited greatly back then from formative talks with Kay Fineran, Victor Golla, Leanne Hinton, Margaret Langdon, Malcolm Margolin, Judith Rock, Bill Shipley, and Brian Swann. They helped give me a sense of what this volume could become and what it might include.

On a wide range of more specific queries and problems, I am indebted to Linda Agren, Therese Babineau, Tom Blackburn, Parris Butler, Catherine Callaghan, Edmund Carpenter, Jim Collins, Beverly Crum, Scott DeLancey, Jeffrey Ehrenreich, John Johnson, Richard Keeling, Kathryn Klar, Arnold Krupat, Julian Lang, Sally McLendon, Marian Olivas, Nancy Richardson, Alice Shepherd, Mary Stieber, and Suzanne Wash. The community of California scholars and friends, to which most of these people belong, is a giving one—so much like a family that it's easy to forget: no one *had* to "take me in" when I came calling for assistance; but these people did, often time and again.

By far my biggest debt of gratitude goes to Brian Swann, who had the idea for this book in the first place. When I started, I was alarmingly naive and new to the business of editing anthologies. Each step of the way, Brian showed me the ropes. Without his patient guidance, sound advice, and moral support across the years, this book would never have come to be.

Three anonymous reviewers for the University of California Press gave me valuable input on the manuscript—feedback that I trust I have put to good use. I am grateful for their scrutiny, and hope that, by acting on most of their suggestions, I have given them some measure of job satisfaction.

At the University of California Press, I'd like to give thanks to two people who proved themselves true friends of this book: to Stan Holwitz, for his encouragement and unfailing good judgment while I was trying to pull the manuscript together for final submission and review; and to Rachel Berchten, project editor for the book, for being so perceptive and careful and patient through the giant process of nudging all the mountains and molehills into place: more than anyone else, she helped this sprawling manuscript become a book. Finally, my thanks to Carolyn Hill, who copyedited the manuscript brilliantly, improving it in a thousand ways, with a keen eye for infelicity and bilge.

Closer to home, I would like to thank Judy Bowser and the other reference librarians at Clarion University for not locking me out of their offices when they saw me coming, even after the first hundred interlibrary loan requests; my department secretary, Carole Pasquarette, for putting up with a lot of weird text entry and scanning projects; my dean's office for photocopying support; and the College of Arts and Sciences for one-quarter release time in the fall semester of 1994 "to finish the book." Two small grants from the Clarion University Foundation in 1994 and 1995 enabled me to travel to conferences and do research at the Bancroft Library and Hearst Museum on the University of California, Berkeley, campus.

Finally, I'd like to thank my wife, Kay, for being—always, somehow—there. Without her . . . well, it's unsayable.

PRONUNCIATION GUIDE

Because this is a book of translations, not bilingual texts, pronunciation is not as pressing an issue as it might have been. Nevertheless, stray words and names and places crop up in these pages, and readers who like to meet a challenge head-on, or don't want to have to mumble and squint, may appreciate a brief, generalized guide to pronouncing tribal and linguistic orthographies. I say "generalized" because, in a land of such profound linguistic diversity as Native California, there is no such thing as a shared orthography common to all languages. The rough outlines of the various systems are fairly consistent—most are based on the phonetic alphabet, after all. But because most contemporary orthographies are phonemic (meaning that it takes a degree of "insider knowledge" to interpret the symbols with certainty), the phonological particulars and eccentricities of the individual languages work to limit the consistency of the alphabet used.

At any rate, and for what it's worth, here are some pointers for pronouncing the native-language words and names that readers will encounter in this book. Following them won't guarantee that you'll be right, just that you won't be egregiously wrong—a plausible rendition, if not a perfect one. For details on any particular language, consult the "Further Readings" section following each selection, which supplies references to grammars and teaching aids (if there are any for the language in question).

Most accepted orthographies for Native American languages are based on the Americanist Phonetic Alphabet (a North American variant of the International Phonetic Alphabet). Therefore the following suggestions will be valid for most of the Indian words you find in this (or any other) book.

The letter ʔ and the apostrophe both represent the glottal stop (the catch-in-the-throat sound spelled by the hyphen in "uh-oh!" or in the Cockney pronunciation of *bottle;* most likely your pronunciation of the word *apple,* when spoken forcefully in isolation, begins with this sound as well).

The letters *č* and *ǰ* represent the sound of the "ch" in *cheap* and the "j" in *jeep,* respectively.

The letter *c* may be pronounced either as "ch" or as "ts" (like the "zz" in *pizza*), depending on the language. (In old turn-of-the-century transcriptions, such as Sapir used for Yana, the *c* was used to represent a "sh" sound.)

The letters *p', t', c', č', k',* and *q'* are glottalized stops, pronounced as the base letter plus the simultaneous articulation of a glottal stop; likewise the letters *m', n', l', w',* and *y',* although these are sometimes written *'m, 'n, 'l, 'w,* and *'y.* (If you say the phrase "Up-up-and-away" carefully, the first of the two *p*s you produce will come out sounding something like the glottalized *p';* likewise the negative murmur "Mm-mm" contains a glottalized *m'* in the middle.) These sounds are not easy to imagine, much less to produce, without first hearing someone do it.

The letter *q* stands for a voiceless uvular stop—somewhat like the "k" sound in English *car,* only farther back.

The letter *r* is usually pronounced as a flap, like the "r" in Spanish *María.*

The letter *x* represents a harsh "h" sound, like the "ch" in German *Bach.*

Raised or superscript letters can signify a variety of things. (1) A raised ^{h} following a consonant indicates that a small puff of air (what phoneticians call "aspiration") accompanies the sound, like the "p^h" in English *poor.* In orthographies where the ^{h} is written, its absence (for example, plain *p* as opposed to *p^h*) implies an absence of aspiration. (2) A raised ^{w} following a consonant indicates the presence of lip-rounding or labialization, like the "k^w" in English *queen* or *coop.* (3) A raised ^{y} following a consonant indicates the presence of palatalization, like the "k^y" in English *cute* or *keen.*

A dot underneath a consonant (primarily *ṭ, c,* and *ṣ*) indicates that the sound is retroflex—that is, the tongue is curled back in a slightly *r*-like fashion, like the initial consonants of English *tree* and *shrew.*

Other consonants should be pronounced more or less as expected.

VOWELS

Most vowels have their continental values: *a* as in *aha!*, *e* as in *gray*, *i* as in *bee*, *o* as in *show*, and *u* as in *boo*.

There are also three commonly found diphthongs, or complex vowels: *ay* as in *cry*, *aw* as in *cow*, and *oy* as in *coy*.

Some unfamiliar vowel symbols that you may encounter include the "barred" letters *i* and *u*, both of which represent a high back unrounded vowel (try saying *moo* while smiling), and the umlauted vowels *ü* and *ö*, which may be pronounced like their French and German counterparts (try saying "e" or "a" while rounding your lips as if to blow out a candle).

Many languages have a distinction between long and short vowels (a term that in phonetics refers to actual duration—long vowels are held longer than short vowels are). There are two common ways of indicating length: a colon or raised dot (*ba:nu* or *ba·nu*), or simply doubling the vowel (*baanu*). (*Baanu* is the Yana word for *basket*.) A few older orthographies use the macron for length.

Some orthographies indicate stressed or accented syllables with acute accents over the vowel (*á, é, í, ó, ú*, etc.) or immediately following it (*a', e', i', o', u'*). Others don't mark stress at all, in which case you'll just have to guess, unless you can locate a grammar that explains the rules for stress placement. (In a few languages, such as Karuk and Achumawi, the accent mark indicates high pitch rather than stress.)

An italicized or superscript vowel (*pat^{i}*) usually indicates that the vowel is whispered.

SURVIVING THROUGH THE DAYS

My heart, you might pierce it and take it,
You take it, you pierce it, you take it,
You might pierce it and take it,
You my older brothers here,
You Bear here,
You Mountain Lion here,
You Wildcat here,
You my older brothers,
My heart, you might pierce it and take it.

Song from a Quechan myth
Abraham Halpern
"Kukumat Became Sick"

General Introduction

CALIFORNIA'S ORAL-LITERARY HERITAGE

When this volume was in its planning stages, I always described it to colleagues and editors as a "reader," a reader in the field of California Indian oral literature. It was to be a comprehensive anthology of both classic and contemporary works in translation, whose selections would feature as many of California's cultures and languages as possible. Indeed, my working title throughout these many years of putting it together was simply *A California Indian Reader.* The book has turned out pretty much the way I first saw it in my mind's eye, but the title itself has since then suffered a demotion. The reason why is worth the telling.

In truth, it wasn't long before I grew uneasy describing this book as a "reader." The term seems to promise that the book in hand will contain all of the essential readings on a given topic. And I will admit to believing, when Brian Swann first suggested I think about undertaking such a project, that this book could and would do just that. I actually thought I could examine and absorb *all* of what there was and select the essentials from a complete picture of the recorded literature. Looking back, bemused, I can only shake my head at such naïveté. There is so much material in so many sources, in so many different forms and places, that after many years of going through libraries and collections, talking to singers and storytellers, linguists, and archivists, and wearing out my welcome at my once-willing interlibrary loan department, I've still seen only a portion of what exists. What's more, I'm thrilled to admit it. My notion that this volume could actually *be* a reader, in the most restrictive sense of the term, is gone. In retrospect, I see that what I've really been putting together is more of a "sampler"—and that is the genre I have tried to make good.

There are several reasons why the task proved so overwhelming. The first thing to consider is the astounding diversity of language and culture that is Native California. Four markedly distinct culture areas—Pacific Northwest, Central California, Southern California, and Great Basin—lie within the cartographic confines of the state. With some seventy-five to one hundred distinct languages and tribal groups at the time of European contact, California was the single most populous and linguistically diverse area in all of North America. Indeed, Native California stands out as one of the richest, most linguistically complex areas in the world.[1] To find a corresponding depth and richness in its oral traditions and literatures should not be surprising. The sheer number of traditions alone makes any attempt at exhaustive coverage impossible in a single volume. A look at map I (p. 573) will show how much of the region has in fact been represented but will also reveal just how much has not.

Second, the University of California at Berkeley has been home to two of the most active Native American research programs in the country, in anthropology and linguistics. A. L. Kroeber took command of the newly founded Museum and Department of Anthropology in 1901 and, in his forty-five years as chairman of anthropology at Berkeley, wrote hundreds of articles and dozens of books and either sponsored or coordinated four decades of research by many of the great scholars and collectors of his time. In 1953, Mary R. Haas, the great Americanist, helped to found the Department of Linguistics, also at Berkeley. This program has had a major impact on the study of Native American—particularly Californian—languages. Both these scholars had the gift to inspire not just one but two or even three generations of students (many of whom serve as translators in this book) and, in the process, sent scores of researchers into the field to study California cultures and languages.

But the work on California language and literary traditions has never been an exclusively academic pursuit; it has come from within the Native community as well as without. Elders throughout the state have led family and tribal efforts to preserve local traditions, revive their languages, and tell their histories. From Lucy Thompson, the aristocratic Yurok elder who wrote *To the American Indian* in 1916—the most widely known example of this kind in California—to the latter-day efforts of people like the late Ray Baldy (Hupa), Villiana Calac Hyde (Luiseño), Goldie Bryan (Washoe), and Bun Lucas (Kashaya), to name just four out of so many little-sung heroes, California Indians have long been active in trying to sustain and document their own cultural and linguistic heritage.[2]

As a result of all this academic and grassroots activity, most of California's many cultures have received at least some documentary attention, though some to much greater degree than others. (Wintu and Yurok, for instance, have a rich, varied, and continuing history of documentation going back more than a hundred years, whereas so little is known of Esselen and Saclan that the extant materials on these languages amount to little more than a sheaf of papers.) Of course, only some of this wealth of material concerns traditional storytelling and song, but that fraction still turns out to be a great deal. In short, if a particular culture is not represented in this volume, it is not usually for want of material—though for all too many (Huchnom, Esselen, Tataviam, and Northeastern Pomo, to name a few) the shock of contact destroyed the continuity of language and tradition before anyone took an interest in trying to preserve or write down the literature.

Third, however long the bibliography of published accounts of Native California anthropology and linguistics, still more lies unpublished. Active fieldworkers generally gather far more material than they can ever hope to work up in a lifetime. The ultimate case in point is the legacy of John Peabody Harrington, whose fifty years of ceaseless fieldwork for the Smithsonian Institution focused almost exclusively on California. Harrington left behind not mountains but whole mountain *ranges* of information about California Indian cultures. The Smithsonian collection of his California and Great Basin fieldnotes (those that have been found, that is, for he was secretive and given to caching his notes in unlikely places) runs to 283 reels of microfilm—hundreds of thousands of pages. Very little of this work has ever been published, even now, some thirty-five years after his death.[3] It is only in the last few years, with the inauguration of the annual J. P. Harrington Conference, that researchers, Native and otherwise, have begun to sort through these priceless notes to see what they contain.

Harrington, of course, was an extraordinary case. In the last fifty years, though, hundreds of men and women have done work on California cultures, collecting photographs, recordings, notes, and artifacts. But scholars are just like everybody else. They get busy, or sidetracked, or interested in other things. They get burned out. They get discouraged and quit the field. They get married, find jobs in other sectors, or move away. The archives are overflowing with recordings and photographs and cartons of original fieldnotes going back to the early part of this century, much of which has never been published. And who knows how much material is dusting away in attics and offices across the country, saved for posterity, for a rainy day that never came, for the illusory free time of retirement—or just plain forgotten.

The same is true on the Native side of the equation. Affordable cameras have been around for sixty years at least, tape recorders for forty, and camcorders for ten or more. How many sons and daughters, how many grandchildren, have had the urge to document something of their parents' or grandparents' lives—record their stories and songs, their life histories, photograph them basketweaving or leaching acorns or dancing? Usually these private documentations are treasured and saved. Some even get made into locally distributed pamphlets or tribal learning materials. Often, though, human nature being what it is, the photos curl in a box somewhere, the tapes get jumbled up with the country-western or heavy metal or rap, always just a step or two away from destruction or loss. And because human life and times are always in a state of passing, all of it—everything we know, everything we have learned or gathered against the future, everything we are in danger of forgetting—is precious, no matter who we are.

There is a fourth reason, most important by far, why this volume cannot hope to draw from an exhaustive consultation of the literature: *the traditions are still alive, still growing.* Despite more than two centuries of occupation, assimilation, and outright genocide, they have never been fully stopped. (Hence the choice of title for this volume: *Surviving Through the Days.*) People adapt, and the appearance of things may change, but there's a deeper current, a continuity of difference, that the Native peoples of California have fought hard and paid dearly to preserve. New ways come to mingle with the old.

As a graduate student, I once attended a conference, the Fifth Annual California Indian Conference, in Arcata in the northwestern part of the state. On the last evening of the conference, the organizers arranged a traditional-style Yurok salmon roast at one of the beaches. Perhaps a hundred people attended, so this was not a small affair—the Yurok man (husband of one of the organizers) who put it on had been fishing for days prior to the feast. The charcoal pit was in fact a trench about fifteen feet long and a yard wide, banked with alder logs and ringed with dozens of slender, blade-like cedar stakes about eight inches apart around the entire perimeter of the fire. The stakes were stuck in the sandy ground like the pickets of a fence and spitted with huge chunks of salmon and snaky loops of eel. There was harmony everywhere: the red-orange glow of the fire matched the glow in the sky after sunset; the surf, and the breezes combing through the dark bank of pines and redwood along the hill leading down to the beach, alternately matched and masked the quiet sizzle of salmon juices pressed out by the heat of the coals.

Of course, I'm describing a still life here—a static scene, wonderfully idyllic for those of us enjoying the feast, and one that I have always remembered. But the reality was more than a simple picture postcard: it was a *performance,* and a masterful one at that, made possible only by a prodigious amount of labor and traditional skill on the part of the organizer's husband. But it is this scene that sets the background for the part of the story I'm really trying to tell.

Later, I wandered away from the party and walked along the beach. It was dark and a bit chilly. Down in a hollow between dunes I came across a little circle of people from the conference party—adults and a few youngsters, a mix of Indians and whites—sitting around a small driftwood fire. I stopped to say hello. One of the women had just finished telling a story as I walked up. After the silence ripened again, another woman, older than the first, began telling a new story. As I listened, I realized to my surprise that I knew the story she was telling: the traditional California tale of the Rolling Head. I recognized it because, by chance, I was in the process of translating a 1907 version of that tale from Yana, called "Rolling Skull."[4] Hers was definitely the same story, but different from the version I was familiar with in all sorts of interesting ways. Grad student that I was, when she was finished I mentioned the coincidence and described some of the differences. Before I knew it, I had been invited to contribute a story of my own to the circle. Lacking the skill and experience of telling a traditional story aloud, I knew I would make a hash of any tale I might try, so wisely but somewhat sheepishly, I declined the invitation. The point of all this is that the two women in that firelit circle *did* possess that skill. In another time, they would have been telling their stories in Karuk, say, or Yurok, but because of the mixed and mostly younger audience and the sad course that history took in Northern California, that night found them performing their repertoire in English. And so the traditions are still being carried forward—sometimes in English now instead of Karuk or some other Native language, but carried forward nonetheless.

So much of the spirit and particularity of a culture is embodied in its language that, when language is lost, in many and indefinable ways the patterns of the culture, of its poetics and worldview, are lost as well, or transformed. At the same time, koan-like, there is so much that transcends the particularity of language that in many and indefinable ways the culture flows on just as before. As a linguist, I mourn the loss of language more than anything—but people have to conduct their lives in whatever language they happen to share. If that language is now becoming English, where once it was Karuk (or Kawaiisu, or Konkow, or Kitanemuk), then so be it. At least the stories—their excitement, wisdom, and spirit intact—are still being told. As long as this remains true, as long as the precarious flame of tradition passes to a new generation, the body of Native California oral literature will remain open-ended and continue to grow.

So, all things considered, there is a tremendous wealth of material on the oral literatures of Native California, in libraries, in archives, in attics, and in the living minds of the people whose religious and literary heritage it is. Yet consider this: however overwhelming this literary wealth may appear to an unsuspecting scholar out to master the field, those same riches seem to dwindle when compared to the body of, say, Irish literature, or Persian or Japanese. Despite my mad, naive campaign to read and hear "all there is" in the oral-literary fields of Native California, I am left, in the end, with a sudden, keen perception of the rarity of material. Such rarity makes every scrap precious. And every piece of tradition that has been passed on, recorded, or written down is made that much more valuable, as it becomes—in consequence, for better or worse—emblematic of all that was not.

PRINCIPLES BEHIND THE SELECTION

Surviving Through the Days presents the reader with a solid sampling of these riches. As befitting a sampler, you will find something of nearly everything in this book. Though it is an impossible task in a collection this size, I have tried my best to cover the state geographically as thoroughly as possible—patchy though the result may be. And I have tried to represent as many different genres as possible, though here I faced my most intractable problems. I have also tried to represent different translational styles, different eras and methods of collection—even, in some cases, different versions of the same tale. Lastly, I have tried to feature at least a few of the best-known personalities in the field of California oral tradition, from its most indefatigable collectors to its most important singers and storytellers. (There was far from enough room on the ark for everyone, though . . .)

Yet all that I have tried to accomplish in making the selections for this book has been constrained by one overriding imperative: that each piece chosen, whatever its genre or translation style, be grounded in an actual performance—that there be an authoritative text behind each presentation, backing it up.[5] This means that every translation in this book (with two rather complicated exceptions) is both *verifiable* and *replicable*.[6] Not replicable in the scientific, experimental sense, of course, but replicable in the sense that there is an original text upon which to base a new translation, should anyone desire to do so. And verifiable in the sense that serious literary and linguistic scholars can examine the native-language text to judge the peculiar blend of conservatism and liberty in an individual translator's style, or examine the original language underlying some crux in a song or story.[7]

The reader may therefore be certain that these are honest, authoritative translations of authentic oral performances.[8] The singers and storytellers whose work is represented in these pages are all knowledgeable, sometimes even renowned, proponents of their cultural traditions, and finely skilled in their art. Likewise, their translators are all acknowledged experts in the language at hand—either native speakers themselves or linguists with a deep insight into its grammatical structure.

I had a second imperative, which was to follow the laudable standard of presentation established in Brian Swann's recent anthology, *Coming to Light* (1994). Too often, Native American and other oral literatures have been presented without context other than tribe of origin. Nothing is given of cultural background, the identity of singers or storytellers, the circumstances of collection, the methods of translation or transcription, clues as to significance and interpretation, and the like. Each selection here is therefore accompanied by an introductory essay providing background and contextual information helpful for approaching and appreciating the work.

Oddly enough, though, this documentary requirement—which I think an essential one—has led to a crisis in choosing materials for this book. The reader will notice that, while the narrative genres—myth, legend, folktale, and reminiscence—are amply represented, there are only a few selections of songs, and oratory is not represented at all by formal selections. Although there is very little authentic extended oratory in the California corpus to begin with, which explains its near absence here, there is a lot of song. Open almost any ethnographic treatment of California tribes, and you will find a few scattered songs and maybe even a snatch of oratory accompanying the description of a ceremony. This presents a problem: it is hard to justify space for a selection that consists of a four-page introduction followed by one or two couplets of song, yet that is precisely what the documentary spirit of this volume and its format requires. Unfortunately, there are very few extended collections of song, and those that do exist are either already well-known or were so poorly glossed and contextualized at the time as to defy reliable translation today.[9] Until quite recently, most songs were neither collected nor presented in the exemplary style that Alice Shepherd and Leanne Hinton have developed for the Wintu songs of Grace McKibbin (#13). So the genre of song, which is scattered everywhere in the notes and pages of California's many ethnographers, does not receive its full formal due in this volume. The same shortcoming holds for the bits and pieces of oratory that stud the ethnographic literature.

To compensate, I have sprinkled the volume with songs and speeches and quotations, unannotated except for the bare essentials of who, what, when, and where. As Beverly Crum, a well-known Shoshone singer and anthropologist, once said to me, sometimes the beauty of a song should be appreciated all on its own, just the sheer poetry of it, without the millstone of analysis and interpretation—in short, let the bare words speak for themselves. To honor that minimalist impulse in a book that otherwise goes out of its way to contextualize its selections, as well as to increase the presence of these slighted genres in this collection, I have gathered up handfuls of such gems and tucked as many as I could into its nooks and crannies to serve as epigraphs, as verbal artwork.

Some final words of caution. The reader should not presume that the selections in this volume necessarily represent what is typical of Native

California oral traditions. Some do, some do not. William Benson's "Creation" (#16) is not a typical Central California version of the Beginning, for instance, though its roots nevertheless reach deep down in Pomo cultural tradition. And James Knight makes no bones about how he has changed his telling of the widespread California Orpheus myth in "The Dead People's Home" (#19). The Orpheus myth is much more conventionally rendered in the Chawchila Yokuts selection, "Visit to the Land of the Dead" (#20a), yet even so, there are elements here (the startling cause of the young bride's death, for instance) that simply come shining out of nowhere. Outstanding works of verbal art may often be highly individualistic, while still evoking the tradition from which they emerge.

Nor should the reader presume that this book presents "the best" of California oral literature. It does not, it could not. Rather, you will find in these pages only *some* of the finest songs and stories that the Native cultures of California have to offer. Easily a dozen volumes of material could have been selected (and in time no doubt will be). Ultimately, despite all my earnest considerations and constraints, this is my own very personal selection of works—stories and songs that struck me, in one way or another, with their power, their subtlety, their humor, or their beauty.

A GUIDE TO THE BOOK

The order of selections could have followed any number of different organizations: genre, tribe, theme, language family, date, culture area, recording method, and so on. In the end, though, I chose to follow a geographic arrangement—not despite, but actually because of the artificiality of such an organization. That artificiality has one virtue: that it introduces an appealing randomness to the sequence and arrangement of the selections. (The cartographic approach—the book runs generally from north to south—is not entirely random. Neighboring cultures often, though not always, share cultural patterns and motifs, and geographic proximity lends a shared landscape to passing sections of the book. In any case, the book's division into regions—"Northwestern," "Southern," and the like—is based more on geography than on culture areas per se.) Readers interested in charting a different path through the material may certainly do so. To that end, tables 1–4 offer nonrandom ways of organizing the book's main selections—by genre, recording method, date of performance, and language of narration.

Since few readers will actually read this book through consecutively from beginning to end, let me say a few things about Darryl Babe Wilson's opening contribution, "Kwaw Labors to Form a World," which stands separate from the rest of the selections in two key ways. First, it has no introduction of its own, save this mention here. More important, it is not an oral composition. Darryl, a Native California writer of great power and ability, sent me this piece as part of his introduction to the story of "Naponoha" (#9). But I was so struck by the self-contained elegance of this section that I asked him if I could use it as a kind of narrative "myth-preface" to the body of the collection as a whole. He agreed, so that is where it now stands. All readers should enter the collection, whatever paths they choose to take inside, through this opening selection.

As for supporting materials, I have tried to be generous in providing critical, historical, and linguistic information on California languages and literatures. Immediately following this introduction is an essay, "Making Texts, Reading Translations," that examines the processes by which oral-literary texts are typically collected and produced and discusses the various schools and philosophies of translation that help shape the selections you will encounter here. This essay ends with a section, designed with beginning students of oral literature in mind, that explores some of the aesthetic features of Native American storytelling that new readers are sure to wonder about.

Following the translations themselves comes a suite of essays. The first, "A Brief History of Collection," offers historical background on text-collecting and fieldwork in California. The second, "Notes on Native California Oral Literatures," provides an overview of the distribution and stylistic characteristics of California oral literatures, including sections on genres of narrative, oratory, and song. The third, "Notes on Native California Languages," offers information on California language families, provides a historical perspective on the tragedy that has befallen California languages and their speakers in the years since European contact, and reviews contemporary efforts toward language revival. After the essays comes a section containing maps of California tribal territories, linguistic diversity, language families, and language endangerment. The bibliography section contains an article, "Selected Resources for Further Study,"

Table 1. Selections: Genre

Origins	"Kwaw Labors to Form a World" (#1)
	"Test-ch'as (The Tidal Wave)" (#2)
	"The Boy Who Grew Up at Ta'k'imiłding" (#6a)
	"Creation" (#16)
	"The Creation" (#23)
	"An Account of Origins" (#27)
Myths	"The Young Man from Serper" (#3c)
	"Naponoha (Cocoon Man)" (#9)
	"Loon Woman" (#12)
	"Mad Bat" (#15)
	"The Trials of Young Hawk" (#17)
	"The Dead People's Home" (#19)
	"Visit to the Land of the Dead" (#20a)
	"Condor Steals Falcon's Wife" (#20b)
	"From 'The Life of Hawk-Feather'" (#25)
Coyote stories[a]	"Coyote and Old Woman Bullhead" (#4)
	"The Contest between Men and Women" (#21)
Tales	"The Devil Who Died Laughing" (#5)
	"The Stolen Woman" (#6c)
	"It Was Scratching" (#6d)
	"The Bear Girl" (#7)
	"A Story of Lizard" (#10)
	"The Dog Girl" (#22)
Songs	"A Selection of Wintu Songs" (#11)
	"Four Songs from Grace McKibbin" (#13)
	"A Harvest of Songs from Villiana Calac Hyde" (#24)
Personal reminiscences	"Blind Bill and the Owl" (#3a)
	"Ragged Ass Hill" (#3b)
	"Grandfather's Ordeal" (#6b)
	"How My Father Found the Deer" (#8)
	"How I Became a Dreamer" (#14)
	"The Woman Who Loved a Snake" (#18)
	"The Dead People's Home" (#19)
Historical epic	"In the Desert with Hipahipa" (#26)

[a]Other selections involving Coyote as an incidental or supporting character include numbers 1, 3 ("The Young Man from Serper"), 15, 20 ("Condor Steals Falcon's Wife"), and 23.

Table 2. Selections: Recording Method

Tape recording	"Blind Bill and the Owl" (#3a)
	"Ragged Ass Hill" (#3b)
	"The Young Man from Serper" (#3c)
	"'The Boy Who Grew Up at Ta'k'imiłding' and Other Stories" (#6)
	"How My Father Found the Deer" (#8)
	"Four Songs from Grace McKibbin" (#13)
	"The Woman Who Loved a Snake" (#18)
	"The Dead People's Home" (#19)
	"The Creation" (#23)
	"A Harvest of Songs from Villiana Calac Hyde" (#24)
	"From 'The Life of Hawk-Feather,' Part 1" (#25a)
Phonetic or verbatim dictation	"Coyote and Old Woman Bullhead" (#4)
	"The Devil Who Died Laughing" (#5)
	"The Bear Girl" (#7)
	"Naponoha (Cocoon Man)" (#9)
	"A Story of Lizard" (#10)
	"A Selection of Wintu Songs" (#11)
	"Loon Woman" (#12)
	"How I Became a Dreamer" (#14)
	"Mad Bat" (#15)
	"Creation" (#16)
	"The Trials of Young Hawk" (#17)
	"Visit to the Land of the Dead" (#20a)
	"Condor Steals Falcon's Wife" (#20b)
	"The Contest between Men and Women" (#21)
	"The Dog Girl" (#22)
	"From 'The Life of Hawk-Feather,' Part 2" (#25b)
	"An Account of Origins" (#27)
Interpreter translation	"In the Desert with Hipahipa" (#26)
Written composition	"Kwaw Labors to Form a World" (#1) [English]
	"Test-ch'as (The Tidal Wave)" (#2) [Tolowa]

Table 3. Selections: Date of Performance

1900s	"Mad Bat" (#15) "In the Desert with Hipahipa" (#26) "An Account of Origins" (#27)
1910s	"The Dog Girl" (#22) "A Story of Lizard" (#10)
1920s	"From 'The Life of Hawk-Feather,' Part 2" (#25b) "The Bear Girl" (#7) "Loon Woman" (#12) "A Selection of Wintu Songs" (#11)
1930s	"Creation" (#16) "Coyote and Old Woman Bullhead" (#4) "Condor Steals Falcon's Wife" (#20b) "Naponoha (Cocoon Man)" (#9) "Visit to the Land of the Dead" (#20a) "The Contest between Men and Women" (#21) "How I Became a Dreamer" (#14)
1940s	"The Trials of Young Hawk" (#17)
1950s	"The Devil Who Died Laughing" (#5) "The Young Man from Serper" (#3c)
1960s	"From 'The Life of Hawk-Feather,' Part 1" (#25a) "The Creation" (#23) "'The Boy Who Grew Up at Ta'k'imiłding' and Other Stories" (#6)
1970s	"How My Father Found the Deer" (#8)
1980s	"The Dead People's Home" (#19) "Four Songs from Grace McKibbin" (#13) "Test-ch'as (The Tidal Wave)" (#2) "Blind Bill and the Owl" (#3a) "Ragged Ass Hill" (#3b) "The Woman Who Loved a Snake" (#18)
1990s	"A Harvest of Songs from Villiana Calac Hyde" (#24) "Kwaw Labors to Form a World" (#1)

Table 4. Selections: Language of Narration

Achumawi	"How My Father Found the Deer" (#8)
Chimariko	"The Bear Girl" (#7)
Cupeño	"From 'The Life of Hawk Feather'" (#25)
English	"Kwaw Labors to Form a World" (Atsugewi) (#1) "Blind Bill and the Owl" (Yurok) (#3a) "Ragged Ass Hill" (Yurok) (#3b) "Naponoha (Cocoon Man)" (Atsugewi) (#9) "Four Songs from Grace McKibbin" (Wintu) (#13) "How I Became a Dreamer" (Nomlaki) (#14) "The Woman Who Loved a Snake" (Cache Creek Pomo) (#18) "The Contest between Men and Women" (Tübatulabal) (#21)
Hupa	"The Boy Who Grew Up at Ta'k'imiłding" (#6a) "Grandfather's Ordeal" (#6b) "The Stolen Woman" (#6c) "It Was Scratching" (#6d)
Karuk	"Coyote and Old Woman Bullhead" (#4) "The Devil Who Died Laughing" (#5)
Lake Miwok	"The Dead People's Home" (#19)
Luiseño	"A Harvest of Songs from Villiana Calac Hyde" (#24)
Maidu	"Mad Bat" (#15)
Mojave	"In the Desert with Hipahipa" (#26)
Pomoan	"Creation" (Eastern Pomo) (#16) "The Trials of Young Hawk" (Southern Pomo) (#17)
Quechan	"An Account of Origins" (#27)
Serrano	"The Creation" (#23)
Tolowa	"Test-ch'as (The Tidal Wave)" (#2)

Table 4—*Continued*

Wintu	"A Selection of Wintu Songs" (#11)
	"Loon Woman" (#12)
	"Four Songs from Grace McKibbin" (#13)
Yahi	"A Story of Lizard" (#10)
Yokutsan	"Visit to the Land of the Dead" (Chawchila) (#20a)
	"Condor Steals Falcon's Wife" (Yowlumni) (#20b)
Yurok	"The Young Man from Serper" (#3c)

where interested readers may find an annotated list of important books, articles, websites, and other resources on California languages and literatures. This list prefaces the reference section, which collects full citations for all the works referred to in the essays and individual selections of the book.

NOTES

1. Johanna Nichols's *Linguistic Diversity in Time and Space* (1992) demonstrates this observation in great technical detail.

2. Nor is it just the elders who give their energies to rescuing their native languages and traditions. Parris Butler (Mojave), Nancy Richardson (Karuk), Terry and Sarah Supahan (Karuk), the late Matt Vera (Yowlumni), and Linda Yamane (Rumsien) are only some of a growing younger generation working hard to revive their languages and sustain their cultural traditions.

3. Harrington's Chumash notes alone run to nearly half a million pages, by most estimates. See Kathryn Klar's introduction to "The Dog Girl" (#22) for more information on Harrington's life and work.

4. This translation appeared along with another Yana tale in Brian Swann's *Coming to Light* (1994).

5. I very much would have liked this book to have been in a bilingual format, with the English and native-language texts on facing pages, but the realities of publishing and marketing such a volume—consider that its size would

have been nearly doubled—made that option impossible. I hope to see bilingual formats become the norm in this field someday.

6. The exceptions are selections #26, "In the Desert with Hipahipa," and #27, "An Account of Origins," which were interpreted from Mojave and Quechan, respectively, but recorded only in English.

7. Many of the stories here have been previously published, and their native-language texts are accessible or are stored in archives, as noted in their respective introductions. However, many of the newly commissioned translations are based on unpublished texts. Scholars wishing to examine the originals in these cases will have to get in touch with the individual translators to see if interlinear versions of the texts are available. As for the handful of stories narrated originally in English (see table 4), the version presented here *is* the text, for all practical purposes.

8. It must be kept in mind, though, that stories are rarely recorded "live" at actual ceremonies or storytelling sessions where the presence of a linguist with a tape recorder tends to be intrusive or even unwelcome, but instead are generally recorded "in the studio," as it were, where the researcher can better control sound quality and focus the interview. Not all storytellers can deliver living, natural performances under such circumstances, but many do rise to the occasion, as evidenced by the performances in this book. (For scholarly discussions of the differences between "live" and "studio" performances, see Hymes 1981, Sherzer 1987, and Tedlock 1983.)

9. An example of the former case would be the famous Wintu Dream songs collected by Dorothy Demetracopoulou and excerpted here as selection #11; an example of the latter (which I owe to Margaret Langdon) would be the Diegueño Eagle Ceremony songs published by T. T. Waterman in 1910, which do not appear here as a selection for precisely this reason.

Making Texts, Reading Translations

In books like the one in hand—monolingual in format, without the presence of an original native-language text on each facing page as a reminder—it is entirely too easy for readers to forget that they are reading translations, that the performances behind most of the stories and songs they are reading were given first in another language, and that therefore the words they are reading are not the actual words of the singers and storytellers but approximations of them created by scholars who happen to speak or study those languages and who are presenting or "packaging" the works for their perusal. Just what and how much is inevitably lost in the process of translation is difficult even to imagine. It's not so much that information is lost—the journalistic facts of "who, what, where, and when" come through in any translation—but *sound* is lost, *nuance* is lost, the very substance of verbal art goes missing. If, as Pope once said, "The Sound must seem an Echo to the Sense," pointing to the interdependence of sound and meaning in a work of art, then when the sounds and connotations of English words replace the sounds and connotations of Chumash words or Pomo words or Karuk words, the "sense" in English can never be quite the same as it was in the original language, no matter how good the translation. Different sounds and rhythms and nuances take the place of the original.

For a translator, though, that is the challenge and the real pleasure in doing the work: learning how to carry into English the fullest possible share of what is present in the text. But that goal presumes being able to recognize what is there in the first place—what is said and what is unsaid, how it is said or unsaid, and why it all hangs together. And so the process of translation is always a voyage of discovery. Each word is a step along a trail that leads deeper and deeper into the unexplored country of the language and the culture that cradles it. Translation, therefore, makes an excellent discovery procedure for all aspects of linguistic study, as all the facets and resources of a language are brought to bear in making verbal art. The act of translation, then, forces the translator to grapple with the entire range of these resources and often leads to a deeper understanding of the linguistic patterns of the source language itself. At the same time, translation stretches the limits of the English language to embrace the resources of that other linguistic world—so it's a voyage of discovery into English, my own beloved language, as well.

Translations get made in a number of different ways, and in this collection I have tried to represent the most important of them. Perhaps the most primitive of these methods, from the point of view of accuracy, is what I will call *interpreter translation*. Common in the days before tape recording, this method was employed by collectors who either lacked the phonetic skill to take down texts in dictation, or who were too pressed for time (phonetic dictation was an exhausting and laborious process) to do so. Three parties are involved: the narrator and the collector (often monolingual speakers of their respective languages), and a bilingual interpreter who mediates between the two. Jeremiah Curtin's early collection of Yana and Wintu narratives, *Creation Myths of Primitive America* (1898), was made in this fashion.

In this volume, the Mojave migration epic, excerpted as the episode "In the Desert with Hipahipa" (#26), was collected this way, too, as was "An Account of Origins" (#27). Alfred Kroeber, who made the handwritten record of the former, is quite frank about the limitations of the process in his commentary (A. Kroeber 1951:133):

> In spite of my best efforts to record the full translation of the story, it is evident that I did not altogether succeed. It now contains between thirty and forty thousand words, whereas Inyo-kutavêre in six half-days must have spoken the equivalent of a hundred to a hundred and fifty thousand English words. I have already mentioned [see Kroeber's introduction to #26, this volume] that some of the shrinkage is due to my omitting verbal repetitions and otherwise trimming redundancy, primarily in self-de-

fense in trying to keep up with the interpreter—I wrote only in abbreviated longhand. Perhaps a fair estimate would be that the other half was a regrettable loss of vividness, concrete detail, and nuance. In short, condensation compacted the manner of telling, but also diminished something of such virtues of quality as it possessed. Verbal style in particular had little chance of penetrating through the double screen of Englishing and of condensed recording.

In this process, it is actually the Native interpreter—John Jones in this case, working on the fly without the opportunity for reflection or refinement—who should really be credited for the translation. It is the interpreter who does the hardest work, and whose linguistic and mnemonic skills primarily determine the integrity of the finished product. The collector merely writes it all down as best he can and edits the transcript later. Because the original text has thus had to pass through two different filters on the way from performance into print, narratives recorded by this method have to be appraised carefully. In addition, because no record of the original language is made or kept—it vanishes immediately, replaced by the interpreter's English rendering—such texts are unfit for all but the coarsest sorts of stylistic studies, however impressive and culturally sound they may be in other respects.

Almost any method of recording oral literature (save hearsay, I suppose, or hazy recollection) is preferable to interpreter translation, at least as far as the study of poetics is concerned. Texts taken down by *phonetic dictation* (or "verbatim" dictation if the text is given in English) are much more desirable, because they preserve the exact words of the original performance, in the exact order in which they were spoken. Before tape recorders became widely available, this was the preferred method for collecting texts. Once the story had been dictated and an accurate phonetic transcript made, the collector would read it back to the narrator, word by word or phrase by phrase, verify it, and obtain a running gloss of the meaning.[1] Needless to say, this second stage of the process could take even longer than the first—sometimes several days or weeks for a long story. The translation itself (and a great deal of linguistic analysis as a byproduct) is produced by working back and forth between the phonetic text and this initial gloss. Roughly half of the stories and songs in this collection were taken down this way (see table 2 in the "General Introduction" for a complete list of selections categorized by method of recording).

The emergence of *tape recording* in the latter half of the century as the new (and still) primary method of documentation changed some aspects of the collection process drastically, and others not at all. Once the taped record of a performance has been made, the process of working it up as a text is largely similar to that of phonetic dictation. A phonetic transcription is made by listening (endlessly, endlessly!) to the tape, usually with the help of the narrator or another native speaker. Next, a running gloss of the text is made, this time with the crucial help of a native speaker, by playing the tape back a phrase or sentence at a time. (These two steps may, of course, be combined.) The process of translation itself works just the same as it did with the older method, except that in recent years it has become more common for contemporary singers and storytellers to take an active or collaborative role in producing the final literary translation of their work.[2]

Marianne Mithun's obituary remembrance of Frances Jack, a Central Pomo elder who died in 1993, while canted more toward the linguistic side of fieldwork, reveals something of what this kind of work is like and the closeness and warmth that can develop between people involved in the process of documentation (Mithun 1993):

> Her knowledge of her traditional language, Central Pomo, was rich and vast. She was an exquisitely skilled speaker; her style could be dramatic and spellbinding, as she told of events from the past, or quick and full of wit, as she conversed with friends. Over the past nine years, as we worked together on a grammar and dictionary of the language, we certainly never came to the end of what she knew. Her memory was astounding. She easily came up with words that no one had used for decades.
>
> At the same time, she was highly articulate in English, able to explain intricacies of the Central Pomo language in ways that few others could. She was aware not just of what could be said in her language, but also of what had been said, and under what circumstances.
>
> One day we were discussing a suffix, *-way*, whose meaning is something like 'arrive.' This suffix appears with the verb root *mó-* 'crawl' in the verb *mó-way*, for example, to mean literally 'crawl-arrive.'
>
> As she explained the meaning of that word, however, she went well beyond that definition, as usual, noting it would be used if someone feels sorry and crawls over to you like a dog, in a pitiful way.
>
> She explained that *čá-way*, literally 'run-arrive,' would be used if a gust of wind hit you, or a child ran into you. The word *hlí-way*, literally 'sev-

eral go-arrive,' would be used for moving in on someone, as when a woman sees a man sitting on a bench, sits down next to him, and moves in on him.

She was dedicated to creating as full a record as possible of her language. We found we worked best by staying together for four or five days at a stretch every few weeks, working steadily. What a tireless worker she was! First thing in the morning she would be eager to begin, brimming over with things she had thought of during the night. We would work late into the night, stopping only when I could no longer hold a pen.

The best working relationships have always been based on mutual respect and admiration, and that goes for linguistic fieldwork as well as anything else. But I think what shines through here most of all is the genuine love of the work itself, and the immense sense of commitment and urgency that both workers brought to this self-appointed task of documentation—the drive, not so much to "get it all" for posterity, which can never be done, but to get as much as humanly possible, and then to get it right, before it's gone. After preserving life itself and passing the seed of culture and language on to the next generation, no work is more important than this for Native American cultures at the beginning of the twenty-first century. It demands great knowledge and great skill to begin with, but ends as a labor of love.

SCHOOLS OF PRESENTATION

Of course, there is a big difference between the literal translations produced for linguistic publications and the literary translations created for a wider audience. In the earliest days of text publishing in California, in volumes of the old *University of California Publications in American Archaeology and Ethnology* series, the format was an interlinear one, where the native-language text was accompanied by a running word-for-word gloss. The following example from the story "Grizzly Bear and Deer" in Sapir's *Yana Texts* (1910), taken down by phonetic dictation, serves to illustrate this format.[3]

bama´du   wa´wi   t'e´nna   mīk!a´iᵋi   djū´tc!ilᵋaimā´dj
Deer place | house. | Grizzly Bear | she was angry. | "Cut it off for me

aidju   ba´cⁱ   mô´yau   djô´tc!il ͤ aitc‘it ͤ atdi´*n*ͤ t‘i
the your | flesh. | I shall eat it." | Now she cut it right off,

mô´citdi*n*ͤt‘ê ͤᵃ   mô ͤatdi*n*ͤt‘   djī´kithī´s   ‘itdjiha´m ͤ
now she roasted it, | now she ate it. | "It tastes good." | "I looked for your lice."

auwi´tdi´*n*ͤt‘   dji´na muitc!ila‘u ͤatdi*n*t‘   baru´ll o‘pdji*n*ͤ t‘
Now she got hold of it | louse | Now she bit her | neck, | she killed her.

djô´t!alditdi*n*ͤ t‘   mô´ba*n*ͤ t‘   mô´ba*n*ͤ t‘ⁱ   dan ͤma´un
Now she split her up, | she ate up all, | she ate up all | being much.

o´pdjiba*n*ͤ t‘
She killed all.

Because the glosses are not, strictly speaking, "readable" with any fluency or certitude (much less enjoyment), texts presented in this manner were generally also accompanied by a "free" translation, wherein considerable liberties might be taken to bring the story into conventional English storytelling prose. Here is Sapir's turn-of-the-century free translation of the preceding passage:

> There was a house in which dwelt Deer. Grizzly Bear was angry. "Cut off some of your flesh for me," (she said to Deer). "I am going to eat it." Then (Deer) cut some of it right off and roasted it. (Grizzly Bear) ate it. "It tastes good," (she said. Some time after this, she was lousing Deer, and scratched her. Deer protested; but Grizzly Bear said,) "I was lousing you." Now she caught hold of a louse; now she bit (Deer's) neck and killed her. Then she cut up her belly and ate her up, ate up much. All (the Deer people) she killed.

Some of the liberties are obvious: the first sentence has been considerably contextualized, as has the clause *djô´t!alditdin ͤt‘* 'now she split her up, it is said'; and near the end, the exact repetition of *mô´ban ͤt‘(ⁱ)* 'she ate her all up, it is said' has been obscured, thanks to a misreading of prosodic junctures (the word *dan ͤma´un* goes with *o´pdjiban ͤt‘*, not with *mô´ban ͤt‘ⁱ*). The remote-past quotative element -*n ͤt‘⁽ⁱ⁾* 'it is said' has not been translated at all, either in the translation or in the gloss line. Still, these liberties, good or bad, are afforded precisely because the native-language text has been presented in this fashion—it's there to check the translation against, since the interlinear presentation provides a running gloss of the forms and their meanings.[4]

Texts made and presented this way are often referred to as *ethnolinguistic* texts. Their practitioners, from Kroeber and his early Californianist colleagues all the way through to present-day scholars, all share the central Boasian belief in the primacy of the native-language text. Along with that insistence, however, often came a corresponding lack of interest in the translation of the text as an entity in itself—except insofar as it should reflect accurately the semantic and syntactic structures of the original. In short, the translation is just there as a "crib," a convenient key to the native-language text. And because Boasian ethnolinguistics focused on the ethnographic and linguistic aspects of the texts collected, not so much on their aesthetic or poetic aspects, the aesthetic and poetic dimensions are only indirectly reflected in the translations of ethnolinguistic texts.[5]

Over the last couple of decades, there has been a change—some say a revolution, others merely an evolution—in the way scholars go about collecting, translating, and presenting Native American texts. Today, we refer to this new approach as *ethnopoetics,* in explicit contrast to the more classically oriented school of ethnolinguistics. Pioneered by Dell Hymes and Dennis Tedlock in the 1960s and 1970s, ethnopoetics brings together the overlapping interests of linguistics, literary criticism, folklore, and anthropology. It makes the claim that a disciplined understanding of the aesthetic properties of an oral text, be it song or story or reminiscence, is essential to making a proper analysis—that there is an interplay between form and meaning that is ignored only at the risk of misinterpretation, misrepresentation, or both.[6] Such claims are taken for granted with written literary traditions. It should not be surprising to learn that these matters are just as relevant to oral literary traditions. Despite vast differences, both modes, written and oral, fall within the broad domain of verbal art.[7]

The criticism raised against older ethnolinguistic treatments is that they tend to ignore poetics—those aspects of structure, style, and performance that make a text a work of verbal art. Ethnopoetic approaches seek to reverse this tendency. (Contemporary ethnolinguistic translators, of course, are much more conscious of the aesthetic and rhetorical dimensions of their texts.) To illustrate some of the characteristics of an ethnopoetic approach, let's return to Round Mountain Jack's version of "Grizzly Bear and Deer." This time, the translation is my own and proceeds from Hymesian principles of ethnopoetic presentation and analysis. (To provide more in the way of illustration, I have gone beyond the short passage of interlinear glosses and translated the entire opening scene of the story. The right-margin notes supply interpretive information that is not present in the native-language text.)

1 There was a house at Deer's place.
   Grizzly Bear,
     she was angry:
    "Cut me off a piece of your flesh—   *Grizzly said to*
      I'm going to eat it."   *Deer*

2 Now right away she cut off a piece, they say.   *Deer did*
   Now she roasted it.   *Grizzly did*
   Now she ate it.

3 "It tastes go-o-d!"

4 "I was just grooming you!"   *Grizzly protest-*
                      ed, when Deer
                      complained of
                      roughness

5 Now she plucked up a louse.
   Now she bit her through the neck—   *Deer's neck*
   she killed her.

6 Now she carved her up.   *Grizzly did*
   She ate her all up,
   she ate her all up, they say.

7 There being so many, she killed them all.   *so many Deer*
                      people

8 She went off looking for them.   *for Deer's two*
   She didn't see them.   *children*
   She came back.

9 She went down into the south.
   She killed everything.
   She came back north.

10 Off in the west she ate up all of the deer.
   She came back east.

11 Off to the north she ate up all the elk.
She ate them all up,
she killed them all.

12 She headed back, they say, into the east.
She killed all of the deer.
She stood still, they say.

13 She looked around.
"I have killed them all," she said.
"Now then!" she said.

14 Then she went back home, they say.

The most obvious difference, of course, is the typographical format: this translation is presented in broken lines—akin to poetry, not to prose. Furthermore, many of the lines are grouped into units that look like stanzas or verses, making the result superficially even more like poetry. I will have more to say about the nature of this resemblance later on; for now, I merely want to point out a few of the oral-literary features of the Yana story that are reflected in this excerpt.

In making the translation above, I used syntactic constituency as my main criterion for dividing the text into lines. Each line of translation, therefore, represents a clause or predication in the original Yana. When I then looked more closely at the sequence of lines, I noticed that some of them seemed to be more tightly linked together than others in terms of thematic unity. To reflect that observation, I used blank lines to represent the existence of these groups of lines (numbered in the left margin to facilitate discussion) on the page. Groups 5 and 8, for instance, form units on the basis of related action: in 5, it's the tight action-sequence of plucking, biting, and killing that defines these lines as a single rhetorical entity; in 8, it's the sequence of going, looking around, and returning that defines them as a unit.[8] In fact, all of the line-groups in this excerpt are defined by patterns of action or speech, as examination will reveal. What is interesting is how frequently these units seem to come in triplets. Eight of the fourteen line-groups in this passage contain three clauses each—a high enough proportion to speculate that this pattern represents some kind of rhetorical ideal, one that the narrator actually strove for in his oral composition of the work. (Indeed, a preliminary examination of the entire text suggests that the overall proportion of triplet line-groups is even higher than in this excerpt.)

Furthermore, the four "singlet" groups (3, 4, 7, 14) seem all to carry a special rhetorical force: by virtue of their brevity, their singularity, they tend to punctuate the rhythm and add dramatic highlight to the information they convey. In contrast, the lone "doublet" group (10) simply seems underdeveloped, in that it fails to realize the three-fold rhetorical pattern established in group 8, of going, doing something, and coming back. Groups 9 and 12 fulfill this template (though in 12, "standing still" takes the place of "coming back"), while group 11 appears to be an incomplete variant of the basic design, perhaps deliberate, perhaps not.

Sometimes this latent trinary patterning even plays out at higher levels than the line-group, as in this passage translated from the middle of the story:

1   "Where are they?" she said.

Grizzly, looking for Deer's children

2a   She asked a poker;
    it didn't answer.

2b   She asked a stone;
      it didn't answer.

2c   She asked the earth,
        she asked the stick,
        she asked the fire.

3a   She asked the coals:

3b   "Yes, indeed," they said.
      "They have run south," they said.

3c   "Aha!" she said.

4   She bit the stone, angry.
    She bit the stick.
    She bit the fire.

5   She went right out.

Only two of the nine separate sets of line-groups in this passage (2c and 4) are actually triplets in their own right, but it is easy to see the way the overarching structure of the passage involves a three-fold organization of line-groups. Set 2 is defined by a three-stage action-sequence (the interrogation of various nonrespondent objects), just as set 3 is defined by the three-stage interrogation of the responding coals (the three stages being Grizzly's question in 3a, the coals' answer in 3b, and Grizzly's response in 3c). Similar complex hierarchical organizations may be found throughout the story.[9]

This type of organic literary patterning, which Hymes (1976) has termed *measured verse,* is obscured in the typical prose-format presentations of the ethnolinguistic school but is nicely revealed by the broken-line presentations of the ethnopoetic school. On the whole, ethnopoetic texts and translations are more amenable or accessible to stylistic analysis than the typical ethnolinguistic text—in part because considerable rhetorical analysis has gone into working up the text in the first place.

While some ethnopoetic presentations try to make explicit the underlying rhetorical and compositional patterns of the text, others try instead to capture various "live" aspects of the performance itself—such dynamic features of the living human voice as intonation, vocal quality (shouting, whispering, and the like), and pause-phrasing. Hymes is most often associated with the former, Tedlock with the latter. I often refer to these two different ethnopoetic styles, respectively, as the *structural* and *prosodic* approaches to the poetics of oral literature. Structural approaches focus on the rhetorical architecture of the narrative and are most common with texts taken down earlier in the century by the method of phonetic dictation, whereas prosodic approaches focus on the voice and necessarily require texts that have been tape-recorded or videotaped, because only taped performances can capture and hold the sound of the voice itself in delivery.[10]

As it happened, the first scholar to try for a synthesis of these two methods, William Bright, was himself a Californianist, working with Karuk myths. Today most ethnopoetic practitioners who have the luxury of working with tape-recorded texts aim for some combination of the two approaches. The following translation, the middle section (Bright calls them "acts") of a three-part myth, illustrates an integrated approach. The original was told in Karuk by Julia Starritt and translated by Bright. The story is a widespread myth, well-known in California and elsewhere in North America, called "Coyote Steals Fire." In this presentation, Bright uses a number of typographical conventions to represent aspects of his ethnopoetic analysis (1979:94–95). Capitals, for instance, represent "extra-loud material," and italics represent "extra-soft material." Each line-group ("verse" in Bright's terminology) starts at the left margin, with each succeeding line indented. Intonation contours are indicated by punctuation: falling final intonation by a period, marking the end of a verse; falling but nonfinal intonation by a comma or dash; final high or mid-pitch intonation by a colon. In act 1, Coyote devised a plan for getting back the fire the "upriver people" had stolen. Here, in act 2, he puts his plan into action:

SO THEN THAT'S HOW THEY WENT UPRIVER.
And Coyote arrived upriver.
And he saw it was empty.
And in the mountains he saw there were fires,
    there were forest fires,
        up in the mountain country.
And he went in a house.
And he saw only children were there.
And he said:
    "Where have they gone?
"Where have the men gone?"
And the children said:
    "They're hunting in the mountains."
And he said:
    "I'm lying down right here,
       I'm tired."
And he said to the children:
    "I'll paint your faces!
"Let me paint your faces.
"You'll look pretty that way."
And the children said:
    "Maybe he's Coyote."
They were saying that to each other.
And they said to him,
    to Coyote:
        "Maybe you're Coyote,"
And he said: "No.
"I don't even know
    where that Coyote is.
"I don't hear,
    I don't know,

> *the place where he is.*"
> And he said:
>> "Let me paint your faces!"
> And when he painted all the children's faces,
>> then he said:
>>> "SEE, I'VE SET WATER DOWN RIGHT HERE,
>>> SO YOU CAN LOOK INTO IT.
> "Your faces will look pretty!
> "BUT I'M LYING DOWN RIGHT HERE,
>> I'M TIRED."
> In fact, he had stuck fir bark into his toes.
> And then he stuck his foot in the fire.
> And then finally it caught fire well,
>> it became a coal,
>>> it turned into a coal.
> And then he jumped up again.
> And he jumped out of the house.
> *And he ran back downriver.*
> And when he got tired,
>> then he gave the fire to the next person.
> *And he too started running.*
> And in the mountain country,
>> where there had been fires,
>>> then they all were extinguished.
> And then people said,
>> "Why, they've taken it back from us,
>>> our fire!"

In an ethnopoetic presentation, the typographical layout of the text on the page (line breaks, indentations, font effects, and the like) is used to convey linguistic information (intonation boundaries, syntactic structure, pauses, voice quality, and so on)—information that is primarily of interest to the specialist. At the same time, though, it offers the nonspecialist a visually intuitive way into the flow and structure of the text as a verbal performance. Notice how the broken-line format of Bright's presentation works to slow the eye as it follows down the page and helps to re-create the pace or rhythm of the original. The vocal cues signaled by italics and caps add texture to the result.

The notion that oral storytelling is delivered in lines—which in turn are organized into units resembling verses or stanzas, which in turn may be organized into larger and larger units resembling "scenes" and "acts"— is one of the foundational insights of modern ethnopoetics. It is also one of the most widely misunderstood. In ethnopoetic theory, the line is the basic unit of oral-literary composition, comparable in most respects to the cognitive-prosodic units of ordinary speech production (breath groups, intonation units, pause groups, idea units, and so on) that have been identified by linguists doing discourse analysis on conversational speech more generally (see Chafe 1980, 1994).[11] If you listen closely to the sound of people telling stories, lecturing, or just plain talking, you will notice that their speech doesn't come forth in a long, smooth, unbroken flow, like a river. Instead, it comes in pulses, rising and falling like waves on a shore, with each new spurt or "parcel" of information riding in on the crest of its own wave. The lines in ethnopoetic texts are meant to represent these waves or pulses of language.[12]

The misunderstanding comes about because, when these lines are delineated typographically by line breaks and further grouped into "stanzas" by means of blank lines or indentation, the resulting text looks like modern written poetry. Looking at a story presented in this fashion, it's easy to jump to the conclusion that Native American myths and stories are not prose but poetry. But in fact they are neither. Prose is a written category, as is our default conception of poetry. Whatever *poetry* (or *prose*, for that matter) might mean in the context of oral storytelling, it is simply not the same as what it means in the context of Western written literary tradition. All this is not to say that Native American storytelling is not poetic—it most certainly is, often densely and intricately so. But I particularly wish to avert the conclusion, implied by the broken-line formats of most ethnopoetic presentations, that it is poetry in the sense that literate Europeans and their cultural descendants typically understand that term. The purpose of presenting texts and translations in broken-line format is to highlight the poetic and rhetorical structures organic to the original language and performance patterns of the text—not to suggest potentially misleading cultural parallels between oral and Western written traditions.

And yet, over the years there has been considerable, sometimes even acrimonious, disagreement over these ideas, and ethnopoetics remains somewhat controversial even to this day.[13] Both paradigms continue to stimulate useful contributions to the discipline. For that reason, in addition to presenting classic examples of ethnolinguistic work from the past, I have made it a point to represent a range of contemporary approaches, both ethnolinguistic and ethnopoetic in orientation, in the selections for this volume. In these pages, Dell Hymes's retranslation of the Wintu "Loon Woman" myth (#12) is a prime example of a structural ethnopoetic presentation. There are also two essentially prosodic presentations: Ken Hill's Serrano "Creation" (#23), and the second of Jane Hill's two Cupeño episodes in "From 'The Life of Hawk Feather'" (#25b). Other ethnopoetic treatments here include William Bright's "The Devil Who Died Laughing" (#5) and Leanne Hinton's "Four Songs from Grace McKibbin" (#13). On the ethnolinguistic side of the equation, we have Victor Golla's presentation of "'The Boy Who Grew Up at Taʾkʾimiłding' and Other Stories" (#6), Robert Oswalt's "The Trials of Young Hawk" (#17), Catherine Callaghan's "The Dead People's Home" (#19), Bruce Nevin's "How My Father Found the Deer" (#8), and Darryl Wilson's "Naponoha" (#9). The other contemporary translations in this volume steer more towards Bright's synthetic middle ground—for example, Luthin and Hinton's "A Story of Lizard" (#10), William Shipley's "Mad Bat" (#15), Richard Applegate's "The Dog Girl" (#22), and Ermine Wheeler Voegelin's "The Contest between Men and Women" (#21). Translations made prior to the 1970s, before the real advent of the ethnopoetics movement, are by definition ethnolinguistic presentations.

Both modes of translation are in active use today. Readers interested in comparing these two approaches will find that the difference between the two camps has nothing to do with their literary quality. All the translations in this volume are literary translations, after all—carefully crafted with the intent of re-creating as far as possible in English the style and artistry of the original songs and stories.

WHEN AESTHETIC WORLDS COLLIDE

First-time readers of Native American oral literature often feel confused, even alienated, by the narrative worlds they have entered. Without guidance and preparation, they may even turn away in bewilderment. The motivations for behavior may seem opaque; the timing of stories may seem "off"; their sense of outcome, of dramatic resolution, may seem to be missing entirely. By and large, these problems are simply due to a different style of storytelling—so similar in some ways to the fantastical myths we know from the Bible, or to the European folktales most of us know from childhood, yet so very different in others.

Sometimes the initial strangeness can obscure the common ground. In Ishi's "A Story of Lizard" (#10), when Lizard cuts open Grizzly Bear's stomach to rescue the gobbled-up Long-Tailed Lizard, try thinking of "Little Red Riding Hood." Or again, in the story behind "Sapagay's Song" (see pages 533–34), when Sapagay dives down into a pool to discover a shaman's underground realm, try thinking of Beowulf diving into the lake to confront Grendel's mother. At other times, the sensation of familiarity can obscure what is truly different. For instance, the average American reader will take the ending of the Yurok story "The Young Man from Serper" (#3c) right in stride:

> And so for this we say that it is not good if a person thinks too much, "I will have everything." But a man lives happily if somewhere he has plenty of friends, and has his money; then he does not go around thinking that he should have everything that does not belong to him, and wishing it were his own.

Most will automatically absorb this moral thanks to its familiar ring, so congruent with European folk wisdom regarding wealth and ambition. And in truth there is much here that can be taken at face value from Yurok into English tradition. But the idea and function of money, of personal wealth, in Yurok culture is ultimately quite different from its Western counterpart, and so this feeling of transparency is partly an illusion.

Other difficulties readers may encounter are caused by the nature of oral literature itself.[14] True oral storytelling—as opposed to reading aloud or acting out a story one has memorized (the usual fare at "story hour" in libraries and schools across the country)—is something that most of us in America today are completely unfamiliar with. When a child hears the story of "Goldilocks" or "Snow White" over and over again at bedtime, it's the same every time. Different readers may have different voices, some more animated than others, but the words written down are always the same. True oral storytelling very seldom involves the redaction of a fixed text, but rather, involves the re-creation of a living one. While some storytellers can produce versions of their stories that remain remarkably constant even when many years separate the tellings, others may dramatically alter the structure and even substance of their stories from one occasion to the next. Depending on factors such as audience, mood, setting, and personal style, oral narrators tailor their performances to suit the moment, expanding an episode here, truncating an episode there, highlighting this or that aspect to reflect what's going on in the here and now. Thus, in a living oral culture, there could never be just one "Goldilocks." Instead, there would be a different "Goldilocks" for every storyteller—with a great deal of consensus among the versions, to be sure, but with divergent versions as well. On top of that, each version will have its own variations, slight differences each time the story is told. In a sense, there is an ecology to what we find here, for in this very diversity lies the health of an oral tradition.

Native American stories will strike readers in many different ways. When you think about it, though, these stories *should* feel different. Native American traditions and cultures are as much a part of the grand galaxy of world human culture as any other group. But Native American cultures have also been growing independently on the American soil for at least fifteen thousand years. (By way of perspective, that's seventy-five thousand generations—at least ten times longer than the mere fifteen hundred years the English have dwelled in Britain.) In that wash of time, they have found their own paths of custom and philosophy, made their own worlds, alike yet unlike any other. So we must expect to encounter differences alongside the similarities. Therein lies what is special about Native American cultures and traditions.

Of course, Native American cultures are different enough from each other, let alone from other cultures around the globe. Even while we may speak of "European" culture, we are mindful of the differences between Germany and France, Hungary and Spain. So, too, with Sioux and Hopi, Nootka and Cherokee. If you, as a reader, come from some other tradition—European, Asian, African—and Native American stories *don't* seem just a little strange and different, then you should wonder whether the translator has gone too far in translating the stories into English.

The contributions to this book strike a balance between the need of the general reader to connect with the stories and the rights of the storytellers to be heard in their own voices. Here, then, are a few of the stylistic highlights that novice readers may look forward to when encountering Native American oral literature for the first time.

Anthropomorphism

Anthropomorphism, where animals and even inanimate objects take on characteristics and capabilities of human beings, is probably the easiest feature of Indian myths for contemporary Americans to adjust to. After all, anthropomorphism is nearly ubiquitous in our own culture today, from children's books and fairy tales to movies and advertising campaigns on TV. But it is important to understand the nature of Native American anthropomorphism, which is significantly different from what European descendants are accustomed to. In Western cultures, so very long separated from their mythic, animistic pasts, anthropomorphism carries largely an allegorical value, and today it performs the function of entertainment more than anything else. In the old-time Native American traditions, though, anthropomorphism is much more: it is also a consequence of cosmology and religion. Most Native cultures look back to a remote time when the difference between people and animals was blurred, before humans emerged as a distinct race of beings on earth. Animals (or "animal people") were thus our forerunners on this earth. The hard dichotomy between Man and Beast that characterizes Western worldviews is largely absent in Native America. People are distinct from animals, to be sure, but there is still an ancient kinship between them; the relationship is not one of alienation and dominion.

Annie Burke's way of opening her Southern Pomo story, "The Trials of Young Hawk" (#17), sums up the situation with a minimum of fuss: "A group of small birds and animals, who were all also people, used to live together in a big community," she begins. That's why, in so many myths and stories, it can be difficult to decide whether a character is an animal with human characteristics or a person with animal characteristics— or both, or each in alternation. In the end, the distinction is somewhat meaningless; at best, it is a sliding scale. Traditions, even individual narrators within local traditions, vary on how "human" or "animal" their characters appear to be. In "The Trials of Young Hawk," for instance, the characters are fairly concrete, remaining close to their animal natures. Thus Young Hawk has a "perch" high in his older brother's earthlodge, and the beaver brothers "gnaw" new eyes for him, and the fieldmouse sisters "nibble" off his hair. (Note that Young Hawk has hair, though, not feathers.) But in other stories, there is often little that is specifically "animal" about the characters, beyond their names, personalities, and a tendency to dwell in surroundings appropriate to the natural habitats of their namesakes, like Ouzel at the end of the Maidu story "Mad Bat" (#15). There is perhaps a tendency for minor characters to display more animal-like traits than do main characters, possibly because of the greater range of actions main characters are called on to perform, with the consequent drain that maintaining such restrictions (lack of hands, particularly) tends to place on the task of narration.

The core personalities of anthropomorphic characters are often drawn at least tangentially from the Book of Nature. Not surprisingly, there are parallels to be made between Native American folklore and the folklore of ancient and medieval Old World fables and beast tales (the *Panchatantra,* for instance, or closer to home, the fables of Aesop and a variety of Middle English poems, like *The Owl and the Nightingale,* "The Fox and the Wolf," and Chaucer's "Parliament of Fowls"). Just as, in a European folktale, when a fox or a nightingale comes on the scene, we already know what to expect from that character in terms of behavior and personality, so it is in Native American stories when Coyote or Eagle or Bluejay comes on the scene.

Coyote makes a superb example of a character whose behavior—curious, tricky, insatiable, and by turns noble and foolish—is based in part on close observations of the natural world. The Bear Girl in the Chimariko story (#7) is another example—she is crabby, unpredictable, and violent, just like a real bear. Still, different cultures can read the Book of Nature differently. There's a degree of arbitrariness in all bodies of folklore, so what we know about animal figures in one tradition is not always transferable to another. For instance, the loon is a giddy minor character, little more than a walk-on, in American folklore. (As our saying goes, "crazy as a loon.") But in the native folklore of Northern California, Loon is a much darker, much more serious character—a heavy. And the wolf, far from being the evil, rapacious killer that salivates its way through European folklore, is a stalwart, dependable character—a strong leader and good provider, maybe even a bit dull and unimaginative—in much Southern California mythology. Readers should look for both similarities and differences in the animal characters they meet in these stories.

All cultures, and especially oral cultures, make use of anthropomorphism. The mythologies of animistic hunting-and-gathering societies in particular are often heavily and crucially anthropomorphic. As the anthropologist Claude Lévi-Strauss once pointed out, animals are "good to think with." In Native California, animals have long been used, through systematic anthropomorphism in mythology, folklore, art, and religious ceremony, to express deep patterns of thinking about the world. It's a common mistake—and one the reader should guard against—to interpret anthropomorphic myths and stories as merely "children's fare"; they are not. These narratives are amenable to multiple levels of interpretation, at any degree of sophistication their audiences—traditional or modern—care to approach them with. In truth, anthropomorphism has always provided humankind a primary means for exploring one of the most enduringly important themes of inquiry and spirituality: the relationship between ourselves and the natural universe.

Repetition and Parallelism

Somewhere along the road to written culture, in becoming readers rather than listeners, we have lost our patience for repetition, or at least think we have. Yet some of our oldest and most fundamental literary texts—the books of the Old Testament Bible, for example—are alive with repetition, at all levels of rhetorical structure. That's because the writings of the Bible, like Homer, like Gilgamesh, are intimately grounded in oral tradition—and repetition is a cornerstone of oral composition.

In cases of *episodic repetition,* entire scenes or plot motifs get repeated, wholesale or piecemeal, sometimes with only minimal variation. Anyone raised on the Brothers Grimm knows all about episodic repetition. In "Cinderella," when the Prince takes the glass slipper on the road, searching for the foot that wore it, there's a scene at Cinderella's house where he tries it on the eldest sister's foot to no avail. This "Foot Trial" episode is repeated twice more. The first repetition, with the second sister, is virtually identical to that of the eldest sister's trial—except that where the eldest sister amputates her toe to make the slipper fit, the second sister amputates her heel. Both times, the slipper fills up with blood, and the Prince returns the impostor to her family. The third time around, of course, it's Cinderella's turn, and the outcome and content of this episode is significantly different from the first two—indeed, the third trial marks the culmination of the whole sequence and leads to the resolution of the tale. But this is often how episodic repetitions work: a sequence of more-or-less parallel episodes culminates in a final episode where it "all works out," where the tensions generated by the preceding episodes are resolved and their expectations gratified.

The Cinderella example points to an important ingredient of episodic repetition, namely, *pattern number*. In European and many other traditions, things happen in threes: three wishes, three obstacles, three magical helpers, and so on. The influence of the pattern number pervades not just our literature but also all aspects of our symbolic life, from sports (three strikes, three outs; the gold, silver, and bronze) to folk superstition ("third time's a charm," "three on a match," "disasters come in threes") to religion and poetry (the Trinity, Dante's *terza rima*), and all points in between.[15] Pattern numbers may be found in all the world's cultures, a predisposition that stems, perhaps, from a still more fundamental numeric capacity—part of our innate human cognitive endowment. After the manner of language itself, numbers provide human beings with an instrument for perceiving and controlling their world—for structuring and hence manipulating it. Indeed, the old Whorfian arguments concerning linguistic relativity and universalism may be just as apt (or just as overstated) where basic numerical perception is concerned.[16] But even though all cultures appear to possess a dominant pattern number, that number varies from culture to culture—that is, it is acquired through cultural transmission. In the Americas, fours and fives are more prevalent than threes, and this is true in Native California, too.

Examples of episodic repetition are everywhere in this volume. Myths like Ishi's "A Story of Lizard" (#10) and William Benson's "Creation" (#16) involve repetition at the macro level, with entire chapter-like structures repeated with either very minor or very major variation, respectively. Annie Burke's "The Trials of Young Hawk" (#17) is another story where episodic repetition forms a prominent feature of the narrative landscape. But really, this important rhetorical device is present at least in some measure, on large scales or small, in almost all the selections. Sometimes the patterns are played out in full, very strictly; other times, narrators choose merely to summarize some of the sequences. In this passage from Jo Bender's "Loon Woman" (#12, lines 52–89), the repeated episode begins with the mother's question about which brother to take for a companion and concludes with Loon Woman's rejection (or final acceptance) of the mother's suggestion:

Thinking of the man,
    "This morning I shall go west," so says that woman.
      "I want to take someone along to guide me.
"I am going to go," so she tells her mother.

"I am going to go west," so she says,
    thinking of the man, so she spoke.
"Hm," [her mother] says.

"Whom do you want to take with you?" she says.   *[first suggestion]*
She will not tell whom.

The old woman,
    "Well, surely take this little one, your younger brother."
Now that woman says,
    "I don't want to take him."

"Whom will you take with you?" so she says.   *[second suggestion]*
"I want to take another one with me."

"Take this one then."
"I won't," so said that woman.

She does this for a long time,   *[third and*
    she goes through them all.   *fourth suggestions,*
He-who-is-made-beautiful alone is left,   *conflated]*
    He-who-is-made-beautiful.
The little old woman sits,
    sits pondering it all, the old woman.

That woman measures that hair like that.
The hair of the rest does not match.
The one hair she had found is longer.

The old woman sits,
    sits pondering it all.
Suddenly,   *[fifth suggestion]*
    "Yes, surely take this one,"
      so she says,
        "He-who-is-made-beautiful,"
          her son.
"Yes," so she said.

The woman is happy she is going to take him along.
She measures the hair,

that hair matches.

"I'm going to take this one," she says.

From other evidence, the Wintu pattern number appears to be five, but here the full potential run of five episodic repetitions—four rejections capped by the final selection of He-who-is-made-beautiful—has, for one reason or another, been truncated in this telling.[17] (See Dell Hymes's introduction to the myth for a more detailed discussion of the numerical patterns operating in this complex narration.) As is often the case, the final episode here is considerably more elaborated than the lead-up episodes. In the hands of a skilled narrator like Jo Bender, episodic repetitions are far from mechanical.

For readers coming from a European or Europeanized background, pattern number is a common stumbling block.[18] Stories can seem repetitious simply because they are playing out a different pattern, a pattern based on fours or fives instead of threes. We are seldom consciously aware of the ways in which our sense of timing, of suspense and expectation, is in thrall to these deep-seated rhetorical patterns. Forewarned, though, readers can take an interest in looking for these cyclical patterns in myths and stories. Some of the translators have pointed out the presence of these patterns, where they are known or understood, in their introductions. Often, though, this aspect of linguistic structure hasn't even been studied yet for the narrative traditions in question. An astute reader may well spot rhetorical patterns in these translations that no one has yet described or documented.[19]

Another pattern, *formulaic repetition,* is found where a single phrase or line gets repeated several times, with or without slight variation. A typical example is this one from a Central Yana story I translated several years ago, called "Rolling Skull" (Luthin 1994). In the story this passage is taken from, Wildcat is up in a tree knocking pine cones down to his wife:

> He knocked one loose down to the east,
>   he knocked one loose down to the west,
>   he knocked one loose down to the north,
>   he knocked one loose down to the south.

Formulaic repetitions frequently involve an action repeated, as here, to each of the cardinal directions. The repetition suggests almost a ceremonial quality and often seems to mark the event it highlights as having special significance. (Here it foreshadows another action still to come, the real turning point in the story.) In part, this highlighting effect is a consequence of the simple, temporal "physics" of repetition itself: an action repeated twice formulaically is kept before the listener's consciousness twice as long; an action repeated four times, four times as long; and so on. The rhetorical device of repetition thus provides the narrator with a straightforward means of dwelling on the event in question—of slowing the action, and the story, down. However, it is not only strict formulaic repetitions that have this "lingering" effect.

Under the heading of *poetic repetition*—a rather loose and deliberately general term—come patterns of repetition that, through a variety of effects, seem especially to increase or enhance the linguistic resonance of the passages they adorn. In the "Loon Woman" passage cited previously, there's a great deal of such poetic repetition going on, even apart from the basic episodic patterns. Right at the outset, two lines, "Thinking of the man" and "This morning I shall go west," are repeated, but in reversed order—ab . . . ba—a simple chiasmus. A little later, the name "He-who-is-made-beautiful" is repeated, purely for the poetic and rhetorical effect of the echo. The next pair of lines, "The old woman sits, / sits pondering it all," is also repeated, with slight variations, the two occurrences separated only by the image of Loon Woman measuring the telltale hair—an image that is itself repeated at the end of the scene.

These repetitions serve to enrich the telling—phonetically, of course, since all these echoes make the language reverberate, but also in other ways. There is a cyclical, replay effect created by these repeated lines, as if the narrator were forcing us to linger in the scene by circling back through it again and again, visualizing and revisualizing key images, like the measuring of the hair, or the old woman sitting. It's a haunting, almost cinematic effect—though one that can be confusing to readers who aren't yet sensitized to the value of repetition in oral storytelling.

Akin to repetition, or a subset of it, is the literary device of *parallelism*. Although parallelism necessarily also involves some element of repetition, what I'm referring to here has more to do with iterated syntactic and semantic patterns than with exactly dittoed phrases or episodes. The emphasis is more on the variation than on the identity. This passage from Sally Noble's Chimariko story, "The Bear Girl" (#7), makes for a good illustration:

Her mother hired a good Indian doctor to ask
    what was the matter with the girl.
She was not like people.
She was not like our flesh.
She was not a person.
She was not a human woman.
She was going to turn out to be a bear.
That's what the matter was.

The parallelism of these four middle lines is straightforward, uncompli-
cated by other phenomena—in effect, a small litany. But things are not
always so clearly laid out. The following passage, taken from María Solares's telling of the Chumash "Dog Girl" (#22), is one of the most complex and richly ornamented passages in this collection:

As for the dog girl:
    she had a bracelet,
        a bracelet of fine beads;
    she had a necklace,
        a pendant,
            a pendant of *apɨ* beads,
                of *apɨ* beads;
        a nose stick;
        a basket hat;
    she had many ornaments.
Her hair was all fixed up in a braid wrap—
    she had braid wraps—
        and her apron,
            her apron was of otterskin.
His wife was well dressed,
    she was adorned.

Notice how much of all this sheer poetic repetition is contained and
organized within the framework of a single syntactic pattern—the template "she had _____" that introduces the various adornments in
the Dog Girl's possession. This syntactic frame leads internally to a run
of parallel object noun phrases in the sequence "she had a necklace, /
a pendant . . . / a nose stick; / a basket hat." Though some storytellers
and stylistic traditions employ more of this type of parallelism than

others, there are numerous examples to be found in this volume's selections.

Finally, in this same "Dog Girl" passage, there's another pattern, *incremental repetition,* that has been exploited here by María Solares three separate times. First, "she had a bracelet, / a bracelet of fine beads"; then, "a pendant, / a pendant of *apɨ* beads"; and lastly, "and her apron, / her apron was of otterskin." Each of these repetitions takes the incremental form "X / X + Y," where the second line of the pair repeats the key element of the first and expands it with additional detail. Incremental repetition is a common feature of oral storytelling, and, along with formulaic repetitions, is often found in song as well. (For a more extended discussion of song aesthetics, see the "Notes on Native California Oral Literatures.")

I have tried to be indicative, rather than exhaustive, in this thumbnail sketch of repetition and parallelism in oral poetics. Certainly, there's no single function that repetitions and parallelisms serve. But with close attention and a bit of literary sensibility—a feel for rhythm, scene, and poetry—the careful reader can probably figure out some of the dramatic and rhetorical effects that the narrators are striving for in their performances. Suffice it to say that oral poetics can indeed be extremely intricate and that repetition is an important device in the narrator's toolkit.

As to why this might be so, why repetition, parallelism, and numerical patterning are so pervasive in oral literatures the world over, there is no simple, single reason. Their prevalence stymied nineteenth-century critics of Native American song and narrative, who typically saw these elements as signs of "primitivism" and inferiority. Even pioneering early-twentieth-century critics like Nellie Barnes lacked a sufficiently sophisticated theory of poetics to see them properly. It wasn't really until the 1950s, with Alfred Lord's work on the oral composition of epic poetry (*The Singer of Tales,* 1960), later augmented by developments in performance theory and ethnopoetics led by Hymes and others, that we have finally come to appreciate the significance of these devices, to understand their dynamic role in the process of oral composition itself.[20] For clearly one of the key functions of repetition, especially when abetted by numerical patterning, is to assist narrators in maintaining the structure of their compositions, in terms of both storage in memory and delivery in performance. This is most obviously true of the larger-scale episodic patterns, where the coarse mechanics of plot sequencing come into play, but scholars are increasingly amazed at how fine-grained the rhetorical patterns of oral composition really are. At least some of the smaller-scale repetitions—the poetic and formulaic repetitions, the syntactic parallelisms—may actually be motivated by subtle structural patterns operating at considerably more local levels, in keeping with what Hymes has called *measured verse*.[21] This possibility, though, does not diminish the other roles that repetition plays—in controlling flow, in heightening dramatic effect, in highlighting actions, and in elevating the sheer poetic resonance of the narrative language. Is it art or architecture? Improvisation or design? Poetry or technique? At some point, in the hands of a skilled narrator, the question becomes one of the chicken or the egg. Repetition and parallelism add dimensions of both beauty and intricacy to the performance of verbal art.

Motivation and Characterization

Motives for behavior are often taken for granted, because they are obvious within the culture. After all, when Jack grabs the golden goose and hightails it out the door, the story doesn't stop to explain why he does so. A European audience already knows it's because gold is valuable in that society; the audience shares the ever-present dream of getting rich. The same is true in Native American stories: storytellers don't bother to explain what is plainly understood by all. In fact, when we encounter stories that *do* provide this kind of explanatory information, it can sometimes be a clue that the story was performed in front of a mixed or nonnative audience, or before native listeners who weren't raised traditionally—or even before a solitary linguist.

One of the purposes of providing an introductory essay for each story is to anticipate such confusions and fill in some of the cultural gaps. Sometimes even the storytellers themselves try to do this. Loren Bommelyn added the opening section of his Tolowa story, "Test-ch'as (The Tidal Wave)" (#2), to remind people what precipitated the events he tells about. Over the phone one day, as we were talking through details of his translation, Loren suddenly realized I had been misinterpreting a key passage of dialogue. As a result, he decided to back the story up a bit, in order to frame the myth more formally. Apparently, the old-time narrators Loren learned it from, counting on other Tolowas' familiarity with the myth, picked up the storyline a bit further along, beginning in medias res. But now, thanks to his additions, we can know what happened: the improper behavior of some partying villagers triggered a cataclysmic imbalance of nature, in the form of an earthquake and tidal wave. The arrival of the widow, who should have been in mourning, was the last straw, scandalizing even the dog.

So characterization is often assumed, or "referred to," rather than being explicitly developed as it would be in a novel. Where traditional myths and stories are concerned, the audiences by and large already know what happens and are well acquainted with the quirks and motives of the characters taking part in them—a factor that gives narrators a great deal of latitude in shaping their performances. One consequence of stories being so familiar and oft-told is that characters can seem to behave as they do simply because they are destined to do so, being eternally in the process of acting out the events of the story they are in. Often they seem to have an eerie foreknowledge of their own fates, as if they already "knew their own stories." This quality probably stems from the nature of oral literature itself.

In the end, the stories and songs are just the tip of the iceberg. Many songs are specific to certain dances or ceremonies, performed only at the appropriate point of that one ceremony, whenever it might be held in the annual cycle. And storytelling, particularly of myths, is typically restricted by general cultural prohibition to certain seasons of the year—the rainy winter months in most California cultures. But there is a kind of running, ethnocritical discussion that's carried on by the people in the culture at large—a whole metaliterary conversation—that constantly explores and reexplores the themes of its great stories and the meanings that are to be taken from them. Oral storytellers draw and depend on this ongoing conversation at least as much as they contribute to it.

So human is this tendency to dwell on and in our stories, that it is even possible, with faith, imagination, and hard work, to revive that conversation once the flame has gone out. Ohlone culture, its language and oral literature along with it, was an early casualty of the Contact period in California. Its stories now are known only through the archived fieldnotes of collector J. P. Harrington and a handful of others. Linda Yamane, a Rumsien Ohlone artist, storyteller, and writer living in the Bay Area, speaks movingly about how those scratchy pages have begun to come alive for her, enriching not just her perceptions of nature, but her sense of place in the universe:[22]

Finding these stories has changed the way I see the world. I can see it like a picture in my mind . . . [N]ow when I go hiking and see Crow, it's not just a crow, it's Crow person from the story, who did these things from our history. It's the same with Hawk—it's not a hawk from a natural history field guide, but Hawk, who with Eagle's help planted the feather in the earth at the bottom of the floodwaters, causing the waters to recede. I recently saw Golden Eagle for the first time, very close up, near my ancestral village site. I could see Eagle and it was just how I pictured him saving the world. The same with Hummingbird, it's all a part of our history.

It's a connection to the ancestors and to this place, to this land where I live and where my ancestors lived. In the course of the work I have been doing [with Harrington's fieldnotes], what feels most important to me is that these stories can now be out in the world for other Ohlone people, so that they can have the same experience. It strengthens our sense of cultural community. . . .

I think in a similar way the stories help non-Indians[, too]. It's not exactly the same, because there is not the ancestral connection, but it's similar in that the stories can help people to feel more connected to the place where they live. Feeling more connected to a place gives them a better understanding—not just a mental understanding, but an emotional understanding. An emotional understanding and connection helps people to feel they are more a part of things and to care for a place. It's easier not to care when you don't have a connection to a place.

In the final analysis, stories must have a place in people's hearts and minds, not just on their lips or in the pages of their books, to be truly part of a living tradition.

Stories are always more than just entertainment. Much of the conscience and philosophy of a culture is expressed, either directly or indirectly, in the myths of its people. It's no different than with the stories and characters of the Bible, the Koran, the Torah: if you are a Christian or a Muslim or a Jew, you have probably *heard* much more about the central events and characters—about Joseph or Mary Magdalen, Adaam or Gibreel, Eve or Noah, their thoughts, their feelings—than is written in the pages of the holy books themselves. Almost anyone raised in a Christian, Islamic, or Jewish culture could provide a more embellished account of the Flood than is actually given in Genesis. The same is true of aspects in Hindu tradition, or any other. No matter how rich the literary canon of a culture may be, the oral tradition that it grew out of, and that embeds it still, is richer by far. And the oral tradition surrounding an oral-literary canon is no different than that of a literary one in this respect.

As you read the translations in this book, then, remember: these are *traditional* songs and stories, most of them, heard time and time again in the course of a lifetime. Except when visitors from afar might be invited to give a telling in the roundhouse or sweat lodge (or in later days, around the kitchen table at home), most traditional stories were not new to their audiences, only newly told. And everybody—except for children, to whom everything is new, and for those readers encountering Indian stories here for the first time—everybody already *knows* what's going to happen, and who does what, and why.

The people these stories were originally intended for were wholly immersed in their world, at home with their own traditions. Readers should not figure they can play catch-up with California cultures—not really, anyway, and maybe not ever.[23] Even cultural outsiders, though, can listen in on the songs and stories as they are translated here—enjoy them and learn from them. The introductions will help readers through the roughest patches, and the notes on suggested readings will carry them further where problems nag or an interest is kindled. In the meantime, Jaime de Angulo's trademark advice to *his* readers may prove indispensable: "When you find yourself searching for some mechanical explanation, if you don't know the answer, invent one. When you pick out some inconsistency or marvelous improbability, satisfy your curiosity like the old Indian folk: 'Well, that's the way they tell that story. I didn't make it up myself!'" Sure, he's being a *bit* disingenuous. After reflection, you will want to know if your guess, the sense you have made of something puzzling, was on the mark. When that happens, you suddenly find yourself right back where you started from—but with one important difference: while you were pondering, you moved on. Keep reading, and after a while, you'll start to get the hang of it. And then, bit by bit, these worlds of song and story will open up for you.

1. Actually, good storytellers often don't have the patience for the work of analysis and translation that comes after the dictation is finished; in such cases, the collector usually works with a friend or relative of the narrator to make the translation.

2. Certainly this is true, in this volume, of Villiana Hyde's collaboration with Eric Elliott, from which is drawn her "Harvest of Songs" (#24). Indeed, we have finally reached a milestone stage of development—long overdue—in California, where some performers (Julian Lang and Loren Bommelyn spring to mind) have begun to translate themselves.

3. In Sapir's early Americanist orthography, *c* and *j* represent "sh" and "zh" sounds, respectively; the ^ε represents a glottal stop; a *!* (exclamation mark) glottalizes the preceding stop or affricate; and the ' (open single quote) indicates aspiration. Both macron and circumflex indicate vowel length, and superscript vowels are "whispered."

With the exception of the first two lines, all the narrative verbs in this excerpt contain a quotative suffix, "they say" or "it is said." This element has been translated only in those lines where it appears to receive a special emphasis.

4. In later years, when typesetting costs began to chip away at the budgets of publication series like the *UCPAAE* and others, editors switched to another design format, that of facing pages. This format became the standard for subsequent text series, like *UCPAAE*'s successor, UCPL. In consequence, the translation portion was constrained to become much more literal, because the loss of the interlinear element of the old-style format meant that the single, facing-page translation now became the only avenue to an accurate interpretation of the original. The result was the rise of a series of purely technical publications that were drastically less accessible and appealing to the casual reader or the student of literature than the interlinear publications of old (not that the latter were not technical and arcane-looking as well). Their volumes now contained only linguistic translations, not literary ones, despite the best efforts of most authors to serve both masters. As William Shipley says in the introduction to his 1963 *Maidu Texts and Dictionary* (UCPL 33), "Although I have done my best to practice the art of translation, . . . I have subordinated such efforts to my responsibility as a linguist—to the providing of a key for the forms of the original" (8). In the end, the need for utmost fidelity toward the source language will always outweigh considerations of aesthetics and felicity in the target language—and rightly so, where that choice must be made. But a price is always paid.

5. Indeed, some have claimed (Hymes 1981, Tedlock 1983) that such translations can actually impede our understanding of Native American songs and stories as works of verbal art.

6. Hymes argues this case very strongly in his book *'In vain I tried to tell you': Essays in Native American Ethnopoetics* (1981), as does Tedlock in *The Spoken Word and the Work of Interpretation* (1983), though the two writers come at the problem from very different directions. There are several important anthologies of ethnopoetic writings and translations: Brian Swann's *On the Translation of Native American Literatures* (1992) and *Smoothing the Ground: Essays in Native American Oral Literature* (1983), Swann and Arnold Krupat's *Recovering the Word: Essays on Native American Literature* (1987), Karl Kroeber's *Traditional American Indian Literatures: Texts and Interpretations* (1981), and Joel Sherzer and Anthony Woodbury's *Native American Discourse: Poetics and Rhetoric* (1987).

7. In short, the literary value of a text is inextricably intertwined with its formal poetic structure, which is in turn intertwined with the circumstances of its performance. Any treatment of a song or story that does not begin with the recognition that it is a work of verbal art, and does not recognize the effect of performance dynamics on form, and does not try in some way to reflect performance features in terms of presentational form, is bound to misrepresent the text on those levels.

8. Both these units, and many of the others besides, exemplify a common American Indian rhetorical pattern that Dell Hymes (1977) refers to abstractly as "Onset—Ongoing—Outcome." In group 5, the plucking is the Onset (it's the action that pushes Grizzly Bear over the edge), the biting is the Ongoing (the action of the group as a whole, seen in progress), and the killing is the Outcome. Such rhetorical "templates" help oral performers structure their compositions.

9. Dell Hymes's hypothesis (1981) that the world's oral-literary traditions tend to prefer rhetorical patterns based on groupings of threes and fives, for some, and twos and fours, for others, has been tested many times by many different scholars (for instance, Bright 1982 and Kinkade 1987). The evidence for Yana, to my mind, is somewhat ambiguous, though a tendency toward threes and fives (as in the passages under discussion here) is frequently apparent.

10. However, Luthin (1991) presents a methodology for recovering or reconstructing at least some live prosodic information from dictated texts.

11. Different practitioners have different criteria for defining lines, so this statement is meant to be a general one. Tedlock, for instance, typically works with a pause-based line defined by silence, whereas Hymes works with a syntactically based line defined largely by clause boundary. Others (Woodbury 1987, McLendon 1982) work with intonationally defined lines. Woodbury (1987) points out that all three of these phenomena (and others besides) are in fact interlocking components of a language's overall rhetorical system and that any ethnopoetic analysis of a text that does not take all such aspects into account is bound to be inadequate.

12. In the case of ethnopoetic analyses done on texts taken down by phonetic dictation, the lines are technically only reconstructions of what the actual lines of the original performance must have been, based on syntactic and structural clues such as repetition, particle placement, and the like.

13. For an extended discussion of some of the parameters of this disagreement and of the development of the ethnopoetics movement in general, see my *Restoring the Voice in Yanan Traditional Narrative* (1991).

14. We are not used to seeing genuine spoken language in print. Most interviews in books and magazines are either heavily edited or are given by people—politicians, actors, novelists, academics—who are professional writers or speakers themselves, whose speech is very "written" to begin with. Of course, storytellers are professional talkers, too, but their craft is entirely an oral one, not channeled into written grooves.

15. It's not that we don't have other significant numbers—sevens, fours, fives, twos, tens, and dozens all have roles to play in Western symbolism. It's just that the number three has premier cultural dominance; other numbers are subordinate to it.

16. I refer here to the dialectic between the Chomskyan theory of linguistic universalism and the earlier theory of linguistic relativity, also known as the "Sapir-Whorf Hypothesis"—surely two of the most exciting intellectual conjectures in the history of human thought, even given the ultimate failure of relativity in its strong form.

17. Our long-standing literary tradition has made us fairly impatient with full-blown episodic repetition, and there is a strong tendency in written literature for the second and third episodes in a sequence to be progressively truncated or even dropped entirely. The example here shows that the same thing can happen in oral performance. But whether the choice to do so stems from an intrinsic impatience (perhaps the mood of the storyteller or the attentiveness of the audience controls this) or marks a concession to presumed European narrative tastes (linguists and anthropologists must often seem to Native storytellers to be glancing at their watches—and they even pay hourly rates!), it is difficult to know.

18. More precisely, what we're talking about here is *global form/content parallelism,* in current ethnopoetic terminology (see Hymes 1981 and Sherzer and Woodbury 1987 for further discussions of this and related concepts).

19. Keep in mind, though, that you're just dealing with translations in this volume; if you really think you are on to something, the only ultimate arbiter is the original-language text.

20. These in turn built on Propp's earlier codification of episodic and motif patterning, *Morphology of the Folktale* (1968 [1928]).

21. The best single source for treatment of this notion is Hymes's *'In vain I*

tried to tell you': Essays in Native American Ethnopoetics (1981). Sherzer and Woodbury's *Native American Discourse: Poetics and Rhetoric* (1987) makes a good source as well.

22. Linda Yamane, quoted in excerpt from Lauren S. Teixeira, "Like the Air We Breathe," *News from Native California* 9.4 (1995): 50.

23. As Bill Bevis (1974) has rather famously said, "We won't get Indian culture as cheaply as we got Manhattan."

— Shows the belief in a →
deity.
A super power above
all creations.

I

SELECTIONS

Who is tending this sun, [this] moon?
Who moves them around?
There must be somebody to look after this world . . .

Nisenan prayer
Ralph Beals, "Ethnology of the Nisenan"

CREATION SONGS

1 A

Deserted it was,
Deserted it was,
Deserted, the earth.

First they appeared,
First they came out,

First Mukat,
First Tamayowet,

First the chiefs,
First the ancients.

1 B

His heart roared,
His heart thundered,
Water and mud roared.

Then outside, toward the door,
Themselves they lay down,
Mukat outside,
Tamayowet then,
Themselves they lay down:

Where it was bare, where it was lonely,
Themselves they laid down,
Where dust was, where mist was.

Cupeño song, Salvadora Valenzuela, 1920
Paul Faye, collector

[handwritten annotations:] Animals created first. Rankings. Men created later.

Animals

There, they existed with no problems or preocupation.

1

Kwaw Labors to Form a World

ATSUGEWI
1996

DARRYL BABE WILSON

creation story.

It is said by the old ones that a thought was floating in the vastness. Thought manifested itself into a voice. Voice matured into Yeja, an everlasting medicine song. Song sang itself into being as Kwaw, Silver Gray Fox. By continuing the song, Kwaw created all that we know. He sang the universe into being. His singing spawned Reason, but not sufficiently, so we shall never know all that moves within this universe.

It was Song, infusing itself with both beauty and power, that caused the outer world to tremble and the inner world to quake, and instructed the stars to become one with the vastness and the vastness to become one with the stars.

The "new" universe created a new kind of emptiness, within which Kwaw grew lonesome—wanting somebody to talk with. Laboring over what to do with so much nothingness, he decided to make another being, much like himself. Some haste on Kwaw's part caused that being to be created with a defect: vanity. That being came to my people as Ma'kat'da, Old Coyote.

Kwaw instructed Ma'kat'da to sleep while he busied himself with making "something shiny." Kwaw sang for a million years or more, and in the distance something shiny appeared, a mist. Mist contained no voice and no song, but it possessed a magic.

Kwaw kicked Ma'kat'da awake, showing him the shiny mist. They sang together and Mist moved ever to them. It approached silently, like a soap bubble on a summer afternoon, floating upon the breeze. Kwaw caught it in his hands and it rested there. Ma'kat'da thought that Kwaw could not possibly know what to do with Mist, so he grabbed for it. There was a struggle. In the conflict, Kwaw dropped the mist. Ma'kat'da and Kwaw wrestled over the possession of Mist for eons. Meanwhile, Mist dropped slowly down, ever down. And, just before Mist struck Nothingness, Kwaw broke free from Ma'kat'da, reached under it, and gently nudged it back into the safety of his hands.

Here, then, if there ever was one, is "the beginning," according to the keepers of our ancestral knowledge. For it was from the birth of the mist sung into being that all of the stars and moons of the universe were created; earth, also. Our earth, they say, is an infant, being fulfilled after all of the rest of the universe.

It is said that Mist took on substance, forming into something much more solid. It became more pliable, like bread dough, and they kneaded it and stretched it as they sang and danced. They danced harder and fragments separated from the mist-gel and moved out in a vast circle, tumbling ever away. These became the stars and the Milky Way.

Kwaw labored to form a world. But everything he created, Ma'kat'da changed. Vanity caused Ma'kat'da to think that he knew best. Kwaw created, Ma'kat'da changed. Then Ma'kat'da grew angry because all he could accomplish was "change." He became destructive.

Seeing that he could not teach Ma'kat'da, Kwaw decided to remove himself. He entered his *chema-ha,* his sweat lodge, lifted the center post, and dropped down through into this world, carefully replacing the center post so Ma'kat'da would not see where it was disturbed. When he arrived here, there was only water. Kwaw sang land into being, then sang a *chema-ha* to rest upon the land. He created himself a fresh home upon new earth—with no Ma'kat'da!

Then Kwaw set about making the world as we know it today, thinking that Ma'kat'da would be satisfied with the world beyond the sky and would never come to this one. He made all that we know: the geese and salmon, the mornings and the mountains, the rivers and streams, the seasons and the songs of all the birds. He made it wonderful and, it is said, he made it good.

Ma'kat'da searched for Kwaw in the world beyond the sky and could not find him. So Ma'kat'da, whose best power is fire, found a little basket in Kwaw's abandoned *chema-ha* and threatened it with cremation if it did not tell. Little Willow Basket, not wanting to perish in flames, said, "He went through there," pointing to the center post of the *chema-ha*. So Ma'kat'da, employing his own magic, came to this world like Kwaw after all . . .

This explanation came to me through Ramsey Bone Blake, who received it from White Horse Bob. White Horse Bob was given the song that Kwaw sang upon the inception of Life. The song was his *damagoomi,* his spirit helper. Ramsey couldn't remember the whole song, but often recalled fragments of it. However, he was not allowed to sing it, for the song already belonged to White Horse Bob.

Within this magic my people dwelled just a short time ago. More recently, our home has become the legal possession of strangers. We have been restricted from approaching our places of power and spirit. We have become mute witnesses while others despoil the air, the land, the wildlife, the rivers, and the ocean waters. It is said that Kwaw created this world for original native people, not for wanderers. But it is the wanderers who have brought a different rule, saying that our ancient laws are of no value.

This may be one of the reasons why we are in a spiritual quandary: not knowing how to become a functioning part of the invading American society, not remembering how to sustain a strict connection with the "knowing" that is our origin—and trembling in the presence of both.

With these thoughts in mind, then, proceed through the following "lesson-legends" realizing that it was not long ago that there was great magic in the land of my people—of all our Native people. That there was a wonder in the patterns of everyday life, and that there was much singing and dancing. For these were our instructions when the earth began turning around the sun, and the sun began moving with the universe, to a destination that may never be known to any of us but Kwaw.

NORTHWESTERN CALIFORNIA

You come upon a place you've never seen before,
and it has awesome beauty.
Everything above you,
    below you,
        and around you is so pure—

    that is the beauty we call *merwerksergerh,*
    and the pure person is also *merwerksergerh.*

                Yurok, Florence Shaughnessy, at Requa
                Peter Matthiessen, "Stop the GO Road"

Why is the water rough,
  by Rekʼʷoy at the river mouth?
Why is the water rough,
  by Rekʼʷoy at the river mouth?

By Rekʼʷoy at the river mouth,
  that is why they watch it,
    by Rekʼʷoy at the river mouth.
Near the houses the surf runs further up,
  by Rekʼʷoy at the river mouth.

Why is the water rough,
  by Rekʼʷoy at the river mouth?
Near the houses the surf runs further up,
  by Rekʼʷoy at the river mouth.

Why is the water rough,
  by Rekʼʷoy at the river mouth?
Near the houses the waves break further up,
    by Rekʼʷoy at the river mouth.

High in the air by Rekʼʷoy,
  that is why they watch it,
    by Rekʼʷoy at the river mouth.
Near the houses the surf runs further up,
    by Rekʼʷoy at the river mouth.

Why is the water rough,
  by Rekʼʷoy at the river mouth?
Near the houses the waves break further up,
  by Rekʼʷoy at the river mouth.

Yurok doctor dance song
R. H. Robins and Norma McCloud
"Five Yurok Songs: A Musical and Textual Analysis"

2

Test-ch'as (The Tidal Wave)

TOLOWA
1985

LOREN BOMMELYN, AUTHOR AND TRANSLATOR

INTRODUCTION BY LOREN BOMMELYN

The Tolowa are a Pacific Coast Athabascan-speaking people of Northern California and Southern Oregon. Their terrain is heavily wooded with climax redwood and Douglas fir forests and accustomed to heavy rainfall. The rivers of the past were choked with trout, steelhead, and several species of salmon. The ocean provided whale, sea lion, and innumerable species of fish. The coastal tide-pools produced a rich diversity of crustacea and bivalves. The land, too, yielded its plenty: the annual harvest of fruits, nuts, and herbs. The control-burned forests and prairies of the hills ran with great herds of elk and deer. And the skies were blackened with hundreds of thousands of fowl from the Pacific flyway.

The rich food supply afforded the Tolowa a heavy population and encouraged the development of high customs, elaborate protocol, and a complex legal system. They built their homes from hand-split and hand-hewed redwood planks. The Tolowa seagoing canoes were famous up and down the coast. Their exogamous marriage customs resulted in a multilingual society with a diverse system of religious practices. The Headmen controlled and protected their village districts, where dentalia currency ranked supreme in deciding all legal matters—torts, damages, marriages, and all the rest of it. These men were responsible for implementing and carrying out the high ceremonies surrounding our foremost responsibility: for men and women alike to walk in balance with creation.

But the life of the Tolowa changed forever in the 1850s with the arrival of the Europeans. Their rapacious passions and disease destroyed the Tolowa and their neighbors. Thousands of people perished. The Europeans pushed and drove the Tolowa population into two separate concentration camps, one at Siletz, Oregon, and the other at Hoopa, California. The Tututni and Chetco people are our northern divisions. The residual population—of no more than two hundred individuals who escaped the camps and returned to their homeland—established the basis for the current Tolowa population. Out of this painful past the Tolowa have survived. My great-grandparents survived the seven-year holocaust that began in 1853. Their children were born at the end of the nineteenth century, their children's children (my parents) in the 1920s and 1930s. I was born in 1956.

Aunt Laura was nineteen years older than my mother and served as my grandma. Auntie and Mom did everything together. The annual food cycles followed one after another. First was the spring routine of gardening, seaweed drying, beef fattening, and salmonberry and thimbleberry picking. Next was the summer routine of smelt drying, clamming, strawberry and blackberry picking, and peach, apricot, and pear canning. And last came the fall routine of acorn and herb gathering, the making of deer jerky, huckleberry picking, and the netting of steelhead and Chinook salmon. Every day after school, we would run down to Auntie's house. She fed us, and we played continental rummy and cribbage. Then Auntie would tell us stories. I could envision how our village looked during her youth. I could see how our village looked when Grandma Alice was young and when Great-grandma Deliliah was alive. Many times it would get dark, and we would sleep at Auntie's.

The fall nights were gillnet-setting time. The State of California had long since illegalized our livelihood, but this made no difference to us. "Paddle quietly. Never smoke out on the water: the game warden can see the red cherry from a long way off. Wear a sweatshirt: the buttons of a shirt will hang up in the net and drown you. Club the fish with a quiet sock to the head." No one could gut and fillet a salmon with the skill and finesse that Auntie and Mom had. Each salmon was carefully washed and scaled. The stomach was split open exactly, and the entrails and black blood removed with precision. The salmon's head and fins were removed, and then it was filleted. They stripped the fillets with care. Each jar was packed to perfection. They hung long strips of salmon in the smoke-house. A small, cool alder-wood fire sent the curing smoke wafting through the salmon strips. My favorite dish at fish-cleaning time was salmon-head and egg chowder.

The winter rains of Del Norte County were extremely marked during my youth. The rain would pelt out of the skies for ten days and nights from its high ceilings, while powerful winds and clouds cloaked the coastal plain. These winds pounded the top of Milichundun Mountain across the Smith River from our home place, Nelechundun. The air was warm and magical, astir and wild. Back in the eastern mountains at the headwaters of the river, the annual rainfall could reach twelve feet at Bear Basin Summit. These rains would send us scurrying over mountains, through redwood forests, fields, and the riparian habitats of the river and estuaries. Soaked to the bone, we panted, cheeks flushed and red, lost in time, lost to the eternity of our ancestors. Aunt Laura counted the days of rain and the swift slapping waves of the river to predict if it would flood.

"Gee, maybe we'll have the Great Flood again," she might say. "One time the people began to go against the laws of the Creator. That was the time when Dog spoke to the people. This is why in Grandma Deli-liah's time you did not talk to dogs. If they were to answer you, the world might come to an end." You see, a dog speaking to humans is an indi-cation of catastrophic destruction. A few years ago, someone had recorded the Christmas carol "Jingle Bells" with a dog barking out the tune of the song. The radio station owner, Bill Stamps, played it over the air. Ella Norris, one of our elders, called him up and chewed him out. "What are you trying to do, make the world come to an end?" (This belief had changed in my family during Grandpa Billie Henry's time, though. He and Grandma Alice always used to "dog talk" with the dogs. And we still "dog talk" with our own dogs today.)

The following account of Test-ch'as is an illustration of the powerful ethical values of the traditional Tolowa. The outside pressures of modern American socialization and religions are eroding these values. But the traditionalists have a strong sense of what living right means. "If you can't do it right, don't do it!" Each activity of daily life is presided over by the "One Who Watches Over Us." At the time of our genesis, K'wan'-lee-shvm laid out the universe and the laws we are to live by. To live correctly brings us blessings. To live outside these laws is to invite strife and trouble into one's life. The Test-ch'as account is a testimony and a warning to us of what happens when we fall outside the balance of the universe.[1]

The Test-ch'as account is a template of inspiration and replenishment. From the nearly complete annihilation of the Tolowas from the face of the earth during the 1850s, our population has now reached more than one thousand members. It has happened again as it did in Test-ch'as: that a man and his wife live together.

NOTES

1. The opening section of this story, set in italics, comes from a different version of the myth than that on which the rest of the translation is based. Because the main version of the story presented here begins with the disaster itself, leaving the "why" unspoken, Bommelyn added this scene onto the beginning to explain the events that precipitated the disaster.

The Tolowa place-name *Enmai* ('Big Mountain'; rhymes with "Hen-my") corresponds to the peak known as Mount Emily on maps of the region. ("Emily" is an Anglicization of the original Tolowa form.) The word *Chit-dvn* is pronounced "Cheat-done."— HWL

FURTHER READING

Philip Drucker produced an excellent ethnography of the Tolowa, *The Tolowa and Their Southwest Oregon Kin*. Richard Gould's article,

"Tolowa," in the California volume of the Smithsonian *Handbook* presents a useful summary. Jack Norton's *Genocide in Northwestern California* provides information on how the Tolowa fared in the post-Contact period. Bommelyn has two books of language-teaching materials, *Now You're Speaking Tolowa*, and *Xus We-Yo': Tolowa Language* (with Berneice Humphrey). (The latter contains the glossed Tolowa-language version of the story translated here.) Allogan Slagle's article, "The Native American Tradition and Legal Status: Tolowa Tales and Tolowa Places," explores the legal standing of territorial references contained in traditional tales. Finally, Bommelyn may be heard singing Tolowa songs on a recording made by Charlotte Heth, *Songs of Love, Luck, Animals, and Magic.*

TEST-CH'AS (THE TIDAL WAVE)

At Chit-dvn Village, all the young men and young women, they were partying there, at the center of town. At dusk they had partied. One alone of all of them told his sister, "Our grandmother teaches us, 'Don't you go outside at dusk.'"

A widow also joined with them, then. She, too, started laughing around with them there.

Truthfully, then, a dog sat up and spoke out loud: "You all will see what's going to happen!"

The young man and the young woman, they ran to their home.

"Gram! A dog has spoken here!"

"I knew it was going to happen this way," their grandmother said. "You two go to Mount Enmai now. Grab some dentalia, and a smelt net also. To Enmai you must go—quickly, both of you! Wait for no one."

"Gram, what are you going to do?"

"I am old. I am going to die. You must go quickly now, both of you . . ."

It was during the fall when the ground shook. Twice the ground had shaken.

"Well now! Something bad is going to happen. You had better go look now," the man said.

Then the ground shook again.

"You two run to the beach," he told the boys. "You two paddle the boat out to sea. Should the boat run aground on the sand, the ocean tidal wave will come that way. If it happens like that, you two return again quickly to this side. Then we will know what is going to happen."

The ocean was extremely smooth. Not a bit of wind blew. When those two paddled toward the beach, it happened just that way.

"We ran ashore almost to the sand," they said.

Then they put all the canoes in a safe place. Then the ground shook again.

"If it shakes the ground from east and west, the ocean will rise up."

Then the ground shook from the west. Everything standing on the ground fell over. The water began to rise in the rivers. The river ran over its banks.

One teenage girl amongst them was having her time of the month. With her brother, she ran up into the mountains. They kept looking behind them as they were running. As they ran, the ocean nearly caught them. Everything that lived there turned into snakes. The snakes all slithered into the ocean.

These two people ran up on top of a ridge. The water, rising up in a tide, nearly ran them over. Everyone who lived upon the earth ran toward the mountains. The water, too, rose up the mountain from the east—all the rivers were running over, is why. Everything alive was floating alongside the mountain. When the water ran over them, they all turned into snakes.

"Let's run along the ridge now," he told his sister.

Then they ran to the top of Mount Enmai, and saw that the water had flooded over the Earth. Then all this water began to boil.

When the water had run almost over the top of Mount Enmai, the boy told his sister, "Stick your nose ornament into the ground. The water will rise up no further than there."

Then she stuck her flicker feather in the ground. Really, the water rose up no further! The young man built a fire. Then all who did not drown stood on the mountaintop. The Eastern people, the Western people, all perished.

Everywhere the fog came in. Nowhere could land be seen. All night they could not sleep. All night they kept the fire going. When it was morning everywhere, they looked around. Only mountaintops were sticking out of the water. Mount Enmai's peak floated southward. These two stayed there ten nights.

All those dangerous ones who live in the forest, they, too, were standing on Mount Enmai's peak. All of them were afraid—they didn't want to go down to the foot of the mountain. Ten days passed by. The young man went to the foot of the mountain.

When he returned, he told his sister, "Many large creatures and small creatures are lying around everywhere."

The ocean had left them there.

"You and I will go down the mountain."

His sister told him, "All right."

They descended to the valley. The girl was afraid, until her brother told her, "Nothing will harm you. All of them everywhere are lying dead. Do not be afraid of it. Let's seek out our home."

When those two found their way back there, everything was nothing there. Their house was also gone. Everywhere only sand was lying. They recognized nothing. There, where they used to live, there was nothing. Everywhere they went, the dead ones had started to stink.

"Where will we live?" one asked. The other said, "Anywhere we live is going to be good."

Then this teenager told his sister, "You sit here. Wait for me. I am going to the bottom to see what I can see. Perhaps some people are living there."

Before he went, he prepared food. He took it there to a safe place. They found a piece of fresh whale tail. The whale meat was cut up for drying.

"This meat will be good for you," he said.

Then the young man walked to the south. He looked for people everywhere. As he was walking, he saw only dead ones. He walked far into the south. He saw not a soul still alive. Then he walked to the east. He walked all night and all day. He saw only small lakes. Then the lakes became a gully in there. In the east, he walked along the border of his land. There, also, he found not a soul alive. He also saw no deer tracks. He walked far to the north there. He saw coyote tracks there.

Then he thought, "I suppose another mountain poked out. Different people must still be alive. It will be good if I see some people."

He saw nothing. Then he walked to the beach. The beach was covered only with sand. As he walked southward, nothing stood. Not a fir tree stood. Finally he found one tree, a crabapple. It alone had not become a snake when the ocean washed over it. Then again he walked southward. He had walked almost to his home when the ocean began to look like blood.

Finally, he returned there to where his sister was living. He told her, "Nowhere did I see a man. Everywhere all of them were drowned, I suppose. I walked ten days and ten nights. I walked continually. All the water running down is not good. On the tenth night I thought, 'I wanted to find a man alive for you to marry. Also, I wanted to find a woman alive for me to marry. That is the reason I walked over the whole earth.' So let us marry each other. There is no one else anywhere still alive for us to marry."

They dug a round depression in the ground for a house. There they lived, those two, together.

In time she gave birth to a son.

"We shall make a better house. Let's go down to the beach," the man said.

Something was floating out on the ocean. All day they watched it. When it was about sunset they could still see it. Then they went together to their house.

"Let us look again," the man said.

When it was growing daylight outside, they went together. Really, there was a redwood log there! They went together to the edge of the shore. There were whale ribs and body bones piled there.

"Let's split the log," the man said.

They split the log into boards with the whale bones. They pounded the wedges with rocks. They made many planks. They packed the boards to the bank. There they built a house, a good one.

One day, he dipped for smelts there. Another woman came paddling along from the south in a canoe. They too married.

When again another year had passed, the head wife gave birth to another one. She gave birth to a girl child. When these two in turn became man and woman, they married. When it happened again and again this way, there came to be a great number of people. They scattered all over, everywhere. In every place, all the men lived together with their wives.

3

"The Young Man from Serper" and Other Stories

YUROK
1951, 1985–1988

FLORENCE SHAUGHNESSY, NARRATOR

R. H. ROBINS, COLLECTOR AND TRANSLATOR

JEAN PERRY, COLLECTOR

INTRODUCTION BY JEAN PERRY

These three stories come from the Yurok Indians, who still inhabit their ancestral homeland along the lower forty miles of the Klamath River and the surrounding coastline in Northwest California, near the Oregon border. Here they continue to harvest salmon, eels, and winter steelhead, to hunt deer and elk, and to follow many of the old lifeways and traditions along with other more modern pursuits.

All of these stories were told by Mrs. Florence Shaughnessy, a Yurok elder who was born in 1902 and lived in Requa, near the mouth of the Klamath. In 1951 Robert H. Robins was recruited as a young Ph.D. by the Survey of California Indian Languages at the University of California at Berkeley to come from London and do fieldwork on a California Indian language. Mary Haas assigned him to do a grammar, lexicon, and collection of texts of the Yurok language. He came to the

Klamath and worked with Mrs. Shaughnessy during the winter and spring of 1951, left for a time, then returned in the late summer, during the height of the salmon run, to finish his work. In 1958 he published *The Yurok Language.*

When I met him in 1986 and talked to him about his fieldwork, he still remembered the place, the people, and much of the language in detail and with great fondness. He told me many things about the circumstances of his work that year—that he spent part of his time in Michigan at the Linguistic Society of America's Summer Institute working up the grammar, lexicon, and texts, and that he used his return visit to check the details and fill in the gaps in his data. During that year the Survey was able to purchase its first tape recorder, which was shared among all the researchers in the field. He said that he (along with Bill Bright, who was then working on Karuk just upriver) was able to keep the recorder for two weeks, rather than the usual one. He told me that on his return visit, Mrs. Shaughnessy was very busy working on the Ark, her floating restaurant, and that he was worried that he might be bothering her, so he tried to minimize the bother. (Ironically, she once told me that Robins was sometimes in too much of a hurry to take down detailed explanations, that he would run into the kitchen and say, "What's the word for so-and-so?" and then run back out again.) "The Young Man from Serper" is one of the stories that Robins recorded with that tape recorder in the Yurok language and translated into English.

I, too, worked with Mrs. Shaughnessy, although much later in her life, from the end of 1985 until she passed away in 1988. I, too, was working for the Survey when I first came to Yurok country. The first goal of our work together was to record stories. The two stories I have selected here are reminiscences from her childhood, in contrast to the old, formal, and mythical "Young Man from Serper." Though she told them to me in both Yurok and English, I have decided to use the English versions here, because they directly reflect her voice and storytelling style in English, without the mediation of a translator. They are transcribed verbatim, with only minor editing.

When she told me the story about Blind Bill, we were sitting in her room, looking out the window at the hillside where it happened, and she was pointing out where the buildings once stood (most of them are gone now). So this story has always held a sense of immediate reality for

FIGURE I. Florence Shaughnessy.
Copyright 1988 Jean Perry.

me, and conveys a feeling of Requa in its boomtown days when the canneries were still in operation, with the old Indian way of life mingling with that of the newcomers. The owl in the story, of course, foretells death, and one way to circumvent that message is to "kill the messenger," the owl.

"Ragged Ass Hill" is a steep mountainside leading down to the beach south of Crescent City, California. The name is derived from the experience of a settler in the 1860s. Wagon drivers would usually tie a log to the wagon to hold it back. The present Highway 101 is slightly east of the wagon road described in this story but is still quite steep. Nowadays as I drive through that area, I think of my daughter, who is Mrs. Shaughnessy's niece and who is about the same age as Mrs. Shaughnessy was then, and I wonder how she would manage such a trip. These stories show how rapid—just a few generations—the transition from the old ways to the frontier to modern times has been in this region of California, one of the last areas of the Continental United States to be settled.

"The Young Man from Serper" was one of Mrs. Shaughnessy's favorite stories. Her mother was from Serper, and this story was handed down within her family. I believe Mrs. Shaughnessy learned it from her grandmother, who spoke only Yurok. It is a mythical tale, a journey across a mythical geography during the time long ago when animals were like people and the idealized world that parallels this one on earth was more readily accessible than it is now. Such journeys often provide the framework for Yurok myths.

In the myth, the notion of the white deer is highly significant, because the Yurok regarded them as sacred. Likewise, the white sand on the other shore signals that it is a special place, since our local beaches have sand that is dark gray to black. Oregos is a tall, upright rock that stands at the mouth of the Klamath River. It is considered to have once been a person, a very long time ago, and there are stories about it as well. Going out the mouth on the eleventh breaker is not a case of number symbolism; the eleventh breaker is simply said to be the smallest one, the one on which it is easiest to pass through the rough place where the river current and the surf collide.

Oddly enough, Mrs. Shaughnessy was not entirely satisfied with the version of this story as it appears here, as she told it into Robins's tape recorder. Her main criticism was that parts of the story had been left out. Early in our work together, she told me a very different version of it in English. It seems that when the young man was leaving to return home, a few of the people there wanted to rescue Coyote, so "all the animals with teeth" went and chewed holes in their boats so that Coyote would be sure to leave. And when the young man returned home, his grandmother (and a grandfather) were still alive. The moral of the story as she told it to me was that it is good to take care of the old people—very different from the moral of the Robins version, which is that one should not want too much. We continued to work on this story on and off during our time together but never really completed a definitive version. It is clear to me that Mrs. Shaughnessy knew several different versions of this story.

These three stories are but a very small sample of the wealth and variety of Mrs. Shaughnessy's repertoire. She, in turn, was but one of a number of valued Yurok storytellers from her generation. Although the Yurok oral tradition continues on in various ways, the Yurok language is severely endangered today, because only the oldest people speak it fluently. And as the language is endangered, so this repertoire of stories—indeed, a whole way of *telling* stories—is endangered, too.

For a cultural overview, start with Arnold Pilling's article "Yurok" in the California volume of the Smithsonian *Handbook*. R. H. Robins combines grammar, eight texts (including "The Young Man from Serper"), and a Yurok-English vocabulary in *The Yurok Language: Grammar, Texts, Lexicon*. Alfred L. Kroeber's *Yurok Myths,* published posthumously, is a rich and important collection of traditional narratives, mostly told in English, drawn from a wide variety of Yurok storytellers; it includes some stylistic and folkloristic analysis of the texts.

"THE YOUNG MAN FROM SERPER" AND OTHER STORIES

BLIND BILL AND THE OWL

In the old days,
right up there,
there used to be a flat.
Brizzard's used to have a store there.
Above there they have a salt house,
and then above that they had a big hall house where people
   would dance.
They put on Christmas plays and everything in there.
And a little above that was a jail house.

When an owl comes and starts making noise around your home,
it's bad luck.
Mama's cousin was Blind Bill,
Starwen Bill.
He lived with us.
She came and got him.
She says,
   "There's an owl, now,
    making noise right out here."

And he says,
    "Pick me up some flat rocks,
    like that.
    I want three,
    three rocks."

So she went out with the lantern and picked up the rocks.
He said,
    "Don't bring them in the house.
    Give them to me when I get out there,
    and then you show me the direction,"
        because he was blind.
    "Show me the direction."

While he was getting his directions this owl made noise again,
so he knew right where.
I guess he had already said something to those rocks,
blessed them or whatever.
He threw them down there,
and then there was not another sound.

Early in the morning,
as soon as he got up,
he told Mom,
    "Get those kids up.
    I want them to get that owl."
And so we got up and went around there.
We looked in the hall there,
and we looked around by the jail,
all around.
And we found it,
we saw it.
By golly, he killed that owl!
That blind man killed that owl in the nighttime.

RAGGED ASS HILL

With us,
we lived here,

and it was only toward the last that we had hard times.
But at first Dad used to go out and gamble.
Sometimes he'd go to Crescent City and stay three or four nights
    playing Indian cards.
He'd take his drum,
and he was a good singer.
He'd take his team.
They'd go up there and play the Smith Rivers.
There were two or three different tribes of Indians up there all in
    the same area,
but they spoke their own different dialect.
They'd go up there and play them.
Sometimes they'd lose and come home pretty poor.
But then Dad had a lot of friends in Crescent City.
He always took his wagon and the team when he went.
So then he'd stop and borrow money from the friends,
and then stop the wagon and make all the friends walk up.

Oh! You don't know what they would call it—
Ragged Ass Hill!
Boy,
to bring freight up that hill!
Oh my goodness!
You almost had to get out and help the horses.

I must have been eight or nine years old,
because I was always a big girl for my age.
Something went wrong with Dad's eyes.
And there was nobody that could drive.
We had a little buggy,
one with those little tops like you see in pictures now,
a little black buggy.
Well, they said,
    "Florence is the only one that can drive,"
because I used to drive the team getting the hay in.
    "She can drive."

Well,
Dad said,

"What about Ragged Ass Hill?"
They said,
    "Florence will drive,"
and he had to take me because there was no one else.
His eyes were blind then,
they were hurt so bad.
So somebody said,
    "Jimmy,
    why don't you cut down a good-sized pine tree up at the top
        there?
    Take your saw and your axe and yank the rope and tie that in
        the back.
    Then the horses will have to pull that."

So that's how,
using the brakes,
I got down that hill.
We got down to Cushing Creek,
and even then we had Indians living there.
There used to be three little huts there,
and there were three Indians,
one old man and two women.
They looked like they were blind to me.
But Dad talked to them;
they knew Jimmy.
And they blessed him and wished him luck.

We still has five miles to go.
They say that beach is five miles long.
You see,
we had to make that beach while the tide was out.
Because at high tide you had to seek the sand roads in the back,
and sometimes they weren't even passable.
You'd get stuck.
So we had to hurry across there.
But we made it.
I got to the stable.

All I know is that they called that hill Ragged Ass Hill.

It seems that some men came down through there,
and it was so brushy that they just tore their pants to shreds
    by the time they got down to the bottom of the hill.
That's why they named it Ragged Ass Hill.
It was a bad one.
It's still there.

THE YOUNG MAN FROM SERPER

Once upon a time an old woman lived up the river, and she had her grandson there with her. It was difficult for her to look after her grandson. The boy was very small, but as he began to grow up it turned out that all he would do was to go down to the water's edge and was never done with fishing for trout; whatever he caught he gave to his grandmother. And then the old woman began to live better because the boy was always catching something in his fishing. He began to get bigger and then he would catch all sorts of birds, and the old woman would say, "Child, this one's feather is pretty; you will make something with this; we will put it away."

Then he quite grew up and became a young man, and it so turned out that all he did was to hunt. And once it seemed as if something said to him, "Go way up into the hills," and he saw lying there a tiny white fawn. He took it and carried it away and felt very pleased. He said, "Look, grandmother, I have caught this and will make it a pet." The old woman was very glad. It so turned out that his pet ran around there; whenever the young man went anywhere his pet would often run right on ahead of him. The pet grew up and it often happened that it disappeared in these runs. He would look for it and frequently found it high up in the hills.

Once the young man woke up, looked, and searched in vain for his pet. It was not there. Then he ran straight off to look where else it could have gone. He also asked his grandmother, "Haven't you seen my pet, Grandmother?" She said, "No, child, I have not seen anything here this morning." Then he ran off; and he had a friend, and so he went to him. He said, "Let us both go together and look; my pet has disappeared."

And for a long time they looked everywhere, and they came back and lay down. In the evening he thought, "I believe that maybe it will come back now."

The following morning they looked for it again; but no, there was nothing moving about there. So it went on, and the young man mourned its loss and came to pine for his pet. Then one night it seems he was not sleeping soundly, and he heard something apparently talking to him. He was told, "Wake your friend up, and both of you go down to the water. Your friend is to sit in the front of the boat, and you stand behind. Don't touch your paddle; you are just to stand there."

So he did just as he was told. His friend woke up, and they went down to the water. His friend sat in the boat in front and watched; they did not speak. Then the boat moved and slid down into the water, and then sped along. The boat passed through patches of very rough water as though it was quite smooth as it seemed to move along on top of the water. Then he saw that it was being taken down the river.

From up in the hills Coyote had seen where something was moving along and had heard tell that the two young men were being carried down from across the river. Coyote thought, "Well I will not be left behind. There is bound to be plenty more to eat wherever they are going. Shouldn't I go too?" He ran along the bank, and whenever he got to any point on the riverside the boat was passing near him. And in this way Coyote jumped along and saw the boat floating down and moving toward the mouth of the river. Then Coyote ran and came along the bank to Hop'ew [Klamath]; he jumped and saw the boat already moving far down stream. Then Coyote ran for all his might along the bank to pass it and chased after the boat.

Then he leaped on to the rock Oregos as the boat was first breasting the breakers. It was just going to pass the rock, and Coyote jumped in and came crashing down from high up into it. Then he said, "Yes, my grandchildren, I will come with you wherever you are going, for I think you will not get on well if there is no one who will speak on your behalf wherever you may go."

Then the boat sped on; eleven times it broke through the waves at the mouth of the river, and then went on its way. So it was that it sped on; it sped on toward the west. Then it was dark for a long time, and the boat still sped on.

The next morning they looked and fancied they saw some things swimming ahead of them. Even Coyote was now afraid and did not talk, because he had been chattering and at last had felt drowsy where he was sitting, and was not the first to see that it looked like land in sight. Then they saw that it really was land lying right out in the ocean. And the sand was all white, and a crowd of people were standing on the shore to watch the boat bounding in there.

Then they landed. When they landed they saw that there were seals going ashore, and that it was they that had towed the boat. And then two girls arrived there and one said, "Come to our house; we will be going. I am sure you are tired, for your voyage here has been long."

Coyote went on ahead and ran to see how the people lived who lived there. The two young men went up to the house and entered, and there stood another young man. Then he said, "I am glad that you have come, Brother-in-law," and then he said, "Let us go and bathe ourselves." They went outside and were all together at the young man's dwelling.

Then Coyote thought, "How very pretty that girl is. I think I will get acquainted a little with her." They were sitting by the fire when the cooking was finished, and Coyote sat down right in the middle. No notice whatever was taken of him where he sat.

The two who had arrived had a meal when they came in. They could not but feel strange wondering where on earth they had come to at this place, for the sand was all white, and they had never seen people living like this. Then one of the girls said, "Now I will tell you in full why you have come here. I am your former pet. For a long time I stayed outside, and then I saw how you lived. I saw that you were good and loved you for it. It was I who engaged the seals, saying to each of them 'Go and fetch him.' I have a sister. I thought too that you would be lonely here if you did not bring your friend; and my sister may be his wife." He thought, "Well," and then he thought, "So this girl is my former pet, and that is why I loved her so much." Then they loved one another well, and were married, and lived long and happily, and had children.

Then gradually the woman noticed that it happened that her husband would go far up in the hills and sit somewhere there. For a long time he would gaze out over the water. And one day the woman followed him and said, "Alas, my husband, you seem to have something on your mind." He said, "No, I sit here, but I have nothing on my mind." Then his wife said, "I think, no I know, how you are; you keep sitting here and gazing. I think you are homesick here. Do you want to go back home?" Again he said, "No." She said, "Well, I know that really you are homesick. And I will tell you that if you decide to go home, I will arrange it that you shall go home."

Then he thought, "I will go and tell my friend, and I shall go home." He went in where his friend lived and said, "Let us both go home. Arrangements can be made for us to go home." Then his friend thought, "No, friend, I will not go with you. I now like living here; I have my children and I will not leave them." The other said, "Well, I shall go home; I shall return. Alas, alas that my grandmother's life is a burden to her, as I fear she does not know where I have disappeared to."

And so it came about that the boat was launched. And then they saw there was a crowd and that something was being dragged along there. It was Coyote being dragged along; he was all tied up, and thrown into the boat, because people were fed up with Coyote ever since he had been there. Whenever anyone was at home he leaped into the house and said, "Grandmother, isn't there anything lying here for me to eat?" And he was told, "Be off outside! Who are you and what on earth are you doing here?" Coyote ran up again; "Aha," he said. "It seems there is some soup in the pot here. I think I will have some." Then he gobbled it all up and heard the old woman pick up her stick. "Be off! You are just going to steal again. Ugh! I hate you. Don't come here again! Don't come to the house again to steal something!" So he was now hated by everyone, and therefore he was thrown into the boat. After a shout the boat was thrust out into the sea.

Then the young man came back again to this part of the world. At once he went up the river, and when he arrived there he saw that it was now a long time since his grandmother had died. His house was no more; it had fallen down, and nothing remained. Then he thought, "What a terrible thing has befallen me! Now I have come to be here alone. How happily I was living across the water, and I have left it all."

And so for this we say that it is not good if a person thinks too much "I will have everything." But a man lives happily if somewhere he has plenty of friends, and has his money; then he does not go around thinking that he should have everything that does not belong to him, and wishing it were his own.

4

Coyote and Old Woman Bullhead

KARUK
CIRCA 1930

MARGARET HARRIE, NARRATOR
HANS JØRGEN ULDALL, COLLECTOR
JULIAN LANG, TRANSLATOR

> *Springtime comes more quickly when we recite our creation stories.*
> *We lay down together for a long time*
> *and recite the stories to each other in turn.*
> *We answer each telling with a telling.*
> *And when we recite creation stories long into the night,*
> *daylight comes more quickly.*
>
> A Karuk elder's commentary, 1920s

INTRODUCTION BY JULIAN LANG

The Karuk are a Hokan-speaking people living in mountainous North-western California. Traditionally, they lived along the Klamath River be-tween their territorial boundary with the Yurok and the California-Ore-gon border. They lived by hunting, gathering, and especially fishing. Salmon and acorns were the staples of life, because these were what the land gave in abundance, as everywhere in Northern California. They were closely allied in social structure and worldview—though not in linguis-tic affiliation—with the Hupa and Yurok.

Then came the Europeans. The American "gold fever" of 1850 ended nearly as quickly as it began. It left behind widespread disruption of Karuk culture, destruction of many village sites and other lands, and death for many. As the placer mines petered out, the miners left in droves, leaving behind the Karuk to resume their lives, in relative peace, and still living within their aboriginal homelands. Today there are about twenty-eight hundred tribal members. Important religious and healing ceremonies continue to be held annually at the same sites ordained by the spirit race known through the tribal creation stories.

In pre-Contact times (prior to 1849) a Karuk creation story possessed a unique power to transport the teller and the listener from their present into myth-time. The word *uknîii* was a signal that a *pikva*, or creation story, was about to be told, and that the present was about to become one with the creation. The awesome power and energy of the Ikxaréeyav, the spirit inhabitants of myth-time, was unleashed with the telling. Cultural protocol insisted upon silence while the story was recited. Often recitations lasted well into the night. When special guests visited, the best *pikva* were recited: the stories of Ithyarukpíhriiv ('Across-the-Water-Widower'), Ikmahachram'íshiip Veekxaréeyav ('Sacred-Sweathouse-Spirit'), and Kahthuxrivishkúrutihan ('One-Upriver-Who-Carries-the-Network-Sack'). The best *pikva* were rarely told in mixed company, being considered the highest form of tribal knowledge. Only the wealthiest and most spiritually endowed families possessed such stories.

There are very few *pikváhaan,* or storytellers, today, in the pre-Contact sense. Rarely used to invoke the creation, today the *pikva* have become grist for elementary school education. For instance, in California the study of California Native peoples occurs during the fourth grade (when students are ten years of age), and only at that time. An arbitrary and distinctly non-Indian educational framework forces the conformity of *pikva,* trivializing medicine formulas and other important, orally transmitted cultural knowledge.

The very origin and design of the Karuk worldview is delineated by the *pikva.* They are the verbal chronicle of the prehuman era of the Ikxaréeyav, the Immortals, and their world, the Pikváhahirak ('Place-of-the-Creation-Stories'). As Yaas'ára, or Humanity, was about to come into existence, the Immortals were instructed to transform themselves into what is now the diversity of the Karuk natural world. Individually named and motivated, each Ikxaréeyav metamorphosed into an animal, a bird, a plant, a mountain, a constellation. Sometimes an Ikxaréeyav family transformed together. Whether alone or as a group, the Ikxaréeyav left behind their "story" (that is, their insights and instructions) for the benefit of Humanity.

The initial religious Karuk ceremony of the year, the First Salmon Ceremony, prominently featured *pikva* storytelling. In April of each year a spring salmon was ritually caught and cremated. The rising smoke of the fire served as Humanity's signal to the Heavens requesting that all eating and hunting taboos be erased, and that good fortune and good health descend upon the Earth. The Salmon Ceremony ritual was preceded by a month-long period during which the adolescent boys stayed in the sacred Ameekyáaraam ('Where-They-Make-the-Salmon') Sweat House, learning the *pikva* of Hookbill Salmon, Spring Salmon, Steelhead, Lamprey Eel, Summer Salmon, Fall Salmon, Trout, Sucker, the Old Spinsters, Buzzard, Grizzly Bear, and many others. Of these sweat house stories it was said, "*Kóovura vaa kooka píkva, áas va'avahapíkva*" 'all that kind of stories, stories of food from the river.'

The story included here concerns the now-familiar figure of Pihnêefich, Coyote. In Northwestern California, Coyote was regarded as "the craziest and nastiest man." Usually the stories told about him reveal his buffoonery and lascivious nature. This story is unique because it presents Coyote's darkest side. When recited, the story invariably causes both Native and non-Native audiences to squirm uncomfortably in their seats as their well-known, funny, crazy Coyote murders a child in cold blood, greedily eats the child's food, and physically and verbally abuses an old woman who has come to avenge the murder of her grandson. When finally she overcomes Coyote, she transforms.

This *pikva* was recited by Margaret Harrie, known as Mâakich (a diminutive of the English "Maggie"). She was from the village site of Asánaamkarak (Ike's Flat) on the Klamath River, which was the site of the First Salmon Ceremony. Her son, Benonie Harrie, became a highly respected *êem*—a shaman. The Danish linguist Hans Jørgen Uldall recorded the story in the early 1930s at Harrie's home in the Quartz Valley near Ft. Jones, California (see Lang 1994). Uldall, a noted phonetician of the day, was invited by Alfred Kroeber, the head of the anthropology department at U.C. Berkeley, to study California Indian languages and, incidentally, to trace the footsteps of the Spanish physician-linguist Jaime de Angulo, who had transcribed several creation stories from Margaret Harrie and texts from her son. I translated Uldall's phonetic transcriptions after finding them—handwritten, in pencil, on lined "filler" paper—in the archives of the Survey of California and Other Indian Languages in 1989.

Each *pikva* opens with the word *uknîii,* its only functional usage. The word means 'a story from the time of creation is about to be recited'. Once uttered, there should be no talking among the listeners, and no interruptions, because the *pikváhaan,* the *pikva*-teller, must render the story verbatim, just as it was previously taught to him or her. All creation stories take place during the era known as Pikváhahirak ('Place-of-the-Creation-Stories'). The word *kupánakanakana* (its only functional usage) ends the creation story and alerts the listeners that they have been returned to the present time. After bringing us back, the teller usually reminds us of the most significant deed of the story's protagonist. Finally, the teller recites a kind of word-medicine which she or he must speak after every recitation in order to hasten forth the springtime (stories are reserved for the winter months, as is the case with many tribes), by beckoning forth Spring Salmon and the brodiaea plants. The recitation also attests that the teller has been punctilious in his or her telling of the story. A sloppy telling might result in the teller having a *vasíhkuun* (a crooked back) in old age, or some other bad luck, such as a snake bite or broken leg. Some tellers elaborate their recitation (in fun) by saying that their "asses are wrinkled and shriveled" from lack of food.

The conventional recitation:

Cheemyâach ik Ishyâat imshiríhraavish!
Spring Salmon, you must shine upriver quickly!

Náyaavheesh ik!
You must hurry to me!

Cheemyâach ik Ataychúkinach i'uunúpraveesh!
Brodiaea, you must sprout upriver quickly!

Náyaavheesh ik!
You must hurry to me!

Nanivási vúra veekináyaach!
My back is straight!

The self-mocking coda:

Afupchúrax taneemchitátkoo!
My ass is all wrinkled and shriveled!

FURTHER READING

For a concise anthropological orientation to Karuk culture, the reader should consult William Bright's "Karok" article in the California volume of the Smithsonian *Handbook*. ("Karok" is an older spelling of the tribal designation.) Bright also has written a grammar, *The Karok Language*, and translated several Karuk stories into English, including "Coyote Gives Salmon and Acorns to Humans," "Coyote's Journey," and "Coyote Steals Fire." Harvey Pitkin presents a Wintu version of "Coyote and Bullhead" that is strikingly different from this one yet is not without parallels. More texts may be found in A. L. Kroeber and Edward Gifford's *Karok Myths*. Julian Lang's book, *Ararapíkva: Creation Stories of the People*, contains an introduction discussing Karuk culture and storytelling traditions, a pronunciation guide and notes on Karuk grammar, a glossary, and interlinear translations of six traditional stories and personal reminiscences.

COYOTE AND OLD WOMAN BULLHEAD

Uknîii . . .

A person lived there. He thought, "I'm going upriver. I'm tired of living here! I feel lonesome."

So, he left. He went a long ways upriver, to where a big creek flowed down. He looked up the creek, when suddenly he saw a boy walking about. The boy carried lots and lots of trout.

The man looked at the boy and said, "Geez, I like eating trout, I wish I was eating some of his." The man went over to the boy.

"Where did you find that trout?"

The boy said, "I caught them."

"You couldn't have caught that many fish! I bet you've been traveling with someone else!"

The boy said, "No-o-o. I have a willow seine. I was just there to see it. That's where I caught the trout."

Then the man said, "Are you telling me the truth?" The man was thinking to himself, "I'm going to murder him." And then he killed the boy.

"Hooray! I'm gonna eat trout!" The man built a fire, a big fire. Then he hid the one he had just murdered. There was a logjam nearby, and he hid the body under a log.

Then he went back to his fire, and he roasted the trout. He picked some herbs, and added them to his cooking.

Then he ate, finally devouring all the trout. Then he thought, "Hooray! I'm just full! Now I can travel a long ways upriver!" He said to himself, "I'm going to paint myself."

He saw smoke rising when he looked upriver. "Hey, I'm about to arrive at a village!" So he painted himself up good with red-earth paint.

Then he decorated his buckskin shoes. He painted red stripes running down his leather leggings, and he painted his buckskin blanket completely red with the earth paint. He put on an Indian-money necklace, and then he put on a new man's basketry cap.

Then he walked upriver.

After walking just a little ways, he looked upriver and saw an old woman standing in the trail. She was crying.

The man arrived where she stood, and asked her, "You're crying HERE, in the path?"

The old woman refused to answer him.

"Why don't you answer me!" the man asked. The old woman just kept on crying. Then he said, "YOU can't beat me up!"

The man started to walk upriver. He barely passed her by, when she grabbed him around the waist.

"Hey, let me go! Why did you grab me?" He tried hard to pry apart her grasp-hold, but he couldn't do it. She was slippery. He gave it his all, but she still held onto him.

Suddenly there were dark clouds! Before too long it was raining. The rain just flowed down. When he looked downhill toward the river, the water was rising.

And Coyote thought, "It's all right now! She'll let me go now, as soon as the river rises up to us here. She's so short! It's all right now."

Finally, the river rose right up to where they stood. The man said, "Hey! My nice shoes are getting wet! My little leggings are getting wet! Let me go!" She refused to answer; the water hit them. "It's all right now!" the man thought. "She'll let me go when she disappears under the water!"

Finally the water was up to her knees. He kept thinking, "I wish she'd let me go." He tried hard to pry her hands apart again. It was no use.

Finally the water was up to *his* waist. "All right! She'll be under water any moment!" Then she disappeared under the water.

Coyote started crying then—still she held onto him. Finally both of them disappeared under the water. The river rose to uphill of where they were. *Then,* she let him go.

The old woman poked her head out of the water. "Let it be so, that I become transformed here in the water!" And then she turned into Bull-head Fish.

As for Coyote, he drifted far downriver. The old woman found him stuck in among some willows. When the high water receded, the old woman hauled him out of there.

As for the old Spirit Woman, she came back to this world.*

And Coyote, he came back to life again!

Kupánakanakana.

Coyote did that. He killed the old woman's grandson . . .

Spring Salmon, you must shine upriver quickly!
You must hurry to me!

Brodiaea, you must sprout upriver quickly!
You must hurry to me!

My back is straight!

* That is, she came back to this mortal world, transformed as Bullhead.

5

The Devil Who Died Laughing

KARUK
1950

MAMIE OFFIELD, NARRATOR
WILLIAM BRIGHT, COLLECTOR AND TRANSLATOR

INTRODUCTION BY WILLIAM BRIGHT

My principal fieldwork on the Karuk language (previously called
"Karok") was done in the spring of 1949 and the summer of 1950. During the latter period, in search of Karuk speakers who could tell traditional stories, I visited Mrs. Mamie Offield, an elderly woman living at
her summer home on the slope of Mount Offield, near Somes Bar, in
Siskiyou County. (During the winters, she lived in Los Angeles.) Some
years before, she had served as a translator and consultant for the ethnographic fieldwork of Professor Edward W. Gifford, of Berkeley; people
told me that she knew a lot, but that she was "kinda mean"—that is,
unfriendly or uncooperative. I was apprehensive, but in fact she proved
to be knowledgeable, friendly, and very cooperative. During that summer she dictated eighteen stories and helped me translate them. Most
were myths, about the deeds of Coyote and the other Ikxaréeyavs—the
First People who inhabited the earth before humans came into existence.
But others were stories with human characters—sometimes involving

supernatural occurrences, but believed to have happened in "modern" times.

Among these, the anecdote that I have called "The Devil Who Died Laughing" has always been one of my favorites. It involves no superhuman characters and no moral lesson: it's simply a funny story, which I have enjoyed retelling, and my Karuk friends have enjoyed hearing, for the last forty years. Years ago, I published the text (Bright 1957:274–75; there is a photo of Mrs. Offield on page 155) in a technical transcription system for linguists and other specialists. The spelling for Karuk used in this introduction is a more practical system, which I have recently developed for the Karuk tribe's language program.

To understand the story, one needs to know what the Indians of Northwestern California mean by a "devil" (Karuk *apurúvaan*). The term has nothing to do with demons from Hell, but rather refers to sorcerers: human beings, male or female, who practice malicious magic. (One could use the term "witch" except for the female connotation of the English word.) Devils get their power from magical objects called *ápuroon* 'devil machines'; armed with these, they prowl around human dwellings at night, sometimes emitting *machnat,* or small flashes of light (will-o'-the-wisps?), spying on the inhabitants and choosing their victims.

In Mamie Offield's story, a pair of devils come to spy on a man and his wife, who are occupying a temporary house in an acorn-gathering area. But the devils get a surprise and never have a chance to practice their sorcery. Stories in which devils are thwarted seem to be a recognized genre; Mrs. Offield told me three such stories on a summer afternoon in 1950 (see Bright 1957:274–77). The humor of such stories is perhaps enhanced by being at the expense of a hated and feared class of people; we might imagine a similar modern story in which the prowlers were tax collectors.

In spite of its secular nature, the story shows an ethnopoetic structure similar to that of Karuk myths and other narratives. It consists of fourteen "verses," most of which begin with a sentence-initial particle construction—usually *kári xás* 'and then', indicating sequentiality. As is typical in Karuk storytelling, the initial verse lacks this element. The following central passage shows a variation in the use of initial particles: verses 11–12, at the climax of the action, begin not with *kári xás,* but with the word *hínupa* indicating a surprise, translatable as 'and there . . . !' This initiates a kind of freeze-frame effect: the sequence of actions is suspended and previously unknown features of the situation are revealed.

5   Kári   xás   chámuxich   ú-ykar.
    And   then   sucker   he caught it.
    And then (the husband) caught a sucker.

6   Kári   xás   pa-asiktávaan   u-piip,   "Chími   kan-thimnûup-i."
    And   then   the woman   she said,   "(intention)   I'll roast it."
    And then the woman said, "I'm going to roast it."

7   Kári   xás   u-thímnup,   pa-chámuxich.
    And   then   she roasted it,   the sucker.
    And then she roasted it, that sucker.

8   Kári   xás   pá-faan   u-yhúku-rishuk.
    And   then   the guts   she ripped them out.
    And then she ripped out the guts.

9   Kári   xás   pa-mukun-ikrívraam   u-súru-ruprin-ahi-ti,   yítha-kan.
    And   then   their house   there was a hole through,   at one place.
    Now then, there was a hole through their house-wall, at a certain place.

10 Kári   xás   vaa   kaan   u-ákith-rupri,   pá-faan.
    And   then   that   there   she flung them through,   the guts.
    And then she flung them through that hole, those guts.

11 Hínupa   vaa   káan   u-t-nûuprih-ti,   yítha   pa-apurúvaan.
    And there   that   there   he was peeking through,   one   the devil.
    And there he was peeking through that hole, a certain devil!

12 Hínupa   yúp-yaach   t-u-ákith-tir.
    And there   smack in the eye   she had flung them.
    And there she had flung them right smack in his eye!

Apart from the initial particle constructions, features of ethnopoetic structure in this passage include the following:

Word Order

There is regular alternation of preverbal and postverbal position for nouns to indicate new and old information, respectively. Thus we have, in verses 5–7, "He caught a sucker [NEW]—And then she roasted it, that sucker [OLD]"; then, in verses 8–10, "She ripped out the guts [NEW]— And then she flung them through that hole, those guts [OLD]." Along with the repeated *kári xás,* this pattern suggests an atmosphere of routine activity or "business as usual," serving as a background to the surprise that comes in verses 10–11.

Repetition

There is repetition of the verbal suffix meaning 'through a hole', with the three variants *-ruprin ~ -rupri ~ -nûuprih:* (9) "There was a hole through their house-wall"; (10) "She flung them through that hole, those guts"; (11) "He was peeking through that hole." Apart from the poetic echo effect of the partial phonetic repetition, the reiterated semantic element gives extra cohesion to the narrative at this point of climax.

For a translation of this text, I would have liked to present Mrs. Offield's own English version, but unfortunately, I have not preserved that—either in a verbatim transcript, or in an audio recording—so I've done my best to reproduce features of her colloquial storytelling style, as I remember it: short sentences, informal but totally clear vocabulary and syntax, and certain Karuk stylistic devices such as the movement of old-information noun phrases to the end of the sentence ("And then she roasted it, that sucker"). Where the Karuk text uses repetition, I've tried to reproduce that faithfully in English. Finally, at several points where the Karuk uses vocabulary items that are highly distinctive, semantically or phonologically, I've attempted to find correspondingly colorful English vocabulary. Thus, in verse 8, the verb-form *uyhúkurishuk* means 'she pulled (something) out' but can refer only to the guts of an animal; I translate "she ripped out the guts." In verses 10 and 12, the verb stem *ákith* means not simply 'to throw' but 'to throw something soft'—such as mud, dough, or (in this case) fish guts; I propose the translation "to fling." In verse 12, the alliterative *yúp-yaach,* literally 'eye-ex-actly', suggests not just 'right in the eye' but the more vivid "smack in the eye."

FURTHER READING

For an overview of Karuk culture, see William Bright's article "Karok" in the California volume of the Smithsonian *Handbook.* Concerning sorcery in Native Northwest California, see William J. Wallace and J. S. Taylor's article, "Hupa Sorcery." A Karuk grammar, text collection, and dictionary are presented by Bright's *The Karok Language.* For ethnopoetic analyses of Karuk narrative, see Bright's "A Karuk Myth in 'Measured Verse'" and "Coyote's Journey," both collected in *American Indian Linguistics and Literature;* see also Dell Hymes's "Particle, Pause, and Pattern in American Indian Narrative Verse."

THE DEVIL WHO DIED LAUGHING

1 A lot of people were gathering acorns,
     up in the mountains,
     in acorn season.

2 And then they had gone home,
     all those people.

3 Only one man was left,
     he and his wife.

4 And then he said,
     "I think I'll go spear some fish."

5 And then he caught a sucker.

6 And then the woman said,
     "I'm going to roast it."

7 And then she roasted it,
     that sucker.

8   And then she ripped out the guts.

9   Now then, there was a hole in their house-wall,
        at a certain place.

10 And then she flung them through that hole,
        those guts.

11 And there he was peeking through that hole,
        a certain devil!

12 And there she had flung them right smack in his eye!

13 And then that other devil burst out laughing.

14 And then he just laughed himself to death;
        the next day his friend saw him,
            he was lying there,
        he was still laughing,
            even though he was dead.

15 So then the other one told what happened.

6

"The Boy Who Grew Up at Ta'k'imiłding" and Other Stories

HUPA

1963–1964

MINNIE REEVES AND LOUISA JACKSON, NARRATORS

VICTOR GOLLA, COLLECTOR AND TRANSLATOR

INTRODUCTION BY VICTOR GOLLA

Together with their close neighbors the Yurok on the lower Klamath River, and the Karuk further upstream on the Klamath, the aboriginal Hupa of the lower Trinity River subsisted (and subsisted well) on the abundant spring and fall runs of salmon, which they supplemented by gathering acorns and berries, trapping eels, and hunting deer and small game. The modern Hupa people have been able to preserve a close attachment to this rich environment, since they are fortunate to possess a large reservation that includes the center of their traditional territory, Hoopa Valley. This spectacularly beautiful eight-mile-long stretch of bottomland, studded with oaks, is located on the Trinity a few miles above its confluence with the Klamath. In the Hupa language it is called *na:tinixw* 'where the trail goes back', and its geography is closely interwoven with traditional Hupa religion and story.

In addition to the people of Hoopa Valley (*na:tinixwe* 'those of *na:tinixw*'), there were several Hupa-speaking tribelets, all virtually identical in language. Two of these tribelets (known ethnographically as the Chilula and the Whilkut) were located on Redwood Creek, west of Hoopa Valley. There was at least one tribelet upstream on the Trinity River, centered on the village of Łe:lding where the Trinity and South Fork join.

Shortly before the turn of the century, Pliny Earle Goddard came to Hoopa as an interdenominational missionary. He built a church, which still stands, and learned Hupa sufficiently well to be able to preach in it. In 1900, however, he abandoned religious work to become an anthropologist. His ethnographic sketch "Life and Culture of the Hupa" is a classic, and he also published an important volume of traditional Hupa narratives, "Hupa Texts." These studies, together with Goddard's numerous publications on the language, made the Hupa one of the best described Indian cultures of California in the early decades of this century. In 1927 the great anthropological linguist Edward Sapir added even more to the documentation of Hupa traditional culture in a field study that focused on language and literature. He collected seventy-six narratives, some of them quite long and most of them full of cultural detail. This important collection is now being readied for publication in a forthcoming volume of *The Collected Works of Edward Sapir.*

I began my own work with the Hupa in the 1960s. My work was primarily linguistic, but I also collected a number of narrative texts. The four Hupa stories included here are translations of narratives collected on tape in 1963 and 1964 from Mrs. Minnie Reeves and her younger sister, Mrs. Louisa Jackson. Minnie Reeves (1880–1972) was well past eighty at the time, and Louisa Jackson (1888–1991) was in her late seventies. Although married into Hoopa Valley families, Minnie and Louisa were actually from the Chilula tribelet. Their father, Dan Hill, and grandfather Tom Hill had refused to resettle the family on the Hoopa Valley Reservation after its establishment in 1864; they continued to live in the traditional village of Nolehding ('waterfall place') on lower Redwood Creek, a few miles northwest of the reservation boundary. The family moved to Hoopa in 1888, and both sisters attended the boarding school there.

Minnie Reeves was a talented narrator, and her carefully told stories span several genres. Her sister Louisa Jackson had a smaller repertoire, but a vivacious style.

"The Boy Who Grew Up at Taʼkʼimiłding" is the sacred charter of the two principal World Renewal dances. These ceremonies, the Hupa term for which is *chʼidilye,* are unique to the traditional cultures of the Yurok-Karuk-Hupa area and continue to be performed today. They focus on maintaining the equilibrium of the physical and social world through songs and dances pleasing to the *kʼixinay,* the supernatural inhabitants of the world before humans arrived who still exert influence on human affairs from a Heaven beyond the sky. The ceremonies are performed in two ten-day cycles, the White Deerskin Dance (*xonsił chʼidilye* 'summer World Renewal') and the Jump Dance (*xay chʼidilye* 'winter World Renewal'). The White Deerskin Dance takes place in August or early September at a series of dancegrounds in Hoopa Valley. The Jump Dance is performed in late September at a single site about one hundred yards upstream from the village of Taʼkʼimiłding ('acorn cooking place'). Formerly the two dances may have been annual events; today they are biennial, held in odd-numbered years.

The story that Minnie relates is not in the strict sense a myth. Hupa myths relate events that happened in the days when the *kʼixinay* were still on earth, whereas this story has the character of a religious legend set in human times. In it the World Renewal dances are said to be the inspiration of a specific young boy, a child of the family that owns the *xontah nikyaːw* ('big house'), the largest and most prestigious house in the principal Hoopa Valley village, Taʼkʼimiłding. This boy is well-behaved and "sings all the time," an indication that he has been chosen by the *kʼixinay* as a vehicle of spiritual power. Then one day he disappears in a cloud to join the *kʼixinay* beyond the sky. After a long absence he briefly reappears to his father to convey to the Hupa people how and where the *kʼixinay* want the World Renewal dances to be performed. "I will always come back. . . . I will always be watching," he both promises and warns.

Minnie Reeves's telling of this sacred story was appropriately solemn and serious. Although her version was abbreviated and broken here and there by a hesitation or groping for words, it was clear that she was reciting well-known lines and phrases—a sacred text in the most real sense. (See the "Hupa Language Sample" at the end of this introduction for a closer look at the language behind the translation.)

The incident that Minnie Reeves relates in "Grandfather's Ordeal" probably occurred in the 1850s or early 1860s, when hostilities between white settlers and Hupas—particularly the Chilulas—were at their worst. Minnie's maternal grandfather and the Indian doctor he was escorting were by no means the only Indians gratuitously killed or wounded by whites on the trails between Hoopa Valley and the coast. The need to import a shaman from Hoopa Valley underscores the peripheral status of the Chilula tribelet.

"The Stolen Woman" is one of many legends whose theme is a raid on a peaceful Hupa village by "wild Indians" from the south. There is undoubtedly a historical kernel to these stories, and the raiders (usually called *mining'wiltach'* 'their faces-tattooed') may be either the Yuki of Round Valley or the Hayfork Wintu. A particular twist to this story is the implication that the wealth of Me'dilding, the leading village of the upriver (southern) half of Hoopa Valley, is based on stolen treasure. Not surprisingly, Minnie's connections were largely to Ta'k'imiłding and the downriver (northern) half of the valley.

"It Was Scratching" was told to me by Louisa Jackson. It belongs to a popular genre of "Indian Devil" stories, based on a widespread belief in witchcraft practices (*k'ido:ngxwe*). Devils are said to sneak around houses and graveyards in the night, peering through windows or catching people when they venture outside alone. They insert "pains" into people, causing illness, bad luck, and even death. Note how the woman in the story accuses the devil of having killed off her entire family (*ch'e'whinełya:n* 'he ate me up' is the Hupa idiom). In traditional times, suspicions and accusations of deviling were quite common, giving social life a distinctly paranoid tinge.

Hupa Language Sample

The following lines of Hupa, with their glosses and translations, come from the beginning of the first story presented here, "The Boy Who Grew Up at Ta'k'imiłding."

Ta'k'imiłding   nat'tehłdichwe:n,
at Ta'k'imiłding   he grew up
He grew up at Ta'k'imiłding;

xontah   nikya:w   me'   ts'isla:n—   kile:xich.
House   Big   in   he was born   a boy
he was born in the Big House—a boy.

Haya:ł   ang'   łahxw   na'k'iwing'ah   wehst'e';
then   it was only/nothing but   he sang   continually
He would do nothing but sing all the time;

na'k'e'a'aw.
he would keep singing
he just kept singing.

Haya:ł   hay diydi   'a:ya:xołch'ide'ine',
then   whatever   they would tell him
Then, whatever they would tell him,

'aht'ingq'a'ant'e: mida'   q'eh   na'a'a'.
everything   its word/mouth   after   he carried it about
he minded it.

'e'ilwil   na'ky'a'ah'xw,
it would get dark   as he sang,
He would sing all day long,

xontah   nikya:w   me',   Ta'k'imiłding.
House   Big   in   at Ta'k'imiłding
in the Big House at Ta'k'imiłding.

FURTHER READING

Readers should consult William J. Wallace's entry, "Hupa, Chilula and Whilkut," in the California volume of the Smithsonian *Handbook*. For a more in-depth ethnography, there is Pliny Earle Goddard's classic "Life and Culture of the Hupa." Goddard's "Hupa Texts" is also an important collection of Hupa oral literature. The stories presented here are taken from *Hupa Stories, Anecdotes, and Conversations,* a booklet prepared by Golla for the Hoopa Valley tribe in 1984.

"THE BOY WHO GREW UP AT TA'K'IMIŁDING" AND OTHER STORIES

THE BOY WHO GREW UP AT TA'K'IMIŁDING

MINNIE REEVES

There once was a boy who grew up at Ta'k'imiłding—born into the Big House there.

He did nothing but sing all the time. He would always be singing. He was a good boy and did what he was told, but he would stay there in the Big House at Ta'k'imiłding, singing all day long.

One day his mother went down to the river to fetch water, leaving the boy singing in the house. She dipped up some water, and was on her way back up to the house when a sound stopped her. It sounded like someone was singing inside a cloud that hovered over her house. She put her water basket down and listened. She could hear it clearly: someone was singing there inside the hovering cloud. After a while the cloud lifted up into the air. She could still hear the singing. Eventually it vanished into the sky.

She went on back to the house. When she went inside, the boy was gone. It was clear that he had gone off inside the hovering cloud.

When her husband returned from hunting she told him what had happened. They had loved him very much, and they cried and cried.

A long time passed and there was no sign of the boy. Then, one day, many years later, the man went up the hill to hunt. After hunting for a while he got tired and decided to rest under a big tan oak. As he sat there smoking his pipe he was suddenly aware of a young man walking toward him out of the forest. Looking more closely he saw that it was the boy, now grown up. He leapt to his feet and ran to embrace his son.

"Stop there, Father! Don't come toward me," the young man said. "Don't try to touch me. I can't bear the scent of human beings any more."

Then he continued, "The only reason I have come back is to tell people the way things should be done in the future. When I went off to Heaven in that cloud, I found them dancing there, dancing without ever stopping, dancing the whole day long.

"And that is why I have returned—why you see me now. I have come to tell you about the dances. I am here to tell you the ways they should be danced, and the places where they should happen.

"You will dance downstream through Hoopa Valley, you will finish the dance over there on Bald Hill: that is where the White Deerskin Dance is to be danced.

"Ten days after the White Deerskin Dance is finished, you will dance the Jump Dance for another ten days. There behind the Jump Dance fence I will always be looking on. I will always come back for the Jump Dance, although you won't ever see me. Because I will be looking on from there, invisible though I am, don't let anyone go back of the fence, don't even let a dog go back there.

"I will always be watching."

That is the end of the story.

GRANDFATHER'S ORDEAL

MINNIE REEVES

I will tell you now about how my grandfather—my mother's father— got shot, a long time ago.

His mother had gotten sick. The Chilula Indian doctors who were treating her told him that she probably wouldn't pull through. They told him that he should go get this Indian doctor from Hoopa who had a good reputation. She might be able to save his mother.

My grandfather immediately set out on foot for Hoopa Valley. He found the Indian doctor and the two of them started back toward the Bald Hills.

The Indian doctor carried a lot of stuff in a pack basket, and my grandfather carried another pack basket. They crossed Pine Creek at the ford called Soaproot (*qos-ding*) and went up the Bald Hills past Birds Roost (*k'iya:wh-nondiłding*).

As they were heading down the far slope, my grandfather happened to look back along the trail and caught sight of a party of whites on horseback. The whites had seen the two of them and were pointing their rifles at them. My grandfather tried to raise his hands—he raised them straight up—but it did no good: the whites shot at them anyway. A bullet hit the Indian doctor and she fell down dead. Another bullet tore through the upper part of my grandfather's back. It didn't kill him, but his legs got caught in some berry vines and he too fell to the ground. Thinking that they had killed both of the Indians, the whites went off downstream.

My grandfather dragged himself back up the trail toward the ridge. He remembered that there was a cedar-bark hunting shelter up there. He finally found it and crawled inside, where he collapsed and fainted.

Meanwhile, the people back at home were getting worried. "They should have gotten back long before now," they thought. "Maybe something has happened. Somebody should go out looking for them." So a party went off to search for them. When they got to the hunting shelter, they saw my grandfather lying inside. It looked like he had been dead for some time. They took a piece of bark from the shelter and were going to lay him out on it, like a corpse, to carry him home for burial.

But when they started to handle him, he jumped up. The moment he leapt up, blood and matter spurted out of his wound and he started gasping for breath. He had been in a deep coma, near death, but he had seen a vision of a white grizzly bear pouncing on him and tearing open his infected wound. He had trained for power and had acquired a lot of it—he was a strong believer in all of those things. A vision came to him from Heaven, and he survived.

They carried him back home, where he recovered. And that is the end of the story.

THE STOLEN WOMAN

MINNIE REEVES

A long time ago, they were having a Brush Dance at the village of Me'dil-ding. In the middle of the night, when the dance was going strong, an extraordinarily handsome man showed up, carrying two valuable fisher hides. He went right into the pit and danced between two girls.

As they filed out of the pit at the end of the set of dances, he caught hold of one of the girls and ran away with her. He took her far off. She had been kidnapped.

He took her along with him from place to place, across the mountains. After a long while they arrived back at his home—a bark house, located at the base of a large rock. They lived there together, and eventually she had a child—a little boy.

When the man went out hunting he would take the woman with him. When he saw a good-sized deer, he would point a magic Jump Dance basket (*na'wehch*) at it and wiggle it around, and instantly the deer would fall over dead. He was always careful to keep the woman with him and would never let the magic basket out of his sight. They would then go back home. After the venison was all eaten up they would go out hunting again.

One time when they were doing this, the man incautiously put the magic basket down while he went to pick up a fallen deer. The unhappy woman thought that she saw a way of getting home to Me'dilding. She picked up the magic basket and pointed it toward him, wiggling it around the way he did when he was killing a deer. He didn't see her do this, and they went back home. That evening he complained of a headache, and before the first light of dawn appeared he was dead.

The woman searched the man's house. She found her child, now grown to be a fair-sized young man. She also found that the man had a large number of valuable things that he had stolen from people. She fixed up a pack basket full of such things and then she and the boy set off for home.

She thought hard about how they had come when she had been kidnapped, and the two of them traveled for several days. Finally they reached Me'dilding. The boy had never seen so many people before. It scared him, and he would run and hide behind the houses.

This is how there came to be rich people at Me'dilding. The kidnapped woman had brought back all sorts of valuable things.

This is the end of the story.

IT WAS SCRATCHING

LOUISA JACKSON

Once, a long time ago, when the harvest season came, a group of women went off to gather acorns. They camped in a bark hut at the place called Mortar Lies There (*me'ist-sitang-xw*). They had gathered lots of acorns, and when it came time to pack them home they decided it would be best to fetch a man to help. So they went back for someone, leaving one woman to stay with the acorns.

She spent the night alone in the bark hut. In the middle of the night she heard something making a noise, like an animal scratching the outside of the hut. She didn't get concerned about it. But when she got up in the morning she thought she'd look, and discovered scratch marks outside the hut next to where she had been sleeping. In spite of this she went out and spent the day gathering more acorns.

That evening she got ready to spend another night in the hut. Thinking that perhaps someone was trying to devil her, she placed a log where she had slept before. She covered it with a blanket and sat down beside it. In the middle of the night she again heard the noise of something scratching. As she watched, she saw someone put his hand into the hut. He kept pushing it in until his arm reached the log that was lying there like a person in the blanket. At that instant, the woman caught him around the wrist, held his arm down, and sawed it off with a knife. When it was severed, she hurled it aside.

When she got up in the morning she decided to go back to the village. She gathered some ferns and stuffed them in her pack basket. Throwing the severed arm on top of the ferns, she set off for home.

As she was coming down the ridge past the village of Xonsahding, she heard the sound of people crying. She wondered what was going on and decided to go down and see. When she got there she found a man laid out for burial and people mourning him. She asked what had happened.

"That poor man met with a great misfortune," they told her. (They also mentioned his name, but I won't repeat it here.) "A tree limb fell on him out in the woods."

"Yes," she said. "Of course. A tree limb fell on him."

She took her pack basket down, felt around in it, and pulled out the severed arm. She threw it on top of the body.

"This too," she said. "This too is his. He was the one who was coming after me, trying to devil me. Now I know who it was who killed off my family!"

And suddenly the mourners were silent.

7

The Bear Girl

CHIMARIKO
1921

SALLY NOBLE, NARRATOR
J. P. HARRINGTON, COLLECTOR
KATHERINE TURNER, TRANSLATOR

INTRODUCTION BY KATHERINE TURNER

The Chimariko language was once spoken on the Trinity River in Northwestern California, a heavily forested and mountainous country. Chimariko is classified by linguists as a Hokan language, but it is only distantly related to some of the other languages spoken in prehistoric California. To the west and northwest their neighbors were the Athabascan Whilkut and Hupa. Their neighbors to the south and east were Penutian-speaking Wintu people.

Sally Noble was the last known fluent speaker of the Chimariko language. She told the story of "The Bear Girl" to John Peabody Harrington in 1921. Mrs. Noble told Harrington several Chimariko stories as well as recounting historical events, describing customs such as tattooing and doctoring, and giving her personal reminiscences. There is no place in Harrington's notes of his work with her where she told a single story from start to finish. Sally Noble was remembering these stories from long before she told them to Harrington, and each time she told a story she would remember another detail or episode. Although she knew Chimariko, she had seldom spoken the language as an adult. By the time she told this story, she had not spoken Chimariko for many years, so she told it in many overlapping fragments. This story was pieced together from those fragments.

J. P. Harrington amassed more data about North American languages and cultures than any other person. An ethnographer and linguist, he was employed by the Bureau of American Ethnography. He recorded his notes on the Chimariko language from Sally Noble between September 1921 and January 1922. His notes are stored in the Smithsonian Institution in Washington, D.C. They have been photographed and microfilmed, making them more accessible to libraries around the world. By January 1922 Harrington had compiled several thousand pages of notes on Chimariko, and he planned to return to his work with Sally Noble in May. Mrs. Noble died in February 1922.

The story of "The Bear Girl" told here is my translation of Mrs. Noble's Chimariko, not her English versions of the story. She spoke in English at first, then in both Chimariko and English, and, finally, in Chimariko with an occasional English word or phrase. When she spoke English, Harrington wrote it down in English, and when she spoke Chimariko, he wrote it down phonetically because there is no alphabet for Chimariko. As Sally Noble got into the story of "The Bear Girl" in her own language, she added a wealth of detail absent from her English tellings.

In Chimariko the story is lyrical through its use of repetition to unfold the plot gradually. There is a majestic beauty in the repetitions. For most of the story, Mrs. Noble speaks one phrase and then partially restates it, adding just a little more detail before moving on to the next sentence. This is such a prominent feature that it is quite noticeable when Mrs. Noble does not exploit this device but moves straight ahead with her story, adding new information with each new sentence. For instance, in the scene where the Bear Girl abandons civilization for good (lines 60–73), there is very little repetition, and its absence underscores one of the climaxes of the story. We find the same pattern again near the end of the story (lines 96–104) at another dramatic moment, the scene where her brother shoots the Bear Girl.

FIGURE 2. Sally Noble.
Courtesy of the Bancroft Library,
University of California, Berkeley.

A few additional notes about the translation of Chimariko may be in order. First, there is no difference between *he* and *she* in Chimariko, so I have supplied the distinction for English-speaking readers; it would look and sound odd had I translated the Chimariko pronouns as *it*. Second, I have changed the order of the words from Chimariko word order to that of English and moved descriptive words to where they would occur in an English sentence.

This story gives us a glimpse of Chimariko culture and beliefs, as in the concept that there was a time long ago when a person could grow up or "turn out" to be an animal. In translating this story into English, I have tried to reflect the style and phrasing as Sally Noble told it in Chimariko. The line breaks are an attempt to suggest the controlled, rhythmic pace of delivery that seems implicit in the language of the original. I have not elaborated or filled in blanks, because that would alter the story told and add nothing of significance. This story speaks for itself.

FURTHER READING

Little is known about the Chimariko. Two articles in the California volume of the Smithsonian *Handbook*, Shirley Silver's "Chimariko" and William Wallace's "Hupa, Chilula and Whilkut," supply the most up-to-date information we have about the Chimariko people, their language, and their culture. Roland Dixon's "The Chimariko Indians and Language" provides an earlier but more extensive ethnography. C. Hart Merriam's "The New River Indians Tol-hom-tah-hoi" may also be of interest. James Bauman's "Chimariko Placenames and the Boundaries of Chimariko Territory" takes an interesting look at Chimariko ethnogeography. In addition to the few published sources, the Bancroft Library at the University of California at Berkeley has two small notebooks of fieldnotes on the Chimariko language recorded by A. L. Kroeber in 1901–1902. The American Philosophical Society in Philadelphia has the small amount of Chimariko linguistic data recorded by Edward Sapir in 1927.

THE BEAR GIRL

Long ago there was a cross Indian girl.
She was cross and angry all the time.
She did not like people.
She had no appetite for food.
She did not like the food her mother fed her.   5
She did not eat the food she was given.

They were afraid of her.
They could do nothing with her.
They wondered what she would amount to.
Everybody wondered how she would turn out. 10

Her mother hired a good Indian doctor to ask
    what was the matter with the girl.
She was not like people.
She was not like our flesh.
She was not a person.
She was not a human woman. 15
She was going to turn out to be a bear.
That's what the matter was.

Everybody was afraid of her because she was so cross.
She was always slapping.
She did not use a stick, not ever. 20
She always slapped with her hand.
She was not like the other children.
She always slapped.
When good children play,
they do not slap with their hands but use a stick. 25
Their mother told the children: "Don't hit her.
I am going to punish you if you hit the bear girl."
But they would sometimes hit her with a rock because she was so
    mean.

When she was still a little girl,
she already slept alone in a little house, 30
because everybody was afraid of her because she was so cross.
When the hazelnuts and berries got ripe,
she gathered wild blackberries,
but she did not eat them in the house.

She had only one brother. 35
Her brother watched his sister as she got a little bigger and
    crosser every year.
Everybody kept a watch on her.
Every year she got worse and worse.

When the old women went to gather hazelnuts,
she went with them.   40
Each time she went a little further.
She watched other people cracking the hazelnuts
and learned how to crack them too,
though she had been told not to.
She gathered lots of hazelnuts and cracked them,   45
but she did not eat them in the house.
Maybe she ate them out in the woods.
In the house she threw everything around.
She got worse and worse every year—bigger and crosser.

When the women went out to gather hazelnuts,   50
the girl went to get a drink further upstream.
When it was time to go home, the women called out:
"We are going home."
They called to her and hollered,
"Come on, let's go."   55
They hollered but she did not answer.
She went a little further every time.
She went further into the brush.
Finally she set the basket down on the trail and just kept going.

They say her brother followed her through the thick brush, 60
and found the basket.
She kept going, up into the mountains,
and she threw away her apron.
But she wore a nice fancy dress, well fixed up.
Her brother found the apron and put it in the basket.   65
She kept going, climbing higher and higher.
Her brother found her nice fancy dress.
He put it in the basket, laying it across her apron.
Then he found her hat.
Her brother kept following her upstream through the brush. 70
Finally he caught up with her.
She had already changed into a bear.

She looked back.
She said:

"My brother,   75
I thought I was a natural born person,
but I am a big bear.
Now I get where I want to go,
now I turn out to be a bear,
so that's how I turn out.   80
I have turned out to be a bear,
a cross female bear.
Remember what I say:
You will see me in a clover patch with lots of other bears.
I will be the biggest black bear.   85
I won't run.
That will be me.
Don't shoot."

She had become a bear, she ran away as a bear.
That is the reason why the little girl was so mean.   90

Her brother returned to the village and told the people what she
    said.
"I am going to be big and black,
don't shoot me," she told him.

Then, after a while, that boy got to be an old man.
All the men went bear hunting.   95
The old man saw a big patch of clover and went to look at it.
He saw lots of bears.
He shot one.
He shot a black bear twice.
Then he heard her:
"Don't you recollect?   100
I told my brother not to shoot me!"

The bear got away through the snow high up on the mountain.
The man looked for her,
but he never knew whether the bear died or not.   105
But that bear could talk Indian.

Finally, the man went home.
At supper time he wouldn't eat or say anything.

He looked like he'd been crying.
He wouldn't say anything. 110
He lay in bed for two days looking sick but saying nothing.

His wife asked him,
"What's the matter? Are you sick?"
But he wouldn't say anything.

After a while he told his wife, 115
"I shot her. I shot her twice."
And his wife said,
"Don't tell the old folks. Don't tell them."
His wife said,
"Well, what's the use to cry, you can't help it, 120
that part of it is done already,
that part of it is gone," she said.
"She is alive and that's all."

So, he never told any people at all.
He told nobody else. 125
He told only his wife.

NORTH-CENTRAL CALIFORNIA

Winter mosquitos go,
Summer mosquitos come—
Spring, hurry up!

> Traditional story-closing
> formula, Wintu
>
> Dorothy Demetracopoulou
> and Cora Du Bois, "A Study
> of Wintu Mythology"

SPELL SAID BY A GIRL DESIROUS OF GETTING A HUSBAND

S·uwā′! May you think about me to yourself! May you turn back to look! Would that I might stand before his face! I just cry to myself. Would that I might see him every day!

I do just as you do. Sometimes I dream of him, and I rise when it is daylight, and I look about. Now, as I see him, my heart flutters. I look at him without raising my eyes. He gives me trinkets, and I take them, and I wear them for some time, until they are worn out.

Northern Yana, Betty Brown, 1907
Edward Sapir, *Yana Texts*

8

How My Father Found the Deer

ACHUMAWI
1970

LELA RHOADES, NARRATOR
BRUCE NEVIN, COLLECTOR AND TRANSLATOR

INTRODUCTION BY BRUCE NEVIN

Probably they ought to be called the Is, or the Ish, their word for "people."
Anthropologists call them the Achumawi, from their word *ajúm:á:wí,*
meaning dwellers on the *ajúm:á* or 'river', though the people themselves
applied that term only to families who lived in the valley midway up the
Pit River where the Fall River flows into it from the north. We will call
them the Pit River people, for that is what they call themselves today.

Their territory overlaps two ecological zones. Traveling up the Pit
River, one passes from deeply wooded intermountain declivities through
valleys that are progressively higher, broader, and drier. Downriver from
the place called *wíní'ha:'lí'wa* 'where it [the salmon] turns back', below
the junction of the Fall River, one finds typically Californian deer and
salmon, pine and oak. Upriver from that point, the land opens out to
the high plateau ecology of sagebrush and juniper, jackrabbit and elk that
one associates with Nevada and Eastern Oregon.

The people trapped animals in pits, hence the name. European explorers surely saw too the people's semisubterranean, earth-covered homes.

The ancestors of the Pit River people were evidently among the earliest settled inhabitants of California, speakers of Hokan languages whose descendants include Yana to the south, Shasta, Chimariko, and Karuk to the west, and others which are now separated from this northern group by intervening populations, such as the Pomo and Yuman groups of languages.

From ancient times they have maintained an annual cycle of land use: descending to the great rivers to fish for salmon in the spring; scattering to small family camps in the cooler foothills and mountains in the summer and autumn to hunt and to harvest crops planted for them, as they saw it, by the hand of God; retiring for the winter (*asjúy*) to separated villages of permanent earth-covered homes (*asjúy*) in sheltered mountain valleys; then returning to the riverside for the salmon run, cycle after yearly cycle of life in the Garden.

After centuries, or perhaps millennia, speakers of Penutian languages, whose descendants include the Wintu and the Maidu, brought different forms of land use and social affiliation. They occupied their riverside villages throughout the year, making expeditions for hunting and for the gathering of particular foods or craft supplies. When the Hokan people returning in the spring found a small Penutian settlement at some choice fishing spot, they shifted to another just as good, or almost as good. But the newcomers spread along the river into chains of villages whose inhabitants responded with quick allegiance to ties of blood and marriage if conflict arose with returning Hokan fishermen. The autonomous families and bands of Hokan speakers could not compete. Gradually, but with no evidence of settled warfare so far as we can tell today, the Hokan people retreated from the great Sacramento Valley to its periphery and outlying regions, where they continued their way of life, adapting to changed ecological conditions where they needed to.[1] The annual reunions for the spring salmon run, in which now both peoples were represented, continued to be the occasion of celebration, with feasting, dancing, singing, and gambling at the stick games.

At such a "big time" much trading was accomplished, and much courtship, for these were exogamous communities, proscribing marriage to relations calculated to a degree of remoteness that concerns only genealogists among us today. It was not uncommon for one of these small Pit River communities to include Modoc or Maidu or Wintu in-laws, and indeed one of these in-laws has an important role in our story. The fabric of communal life is woven of a thousand expectations and commitments that are as important to survival as the implements of hunt and harvest are for a small, highly interdependent community such as the one in which our story is set. So long as these mutual expectations are met, they scarcely rise to awareness. But this fabric is easily torn, and rifts put all parties at risk of privation and even death. As we shall see, the healing of relationships, the mending of reliability and reliance, was one of the responsibilities of a doctor or shaman.

Mrs. Lela Rhoades, whom it was my privilege and delight to call "Grandma," told me this story about her father's work as a shaman on November 28, 1970, at her home in Redding, California, when she was about eighty-seven years of age. I had met her that summer, not long after the beginning of my first experience of linguistic fieldwork. She lived alone in a large trailer home south of town. I say "alone," though her daughter and granddaughter were much present, her two sons lived nearby and visited, and before long her great-granddaughter's cradle was often at her feet as we sat and worked at her kitchen table—I with my tape recorder and notebook, she with her seemingly endless fund of stories and songs remembered from childhood. Once, she was singing me a song, remembering it, with her eyes closed, and she stopped suddenly and would not go on. "Something's looking at me," she said—a spirit animal, such as her father worked with. "I don't want to catch it." She explained that she could have been a doctor too, but she didn't want it, because it was an all-consuming profession. "People always want something from you," she told me, "or blame you for something."

Her father, Samson Grant, was of the Atsugewi or Hat Creek tribe.[2] These are close relatives of the Pit River people, living immediately to the south of them. Like many Atsugewi, he spoke both languages. Around 1852, when he was only a young boy, the majority of the Pit River and Hat Creek people were force-marched by soldiers to the concentration camp in Round Valley, Mendocino County. Indians from all over the state were confined there. After his parents died in the camp, he made his living by hunting and fishing for an elderly widow, who in turn cooked and provided a home of sorts. In his early teens he worked in various places around the Sacramento Valley as a ranch hand.

He knew that not all of his people had been captured. After a few years he returned to Pit River country. He found Buckskin Jack, the Hat Creek chief, who later arranged his marriage to Lela's mother. Her family had hidden themselves at Wé:'lá:mugí:'wa 'it gets shadowy early', a remote place near Goose Valley, north of Burney. To the north and west of this valley stands Yét, great Mount Shasta—"Lonely as God," in the celebrated words of Joaquin Miller, "and white as a winter moon." Southward, beyond lesser heights, stands its companion Ye:dí:jana 'the other Yét' (Mount Lassen). Except for the remoteness of their valley, and the fact that they were there year-round, they were much like other Pit River family groups that had dwelt under the watchful guardian spirits of the mountains for more than ten thousand winters past.

When Grandma Lela told the story to me in the Pit River language, it was somewhat as it might be told to one who knew the participants and their motivations, who was familiar with the customs and expectations of the community—the easiest and most natural way to tell it in Pit River. But when she retold the story in English, she provided background information interpreting one culture to the other—the easiest and most natural way to tell it in English. For example, in English she had to explain how Uncle Jack called Samson his son-in-law. In Pit River, she merely used a kinship term that, like many in the language, happens to apply reciprocally to both the elder and younger member of a relationship. This sort of difference of rendition is one of the thorniest and most disputed of the translator's problems. To present a story that is meaningful for English speakers, yet still reflects faithfully the teller's intentions and narrative skill, I have begun with her English rendition and have made it conform more closely to her Pit River rendition. Where new participants or new themes are introduced, the English version interjects more detail, some of which I have kept. This is especially obvious at the very beginning of the story. Here are the first few sentences, for comparison:[3]

Háné'gá	tól	chgí'wá:lujan	twijí:ní
Thence	for long	doctor	he was

qa	itú	wa'y:í:wílóo.
the	my	late father

A long time ago my late father was a doctor.

Wíy:úmji	twijí:ní.
One who dwelt	he was

[An old Wintun man] was living there.

'Amqhágam   qa   dó:si   dét'wi,   dí:qá:lami,
When   a   deer   kill   carry home

  'lá:sa'ch   duji.
  happy   to do

When someone killed a deer, packed it home, he was happy.

The word *wíy:úmji* 'one who [characteristically] dwelt' has perhaps a bit of the sense of a "roomer" or "boarder" in English. The old Wintun doctor was around seventy years old. The elderly were dependent on relatives for sustenance. In the opening two paragraphs of the English rendition we are told much more about him, about Uncle Jack, and about their relationship.

The example shows the characteristic verb-subject-object word order of this language, but scarcely any of the complexity of pronominal, adverbial, and other prefixes and suffixes that Pit River verbs frequently have (for instance, *twijí:ní,* t- 'EVIDENTIAL', w- '3RD PERSON', -jí- 'be, do', -n 'DURATIVE PAST'), and only hints of the sound system, with its tones, its laryngealized consonants, and its uvular (q) sounds pronounced at the back of the throat; but these are after all matters for another kind of discussion. A particular problem for translation is ambiguity as to the reference of pronouns. In this narration, Mrs. Rhoades makes frequent use of a narrative infinitive construction, with no pronouns at all. This ambiguity was also a characteristic of the English rendition, which I have tried to remedy without disturbing the vernacular tone of the original.

Three details in the story may require clarification. First, when Samson Grant accepts and smokes the tobacco, it seals a contractual agreement. In earlier days, it would probably have been in a pipe (*s'qoy'*), but this was a rolled cigarette. Having served its ceremonial function, the tobacco cannot be used further, so the grandfather returns it to the earth. Second, in the matter of who is at fault—the uncle or his wife—for neglecting the old man's portions, I would accept at face value the uncle's claims about responsibility for the distribution of meat; he had presumably expressed his feelings to his wife about their elderly neighbor, and she may well have shared those feelings. Third, a doctor commonly worked with an assistant who "interpreted" the words of his song, but Samson Grant did this for himself.

Mrs. Rhoades's gifts as a storyteller, long whetted on the myths and traditional stories of her people, are applied here to a piece of family history with grace and skill. Regardless of whether these events could be proven or disproven to have happened exactly as told, her narration is a true and vivid representation of the concerns and values of the community in which it arose.

NOTES

1. This account, which seems entirely plausible to me, is based on the work of Christopher Chase-Dunn of Johns Hopkins University and S. Edward Clewett and Elaine Sundahl of Shasta College in Redding.
2. "Atsugewi" is the anthropologists' term for this tribe, on analogy with the name "Achumawi." The actual Hat Creek word is *acug:e*, or "Atsuge."
3. The Achumawi forms cited in this article are given in a practical orthography, not a linguistic one.

FURTHER READING

A brief account of mostly physical aspects of Pit River culture is given in Alfred L. Kroeber's *Handbook of the Indians of California.* Jaime de Angulo's popular *Indians in Overalls* retells stories of his youthful encounters with a society in tragic disarray. He was primarily a raconteur, and his tales are colored by his personal preoccupations and his notions of "primitive psychology." The grammatical sketch of the language that he prepared with the help of L. S. Freeland ("The Achumawi Language") is not reliable. David Olmsted's *Achumawi Dictionary* is a compilation of earlier records, mostly de Angulo's, with elements of at least one other language mistakenly interspersed. Nevin treats the Achumawi sound system in his dissertation, "Aspects of Pit River Phonology." James Bauman's *Pit River Teaching Dictionary* represents upriver dialects.

HOW MY FATHER FOUND THE DEER

A long time ago my late father was a doctor. There was an old Wintun man who lived with us. He was married to my grandfather's sister. He didn't know how to talk Pit River, just a few broken words, but when he would sing for somebody, his words were just clear. He used to live aside of my uncle, my mother's brother, who had a lot of children.

My uncle used to be a good deerhunter. He didn't like this old fellow because he was a doctor. A doctor can do things to you, by just looking at you. He knows what you're going to do tomorrow, and who you did something to yesterday. He'd sing first, and his power would look back, trace you back. Then he'd tell you what you did and did and did, he'd pick up the tracks. He could see ahead too, maybe four or five years ahead, what you're going to do. But they don't do that until they sing.

So my uncle went out and killed a big deer. And the old man was happy, he was so happy. "We'll eat some meat tonight, they're going to give us a piece of meat." But no one came, they never gave him any meat. "He has to feed a lot of kids," he thought, so he didn't say anything, he didn't think anything about it, he didn't have bad thoughts.

In a week or so, my uncle brought in another deer. The old man was feeling very happy again. "This time he'll give us a piece of meat," he thought. And he was looking forward to sundown, for the evening meal. "I'm going to eat good tonight!" he thought. But he went to sleep without eating deer meat. And then in the morning no one came. That night, and next morning, no one came, and he didn't have any to eat. It went that way three times. And he thought, "Why does he do that? What's the matter, that he doesn't give me any meat?" And it grieved his heart, and then he cried.

"You won't eat, you won't eat deer meat," he thought. And then he sang, that night he sang. He called the *mák'má:ga,* the pileated woodpecker. He sang, "Drive away these deer and hide them! He didn't give me any," he sang, as though talking to the woodpecker. And then the woodpecker drove all the deer away and hid them.

After that, when my uncle went out, he didn't kill a deer. He didn't kill any deer all winter long. They went out, and none of them could find a deer. My father went out to hunt, my grandfather went out to hunt, they couldn't find even a track. And my uncles went out, but they couldn't find a track. For almost two years we never got any deer meat, we didn't eat any deer meat.

My uncle Jack's father, he knew something was the matter. "Something is wrong," he said. "Something is wrong someplace. I'll go and see my son-in-law." He called my father "son-in-law" because it was his brother's son-in-law. Of course, he knew my father was a doctor.

Just after dark he came, and he came in where we were all sitting around. He didn't come right in and sit down, he came in and stood. He rushed right in, talking, without stopping he talked. When he pulled out his tobacco, we knew something was wrong. He rolled some tobacco. He took just three puffs.* Then "Bi!" he said, "Here!" holding out his hand. My father looked at him. "What for?" he said. "You know what for!" he said. "There isn't any food, there isn't any meat, there isn't anything. There's no sign of a track," said my grandfather. "We haven't had any meat! What's wrong?" he said. "What's wrong with our country," he said, "that we don't have any meat? We've been hunting all winter, all this summer, and now we haven't got any meat, we can't find any meat. What's wrong? Look for it," he said. "I want you to have it searched for. That's why I've come in the evening," he said. And then he held out the tobacco again.

This time my father took the tobacco. He only drew three puffs, and he gave it back to him. After my father tasted it my grandfather didn't smoke it, he destroyed it. My grandfather never even sat down. And my father says, "You sit down and eat before sundown," he said. "I'll help sing right here," he said, "in my own house. Just before sundown I'll sit down. But don't invite anybody," he said. "Just you and your son and his two brothers, that's all." And that's all that came. But they didn't invite this old man, because he was a medicine man. "Before sundown, you eat. Then just before the sun touches the mountain, I'll sit down." And then without sitting down my grandfather went out and went home.

The next day in the evening they all came, they came to our house. And then, when the sun was just striking the mountain, my father went out. When he stepped out, they all came in, the three brothers, and sat

* Here, Mrs. Rhoades puffs three times.

down. We already had wood piled up inside, and pitch wood already split up and ready for us to use; my father had a chimney. They didn't allow a lamp to be lit, just the pitch. Then my father went out. I don't know where he went to. He just went out in the timber. And then when the sun was just about to disappear behind the mountain, he came in and sat down. Everything had to be very quiet. We were all to sit and be quiet, we couldn't even whisper. We children all sat in bed and watched.

Then he sang. Then he said, "I'm ashamed to say it. I'm ashamed to tell about it. I don't know," he said. And my grandfather said, "Don't be ashamed to tell us," he said. "Tell us," he said. "Tell us, tell us, tell us. We want to know," he said.

"Well," my father said, "OK, there's that old man, he was your brother-in-law, lives right there by you." He said, "He was sitting outside there, and he saw your son. This man," he said, "brought in a deer. And that old fellow was so happy that he was going to have some deer meat too. He thought maybe you'd give him a little of the ribs or something. But you didn't give it to him. You didn't take him over a piece of meat that evening, or the next day, or the next day. You didn't give him any. Then he thought, 'Well, he's got a big family, he's got lots of kids to feed. And of course, me, I'm nothing. So I guess that's why he didn't have any meat left over to give me any,' he thought. So he never thought any more about it. He forgot about it," he said. "He didn't think any more about it," he said.

"Then the next week, you killed another deer," he said. "You brought it in. He was happy when he saw you come in, he laughed to himself, he was so happy inside," he said. "And he thought he was going to get a piece of meat. But the same thing happened. You didn't give it to him. Three times you killed meat and he saw you. And you never gave any to him. And he cried," he said, "that night he cried. And he sang a song," he said. "He sang a song with *mákʼmá:ga*. He sang this song," he said, "and this *mákʼmá:ga* drove all the deer away and hid them. He's hiding them," he said, "and we can't find them."

And my uncle Jack said, "Yes, I did that. But I guess my wife never gave him anything," he said. "I have got nothing to do with it after I come home with that deer," he said. "She's the boss of the meat," he said.

Then my grandfather came again next night. They went home that night, and he came again, the same way. And then they knew something happened again, something was wrong again. My mother got kind of scared. Maybe he wanted my father to kill that old man, or maybe Uncle Jack killed him, or something. And he came again and he rolled that tobacco. And he gave it to my father. And my father says, "What for?" "Well," he said, "I want you to look for that meat and bring it back," he said. "Bring it back!" he said. "Where did he hide it? You look for it!" he said. "You, you're that kind too," he said. "Track that *mák'má:ga,*" he said. So my father took the tobacco, and he tasted it. "Yeah," he said. "The deer are still alive," he said. "They're still alive," he said. "They're not dead. He's just hiding it." And he gave the tobacco back, and my grandfather destroyed it.

Then, the same way, he had to sit down the same time. The same way, and that's why we had supper early, and they came again. They didn't invite the old Wintun man. And he sang that song again. And he couldn't find it. He hired this little screech owl spirit. "Did you see it go?" he asked, and he sent it out, and this little screech owl went out and looked for what was hiding the deer. And he said that the little screech owl said, "I can't find it." In just a short while, he came back. He says, "I can't find it. I can't even see the tracks," he said. Then he got another animal, I can't remember what. And that one came back right away, and said he couldn't find it either.

So then he sent out this little burrowing snake. It travels under the earth, like a mole burrowing, humping up the earth. He told it to go along under the earth. "Now go look for him, you go look for him in your earth," he said. And that little snake went along, and before long he came back. "It's there, I found it," he said. He found the deer bones. "But it's hot," he said. A big man was roasting all the deer bones in his *asjúy,* his winter house, that's how he kept the spirit of the deer there. "He's got it roasted," he said. "He's got it so hot that I can't pull it down," he said. "And this man was watching, and he had his bow ready and an arrow half drawn, ready to shoot anybody that looked down, looking for that deer meat. He was ready for him with his bow. He was ready to shoot," he said. "I just peeked in there, but it's too hot," he said. "I just peeked and I burned one of my eyes," he said. "I'm blinded in one eye." Blinded from the heat.

"Go again," my father said, "and take ice along with you. And as soon as he's not looking down," he said, "you look first, be very careful, don't make any noise," he said. "Look those bones over good, and you pull that one," he said, "you pull that bone down in the ground." He named a main bone in the deer's body, a special bone, but I don't remember what it is. "Take that bone from the fire with your mouth, holding it in your mouth," he said. So this little fellow went back again. He sang the song again, and it sounded like he went, that little snake. I heard that he went.

This little snake spirit went, he went under the ground. Then he peeked up with one eye, and he saw that man was looking right straight up there. While he was looking, he saw those bones, and with his one eye he saw that bone, the one to take. So he went out there and, holding ice in his mouth, he pulled it out from the fire and drew it down. He slipped the bone down under the ground, and that man never noticed it. He brought it back under the ground, though it was burning him, even as my father was singing. And he danced, he danced around the fireplace. They lit a stick of pitch. He had no shirt on, just his pants, barefooted, and he was dancing right by the chimney there. When that little snake was going to pull the bone down, my father had to be in that hot place there too. Then blood gushed out of my father's mouth, it just streamed down his mouth. The little snake was the one that was burned, that was what made blood come up. That's when the snake burned his mouth, that's why he did that. Then it looked like he came back. When he brought that bone back, "Here!" he said, and he gave it to my father. And he reached out and took it, it looked like he reached out and grasped something. My father took it. We couldn't see it. And he fainted, my father fainted. They had a bucket of water there, and they stuck that arm in the water, and they put water on his face, and he came to.

And then he sang and talked to the snake. And he said, "Now he brought back the deer." Then he said, "Treat that man good. Next time you kill meat, even a small one, don't be stingy, give him a ham. Even a ham, going to him with it, say 'Have some for breakfast,'" he said. That's what he said when he sang. And then he told it, he was the one who told about it, he didn't have an assistant to interpret for him. And he said, "Don't think anything bad, but doing in the right way, have compassion, treat him well. You should give some to him first," he said. "Not to us," he said. "We're young men yet, we can still hunt for ourselves, so don't think about giving meat to us. That one, you two give to that one," he said. "Well," said my uncle, "I'll tell my wife." And I guess he did.

The woodpecker was the one who drove all the deer away and hid them, piled the bones up in a ring of fire, piled the bones inside the fire so nothing was able to touch them. And he was waiting for someone to look down through the doorway in the roof of the *asjúy,* ready to shoot him in the heart, watching, determined not to give up the deer bones. That's why the screech owl was afraid, and the other one also was afraid, so he came back. But this little snake, burrowing through the earth, he's the one that brought back the deer.

And then we ate deer meat again. "For three days, you wait, and then you go hunting," said my father, "and you'll get your deer." So Uncle Jack went out there and he got his deer, and Uncle Jim went out there, and they all got deer. My father killed one deer. And so they gave the old Wintun man meat, and he was happy.

So I saw this, I saw it while I was still pretty young, but old enough to understand, and that's how it was that I listened. That's how my father used to do.

9

Naponoha (Cocoon Man)

ATSUGEWI
1931

JOHN LAMARR (DIXIE VALLEY), NARRATOR

SUSAN BRANDENSTEIN PARK, COLLECTOR

DARRYL BABE WILSON, EDITOR

INTRODUCTION BY DARRYL BABE WILSON

In 1931, Susan Brandenstein Park had just graduated from the University of California, in Berkeley's anthropology program, and had applied to be a part of an expedition to the Fiji Islands. She placed her name on the sign-up sheet, "somewhere near the bottom, but not off of the roster by any means whatsoever."[1] Then she, along with all the others, anxiously awaited its posting. Daily she rushed to the anthropology department. Finally, the roster was hanging on the door.

"There was a crooked line through my name. It was as if somebody had cut me across the heart with a knife. I never quite fully recovered." Although slashed, Susan was not defeated. Dr. Kroeber and her advisor, Robert Lowie, had strongly hinted that, if she first could accomplish some fieldwork, she would then have a good chance at the next Fijian expedition.

She dreamed of Fiji. Of the perfume from the jungle flowers in the morning sun, and the waves rushing in and smoothing back out. Of birds of every color flitting through the sunlit forest while she walked in the silver sand hunting seashells. Of listening to the drumming and singing in the night and watching the stars move softly across the powdery, warm heavens.

But Dr. Kroeber had advised her to cut her teeth on a "simpler culture" and directed her to the mountains of Northeastern California to work with the Atsugewi, my father's people, with the admonition that information that is not published "is worthless." So she packed her little coupe and headed north from San Francisco.

The Atsugewi ('People Who Live in the Pine Forest') live along Hat Creek, east of Mount Lassen and south of Mount Shasta, about sixty miles east of Redding. Susan found herself in very wild country, with lava beds, rattlesnakes, bears, mountain lions, and coyotes. "To me, it was like going to the moon," she said. This was because there was such disparity between American society and the Atsugewi culture. She was surrounded by huge mountains, rushing rivers, wild animals, some not-so-tame natives, and some not-so-civilized whites.

She rented a shack so the Atsugewi would not think of her as needing too many comforts. Then, after learning that the Cassel Post Office was the place to find "Indians," she walked there in the morning.

"There were many Indians there, sitting around. Not talking, just sitting. I do not know what they were waiting for, they never seemed to get any mail," Susan told me. She did not know that the post office was the local "Department of Employment" and a place for people to exchange news and information. Whenever a farmer wanted a fence built, he picked up an "Indian" from the post office. Loggers, ranchers, and construction companies all did the same.

Susan "did not know where to begin," so she simply talked with the first person who seemed to be friendly, Lee Bone. She failed to record her first conversation, but word got out quickly that she was paying a dollar a day for information—the same as the Atsugewi received for hard labor. Contrary to the opinion of her advisor, Susan had discovered that the Atsugewi were "not such a simple culture, after all." Although some people wondered about being paid "just for talk," Susan received many responses, recording over two thousand pages with her Number Two pencil and hardbacked notepads, from the people of Hat Creek, Dixie Valley, and Goose Valley.

One evening she decided to move out of her shack. "I returned to discover that a friendly rattlesnake had taken up domicile under my cot!" She promptly moved to Rising River Lodge and continued her research from there.

In 1989, I met Susan through *News from Native California,* a quarterly produced by Malcolm Margolin in Berkeley, California. Susan had been reading the magazine and had seen my name and my tribal identity, A-juma-wi/Atsuge-wi. "'Atsugewi' just leaped out of the page at me—the very people I had studied long ago," she stated.

Soon I was visiting her in Carson City, Nevada. We looked over the old narratives. There were my elders, peering back at me through the pages and through time. It was exciting to read the transcriptions of the old stories I had heard when I was just a child holding on to my father's legs in the midst of a gathering of grandmothers and grandfathers, in the darkness of winter evenings, long ago.

I asked her one day in 1992 if she had ever made it to Fiji. "No," she said, "I never did, but I hope to. Some day in the future, perhaps." Susan Park was born in 1908 and was in fragile health when we first met in 1989. She often said that she would not make it through the winter of 1993. She did not: she died just before Thanksgiving 1992. If she had lived just one more year, she might have seen her work published at last, in my master's thesis, *Yo-Kenaswi Usji (Necklace of Hearts).*

According to the legends of my people, Naponoha (Cocoon Man) changed into Night-Flying Butterfly during the "great transformation." This butterfly is not to be confused with the moth, but is the huge butterfly that appears to be a moth. Up close, it has all the markings of a monarch butterfly. It could be compared to the black jaguar: upon closer examination, the fur of the black panther reveals all of the patterns and markings of the "regular" jaguar, but black is very dominant.

The Night-Flying Butterfly is beautiful. When viewed in the sunlight, it shines with the most precious colors of camouflaged shadows. The powder on its body is thick, like fur, and it moves so softly! My boy Sonny, when he was five years old, once asked me, "Dad, do you know what happens to butterflies when they get old? I mean, when they get *really* old?" And then he answered his own question: "They turn into moths."

So, Naponoha may be the wise and creative butterfly that turned into something like a moth. But Naponoha is also much more than that, according to our legends. He also helped create much of the world and the universe.

Lela Rhoades, one of the very old wisdom-keepers of our history, gave our nation a song:

Aboni-ka-ha, me-moo-ischi-ee
Aboni-ka-ha, me-moo-ischi-ee
Aboni-ka-ha, me-moo-ischi-ee

She sang the melody three times in a variety of tempos. Then she explained that it meant, "in American,"

Great Wonder, we are your children,
Great Power, we are your children,
Great Spirit, we are your children.

It should not be surprising, then, that Naponoha possesses all of the abilities to dream and to have his dreams fulfilled. He can see all of the world around him. His vision goes through the mountains, deep into the universe, and far into the thoughts of his people. Naponoha is a prophet, a dreamer, a creator, a wonder. In this narrative, Naponoha takes the form of a leader of his people—a warrior.

Latowni is the ceremonial roundhouse at Pittville around which the people lived. The Mice brothers stay awake all night, get into the food, and cache or scatter it. They are mischievous. It is their "way" to stay awake at night and to sleep during the day. Weasel intends to scold the boys for their nocturnal troublemaking. What Weasel does not know is that Naponoha has a mission for the boys.

The Klamath people (Oregon, just north of the Modocs) have stolen three articles: the Pestle, used for grinding seeds and dried foods, and representing the labor of the people; the Sky Knife, a long sword made from clear obsidian, and representing the protection of the nation; and the Diamond, a lucky stone that contains a rainbow and brings goodness to those who honor its power. (Naponoha later uses the Sky Knife while riding his dog during the war, taunting the enemy.) Naponoha tells the Mice brothers that they should go north to the Klamath people and retrieve the tribal materials, which they do.

When the Mice brothers have completed their mission, they return home, make a lot of noise in camp at night, then sleep during the day. Their father is Coyote. The Mice frolic around, play war by shooting at each other, and wind up shooting their father in the ear. They think they are pretty tough.

A few days later, a Klamath man arrives at Latowni and says there is going to be a war to regain the articles. Naponoha sends for Frog to interpret his message, but Frog gets it wrong. When the messenger returns, Naponoha this time asks Lark to translate, which she does. After displaying the recovered articles, Naponoha agrees to have a war to settle the issue. So the Dixie Valley people and the Klamath people meet. The war lines are drawn in the Fall River valley. Twins do the interpreting for each side, carrying messages back and forth. Each side constructs rock fortifications in the forest and just beyond the ridge, but they actually meet face-to-face in the valley, the Dixie Valley warriors facing the Klamaths in a long line within arrow range. Naponoha has a huge dog that he rides like a horse, and he has the Sky Knife, which flashes in the sunlight, and his long hair shines. The Klamaths are bewildered. And so the war begins.

The Klamath people have a "witch" with them. Every time the arrow hits the witch, it glances off. Finally, the witch tells how he can be killed, and the Dixie Valley Indians use this information to kill him. The witch turns out to be a turtle, all the Klamaths are killed, and the war is over. Turtle, who is a powerful "doctor," revives. He takes a stick and brings all the Klamaths back to life. The Klamath people agree to abandon their war over the Diamond. Both sides smoke to seal the "word."

Naponoha then declares that the timber line will always be a reminder that there was once a war between the Klamath people and Dixie Valley. He also decides that he and the twin interpreters should stay beside the river for a while, telling the story, so the history might be told properly. Turtle and some of the other Klamaths want to stay in the Fall River valley, which Naponoha decides to allow. So Turtle and some of the Klamath people remain in the Pit River country, which is how the turtle came to be in the Fall River valley. It must have been the first time any of the Dixie Valley people had seen a turtle.

In the end, all of the Dixie Valley people return home to have a big sweat in their sweat house. Everybody gathers together and Naponoha makes a big smoke of many colors and many shapes. It is so beautiful that the people agree that, if there is ever any more trouble, there should be a big fire and a big smoke announcing the event, and all will assemble quickly.

All this was recorded to preserve the history of the conflict between the Dixie Valley and Klamath people and to show that it is not right to steal or claim something that belongs to another. The timber has long since been cut, and the rock fortifications removed by settlers—but the history, like the spirit of the people, remains.

NOTE

1. All quotes attributed to Susan Park in this introduction are drawn from conversations I had with her during the years 1989–1992.

FURTHER READING

See Thomas Garth's "Atsugewi Ethnography" and his "Atsugewi" article in the California volume of the Smithsonian *Handbook*. See also David Olmstead's *A Lexicon of Atsugewi*. Diane Walters presents an Atsugewi story, "Coyote and Moon Woman (Apwarukeyi)," in Victor Golla and Shirley Silver's *Northern California Texts*. Darryl Wilson has edited a collection of some forty-five narratives recorded by Susan Brandenstein Park from Atsugewi and Achumawi storytellers: see his *Yo-Kenaswi Usji (Necklace of Hearts)*. He has also written an autobiography, *The Morning the Sun Went Down*.

NAPONOHA

Naponoha said this: "The Mice in Latowni, whatever grub they had, they changed it around all night. Next morning, Yas, the Weasel, got mad because they took their grub to another place." And Naponoha said, "Leave these boys alone. Don't scold them."

That night Naponoha said to the Mice, "You two ought to go north, get the Diamond and the Pestle. If you could get that . . . " And they listened and they whispered to one another, "What does he mean?" And, he said, "You might, too, get the Sky Knife at the same time. It's back north." And [the] Mice said, "Where about does he mean, anyway?"

They did the same thing that night—made lots of noise, changed the grub again. Along toward daylight they went, and everything was quiet after they left. And they went north, the two little Mice. They were brothers.

They kept going till they got there. They stopped overnight and then would keep going. They got to a great big river and they saw a lot of people on the other side, and the two little Mice said, "Maybe that's the place Naponoha meant. Maybe that's the place. And how are we going to get across?" the two little Mice said.

And they said, "We'll wait till dark comes and maybe someone will cross with a canoe and maybe we'll get across that way. And all night we'll do that."

And some people were waiting, and someone came across, and the Mice hid in the tules, and someone called to the man to come across and he went across. It was dark-time and he came up to shore. "There's a chance, there's a chance," one mouse said. "Now, get ready!"

And the man got in the canoe and the Mice jumped in under the man and they went across, and when they got to the shore on the other side, as soon as they hit shore, the two little Mice jumped out, and these two men didn't know that the Mice were in the canoe.

And the Klamath chief said, "Well, we better have a Big Time tonight. We'll look at the Diamond and the Pestle and the Knife. We better show them," he said.

"Now we got the right place," [the] Mice said when they heard it. Little Mice said, "There's our chance now, we must be sure now." And everybody came all to one place in the *chema-ha,* the sweat house, and they got ready and showed the Diamond and the Pestle and the Knife.

And the two Mice were behind the legs of the people. They hid and no one knew they were there. They watched while the Diamond and Pestle and Knife were being shown.

Oh! there was a big light over the sweat house when they showed the Diamond. And then everybody got through showing it and they put the Diamond and Pestle and Knife away, and the Mice wondered where they put them away.

Nobody went to sleep that night and the Mice began taking the grub that night the same as they did at home. And they went to look for the Diamond and the Pestle and the Knife.

They found them and they took them outside and they went all over the camp, all over where the people were living. They ran across Pi-jko, the Lark, who had a Klamath Indian for a husband.

They said, "Hello," and they pinched her and that woman said, "What's bothering me so much?" And [the] Mice said, "That's us two," and they went up and they talked to her, and she said, "Two bad brothers. How did you get over here?"

Well, they said, "Put us across. We want to go home." They told Pi-jko, and she did, she put them across, and they let her know what they took away, and they went to where the canoe was and all got in and went to the other side. And they said, "Good-bye," to Pi-jko and they came back, the two little Mice, and she went back to the other side in the dark.

And she called, "Brothers, be sure and get back." And the little Mice said, "All right," and they came back. They stopped over night, and they came and stopped and came, and they got home way in the middle of the night, and when they got back they made a noise and the Big Time chief felt everyone in Latowni was sorry. Naponoha was sorry for them, and they made the same noise, and when daylight came they slept.

They had a bow and arrow apiece, and they shot one another and then they shot Coyote in the ear. Coyote was Mice's father.

"Oh!" said Coyote. "You're hurting me." And Mice said, "That's what I'm going to do when I fight." 'Course they went to sleep, them two.

Oh, a few days after that he says, "Friends, *she-me-wolol, she-me-wolol.*"

That time the Klamath Indian came over to tell them they were going to have a war because the Mice stole the Diamond. And the Klamath Indian said, "*She-me-wolol, she-me-wolol.*" And he said this through the smoke hole of Latowni.

And Naponoha asked Ali-yem, Frog, who spoke all languages, what was meant by this. And Yas ran over there to Ali-yem to tell her that Naponoha wanted her to come over and say what the Klamath Indian meant. So, she came there inside, and the Klamath Indian said, "*She-me-wolol, she-me-wolol.*"

And Naponoha said to Ali-yem, "What does he mean?" "Oh," she said, "They are going to have a dance down here, that's what he means." And, of course, after she said this the Klamath Indian went back, and after he went back the Klamath people asked him, "What did they say?" And he said, "They didn't say anything to me."

They sent him back again to Naponoha's place. He came again to the same place and he said, "*She-me-wolol, she-me-wolol*" again. And Naponoha said, "What does he mean? You said he was saying they are going to have a dance. What did he come back for?"

So, Naponoha said, "You get Pi-jko now," and Yas went over to let her know again. So she came over, and the Klamath Indian said, "*She-me-wolol.*" And Pi-jko said, "He says the two Mice stole the Diamond, the Pestle, and the Knife. And he says there is going to be a war. That's what he's saying. They want the Diamond right back; otherwise there will be a war."

And the two little Mice were sleeping all the time. They would not get up. And then the Klamath Indian went back, and Naponoha said, "You two better get up. What did you do with the Diamond and Pestle and Knife? You stole them. We used to lose those things. It's a good thing you have them back. We're going to have a war with the Klamath Indians," he said.

The two little Mice jumped up and they shot their father, Coyote, in the ear again, the same way, and they said, "Yes, sir, right over there." "Go get them then," Naponoha said. "Where are they?"

They went and got them and gave the Diamond and Pestle and Knife to Naponoha, and they untied and untied and held the Diamond up and it was just like lightning. And the Klamath Indian saw it. Oh, the Klamath Indian saw that light, and they sent that same Indian over again, and he said, "*She-me-wolol, she-me-wolol.*"

And Pi-jko said, "You better get ready to fight. Hurry and get ready. If you ain't going to give the Diamond up, there is going to be a war!"

"All right," Naponoha said. Pi-jko can talk any language. And Naponoha, he told Pi-jko, "All right. We are going to have a war." And the Indian went back and he said, "Yes, they are willing to fight, and right away." That's what the Klamath Indian told his own people, and Naponoha's people got ready and they went down on the side of Fall River.

Naponoha's people were in that edge of timber there, and the Klamath Indians were on the other side of that ridge of timber, and each side got interpreters halfway between the Klamath Indians and Naponoha's Indians. There were two twins there and those were the interpreters for the two sides, and they went forth and back with what they said.

The Klamath Indians sent over a man who said, "If you don't give up that Diamond, we are going to have a war."

So then Naponoha's interpreter went back and told Naponoha, and he said, "They said for you to give up the Diamond, otherwise they're going to have a war." Naponoha sent him back. "Tell him I'm not going to give it up. Tell him we'll have a war."

And the interpreter told the Klamath interpreter, "They ain't going to give up. They are going to have a war."

So the Klamath Indians said, "All right, we'll have a war and we'll fight right away." And they all got ready and they fought.

They fought. They shot one another and Naponoha had a great big dog that hunted around, and he used it as a horse and he rode it with his hair flying (and Naponoha had great long hair, bright hair), and he had a great long knife in his hand, and when the Klamath Indians saw him they didn't know what to do.

And he told his people, "Go ahead and fight!" And they killed all the Klamath Indians. They killed every one of them.

But they couldn't kill To-ka-jisa, the witch. They didn't know how to. They shot him and the arrows just glanced off. And To-ka-jisa said like this to Naponoha: "I like this country." And he said to Naponoha, "If I stand straight up and you shoot down at me, that's the only way you can kill me."

So, he stood straight up, and they shot down into his mouth, and that was the only way they could kill him. "I don't like to go back to Klamath. I like this country, that's why I told you how to kill me. If I didn't tell you, I could clean you all up."

And To-ka-jisa took a stick and he hit the Klamath Indians, and they all came back to life. And Naponoha said, "You people better go back." And the Klamath Indians said, "All right. We give up. You whipped us all right."

So he said, "When you were [in] the war lines, [that was] good. That is our timber. It shows that you were Klamath Indians on that side. So it will be on my side, the same way." That's what Naponoha told them and that interpreter.

"Those two twin interpreters will be there along on the river. So the people would know what we did. So they can tell about it in history, what trouble we had, and it will settle it right." That's what Naponoha said. And the Klamath Indian said, "All right." And he said, the Klamath Indian said, "I'm sorry, but I can't help it. I would not think about it anymore. You can have the Diamond and Pestle and Knife for good."

"How about it," Naponoha said to To-ka-jisa. "Why are *you* going to stay here in this country?" And the Klamath chief said, "What can I do if they want to stay here? I cannot kick over them because you whipped us and asked me, that's the reason I have to let my man stay. I can't kick," he said.

"Well, let them stay here," Naponoha said.

And that's the reason that Hap-ej, the Turtle, is in the Fall River valley. Hap-ej belonged to the Klamath and he spread all the way down the Sacramento Valley. And they scattered all over. That was the Klamath Indians. There Hap-ej was, and they scattered him.

They sat down and smoked, and then they said, "Well, I go." And the Klamath Indian went back.

So, Naponoha came back where he belonged, and they got home, all on both sides. So they had a Big Time, Naponoha's people. And he let all his people see the Diamond and the Pestle and the Knife. He said, "We used to have this and we got it back." And Naponoha told his people, "We've got it back."

And it was all right. Everything was settled fine and dandy, and Naponoha was in the *chema-ha,* everybody was in the *chema-ha.* It was a great big sweat house. Naponoha told his people, "I'll show you what I can do." And he filled his pipe with tobacco, Naponoha did, and he smoked and he smoked like a cloud inside the sweat house. It was so pretty, and they all looked, and all the Indians said, "Ain't that pretty?"

It was a pretty color and all kinds of shapes, rings. And all the Indians said, "We'll all have to go back where we belong, and if anything happens let us know." So he said, "Whenever you have anything happen, build a big smoke so we will know."

That's what Naponoha told his people. And the people said, "All right." And they all scattered and went back.

That's what it is, Naponoha's history.

It shows plainly right now in the timber. That was all.

10

A Story of Lizard

YAHI

1915

ISHI, NARRATOR

EDWARD SAPIR, COLLECTOR

HERBERT W. LUTHIN AND LEANNE HINTON, TRANSLATORS

INTRODUCTION BY HERBERT W. LUTHIN

Ishi, the narrator of this story, is something of a legend in the history of post-Contact Native America and is a touchstone figure in California anthropology. His story is well-known—it's been told in books, articles, and films—so I won't do much more than summarize it here. But it's only fair to say that the "legend" of Ishi is nothing if not a conflicted one.

The subtitle to Theodora Kroeber's celebrated Ishi source book, *Ishi in Two Worlds,* provides us with a good starting point in this regard: *A Biography of the Last Wild Indian in North America.* Whatever he may have been to himself, for non-Indians Ishi, quite simply, stood as an icon of the natural man, a latter-day remnant of pre-Contact Native America. The irony, of course, is that Ishi lived anything but a natural human life, was anything but a pre-Contact "natural man."

Ishi was the last Yahi. His tribe (the southernmost division of the Yana group), after decades of conflict with settlers and prospectors, skirmishes with the U.S. Army, and what can only be called the wanton "poaching" of white vigilantes who killed for sport, was all but wiped out along with the rest of the Yana in a concerted campaign of genocide carried out by local militia groups. Ishi was born into this shattered world—probably in 1862—about two years before these "final solution" massacres took place.

Ishi survived because his band survived, decimated but intact, only to be surprised a year later by vigilantes in their Mill Creek camp and decimated once more. Only a handful, perhaps as many as a dozen, escaped—among them the little boy Ishi, his mother, and an older sister. This small group then went into deep hiding, vanishing almost without trace for forty years. Except for a few scattered incidents, as far as anyone knew, by 1872 the Yahi were functionally extinct. But life went on for Ishi's people in hiding. With no births, though (there were no marriageable children in the group when it slipped "underground"), the old just grew older, and the group gradually dwindled. By the time Ishi reached the age of forty, after nearly four decades of hiding, the last member of his group, his own aged mother, had died.

That year was 1908. On August 29, 1911, naked and starving, hair still singed off in mourning three years after the death of his last human companion, Ishi gave himself up outside a slaughterhouse in Oroville. Until he walked out of hiding and into the history of twentieth-century California, Ishi's entire life, from infancy to middle age, was spent in hiding—a sort of backcountry version of Anne Frank's concealment. The stress of that existence, a life of constant hardship and fear of discovery, is difficult for us even to imagine. Ishi was Yahi, all right—purely, deeply, fully so. But the Yahi life he knew was not the free, self-possessing, traditional existence of his ancestors; and it is a mistake to think that Ishi can represent for us—for anyone—some animistic "free spirit" or serve as a spokesman of untrammeled Native American life and culture.

Upon his discovery, Ishi became an overnight media sensation: a "wild Indian," a living Stone Age man—captured in the backcountry of modern California! When the news hit the stands in San Francisco, Alfred Kroeber, head of anthropology at the University of California, dispatched the linguist-anthropologist T. T. Waterman to Oroville to establish communication and bring him to the university. To protect him from exploitation (though let's not forget that Ishi was also the anthropological "find" of a lifetime), Kroeber gave him light employment as a live-in caretaker at the university's new Museum of Art and Anthropology, as a way of providing him with pocket money and safe lodging. His days were often filled with linguistic and ethnographic work, for there was an endless stream of scholars coming to work with him, and other interested visitors seeking audience. And on Sunday afternoons, he appeared as a kind of "living exhibit" in the museum itself, chipping arrowheads, drilling fire, and demonstrating other native Yahi crafts and techniques for the public. Thus did Ishi live out the last five years of his life—in truth, in relative contentment and ease, unlikely though this may seem. Those who knew him and became his friends came to love him. He died of tuberculosis in March of 1916.

Given this extraordinary life, it should come as no surprise to learn that Ishi's stories—which only now, eighty years after their narration, are finally being made available to scholars and the public alike—are strikingly unlike anything else known in California oral literature. In some respects, they are of a piece with known Yana tradition; in others, they are eccentric to an amazing degree. Yet we are extremely fortunate to have them, for they tell us a great deal about Yahi life and custom and even more about Ishi himself.

The story presented here was taken down by the great linguist Edward Sapir, who came to California in the summer of 1915 to work with Ishi in what was to be his last year. Ishi was probably already ill by the time Sapir arrived, but in August, after many weeks of steady work, his illness grew too pronounced to ignore, and he was placed in the hospital, where he died about six months later. Ishi's untimely death was no doubt the main reason Sapir never returned to his notebooks and worked up these texts for publication. And in truth, it would have been a daunting task, for much of the work of translation and verification was incomplete at the time Ishi was hospitalized. Sapir called his work with Ishi "the most time-consuming and nerve-wracking that I have ever undertaken," noting that "Ishi's imperturbable good humor alone made the work possible" (Golla 1984b:194).

Sapir recorded Ishi's stories the hard way: by hand, in detailed phonetic transcription. All told, he recorded at least six stories, filling five notebooks—more than two hundred pages of text. Most of the pages are only sparsely glossed at best (indeed, two entire notebooks contain only unglossed Yahi text), and this poses a challenge for linguists of the Yahi Trans-

FIGURE 3. Ishi.
Courtesy Phoebe Apperson Hearst Museum of Anthropology
and the Regents of the University of California.

lation Project, who are trying to reconstruct their meaning.[1] I present here
the best-worked, best-glossed text, "A Story of Lizard." Even so, there are
places (duly marked) where we are still not sure exactly what is going on.

Ishi's narrative style is often demanding, at least for those coming from
a Western literary tradition. Readers may well find this to be the most
difficult of all the selections in this volume, thanks to Ishi's stripped-down,
elliptical approach to telling a story, even a long one, and the short, bul-
letlike bursts of his delivery. Compositionally, "A Story of Lizard" is more
of a suite than a story. Rather than a single overarching plot, it contains
a series of episodes and situations, each with its own interior form, all of
which combine to form the larger whole. Some of these episodes and
situations recur cyclically a number of times. For instance, the Ya'wi, or
"Pine-nutting," episode occurs three times, in parts verbatim; and there
are four separate "Arrow-making" episodes, some quite elaborately detailed. The remaining two episodes are unique: one, a "Grizzly Bear" adventure, is essentially a story-within-a-story; the second is a "Night Dance"

episode that is not matched by other elements within the tale. Rather than recounting the story sequentially, I will briefly describe the individual episodes, then explain how they are pieced together to comprise the whole.

Arrow-making

Ishi opens his tale with a glimpse of Lizard making arrows, an activity that provides the background for the entire story. In some sense it is Lizard's unflagging industry that serves as the story's thematic center. Other adventures—the various alarms and excursions that make up the "plot"—may come and go, but the arrow-making is always there.[2] (It is something of a joke among those of us working on these stories, that the real reason Lizard always seems to be making arrows is because he keeps losing them all in his fights with the Ya'wi.) Ishi was himself a master arrow-maker, and reportedly loved to flake arrowheads, experimenting with all sorts of materials. Indeed, the arrowheads he made during his brief tenure at the old Museum of Anthropology in San Francisco are among the finest in the Lowie Museum's collection of artifacts. One can almost learn how to make arrows from Ishi's descriptions of the process in the four Arrow-making episodes.[3]

Pine-nutting

The "Ya'wi" is what the Yahi called the Wintun people to the west—enemies in ancient times. Lizard ventures into hostile territory to collect pine-nuts for his people, and is attacked by a band of Ya'wi warriors. He keeps his cool, pretending their war-whoops are "nothing but the wind," and shoots his arrows "straight into their faces." In the end, he makes it back home with a fresh supply of pine-nuts. The oral-formulaic style of patterned repetitions is very prominent within these sections, based primarily on the variation of Yahi directional elements ('to the west', 'to the east', 'across a stream', 'up a mountain', and so on) against a common stem, especially *mooja-* 'to shoot' and *ni- ~ ne-* 'to go'.

Grizzly Bear and Long-Tailed Lizard

This is the most complex episode of the story—a fully developed narrative in its own right. Lizard runs out of *baiwak'i* sticks for making the foreshafts of his arrows. He sends Long-Tailed Lizard to collect some more. Long-Tail is surprised by Grizzly Bear, who swallows him up and "grows pregnant." When Long-Tail fails to return, Lizard sets out after him. He finds the *baiwak'i* all scattered around, and Grizzly's tracks, and guesses the rest. Gathering up the sticks, he returns home. As a token of mourning, the sticks are not used, but burned. At daybreak, after cutting off his hair and smearing his face with pitch (further tokens of mourning), Lizard sets out to find the bear.

What happens next is unclear, because there are some thorny problems with the interpretation of Sapir's text and glosses throughout this section. But it appears as if Lizard travels to Grizzly Bear's favorite feeding ground and climbs up into a convenient tree toward evening to have a smoke and wait for her. In the morning she comes, as she seems destined to do, to feed on the *k'asna* vines (identified only vaguely as a vine growing near water). Lizard has prepared himself by draping one of the vines around his neck and letting it dangle down, the idea being (we think) that when Grizzly arrives and begins to feed, she will tug on the vine and alert him. In the morning she comes and starts to feed. Lizard puts a loop into his bowstring and lets Grizzly pull him down onto her back, whereupon he slips the loop around her neck and lets the strung bow strangle her. After gouging out her eyes (the revenge against a man-eating bear is always harsh), he slits her open and recovers Long-Tailed Lizard. (As Leanne Hinton points out, this is a familiar motif in folklore: Europeans know it from "Little Red Riding Hood.") In the morning it's back to making arrows.

The Night Dance

One day, as Lizard is "busy with his arrow-making," he breaks a shaft. The break in the shaft foretells a break in the routine: some neighboring people are having a dance. For the next three days, the domestic rhythms of the camp are inverted, as Lizard's people dance all night and—except for one attempt at gathering food, abandoned the next time around as too much hassle—sleep all day. We simply have no idea what all the "excrement" is about: the way the text reads, at the beginning of the Dance episode, Lizard's people are given some excrement (the stem *wak'i-* 'shit' is unambiguous on this point), which they smear all over themselves. After the last night of dancing, Lizard scolds them for being slug-a-beds, whereupon they all bathe themselves clean and get back to work. Life returns to normal, and Lizard resumes his arrow-making.

When we put all these episodes together, paying careful attention to their cycles of repetition, an overall pattern reveals itself—the true architecture of this fascinating tale. If we take the four Arrow-making episodes to be the thematic baseline or rhythmic "pulse" of the narrative, view the Pine-nutting episodes with their Ya'wi attacks as intermittent events that punctuate that baseline, and recognize the unique Grizzly Bear and Night Dance episodes as extraordinary happenings that stand far out against that background "hum," we might represent the narrative structure schematically as in figure 4:

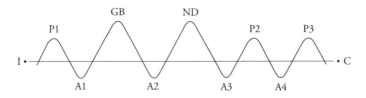

FIGURE 4. Narrative structure of Ishi's "A Story of Lizard." (I = Introduction; P = Pine-nutting; A = Arrow-making; GB = Grizzly Bear; ND = Night Dance; C = Conclusion.)

What seems at first a hopeless déjà vu of motifs and situations proves now to be quite the opposite: a carefully controlled narration of great balance and dignity.

When I first went to work on this story, nearly a decade ago, I felt it to be one of the bleakest accounts of survival I had ever seen—a relentless tale of repetitive drudgery and danger. Now, looking at it anew, I see it in a different light. Like a Beowulf or a Roland in European tradition, Lizard represents the essence of a Yahi culture-hero. Lizard provides for his people—unfailingly. Instead of despair, there is reassurance in these unvarying routines and in Lizard's unflappable reliability in a crisis.

And in truth, I think Ishi, as the only able-bodied man among his lost band of survivors for all those long, lean years of hiding, must have been something of a Lizard himself.

A NOTE ON THE TRANSLATION

Because so much has been said for and about Ishi, and so little has ever come forth from Ishi himself, we have felt a special urgency, in dealing with the records he left behind, to let Ishi be heard in his own voice and words at last. Granted, proclamations like this have a hollow ring when the end-result is a translation. After all, what Ishi *actually* said in "A Story of Lizard" (as in these lines from the very beginning of the myth) was this:[4]

Híri',
    héebil' k^h híri'mawna . . .
K'úllil'.
Niwílji',
    wísdu' gi iwílc^{hi}.   5
Nilóopji'.
Domjawáldi' k^h díitel^{la}
(Hóok'awdubalgu' gi wéeyump^{ha};
dóowayalcidibil' wéeyump^{ha}).
Bóot'an' c^h wísh^i.   10
Júspja',
    jóst'al'^{i}.
Jewóo' c^h yónbal'^{i}.
Jé^{h}duwoo' k^h báan^u.
Busdím' c^h Yáa'^{wi}!   15

Since there is no one left alive who can speak or understand this language, the need for translation is unimpeachable. Still, we have wanted to minimize the degree to which the voices of translation mingle with Ishi's own. So where, in most other literary translations, obscure or ambiguous sentences are silently clarified—with the addition of a phrase or transition here, a "she said" there—we have chosen another tack. Though this is still a literary—not a literal—translation, we have nonetheless tried to convey only what is present in the Yahi text, just as Ishi dictated it to

Sapir in 1915. That means that we have had to explore other methods of providing readers with the interpretive and textual information they need in order to follow the story. We have settled on two devices, footnotes and sidenotes, to help us "buy" this degree of fidelity.

The sidenotes (set in the right margin, in space fortuitously made available by the broken-line format of the translation) are used mostly to supply key missing information—primarily proper names or specific nouns that are referred to only by pronoun in the original, and which the reader might have trouble intuiting. Less-critical information—of a contextual, interpretive, linguistic, or philological nature—has been consigned to footnotes. To illustrate the way the sidenotes work (the footnotes should need no explanation), let's take a look at an excerpt (lines 138–149) from the translation:

> He made himself arrows in the morning.
> He rubbed them and smoothed them. *the cane shafts of the arrows*
> He was busy at it all day—
>   finished.
> As he turned them on the ground,
>   he painted on the bands.
> He finished putting on the painted bands.
> He soaked them in water, *the feathers*
>   wrapped them on with sinew—
>   finished.
> He trimmed the feather-vanes— *with a flint blade*
>   finished.

At line 139, while the reader can certainly deduce that the pronoun "them" refers generally to the arrows of the preceding line, the sidenote allows us to provide a bit more specificity: it's the cane *shafts* of the arrows that Lizard is smoothing, as Sapir's fieldnotes indicate. At line 145, the reader may be forgiven for being puzzled as to the referent for the pronoun "them." But a quick glance to the side supplies that information right when it's needed, and saves us from having to falsify the text by interpolating the missing referent (either with distracting brackets, or, worse, without) into the line: that is, "He soaked the feathers in water." Our unembellished translation makes it clear that Ishi himself, to whom the process of arrow-making was second nature, thought the circumstances too obvious to spell out using the concrete noun. Finally, at line 148,

Sapir's own gloss for the Yahi sentence *Dee-wunii-'* (literally, 'cut some-thing-feather-NARRATIVE TENSE') reads "He cut off vanes with flint," but in fact the information about the flint blade is not there in the Yahi—it's only implied by context and cultural knowledge; the sidenote here allows us to provide this information (useful for helping readers visual-ize the action) without embellishing the translation itself.[5]

NOTES

1. The Yahi Translation Project was constituted at Berkeley in 1986, specifi-cally to prepare Sapir's unpublished Yahi materials for publication. Victor Golla was the project director, and Leanne Hinton coordinated the Berkeley seminar that kicked off the project. Bruce Nevin and Ken Whistler served as special con-sultants. Other researchers who have kept involved in the project over the years include Jean Perry and this author.

2. In other of Ishi's stories, different sets of domestic activities such as leach-ing acorns and going for water take the place of arrow-making yet serve the same narrative function.

3. In order to determine the complete sequence of steps in arrow-making, it is necessary to build a composite sequence based on a collation of steps from the various episodes, because no one episode contains all the steps in the process.

4. This passage is cast in an informal practical orthography devised for the Yanan languages; it balances linguistic needs with the desire to be helpful with regard to pronunciation. Doubled characters represent length, stress is indicated with an acute accent over the vowel, and superscript letters are voiceless. Cer-tain phonetic processes involved with prosody (final aspiration, devoicing, sec-ondary and emphatic primary stress) are preserved in the transcription.

5. The text has been parsed into lines primarily on the basis of predication units (one per line), augmented by reference to prosodic features like final-syl-lable retention and Sapir's own field punctuation (see Luthin 1991 for a detailed discussion of these issues).

FURTHER READING

For an account of Ishi's two lives, Theodora Kroeber's *Ishi in Two Worlds* is indispensable as well as good reading; she covers the brutal years of ex-termination in great historical detail, as well as what is known of Ishi's life in hiding, and describes his last years at the museum. For those interested in Ishi's arrow-making, Saxton Pope's "Yahi Archery" gives a thorough description of the process (Pope was Ishi's doctor and closest friend at the university). The Ishi texts will eventually be published as volume 9 of *The Collected Works of Edward Sapir* (Sapir, forthcoming). Leanne Hinton, with artist Susan Roth, has excerpted this story in a stunningly illustrated children's book called *Ishi's Tale of Lizard*. Finally, there have been two recent films made about Ishi: the HBO production, *The Last of His Tribe* (Hook 1992), starring Graham Green as Ishi, and the Yahi Film Project's excellent documentary, *Ishi, the Last Yahi* (Riffe and Roberts 1994). A fair amount of Ishi collectanea is on more-or-less permanent display at the Hearst (née Lowie) Museum in Berkeley.

A STORY OF LIZARD

He made arrows,
    he was busy with his arrow-making . . .

I.   [PINE-
                                             NUTTING 1]
He wanted to start back.
He went westward across a stream,
    went to gather pine-nuts west across a stream.   5
He went westward up a mountain.
He put his quiver down on the ground.
(He had just gone and gotten some old deer antlers;   *to use as a quiver*
he carried the antlers around on his shoulders.)
The one pine-nutting cracked the cones with a rock.   10
He was getting out the nuts,
    got them broken open.
And then he scooped them up in his hands.
He took up his storage basket again.
The Ya'wi shouted their war-whoops!   15
He took up his quiver again.
The Ya'wi whooped.
He drew his bow from his quiver.
"The wind is blowing," he said,

"It is storming," he said.
They rushed against him.*

Now he shot off his arrows,
 hit them straight in the face.
He went back east down the hill.
He shot off arrows to the north,
 shot off arrows to the south,
 shot off arrows to the east,
  hit them straight in the face.
He went back into the water at the river,
 went back east across the water,
 came out of the water at the river.
The Ya'wi scattered out of sight.

Now he stepped along the trail.
He got back home during the night.
He put his storage baskets away again.

II.

Early in the morning he smooths them down.
He made arrows,
 rubbed the shafts smooth,
 worked at his arrow-making—
  finished.
He fitted the cane shafts tight around the arrow shafts—
 finished.
He socketed the foreshafts.
Turning them on the ground,
 he painted the bands.

Now he was busy all the day.
He fletched the arrows—
 finished.
And then he trimmed the feathers—
 finished.
He charred the feathers black,

marginal notes:
[ARROW-MAKING I]
the arrow shaft canes

on the arrow butts

---

* Literally, "He was rushed at."

bound the shafts together with sinew—
finished.

Now he smoothed the foreshafts.   *with a scouring
rush*
55
He finished and put them aside for the night.

III.   [GRIZZLY BEAR
EPISODE]
"It seems there aren't enough to eat," he said.
(Enough pine-nuts,
    for those coming to him for food.)
The woman shared them out.

"There are no more of my foreshaft sticks," he said.   60
"Let's have Long-Tail get some for me," he said.*
"Let's see you go get *báiwak'i!*" he said to him.†

And then the one getting *báiwak'i,*
    now he went off.
He twisted the *báiwak'i* shoots out of the ground,   65
    broke them off at the roots.
He laid the shafts down on the ground.
"There are plenty of sticks!" said Long-Tail.

Up jumped Grizzly Bear!
And then she eats him!   70
Grizzly Bear swallowed him down and grew pregnant.
She turned around,
    lumbered back down the middle of the trail.

When it was just too dark for gathering *báiwak'i,*
    Lizard took up his quiver.   75 *to go find
out what
happened*
Sure enough, there was the *báiwak'i*—
    it was lying on the ground.

Now he looked around all over.
Sure enough, there was the grizzly bear,
    her tracks.   80
"Little one,
    did you get eaten?" he said.

* Referring to *páat'elwalla,* a long-tailed lizard.
† A type of wood for making foreshaft sticks.

He gathered up the *báiwak'i,*
  carried it back to the house in his arms,
  placed the *báiwak'i* in the fire.*   85

In the morning,
  "What shall I do?" he said.
And then he cut off his hair.   *in mourning*
He took some pitch,
  finished smearing his face with pitch.   90

"Now how long will it take before you return?" he said.   *said Lizard, to*
  "Don't let it be long," he said.†   *absent Bear*
  "Aren't you getting hungry?" he said.

He strung a *k'asna* vine around his neck.‡   *as a necklace*
He smoked, then filled his pipe: 95
  "I'm having myself a smoke!
  How long before your return?
  Don't let it be long," he said.
  "These are your feeding grounds!" he said.
  "This is the one, all right!" he said.   100
He climbed up the *k'asna* tree,
  settled himself up in the grape vines
    as the sun went down.

When the sun came up,
  "I want to go back west," she said.   105 *Grizzly Bear*
  "He may be sleeping there," she said.   *at the* k'asna
                                                           place

Now Grizzly Bear went back west,
  pregnant with Long-Tail.
Lizard heard her to the east:
  "It must be her," he said.   110

Now she came padding from the east after *k'asna.*
The *k'asna* vine was hanging down from the tree,
  the one wrapped around his neck.

---

* Because of the death associated with it, the wood is now tainted and must be destroyed.

† This is just a wild guess as to the meaning of this difficult line.

‡ Sapir identifies *k'asna* as "wild grape."

She pulled down on the vine.
"Pull hard at me, you who bereaved me!   115
   It would be good if you would die," he said.
   "Pull me down on your back!" he said.
He loosened his bowstring.
"Let it be me who gets packed on your back," he said.
The pregnant one started to climb up.   120
He tied his bowstring into a noose,
   looped it back onto itself.
He was pulled back down from above.   *onto her back*
Grizzly Bear climbed down again,
   tumbled back down to the ground.   125
Grizzly Bear's head fell off,
   strangled in two by the bowstring.
He took his stone knife,
   gouged out her eyes.
He picked up his Long-Tail,   130
   placed him in water,
   bathed him.
He picked up his quiver again—
   put Long-Tail into his quiver.

He got back home.   135
He threw away the makeshift "necklace."
He got back home.

IV.   [ARROW-
                                                               MAKING 2]
He made himself arrows in the morning.
He rubbed them and smoothed them.   *the cane shafts of*
He was busy at it all day—   *the arrows*
   finished.   140
As he turned them on the ground,*
   he painted on the bands.
He finished putting on the painted bands.
He soaked them in water,   145   *the feathers*
   wrapped them on with sinew—
     finished.

---

* That is, while holding the brush stationary, he rotates the arrows to apply the paint bands.

He trimmed the feather-vanes—
    finished.

with a flint
blade

Now he charred the feather-vanes,*
    finished putting them away.

150

Now he bound the joins with sinew—†
    finished.
He put the arrows in his quiver.

Early in the morning,
    she took up her fire-making,
        the woman.

155

Now he rubbed them—
    finished.

the arrows

Now he was busy with it.
He finished socketing the arrow shafts.
And then he painted on the bands.
He put them away finished.
He soaked the feathers in water.

160

Now he fletched the arrows,
    wrapped them on with sinew—
        finished.

165
the feathers

Now he was busy trimming the feathers—
    finished.
He charred the vanes,
    put them away finished.

170

Now he went ahead with putting on red paint.

Now he worked at it,
    put on the red paint,
    put them away finished.

175

Early in the morning,
    as he turned them on the ground,‡
        he flaked arrowheads.

made of obsidian

---

* With a hot stick, to "seal" them.
† Where the shaft fits into the foreshaft.
‡ Here, the action seems to refer to pointing arrowheads.

Now he chipped off flakes.
He finished at sundown.

Early in the morning,
    as he turned them on the ground,
        he attached the points to the foreshafts—
           finished.
His deer-horn quiver was slung over his shoulder.   185
He finished,
    put the arrows into it.
At night,
    he finished working.

Early in the morning,   190
    he went after more foreshaft sticks.
He packed home the new *baiwak'i* and put it down.

Now he started scraping the bark off: *with a stone scraper*
    he scraped off the *baiwak'i*.
He finished at sundown.   195

Now he was busy with it—
    he finished working in the dark.

V.   [THE NIGHT DANCE]
Early in the morning,
    he took his arrow shafts,
        spread them out in front of him.   200

Now he rubbed the arrow shafts smooth.
"What's the matter?" he said.
He broke it on the ground,   *the arrow he was smoothing*
    broke it in two on the ground.

Now he just sat there, waiting.   205

"The women are dancing together," she said.*
"The men are dancing together," he was told.
"Aaah, and you would spread the news, too," he said.
    "That smoothing work of mine just broke for no reason."

* Unclear; Sapir's notes say, "not girls but 'story' creatures," whatever that means.

"They are going out there to dance," she said.   210
He put away his arrow-making things.

At sundown:
   "Some funny kind of pitch—
      it smells like that," he said.*
   "They must be dancing," he said.   215
And then the pitch—
   it was given to him,
      the pitch.
"What's the matter?
   Aaah, so that's what this is," he said—   220
      "some funny kind of pitch."
"Evidently what it is, is excrement," a man said.†
He gave him the excrement.   *gave Lizard*
Lizard smeared it all over,
   smeared the excrement smoothly over himself—   225
      finished.
"Build a fire!
   I'm going to dance and play!" he said.

Now they danced:
   the young women danced, it is said,   230
   the young women rested, it is said.

Now he sang out,   *Lizard did*
   he went to sing the lead.
He called out the dance.‡

Now he sang along.   235
They danced.
"I'm just going to let it down, children!" he said.   *i.e., 'stop
                                                                dancing'*

"Dance and play!" he said.
   "Say it!" he said—
      "your play-dancing song!"   240

* The smell is coming from where they are dancing.
† It's not clear who's speaking here.
‡ Or 'accompanied his dance-song with whispered shouts'.

The play-dancers sang.*
"Now the women shall dance," he said.

> "*Henééyah, paneyáh,*   *[singing]*
> *Henééyah, henééyah, hiiyaa!*"

"Say it!"   245
He called for a dance:
   "Children!
     Say your song!" he said.

Now they were dancing, dancing.
   "Say it!" he said.   250
    "Children!"
They're dancing to the south,
   they're dancing to the north,
    they're dancing to the south,
     they're dancing to the north.   255
"*Hiiyaa!*" he said.
He called for a dance:
   "Say it, children!" he said,
    "your play-dancing song," he said.
"I'm just going to let it down," he said.   260   *i.e., 'stop dancing'*

Early in the morning:
   "Everybody go off to the woods!" he said;   *to gather food*
   they all went off and headed into the woods.

At night:
   "Dance, children!   265
   Dance!" he said.
[Then:] "To sleep, all of you!" he said.
   "Children!
   Let it down," he said.

Early in the morning,   270
   they got up.
"Guess I'll just stay home."   *said Lizard*
The young women danced.

---

* Or 'They sang and danced'.

At sundown:
　"Dance and play, children!" he said.
Again the dancers danced.

Early in the morning,
　they got up.
"All this sleeping is a bad thing," he said,
　"it's not good," said Lizard. 280
The woman went back home.*
They bathed themselves. *Lizard and the*
He took up his arrow-making again. *woman*

VI. [ARROW-
MAKING 3]
He rubbed the arrows smooth all on his own.
He socketed shafts throughout the day— 285
　finished.

Now he painted on the bands during the day,
　put them away when they were finished.
He soaked them in water. *the feathers*

Now he fletched the arrows—† 290
　now, while he was busy at it,
　　he fletched the arrows—
　　　finished.
He turns them on the ground.
He trimmed the vanes— 295
　finished.
He charred the feathers—
　finished.
He put them away when they were finished.
He carried the deer antlers slung over his shoulder. 300
(That's what made his quiver:
　he just cut deer antlers off at the stump.)
He placed the arrows inside.

"Off to the woods, children!" *for food*

---

* Sapir's gloss regarding the woman notes "little, but not child."
† By attaching the feathers with strips of sinew.

He took up his flints,*　　　　　　　　　　　305
　　chipped off a piece.

Now he flaked away during the day.
He scoops the loose flakes into a basket.

"Eat, children!" he said at night.

Now they began eating their meal:　　　　　　310
　　they ate it,
　　　　they finished eating.

"Off to the woods, children!" he said.　　　　　*for food*
They went off and gathered food.
He inserted the arrowheads—　　　　　　315　　*into the*
　　finished.　　　　　　　　　　　　　　　　　　*foreshafts*
He put his finished pointed shafts away.

"Eat, children!"

VII.　　　　　　　　　　　　　　　　　　　　[PINE-
Early in the morning,　　　　　　　　　　　NUTTING 2]
　　he took up his quiver,　　　　　　　　320
　　he took up his net bag.

Now he went westward,
　　went west across the water.
He put his quiver down on the ground.
He climbed up after pine-nuts,　　　　　　325
　　climbed back down.
And then he pounded out the cones.

Now he kept on pounding—
　　finished.
He took up his net bag and scooped them in.　330
And he filled one up—　　　　　　　　　　*his net bag*
　　finished.
And then his other bag—
　　finished.

---

* *Xaka* 'flint' probably represents chert or obsidian.

Now, as they were spilling,
    he scooped them up from the ground. 335   *the pine-nuts*
They made a sound like the wind there, and the sound came
    down:
    the Ya'wi,
        they howled their war-whoops at him.
"I'll presume you're not just the wind blowing," he said.   340
He picked up his net bags,
    tied both his net bags together to carry home.
He reached for his bow.

Now he stepped along the trail.
He shot off arrows—   345
    shot to the north,
    shot to the east,
        hit them straight in the face.

Now he stepped along the trail,
    fired his bow down into them.   350
"You are just barely visible,
    scattered all around me," he said.
He shot to the south,
    shot to the east—
        he killed them off, these Ya'wi.   355
He went back home through the water.

Now he stepped along the trail.
He arrived back home at sundown.
"Here is plenty to eat, it seems," he said,
    as he was asked for food.   360
"It looks like it's really raining down out there, with the wind,"
    he said.

VIII. [ARROW-
MAKING 4]
Early in the morning,*
    "Off to the woods, children!" he said. *to gather food*

Now he was busy trimming feathers all day.

---

* Line inserted by translator.

At sundown he finished it,
    his feather-trimming. 365

Early in the morning:
    "Off to the woods, children!"
He took up his cane shafts,
    spread out the canes. 370

Now he rubbed them smooth—
    finished.
Drilling out the cane shafts,
    he bored into them—
        finished. 375

Now he socketed the foreshafts—
    finished.
He painted on the bands,
    put them away, finished.
He fletched the arrows, 380
    soaked the feathers in water—
        finished.

At sundown,
    he trimmed the feather-vanes. *with a flint knife*

Now he was busy with it: 385
    he charred the feathers,
        put them away finished.

"Eat, children!" he said.

Early in the morning,
    he took up his sinew-binding,* 390
        put them away finished.

Now he was busy with it:
    he smoothed the foreshafts— *with a scouring rush*
    finished.
He slung the quiver over his shoulder— 395
    finished.

---

* Binding the juncture of the cane shaft and foreshaft with sinew.

At sundown,
    those who had gone to the woods came home.
"Eat, children!" he said.

Now they started eating their meal.   400

Early in the morning,
    as he turns his arrows on the ground,
        he flaked arrowheads.
He finished at sundown.

Now he was busy with it.   405

Early in the morning:
    "Off to the woods, children!" he said.   *to gather food*
    "I won't be doing like the rest of you,
        as for myself," he said.

And he smoothed the arrow shafts: 410
    early in the morning,
        as he turns them on the ground,
            he smoothed the arrow shafts.

Now he rubbed them smooth.
He finished during the day.   415

Now he was busy,
    he bored holes into the cane shafts—
        finished.
He socketed the foreshafts,
    put them away, finished.   420

Now he was busy with it;
    he finished with the painted bands.
He soaked feathers in water.

Now he was busy with it:
    he finished and trimmed the feathers.   425
He put down his arrows—
    finished.

Now he charred the feathers.

"Eat, children!" he said.

Early in the morning,   430
   "Off to the woods, children!" he said.   *to gather food*
   "I won't be doing like the rest of you,
      as for myself," he said.
He finished his sinew-binding.

Now he was busy inserting the flaked arrowheads.   435
He put them away finished.

IX.   [PINE-
Early in the morning,   NUTTING 3]
   he took up his net bag.

Now he went westward,
   went west across the water,   440
      went westward up a mountain.
He put his quiver down on the ground.
He climbed up after pine-nuts,
   climbed down again.
And then he piled pinecones all around the fire.   445

Now he was busy with it,
   now he started pounding.
He pounded out the nuts—
   finished.
He took up his net bag,   450
   he took up his other net bag.

(*Not yet . . .*)*

Now, as they were spilling,   *the pine-nuts*
   he scooped them up from the ground.
They made a sound like the wind there, and the sound came
   down: 455
   the Ya'wi,
      they howled their war-whoops at him.
"Ho, I'll presume you're not just the wind!" he said.
   "It really looks like it's raining down, now—

* Perhaps a foreshadowing device: Lizard (and Ishi) anticipating the Ya'wi rush.

maybe I'll sit and shell some pine-nuts," he said. 460
He took up his net bags.
    "I have just seen you, everywhere down on the ground," he
        said.
He slung the bags over his shoulder again.
He took up his bow.

Now he stepped along the trail. 465

Now he shot at them:
    he shot to the east,
        he shot to the south,
            he shot to the north.

Now he stepped along the trail. 470
He fired his bow at them,
    hit them straight in the face.
He went into the water again,
    came back out of the water.
The Ya'wi scattered away. 475

Now he stepped along the trail at sundown.
He came into the clearing.   *where his camp*
"Here is plenty to eat, it seems," he said.   *was*
"It really looks like rain, coming down out there on the wind,"
    he said.

[*To Sapir:*]

"Be gone, now!" as they say. 480
Now he has finished talking . . .

11

A Selection of Wintu Songs

WINTU
1929–1931

FANNY BROWN, JENNIE CURL, HARRY MARSH,
SADIE MARSH, AND EDO THOMAS, SINGERS
DOROTHY DEMETRACOPOULOU, COLLECTOR AND
TRANSLATOR

INTRODUCTION BY DOROTHY DEMETRACOPOULOU

The songs presented here were collected in the summers of 1929, 1930, and 1931, during three field trips that were conducted under the auspices of the Department of Anthropology of the University of California.[1] I recorded them intermittently, chiefly as an expression of literary art, partly for their ethnographic value, partly for linguistic purposes. I secured them in text and translated them as literally as the discrepancy between Wintu and English would permit.

The Wintu who sing them live in California, along the northern reaches of the Sacramento, the Pit, and the McCloud. These rivers are in reality only mountain streams, swift and narrow, forming steep little canyons in the mountains. The mountainous country affords almost no valleys and only a few "flats" where the people could build their brush houses. The drainage runs north and south, and perhaps because of this, directional terms are indispensable to the Wintu when any purposeful going is to be described. One goes north along the river, south, east uphill, west along the ridge; or one just walks.

The songs that are sung most by the Wintu today are the so-called dream songs. At one time they formed the chief feature of the Dream Dance cult that was introduced circa 1872 and held sway for about forty years. Dream songs were given to men and women in their sleep by the spirit of some dead relative or friend. In the morning the dreamer sang the song and danced to it. The song then became common property, though the name of the dreamer was usually remembered. A split-stick rattle, struck against the thigh, accompanied the song and dance. The rattle, the dance, and the song each followed its own different rhythm.

Since dreaming afforded such an excellent opportunity for exhibitionism, the Wintu seem to have indulged in it, despite the prevalent belief that it brought bad luck and perhaps death to the dreamer. Dreaming stopped about forty years ago, but many songs are still remembered and danced to when Big Times are held. The most recent stimulus to the revival and preservation of the dream songs came when Miss Cora Du Bois and I began collecting them.

The dances of the Dream Dance cult show a wide range of variation, but the songs roughly follow certain set rules; this, despite the fact that they were genuinely acquired in a dream. The words treat of the land of the dead, as for example, the above, the west, the mythical earthlodge of the flowers, the Milky Way along which the spirits of the dead went to their final resting place. Flowers form an important theme. The references to nature are not lyrical expressions but simply an unquestioned conformation to the requirements of the song.

The arrangement of the verses as well as the tune follow a somewhat set pattern. Generally there is the introductory part, consisting of one or two verses that are repeated several times in a low key. Then the first verse with perhaps a new verse is sung in a variation of the theme in a higher key once, and a final verse, the completion or climax, is sung in the original low key.

The following song will serve as an illustration. First come two alternating verses in a low tone:

It is above that you and I shall go;
Along the Milky Way you and I shall go;

It is above that you and I shall go;
Along the Milky Way you and I shall go.

Then we have a variation of the theme in a higher key:

It is above that you and I shall go;
Along the flower trail you and I shall go.

Then we go back to the tune of the first verse:

Picking flowers on our way, you and I shall go.

This tune pattern seems to derive from the Southland Dance cult.[2] The only song that is remembered from the Southland Dance cult is one which is composed of the meaningless syllables *heyoyohene,* sung according to the tune pattern found in the dream songs.[3] Whether this tune pattern originated with the Southland Dance cult or was already present among the Wintu when this cult entered the territory, we do not know. Just now it occurs only in the singing of dream songs.

Individual variation is to be found in the particular arrangement of the verses within the tune pattern. It is not known how much unconscious revision of the words took place. Unfortunately, only one song was secured from two different informants. The two versions show a difference in the tune pattern as well as in the words. Miss Du Bois reports a case where the tune of a song was revised consciously. A singer of some note altered the tune to suit his taste, and it is his version that is known and sung now.

The words of the songs are important in themselves. My informants sometimes repeated them to me, exclaiming over their beauty; this, in spite of the poetic license that allows the dreamer to break from the ordinary Wintu phrasing and makes the meaning often hard to grasp. Miss Du Bois has even recorded a song whose words are remembered and liked although the tune has been forgotten.

NOTES

1. This selection is based on Demetracopoulou's famous 1935 article, "Wintu Songs" (*Anthropos* 30: 483–494). The text of her introduction and song notes

has been excerpted, rearranged, and edited (for continuity) for inclusion in this volume. Of the forty-nine songs included in the original article, twenty-nine have been selected here. The songs retain their original numbering, for the sake of reference.

In her publication of these songs, Demetracopoulou printed only the "gist" of each song, with notes indicating how many times each separate line was sung, and in what order. I have reconstructed the original order from her annotations and present the songs here in their full performance order.—HWL

2. This cult was introduced into Wintu territory circa 1871 and held sway for about a year. See Cora Du Bois, "Wintu Ethnography," for a fuller description. Most of the information about the ethnographic aspect of the songs contained in this essay has been supplied by Miss Du Bois.

3. These syllables may be simply a variation of *heninoiheni,* the introductory and final refrain of the girls' puberty songs, which is sung with slight variations by different singers.

FURTHER READING

Cora Du Bois's "Wintu Ethnography" and Du Bois and Demetracopoulou's "Wintu Myths" are important sources of information, as is Demetracopoulou and Du Bois's "A Study of Wintu Mythology." Demetracopoulou's "A Wintu Girls' Puberty Ceremony" (Lee 1940) might be useful for contextualizing the puberty songs selected here. Harvey Pitkin has published a *Wintu Grammar* and *Wintu Dictionary.*

A SELECTION OF WINTU SONGS

DREAM SONGS

1. Harry Marsh, dreamer; sung by Harry Marsh, 1929*

It is above that you and I shall go,
Along the Milky Way you and I shall go,

---

* Harry Marsh uses the inclusive dual that is found in practically all the dream songs where an address form is used. The song is considered to contain an amorous or at least a romantic flavor.

It is above that you and I shall go,
Along the Milky Way you and I shall go,

It is above that you and I shall go,
Along the flower trail you and I shall go,

Picking flowers on our way, you and I shall go.

2. Anonymous dreamer; sung by Harry Marsh, 1929

Above the place where the minnow maiden sleeps while her fins
    move gently in the water,
Flowers droop,
Flowers rise back [up] again.

3. Anonymous dreamer; sung by Harry Marsh, 1929

WHERE WILL YOU AND I SLEEP?

Where will you and I sleep?
Where will you and I sleep?
Where will you and I sleep?
Where will you and I sleep?
At the down-turned jagged rim of the sky you and I will sleep.

4. Jim Thomas, dreamer; sung by Harry Marsh, 1929*

Above [they] shall go,
The spirits of the people, swaying rhythmically,
Above [they] shall go,
The spirits of the people, swaying rhythmically,

* The word used for "swaying rhythmically" is applied to women swaying with bent elbows and
  forearms pointing forward, as an accompaniment to the dancing of the men. During a performance of the Dream Dance, the men danced in a circle around a fire, while the women stood in
  two lines on either side, swaying and waving flowers or handkerchiefs in their outstretched hands.
  Jim Thomas, a shaman, introduced in his song the dandelion puffs as representing spirits that
  float away. This conception was liked so generally that the song was dedicated to funerals. The
  participants sway, holding dandelion puffs, and then with one accord, blow on them and make
  them float away. Singing at funerals is an innovation and probably was initiated with the first use
  of this song, at the death of Bill Popejoy, some twelve years ago.

Above [they] shall go,
Swaying with dandelion puffs in their hands,
The spirits of the people, swaying rhythmically.

5. Anonymous dreamer; sung by Harry Marsh, 1929

There above, there above,
At the mythical earthlodge of the south,
Spirits are wafted along the roof and fall,

There above, there above,
At the mythical earthlodge of the south,
Spirits are wafted along the roof and fall.

Flowers bend heavily on their stems.

8. Dum Du Bel, dreamer; sung by Harry Marsh, 1931

O me, your brother-in-law
Looks west.
All day long
He looks west.

O me, your brother-in-law
Looks west.
All day long
He looks west.

O me, your brother-in-law
Looks west.
Flowers of daybreak
He holds northward in his outstretched hands.
All day long
He looks west.

9. Mary Silverthorne, dreamer; sung by Harry Marsh, 1931

From the east he came west against the mountains and stopped.
Flowers he picked just now,
Flowers from my grave.
Flowers he picked just now.

11. Sadie Marsh, dreamer; sung by Sadie Marsh, 1929*

Down west, down west we dance,
We spirits dance,
Down west, down west we dance,
We spirits dance,

Down west, down west we dance,
We spirits weeping dance,

We spirits dance.

12. Mary Kenyon, dreamer; sung by Edo Thomas, 1929

From the old camping place
Comes a flash of flowers.

I love flowers.
Give me flowers.
Flowers flutter
As the wind raises them above.
I love flowers.
Give me flowers.

13. Dick Gregory, dreamer; sung by Edo Thomas, 1929†

Daybreak people have been chirping.
Daybreak people have been chirping.
Daybreak people have been chirping.
Daybreak people have been chirping.
Daybreak people have been chirping.

Above on the roof,
Alighting, they chirp.

* Sadie Marsh says that a few years ago her best friend died, and a little after came to her in a dream
   with a company of other female spirits, weeping, dancing, and singing this song.
† The daybreak people are sparrows. The roof is that of the mythical earthlodge.

GIRLS' PUBERTY SONGS*

21. Sung by Harry Marsh, 1931†

Heninoy, heninoy
Heninoy, heninoy

At Bare-Gap-Running-South-Uphill a girl has [come to] pu-
    berty,
We said to ourselves.
So from below, bringing eastward with us,
We brought puberty songs.

Heninoy, heninoy
Heninoy, heninoy

22. Sung by Harry Marsh, 1931‡

Heninoy, heninoy
Heninoy, heninoy

Where the eastern star emerged,
Fire comes up westward over the slope and falls in a shower.
To the edge of the mountains, to the foot of the pointed ridge,
Come southward along the mountain shore to [join] the dance!

Heninoy, heninoy
Heninoy, heninoy

---

* All songs other than dream songs and shamanistic songs are anonymous. There are many girls'
  puberty songs, of which I secured a few. Some time after the first menstruation, perhaps as long
  as three years after, a Big Time was called to give public recognition to this event. This was done
  for the daughters of the most important people. The headman of the village sent invitations to
  other villages, and as each group arrived, they danced down into the celebrating village, singing.
  Song 21 was sung by such a group. All girls' puberty songs begin and end with a refrain of *heninoy* repeated an indefinite number of times.
† When I first recorded this song, I found it impossible to understand since it was sung for me starting with the second verse. Girls' puberty songs are generally supposed to be incomprehensible,
  full of obsolete words and involved as to style. From this generalization must be excepted the sala-
  cious songs that people take care to understand.
‡ This is an arrival song.

23. Sung by Harry Marsh, 1929*

Heninoy, heninoy
Heninoy, heninoy

Up the hill to the northwest
  an obsidian knife whizzes through the air,
    on the west slope.
It is the beautiful adolescent girl;
  to the place where the deer were scared out of the bush,
    listening, may I come back!

Heninoy, heninoy
Heninoy, heninoy

24. Sung by Harry Marsh, 1931

Heninoy, heninoy
Heninoy, heninoy

At the edge of the mountains she [came to] puberty.
Look along the curve of the mountain shore;
Fleas must be emerging!

Heninoy, heninoy
Heninoy, heninoy

26. Sung by Harry Marsh, 1931†
Heninoy, heninoy
Heninoy, heninoy

May I fall into the hole made by digging,
And there, fluttering about, may I remain!

Heninoy, heninoy
Heninoy, heninoy

---

* Songs 23–28. After the groups arrived there was feasting and dancing for several days. During this time, pertinent songs were sung, some of them incomprehensible to the singers, others referring to the fact that the girl was now ready for a lover or a husband. In Bald Hill, some extremely obscene songs were sung, usually upon arrival. Songs 26 and 28 were sung during the feasting period.

† This is a wish to join the girl where she sits.

27. Sung by Harry Marsh, 1931

Heninoy, heninoy
Heninoy, heninoy

In the southeast the adolescent girl comes seducing to get herself
  a man.
She comes crossing Sucker Creek which should not be crossed.

Heninoy, heninoy
Heninoy, heninoy

28. Sung by Harry Marsh, 1931

Heninoy, heninoy
Heninoy, heninoy

To the north behind the snow mountain,
Going up a bare ridge, feathers* are visible.
Going up a bare ridge north behind the snow mountain,
Going up a bare ridge, feathers are visible.

Heninoy, heninoy
Heninoy, heninoy

LOVE SONGS†

36. Sung by Harry Marsh, 1931

Hinini, hinini
Hinini, hinini

Where he walks about, where he walks about,
Pushing the deer decoy back away from his face,
Right there in front of him

---

* The feathers presumably belong to the headdress of a potential lover.
† The rest of the songs that I collected are love songs and songs from forgotten stories. Love songs
  are known as *nini,* from the introductory and final refrain *hinini,* which is repeated an indefinite
  number of times. They are complete in themselves or simply songs coming from love stories,
  which also are known as *nini.* These latter are often hard to understand, as they refer to incidents
  in the story. *Nini* tunes were sometimes played on a flute.

May I come gliding down and fall!

Hinini, hinini
Hinini, hinini

37. Sung by Harry Marsh, 1931

Hinini, hinini
Hinini, hinini

Please,
Teach me a word I don't know!

Hinini, hinini
Hinini, hinini

38. Sung by Harry Marsh, 1931

Hinini, hinini
Hinini, hinini

Long ago I wept for you,
But now I weep
For him who lives west, further west, I weep
For him who dwells in the west,
Under the sharp pinnacles of Lime Rock.

Hinini, hinini
Hinini, hinini

39. Sung by Harry Marsh, 1929

Hinini, hinini
Hinini, hinini

The sleeping place which you and I hollowed out will remain
    always,
Will remain always, will remain always, will remain always.

Hinini, hinini
Hinini, hinini

41. Sung by Fanny Brown, 1929

Hinini, hinini
Hinini, hinini

Before you go over the gap of the snow-mountain to the north,
Downhill toward the north,
O my, do look back at me!
You who dwell below the snow-mountain,
Do look back at me!

Hinini, hinini
Hinini, hinini

42. Sung by Fanny Brown, 1929

Hinini, hinini
Hinini, hinini

For some reason I dislike you.
I do not love you.

I dislike you because,
Like a snipe hopping on,
You crossed creeks ahead of me.

Truly I dislike you for good.
I love one who dwells there in the west.

Hinini, hinini
Hinini, hinini

43. Sung by Sadie Marsh, 1929*

Of course,
If I went to the McCloud
I might choke on a salmon bone . . .

---

* Songs 43–44. These two songs are referred to as *nini* sometimes. They are derisive songs. The
McCloud woman, who has been nurtured on juicy salmon and has to live on grasshoppers and
such small fry in the Stillwater subarea, sings to her husband.

44. Sung by Jennie Curl, 1930*

Of course,
If I went to Stillwater
I might choke on a grasshopper leg.

Yeah, but—
If I went to the Upper Sacramento
I might choke on the bone of a fawn . . .

SONGS FROM FORGOTTEN STORIES

45. Sung by Harry Marsh, 1929†

Down in the west, lying down,
Down in the west, lying down,
A beautiful bear I found,
Tearing up clover in fistfuls.

46. Sung by Jennie Curl, 1930

SONG OF THE PREGNANT WOMAN

On the north slope of Baqakilim
I was deserted.

Some flower made me heedless
And I was deserted.

A wild orange blossom made me heedless
And I was deserted.

---

* Another McCloud woman refuses her suitors with this ditty.
† Songs 45–47. The last three *nini* are songs coming from love stories. The stories, as myths, are forgotten or perhaps never have had any existence. Nowadays, they are told informally, only as explanations of the songs. There are *nini* tales containing songs that are told formally, but in these, the interest lies in the narrative and the song is merely part of the story, sung in the appropriate place.

Song 45. This is, to my knowledge, the most popular Wintu song. It is said to have been composed by a lover rejected for his poverty, when he found his old love in circumstances so reduced that she had to live on a diet of clover. It is a song of derision, and the Wintu find it amusing.

47. Sung by Jennie Curl, 1930

SONG OF THE FORSAKEN BROTHER

Do not weep,
Do not weep,
Younger brother, do not weep.

She would have gone about,
She would just have gone about in the flat below.

Do not weep.
Do not let her come in front of the north side of our dwelling;
That is where Bead-bear will go about.

Do not let her get tiger-lily bulbs.
Do not weep, younger brother.

49. Sung by Sadie Marsh, 1929*

SONG OF THE QUAIL

I stroke myself, I stroke myself;
East of the camp site, where the earth is heaped,
On my back I lie.
I lie stroking myself,
In the summer, when sunshine falls deep in the northern
    canyons.

* The last song in this collection comes from a forgotten myth.

12

Loon Woman

He-who-is-made-beautiful, She-who-becomes-loon

WINTU
1929

JO BENDER, NARRATOR

DOROTHY DEMETRACOPOULOU, COLLECTOR

DELL HYMES, TRANSLATOR

INTRODUCTION BY DELL HYMES

This dramatization of incest, death, and renewal has drawn repeated attention since its publication in 1931.[1] It has been the focus of a special article (Demetracopoulou 1933), retold in a popular book (T. Kroeber 1959), and addressed at length in a major analysis of myth (Lévi-Strauss 1981).

The Source

We know the text because of the work of two women at the start of their careers, Dorothy Demetracopoulou (Lee) and Cora Du Bois. Both went on to become well-known for other work, Demetracopoulou-Lee for essays on languages as forms of thought (Lee 1944, 1959), Du Bois for study of culture and personality among the people of Alor (an island of Indonesia) and as the first woman professor of anthropology at Radcliffe (Harvard). In the summers of 1929 and 1930 the two women joined in an inquiry remarkable for its time. Among the Wintu, living along tributaries of the Sacramento River north and northwest of present Red Bluff, they sought not only good storytellers, but tellers of different abilities, under varied conditions, so as to shed light on change and stability. Because of this, we have converging perspectives on a community tradition, with specific information about tellers and their circumstances.[2]

Formerly myths were told only on winter nights. A good teller would have a good memory and be a good singer; evidently one could change voice with a change in characters or situation, and animate narration with gesture (Demetracopoulou and Du Bois 1932:376, 379, 497). The "Loon Woman" myth was told in the summer of 1929 by Jo Bender (Upper Sacramento). He was about eighty-five, esteemed as a teller by other Wintu (Demetracopoulou and Du Bois 1932:496, 498, 499) and by the two young anthropologists (379, 392).

I should explain this new translation. Demetracopoulou's transcriptions of Wintu texts are unpublished, and their location was not known to Herbert Luthin, the editor of this volume, or myself. Fortunately, Alice Shepherd had the text of "Loon Woman" and sent a copy to Luthin. It had only Wintu, no English, so the original translation must have been done separately. That translation was published twice, but the two are not quite identical.[3]

Thanks to the grammar and dictionary of Harvey Pitkin (1984, 1985), supplemented by the dictionary of Alice Shepherd (Schlicter 1981), I was able to match Wintu elements with English meanings and identify their grammatical roles. I could then look for further relations among them.

When "Loon Woman" was transcribed, such stories were thought to be prose. Division into larger units (paragraphs) was ad hoc. Recently it has been realized that stories may indicate ways of their own of going together. Intonation contours may indicate units (verses), which enter into longer sequences (stanzas, scenes). For "Loon Woman," the manuscript shows no contours, but patterns do emerge. It is common in stories for some sentence-beginning words to mark units, and that turns out to be true of "Loon Woman." So as to carry over the effect of the original, each such word has been translated always the same way, and each differently from the others: note "After," "After that," "And then," "At last," "At that,"

"For that," "Now," "Suddenly," and of course expressions such as "Next morning." (Interestingly, when "And then" [*uni-buha*] occurs, it tends to be second of a pair of units, or third of three. Parallelism is also a factor in particular cases. Repetition of a common verb of "being, residing" [*buha*] initiates the two opening scenes in part 1.)

Fundamentally, interpretation of the shape of the whole depends upon the hypothesis that, like many other oral narratives, Native American and English, the story makes use of certain kinds of sequence. The common alternatives among traditions are relations of three and five, or of two and four. A narrator may shift between them, to be sure, and one set may include something of the other. Awareness of such relations contributes to an appreciation of the rhythms of a story. This translation attempts to display them on the page.

Some texts in Shepherd (1989) suggest that Wintu narrators use relations of three and five; "Loon Woman" certainly does. But sequences of three and five are sometimes sequences of pairs: the scene in which the elder sister discovers the heart of the hero (part 3, scene [1]), and the final two scenes of the story as a whole, have each five pairs of stanzas (sets of verses). When units are paired, I put a single closing brace in the right margin to mark the end of the pair.

In such patterns a turn at talk is always a unit, and a sequence may consist of alternating turns, as in five pairs of interaction between mother and daughter (lines 56–68). Speeches count as a single unit (turn at talk) in large sequences, but may have internal patterning of their own. The long speech by the helpful bird in act 6 has three parts, each ending with a verb of speaking. (I mark these internal parts with the designations "E/1," "E/2," "E/3.")

Sometimes a three-step sequence has a sense of the onset, ongoing, then outcome of an action, or an object of perception, as when the daughter matures (21–23) and discovers a long hair (cf. 27–29, 30–32 and 33–35, 36–38). Repetition of words sometimes has one pair enclose another—what is called "chiasmus," as in lines 19–20, 234–35, 258–60, 497–98. Sometimes members of a pair alternate, as when twice the mother ponders and the daughter measures (73–74, 78–79 : 75, 87–88).

A run of three or five can elaborate a single action or activity. When the two boys set out, they "play, play, play" (430–32). The second time Loon Woman cries for her parents, she "cries, cries, cries" (236–38). When earlier she prepares a bed for herself and her brother, repetitious wording in a doubled set of five-line stanzas (122–31) seems to convey confusion, urgency, and excitement.

Translation as Retelling

Mr. Bender evidently controlled patterns in English as well as Wintu, and his translating was also in part retelling. When the sister first says, "Whose hair?" (34), the next line in Wintu means literally "she wants to know." Bender's translation is more dramatic: "I want to know."

When the sister and brother go, she calls for evening to come quickly, and then the two are said to "go" six times (given the doubling of "go" elsewhere, this presumably constitutes three pairs). The English has five verbs, not six: "They went, and went, and went, and went, and went."[4] Evidently Mr. Bender knew that English does not ordinarily multiply pairs but does multiply single words, and so he substituted a run. Even so, a run in English would usually be three; Mr. Bender goes to five. I suspect that in Wintu three pairs was a maximal effect, and that a run of five seemed an equivalent maximal effect in English.

In the five pairs of lines in which the brother wakes and leaves his sleeping sister, the third and fifth pairs (166–67, 170–71) exist in English only. The additions extend and do not disturb the pattern of the stanza.

It remains to be seen to what extent other Wintu narrators and translators have made use of possibilities such as those mentioned here.

Proportion

The whole of a story has to make sense in terms of a pattern of relations, and Jo Bender's "Loon Woman" does. Its verses, stanzas, and scenes combine into six acts, paired in three parts. (For other work of this kind, see Hymes 1992, 1994a, 1994b, 1995.) Recognition of such connections of form and content makes clear the proportions and emphases of the telling.[5]

Two acts present a beautiful boy, hidden, then discovered (part 1). Two central acts present incest and destruction (part 2). Two final acts present restorations and retribution (part 3). Within each part something accidental prompts what happens. The sister discovers a hair fallen from her brother's head, and so prepares for incest (act 2); Coyote, although warned, looks down as the family escape upward, and so they fall into the fire (act 4); the two boys wound a bird who tells them about the Loon, and so she is killed and the lost hearts recovered and restored (act 6).

Interpretations

Some of the meaning of the story involves understandings that members of the community would take for granted. Many are shared with other Native American traditions. Here are several such.

The opening and closing—"many people came into being" and "So they say it ends"—are conventional and show that the story was told by someone still conversant with such devices. (Young narrators were becoming less conversant during the period in which the story was taken down.) The opening sets the story in the earlier time when the human age was given shape. The closing indicates that the story is vouched for by what others have said. If it had been told in winter, someone would have followed the closing with words wishing for spring.

The sister's attention to a hair fits the first requisite for physical beauty, long, thick, shiny, black hair (Du Bois 1935:59; cf. restoration of such hair in Hymes 1983, and Lévi-Strauss 1981:389).

That the daughter goes west may foreshadow her transformation into a dangerous being. The word *nom-yo* ('west-?') describes persons likely to become animals, or "werebeasts" (Du Bois 1935:5).

When the mother at last accedes to the daughter's refusal to go except with the eldest son, it is not because she cannot recognize danger. One cannot forever refuse a kinsperson or partner.

That it is Coyote who looks down, causing escape to fail, is no surprise. He is the father in some versions of the story, but not here, and is not restored to life at the end. Having an isolated Coyote at just this point, a sort of walk-on numskull, fits well with the story's view of the family as not to blame. Given a boy so beautiful as to cause (illicit) desire, they hide him. That the daughter finds a telltale hair is accidental. A proper mother cannot at last keep her daughter from choosing her brother. The son leaves the sister as soon as he can awake, and the family do at once what he runs to tell them to do. A new generation kills what the daughter has become.

As for the two women who find the oldest son's lost heart, they are shown to be good at the very start (of act 5): they do useful work every day. And their first line inserts "human" (Wintu) before "women," contrasting them with what the woman just-mentioned, the sister, has become.

That the son's heart has song shows power. That there are deer tracks where it is found indicates a prototypical male power, hunting deer. Another version has his tears create a salt lick that attracts deer. Absence of that here may indicate that deer recognize power as such.

That the restored son has two women as wives indicates high status. Usually co-wives were sisters, and their husband slept between them.

Instruction from a wounded bird is a popular device in many traditions. The bird goes unnamed here, but perhaps its cry is an identification. The cry "Tuwétetek" is like a name for killdeer in the neighboring and related language, Nomlaki, *te-wé-dé-dik*.[6] Notice that the usual step of bandaging the wound, and being given advice in return, is absent. The bird is already on the side of the boys, somehow related to them, referring like their father to "she who made *us* kinless."

Title

In the manuscript and publications of the myth, the title has the name of the older brother in Wintu, but "Loon Woman" in English. In the story he is named, but she is not; not even a word for "loon" occurs. Perhaps that is because no loon survives. The story does not tell, actually, why a loon will look as it does in a world to come. One would have to speculate about that; this loon is different. The distinctive necklace has been taken back, the hearts are human beings again. So far as the story goes, the loon is an evil forever gone.[7]

I translate the hero's name with one of its possibilities (cf. Pitkin 1985: 36, 37, 38, 271). Shepherd (personal communication) says that the name could suggest most or all of those possible senses. Since the story is about what a sister as well as a brother becomes, lacking a Wintu name for her, I use "become" for her in the title.

Other Discussions

Demetracopoulou (1933) analyzes versions of "Loon Woman" in terms of some eighteen incidents and their distribution among versions from the Achumawi, Atsugewi, Maidu, Karuk, Modoc, Shasta, Wintu, and Yana.

She finds the story to have a sharply defined character in a limited area, integrating incidents intrinsically unrelated. Two incidents do seem original—that of the lost hair and the revivified heart—but neither would account for the story itself. The sequence of incidents, their dovetailing and remolding, is based first of all on the theme of catastrophic incest and secondarily on the punishment of the prime actors, linked with the widespread theme of a son revenging and reviving his father.

Theodora Kroeber (1959:39–65) reframes and retells the story, drawing on several of the same versions (Achumawi, Atsugewi, Karuk, Maidu, Shasta, Wintu, and Yana).

Lévi-Strauss (1981) makes the Loon Woman story an essential part of his great enterprise, to show the unity of myth throughout the New World. By way of a recently published Klamath myth, he connects the Loon Woman stories of Northern California to the bird-nester theme in South America, with which he began the four volumes of his *Mythologiques*. He takes the hidden child in Loon Woman to be an inversion of the bird-nester, and by a series of further inversions, oppositions, and transformations, he finds that "the whole northern part of North America is the scene of a vast permutation" (215), reaching as far as the Wabenaki of New England. His argument takes Demetracopoulou to task at several points (e.g., 60–62, 388–89)—for instance, for treating the hair incident as arbitrary and specific (389).

Lévi-Strauss's work is indispensable for its vast command of detail, its attention to natural history and geography as factors, and its recurrent sensitivity and insight. At the same time, its conception of mythical thought as often a playing out of formal possibility, its overriding concern for indications of the emergence of culture out of nature, and for certain kinds of coding—astronomical, gastronomical, and so forth—omit what may be perfectly good reasons for a story to be the way it is. In the case of Jo Bender's telling of Loon Woman, one reason may be pain felt for an intelligent, determined child cleaving to a fatal course. Another is to fit with a cultural cognitive style.

The two Wintu versions, this by Jo Bender, and another by Sadie Marsh (Du Bois and Demetracopoulou 1931:360–62) can be understood as alternative ways of portraying and thereby thinking about lust as a woman's motive. The daughter in the Marsh story is immediately impulsive, aggressive, and ultimately cannibalistic. The denouement takes little time. The denouement in the Bender story takes a generation. This daughter is complex. She holds to her goal in extended interaction with her mother, she plans and works and uses magic to make it happen, and later she grieves at length for the loss of her mother and father.

As to hair, having found the hair, she looks and looks, and later matches and measures. All this is in keeping with a Wintu concern for bases of knowledge, expressed in a recent development of a system of evidential suffixes (see the lucid analysis in Schlicter 1986). The first major action of the story is the scenes in which the daughter looks and looks to be sure of the source of a hair (act 2, scenes [1] and [2]). Visual knowledge, the kind most assured, is again in focus in lines in which her counterpart sees and hears speak the lost heart of that source (319–30). Even so, her conclusion as to who it must be (329) is marked as inference (-re:m). Sight is again in focus in the lines in which her younger sister sees what she has discovered (388–96), and when the boys who have killed Loon take their father to see. Hearing, to be sure, begins the long process by which she discovers, then nourishes, He-who-is-made-beautiful. The women at the center of the first and third parts, she who destroys and she who recovers, are akin in deliberate response to evidence.

In this respect the hair incident is indeed "important aesthetically to the form of the myth" (Demetracopoulou 1935:121) and is to be explained, not by distant analogues (Lévi-Strauss 1981:389), but from within Wintu language and culture. The myth as a whole is distinctive in its steady marshaling of detail to show a family almost destroyed and in the end surviving evil.

Native Language Passage

Here are lines 24–35 in Wintu, with word-by-word glosses and translation. The lines, in which the sister, She-who-becomes-loon, discovers the fateful hair, are taken from the incident that precipitates the main events of the story.[8]

'uni-r	p'o·q-ta	k'éte	hima	me·m-to·n	hará·,
they-say.SCA	woman-that	one	morning	stream-that.LOC	goes

After that one morning the woman goes to a certain stream,

me·m-tó·   me-s-to·   pi-to·n   hara·,
stream-that.OBJ   water-GEN-that.OBJ   she-that.LOC   goes
she goes to where they get water,

kén·ła·   pi   p'o·q-ta.   Pómin-winé,   wine tómoi,
sits-down she woman-that ground-looks.at sees hair
she sits down that woman. She looks at the ground, she sees a hair,

číne·.   Wine·,   wine·   tómoi,   k'ete·m   tómoi.
catches/takes.it looks.at.it looks.at hair   one.OBJ hair
she takes it up. She looks, she looks at the hair, one hair.

Tómoi   niqa·'a   wíne: "Héket-un tómoi?"   t'ipna·-s-kuya.
hair   find-STA   look.at who-POSS   hair   know-STAT.INT-want
She looks at the hair she has found: "Whose hair?" she wants to know.

NOTES

1. I am indebted to Herb Luthin for inviting me to take on this challenging and rewarding task, and to Alice Shepherd for information and encouragement. She has caught mistakes and sparked recognition of the striking relation between categories of the language (Schlicter 1986) and the shape of this telling.

2. An example of such information as it bears on the present translation: to heighten action Mr. Bender used a special arrow-release gesture (not the one normal for arrow-release), whether or not an arrow was released in the story. The oldest teller, Jim Fender, age ninety, also actively used gesture, especially for directions and arrow-release. On the strength of this, two otherwise odd uses of a word that can mean "thus, like this" are taken here as marking gestures to show how Loon Woman scratched for hearts (lines 260, 264).

3. There is evidently incidental editing in the second publication (Demetracopoulou 1935) and slippage in the course of its reaching print. Part of the speech of the wounded bird is missing. Lines 456–68 here are in the first publication (Du Bois and Demetracopoulou 1931:359, lines 19–25), but absent in the second (Demetracopoulou 1935:107, line 3).

4. Wintu does not explicitly mark tense in the verb, and the past is the normal English narrative tense. In the translation itself (lines 111–13), I have used the present tense "going" at this point, thinking that it avoids the implication that the Wintu is the same as English, and because it has a certain freshness.

5. Following conventions I have established elsewhere (see Hymes 1992, 1994a, 1994b, 1995), I employ capital roman numerals (I, II, III) to designate

"acts," lowercase roman numerals (i, ii, iii) to designate "scenes," capital letters (A, B, C) to designate "stanzas," and lowercase letters (a, b, c) to designate "verses."

6. The information here comes from Alice Shepherd. Lévi-Strauss notes an analogous role for Killdeer in Klamath and Yana versions of the story (1981:49, 95) and for Meadowlark among the Shasta (133).

7. A giant bird called *wukwuk* was known among the Nomlaki, who live to the south of the Wintu and are their linguistic relatives (Goldschmidt 1951:353). The account of the bird that Goldschmidt obtained from Jeff Jones does not connect it with the loon or a myth.

8. The abbreviations used in this passage are as follows: GEN = 'generic', INT = 'intensive', LOC = 'locative', OBJ = 'objective', POSS = 'possessive', SCA = 'subordinating causal anterior', STA = 'subordinating temporal anterior', STAT = 'stative'.

FURTHER READING

The introduction points to numerous sources and readings. Frank LaPena's article "Wintu" in the California volume of the Smithsonian *Handbook* provides useful ethnographic background. Dorothy Deme-tracopoulou's "The Loon Woman Myth: A Study in Synthesis" is an essential comparative study. Theodora Kroeber, in *The Inland Whale*, retells the story in formal literary style. Lévi-Strauss, in *The Naked Man*, analyzes the myth from a structural perspective. For more on ethnopoetic approaches to oral literature, see Hymes's *'In vain I tried to tell you.'*

LOON WOMAN: HE-WHO-IS-MADE-BEAUTIFUL, SHE-WHO-BECOMES-LOON

[PART ONE]
[The Beautiful
Boy]
[I] [Hidden]

They live there,
many people came into being.

After that two,
 a pair,

a man and wife live there,   5
    they have many children,
        a lot of children,
    nine boys,
        one girl,
            ten children.   10

The first born [is] a beautiful boy.
And then they leave him put away inside.
He-who-is-made-beautiful is what they name him,
they leave him put away inside,
they leave him to stay rolled up in a bear hide.   15

[II] [Discovered
and Desired] [i]
They live there,   A
    live there,
        live there,
    some of the children walk around,
        children play around.   20

That "girl" lives there,   B
    the girl grows bigger,
        turns into a woman.   }

After that one morning the woman goes to a certain stream,   C
    she goes to where they get water,   25
        she sits down, that woman.
She looks at the ground,
    she sees a hair,
        she takes it up.
She looks,   30
    she looks at the hair,
        one hair.

She looks at the hair she has found: D
    "Whose hair?"
        she wants to know.   35
She looks at it long,
    looks at the hair,
        one long hair.

That woman thinks,
   she thinks, "Whose hair?"   40 }

That He-who-is-made-beautiful goes every morning to bathe.   E
No one has any idea that he goes to bathe.
That He-who-is-made-beautiful goes to that water,
   bathes,
      comes home.   45

One hair has come loose,   F
   comes off his head.
The woman finds it, the hair,
   finds the hair at the flat where they dip up water.
"I want to know whose hair it is," so she thinks.   50
   That woman keeps that hair.   }

Thinking of the man,   A(ab) [ii]
   "This morning I shall go west," so says that woman.
      "I want to take someone along to guide me."
"I am going to go," so she tells her mother.   55

"I am going to go west," so she says,   (cd)
   thinking of the man, so she spoke.
"Hm," [her mother] says.

"Whom do you want to take with you?" she says.   (ef)
She will not tell whom.   60

The old woman,   B(ab)
   "Well, surely take this little one, your younger brother."
Now that woman says,
   "I don't want to take him."

"Whom will you take with you?" so she says.   65   (cd)
"I want to take another one with me."

"Take this one then."   (ef)
"I won't," so said that woman.

She does this for a long time,   C
   she goes through them all.   70
He-who-is-made-beautiful alone is left,

He-who-is-made-beautiful.
The little old woman sits,
   sits pondering it all, the old woman.

That woman measures that hair like that.   75   D
The hair of the rest does not match.
The one hair she had found is long[er].   /

The old woman sits,   E
   sits pondering it all.
Suddenly,   80
   "Yes, surely take this one,"
      so she says,
         "He-who-is-made-beautiful,"
            her son.
"Yes," so she said.   85

The woman is happy she is going to take him along.   F
She measures the hair,
   that hair matches.
"I'm going to take this one," she says.   /

After that the woman prepares herself attractively,   90   [iii]
   paints herself,
      [gets] food to take along,
         everything—
           acorn soup,
           acorn bread,   95
           salmon flour.
She packs them on her back in a carrying basket.
She goes,
   taking him, He-who-is-made-beautiful, with her.
      (That woman is happy to take her older brother with her.)   100

[PART TWO]
[Incest,
Destruction]
[III] [Incest] [i]

The two go west,   A
   that He-who-is-made-beautiful goes ahead,
      that woman comes behind.

"Dearest, my husband," so speaks that woman.   B
That man, "What?" so he says.   105
"Oh elder brother, don't hurry,
    that is what I am saying to you," so she says.

So that woman says,   C
   "Hwaa," so she says,
      "Evening come quickly," so says that woman.   110

Going, going,   D
  going, going,
    going, going—
Evening comes.

The woman speaks thus: 115   E
   "Let's the two of us spend the night right here.
   It's evening."
"Yes," so he said.

After that she makes a fire.   A [ii]
And then the two eat,   120
  eat supper.

After [having eaten],   B
  she fixes a sleeping-place,
    she is the one who fixes it,
      makes it,   125
        that woman works hard—

Nicely she fixes [it],
  makes a bed,
    she fixes a sleeping-place nicely,
      all kinds of ferns she cuts,   130
        spreads them on the ground.

"Lie down here, elder brother.   C
  I finished making a bed for you to lie on,
    I finished making it."
After that,   135
  so she said,
    "As for me, I'll sleep anywhere on the ground."

After that the two lie down,   *A [iii]*
  He-who-is-made-beautiful lies down,
    sleeps,   140
      near the fire lies He-who-is-made-beautiful.
The woman lay there on the ground.

After that the woman says,   *B*
  "Hiwaa, go to sleep,"
so the woman says to He-who-is-made-beautiful,   145
  ["Go to sleep"].
They say then he sleeps,
  He-who-is-made-beautiful sleeps.

The woman, having gotten up,   *C*
  looks,   150
    he is sleeping.
Softly now she goes,
  lies on the ground,
    takes He-who-is-made-beautiful in her arms,
  on the ground now,   155
    that woman lies.

      [IV]
      [Destruction]
      [i]
He-who-is-made-beautiful wakes up,   *A*
  sees he is sleeping in his sister's arms.
That woman is sleeping,
  she lies snoring,   160
    asleep.

He-who-is-made-beautiful gets up,   *B*
    softly having gone and gotten pithy alder wood,
  brings it,
    leaves it on the ground,   165
  gets pithy alder wood
    and leaves it there,
  puts it in her embrace,
    leaves that wood.
[he,   170
  He-who-is-made-beautiful.]

Once he is done,   *C*
    he comes,
    comes toward the house,
        comes,   175
    comes rapidly,
        comes rapidly,
            comes rapidly.

The woman sleeps a long time.   *A [ii]*
That man comes,   180
    comes rapidly,
and then reaches the house,
    his mother's home,
        his father's home.

After he gets there,   185   *B*
    "Be quick, let's go," he said.
The old woman, the old man,
    "Yes, let's go," they say.
And then they set the earthlodge completely on fire,
    the earthlodge smokes.   190

At last at that spot they go whirling upward with that smoke.   *C*
Coyote they make sit at the very bottom.
"Don't look down!" they say to Coyote.
    "That woman will come and will cry,
        will say all sorts of things."   195
"Don't look down!" thus [they say] to Coyote.
Whirling upward,
    they go above.

That woman in that bed in the west wakes up.   *A [iii]*
Oh, and then she sees   200
    how the bed has held pithy alder.
She is angry,
    that woman is angry.
"I am going to kill you," she says.
She cries,   205
    that woman cries:
        "Anana, ɔñɔñɔñ,

Anana, ɔñɔñɔñ,
Omanuč anana,
Omanuč ɔñɔñɔñ!"   210

Singing, she comes toward the east.   B
Because of that the woman comes rapidly east.
She rushes to that earthlodge and stops,
    she sees the lodge burning,
        she truly doesn't know what to do.   215

She looks all about the country,   C
    she does not see anyone.
There she goes *completely* around the lodge.
Still she sees no one,
    she has no idea where they have gone.   220

She looks all about the country there,   D
    she looks all about.
"Where can Daddy have gone?
    Where can Mama have gone?"
        She thinks about them that way.   225

For that she cries,   E
    cries,
the woman cries,
    cries.

Suddenly she happens to look up,   230   *A [iv]*
    sees them going up,
        her mother, her father, her elder brother,
            she sees them going.

"I want to go, oh Mommy, oh Daddy,   B
I want to go,"   235
    she cries,
        cries,
            cries.   /

They almost get above,   C
    they almost get above into the clear sky.   240
The warned one,

Coyote,
    looks down,
everyone comes there to the fire,
    falls down to the earthlodge,   245
        burns up.

They fall down,   D
    they all fall into the fire.
He-who-is-made-beautiful falls into the fire,
    ah, everyone falls into the fire.   250
He-who-is-made-beautiful's heart pops off.   }

Because of that, that woman keeps walking around,   E
    keeps walking around,
        keeps searching.

It is cold,   255   F
    the fire gone out,
        the earthlodge burned down.   }

Now she takes a stick,   A(ab) [v]
    she searches there,
        she searches like this with the stick.   260
She finds her own mother's heart,
    her own father's heart she finds,
        all her younger brothers' hearts she finds.

Like that surely she scratches with both hands,   B(cd)
    she scratches in the ashes,   265
        trying to find He-who-is-made-beautiful's heart.
She does not find it.

After that, that woman strings the hearts on a cord,   C(ef)
    she strings them,
        hangs them on her neck.   270
She does not find He-who-is-made-beautiful's own heart.

For He-who-is-made-beautiful's own heart has exploded,   D(gh)
    going to another place,
        fallen.
No one knows about *his* kind of heart.   275

That woman,

    "I want to see *his* kind of heart," she says.

The woman, thinking a little,

    keeps walking around,

        hearts hung on her neck.

E(ij)

280

[PART THREE]
*[Restorations,
Retribution]*
*[V] [Rediscovered,
Restored] [i]*

Far away two human women live.

The two go for wood early in the afternoon every day,

    the two sisters.

The older goes off ahead nearby.

The other girl breaks off wood,

    taking it home.

A

285

That older woman goes on ahead nearby,

    she seems to have heard singing,

        strange soft singing she hears.

That younger girl does not perceive

    what her older sister hears.

She listens,

    listens to the singing.

B

290

At last she turns around.

    "Let's take the wood," she says.

The two pack the wood on their backs in funnel-baskets,

    bring it to the house.

In the evening they sleep.

C

295

The next morning they get up,

    eat food,

        go for wood early in the afternoon.

At that, that woman hears singing,

    the singing she hears seems louder little by little.

A [ii]

300

B

]

And then she goes over there,

    she goes listening to that singing,

        she goes and goes.

C

305

That woman goes,   *D*
    goes over there,
        listening to the singing,
        listening ahead,   310
            goes on.   }

Stopping every now and then,   *E*
    she goes,
        comes up to the place,
            sees damp ground.   315
Having come up to it, she looks,   *F*
    she looks at the ground,
        nothing is there.   }

She keeps hearing singing.   *G*
She sees something black on the ground.   320
That black thing on the ground,
    that which sang, says,
        "Woman, come.
        Don't be afraid," it says.
That woman thinks,   325   *H*
    says,
        "This must be,
        this must be the one lost long ago.
        It must be that He-who-is-made-beautiful,"
            so she thinks.   330   }

At that, thinking, the woman looks at the ground.   *I*
The one on the ground says,
    "Ah, woman, don't be afraid of me,
    Come."
Now the woman says, "Yes."   335
At that she looks at the one who is on the ground.   *J*
Many deer had been there,
    it is dusty.
To the east of where that person lies,
    to the west,   340
        there are many deer tracks.   }

As soon as she had looked at him,   *A [iii]*
   she goes to carry her wood,
      where her younger sister is standing.
She goes,   345
   comes up to her.
When she came up to her,
   "Elder sister, where did you go?
   You were gone a long time," she says.
"I was off walking a while," she said.   350
Carrying the wood,
   the two brought it home on their backs.

And then in the evening the two went to bed,   *B*
   the two slept,
      the woman said nothing.   355

The next morning they got up.   *C*
As before they were about to go after wood.
She put a little soup into a basket cup,
   in the basket cup she carried it hidden in her clothes,
      she carried the soup.   360
The younger one gathers wood.
The woman gets the soup,
   carries it,
      does not let the younger sister see she is carrying soup.

She goes on,   365   *D*
   comes over to him there,
      feeds the soup to the one who lies on the ground.
The one who lies on the ground seems a little better,
   he is starting to be a person.
He eats soup,   370
   he eats soup,
      that woman feeds him,
         she feeds him.
Having finished feeding him,
   she gets wood ready,   375
      gets wood ready,
         gets wood ready.

At last she carries it on her back to the house,
    she brings it there,
        she brings the wood.   380

As before it became evening,   *E*
    they all slept.

After that the next morning those two women get up.   *A [iv]*
At last having eaten,
    she goes carrying the soup.   385
Then that younger girl,
    "What is going on?" so she thinks.

Her elder sister having gone,   *B*
    that younger girl follows.
She goes,   390
    she follows her elder sister's tracks,
        wanting to see.
She sees.
Her elder sister is sitting,
    feeding someone soup.   395
The younger girl sees.

At that she ponders about it,   *C*
as she sees she is feeding soup to someone.
"Have you discovered this one?" so says the younger girl.

And then the younger girl, going on,   400   *D*
    reaches her elder sister.
"Have you discovered this one?" she says.
"Yes," so she told her.
"The one who went away long ago,
    the person who was lost,   405
        the person not found,
            this is the one,"
                she said, speaking to her younger sister.
"Let's go home," she said.

The two go home,   410   *E*
    the two getting home,
        they sit.

It gets dark,   *A [v]*
   they eat,
      lie down,   415
    go to bed,
the two women sleep.

In the middle of the night the two women wake up,   *B*
   see a man lying between them,
     a beautiful man is lying.   420

For, they say, he has come back to life,   *C*
   come to the house,
     he who was found by the two women.

[VI] [Retribution
and Family
Restoration] [i]

And then he stays there,   *A*
   a little while he stays.   425
     At last the two women bear children.

The two boys,   *B*
   those their children,
     having grown little by little,
   play,   430
     play,
       play,
   shooting at birds.
Suddenly they see a bird,   *C*
   they shoot at it with an untipped arrow,   435
     they pierce its lower leg.

The bird,   *D*
   "Tuwétetek, tuwétetek!" it shrieks.
   "Oh why do you shoot at me, cousins?"
   "Come, you two, there is something I should tell you."   440

Now the two come to find a woman.   *E*
Having sat down,
   she talks:
     "Let me tell you.   *E/1*
       You two are getting older.   445
         There is a pool over there.

"You two, having gone to look,
    there will in fact be a raft,
        right there indeed on that deep pool.

"You two are *not* to shoot with this.   450
    You are to prepare good untipped arrows,
        You are to prepare good untipped pitchwood
            arrows," she said.

"There, to that deep pool, comes always every evening   E/2
    she who made us kinless.
        For that she comes from the east round the hill.   455

"You can hear her coming,
    there above she comes rushing,
        up there she'll come.   }

"She'll alight on that pool of water,
    she alights on the water,   460
        she alights,
            she who makes [us] kinless.
                There she glides on the water.

"After that she goes, 'Wuuuuk,'
    flaps her wings up in the air.   465 }

"And then she dives.

"And then she comes out of the water there near that raft.
    she always comes out close to it," she tells the two young
        men.   }

"And after she comes out,   E/3
    this is what she does,   470
        she always flaps her wings up in the air.

"Now look her straight in the eye, you two,
    and shoot.
Look carefully, you two,
    and shoot.   475
Just don't miss, you two, with your untipped pitch wood
    arrows.

"Do *not* miss, you two;
　　Look her straight in the eye, you two,
　　　and shoot!"

When she is through talking,　　　　　　　　　　　480　　*F*
　　the two boys go to the house,
　　　come to their home,
　　they come to the house playing.
　　　They do not say anything.

They stayed home the next day.　　　　　　　　　485　　*A [ii]*
The next day, having gotten up,
　　they eat,
　　　go,
　　　　the two amuse themselves,
　　　　　the two amuse themselves.　　　　　490
And then the two arrive there at the pool.

At last it grows dark,　　　　　　　　　　　　　*B*
　　the sun goes in.
　　　The two boys get up on the raft,
　　　　row themselves about,　　　　　　　　495
　　　　　shooting at the ducks in the pool.　*/*

Suddenly they hear her coming with roaring wings.　*C*
"Here she comes, listen," they say.
She who is coming alights on the pool.
"Wuuuuk," she says.　　　　　　　　　　　　　500
And then she dives.

Those two boys, already prepared,　　　　　　　*D*
　　sit watching, those two.
She comes close,
　　gets out beside that raft.　　　　　　　　505
And then, having gotten out,
　　she flaps her wings in the air.　　　　　　　*/*

The two boys are fully prepared,　　　　　　　　*E*
　　keep her in sight all the time,
　　　shoot with the untipped arrows of pitch wood　510
　　　　exactly at the hollow of her armpit,

shoot,
    hit her.

Now she dives,   *F*
    into that pool she dives.   515
        The [two little] boys stand watching.   *∤*

Suddenly she comes to the surface,   *G*
    rises bloated,
        dead.

Now the two take hold of her,   520   *H*
    drag her there to the edge of that raft,
        throw her on top,
    the two drag her out,
        the two throw her on top.   *∤*

And then the two, having left,   525   *I*
    come to the house.
        The two finish eating.

And then they speak.   *J*
"Father," they say.
The old man says, "What?"   530
"We killed her," they say, "the Wukwuk."
The old man says, "Oh."   *∤*

Early in the morning they have gotten up,   *A [iii]*
    the old man goes,
        the two boys go,   535
            leading their father,
                to show him the one they had killed.

They go,   *B*
    the old man sees who lies on that raft.
        "Yes," he says,   540
            "this is she who made us kinless," says the old man.   *∤*

And then he takes hold of her,   *C*
    sees she has on a necklace,
        she has on a necklace of human hearts.

At last the old man unties his father's heart,   545   D
   his mother's heart,
      the hearts of his younger brothers.   }

And then cutting the flesh into strips,   E
   he leaves it.

And then he goes,   550   F
   he cuts it into strips, leaving it,
      he goes to the house, his home.   }

He brings the hearts of his mother,   G
   his father,
      his younger brothers,   555
   he brings them to the house.

And then he weighs them down in water [with stones],   H
   he lies down in the evening.   }

In the morning, at dawn,   I
   his mother,   560
      his father,
         all his younger brothers,
            arrive,
   having come to life,
   those who had been soaked in water arrive early in the
      morning.   565

So they say it ends.   J}

13

Four Songs from Grace McKibbin

WINTU
CIRCA 1982

GRACE McKIBBIN, SINGER AND NARRATOR

ALICE SHEPHERD, COLLECTOR AND TRANSLATOR

LEANNE HINTON, ANALYSIS AND TRANSCRIPTION

INTRODUCTION BY LEANNE HINTON

Grace McKibbin was a great singer, with knowledge of hundreds of traditional Wintu songs. While there were many Wintu songs of ceremonial significance to be sung by trained religious leaders, the four songs transcribed and translated here are secular in nature and sung by plain folks. People among the Wintu and other tribes used to make up songs to express strong emotions in situations of great joy or pain. Three of these songs Grace called "love songs," and one was a "cry song." Although love songs sometimes speak about romance between a man and woman, they are more often about the strong bonds of family. Two of these songs express the pain of parents when their daughters leave them to marry; and the other love song displays the pride of a young girl in her brother-in-law. The cry song is also about family love: the lament of a newly widowed man trying to figure out what to do with his three small children.

FIGURE 5. Grace McKibbin.
Courtesy Alice Shepherd.

When Grace sang for Alice Shepherd, she always prefaced and ended her songs with some description of their history and meaning. I consider her words about the song to be part of the performance. Indeed, it must have been the case that even for Wintu listeners, most singings of these songs were also accompanied by explanations, because they were sung by people for generations after their first composition. I have therefore included Grace's explanations here as integral parts of the performance.

Since Grace was talking to an English-speaker, her explanations were in English, and are presented here verbatim. The songs were in Wintu, and in keeping with the requirements of this volume, they are presented in translated form. I present the songs with the exact number and arrangement of lines as the original performances. The translation tries to remain as true as possible to the meanings of the Wintu lines. When the lines contain vocables (meaningless syllables), they are presented as they are pronounced in the song. The spoken song explanations are formatted in keeping with pauses and sentential intonation (and punctuation therefore reflects phrasing rather than the conventions of English grammar). After each sentence-final falling intonation (whether terminal or not), a new left-adjusted line begins. A nonfinal pause at a clause boundary is signaled by a line break with the new line indented. A pause within a clause is signaled by a line break with the new line beginning just below the end of the previous line. Loudness is represented by capitalizing the words spoken loudly; italics indicate emphasis.

In general the song consists of only one or two different lines of text plus a line of vocables, sung to a longer melodic form (see p. 225). The same small set of lines is repeated many times in the song in different orders. Much of the artistry and listening pleasure comes from the weaving of the text lines into the different melodic phrases. Of course, no written transcript of a song text can do that song justice. Missing are the lilting melody, the startling rhythms, the fine glides and bursts and vocal ornaments that accompany the song performance. Songs on paper can sometimes seem strangely repetitive and dull. Nevertheless, the ideas being presented in the songs are profound. The line of text is an epigram, an epitome of a feeling, woven over and over into a melodic frame.

NOTES ON THE SONGS

1. First Love Song

Three brothers from a tribe in Oregon came to a Big Time, an intertribal celebration held in Wintu country and neighboring areas. They were the sons of Elc'o:di, named in the song as the "younger Elc'o:dis." They danced the *hisi* dance, and a young Wintu girl fell in love. As Grace McKibbin put it while explaining this song on another occasion:

And this young girl
    she fell in love with these brothers,
'Cause she didn't say which one she liked,
    but she
        she felt an awful lot for all three of them, I guess.

She decided to go home with them to Oregon, and this song is her farewell song to her father.

Love songs have a typical melody and rhythm that differ from *hisi* songs; but in this case, the young woman who made this love song used a *hisi* melody to frame her words, in commemoration of the event that caused her to fall in love. Two sets of vocables are used in the song: *henini ninini* is one variant of the standard vocable set used in love songs; and *heyano heyano* is the set used in *hisi* songs. In fact, after an earlier performance of this same song, Grace talked about the dual nature of the song and reminisced about the dancing itself:

> It's a love song through *her,*
> > but it's a dance song otherwise:
> > > *hisi ča:wi.*
> They just go front,
> > and backwards.
> And the front [ones] go back,
> > so that they—
> > > > they *hold themselves same way:*
> > my dad say they were,
> > > when they dance like that,
> > > they hold themselves SO straight,
> > > and so EVEN when they dance,
> > > > they *step* even,
> > > > step, go forward,
> > > > and step back, you know?
> They STEP EVEN.
> They go side by side,
> > whole big row of 'em.
> That's just the way they dance that song.

2. Second Love Song

This love song shows the depth of family feeling among the Wintu and the joy that accompanies work in a well-integrated culture. The child who sings the song is expressing her pride in her brother-in-law who has killed a buck and gone with the girl's sister to bring it home. The girl is asked to take care of the cooking while the sister goes with her husband, and unlike children many of us no doubt know, this girl responds to the request with joy. She feels proud of her ability to help the family with adult tasks, and she sings with a welling sense of love. I have found a similar song and accompanying story among the Havasupais in Arizona, which makes me suspect that the song-type is very old and widespread among hunting cultures.

3. Third Love Song

In the first love song, a daughter sings a song of empathy for her father, who will be left alone without her when she heads off with her newfound lover. In this song it is the mother who sings to her daughter. This woman's daughter also met a man from a northern tribe and will go away with him. The mother likens the northerners to migrating geese, envisions the daughter flying north with the geese, and implores the daughter for one last backward look before she flies away. (Notice, by the way, that in Wintu one travels "down" north, rather than "up" north. The prepositions we choose to accompany the cardinal directions are culture-specific.)

4. Cry Song

Vocables (so-called nonsense syllables) actually carry some meaning. One aspect of their meaning is that they signal what kind of song is being sung. The vocables *hinini* are diagnostic of love songs. Cry songs are characterized by the lamenting exclamation *ani:*, or *ani: yo:*. In this cry song, there is a line of vocables sung many times, and then two lines of real words. The words are plain: "Which trail should I take to go over the hill? I guess I'll take the south trail over the hill." But meaning is multileveled: this grieving widower is trying to take his young children on a dangerous trip over the snowy mountain by horseback, and the wrong trail could mean the difference between life and death. On yet another level, he is expressing a general sense of being lost, not knowing what he and his family will do now that the mother of his children is dead.

FURTHER READING

Two essays in Hinton's *Flutes of Fire*—"Songs without Words" and "Song: Overcoming the Language Barrier"—should make good starting points for those interested in California Indian singing traditions. Cora Du Bois's "Wintu Ethnography" and Du Bois and Dorothy Demetracopoulou's "Wintu Myths" are both important sources of cultural information. Harvey Pitkin has published a *Wintu Grammar* and *Wintu Dictionary*. Alice Shepherd's *Wintu Texts* presents narratives in Wintu with English translations. Finally, there is the collection of McKibbin's singing and storytelling, *In My Own Words: Stories, Songs, and Memories of Grace McKibbin, Wintu*.

THREE LOVE SONGS AND A CRY SONG

1. LOVE SONG: "OH MY FATHER, WHAT WILL YOU DO?"

A good-size girl, must have been about seventeen or eighteen,
She fell in love with one of the guys
   and they had a Big Time
   and they belong some place up in Oregon, I guess,
     Oregon Indians it must have been.
And she fell in love with one of them
   and she was going to foller them,
   go where they go with them.
And she sing this song.
Told her dad, she said,
   "Dad," she said—
   "Name those guys's name,
   Indian name,"
   and she said, "I'm going too,"
   she said, "They're going up," she says,
   "My Dad," she say, "I don't know," she say,
     "don't know what you're going to do," she say.
   "I'm going to leave you."
And she sung this song:

henini ninini
henini ninini

EX. 1. Musical transcription of first love song.

EX. 2. Musical transcription of second love song.

EX. 3. Musical transcription of third love song.

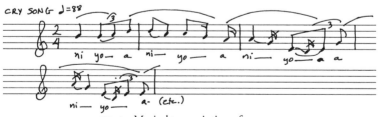

EX. 4. Musical transcription of cry song.

henini ninini
henini ninini

henini ninini
henini ninini

Oh my father, what will you do?
Oh my father, what will you do?

The younger Elc'o:dis danced, and I'm going north,
The younger Elc'o:dis danced, and I'm going north.

Oh my father, what will you do?
Oh my father, what will you do?

Heyano heyano. Oh my father,
Oh my father, what will you do?

2. LOVE SONG: "THERE! THERE! HE'S COMING!"

Well I'll sing that little girl's song again.
One that's maybe a love song for the brother-in-law . . .

hinini nini nini nini
hinini nini nini nini

hinini nini nini nini
hinini nini nini nini

There! There! He's coming!
There! There! He's coming!

My brother-in-law, my brother-in-law, he's coming,
There! There! He's coming!

Southwest upstream on the side of the hill,
Southwest upstream on the side of the hill.

My brother-in-law, my brother-in-law, he's coming,
There! There! He's coming!

My brother-in-law, my brother-in-law, he's coming,
There! There! He's coming!

hinini nini nini nini
hinini nini nini nini

hinini nini nini nini
hinini nini nini nini

My brother-in-law, my brother-in-law, he's coming,
There! There! He's coming!
Southwest upstream on the side of the hill.

Southwest upstream on the side of the hill,
My brother-in-law, my brother-in-law, he's coming.

There! There! He's coming!
There! There! He's coming!

hinini nini nini nini
hinini nini nini nini

My brother-in-law, my brother-in-law, he's coming,
There! There! He's coming!

Southwest upstream on the side of the hill,
There! There! He's coming!

[Alice Shepherd: That's one of my favorite songs.]

[*Laughter*]

That little girl she must have been about ten or twelve years old.
Her sister told her her husband killed this big buck
                                    way up in the canyon
And came home, said he wanted her to go [help him]
                              pack that buck,
And his wife had acorn soup,
She was takin' the bitter out of it
   puttin' the water in it you know?
So she left her little sister to stay home,
   says, "I'm gonna help him pack this big buck,"
And she said to her,
   said, "You pour the water into the acorn soup,
   so it'll take all the bitter out."

She said it'll be late when they get back.
Meantime she said, "Try to get some wood,
    get some wood before it's dark."
So she's gatherin' the wood up
    and puttin' water in the acorn soup,
And she start about this song,
Make up this love song about her brother-in-law
    killin' that big buck, she's tickled. [*Laughs*]

So that's where brother-in-law's comin',
Around that hillside.
West Canyon,
She said he's comin' in,
He killed that buck,
That's where he's coming.
She's sing away.
And when they was comin' down close they could hear her sing,
Just as loud as she could sing.

[*Laughter*]

3. LOVE SONG: "FLYING NORTH WITH THE GEESE"

This is what old mother sing,
Kind of a sad song, I guess,
    she felt bad 'cause her daughter went off and left her,
Went to Klamath someplace.
She's gonna leave,
    she's leaving, and this
                            mother
        start to sing this song.

[*Hums*]

This song.

hiní niní niní ní niní
hiní ní niní niní ní niní

hiní ní niní niní ní niní
hiní ní niní niní ní niní

hiní ní niní niní ní niní
hiní ní niní niní ní niní

Flying down north with the geese,
Oh, my child, stop a while and look back at me!

hiní ní niní niní ní niní
hiní ní niní niní ní niní

hiní ní niní niní ní niní

hiní ní niní niní ní niní
hiní ní niní niní ní niní

Flying down north with the geese,
Oh, my child, stop a while and look back at me!

Oh, my child, stop a while and look back at me!
Flying down north with the geese,

hiní ní niní niní ní niní
hiní ní niní niní ní niní

hiní ní niní niní ní niní
hiní ní niní niní ní niní

Flying down north with the geese,
Oh, my child, stop a while and look back at me!

Oh, my child, stop a while and look back at me!
Flying down north with the geese.

hinini

[*Laughs*]

It's 'cause she done the same thing the girl [in the first song] did.
She had a boyfriend she's following and went down
                        north someplace.
Klamath Indian, I guess.

And this mother said,
  called them guys that,
  the way she sing called them guys that [were] there,
    GEESE.
Geese, when the geese fly down,
  the geese fly down
    north, she said—
      she's follerin' them, you know,
        her daughter is follerin' them,
  she said,
"Please look back before you go."
Said, "Please look back."
Yole means
  'Look
    back a while.'

4. CRY SONG: "WHICH TRAIL SHOULD I TAKE TO GO OVER THE HILL?"

My grandpa's song that he
              lost his wife,
And he had—
  my dad was about four years old I guess, four to five years old,
  and my uncle must have been just about,
    no, my aunt was about
              three,
  and my uncle was about,
    must have been going on two, he was a baby.
So he was living on the Wildwood Road, then he sold his horses,
  most of them,
And he sold his
          two cows he had;
Then he loaded up,
  he couldn't do nothing you know with them three kids;
  while he had his brother-in-law with him he babysat,
  and he sold his horses and cows,

And he
        got ready, and he
                    went to Shasta County with them
                    where his sister was.
Then they was going over the
                    mountain,
    up towards East Fork, and he couldn't go up there,
        on Chilula Trail
        over to Harrison Gulch, Shasta County, you know?
He went up the Wildwood, but,
There was snow,
    four foot of snow;
    hard to see where the horse stepped.
And he—
    he said,
    he telling me after I grew up, he said he didn't know what to do.
And he said he just started thinking about this song,
    singing a song,
    going over the mountain.
So he sing this song,
    about himself you know,
    which road,
    which trail would he go over,
    on the Hazelpatch Ridge or the
                    Wildwood Road.
South Trail,
And,
    he said he think he'd better take the South Trail,
        that's the way this sounds,
        the word is.
"I guess I'll take the South Trail and go over the hill.
I wonder which trail shall I take?"
So he took the Wildwood trail,
    the lower one you know,
    a little ways to go over the heavy snow.
He had
        one of the oldest boys,

packed right into the
                    pack horse, you know?
  Right in the middle, and had him tied down,
  bundled him up
    and tied him down.
Then he had the littler one sitting in the front of him,
  all wrapped up;
And one of them behind the saddle,
  all wrapped up.
So that's the way he led them.
He led the horses,
  the one the little boy is riding, my dad's riding.
And then one of the pack horses packing, and he followed.
So that's the way he went.
And
    he sing this song . . .

ní:yo: aní:yo:
aní:yo: aní:yo:

aní:yo: aní:yo:
aní:yo: aní:yo:

aní:yo: aní:yo:
aní:yo: aní:yo:

Which trail should I take to go over the hill?
I guess I'll take the South Trail over the hill.

Which trail should I take to go over the hill?
aní:yo: aní:yo:

aní:yo: aní:yo:
aní:yo: aní:yo:

Which trail should I take to go over the hill?
I guess I'll take the South Trail over the hill.

aní:yo: aní:yo:
aní:yo: aní:yo:

Which trail should I take to go over the hill?
I guess I'll take the South Trail over the hill.

aní:yo: aní:yo:
aní:yo: aní:yo:

Which trail should I take to go over the hill?
I guess I'll take the south trail over the hill.

I guess I'll take the south trail over the hill.
I guess I'll take the south trail over the hill.

Which trail should I take to go over the hill?
I guess I'll take the south trail over the hill.

Which trail should I take to go over the hill?

He didn't know which way to go.
Thinking about his little kids,
    little bitty ones.

He made it, though.

Snow was deep.
And he buried his wife in the deep snow, you know.
And there someplace where the
                        sun hit and thawed out,
    under the trees,
    and he buried my grandmother up there,
        Wildwood Road,
        up there at
                    oh, Fox Farm,
        that's where he was staying.
To this day—
    well, before I got blind,
I tried to find that place, I couldn't find it.
He said it was at the other tree.
People lives there, I think they builded a shed on that grave.
But the Forest Service asked me if I
                        know where it was

they'd put a fence around it.
Only way to do is dig 'em out, I guess,
    and find out.

I don't know what she died from.
Just
    died.
Them days there used to be a lot of sickness you know.

14

How I Became a Dreamer

NOMLAKI
1935

CHARLES WATHAM, NARRATOR
CLARENCE CAMPBELL, COLLECTOR

INTRODUCTION BY BRIAN BIBBY

Late one evening, as I was conversing with Nomlaki elder Wallace Burrows in his home on the Grindstone Creek Reservation, nestled among the blue oak and bull pine that dot the rolling hills of western Tehama County, he brought up the name of Charley Watham. He had known Charley. Charley was a dance man who participated in the ceremonial life at Grindstone. He was also known for his regalia and, more specifically, as a maker of woven feather belts.

Wallace told me he remembered that Charley had owned a fine sheep dog who could manage a herd of sheep just about all by itself, leaving Charley free to relax, take a nap, eat lunch, or maybe make a feather belt. Sure enough, while the dog was watching the sheep, Charlie would sit up on a hillside where he had a good view of the animals and work away on his belts. These were woven in what is often described as a warp-face weave, using two-ply cordage. Although formerly the belts were made from native hemp, it's more likely that during this period of Charley's life he was using jute fibers he had unraveled from gunnysacks and then retwisted in the old style.

Tiny, brilliant scarlet-red feathers from the scalp of acorn woodpeckers and the iridescent green feathers from the head and neck of mallard ducks were woven securely into belts some five feet in length and often six to eight inches in width. White glass beads were woven into geometric patterns set against the sections of red feathering. This was no idle pursuit: the making of a woven feather belt required some very meticulous and demanding manipulation of thousands of feathers, usually less than a half inch long each. Feather belts were used in the Hesi ceremony and dance. In a photograph, one of several taken during the Hesi dance of July 1907 at Stonyford, a man identified by some as Charley Watham is wearing one such belt, perhaps of his own manufacture.

When the text of a 1935 interview with Mr. Watham recently came to light, I was greatly interested.[1] The only previous references to Watham I had heard were from a few people who had known him. All I really remembered, aside from the great sheep-dog story, was that he was a dance man. The places Charley went to dance are the same places I have heard about from other elders. These ceremonial dance houses—at Chico, Noweedehe (at Grimes), and Wyteedesla (near Princeton)—have long since ceased to exist. Only a few songs and the roundhouse at Grindstone still exist from his time.

There were some wonderful dances in those old places. Each of these communities had developed its own particular attributes relative to its ceremonial and religious life. Each had its own distinct flag (or flags) that flew during the Hesi. Cloth banners, reminiscent of the American flag in shape, materials, colors, and the use of stars and stripes, featured designs symbolic of images seen in a dream by the flag's originator. These villages also possessed their own songs for the Hesi: songs for each ceremonial outfit, songs for the flags, finishing songs, around-the-fire songs, and so forth. These songs were all born of dreams. Collectively they form a song-map of the region, part of the indigenous soundscape of the upper Sacramento Valley.

Remarkably, much of this fragile nineteenth-century oral literature has survived, and appears to be floating on into the twenty-first. The songs Charley Watham heard, and perhaps danced to, at Chico, Noweedehe,

FIGURE 6. Dancer believed to be Charles Watham.
Courtesy Phoebe Apperson Hearst Museum of Anthropology
and the Regents of the University of California.

and Wyteedesla continue to resonate in the four ceremonial roundhouses
that still maintain the Hesi tradition. I remember very distinctly that,
upon conclusion of a song, Wallace Burrows would always identify it according to its village-specific lineage. This was an important thing to
know about a song, an essential aspect of a singer's professional knowledge. Moreover, Wallace often added his own personal remembrances of
the songs: "You should have heard old So-and-so sing that," or "People

used to dance that a lot in the old days," and so on. The association of a particular song with a particular place or individual is very strong in this tradition.

Charley Watham, like many before him and many since, was an initiated member of a dance society. At Chico, where he was of high standing or rank, the dance society was called the *Kumeh* (literally, 'of the dancehouse'). The term for a fully initiated member is *yeponi*. Participating in ceremonial dances such as the Hesi requires membership in the dance society. It is really quite a different experience from the contemporary powwow scene, where anyone with an outfit of any sort may participate. In other words, you didn't show up and dance, or even join; you were brought in at the discretion of the dance society's members and leadership.

As the autobiographical story told here suggests, dreams were a central and guiding factor in Charley Watham's life. Dreams played an important role, too, in the lives of the Native peoples he lived amongst. At one point in his narrative, Watham's wife tells him to reveal his dreams to a friend, because it would be better to have a confidant. By doing so, she says, he will not be bothered by troubling dreams. A special class of "doctor" among the Konkow was the *yom nedi*, or dream doctor. Such an individual helped interpret a dream's significance and advised the dreamer on how to take steps to follow the dream's directions. The *yom nedi* might also help the patient with advice on how to alleviate bad or troublesome dreams.

Within the religious society and the dance societies, the role of the dreamer was particularly significant. Dreams were the origin of most songs and dances, and certain people were more disposed to this kind of dreaming than others, although anyone might receive a dream about a song or a particular dance. The highest rank within the dance society was that of the Moki. The Moki wore a cloak of raptor feathers that covered the dancer's body from head to toe. A central part of the Moki's performance, given at intervals during the Hesi, was to relay messages and prophecies from the Creator and other spiritual entities. Much of this is connected to dreaming.

The reservation Charley Watham was probably born on was one of the first ever established in Northern and Central California. Nome Lackee Reservation was indeed located in Nomlaki country, although Native people were brought there forcibly from other tribal regions beginning in 1854. It is important to remember that Nome Lackee Reservation was established scarcely more than five years after most Nomlakis' first-ever encounter with European Americans. The corruption within this reservation is legendary and well documented and obviously led to its early demise. However, with the establishment of Round Valley a second and more devastating blow was dealt to Native people in Northern California. The "drive" to Round Valley, beginning in 1863, was brutal and deadly. It further removed the majority of Native people out of the upper Sacramento Valley, leaving it open to homesteaders and farmers who sought its fertile soils and plentiful waterways. It is unclear, in Watham's narrative, whether he and his father took part in this drive. He only states that his father "moved" to Round Valley around 1862.

When I visited with Wallace and Edith Burrows at Grindstone in the summer of 1976, Wallace told me that he had heard a rumor that Charley Watham might be living in Sacramento. Someone had supposedly seen him in the downtown area. At first I thought Wallace was pulling my leg again, but he was serious. Someone had seen Charley in Sacramento, and recently. We debated this unlikely news and later talked about traveling down the valley to find him. But we never made the trip.

Charley Watham's reminiscence was collected as part of a statewide Depression-era program (State Emergency Relief Administration Project) designed to provide temporary jobs for unemployed workers. While some such works-projects programs paid artists to paint murals in post offices and other public buildings, or laborers to cut trail in national parks and forests, this particular program—miraculous in its foresight and creativity—paid interviewers and translators to do "salvage ethnography" with knowledgeable Native Californians (Valory 1971: fn. 79). Frank J. Essene was the project supervisor for the Relief Administration and must have pursued his undertaking intently, for the Essene papers in the Bancroft Library Ethnological Archives amass some eighty cartons of ethnographic and oral-historical materials collected during this period.

Watham's interview was taken down by a man named Clarence Campbell, near Pinoleville, California, on the seventh and thirteenth of June 1935. Nothing is known of Campbell—where he came from, what his background was, or how he fell on hard times and came to seek out Charley Watham. Perhaps Campbell was a local resident, hired to conduct salvage ethnography in his own area, or perhaps he was merely directed by Essene to travel to Pinoleville and conduct an interview; we simply don't know, though we may now be grateful to him for performing—and to the inventive Roosevelt-style social programs of the thirties for offering—this service in a time of great hardship and need.

NOTE

1. This interview—a carbon typescript from original fieldnotes whose whereabouts are unknown (at least to me)—was found among the extensive Frank J. Essene papers in the Valory collection of the Bancroft Library at U.C. Berkeley. I've manipulated the original text of the interview in a number of different ways: (1) by supplying the title; (2) by reparagraphing the text, though location of the original paragraph boundaries is indicated by an extra line space between paragraphs; (3) by setting the first paragraph in italics, to reflect the fact that this paragraph is clearly in a different voice (the collector's alone) from the remainder of the text (a blend of two voices, narrator's and collector's, with the balance much in favor of the narrator—though that, of course, must remain a subjective assessment); and (4) by altering punctuation where needed for the flow or sense of the story. Other features of the text, including certain variant or nonstandard spellings and capitalizations, are presented as is.

The heading on the typescript in the Bancroft Library reads as follows:

> BOOK 1 pp. 1–133
> Charles Wathem, informant, age 77. Half or 3/4 breed Nom'laki
> Clarence Campbell, reporter
> Pinoleville, Calif.
> Work assignment from June 7, 1935 to—
> God Indian name Yeaphony.

Note that "Yeaphony" is not really Watham's "Indian" name, as Campbell mistakenly believed, but merely his title (*yeponi* 'initiated member') in the dance organization. There is also considerable variation in the spelling of Watham's name as found here and in other documents. ("Watham," "Wathen," "Wathem," and "Warthon" are all attested in the ethnographic literature.) Brian Bibby and I have regularized it in his introduction to the most common variant, "Watham."—
HWL

For general information on the Nomlaki, begin with Walter Gold-schmidt's article "Nomlaki" in the California volume of the Smithsonian *Handbook;* there, too, will be found Lowell John Bean and Sylvia Brakke Vane's "Cults and their Transformations," with information on the Hesi and various other dance ceremonies. Cora Du Bois's fascinating research on "The 1870 Ghost Dance" includes interviews with Charley Watham ("Charlie Warthon" in her article). Robert Heizer and Alan Almquist's *The Other Californians* and James Rawls's *Indians of California* both contain information about Nome Lackee Reservation. Indian regalia of Northwest California was the focus of a full-color issue of *News from Native California,* which included Julian Lang's "The Dances and Regalia." Brian Bibby has written a richly illustrated book on California basketmaking, *The Fine Art of California Indian Basketry,* and had a number of articles in *News from Native California* concerning the roundhouses and dance ceremonies of Northern California, including one on "The Grindstone Roundhouse."

HOW I BECAME A DREAMER

A true story of an aged Indian, Charlie Wathen. Charlie's father arrived in California in the year 1849. He resided near the town of Weaverville until 1855 or 1856. He then moved to the Sacramento Valley near the old Nomlaki reservation. There he went to work for the government as an interpreter and stockman or cowboy. He could speak the Indian language as plainly as any Indian in the Tribe. "There he took up with my mother . . ."

[June 7, 1935.]

[First Day's Work.]

I was born during the year 1857, and shortly after my birth the Indian reservation was disbanded. My father moved to Round Valley some five or six years after this. This was somewhere between 1861 and 1862.

Now five years later, which brought my age up to about eleven, there came a call for what is known as catch-weight in racehorse riding. My father, being a horseman, owned some racehorses. I was successful in winning two races for my father that day. Then two years later, there was a man by the name of Max James, who picked me up and brought me here to Ukiah. He started me riding racehorses right; according to rules. I rode for thirty years during horse race seasons. These seasons took place in the fall of the year. My jockey days were spent all over the state of California, Nevada, and eastern Oregon.

Then after my jockey days I came to Chico to live. There I made the acquaintance of my first wife, whom I married. Two years later, I lost my wife through childbirth. After this had happened my life was very much changed.

Because of some strange occurrences, I took up the Indian ways. This I will try to explain.

I then went to dreaming. It made no difference what I did or where I went, these dreams came on every night. In these dreams, I and my wife were together all of the time. We would be going riding in our same buckboard driving the same horse. I had sold these belongings, but in my dreams they still lived. We would be going to an Indian dance or "Quomdee," this being a place to give sermons.* And always when we entered, we would be coming down through the top instead of through a side entrance. Somehow we would always find people dancing with no songs or music of any kind.

Being haunted with these dreams, I decided to leave my home, thinking this better for myself. I went to another rancheria, by the name of Noweedehe. There I remained for one year. But I went back to my former residence every year to shear sheep. While in Noweedehe, I instructed the younger folks in playing baseball. The reason for me doing this was that I tried in every way to fight off these dreams that had been with me. They troubled me very much, almost driving me insane.

---

* "Quomdee" is Campbell's untrained attempt at spelling *Kumdi* (pronounced "koom-dee"). *Kum* is the term for the ceremonial roundhouse.

At that time I knew nothing about the Indian ways, for I had always been among the white people and felt very much like a white person. But the Indian blood in me seemed to say that I must go back to the Indian ways.

Now, while I lived in Noweedehe there was a ceremonial dance every Sunday called the Ball Dance.* There was a feast or dinner connected with this, also brought in in a religious way.

So after these dreams, my conscience led me to begin to think over the Indian ways. Having lived among the Indians on a few reservations, I had a fair knowledge of how they conducted themselves and knew their habits and ways. But at that time I, myself, never took any part in their ways.

However, while my wife was living, she had told me to reveal my dreams to some friend, as it would be better to have a confidant. By doing this, she told me that I never would be bothered in any way.

She also told me to mourn her for only two months.† After that I could get married, do what I pleased, have any fun which ever I desired. She told me especially to dance, to go to the dances and enjoy myself. This I told her I could hardly do under two years' time.

She also told me to buy beads. So I went to Noweedehe to secure them. I bought over two hundred dollars' worth of beads. After making my purchase, I started to gamble‡ with the people of Noweedehe. I won two

---

* In the manuscript, there is a margin note regarding the name of this dance (two lines, penciled in by hand): "xxx [undecipherable] / bull-head." However, the Bullhead and the Ball are two separate dances. The Bullhead is equated with the Hesi; the Ball Dance was a more secular dance sometimes associated with Hesi ceremonies.

† Either Watham's wife had had early complications with her pregnancy, or she has had some premonition of her death. (Perhaps she herself was a dreamer.)

‡ The gambling Charley participates in is undoubtedly the traditional handgame played with two sets of bones, usually three inches in length, from the foreleg of a deer. Each set contains a marked bone and an unmarked one. Opponents try to guess which hand holds the marked bone, while the team holding the bones sings good-luck songs. Bets are placed before the game begins, each side putting into the center amounts of equal value. In Watham's day, people were still using clamshell disc beads as "property" or money.

hundred dollars' worth more of beads. When the gambling games broke up it was three o'clock in the morning. I retired for three or four hours, and while asleep I had a dream.

I dreamed that I went hunting and in this dream I saw two ducks come flying along. I raised my gun and fired. The two ducks came falling down to the ground. While falling they came down in a fast whirl. They fell near me. They were the most beautiful birds I had ever seen.

Having this dream interpreted by one of the dreamers of Noweedehe, I found out that the dream meant very bad luck for me. [So] I had my breakfast that morning about six o'clock. Before me, I had a trip of seventy-five miles to make before I reached home. This trip was made with a horse and small buggy called a buckboard. I had to drive my horse very fast and hard to make home by ten o'clock that evening.

On my return, I found my wife was very sick—on her deathbed. I went in and sat down by her bedside. She was asleep. There were some lady friends present who were taking care of her. They told me that some time before I had arrived, she was singing some Christian songs. After she had stopped singing, she told them that I was very near home, and that as soon as I arrived, she would bid me farewell and be on her way home. As soon as these ladies finished telling me the sad news, my only and dearest wife turned her head over to me, gave me her hand, and said, "Good-bye."

After my hard luck and the loss of my wife, I sold my horse and buckboard. The rest of my things I gave away. About two months later I left there thinking I could overcome these dreams. I moved to Noweedehe and, being a baseball player, I instructed the people in the game there. I made my home at that place about six months later.

Later, I made up my mind to start in the Indian way, by taking up the Indian dance ceremonies. The first dance I undertook was the Ball Dance. After my first experience at dancing, my dreams suddenly stopped.

After this event, I made up my mind that this is what my wife wanted me to do. So I danced with those people for several weeks doing the Ball Dance every Sunday. But I was not a success at this.

Now, the chief of this place took me and many mares out on a goose hunting trip. The meat was to be dried for winter, the oil saved, and the feathers. We were out on this hunting trip for one month.

One night I had a dream. I dreamed there were five little old people who took me into a dance house. They had a large basket, and we all sat around the basket. They sang a song and each was instructed to take it (the song) from one another and sing it all around the basket. Then one of these fellows told me to go over and take the drums and do the drumming while they sang. Then he told me to go to the floor and dance. Then one of these fellows took me by the arm with his two hands. He took me over to my place and told me to sit down and that I was all right then. This being a dream, on awakening, I gave it much thought.

Now, after this hunting trip, there came word from Wyteedesla calling for a big dance. So we went, a whole party of us. When we got to this place, Wyteedesla, the people from Chico had also come. The people from Wyteedesla had already taken me up to dance with them, but after the Chico people had seen me, they took me away from the Wyteedesla people and claimed me. So I had to dance with the Chico people.

Shortly after this dance at Wyteedesla, I went back to Chico and worked under those people for over seven years straight. They put me in a high standing or rank about the same as any white man's lodge would do. The first year I worked on the floor as leading dancer. This was to make me into a dance instructor. Then I began dancing Hessie.* Hessie was one of the leading Indian names for this one special ceremonial dance which took place in the spring of the year and in the fall of the year. We danced a different dance every two weeks during the seven years that I danced with them.†

* Campbell's spelling of *Hesi*.
† Some of the narrator's comments about rank and standing might at first blush seem like simple boastfulness. But the Hesi societies were in fact very rank-conscious: "Within the Hesi society there were as many as 10 or 12 ranks to be achieved by payment and performance. Members were

These people tore down the dance hall so as to fix it over, but got into a mixup and never did fix it. So I got discouraged there, and went to another place, a dance hall among my own people. They put me at the head of that hall and I remained there for five years.

[Stopped work at six o'clock.]

[Thursday, June 13.]
[Started work 8 o'clock A.M.]

This dance house which I was in charge of was located at Grindstone, another rancheria, of my people.

Now, while dancing at Grindstone, I would every other year have to go to the mountains to gather acorns. On the trip we would start out with a wagon, but on nearing the mountains we would have to leave our wagon and pack our horses. We had three pack animals. Getting to where we wanted to go was over deep canyons. After arriving at camp we would put in several days gathering acorns. When we had gathered enough and packed our horses, we would have to take another route home. This was through the high mountains.

On this [particular] trip back, we reached the summit after sundown and were forced to camp overnight. We staked our pack animals, made a quick meal, and retired for the night.

As I fell asleep, a dream came over me. I dreamed that the chief from Wyteedelso took me into a dance house and there showed me some of the most beautiful dancing customs that I had ever seen.* This man who

---

paid for enacting ceremonial roles, the acting not requiring the acquisition of esoteric knowledge; they paid to learn the esoteric knowledge that permitted them to direct performances and for the right to sit in a hierarchy of seating sections within the dance house" (Bean and Vane 1978:667). Bean and Vane also comment on the "bewildering variety of dances" performed in the course of the ceremonies.

* "Customs" is undoubtedly a misspelling for *costumes*. Bean and Vane note that "the dance costumes [of the Hesi] were extremely elaborate" (1978:667).

showed me this outfit was a dead man from Wyteedelso. After this man had shown me this paraphernalia I dreamed that I fell asleep.

Another time, not long after this, I was herding sheep [on] the same mountain. While in camp one cold night, I retired early and fell right off to sleep. And another dream came over me. This time I dreamed that I was looking for my mule. I was tracking him along the ridge of a high mountain. While on this errand, I came across a very large snake track which was about twenty inches wide. Looking in the direction which he went, I saw him moving very slowly down the hill. His head was high in the air. It seemed to be about twenty feet high. As he crawled along he made a very loud noise. It sounded like a large body of water rushing through dry leaves. He was going down through a deep canyon, and just beyond him was a very big cliff of rocks. This cliff was just across the canyon from him. I stood there and watched him go. He seemed to run against this cliff of rocks and make a noise just the same as that of loud thunder. After this I crossed his track, lay under a shady sugar-pine tree, and fell off to sleep.

There are many other dreams that I could tell of, and what they meant to me. Some of these dreams put me where I am today, an Indian doctor.

15

Mad Bat

MAIDU
CIRCA 1902

HÁNC'IBYJIM (TOM YOUNG), NARRATOR
ROLAND DIXON, COLLECTOR
WILLIAM SHIPLEY, TRANSLATOR

INTRODUCTION BY WILLIAM SHIPLEY

One of the great adventures of my life began, during the winter holidays of 1954, when I went up into the Sierra of Northern California to seek out the last speakers of a dying California Indian language known as Mountain Maidu. I was a graduate student at Berkeley then, in the newly inaugurated Department of Linguistics. Research funds had been made available by the California State Legislature for sending qualified students out into the field to learn, record, and analyze data on as many native languages of California as possible before they all disappeared forever. Over the next few years, I got to spend some of those funds.

I found the speakers I was searching for: Lena Benner, who was ninety-something, and her daughter, Maym Benner Gallagher. It was actually Maym who turned out to be my great friend and teacher. She fully understood what I wanted to accomplish; she bonded enthusiastically with me in the service of our common enterprise. She put all her knowledge and talent at my disposal. I did the same for her in return. We had wonderful, vivid, and exciting times together and remained close friends until she died, many years later.

Before I started my work with Maym, I learned about the researches of Roland Dixon, a scholar who came out from the East at the turn of the century and investigated various California Indian languages, mainly Maidu. Among other things, he published, in 1912, a collection he had made of Maidu myths and stories, written in both Maidu and English on facing pages. He had collected this material in 1902–1903 from a young Maidu man whose American name was Tom Young. Dixon's achievement was truly remarkable in view of the inchoate state of ethnolinguistics at the time and the lack of any adequate mechanical recording devices.

When Maym and I were well along on our study of the language, I took Dixon's book up to the mountains with me. Maym remembered Tom Young very well, told me that he was noted among the Maidu as a storyteller, and said that his real name was Hánc'ibyjim (pronounced approximately like "HAHN-chee-buh-yim"). We looked through the book, noted the inadequacies of Dixon's Maidu transcriptions, and decided to reconstitute the section called "Coyote's Adventures," an example of what's known as a Trickster Cycle—a picaresque chain of short anecdotes. That was Maym's choice, actually. She and her mother were unspoiled pagans. I'm sure she was attracted to the bawdy, sexy subject matter so characteristic of Coyote stories all over North America. Unfortunately, we never worked through the rest of the book. I reconstituted, translated, and published most of the other stories in later years, including an unbowdlerized version of the Trickster Cycle (Shipley 1991).

"Mad Bat," however, was not among the stories that I translated. It appears here for the first time. Earlier on, I was daunted by some of Bat's speeches, which, as you will see, are essentially like the "word salad" talk of some schizophrenics and aphasics—an assemblage of valid bits and pieces of the language, jumbled together in an apparently meaningless potpourri. But as soon as I decided how to deal with those particular utterances, the rest of the translation came easily along.

The denouement of "Mad Bat" exemplifies a fairly common theme found in many Maidu stories: a powerful and malevolent creature—Bat, Frog Old Woman, and Muskrat are examples—finds himself deprived of his power and shrunken down to a small and innocuous animal. In this story, Bat commits murder and mayhem with grotesque abandon and without any immediate retribution or revenge, perhaps because the other people believe that his madness exempts him from responsibility for his actions.

My first impulse was to include only the first, longer and more elaborate, episode in the translation because the later—and much sketchier—adventure with Cloud and Ouzel seems, on the face of it, unrelated to what has gone before. However, it became clear to me that these later events resolve Bat's madness and restore order to the world. His death, followed by his demotion by Ouzel in the (Maidu) classical manner, involves what is, for us, a paradoxical situation. As Bat the individual he is dead, but as a stand-in for bats in general he lives on in the modern world, stripped of his power to do harm.

I should comment, parenthetically, on the brief irrelevant presence of Coyote in this story. Despite his appearance, this is not really a Coyote story; he's just here to liven the tale, a device which Hánc'ibyjim often used. Even the mention of Coyote could, in my day, move my Maidu friends to laughter. No matter that Coyote often "dies"; he always comes irrepressibly back to life again.

There are also a few contextual things that need to be explained or defined in order that the story may be more fully appreciated.

West Mountain (Táyyamanim) is the Maidu name for what is now called Mount Lassen, the southernmost peak of the Pacific Cascade range, a live volcano that dominates the skyline to the northwest of the Maidu homeland. It was thought that saying the name of the mountain out loud would cause it to erupt. Nakam Valley is the modern Big Meadows.

The ouzel, a bird that many people don't know about, is often called a water ouzel or a dipper bird (the Maidu name is *mómpispistom*). It lives along mountain streams and behind waterfalls and has the curious habit of walking along underwater in search of food. It is smallish and brown with a little white breast and a short tail.

There are four Maidu customs that appear in this story and require some explanation as well.

First, there is the way in which Bat and his brother seem to think of wives as (from our point of view) interchangeable objects. This is probably to be taken as part of Bat's heinousness. In fact, it seems certain that, in the old days, the woman's consent to a marriage was essential, though there was always a bride-price, and there were men who had two, three, or even four wives.

Second, the staple food all over Northern and Central California was prepared from ground and leached acorns. It was eaten as soup, bread, or mush. Therefore, it was perfectly reasonable for Bat's sister-in-law not to have gotten around to providing acorn soup. It's another example of Bat's madness.

Third, when people wanted to get various people together from some distance away, they sent out knotted buckskin strings with the knots matching the number of days before the event. The messengers and the recipients would untie one knot every day. That way, everybody came together on the same day. These strings are what I have called "invitation strings" in the story.

The fourth custom has to do with gambling. By contrast with our view of gambling as vaguely immoral or, for most people, trivial and peripheral, the Maidu held in high esteem an elaborate pastime known as the grass-game. It was more than a recreational event. Charms for luck in gambling were highly prized. A single game could go on continuously for many days and nights, sometimes with enormous wagers.

And now, here is how Hánc'ibyjim opened his telling of "Mad Bat," in Maidu, nearly a century ago:[1]

pótc'odem   májdym   sámbojekytom   hedéden
bat   person   sibling.group   very.close

mym   ínk'i-di   hybó   ky-dom;
that   alongside.place-at   house   make-ing

amá-di   myjím   bomóm-di-'im,
then-at   that. [HUMAN]   group-in-ish

syttim   májdym,   tetét   wasó-sa-pem   májdym,
one   person   very   angry-always-ish   person

ohéj-c'oj-am.
one.in.a.group.they.say.he.was

A very literal translation of these two sentences might read something like this:

A bat-person sibling-group making houses very close alongside each other; then, among this bunch of people, a very always-angry person was one of them, it is said.

Finally, here is the same opening passage in "good" literary English, as I have translated it for this collection:

Bat and his brothers built their houses right next to each other.
Now, among all the people around, there was one bad-tempered man.

A last suggestion. This story, of course, was always told and not written, and was, therefore, more like our theater than like our literature. I have tried to maintain this spoken quality in my translation, breaking the text into phrases, or lines, that suggest how Hánc'ibyjim may have told it. The best way to enjoy the story is to read it out loud, even if only to yourself.

NOTE

1. In Maidu, the letter *j* stands for a "y" sound, and the letter *y* stands for an umlauted vowel, "ü." Stressed vowels are marked with an acute accent.

FURTHER READING

For other Maidu myths and stories, see *The Maidu Myths and Stories of Hánc'ibyjim,* edited and translated by William Shipley and with a foreword by Gary Snyder, which contains most of the textual material collected at the beginning of the twentieth century. For a look at the original source materials from which *Maidu Myths* was reconstituted, see *Maidu Texts* by Roland Dixon. The only extensive ethnographic description of the Maidu is Dixon's beautifully illustrated "The Northern Maidu." For grammatical and lexical information, see Shipley's *Maidu Texts and Dictionary* and *Maidu Grammar.*

MAD BAT

Bat and his brothers built their houses right next to each other.
Now, among all the people around, there was one bad-tempered
  man.

Of all those pleasant folks, the mean and grumpy one was Bat!

One of Bat's brothers went off to find a wife.
But then, he never came back.   5
Bat just stayed there with his other relatives.

One of them said: "Let's go hunting!
We can make camp overnight somewhere and then come back.
But let Bat come along later behind us.
If he's with us, he'll just make trouble.   10
Let's go when everyone feels like it."
So they set off together, but Bat came along behind.

Now, when they got to the camping place and were all sitting
    down,
Bat arrived.

In the morning, they went off hunting here and there.   15
Along toward evening, one by one, they came back.
They skinned out the deer and divided up the meat.
It was a sight to see. But they didn't give Bat any.
They divided it among themselves. They didn't give Bat any.
When they had divided it up and tied it into bundles,   20
they went back home.

Later on, Bat came home too, following behind them.
Then he spoke to his sister-in-law.
"Make me some acorn soup," he said.
But the woman said: "Wait—the acorns aren't leached yet."   25
So he just shot her with an arrow!
He killed that woman! He killed his sister-in-law, just like that!

Later, as it began to get dark, his brother was crying.
And when his brother cried, Bat felt sorry for him.
And when his brother didn't stop crying, he too cried.   30
"Watery draggety, watery draggety, my dingalong," said Bat.
"Stop mourning for that woman!
I say that I will go and find you another woman to be with!"
So then, in the morning, Bat started off, they say.

He traveled along, coming to many places where people were
    living.   35
He looked all around in each and every dwelling.
And in one house, a couple of very beautiful women were living.
So, when Bat had sat outside the door for a while,
he tossed a couple of arrows in to the father of those women.
"I'll trade you these for the women," he said.   40

And then that old man said, "All right!
You two had better leave," he said.
"You two had better go with him, with this man."

And then the two women packed all their things into pack
    baskets,
and they all three set out,   45
and when they had traveled and traveled, they got there.

"You two go to that house over there," said Bat.
So those two women went over and crawled into his brother's
    house.
Thus Bat killed his sister-in-law,
brought those two women back, and made it up to his brother.   50

And after that, Bat went back to his own house and stayed there.
But, as it was getting dark, some people came along.
And when they had completely surrounded his house,
they burnt it down.

The house kept burning.   55
When it was almost completely burnt up,
Bat came rushing back out of the night shadows.

Then he spoke. "Why are you doing this?" he asked.

Then he shot at them.
And they kept shooting at each other until he had killed them   60
    all.
Then he stayed there.
The rest of the people didn't go away. They just stayed there too.

After a while, one of the men spoke.
"We used to always go hunting deer," he said.

Then the village headman said: 65
"Go hunting, but don't say anything about it.
That Bat fellow is a bad man,
so all of you go but don't talk about it.
Let him stay here."
So they packed up a midday meal and went.   70

But Bat, without their knowledge,
got to their camping place long before they did.
They came there,
and afterward, in the morning,
they went off hunting down the mountain.   75
Along toward dusk, they came back, one by one, carrying deer.
And then again next morning, they went off hunting
and straggled back toward evening.
They skinned out the deer and cut up the carcasses.
It was a fright to see!   80
The next day, they packed up their loads of meat
and got ready to go home.

Then Bat spoke.
"Go along think sinew more or less," he said.
"What do you mean?" they said.   85
He said, "Go along think sinew more or less."
Then one of them untied his pack and gave him some sinew.
He refused it. "Go along think sinew more or less," he said.
"What are you saying?" asked the other.
"Are you talking about this kind of sinew?"   90
He showed him leg sinew. He showed him back sinew.
Bat refused it. "Go along think sinew more or less," he said.
Then they gave him a look at a lung.
"Is this what you're talking about?"
They showed him a heart.   95
"Is this what you're talking about?" they asked.
He said, "No! Go along think sinew more or less!"
"He's bad-tempered. He's just going to say that.
Let him alone and go!"
It was one of his kinsmen who spoke.   100
So, when they had gotten their goods together, they went.

Meanwhile, Bat was flopped down on top of a rock.
Some deer's antlers were hanging down, hanging from a sapling.

The hunters went along until they got home.
When it was dark, they all went to sleep.   105
In the morning, they said,
"That magically powerful man never got back.
He was angry. It seems he must have run away somewhere.
That's the kind of thing he does!"
Then one said, "Well, then.   110
You all better go see what's going on with him." So they went.

They kept going until they got to another place, but he wasn't
    there.
When they looked all around,
they saw the antlers lying a little further on.
And one of them kicked them over.   115
Then, it seemed, Bat sprang up from under the antlers.
Then they set the antlers upright and went back home.
Antlers were the very things Bat was talking about,
but, the way he talked, the other men just didn't understand.
So it seems that when they got home they stayed there.   120

Then someone brought an invitation string and left again.
When a few days had passed, all the knots were untied.
Then, one by one, they went off to the feast.
"You mustn't let that bad man hear about the feast," someone
    said.
"If he knows about it, he'll go with us.   125
Let him stay here! He's a bad one!"

Then they sneaked away.
They went along and, when they were almost there,
they stopped to rest.
When they looked back from where they were sitting,   130
they saw that wicked fellow coming along.
"Why did you go away without telling me?" he asked.
"We came without thinking about it," they said.
So then they all went along and arrived at the feasting place.
They crawled into a large house.   135

Meanwhile,
Bat went across to the house where his brothers were staying.
When he got there, he crawled in. His brothers were there.
When he had crawled in there, he sat down.

Now, his sisters-in-law were there, many of them.   140
One of them put some manzanita berries on a plate
and set it in front of him.
"I'm not going to eat that kind of grizzly shit," he said.
And he gave the plate a kick.
And then those women, with scowling faces,   145
were terrifying to see, standing around staring at him.

He snapped them on the nose,
those who were looking down angrily at him.
Then they grabbed at him, but he dodged aside.
They all jumped to seize him but he dodged aside.   150
He kept dodging. He grabbed his bow and arrow and shot them.
Meanwhile, his brother stayed there and said nothing to him.
He kept shooting and dodging.
Then, after a while, he shot all his arrows. He killed them all.
And when he got over there, he stayed.   155

Taking no notice of him, his other brothers were gambling.
They all went on gambling. It got to be morning.
They gambled all day.
Along toward dark, they stopped gambling and set out for home.

Meanwhile, Bat, having come to the last house in the village,   160
got to the place where two women were weaving baskets.
Then he handed some arrows to the old man there.
"I'm trading you these for the women," he said.
"I'm giving them to you for these two women," he said.

"All right!" said the old man. "You two go now," he said.   165
Then those two packed up their basketmaking gear.

Now all the people were scared of Bat,
but there was nothing they could do.
They couldn't kill him. He was very powerful.
Though lots of people shot at him with arrows,   170

they couldn't hit him. They were very frightened.
Whatever he asked them for, they gave him.
They couldn't refuse him.

Those two women got all their things together,
and they all three went off.   175
And then they got there and Bat gave the women to his brother.
"You're going to stay here and be married to him," Bat said.
So his brother lived across the way from him with those two
      women.

Later, Bat ran a race with Cloud, they say. They raced.
They set out and raced toward where the sun goes down.   180
They raced.

Cloud floated up to a mountain.
Bat flapped up to a mountain further on.
Then Bat flew up to West Mountain,
and then Cloud drifted up to another, further on.   185
After that, Coyote saw Bat.
"Well, now, Cousin," he said,
"It looks to me like you're running a race.
When you're racing with somebody,
I'm not one to run along behind!"   190

Then Coyote got to his feet
and took off as fast as he possibly could.
He ran, staring up at them.

Meanwhile, Cloud drifted to another mountain,
and Bat flew to a mountain further on.   195

Coyote ran as fast as he could,
looking up at them all the time.
Then he tumbled over into a rocky river canyon.

Bat and Cloud hastened on,
but Coyote broke his neck and died.   200

Cloud floated to a distant ridge
while Bat flapped on to another mountain.

They went everywhere.
They came to where the sun goes down.

But they turned back from that place.   205
Bat was not left very far behind,
and, after the race, he went back home and stayed there.

Then, later on, he went somewhere to the south,
and he came to the place where Ouzel was fishing with a net.
Ouzel was netting all kinds of animals,   210
he was netting all kinds of creatures
that came floating down the river into Nakam Valley.

Then Bat went down to the river.
When he had gotten to the great waterfall,
he tried to catch fish as they came to the top of the water,   215
and he swooped and almost touched the water.
Just then, he fell into the net.

Bat died.

After he had killed Bat, Ouzel said:
"You'll never again be one of those people-killers.   220
After you fly around in the dark,
when morning comes, you'll stay in a hole in a hollow tree.
You'll be just an animal.
You'll not bother anyone.

That'll be the end of that," said Ouzel.   225

16

Creation

EASTERN POMO
1930

WILLIAM RALGANAL BENSON, NARRATOR
JAIME DE ANGULO, COLLECTOR AND TRANSLATOR

INTRODUCTION BY HERBERT W. LUTHIN

The work of recording this Eastern Pomo creation myth back in 1930 brought together two of the most remarkable figures in the annals of California oral literature: William Ralganal Benson, storyteller and artist extraordinaire, and Jaime de Angulo, a wild and charismatic linguist who became something of a cult figure in his own lifetime. Benson would have been sixty-eight when he told this myth, and de Angulo forty-three. In the latter's books on California Indian life and lore, Benson (or "Uncle William," as Jaime and his wife, L. S. "Nancy" Freeland, called him) is the model for the character of Turtle Old Man. Because the two men, friends for nearly twenty years, are such important figures in the history of California folklore, I will briefly sketch their biographies before considering the myth itself.[1]

William Ralganal Benson

Benson was born in 1862 at Shaxai (now known as Buckingham Point) near the ancient town of Shabegok on the western shore of Clear Lake. It was, in de Angulo's words,

> a pleasant region of small fertile valleys where wild roots and seeds once grew in abundance; where acorns, laurel nuts, buckeye chestnuts were once plentiful; where the streams were once well stocked with fish; where the hillsides were once covered with numerous bands of deer. The lake itself, surrounded by mountains, teemed with fish, and flocks of aquatic birds of all kinds were constantly flying by. (de Angulo 1976a:103)

Benson was fortunate enough to have lived his boyhood years during the last decade in which Eastern Pomo speakers enjoyed a more-or-less traditional lifestyle. By the 1870s, the social and environmental disruptions caused by a growing local Anglo-American population would make traditional life impossible, as the lifeways of local Indians became increasingly marginalized.

Benson himself was of mixed-blood descent. His mother, Gepigul ("Sally" to local whites), came from a line of hereditary leaders of the Kuhlanapo (Water Lily People) and Habenapo (Rock People) tribes. His father was Addison Benson, one of the first white settlers in the Kelseyville area—by all local accounts, an intelligent and open-minded man who got along well with his Indian neighbors.[2] Indeed, Addison saw fit to learn the Eastern Pomo language of his wife's people, so despite his mixed heritage, William Benson still grew up in a household where Eastern Pomo was the language of choice. For this reason, Benson didn't really learn to speak English until later in his adult life. Something of a renaissance man, he even taught himself how to read and write.

Benson became not merely a tradition-bearer of his culture's arts and literature, but a master of them. Sally McLendon, who has worked on Eastern Pomo for many years and knew Nancy Freeland in Berkeley, tells me that everything Benson turned his hand to—basketry, regalia, storytelling—came out almost preternaturally ornate or beautiful: not just a mask, but a work of art; not just a basket, but the most beautiful basket you ever saw; not just a myth, but the most detailed and skillful version in the canon.

The Pomo were one of the very few California groups where baskets

FIGURE 7. William Ralganal Benson, circa 1936.
Courtesy Phoebe Apperson Hearst Museum of Anthropology
and the Regents of the University of California.

were made by men as well as women. Benson was already a skilled basketmaker when he met and married Mary Knight, a Central Pomo speaker
who was also expert in basketry. Together, they supported themselves by
making and selling their baskets to collectors and museums—perhaps the
first California Indians to make their living exclusively as artisans. They
even had their own exhibit at the 1904 St. Louis World's Fair, jointly weaving a basket that won the fair's highest award. Baskets made by the Bensons may be found not only in California museums like the Lowie in

Berkeley, but in the Smithsonian, the Field Museum in Chicago, and the National Museum of the American Indian in New York City.

An initiate into Eastern Pomo religion and ceremony, Benson, with his deep cultural knowledge and mixed-blood ancestry, was an ideal consultant for academic researchers—brilliant and informed, yet also familiar with the manners and expectations of the white world. Over the years, he worked and shared this knowledge (not without controversy) with a string of the most important figures in California linguistics and anthropology: Kroeber, de Angulo, Freeland, Loeb. He stands today as one of the most prolific and authoritative sources of information on the Northern California Indian world, particularly that of the Pomo.

William Benson died in 1937, at the age of seventy-five. Among the papers he left behind is a lengthy autobiography, written primarily in English, though with passages in Eastern Pomo. Sally McLendon is working on a scholarly edition and translation of this manuscript.

Jaime de Angulo

Cowboy in Colorado; failed silver miner in Honduras; medical student with a degree from Johns Hopkins; cattle rancher; army psychiatrist during World War I; novelist; gifted and largely self-taught linguist-psychologist-anthropologist-ethnomusicologist with a lifelong interest in the Indians of California—Jaime de Angulo was all these things and more. Born in Paris in 1887 of wealthy Spanish expatriate parents, de Angulo got fed up with his Jesuit schooling and came away to America at the age of eighteen, looking for adventure. He proved to have a talent for landing in the thick of things, like arriving in San Francisco in 1906 on the day of the great quake.

De Angulo had long been interested in anthropology, Jungian psychology, and linguistics, but it was through a mutual friend, Nancy Freeland, that he met Paul Radin and Alfred Kroeber at the University of California. (Freeland was then an anthropology student studying under Kroeber.) Kroeber quickly recognized his brilliance and—though the two men had an uneasy relationship throughout their careers (de Angulo's lifestyle was just too exuberantly bohemian for Kroeber's sense of propriety)—helped to get him established, inviting him to Berkeley to give lectures and, later, courses in anthropological psychology. (It was after his first such lecture, in 1919, that de Angulo met William

Benson, who was working in Berkeley that semester as a consultant; they soon became collaborators and firm friends.) In the end, de Angulo was too much of a "wild man" to find or hold a position in academia. For all of that, or because of it, he left a lasting mark on California studies.

During the twenties and thirties, de Angulo, often together with Freeland (whom he married in 1923—his second marriage), did significant fieldwork on a variety of California and Mexican languages, including Achumawi, Atsugewi, Karuk, Shasta, Sierra Miwok, Eastern Pomo, Mixe, Chontal, and Zapotec. But it was Achumawi, the language of the Pit River Indians of Northeastern California, that occupied center place in his life and life's work. From his deep personal and professional involvement with the Achumawi came a grammar, numerous mythological texts, ethnomusicological studies, and what has come to be his best-known book, *Indians in Overalls.*

Jaime de Angulo lived a colorful and in many ways tragic life—a life so rich and varied, so full of good times, hard work, and troubles, that I cannot even begin to portray it here. His work in linguistics and music alone (he was one of the pioneers of Native American ethnomusicology) would make him a seminal figure in California folklore and anthropology. But de Angulo was never merely an academic. He had the gift of a poet's ear, and used it to make books of translations and fictionalized retellings that far transcended other treatments of his day for the music, grace, and fidelity of the language, and for their wide-ranging accessibility and popular appeal.

As a writer, de Angulo managed to capture into English not just the contents of the texts he recorded, but something of their rhetorical style and, beyond that, of the worldview that informs them. It is a voice so distinctive as to be unmistakable among translators of Native American oral literature. Nowhere is this voice more evident than in his fictionalized settings of myths and tales jumbled together from his many field trips around California—in books like *Indian Tales, How the World Was Made,* and *Shabegok* (many of them ostensibly intended "for children"). It might be argued, perhaps, that de Angulo as much invented this voice in English as discovered it resident in the texts. There is something so easy-going, so engaging and seductive, about this voice that the dreary postmodernist inside us is all but incapacitated by its charm. In any case, he used this voice in his books and stories the way a musician uses his instrument, to convey what he perceived, from his long and intimate involvement with California Native peoples, as the key spirit—a kind of pragmatic joie de vivre—of California Indian life. He died in 1950, at the age of sixty-three.

Benson's Eastern Pomo "Creation"

This myth was first published in the *Journal of American Folklore* in 1935. De Angulo's commentary prefacing the text, which was presented first in Pomo and then followed by an English translation, was quite minimal. It is reproduced in near-entirety here:

> The text of this Pomo tale of the creation is in the Clear Lake dialect [of Eastern Pomo] and was dictated by W. Ralganal Benson. The translation was undertaken primarily as a linguistic study. In the first part of the myth [¶1–17] therefore the original Indian text has been adhered to most closely, and practically a literal rendering is given. This will be of advantage to students of linguistics, but a detriment to the general reader and folklorist. The general reader is likely to be repelled by the awkward English, as a result of the too close following of Pomo idioms and style. On the other hand he may perhaps welcome the guarantee of accuracy. If he is curious to know how the Indian mind [read: Pomo mind] shapes its thoughts in language and style, here he will find it. As the work of translation proceeded, it was deemed unnecessary to render the original so literally. The student of linguistics would by this time be familiar enough with morphology and semantics to supply or delete a few words here and there, by comparing with the original text. In this latter part of the tale the general reader will find a rendering that gives in reality a truer equivalent of the original Indian style with its slightly Homeric flavor.

Though de Angulo much later published a fictionalized setting of this text in a still freer translation that smooths away the "literal rendering" of the opening seventeen paragraphs, I have chosen to present the more scholarly version of the myth here because of its closer adherence to the original text. For contrast, though, here's how de Angulo opens the telling of this myth in *How the World Was Made* (1976b:41):

> *After the Kuksu left they were quiet in the Ceremonial-house for a long time. Then Old Man Turtle commenced the long tale of "How the World*

Was Made." He launched into it without any warning, as if he were just mak-
ing an announcement of what had happened the day before.

Then Marumda pulled out four of his hairs. He held out the hairs, he
held out the hairs to the east, he held out the hairs to the north, he held
out the hairs to the west, he held out the hairs to the south. "Lead me to
my brother," Marumda said to the hairs.

Readers who make the comparison will understand both how the overly
literal version submits to change and why the fictionalized version, though
more consistent in tone, was not chosen for inclusion in this volume.

Belying its tight cyclical structure, Benson's "Creation" reveals a
sweeping, almost panoramic vision. Within its five gyres there is a great
wealth of detail, as well as the continuing slight novelty of complex and
nonformulaic variation. The particularity lends immense texture to each
patch or passage of narrative ground, while the variation imparts a
through-momentum to the story that carries it forward rather than backward, so that ultimately it transcends its own circularity. The cumula-
tive effect of all this variation and detail is less déjà vu than daguerreo-
type: as in the development of a photographic plate the longer it is bathed
in solution, with each pass at creation the image of the world fills in with
richer and richer detail.

Though some plot elements exhibit less internal variation than others—
for instance, the meetings between Marumda and the Kuksu are highly
and ornately formulaic—variation is nevertheless the key to understanding the myth as a whole. Notice how each cycle of creation either
involves different methods, focuses on different facets of culture and existence, or works at refining the establishments of the preceding creation.[3]
In some rounds of creation, people are made from sticks or other inanimate objects; in others, like the second, they are simply thought or willed
into being. In some creations, such as the first, Marumda's instruction
is limited to basic survival skills, like what foods to eat and how to prepare them; in others, such as the third and fourth, in addition to survival instruction, Marumda sets up key social and governmental institutions. In some, he explains to people the fate of the previous creation;
in others he does not. In some, he partakes of food with his people; in
others he does not. In some, he establishes a dance ceremonial; in some,
he decrees the division of labor between the sexes; in some, there is comic
relief, like the encounters with Squirrel and Skunk; and so on. Even when

two creations seem to cover essentially the same ground, like the third and fourth, Benson manages to impart to them a wholly different feel—a subtle shift in mood or sensibility.

On another level, Benson's "Creation" may be heard as an extended and unabashed love song to Marumda, the Eastern Pomo Creator. One of the most extraordinary features of this myth is the sophisticated way in which the portrait of Marumda is developed across the successive cycles of the world's resurrections. It is not so much Marumda himself but our perception of him as a character or deity that matures so profoundly during the course of the myth. He is lovingly portrayed as a revered and (for a deity) oddly human figure—not through didactic narration, as a lesser storyteller might have done, but obliquely, by showing the increasing respect, affection, and awe with which he is treated by the succession of peoples he creates and instructs. The belated discovery of generosity in the third creation (¶114–116), which is requited in the fourth (and codified culturally as the ideal of hospitality due a stranger), suggests something of this growth in stature and recognition. By the fourth and fifth creations, children are scolded for making fun of "the Old Man," as well as for fearing him—the knowledge of who he is and what he has done being passed on as lore from generation to generation.

There is ever an air of mystery surrounding Marumda. He always seems to be wandering off once his work is done, never to be seen again, leaving his people, his creations, behind to express their wonder and gratitude. Marumda reaps this loving adulation despite his role as avenging angel. Nowhere is this essential duality of character more evident than in the aftermath of Marumda's destructions, where we find him going along, inspecting the newly scorched or scoured earth, simultaneously ascertaining that no survivors have escaped his destruction *and* expressing shock and grief at their extinction. This behavior may seem quixotic to modern readers, given that it is Marumda who calls down their destruction in the first place. It helps, then, to learn that Marumda is historically an anthropomorphic development of a still more ancient mythological figure, Coyote, known across the whole of the California culture area. Once that connection is made, the disparate points of Marumda's personality begin to cohere into a well-known constellation of traits, and we can recognize in Marumda a reflection of Coyote's complex trickster nature in California religious cosmology.[4]

This is a masterful narration, surely with its place in the canon of world literature. The comments I have made here are merely suggestive of a myriad avenues of inquiry into this myth.

ADDITIONAL NOTES

The Kuksu Religion

The Kuksu religion was, at least in historic times, restricted to a portion of North-Central California, involving in one form or another all the Pomo groups, as well as the Coast, Lake, and Plains Miwok, the Maidu, the Patwin, the Yuki, and several other groups distributed around the northern end of San Francisco Bay and up the Sacramento and San Joaquin Valleys. The Kuksu (based on the Eastern Pomo term *kúksu*) was a godlike spirit figure—the focus of secret societies, initiation rituals, curing ceremonies, and dance cycles where the Kuksu and other spirit figures would be impersonated by society members wearing sacred, highly elaborate costumes. For the space of time that these supernatural figures were brought to life through impersonation during the ceremonies, they "re-created sacred time and in one way or another restored their people to the unsullied state that had prevailed at the time of creation" (Bean and Vane 1978:665). The Kuksu religion (often amalgamated with elements of other, prior or parallel, belief systems) has likely been indigenous to the region for thousands of years, though other more recent religions, such as the post-Contact Bole Maru and Ghost Dance cults, have wholly or partially overwritten its territory in historic times.

Marumda and Kuksu

One characteristic of the Kuksu region is the belief in a true creation of the world, instigated by an anthropomorphic Creator. Unlike the Kuksu, whose name takes essentially the same form throughout the region, this creator figure goes by many different names, including K'ó-doyapè ('Earthmaker') among the Maidu, ʔolelbes among the Wintu, Nagayčo ('Great Traveler') among the Sinkyone, and Taikomal among the Yuki. In the present myth, this figure is Marumda (Ma·rúm'da). But Marumda and the Kuksu, who share in the planning of creation, have sharply different natures—one human-oriented and imperfect, caring but exacting; the other beyond human caring, and largely indifferent. The following passage of dialogue from *How the World Was Made* (de Angulo 1976b: 33–35), based on discussions between Benson and de Angulo, underscores this characterization. (The passage is long, but it happens to provide a prime example of the famous de Angulo "voice" discussed earlier. In the story, Tsimmu is a local boy, and Killeli is a young visitor from a more distant tribe. The character Coyote Old Man both is and is not supposed to be confused with the mythological Coyote.)

That evening they were all sitting around the fire. "Well, Tsimmu," Coyote Old Man was saying, "tonight you will get to attend the Kuksu ceremony, and hear the full story of how the Kuksu made the world. . . . "

"Kuksu didn't make the world," Turtle Old Man interrupted. "It was the Marumda who made the world. It happened like this. The Marumda went to see his elder brother, who was the Kuksu, and asked his advice about making the world. The Kuksu didn't care whether there was a world or not. He just sat in his cloud-house, and smoked his long pipe, and dreamed, and thought, and dreamed, and thought. Now he did give Marumda some wax . . . —but it was Marumda who went out and created the world."

"All right, all right," said Coyote. "Marumda made the world, but it was the Kuksu who first put the idea in his head."

"Has anybody ever seen the Kuksu," Tsimmu asked.

"Oh yes, from time to time," Old Man Turtle replied. "At least some people say that you can sometimes find him in the woods, hiding behind a tree, or at noon-time, just sitting in a clearing on a rock. . . . That was probably the Kuksu we saw hanging from the tree the other night."

"That was surely a frightening-looking figure," Killeli said. "Is the Kuksu a killer, like the Giants and the Imps over in my country?"

"Oh, of course not," Old Man Coyote said. "Why should he hurt anybody? The Kuksu doesn't care about people, one way or another. The Kuksu's no killer."

"But, Grandfather, doesn't the Kuksu take care of the world?" Tsimmu asked.

"No, Child. The world pretty much takes care of itself. When it doesn't, well, that's Marumda's job. Then that Old Man is liable to come along, and kick the world to pieces, and make a new one. . . . That Old Man is always worrying about the People, about whether they are behaving properly or not. . . . "

Bob Callahan, summing up the situation in his notes to the Turtle Island edition of *How the World Was Made,* observes that "the central characters of Kuksu and Marumda in the myth seem to function as the left and right hands, or the sons, of the ancestral Coyote figure of California Indian mythology" (de Angulo 1976b:100).

Incest

"Behaving badly," for Marumda and the Kuksu, means incest. Keep in mind that California's storied richness of habitat afforded high population density and a phenomenal linguistic-cultural diversity. Tribal units, correspondingly, tended to be demographically and territorially small, and the task of observing incest taboos and keeping bloodlines safely untangled was of no small moment. Exogamy was widely practiced (with bi- and even trilingualism a common consequence). It's an interesting subtheme that Marumda, dismayed that his creations keep "going wrong," comes up with one back-to-the-drawing-board remedy after another. In the fifth creation (¶153–154), he decides to make discrete languages, perversely hoping that the ensuing unintelligibility might isolate people into incest-proof groups. (Though clearly reminiscent of the myth of Babel, notice how this motif has an entirely different motivation from the biblical version.) And earlier, in the fourth creation, he thinks to establish *two* communities (¶141), the incest bans presumably being too difficult to uphold when there is but a single community. By the fifth and final creation, Marumda has strewn villages all over the place, thus maximizing the possibilities for exogamy, and the feeling is that this time people are finally going to be able to get it right.

Songs

Unfortunately, de Angulo did not record the numerous songs that embellished Benson's original narration. The reference to "archaic language" may indicate that the songs were in fact untranslatable, which might explain de Angulo's decision to remove them from the text. In any case, only their positions are noted in the myth.

Armpit Wax

I do not, nor does anyone else I've talked to, know what *damá-xahwé* 'armpit wax' really refers to. Clearly a potent mythological substance, its true nature remains a mystery. As in other creation myths, though, where the earth is formed from a dab of mud or sand or mist, the very insubstantiality of the original material serves to emphasize the awesome power of the beings who are able to make a world from such an unlikely substance.

Structure

Because the myth is so long, and because de Angulo was somewhat haphazard with his internal section-headings, here is a more detailed schematic of the text's major thematic movements:

PARAGRAPH	THEME
1–20	Meeting and Planning
21–33	Creation: The Making of the World
34–48	First Peopling of the World
49–57	First Destruction of the World (by Flood)
58–70	Second Peopling of the World
71–86	Second Destruction of the World (by Fire)
87–117	Third Peopling of the World
118–127	Third Destruction of the World (by Snow and Ice)
128–148	Fourth Peopling of the World
149–171	Fourth Destruction of the World (by Whirlwind)
172–239	Fifth and Final Peopling of the World
240–241	Narrator's Close

NOTES

1. Sources for the information contained in the following sketches include Gui de Angulo's "Afterword" to the City Lights edition of Jaime de Angulo's *Indians in Overalls;* Bob Callahan's "Notes" to the Turtle Island edition of Jaime

de Angulo's *How the World Was Made;* Sally McLendon's "Pomo Baskets: The Legacy of William and Mary Benson"; Victor Golla's *The Sapir-Kroeber Correspondence;* and review articles by Paul Apodaca ("Completing the Circle," a review of *My Dear Miss Nicholson . . . : Letters and Myths by William Benson*) and Victor Golla ("Review of *The Old Coyote of Big Sur*").

2. According to Sally McLendon, "Benson grew up in a world that was not 'wild' but seems to have been an interesting bi-cultural world of a few, mostly male, white settlers and their ways of doing things and the native world which had its own very rich and patterned way of doing things. The balance of power only shifted during Benson's adolescence, I think, but his first 13 years seem to have been fairly idyllic: sheltered, loved, protected by both parents, and protected from white racism by the standing of his father" (personal communication).

3. Strictly speaking, there is but one "true" creation here—where the physical substance or framework of the world is created out of wax, and beings are created to dwell on it—and this takes place near the beginning of the myth (¶21–33). Subsequent creations are really more like "re-peoplings," where Marumda adjusts local topography (a spring here, a mountain there) to create a suitable habitat, and then creates the community of people who will dwell in it.

4. In cognate and related myths among other California cultures, including the Pomo, the role of Marumda is sometimes played by Coyote. Indeed, Marumda (Eastern Pomo *ma·rím'da*) is an esoteric name suggesting Coyote, most ancestral and important of all California mythological figures. As de Angulo notes, "Marumda alone, however, does not mean Coyote. Coyote in Lake Pomo, is *gunula.* Marumda is the name of the character in this myth. It may possibly be related to the adjective *maru* which has a series of very loose meanings, i.e., sacred, mysterious, traditional, dream omen, etc." (1976b:100–101).

FURTHER READING

On the Pomo culturally, see Sally McLendon and Michael Lowy's "Eastern Pomo and Southeastern Pomo" in the California volume of the Smithsonian *Handbook* and Edwin Loeb's *Pomo Folkways* (for which Benson was a major consultant). There are several collections of myths, especially S. A. Barrett's *Pomo Myths* (1933), Jaime de Angulo and Nancy Freeland's "Miwok and Pomo Myths"; see also McLendon's important ethnopoetic analysis of the Eastern Pomo myth "Grizzly Bear and Deer" in her article "Meaning, Rhetorical Structure, and Discourse Organization in

Myth." For language, try McLendon's *A Grammar of Eastern Pomo.* The myth presented here appears, with accompanying Eastern Pomo text, as de Angulo's "Pomo Creation Myth" in the *Journal of American Folklore* 48; later, he incorporated the translation into a fictionalized book called *How the World Was Made.* Gui de Angulo has recently written a biography of her father, called *The Old Coyote of Big Sur.* McLendon's article, "Pomo Baskets: The Legacy of William and Mary Benson," provides biographical information about Benson and his wife, Mary, and includes several photographs of the Bensons and their baskets. William Benson's "The Stone and Kelsey Massacre on the Shores of Clear Lake in 1849" is reprinted in Margolin's *The Way We Lived,* and also excerpted in "Notes on Native California Languages" (this volume). Extensive museum collections of Pomo materials may be found at the Milwaukee Public Museum, the Museum of the American Indian in New York, and the Field Museum in Chicago, among others. The Survey of California and Other Indian Languages archives several collections of Pomo fieldnotes by McLendon, Abraham Halpern, and others.

CREATION

THIS IS THE TRADITION OF HOW MARUMDA AND KUKSU MADE THE WORLD

1. He lived in the north, the Old Man, his name was Marumda. He lived in a cloud-house, a house that looked like snow, like ice. And he thought of making the world. "I will ask my older brother who lives in the south," thus he said, the Old Man Marumda. "Wah! What shall I do?" thus he said. "Eh!" thus he said.

2. Then he pulled out four of his hairs. He held out the hairs. "Lead me to my brother!" thus he said, Marumda the Old Man. Then he held the hairs to the east; after that he held the hairs to the north; after that he held them to the west; after that he held them to the south, and he watched.

3. Then the hairs started to float around, they floated around, and floated toward the south, and left a streak of fire behind, they left a

streak of fire, and following it floated the cloud-house, and Marumda rode in it.

4. He sat smoking. He quit smoking. And then he went to sleep. He was lying asleep, sleeping . . . , sleeping . . . , sleeping . . . , sleeping. . . . Then he awoke. He got up and put tobacco into his pipe. He smoked, and smoked, and smoked, and then he put the pipe back into the sack.

5. That was his first camp, they say, and then he lay down to sleep. Four times he lay down to sleep, and then he floated to his elder brother's house. His name was Kuksu. This Kuksu was the elder brother of Marumda.

6. The Kuksu, his was like a cloud, like snow, like ice his house. Around it they floated, four times they floated around it, the hairs, and then through a hole they floated into the house, and following them the Marumda entered the house.

7. "Around the east side!" said the Kuksu. Then around the east side he entered the house, and he sat down, he sat, and he took off the little sack hung around his neck. He took out his pipe and filled it with tobacco, he laid a coal on it, and he blew, he blew, and then he blew it afire. Then he removed the coal and put it back into his little sack. After that he smoked, four times he put the pipe to his mouth. After that he offered it to his older brother the Kuksu.

8. Then Kuksu received it. "Hyoh!" he said, the Kuksu, "hyoh! Good will be our knowledge, good will end our speech! Hyoh! May it happen! Our knowledge will not be interfered with! May it happen! Our knowledge will go smoothly. May it happen! Our speech will not hesitate. May it happen! Our speech will stretch out well. The knowledge we have planned, the knowledge we have laid, it will succeed, it will go smoothly, our knowledge! Yoh ooo, hee ooo, hee ooo, hee ooo, hee ooo! May it happen!" thus he said, the Kuksu, and now he quit smoking

9. Then Marumda sat up, he sat up, and then they both stood up. They stood facing east, and then they stood facing north, and then they stood facing west, and then they stood facing south, and then they stood facing the zenith, and then they stood facing the nadir. And now they went around each other both ways, they went around each other four times back and forth. Then Marumda went to where he had been sit-

ting before, and he sat down; and then Kuksu went to where he had been sitting before, and he sat down.

10. Then Marumda put tobacco into the pipe that he took out of his little dried-up sack. He felt in his little dried-up sack, he brought out some tobacco, and filled the pipe with it. Then he felt in his little dried-up sack and brought out a coal, he put the coal on top of the tobacco, he put it on top and he blew, he blew, and blew it afire. Four times he drew, and then he offered it to his brother Kuksu.

11. Four times he made as if to take it, and then he received it. Four times he drew, and then he offered it back to Marumda. He received it, and put it back into his little dried-up sack. He blew out the smoke four times. First he blew it toward the south, then he blew it toward the east, then he blew it toward the north, then he blew it toward the west. Then he blew it to the zenith, then he blew it to the nadir.

12. Then turning to the left, Kuksu gave an oration: "Ooo!" thus he said, "it will be true, our knowledge!" Then Kuksu poked him with the pipe, and Marumda received the pipe, he received it and put it back in his little dried-up sack.

13. And then the Marumda scraped himself in the armpits, he scraped himself and got out some of the armpit wax. He gave the armpit wax to the Kuksu. Then Kuksu received it, he received it, and stuck it between his big toe and the next. And then he also scraped himself in the armpits, he scraped himself, and rolled the armpit wax into a ball. His own armpit wax he then stuck between Marumda's toes.

14. Then Marumda removed it and blew on it, four times he blew on it. Then Kuksu also removed the armpit wax and blew on it four times, and after that he sat down. Then Marumda went around the Kuksu four times, and then he sat down. And then the Kuksu he got up, he got up, and four times around the Marumda he went. Then they both stood still.

15. Now they mixed together their balls of armpit wax. And Kuksu mixed some of his hair with it. And then Marumda also mixed some of his hair with the armpit wax.

16. After that they stood up; facing south, and then facing east, and then facing north, and then facing west, and then facing the zenith, and

then facing the nadir: "These words are to be right and thus everything will be. People are going to be according to this plan. There is going to be food according to this plan. There will be food from the water! There will be food from the land. There will be food from under the ground. There will be food from the air. There will be all kinds of food whereby the people will be healthy. These people will have good intentions. Their villages will be good. They will plan many things. They will be full of knowledge. There will be many of them on this earth, and their intentions will be good.

17. "We are going to make in the sky the traveling-fire. With it they will ripen their food. We are going to make that with which they will cook their food overnight. The traveling-fires in the sky, their name will be Sun. The one who is Fire, his name will be Daytime-Sun. The one who gives light in the night, her name will be Night-Sun. These words are right. This plan is sound. Everything according to this plan is going to be right!" thus he spoke, the Kuksu.

18. And now the Marumda made a speech. Holding the armpit wax, holding it to the south, he made a wish: "These words are right!" thus he said, the Marumda. And then he held it to the east, and then he held it to the north, and then he held it to the west, and then he held it to the zenith, and then he held it to the nadir: "According to this plan, people are going to be. There are going to be people on this earth. On this earth there will be plenty of food for the people! According to this plan there will be many different kinds of food for the people! Clover in plenty will grow, grain, acorns, nuts!" thus he spoke, the Marumda.

19. And then he blew tobacco smoke in the four directions. Then he turned around to the left, four times. Then he put the armpit wax into his little dried-up sack. After that he informed the Kuksu: "I guess I'll go back, now!" thus he said, and then he asked the Kuksu: "Sing your song, brother!" he said. And then the Kuksu sang: "*Hoyá, hohá, yugínwe, hoyá* [here comes a long SONG in archaic language] . . . "

20. After that Marumda floated away to the north, singing the while a wishing song: "*Hinaa ma hani ma* [another SONG in archaic language] . . . " Thus he sang, the Marumda.

21. With this song he traveled north, the Marumda, riding in his house,

in his cloud-house. He was singing along, holding the armpit wax in his hand and singing the song. Then he tied a string to the ball of armpit wax, passed the string through his own ear-hole and made it fast. Then he went to sleep.

22. He was lying asleep, when suddenly the string jerked his ear. He sat up and looked around but he did not see anything, and he lay down again to sleep. It went on like that for eight days, it went on for eight days, and then it became the earth. The armpit wax grew large while Marumda was sound asleep, and the string jerked his ear. At last Marumda sat up, he sits up, and he untied the string from his ear-hole. Then he threw the earth out into space.

23. It was dark. "What shall I do about it?" said Marumda. "Oh! . . . I know," and he took the pipe out of his little sack. He also brought out a coal, and applied it to the pipe. Then he blew on it, he blows, and set it afire. He sets it afire, and then he held the pipe to the south. Then he blew away the fire that was in the pipe. The fire traveled to the south, it grew large, and over the earth the sunshine spread.

24. Now Marumda walked around all over the earth. He walks around: "Here will be a mountain, here will be rocks, there will be clover, here will be a valley, there will be a lake, there will be crops, here will be a playground, there will be crops, here will be a clover flat, there will be a grain valley, on this mountain there will be acorns, on that one man-zanita, juniper, cherries; on this mountain there will be potatoes, deer, hare, rabbits; on that mountain there will be bear, puma, cougar, fisher, coon, wolf, coyote, fox, skunk; on this mountain there will be rattlesnake, king-snake, gopher-snake, red-striped snake, mountain garter-snake, blue snake, big gopher-snake."

25. Marumda then walked over the hill; on the other side it was dark; he sat down; there was no light. He went on. Up in the sky there was light. Then he rolled the earth over, it turned over, he pushed it over: "This is the way you will perform," said the Marumda, "now it is dark, and now it is light, and now it is sunlight." Thus now it performed.

26. Thereupon he went on: "Here will be a valley, and in it there will be many villages. Here will be a river with water in it wherein the fish will run." Thereupon he went on and made a big pond, and then he

said: "Here the fish will come; this will be a fish-bend, a food larder, this pond." Thereupon he made a river: "This will be a roadway for the fishes," thus he said, the Marumda.

27. And then he went on and made a mountain: "On this there will be sugar-pine." And then he went on and made a pond: "Here there will be all kinds of fowl." And then he went on and made a mountain of flint: "This will be for arrowheads and spearheads." And then he went on and made a mountain of drill flint. After that he went on and made a spring and on either side he put sedges, rushes, redbud bushes: "This will be for the women to weave their baskets; dogwood, white willow, black willow, wherewith to weave." And then he went on and made wild nutmeg: "This will be bow-wood." After that he made another kind of dogwood: "This will be arrow-wood, mountain bitterweed."

28. After this Marumda went on the other way, he went on and on, and then he thought of making Big Mountain. He makes it, and on each side he made a large river: "This will be for the fish to come out to the lake." Thereupon he went on and made a wide valley: "Here will be all kinds of crops," thus he said, the Marumda.

29. And now he arrived at the lake, and going along the shore he made rocks, he makes them, and: "This will be a playground for the water-bears." Thereupon he went on and made a sand-flat, and then: "This will be a playground for people." Thereafter he went on and made a mountain: "Here people will not come! Men! Never approach this place!" thus he said, the Marumda.

30. Thus he was going along by the shore, and he found a river barring his way: "Wah!" he said, "what am I going to do?" he said standing on the shore. "Eh!" he said, and laying his walking-cane across he passed over to the other side. "Eh!" he said, "that was the way to do it, there was nothing else to do!"

31. Thus he walked along the shore making rocks, making sand-flats; thus he went around the lake, performing like that. Now he went back inland, and facing the lake he sat on a log. The water was calm: "Water! You will not be like that!" thus he called to the water. Then he went to the water and he splashed it toward the land: "This is the way you will behave!" he told her. Then the wind blew and the water became rough,

it becomes rough, and ran in waves over the shore, it ran in waves over the rocks: "Hyoh! Good! That's the way you will do!" thus he said. "Hyoh! Now I will go across," he said.

32. "Wah! What am I going to do? How am I going to go across? Wah!" he said. "Eh! that oak over there . . . " and going to a tree standing there he picked up from the ground an acorn shell, he took it to the shore and laid it by the side of the water. The water made waves and thereby the shell was pushed into the water. It floated, it grew large, it grew larger, it floated toward the shore and became a boat. "Hyoh! That's a good boat for us!" thus he said.

33. He felt around in his little dried-up sack and took out his pipe; he filled it with tobacco; he laid the coal on top; he blew on it; he blew it afire; then he blew smoke in the four directions and a thick fog arose. He put the pipe back in his little sack and hung the sack around his neck, then he sat down in the boat and shoved off. It started to float away, it floated way off toward the center of the lake; then he whirled his cane in the air and that boat started to race, it went like a bird, and in no time at all it went across.

34. He sat down by the side of the water and he looked about, and then he thought to experiment at making people. "Wah! What shall I make people with?" he said. "Eh!" he said, and he picked up rocks: "These will be people!" These rocks became people. They spoke a language. They were short-legged, these rock-people. These rock-people lived in the mountains only. They did not walk about in the valleys.

35. Then he experimented making other kinds of people. The rock-people were mean, that's why he experimented making other people. He made people out of hair. These people were long-haired; the hair came down to their feet. They found the Old Man Marumda and came up to him: "What are you doing, Old Man?" they said. "I am eating food," he answered. He was eating clover. He also dug potatoes out of the ground, and ate them. Then the long-haired people took an object lesson and they also ate. "This is your food," said the Marumda, and then he went away.

36. Sitting down on a hill he looked back. After a while he went over to where there was a valley. And now the idea came to him to make another kind of people. He felt inside his little dried-up sack and brought

out some feathers. He split them, he splits them, and he broke them into small pieces. These he scattered over the plain.

37. "These will grow into people!" he said, and he sat down with his back to the valley. Then people also came to life and they too came to the Old Man and asked him: "Where do you come from?" These people were covered all over with feathers, like birds. "What are you doing?" "I am eating," he answered. Then they also took an object lesson and started to eat. "Thus you will eat! This is your food!" he said, and then he went away.

38. Then he experimented making more people. This time he went over to another mountain and he experimented making people out of wood. He gathered small sticks, he split them, and scooping out little hollows here and there, he planted them in [the ground]. "These will be people!" he said. Then he went off and turning his back to them he sat down. Soon he could hear them talking among themselves: "There is an old man sitting over there," they said.

39. They came over to him: "What are you doing, Old Man?" "I am eating," he answered. Then they also took a lesson and started to eat. "This is the food that you will eat! I made it for you!" said the Marumda. Then he departed and went around another mountain.

40. "Wah! This also looks like a good place for people." He pulled four hairs from his arm and scattered them over the plain, here and there, all over. Then he sat down on a knoll and listened. In no time they also turned into people. "Where do you come from?" they asked one another. The nearest one to the Old Man said: "There is a man sitting over there too," and they came up to him.

41. "And you, where do you come from?" they said. "Oh! I came from a distance," he answered. "Are there any other people?" they asked. "Yes, there are other people far away from here. You'll find them after a while." These people were hairy and cloven-hoofed, and they had horns. They were the deer-people. He didn't like their looks. "Eh! Over there I will make another kind of people," he said, and went off.

42. Then he went on, northward, and in the hills, in a little hollow he sat down: "And now I will make other people again," he said, the Marumda. And feeling in his little dried-up sack he brought out some sinew. This sinew he broke into little pieces, he breaks them, and then

he scattered them about over the hollow. "These will be people!" he said.

43. Then he sat down with his back to it. In no time they became people. Then the Old Man stood up: "Come over here," he said. Then the people came over to him. "This is your land where you will live," thus he said. These people were like ourselves; they had no hair, no feathers on their bodies, they were all slick. "Here you will eat your food! There is plenty of food on the ground over there; eat it!" thus he said, and he went away.

44. After this he went over to a hillock. There he took some hair out of his little dried-up sack, and this he scattered over the hill. Then he sat with his back to it and in no time they were people talking among themselves. Then he looked. They were big, hairy people, walking about. These were the bear-people; they had long claws.

45. And now he went over to them: "Here you will eat this kind of food," he said, and plucking some clover he ate it. Then these people they also imitated him and ate. Then he dug up some potatoes. "These also you will eat," he said. "Oo! That's good! And are there any other people around?" they asked. "Yes! There are going to be lots of people!" Marumda answered.

46. After this he experimented making still another kind of people: "Wah! What shall I make them of now?" he said. He went to a big valley toward where the sun rises. Here he made people out of flint. These people were the Gilak people. He made this people on the mountain where there are nothing but rocks.

47. These people were like birds flying in the sky. They used to swoop down on people. They had not been taught to do that way. They were mean people.

48. All these were the first people that the Marumda made.

DESTRUCTION OF THE FIRST WORLD

49. Then he went north to his abode. Time passed, time passed, time passed, time passed, and then Marumda saw in a dream that the people were behaving badly. So he decided to go to his elder brother. Then the

cloud-house started to float. Eight days it floated, the cloud-house, and then it reached the Kuksu's house.

50. Four times he floated around it, and then he knocked at the door. Then the Kuksu opened the door and Marumda went in. Then the Kuksu said: "What is it, younger brother?" thus he said, the Kuksu.

51. Then Marumda said: "Oo! It's all wrong! That's why I have come to consult you. The people that we made are behaving wrongly. They are intermarrying, they are turning into idiots, and their children grow puny. Therefore I will wash them away!" thus he said, the Marumda.

52. Then Kuksu spoke: "Wah! It's all wrong! We never taught them to do this!" Then Marumda spoke: "Our people have become like birds, they have become like deer! They sleep with their own children. This is too bad! Therefore I am going to wash them away!"

53. Then Kuksu: "Oo! That is right! They did not believe our wisdom! Well, you know what you must do!" thus he spoke, the Kuksu. Then Marumda filled his pipe, lit it, and offered it to Kuksu. Kuksu then smoked, he smokes, and he blew the smoke in the four directions. Then he returned the pipe to Marumda. Then Marumda he too smoked to the four directions.

54. Then in no time the skies clouded up, the thunder spoke, and rain began to fall. For four days it rained; it became a flood. Marumda himself was running around among the rocks. Finally he ran for refuge to the top of a mountain peak.

55. But the people followed him there. Then Marumda called for help to his grandmother: "Grandma! Grandma! Quick!" thus he cried running back and forth among the rocks. Then a spiderweb basket floated down to him from the sky, Marumda got in it, and with it he floated away, he floated up to the sky.

56. "Ride and don't look around!" said Old Lady Spider, "or you will fall . . . !" but as she said the words he looked down and out he fell. He falls, but already the Old Lady Spider she had thrown out her net, she caught him, she pulled him up, she pulls him up, and to the Kuksu's house she carried him.

57. She carried him, she carried him up to the door, and Marumda

went in. "Oo!" cried Kuksu, "how did it go? Did you wash them away?" "Yes!" said Marumda. "Oo! That was right!" said the Kuksu. "Now we will make a different kind of people."

58. Now Marumda called his grandmother again, and she sent the basket floating down to him. He got in and floated away. It floated for four days and landed on top of a mountain peak. "Here! Get off!" said Old Lady Spider.

59. Then Marumda got off and looked around the world, he wandered about. Then he gathered some sticks of wood and built a fire. Then he went off to look for people. But he couldn't find a single one. Then he called. Not a single person came out.

60. "Wah!" said the Marumda, "what am I going to do? Eh! On this mountain there will be people!" and he called: "Wulu! Wulu!" . . . But there did not remain a single person to come out.

61. Four times he called, then he went off toward the lake. He walked along the shore, he sat down, and looked around. "Here there will be a large village!" he said. Then he went on, he goes on, and again he returned, and once more he looked around.

62. Where a while ago there had been nobody now a big village existed. There were many people along the shore of the lake. Here goes the Chief-Woman. Boys, children, are playing along the shore. They are chasing one another playing tag. They play tag in the water.

63. Marumda stood watching the village he had made. "Hyoh! They will be good people. They will be healthy. Their village will be healthy. They will be kindly in their manners." Thus he spoke, and he went on.

64. He walked, he walked, he walked. "Eh!" he said, "here there will be a big mountain jutting out into the lake." Then the mountain arose. Then he went on. "Here there will be a valley. In this valley there will be a village and a dance house. In the dance house they will perform their dances, they will enjoy their dances, the boys, the girls, the women, the children, the old people!" Thus he spoke, and then he went away.

65. He goes on, he went on, and then he stood. "Here there will be a hillock!" Thus he spoke, and a hillock arose. Then he stood on the top, he stands, and he looked to where he had wished a village to be. And

now they came out, the boys, the girls, the men, the children, the women, they ran to bathe in the lake. They ran hither and yon along the shore, chasing one another. Out of the dance house they swarmed, the many people, the people whom he had wished into existence.

66. The Marumda sat on the ground. He unslung his little dried-up sack from around his neck, out of it he pulled his pipe, he put in a coal, on top of it he placed the tobacco, on top of that he placed another coal, he blew on it, he blew it afire, he smokes, he smoked and blew the smoke toward the village.

67. Then a fog arose and a drizzling rain began to fall. Then the people started to run toward the house. The older boys are telling the younger boys to run into the dance house. Thereupon the grown-up men started building individual houses out of dogwood. They set them all around the dance house. The houses of that village were so closely set together that a man could hardly walk between them.

68. Then the Marumda quit smoking, and he made a speech to call the people: "Gather for the dance! Gather for the dance!" he called. Then the people went into the dance house, they all went into the dance house. And then the Marumda went to the mountain he had just made. He stood on the top and listened. Soon after they began the ceremony.

69. Then he told the people of the village on the other side of the hill: "Over here they are dancing. Watch it. Come and watch it!" Then the boys, the girls, they came running, they came running over the hill. They ran to the door of the dance house and they peeped in.

70. Then Marumda made a speech. "'Come this way!' thus you must say when a visitor approaches. Claim him as a friend. 'Sit down here!' say to your friend. 'You are my relative! These are your people! Therefore you and I must dance together.'" Thus he spoke, the Marumda, and then he went away.

SECOND DESTRUCTION OF THE WORLD—BY FIRE

71. Time passed, time passed, time passed, time passed, and then the people began again their incestuous ways. And Marumda knew by a

dream that his people were doing wrong. "Wah! That's not the way I taught them to do! I will go and consult my elder brother about this!" Thus he said, and then the cloud-house floated south.

72. Eight days it floated, and then it arrived at the Kuksu's place. Four times it floated around the Kuksu's house. And then it floated to the door on the south side. Then Marumda knocked with his cane.

73. "Ooo!" called the Kuksu, and Marumda also called: "Ooo! Here I have come." "All right! Come in on the east side," said the Kuksu. Then Marumda sat down on the east side. Without saying anything he took his pipe out of his little dried-up sack; he placed a coal in it; on top of that he put tobacco; and on top of that he placed a coal. Then he blew on it, he blew it afire. He smoked four times and then he offered it to the Kuksu.

74. Four times he feigned to take it, then he accepted it, he accepts it, and with the pipe in his hand he went back to his seat. "Hyoh! Sumee!" he cried, "what's the matter? What's happened now? The people are doing wrong! Oo! You must tell me the truth!" Thus he spoke to the pipe before smoking.

75. Now he smoked, he smokes four times, and he gave the pipe back to Marumda. "They are doing wrong!" said the Marumda. "The people that we made, they are not obeying our teachings. They have started again their incestuous ways. That's all wrong! Therefore I will destroy them! This is what I have come to consult you about." Then the Kuksu answered: "Ooo! All right! Later on you will make more people!"

76. "Oh! I'll go back and I'll cook them!" "All right! That's fine!" said the Kuksu. "Right now you are going to do it!" "I am going back over there and I'll burn them with fire!" "Oh! that's good! Oh! that's fine! Go! Go!"

77. Then Marumda replaced his pipe in the little dried-up sack, he hung the sack around his neck, and he went away, he went away riding in his cloud-house. He went away, and the cloud roared like thunder as he went back north to his place.

78. After this he went west. Then he went south. Then he went east, he went east to where the sun rises. That was where the Fire-Man lived.

"You must burn the world!" Marumda told him. "Why should I burn the world?" he replied. "Eh! The people we made on the earth are behaving badly! They are incestuous with their own children! They are wrong! They are acting like animals! Therefore I will burn them!" Thus spoke the Marumda.

79. The Fire-Man was still refusing, saying: "And then, where will I live?" "Never mind! You are going to burn the world! You will start the fire from here. You need have no fear about starting the fire. I will not let it burn your house here!" said Marumda. "When shall I start this fire, then?" said the Fire-Man. "Right now you start the fire!" said the Marumda.

80. Then he took down his fire-bow, he took down his fire-arrows, and he went out. He goes out, and he shot to the north. Then he shot to the west, then he shot to the south, then he shot to the zenith. In the north where he had shot the fire commenced blazing, then in the west where he had shot the fire commenced blazing, then in the south where he had shot the fire commenced blazing, then from the sky where he had shot the fire came blazing down toward his house.

81. He was running around pouring water everywhere around his house. Marumda was crying: "That will not burn!" Then the fire spread in the west. Marumda was running around in his excitement. He ran up the mountain crying: "Grandmother! Grandmother! The fire is raging!" Then, just as the fire was reaching him, his grandmother floated her basket down to him.

82. Marumda dropped in it, and it started to float toward the sky. Then the people arrived down below at that spot after his grandmother had started to pull him up, and they cried to him: "Save us also!" "What can I do? We are all finished now!" he cried back.

83. Then he said to his grandmother: "Take me over there to my older brother's place." Then the Old Lady Spider took him to the Kuksu's house. Four times she floated him around, and then she floated him down.

84. Then he went up to the door. "The people are finished!" he said. "Oh!" said the Kuksu. "The fire spread all over the earth and cooked them!" said Marumda. "Oh! Now you will make a different kind of people!" answered the Kuksu.

85. Then he went back and made his grandmother take him to the Fire-Man. She carried him east to the Fire-Man's house, and when she got him there, "Get out now!" she said, and Marumda got out.

86. Then he found the Fire-Man. "Why! I thought all the people were finished," said the Fire-Man, "how is it that there is somebody left yet?" Marumda came up to him: "Yes indeed! All the people are finished everywhere in the north, everywhere in the west, everywhere in the south, the people have all been cooked!" "Well then, how do you happen to be saved?" "I had my grandmother carry me off, that's how I got saved." "Oh! Are there going to be any more people? Will more people come out somewhere now?" "Yes! You will see many people tomorrow in that valley close by." Thus he said, and he went off north to where there was a big valley.

THIRD CREATION

87. He went along the valley and built a fire . By the side of a river he dug a hole. Then he went off, and breaking off some willow wands he brought them back and planted them around the hole. It was evening.

88. To one of the sticks he tied a string. He passed the other end through his ear-hole and made it fast. Then he lay down with his back to the fire. He went to sleep, and while he slept the string jerked his ear. He sat up quickly.

89. He looked toward where he had planted the sticks, but there was nothing. Then he lay down again, he lies down, and he went to sleep. As he lay, the string jerked his ear. He sat up quickly. He looked toward where he had planted the sticks, but there was nothing. "Wah! Why is it that what I had in mind does not become true?"

90. He lay down again: "Wah! Something has got to happen!" thus he said and went back to sleep. While he was sleeping the string jerked his ear. He sat up quickly. He peered toward where he had planted the sticks: nothing whatever! Then he untied the string from his ear-hole, and going over to where he had planted the sticks he examined them. Some of them had fallen down. "I thought so!" said Marumda, and he planted them again.

91. Then he went back to his sleeping place, and passing again the string through his ear-hole he made it fast. Then he went to sleep. He was sound asleep when it jerked. This time he did not sit up. Then the string jerked and pulled him up.

92. Then he sat up and peered. It was dawn. He thought he could see people moving about. He rubbed his eyes and looked again. It looked like people moving about. Then he said: "Hm! I had better go." He went there.

93. It was little boys playing outside. The little boys saw him: "Somebody over there, coming this way!" they cried and ran into the house to tell the people inside. "Over there some man was coming this way!" they said.

94. Then the people went out also. "It's an old man!" they cried. "Who can that old man be, limping along, leaning on his cane?" He came, he came to the house, he sat near the entrance.

95. "Where do you come from?" one of the people asked him. "I have come a long ways. I camped over there last night. I have come to teach you something. That's what I have come here for, to teach you. The people who lived here before, they did wrong, and they are no more. That's why I have come: to teach you not to be that way."

96. Thus he said, and then he picked out four men: "These men will take care of you. What I am teaching you, you must not forget!" Then he led out the four men and stood them apart. He stood in front of them and spoke: "These four men will guard the law for you, they are your chief's lieutenants." He turned around and pointing to the foremost one: "This one is your Head-Chief. If you behave like the people before you, you also will be destroyed! Therefore, be good people! Keep the law! Do not commit incest! The people before you did it, and they were destroyed; therefore don't do likewise!"

97. Thus he spoke, and then he went off and brought back some straight sticks. One large stick he split, and in a trice he had made a bow out of it. Then he peeled the smaller sticks and made arrows. Then he went and brought back some flint. He warmed it in his mouth and chipped it and made arrowheads.

98. Then he felt inside his little dried-up sack and brought out some

sinew, and he rolled it into a string, a bowstring. Then he felt again, and bringing out some feathers he split them in two. Then in a trice he lashed the arrowheads to the arrows and tied the feathers.

99. Then he strung the bow. "That deer over there standing . . . shoot it!" The men looked at one another. Then the Old Man called a fellow who was standing behind the others: "Come over here! You have good strong arms . . . Try this bow!" The man came out and he gave him the bow. Taking the bow he stood looking at it: "What shall I do with it?" he said. "That deer standing over there . . . try it on him!" and he gave the man an arrow. Then: "Where is he standing?" "There . . . he is stand-ing behind the bush . . . Go out toward that tree and then shoot!"

100. Then he went out and the Old Man accompanied him singing the deer-song while the rest of the people watched them. The deer was standing in a waiting attitude. Then the man went out toward the tree, then he shot and knocked him over dead.

101. Then the man who had shot the deer motioned toward the people, and two men came out, they loaded the deer on their backs and deposited him at the door of the house, but they did not know what to do further.

102. Then the Old Man came up, and taking out a piece of flint he skinned him right there and then: "This is the way!" he said. Then call-ing the man who had shot the deer: "Watch and learn!" he said, and he handed him the flint: "That's the way to skin. You will hunt deer for this village!" Thus he said.

103. After this he led the women to a spring to dig roots [for bas-ketweaving]. He took out the roots, peeled them, split them, and spread them out on the ground. Then he brought out some willow shoots, split them, and commenced a basket. When he was starting to weave the up-right part he called one of the women.

104. "This is what you women will do!" he said, and he gave the bas-ket he had commenced to the woman he had called. That woman started weaving right away. Then the others they too started digging for roots, peeling them and drying them in the sun by the side of the willow shoots they had gathered.

105. Then Marumda built another basket and gave it to the same

woman. This was a pounding-basket. Then he went off and picking up a rock, in a trice he made a pestle out of it. Then he picked up a flat slab and brought it to the woman. "These are your tools for preparing food," he said, and then he went off toward the hills.

106. He looked for a spot where acorns had drifted in a pocket in the creek. "These you will gather, and with them you will make mush!" Then they commenced picking up acorns. They spread them on a rock and cracked them the way he taught them, and in no time they dried them. Then they took them home and commenced grinding them and took the meal out to the water.

107. Then Marumda went with the women. He dug a hole in the shape of a hopper and filled it with sand which he patted down, and over this he poured the meal. Then he brought some water and poured it over the meal. "This is how you must do to make it sweet!" thus he taught the women. Then the women they also dug pits in the ground and poured in the meal. They did as he had taught them.

108. Now the Old Man went back to the house with some willow wands and sat down at the entrance. Then he started a basket, a long fish-trap it was, and in no time he finished it. Then he made a little hoop, he wove it into a trap-inset, and when it was finished he set it in the mouth of the basket and braided it in.

109. The people were watching him. "Have you learned?" said the Old Man. "Yes!" they answered. Now he led them to the riverbank. He cut some fence palings, took them into the water, and stuck them into the bottom. The men were watching him. "This is the way to do it!" he said. The trapdoor that he had made, he blocked it on the sides. Then he took the basket-trap into the water and set it facing downstream, and he made it fast with long poles driven into the bottom.

110. He went ashore and after a while he looked back. "It's already filled with fish!" he cried, and: "Bring the trap ashore!" he cried. Then the young men waded into the water and they brought the fish-trap ashore. It was full of fish. They could hardly bring it ashore. Then more young men helped, and they rolled it ashore, and they poured out the fish.

111. Other men commenced weaving pack-baskets. They did it the

way the Old Man showed them. Now they put down their pack-baskets all around the pile of fish. Then the chief divided the fish. Meantime other men had placed the fish-trap back into the water and returned.

112. They carried the fish home. They built big fires. The women now leached the acorn-meal. They brought rocks, cooking-rocks, to the fire. They mixed the meal with water in a cooking-basket, and when the rocks were hot they threw them in. And in no time the mush was cooked.

113. Other women brought their mush-baskets to the fire and filled them with mush. And now they ate the fish they had cooked with the mush they had put on the fire. Meantime in another place they were eating the cooked venison.

114. They had forgotten that the Old Man also might be fond of food. Then the chief said: "Offer food also to the Old Man! Invite him to eat! Give him some fish, give him some venison!" One of the men who had brought the fish-trap ashore then said: "Maybe he is still over there in the creek . . . I'll go and see!" He went off toward the water but did not find him. Then he searched around, but he could not find him. Then he went back to the beach: "I can't find him!" he cried.

115. Then the boys quit eating: "We will all look for the Old Man!" they said. Along the river, in the brush, they searched for him. But they could not find him. "He may have gone off somewhere!" they said, and they returned home.

116. They returned home feeling badly. The chief harangued them: "That Old Man who went around teaching us, he is the one who made us. He was teaching us things that we did not know. In the same way he must have gone somewhere else to teach. He must have left us to teach other people somewhere else." Thus spoke the chief.

117. After a while the Marumda went back to his place in the north.

THE DESTRUCTION OF THE WORLD—
BY SNOW AND ICE

118. The time passed, the time passed, the time passed, the time passed, and then Marumda saw in a dream that the people he had made were

acting badly. "Wah! What's the matter with the world?" he said, and he lay down.

119. He took his pipe out of his little dried-up sack, he put tobacco in, he placed a coal on top, he blew on it, he blew it afire. He took the coal and put it back in the sack, and then he puffed smoke. "Yoh! Sumee!" he cried, "may this smoke spread like a cloud over the earth!" and then he quit smoking. "I will ask my elder brother why these people that I made are behaving badly." Thus he said, and he went to see the Kuksu.

120. He traveled for eight days, and then he got there. Four times each way he went around the Kuksu's house, and then he knocked at the door. "Ooo . . . !" he cried from inside, "Ooo . . . ! Come in on the east side! Come in on the east side!" thus spoke the Kuksu.

121. Marumda went in on the east side, and sat down in silence. He felt in his little dried-up sack and brought out his pipe. He filled it with tobacco and placed a coal on top. He blew on it, blew it afire, took the coal and put it back in the sack.

122. Then he smoked. Four times he drew, then: "Here, brother, take it!" The Kuksu made a motion four times as if to take it, then he accepted it, and said, "Yoo! Sumee! What's the matter with the world? They ought to be good, but they are acting wrongly! You made them and they ought to behave according to your plan! They are your people, therefore do as you like with them!"

123. Then he smoked. Four times he drew, and then he gave the pipe back to Marumda. Marumda said: "Oh! You have spoken well! You knew! You knew that the people I had made were behaving badly! Now I am going to destroy them with snow and with ice!" "All right," said Kuksu, "you may well destroy them. After a while you will try another kind." "Oh! That is why I came here: to get your approval. And now I will go back, and then I will make it snow!" And right away he left.

124. Then the cloud-house floated back to the north. It floated over above the earth, and the thunder roared in the north. After that snow and hail fell, and in no time the snow mantled the earth. The people were snowed in. Time passed. The people were exhausted from cold and starvation. Time passed. Marumda never looked back. He went on north.

125. After a while he dreamed that all the people were dead on the earth. "Wah!" he said, "I'll go and see if they are all exterminated . . . " and he went south. He went to the place where he had first made people and he looked around. There was no one; only birds walking around.

126. "Where are the people?" he asked the birds. The Thrasher answered: "All the people have been destroyed." The Meadowlark also put in a word: "*Yówal quhlíbi'its,* down they skipped!" he said, the Meadowlark.

127. Then Marumda walked around. "Ooo!" he said, "there will be people here again!"

FOURTH RE-CREATION OF THE WORLD

128. He walked around the valley. By the side of a mountain he made a spring. Then a little ways from there he dug a hole. Then he planted sticks around it. Then he went away from the spring. Then he built a fire, and with his back to it he lay down to sleep. Then he wished: "Over there where I wished it to be, people will be!" and then he lay down to sleep.

129. Just before dawn he woke up. He lifted his head quickly. It sounded to him like people talking. He held his head up and listened, but he could not hear anything. Then he lay down again and went sound asleep. While he was sound asleep some little boys came upon him. "Here is an old man lying asleep," said the little boys.

130. Then the Old Man woke up: "Is that you, little boys?" Then the little boys asked him: "Where do you come from?" "I camped a long way from here. Are there any people around here?" "Yes indeed! Over there there are lots of people!" "Lead me over there!" he said, and then the little boys they lifted him up, they pushed him up, and they pulled him up.

131. Then they led him to the people. The people gathered in front of the entrance to the dance house. "Over there the little boys are leading an old man . . . Where did they find him?" they were wondering. They led the old man to where the men were gathered. "Where did you find

that old man?" "Over there on the hillside he was lying down," the boys answered.

132. Marumda sat down by the entrance. "Men! Gather here!" he called. Then he sat up and walking among the people he took one of them by the hand and led him aside. "Stand here!" he said to him. "Let me teach you! You will be the Head-Chief of these people. You will teach them. You will make plans for them. You will harangue them. You will take care of them. This is your village. And they in turn will take care of you!" Thus he spoke.

133. And now, going again amid the crowd, he took one of the men by the arm. "Come!" he said, "and you also stand here!" And then he went back and took another man by the hand, and he led him to the side of the first one. "Stand here!" he said. And then he went back, and taking another one by the hand he led him to the side of the second one. "Stand here!" he said.

134. "You will be the Lieutenant-Chiefs of all these people! You will take care of them. You will teach them as children. You will take care of this village. Over there on yonder mountain there is deer. In that water over there, there is fish. Over there on that hill there are acorns; there are bay-nuts also; you will eat those. Over there on the lake there are birds; you will eat those. All this is your food." Thus spoke the Marumda.

135. After a while he went and got some milkweed. He laid it down by the fire, and when it was dry he cracked it with his teeth and scraped it. In no time he had rolled the milkweed into a string: "This is the way you must do." He whittled a stick and made it into a mesh-stick, then he made a shuttle out of another stick, and he wound the string on it. After that he tied the string to one end of another piece of wood and strung it in the shape of a bow. On this he commenced a net, and in no time he had it finished.

136. Then he went into the brush, broke off two straight sticks, and came back with them. One was for the cross-bow of the net. The other one was for the long handle. And now he led the people to the river. He took the net into the water. And the young men also helped to hold the net in the water. "Now, now! Splash the water!" he said. Then the young men splashed the water. Then the fish went into the net and filled it.

137. Then he called the young men. They ran to him. They took hold of the net and pulled it shoreward. All kinds of fish. The people who had remained on the bank were watching. Then: "Build a fire! Build a fire!" cried the Marumda.

138. Then they built a big fire. First they laid the fish on the fire. The very first batch they had pulled ashore, once it was cooked, was enough to supply the whole village. They did not know what to do with it. It stood in a pile by the side of the fire like a mountain.

139. Then the Old Man took some of the fish, he laid them on the ground, split them open while the people gathered around him, watching. The Old Man ate the fish, he ate it all up. Then: "That's the way to eat!" he said to them.

140. Then he acted as if he were going out for just a little way. But it was to be forever. After that they never saw him again.

141. After that he went over the hill to where there was a big valley, and he walked around. "Here also there will be a village," he said. He brought some willow wands to the center of the valley, and dug a small hole. He planted the wands around the hole and then he went away.

142. He stood a little way off and he made a wish: "Over there, there will be a dance house! In this dance house there will be people!" Thus he spoke and then he went away. He went away and built a fire on a hillside. He lay down to sleep by the side of the fire. He slept all night.

143. At sunrise the people came pouring out of the house, boys, young men, young women, grown-up men, women, they swarmed out. One of them saw the fire. "Over there . . . a fire!" he cried. Some of the boys ran over there. "Hey! Here is an old man lying down!" they cried. Thus they said and they ran back.

144. They told the grown-up people. Then the grown-up people, they went there. They went. "Why are you lying here?" they asked. Then the Old Man turned over on his side. "Is it you my people?" he asked. "Yes!" they answered. "Come over there and teach us!" they said, and they pulled him up.

145. Then they led him up, they continued to lead him, they led him toward the dance house, they led him into the house. They made him

sit down in front of the center-post. "May you live happily! May the food grow in this valley for you! On that mountain over there, there will be acorns for you, bay-nuts, manzanita, for you to eat, for you to store away. When your friends come, you will eat together. There are going to be many people like this. They may come to visit you from afar. When they come you must greet them thus: "In that river down there there is fish. Eat it! It is food for you. Over on that mountain there are deer. Hunt them! It is food for you. In that pond yonder there are birds. Eat them! They are food for you.

146. "You will build houses in which to dwell. This house will be a dance house in which to perform your ceremonies. Over there on that mountain there is flint. You will make arrowheads out of it so as to hunt deer." Thus he taught them, and then he went out.

147. He watched the boys playing. Then he called the men together. He took one of them by the arm and stood him aside. "This man will be your Head-Chief. He will make plans for you. He will place the knowledge for you." Thus spoke the Marumda.

148. And then he took another man by the hand, led him out of the crowd, and stood him by the side of the other one. Then he took another man by the hand, led him out, and stood him by the side of the last one. Then he took still another man by the hand, led him out, and stood him by the side of the others. "These people will advise you and harangue you. The first one I took by the hand, he will be your Head-Chief. You must not disobey his orders. These four men will take care of you." Thus spoke the Marumda.

FOURTH AND LAST DESTRUCTION
OF THE WORLD—BY A WHIRLWIND

149. Then Marumda went back to his abode. Time passed, time passed, time passed, time passed, and then he dreamed. "What is the matter with the world? Why don't they do as I teach them? They have thrown away the knowledge! Why have they turned again to incest? I forbade them to do that! I will have to see about it." Thus he said, and he started his cloud-house floating.

150. He made it float over the earth, and then he looked down to see what was going on. Then he floated toward the Kuksu. He floated out to the Kuksu's house. Four times he floated around it, and then he floated down to it. Then he got out of his cloud-house and knocked at the door. "Ooo!" cried the Kuksu from inside, and he opened the door. "Ooo! On the east side! On the east side!" he said.

151. Then Marumda went in on the east side and sat down against the wall on the east side. He felt in his little dried-up sack, he took out his pipe, he filled it with tobacco, he took out a coal and placed it on top of the tobacco, he blew on it, he blew it afire, he removed the coal and put it back in the little sack, and then he smoked.

152. Four times he drew, and then he gave the pipe to the Kuksu. "Brother, you test it now!" he said. He went out to him, and four times he made as if to take it, and then he took it, and then he went back to the place where he had been sitting before. "Ooo! Yo Sumee! May our conference be good, may we be well inspired!" Thus he said, and then he smoked.

153. Four times he inhaled, and then he returned the pipe to Marumda, and he went back to where he had been sitting. "Ooo . . . ! Now again they have been doing wrong, the people that we made! Therefore I want your consent to destroy them for the last time. Now, this is what we will do, we will teach them to speak different languages so that they cannot understand each other.

154. "Maybe it is because they speak only one language that they are incestuous with their own children, with their older sisters, and with their younger sisters. That is why they are begetting puny and deformed children. Therefore I want to destroy them!" Thus spoke the Marumda.

155. "Ooo . . . ! That is well. You know your own business. You made these people; therefore it is your right to destroy them. This time you had better blow them away with a whirlwind. You go and get the Whirlwind-Man where he lives in the east under the sun. He will blow them away for you. The people that you destroyed before, maybe they inherit their bad tendencies from the bones in the ground, and that is why they are not quitting their evil ways.

156. "Now therefore you will scatter them with the wind. After that

you will make new people, big ones. You will teach them different languages so that they may not understand one another." Thus spoke the Kuksu.

157. "Oh! That's good! That is what I came to hear. I will wipe off the whole world and then I will come back to you!" thus said the Marumda. "And then we will make a different kind of people. You will make people over there as you like them, and I will make people here as I like. Oh! I will find you somewhere! Oh! Now I will go!" "Oh! Go your way! Go your way!" said the Kuksu.

158. "You watch here! Whatever happens I will come back. If not, then I will call you, and you come to me in the north by the side of the water," thus said the Marumda. "Ooo!" answered the Kuksu, "I will come. Wherever you are I will come!" thus said the Kuksu. "Ooo, go your way, go your way!"

159. Then they separated. Then he got up in his cloud-house, and the house started to race like the wind, going eastward. In no time it arrived at the Whirlwind-Man's house. It stood whirling like a big mountain of smoke.

160. Four times he went around, and then downward he floated to it, and then he knocked at the door. "*Kling!*" it said, and the door opened. "Hey! hey!" said the Whirlwind-Man, "it looks like the Old Man! Must be something wrong that you came. Come in! Come in! On the east side! On the east side!"

161. "Oh! The people have gone wrong, they are acting badly. That's why I have come for you. Over there on the earth you must destroy the people. They are behaving badly. They practice incest with their children, with their sisters. That's why they are becoming puny and deformed, incapable of hunting their food. Therefore I want you to destroy these people. After that I will make different and better people." Thus spoke the Marumda.

162. "Ooo! All right! It's too bad for them to act that way, to disregard the rules, to forget what they were taught, to throw away their knowledge! All right then, I will blow them away!" Thus spoke the Whirlwind-Man. "All right," said Marumda. "Come! You will go with me." "All

right!" Then Marumda went out and got into his cloud-house, with the Whirlwind-Man following him.

163. Then the Whirlwind-Man whirled his cane, he made the cloud-house whirl, he whirled it to the north, and he himself followed. And as he went over the land the water stood up and the trees were uprooted.

164. Now the Whirlwind-Man was in the lead with Marumda following. "Now we are going to destroy! Now we are going to destroy!" he cried as he went ahead. Whenever the Whirlwind reached a village you could not see where the people went. Some ran into the dance house. The Whirlwind blew away the house and scattered the people everywhere. Thus he did and destroyed all the people.

165. Ground-Squirrel came out of his hole. "Why! all the people are destroyed and *titsik!*" he said. The Whirlwind heard him and he came back and pulled him out of his hole. "*Titsik!*" he said and threw him in the water. Then he whirled the water into a spout. Ground-Squirrel scooted back under the ground. "That's the way to treat people when they get fresh!" said the Whirlwind.

166. And now the Whirlwind was returning. The people were destroyed. Whirlwind-Man was going home still on the lookout for people. Then it was that he came across the Skunk. He ran up to him and said: "How do you happen to be walking about?" Then he grabbed him and started to whirl him around. Then Skunk farted, and Whirlwind threw him away. "If you were people I would throw you in the water!" he cried to him. Then he chased him into a hole in the rocks, and then he upturned the rocks. That's the way Skunk beat the Whirlwind with his fart.

167. After this the Whirlwind left him and wended his way north, looking for people that might have escaped, but he found no one. "That's what happens to bad people!" he said, and then he started searching for the Old Man. "Maybe something went wrong with him . . . He was ahead of me . . . and then I didn't see him any more . . . I had better search for him . . ." and he went north. He ran north like lightning, and in no time he arrived at Marumda's house. "Oh! You are here!" he said.

168. "Yes!" said the Marumda. "And you are alive?" "Yes, I am lying down but I am alive." "Well, everything is finished, just exactly the way

you told me to do it." "All right . . . Have a smoke before you go," said the Marumda, taking his pipe out of the little dried-up sack. Then he filled it with tobacco, put a coal on top, blew on it, blew it afire, removed the coal, put it back into the sack, and then he smoked.

169. Then he passed the pipe to the Whirlwind. "Yooo! Sumee!" said the Whirlwind. "May it be well! May his knowledge be right! May whatever he does be fit! When he makes people they will be right, they will be fine, they will be thrifty, they will not practice incest with their own blood! If the people that he makes will listen to these words they will be all right! Yooo! Sumee!" thus he said.

170. Then he inhaled four times, and he gave the pipe back to Marumda. "Oh! That's good, my son, that's good! And now you may go back and you will hear whenever I make those people! Oh! You may go!" Then the Whirlwind got into his house. It made "*Klink!*" and then it raced, the Whirlwind's house, it raced like the lightning, and in no time he got home in the east, and it sounded plain as he went.

171. And now Marumda started to look for people. "Have all the people been destroyed?" he said to himself as he went along. And then: "Eh! What shall I do?" he said, walking along. "Oh! There must be people! This earth cannot stay naked! There are going to be many peoples on this earth. They will speak different languages. They will be different in color, the people on this earth!"

FIFTH AND LAST CREATION OF THE WORLD

172. And then he went eastward, the Marumda. He arrived at a large valley and walked around it. "Wah!" he said, "why are there no people here? Here there will be a village!" Then he brought some willow sticks to the middle of the valley. There he dug a small hole, and all around he planted the sticks.

173. "Yoh!" he said, and then he went off a little way, there he built a fire, and then he went back. And now to one of the sticks that he had planted he tied the end of a string that he took out of his little dried-up sack. Then he went back to the fire and lay down with his back to it after passing the other end of the string through his ear-hole and making it fast.

174. He was just dozing when it jerked, and he sat up. He looked back to where he had planted the sticks. He did not see anything. "Wah!" he said, and he lay back to sleep. He slept. In the middle of the night it jerked him, and he sat up. He looked to where he had planted the sticks, but nothing. He went back to sleep. Toward dawn it jerked him. He paid no attention. At daybreak it jerked and pulled him up. Then he sat up.

175. This time he peered. Where he had planted the sticks it sounded like people talking among themselves. "Eh! What I planned will stand true!" he said, and he went over. As he was nearing the roundhouse a man came out of the door. "Where are you going?" he asked.

176. "I have come to see how the villages are doing. In this valley you will hunt your food!" Then the man called to the people inside and then came out. "How are we to hunt food?" asked the leader.

177. "That's what I have come to teach you. Break off some of that wood over there and bring it here." Then the man who was in front of the others broke off some of the wood and brought it back. "Now break off some little ones and bring them here!" Then that man broke off some little sticks and brought them back.

178. Then Marumda split the large piece of wood and scraped it, and in no time he made a bow out of it. Then he peeled the little ones and made arrows out of them. Then: "Bring some flint from over there!" he said. He chipped the flint with his teeth, and in no time he made arrowheads out of it. Then he felt in his little dried-up sack and brought out some sinew.

179. He twirled a string, tied it to the bow, and pulled. "This is called a bow," he said. Then he felt in his little dried-up sack and brought out some feathers, he split them, and tied them to the end of the arrows. Then he fixed the flint arrowheads. "With this you will hunt deer," he said.

180. Then he said to the women: "Over there there is *kuhum* [basketweaving material]." "What is *kuhum*?" they asked. Then Marumda went to dig some and brought it back. "This is weaving material for you." He also brought some willow roots. "With these you will make baskets. Over on that mountain there are trees with acorns. These are food for you. In that river over there there is fish for you to catch with nets. Thus you will live."

181. He felt in the little sack hung around his neck and brought out a string. Then he started a net and in no time he wove a long one. "This is a *gunam* net [a seine]," he said. Then he wove a *buxal* [fish-trap]. "You will make a dam in yonder river, you will place this trap in it, and then you will drive the fish into it."

182. Then he picked up a rock and pecked it, and in no time he made a pestle. Then he brought out a flat rock. "This is called a *gushi-xabe* [metate], for pounding seeds and acorns." Then after a while he said: "Now I am going. Live righteously and your people will be healthy!" Thus he said, and he went on.

183. In this fashion he went around the world. Wherever there was a good place, there he made a village. He went where he had first made people. "Are you living well?" he asked. "Yes, we are living well. But where have you been?" "Just a little way." "Are there other people like us?"

184. "Yes, lots of them! There are people far from here whose language you don't understand. They speak different languages. They live on the other side of that mountain. They speak nearly like you. You must make friends with them."

185. Thus he said. Then the chief sent two young men over. The two young men went over the mountain and found a large village there, and they came back.

186. After this the Old Man went away somehow, and after this nobody ever saw him again in that village.

187. Then he went off. He went over the hill to where there was a big valley, and he walked around it. "Here also there must be a village!" he said. He brought some willow wands to the middle of the valley, and there he dug a little hole. Then he split the wands with his teeth, he took some charcoal and crushed it. Then he painted the sticks with it.

188. "This one will be the song leader. These will be the chorus. These will be the dancers. These will be the women dancers." He felt in his little dried-up sack and brought out a string. He tied one end to one of the sticks, and the other end he tied to his own ear-hole.

189. Then he lay down with his back to the fire. He was sound asleep when the string pulled him up. Then he got up. It was the dancers. The

people that he had wished, they got up to dance, and then it was that the string jerked him.

190. Then he also started to dance. And the boys, and the girls, and the chorus, they all watched him. They laughed at him: "Hurrah for the Old Man!" But the chief stopped them saying: "Don't do that! This is our Old Man Marumda! He is the one who made us!"

191. Four nights he made them dance. When the sun was high the people got out of the dance house and the chief harangued them: "Now you go and hunt deer so that we may have a feast!"

192. And then the women pounded acorns, and when they were done they carried the meal to the water. They scooped out the ground like a bowl and poured the meal in it. Then they poured water over it to leach it. And the boys brought out a large deer and put it down at the entrance.

193. They had already built a fire in preparation. Now the men quartered the deer. Now the women brought in the dough. The men had already heated the cooking-rocks in the fire. The women soon dissolved the dough. They dropped the cooking-rocks in a basket and cooked the mush.

194. After this the men cut the deer-meat into strings and put it on the fire. As soon as some of the meat was roasted they took it out of the fire and put it on the table while other people cut more venison into strings. Thus all the meat got cooked.

195. And now the chief called: "Gather hither!" Then all the people gathered. The women brought out the cooked mush and the meat. They brought it out, and then the women gathered in one place.

196. Then the chief chose four young men. He took the leader by the arm. Then he [the leader] took the next one by the hand. This one in turn took the next one by the hand. Thus he led them around the food four times back and forth. Then he placed the leader on the south side. The next one he placed on the east side. The next one he placed on the north side. The last one he placed on the west side.

197. Then the chief spoke: "These people I have chosen to be your guardians. They will make plans for you. They will address you in speeches."

198. Then the Marumda spoke: "This is what you people are going to do. You are going to gather your provisions, your venison-meat, your acorns, your valley-seeds. Then you will store it away, and on this you will live in abundance. You will hold festivals. When visitors come from a distance, take them into the house and partake of food with them. When your friends come from somewhere to visit you, that's the way you must provide them with food.

199. "There are going to be many of you people. Therefore you must take care of each other. Therefore you must claim one another as friends, you must claim one another as relatives. Thus you will live in happiness!" Thus spoke the Marumda. And then he departed.

200. Thus it was that people got acquainted with one another. They acknowledged one another as friends and relations. The young men hunted deer and caught fish. They gathered acorns. They married and brought food in dowry, and deer, and fish. Thus they did.

201. Thus he went, the Marumda, making villages on the shores of the lake, and he came around again to where he had made the first village. The little boys found him. "Here lies an old man!" they said. The older boys came near. "Where have you come from?" they asked him. "Oh! I have come from far away . . . Say, little boys, bring me an acorn shell." Then the biggest of the boys said, "I'll bring it!"

202. The boy ran home and came back with an acorn shell. "Are you going to eat it?" he asked the Marumda. "No, give it to me!" The boy gave him the shell. Then Marumda took it and threw it in the water. "Hey!" cried the boy, "what did you throw it away for? Now I won't give you any more. You threw it away! Now I won't give you any more."

203. "Look over there!" said Marumda. The boys went to the shore and looked at the shell. It was floating. Then they also threw in acorn shells. Marumda's shell floated on [the water] and became a boat. The boys' shells did not become boats. "Why is it that your shell became a boat but ours did not?" asked the boys.

204. "Are you going to ride in it?" they asked then. "Yes, I am going across the lake in it." "And you are not afraid?" "What should I be afraid of?" said Marumda. "Won't the water-bears eat you?" "The water-bears are my playmates," said the Marumda. "Look, boys, I am going now."

He pushed the boat into the water, he got in, with his cane he shoved off, then he whirled the cane, and that boat went off like a bird flying. In no time it was out of sight. "Oh, he is gone!" cried the boys.

205. Not far from there, there were some grown-up people watching. "Who was that old man?" asked the boys. "What did you ask him?" said the people. "That was no old man. He just made himself into an old man. And then he grew wings. His name is Marumda. He is the one who made the world. He made the lake. He made everything that you see. You saw how he made a boat out of that shell that he threw in the water. He made this big lake and he can dry it up. He also made us people. He made everything here on the earth. Understand that, boys!" Thus spoke the chief.

206. Marumda's boat was already across. It skidded ashore. There were some boys playing there who saw him land. "Hey! An old man just landed out of the water!" they cried. Then a crowd of people came out, men and women. "Why! Here is our Old Man! Give him food!" cried the chief.

207. Then the women went to the house to fetch food and they came back with meal and mush for the Old Man. "Thank you! Thank you!" he said, "I will freshen [i.e., initiate] the boys for you when I am through eating. Look toward the south!" The boys saw a monster running. "He is running this way!" they cried.

208. The monster approached nearer and nearer, and the boys ran away, but he headed them off. They ran toward the house. He rounded them up in one place and drove them into the house. Then he went around the house, four times to the right, and four times to the left, he went around. Then he went over to where Marumda was sitting.

209. "Oh!" said the Marumda, "that's my older brother the Kuksu!" "Younger brother, how are the people that you made? Are they behaving? Did everything come right as you wished? You haven't missed anything?" Thus spoke the Kuksu.

210. They were sitting facing the lake. "Yes, I made everything as I wanted, and then I crossed over." "Then I am happy! Now you must make the people hold a dance, a four-day dance." "I told them the same thing over there across [the water]. We will watch this dance and when

it is all completed and well performed, we will go over there." Thus said the Marumda.

211. "All right!" said the Kuksu. "You are right, your words are true. Good words, sound knowledge and straight. Therefore make a speech for them so that they may learn from you. Already they have their dancing costumes on." Thus spoke the Kuksu.

212. Then Marumda got up and went toward the dance house. He stood on top of the dance house and harangued the people: "Gather for the dance! Gather for the dance! My people, my boys, my girls! Gather for the dance! Go into the dance house!" Then the people, the boys, the girls, the children, everybody went into the dance house.

213. The men gathered in front of the center-post. The chorus sat down in front of them. And then Marumda came out in front of them. Then the people tried to sing the song, but they didn't know how.

214. Then Marumda himself sang it. [SONG.] "This is the sitting-down-song," said Marumda.

215. Meanwhile the men and the women were fixing their dancing costumes. Now they sang the dance-song. Men and boys together were fixing themselves. Women and girls together were fixing themselves. The dance house was crowded with dancers.

216. In the lead went the Marumda. He performed in front of them. Eight times he danced and stopped, and then they rested. They danced all night for four nights. They carried out the dance till just before dawn. Then they took off their dancing costumes and carried them around the dance house four times.

217. After this the men went to the lake to bathe. The young men went to the lake to bathe. The women went to the lake to bathe. The girls went to the lake to bathe. And then they came back to the shore.

218. Thereupon the singers went to the lake to bathe. They came out and started toward the dance house. The singers walked in the lead. Then came the men, then came the young men, then came the women, then came the girls.

219. Four times each way they went around the dance house, and then they went in. And now they went around the center-post four times each

way. After that they sat down inside the house. Marumda stood in front of the center-post and delivered a prayer. Four times he spoke.

220. Then he commanded: "Make donations of food!" Then everyone in the village brought out donations of food. Now Marumda selected assistant chiefs. He selected four of them to distribute the food. He selected four men, and he selected four women chiefs to distribute the food.

221. They first gave some to Marumda, a ball of mush. In no time he cleaned it up. And then he went off. That was forever that he departed. After that no one ever saw him. No one knows where he went. Thus it happened.

222. In this wise he visited every village, teaching them how to perform the dances. Eight days and eight nights he would perform, and then it was completed.

223. After this he walked about on a mountain, and he called together the coyotes: "You will watch over the villages that are strung out on the land. If enemies should approach, you must cry: *Guhmá a'a . . . guhmá a'a . . .* Enemies . . . enemies . . . " Thus the Marumda instructed the coyotes.

224. After this he called together the wolves of the woods: "You will travel in the woods, hunting your food!" Thus he instructed them. And then he called together the pumas: "You will travel on the mountains, hunting your food!" Thus he instructed them.

225. Then he called together the *wiq'a* [unidentified animal]: "You will travel amid the rocks, hunting your food!" Thus he instructed them. Then he called together the lynxes: "You will travel in the chamise brush, hunting your food!" Thus he instructed them. Then he called together the foxes: "You will live inside hollow trees amid the rocks!" Thus he instructed them.

226. Then he called together the skunks. He came out with his tail over his head. There was some noise, and he squirted in that direction. He made the whole land stink as he came. "You mustn't do that!" said Marumda. "Only if they threaten to kill you, then you may do it! You will live in holes in the rocks and in the trees." Thus he instructed them.

227. Then he called together the raccoons: "You will live in holes in the trees and there you will hunt your food!" Then he called together the squirrels: "You will build your nests high up in the trees and from there you will go and hunt your food!" Thus he instructed them.

228. Then he called together the martens: "Amid the rocks you will dwell. From there you will hunt your food." Then he called together the bears: "On the mountains you will travel. There you will dwell in caves. From there you will hunt your food!"

229. After that he called together the elk: "You will dwell in the hills and you will hunt your food in the valleys." Thus he instructed them. And then he called together the chamise-animals [the deer], and he addressed them: "You, in the hills you will dwell, amid the sagebrush. You are dwellers of the hills." Thus he instructed them.

230. Then he called together the rabbits: "You will live in the valleys and in the mountains." Thus he instructed them. After this he called together the ground-squirrels, the moles, the gophers, the field mice, the wood-rats, the badgers: "You will dwell under the ground, you will live in holes!" Thus he instructed them.

231. Then he called together the rattlesnakes, the large gopher-snakes, the small gopher-snakes, the milk-snakes, the red-striped snakes, the mountain garter-snakes, the snakes with green back and red belly, the big lizards, the common lizards, the salamanders, the giant salamanders, the snails: "You will live in the hills, amid the rocks, in the trees, in holes underground!" Thus he instructed them.

232. Then he called together the birds, the eagles, the condors, the hawks, the falcons, the goshawks, the kites, the big horned owls, the screech owls, the nighthawks, the little horned owls, the ground owls: "You will live in the hills, in hollow trees, in holes in rocks!" Thus he instructed them.

233. Then he called together the bluejays, the blackbirds, the quail, the crows, the flickers, the red-headed woodpeckers, the mountain jays, the grouse, the robins, the mountain robins, the towhees, the black-and-yellow finches, the mountain quail, the roadrunners, the ravens, the sapsuckers, the woodpeckers, the thrushes, the bluebirds, the mead-

owlarks, the orioles, the grosbeaks, the swallows, the black swallows, the shrikes, all of them he called together and instructed them: "You will live in the hills and the valleys, and in hollow trees!" Thus he instructed them.

234. Then he called together the water birds, blue heron, sand-hill crane, white crane, bittern, little green heron, swan, goose, mallard, cormorant, grebe, merganser, seagull, pied-billed grebe, little merganser, mud-hen, he called them together and addressed them: "In the water you will live, in the water you will seek your food!"

235. Then he called together the fishes: "Fishes who live in the water, all of you, come ashore!" Thus he spoke. Then Turtle came ashore first, and behind him came all the fishes. "You are not a fish!" said Marumda to the Turtle. "You will travel on the land. You fish, you are not to travel on land! You fish, you must live in the water. You will eat food from the water. And you too, Turtle!" Thus he spoke. Then the fish went back into the water, and Turtle floated back into the water.

236. Thus sitting on top of a mountain spoke the Marumda. Thus he instructed everything on the earth. How they were to behave, what they were to eat, where they were to live, he told them that way, everything. That's what he called them together for.

237. He sat on a large flat rock on top of the mountain, giving instructions to everything that lives. Then he got off and stood the rock on edge. "People must never come here!" Thus spoke the Marumda.

238. Then he departed. "If people come here this rock will fall and the people will live no longer! If anyone comes here he will die forever!" Thus spoke the Marumda.

239. After that he went to see the Kuksu. He arrived at the Kuksu's place and told him what he had done. "You have done the right thing!" said the Kuksu. "Sing a praying song, older brother!" said Marumda to Kuksu. Then: "All right!" he said. [SONG.] Thus spoke the Kuksu. Then Marumda spoke: "Oh! That's good! Ooo . . . Ooo . . . Ooo . . . Ooo!" And then the Marumda pulled out a song. [SONG.] Then he went back to his own abode. And the Kuksu also went back to his own place.

240. Four times he made us people. First he drowned them in the water. Then he destroyed them by fire. Then he destroyed them by snow. Then he destroyed them by a whirlwind. Thus he destroyed them four times. This tale I was taught by the old men, this tale of world-making, of making people, this is the tale as I was told.

241. This is the tale that I heard when I was little, when I was a boy.

17

The Trials of Young Hawk

SOUTHERN POMO
1940

ANNIE BURKE, NARRATOR
ABRAHAM M. HALPERN, COLLECTOR
ROBERT L. OSWALT, TRANSLATOR

INTRODUCTION BY ROBERT L. OSWALT

Historical Background

The terms *Pomo* and *Pomoan* refer to a family of seven related languages and to their speakers. The divergence among the seven languages is similar to that among the various Romance languages; at the extremes, the divergence is greater than that between English and German. At a more distant level, Pomoan is related to some languages classified as Hokan. The Pomo lived in an area stretching roughly from about fifty miles north of San Francisco northward for ninety miles, and from the Pacific Coast inland for fifty miles to include much of the shore of Clear Lake, with an offshoot to the northeast across the Inner Coast Range.

Estimates of the total population of the pre-Contact Pomo vary from eight thousand to twenty-one thousand. The Southern Pomo, who occupied the drainage system of the lower half of the Russian River, were one of the more numerous of the language groups, constituting about 30 percent of the Pomo total. They were not a political unit but lived in several independent village communities.

Aboriginally all the Pomo lived by hunting, fishing, and gathering plant foods. Acorns were the staple of their diet and required a great deal of preparation: gathering, drying, cracking, grinding, leaching (to remove the bitter tannic acid), and cooking. They clipped and ground clamshells into beads, which were strung and used as a store of wealth. Larger and much more valuable beads were made of magnesite (known as "Indian gold"). To keep account of the wealth represented by these beads, they developed a system for counting up into the thousands. However, the Pomo have been most famed for their basketry, which was woven with great skill in a wide variety of techniques. The women took pride in doing artistic work, often taking months to complete a fine, coiled six-inch basket. There has recently been a cultural renaissance, and a few younger women have learned to produce the fancy baskets.

Beginning in the early nineteenth century the Southern Pomo were disastrously affected by missionization, raids, disease, and settlement of their land by immigrants. By the early twentieth century, in the southernmost region, containing the present cities of Santa Rosa and Sebastopol, the surviving biological descendants of the Southern Pomo had lost their ancestral speech. Further to the north, two dialects survived, with, at midcentury, perhaps two dozen speakers each: Mihilakawna 'West Stream', spoken in the Dry Creek Valley (now filled with vineyards), and Makahmo 'Salmonhole', spoken in the area of the town of Cloverdale. By the early 1960s the number of speakers had dwindled to about a dozen for each of the two dialects. And by 1999, there was one speaker of each dialect. There are hundreds of descendants with some Southern Pomo blood, but they are much assimilated and racially mixed through intermarriage with other Indian groups, with Mexicans, and with white people. In the recent cultural revival many of the younger generations have learned their traditional songs and dances and perform them in public.

Salvage Workers

Into the situation in 1939 came Abraham M. Halpern (1914–1985), to collect, over a one-year period, lexical material and texts with free translations and some word-by-word translations in each of the seven Pomo languages. Halpern had spent considerable time studying Yuma (also called Quechan), spoken in far Southeastern California, and he eventually produced a grammar of that language as a doctoral dissertation. He brought northward with him a phonetic skill that enabled him to record in the Pomo languages the unusual sounds that had escaped the occasional earlier collector. For Southern Pomo, Halpern obtained seven Coyote stories, dictated by the one speaker, Annie Burke.

By 1963, I had completed a grammar and a volume of texts of the neighboring Kashaya Pomo language and turned my attention to salvaging as much as possible of the Southern Pomo language. My first principal consultant was Elizabeth Dollar (1895–1971), speaker of the Mihilakawna dialect, who was able to furnish some Coyote stories, as well as much lexical material. From the mid 1960s and for twenty years, Elsie Allen (1899–1990) and I worked together for a couple of weeks each year gathering lexical and grammatical material on her mother tongue. She did not know any Coyote stories, nor did any other surviving speaker of the Makahmo dialect, and thus those dictated by her mother, Annie Burke, remain the only real corpus for the genre in that dialect.

Annie Burke (1876–1960), born Annie Ramone, was raised in a relatively traditional way, speaking only the Makahmo dialect; she learned English later in life. She married George Comanche and with him had two daughters. She gave birth to her first while working in the hop fields and this child, Elsie, was to become a chief consultant on the Makahmo. Annie's second husband was Richard Burke, and with him she had one son, Salvador. The family lived on the Hopland Reservation, where the language was Central Pomo, a language about as different from Southern Pomo as French from Spanish, and that became the third language that Annie and Elsie learned to speak.

Annie Burke was a master basketweaver. Like many artists, she was also a collector of the creations of other masters in her medium. Earlier tradition had been that personal property should be buried with the deceased; however, Annie Burke requested that this not happen to her baskets and that they be preserved for later generations to see. Her daughter Elsie, who also became a master weaver (and wrote a booklet on Pomo basketweaving), made the same request for preservation, with the result that the family baskets are now on display in the museum in the town of Willits.

Narrative Structure

"The Trials of Young Hawk" is of a class of narratives that the Pomo call "Coyote stories," told of a time when animals had speech and other human attributes. Coyote often is the principal character, but, as here, it is not necessary for him to be a participant for the tale to be a Coyote story.

Ritual Numbers. The magical number among the Pomo and neighboring Indians is four: a ritual (submersion in water, in this story) may have to be performed four times, good or bad luck may come in fours, and the hero of a story may have to overcome four obstacles (compare three and seven in European tales). On occasion, half or twice four has special significance: duality, the occurrence of characters in pairs—two siblings, parent and child, two opponents—is fairly common in Pomo stories. This tale carries out the principle of duality to an exceptional degree. The tale begins with two hawk brothers but quickly turns to following the trials of the younger brother alone. He has encounters with various pairs, even pairs of pairs: two beaver brothers, then two gopher brothers; two red ant sisters, then two field mice sisters. There is a shift toward the end of the tale to two separate attacks from single opponents, an ogress and thunder. The story closes with revenge taken on the older brother.

Personal Names and Kinship Terms. Animal characters are identified in the Native text by species name. In other translations these have often been converted into proper names by capitalizing them. As a convention, that might well have been done here, but it is not, because the designations in Southern Pomo are not proper names. As a term of reference, *k'aʔbek'ac'* 'sharp-shinned hawk' is used of either the older or younger hawk brother, not as the name of one of them. Real proper names of individuals cannot be used in ordinary secular situations; instead, a kinship term is almost invariably employed as a term of address.

Whether the characters are related or not, a kin term suitable to the age difference can be selected: someone two generations older might be called by one of the grandparent terms; a slightly older male might be addressed as "Older Brother." The Pomo languages all have distinct terms for the four grandparents, each of which is more inclusive than is suggested by the English translation; for example, the Southern Pomo term for "mother's father" includes all the brothers of the father of the mother. At two points in the tale the younger brother addresses the older, not by the relationship of the addressee to the speaker—that is, "Older Brother"—but by a tecnonym, a term based on the relationship of the addressee to a child, in this case the adopted hawk: "O Father of his Mother" (one word in Southern Pomo). It might be noted that the two pairs in the story addressed as "Mother's Father" are helpful, as older relatives should be. The two pairs of females are not addressed by a kin term because they are potential mates and it would be incestuous for them to be adopted into the equivalent of a close blood relationship. The single ogress is not a potential mate and can address the young hawk by the deceptively friendly "Grandson."

Sentence Connectors. Southern Pomo has an elaborate system of suffixes for subordinating one clause to another. When attached to the verb *ha:mini-* 'do thus' or 'do so' they form a word that links two sentences together, giving such information as the relative timing of the successive sentences and whether there has been a switch in subject between the prior sentence and the one with the connector. The narrative may proceed through several clauses and sentences with no subject expressed overtly; even so, the appropriate English pronouns can be deduced from the tracking system and supplied in the translation. In the native-language extract that follows, taken from the end of the fourth paragraph of the story, these characteristic features of Southern Pomo discourse are clearly on display.

šin:akʰle he?:e pʰa?s'i-ba,
crown.of.head hair grabbed-having
Having grabbed the hair on the crown of the head,

ma:-ṭ'iki-n, "ka:li-n-hkʰay hu?:uci-n!" nih:iw.
own-younger.brother-to up-to-ward turn.face-IMPERATIVE said
he said to his younger brother, "Turn your face upward!"

ha:mini-ba, ma:-ṭ'iki-n hu?:u-kʰbe ?akʰ:o ba-:ciṭ'.
done.so-having own-younger.brother-to eye-rock two poke-out
Having done so, he poked out his younger brother's two eyeballs.

ha:mini-ba   kʰma:yow,   hidʔa   hwa:-ba,
done.so-having   after,   outside   gone.out-having
After having done so, having gone outside,

ʔahca-n-hkʰay   ho:liw.
house-to-ward   set.off
he set off homeward.

The closest English translations of these sentence connectors are phrases like "Having done so," "He having done so, the other," "While doing so," and "While he was doing so, the other." In the story, some of the connectors are fully translated, to convey the style of Southern Pomo narratives, but others are rendered more simply to avoid being excessively intrusive. "Then" and "and" are common translations but deliver less information than the Southern Pomo connector.

Definite and indefinite articles also are supplied to fit the context. Other major elements that have been inserted to clarify the translation, but are not in the original text, are put in square brackets.

Quotatives. Annie Burke's rendition is curiously at variance with what is typical among all other Pomoan traditional stories: She rarely employs the evidential suffix *-do* 'it is said, they say', used to mark that the narrator has been told of the events by someone else, and that they are not personal experiences. The suffix appears only in the fifth paragraph from the end.

FURTHER READING

The most accessible reference on the culture of the Pomo is the *Handbook of North American Indians,* volume 8, which, in three chapters, covers the seven branches of the Pomo and includes a good listing of sources for more information. Elsie Allen, the daughter of the narrator of this story, wrote a small well-illustrated book, *Pomo Basketmaking*, which also contains a biographical sketch of Elsie Allen by her granddaughter, Linda McGill. S. A. Barrett's *Pomo Myths* contains 108 tales in English only, from the Central, Northern, and Eastern Pomo, together with a motif index, a glossary of words in the three languages, and an introduction with a discussion of such topics as the methods of storytelling and the mythological system, and a description of the many supernatural beings. Robert Oswalt's *Kashaya Texts* contains eighty-two texts in the neighboring Kashaya Pomo language, together with English translations; twenty are Coyote stories, thirty more are tales with some supernatural element, nineteen are folk history, and thirteen are of miscellaneous genres. Oswalt's "Retribution for Mate-Stealing" is a story told by Elizabeth Dollar in Southern Pomo, Mihilakawna dialect, with word-by-word translation, free translation, and a grammatical sketch of the language.

THE TRIALS OF YOUNG HAWK

A group of small birds and animals, who were all also people, used to live together in a big community. A sharp-shinned hawk lived there along with his younger brother. The hawk's younger brother always perched up high in the earth lodge on the side with the fire. The older sharp-shinned hawk was married to a wildcat; his wife was a wildcat woman.

One time many of the people set off eastward to load up on fish. After they all had left, the wildcat woman went to her husband's brother down in the earth lodge and pulled her husband's brother down from where he was perched. Having pulled him down, she dragged him away. Then she scratched him, scratched him everywhere on his face, scratched his body too. When she had scratched him, he fled to where the earthlodge was and ran down in. There he perched up high where his bed was.

Those people who had gone off toward the east now started for home, bringing a load of fish. While they were on their way, the scrub jay told the older hawk, "Your wife scratched your younger brother."

In the morning, the older hawk went down there to the earth lodge. He then said to his younger brother, "Climb down! I'm going to brush your hair." He spread a hide for him to climb down onto. The younger brother, having climbed down, sat down on the hide. The older brother, the sharp-shinned hawk, having sat down near his younger brother, brushed his head hair with a louse brush. All of the head hair he brushed well. Having grabbed the hair on the crown of the head, he said to his younger brother, "Turn your face upward!" Then he poked out his younger brother's two eyeballs. After having done so, he went outside and set off homeward.

The younger brother cried and screamed and screamed, writhing around. But nobody at all saw this; he just suffered it alone.

Now night came on and, when the people all lay down to sleep, he, by crawling around, felt the door, the earth lodge doorway, and through there crept outside.

Now he just crawled away somewhere on all fours. He didn't know where he was crawling to. Weeping he crept along; groaning he crawled this way and that. Falling down into brush, he rolled down a steep incline. Having crawled around in this way, he clambered up onto an earth lodge.

When this happened, a beaver and his younger brother living there together both heard the movement on their earth lodge. The older beaver brother said to his younger brother, "Look outside there! Somebody is groaning a lot out there." When he said this, the younger brother said "All right" and went outside. When he did so, he found the eastern hawk and said, "My poor child! It must be our child who has been crawling around, O Father of his Mother!"

The older beaver brother also ran outside. The two of them carried that hawk down into the earth lodge. When they had done this, the mother's fathers wept. After they had wept, they built a fire and placed rocks in it. They filled a baby-bath basket with water, and, when the rocks had become hot, they dropped those hot rocks into that water-filled baby bath. They dropped the rocks, the hot rocks, into the baby-bath basket, in order to heat the water. When the water had become hot, they washed the hawk's body. They fixed up his hair as well, the head hair that had become so tangled, so full of dry grass, so full of foxtails and burrs. Twigs and leaves were all snarled with that once fine hair.

The two of them, sitting beside that place, fixed him up. They made everything good. After doing this, they next gnawed out round balls from wood and set these artificial eyes into the eyesockets. It didn't look good, because it was white, just white all over.

At night, when his mother's fathers had gone to sleep, he crawled back and forth on all fours and then crawled outside. He crawled away, not knowing where he was crawling. He just crawled here and there on all fours, crawling while crying. Having crawled around in this way, he crawled up onto a gopher's earth lodge.

A gopher lived there with his younger brother. The older gopher said to his younger brother, "Somewhere on top of the earthlodge I hear someone groaning. Go and look up there!" "All right, I'll go look. You are such a coward," said the younger, and he went outside.

When he did so, he found the hawk. He then said to his older brother, "The child must be ours, O Father of his Mother." When the younger said this, the older followed him out. The two of them picked [the young hawk] up and carried him down into the earth lodge. They set him down there where they had spread something out. When they had done this, the two of them wept over their grandchild.

When they had finished crying, they set rocks on their fire and put water in a baby-bath basket. Then, when the rocks had become hot, they dropped those hot rocks down into the water. The water heated up. Then they washed the hawk. They washed that body all covered with blood and scratched with brush. They also brushed his head hair well. They fixed him up good.

Then the older gopher said to his younger brother, "Pick some asters and let us try to make eyes out of them." The younger brother said, "All right" and went outside, snapped off the best aster blossoms, gathered them up, and carried them down into the earth lodge. Some of these flowers they prepared well and set into the eyesockets. They looked at their work and it seemed good. It was good. When they were finished, the hawk said, "I see things well. Thank you, Mother's Fathers, for giving me eyes."

His mother's fathers: "You should live here with us. Don't go away!" The hawk: "No, I will leave. I will just wander about. I will wander wherever I wander." When he said this, his mother's fathers said, "All right, it is good. We will give you presents." They gave him arrows, a bow, a duck-bow. The arrows had been placed down into a quiver.

Having picked these up, the hawk set out.

In this manner—wandering, wandering, wandering—he wandered all day long. Then he spied a small house standing. Two red ant women lived there, an older with her younger sister. Those women caught sight of that man. "Ey, a fine man is coming." The older sister: "He will be my man." The younger: "No, he is mine. You are old; I am the one who will marry him." "Come! Come here!" she said to the hawk. Then she had him come into the house.

The older sister: "I am the one who will marry him. I am the one he will lie down with." When she said this, the younger sister said, "No, I will have him lie with me. You are an old woman; I am the one who will marry him." The older sister: "No, we will have him lie in the middle. We will both marry him."

Having said that, night came, and the three lay down together. When they did this, these women didn't let the man sleep. All night long they were biting him. That's why the man, early next morning, when dawn was just brightening in the east, left. Having left, he wandered around.

All day long he walked. Then he spied a small house, a small house standing.

Two field mouse women lived there, an older with her younger sister. At twilight, this younger sister: "Older Sister, a man is coming. A fine man is coming." Then, having said, "Ey," they went out—both of the women went out.

Then, to the hawk, "Come! Come here! Now, where do you come from? Come on into the house!" They had him sit down in the house. Having done that, the older sister said, "I will marry him." Thereupon the younger sister: "But I saw him first. I am the one who should marry him. You are just an old woman." "No, I am the one who should marry him. You are way too immature."

It became night. [The older sister said], "No, we will lie down together in one place and we will have him lie in the middle." Having said this, they lay down and had that man lie in the middle. Because of this, the man was dying for sleep. Next, those women ate his head hair, chewed up his eyebrows, bit out his eyelashes, chewed up all his face hair, and nibbled off all the hair on his body.

In the morning the man awoke. That erstwhile head of hair was gone when he awoke; he arose entirely smooth. Even his duckbow had been eaten up. The quiver had been chewed up as well. Those women were gone; he arose alone. He tried feeling on himself with his hand for his missing hair, but there was nothing there; it was perfectly smooth. Then he went outside and set out.

Having done so, he discovered a pond lying still. Then he said, "You will cause my head hair to grow." And, "World lying around here, have pity on me and cause my head hair to grow! Four times I will submerge in the water."

Now, after having said that, he went down to the pond and into the water. Then he dove under. When he reached the limit of his breath, he lifted his head up out. There was nothing there when he lifted his head; he lifted a smooth head. Again he dove under; again he lifted his head up out. With nothing there, smooth, he lifted his head up. Again he dove under. When he reached the limit of his breath, he lifted his head up out.

Now that body hair had sprouted, and the head hair had sprouted as well. Again he dove under. For a long time he kept his head in the water. When he reached the limit of his breath, he lifted his head up out. Facial hair had grown. Eyebrows had grown. That head hair had become longer. All over the fine body hair was growing out. That wooden bow had become new. That quiver had become new. Everything was good.

Now he set out. He was just walking along. Looking here and there he wandered around. Then he spied a house, a small house standing.

One old woman was living there. Whoever visited there, she would kill. Of the people who visited that old woman, not even one ever left alive. Of the people who visited her, that blind old woman killed every single one. The old woman was blind.

The hawk arrived there.

"Sit down here! Sit down beside me, Grandson! Who have you been listening to that you come here to visit me, your mother's mother?" The hawk sat down near there. She picked up her rock walking stick and struck at the hawk with it. The hawk dodged, causing her to strike bare ground. The old woman missed.

When she did this, the hawk shot that old woman with one of his arrows. He killed her off, put her to death. After he had done this—put an end to that old woman, now dead in the house—he went outside. He put a torch to the house, burned it up. The old woman was burned up as well.

When he had done this, the hawk set out again. He just set out wandering around, set out looking at things here and there.

Now clouds formed and thunder sounded. It thundered very loud. The thunder man kept on failing to strike the hawk. While the thunder man was missing him, the hawk spied, high on a tree, an open woodpecker hole. When he did so, the hawk crawled away and into the hole. Then, the thunder man hovered around where the hole was. While he was doing so, the hawk shot the thunder in the soft spot above the front of the collarbone. When he shot, the thunder thudded onto the ground with the sound "Chol."

When this happened, the hawk crawled up and out from the hole. He looked at the thunder that he himself had shot. They say that the thunder wore all kinds of blankets: rain blanket, fog-rain blanket, hail blanket, snow blanket, wind blanket, fog blanket. In these, they say, the hawk dressed himself up, having removed them [from the thunder].

Then, next, he set out flying far away to where his own older brother had mutilated him. Having become the thunder, he set out flying.

Then he caused rain to fall where his older brother's people lived. He caused thunder to sound. He caused it to rain a lot. When it had rained a lot, the earth lodge filled with water. When this happened, his older brother knew [the cause].

The older brother: "Younger Brother, Younger Brother, make the rain end, make the rain end! I know it is you, Younger Brother, who make the rain fall." When he said this, he went away; the thunder went away.

That is the end.

18

The Woman Who Loved a Snake

CACHE CREEK POMO
1988

MABEL McKAY, STORYTELLER
GREG SARRIS, COLLECTOR AND NARRATOR

INTRODUCTION BY GREG SARRIS

Mabel McKay was born on January 12, 1907, in Nice, Lake County, California. Her father, Yanta Boone, was a Potter Valley Pomo Indian. Her mother, Daisy Hansen, was a Losel Cache Creek Pomo. Mabel was raised by her maternal grandmother, Sarah Taylor, and always considered herself a Losel Cache Creek Pomo. It was from her grandmother that Mabel learned the Losel Cache Creek language and the rich and extensive history, not just of her tribe, but of many surrounding Pomo and southwestern Wintun tribes.

But this knowledge was not what Mabel would become known for. She became an expert basketweaver, perhaps the finest of her time, weaving brilliantly colored feather baskets and miniatures, some no larger than eraserheads. And she became a medicine woman, what we call locally an Indian doctor. She was a "sucking doctor," the most highly valued of the local Indian doctors, and she would be the last sucking doctor, not just among the Pomo, but in all of California. Every aspect of her life was guided by the dictates of her Dream, her general term for her experience

FIGURE 8. Mabel McKay, October 1, 1971.
Courtesy Herb Puffer.

with and knowledge from the Spirit. These things—her basketweaving
and doctoring—made her famous. Other Indians, anthropologists, and
basket collectors all flocked to her, seeking information about this or that.
But she was uncanny, maddening in her replies.

"What do you do for poison oak?" a student once asked in a large au-
ditorium where Mabel was being interviewed as a Native healer. "Cala-
mine lotion," she answered.

At the time this story was recorded, in 1988, I had known her for more
than thirty years, since I was a child.[1] I was attempting to write her life
story, both because she wanted me to and because I had made her life
story my dissertation project at Stanford. I figured because I am Indian
(Kashaya Pomo/Coast Miwok) and because I knew her so well I would
be able to understand her wishes for her "book," as she called it, in terms
of its content and narrative structure. No such luck. "You just do [the
book] the best way you know how," she said. "What you know from me."

What I knew from her were narratives that circled around and around, connecting with one another in space and time in ways I couldn't make sense of, at least not for a book I might write. And when I countered with questions that might help me order these narratives in a way meaningful for me, I heard the same uncanny responses the student heard about poison oak.

"Mabel, people want to know about things in your life in a way they can understand. You know, how you got to be who you are. There has to be a theme."

"I don't know about no theme," she said.

"A theme is a point that connects all the dots, ties up all the stories," I explained.

"That's funny," she said. "Tying up all the stories. Why somebody want to do that?"

Eventually, I came to see and feel what she meant. The stories cannot be tied up, disconnected from one another, not her story, my story, any story. Stories live and change in contexts, with changing hearers and tellers. Mabel reminded me of this every step of the way. I became a part of the story the moment I heard it. In hearing stories, we begin to interpret, or "make sense," of them, and Mabel always seemed to remind me of that fact. Just as Mabel broadened the student's notion of a Native healer, letting the student understand that as an Indian doctor Mabel was also a contemporary woman, so Mabel continued to open my eyes, reminding me of who I was and what I was thinking as a participant in her storytelling. It was important that I remembered my life, my presence and history, as I attempted to understand Mabel.

As I learned more about Mabel, I learned more about myself. The stories, and the dialogue about the stories, served as a way to expose boundaries that shape and constitute cultural and personal worlds. Thus, I understood how I might write her story and her book. I had to chart not just her "story," but the story of my hearing her story. I had to expose the ever-widening world the story comes from and becomes.

Scholars familiar with my work with Mabel often question the fact that my conversations with her were always in English. Would the situation and outcome of the storytelling event be the same or different if she spoke Pomo? Of course, I don't know for certain, because I only know a few words and phrases of her language and could never converse with her at length in that language. But I suspect not. What Mabel invoked and inspired was an awe and respect for everything around her, a way of reminding oneself that the story, like everything in the world, was always more than what you thought, and perhaps more than you could ever imagine. More than the interesting facts of her life as a basketweaver and medicine woman, Mabel wanted to teach me that. English seemed to work just fine.

Others have asked if Mabel's talk—her narratives, conversations, and responses to questions—are typical of older, say traditional, Pomo-speakers. It seems in many ways Mabel was unique as a speaker, but I am not certain. I have known other Pomo storytellers who remind listeners of the context in which they are hearing stories. I have also known Pomo storytellers to implicate their listeners in what they are saying. None of the speakers I have known, however, was as consistent in these matters as Mabel. But I have not done a study or comprehensive survey. I have only looked at Mabel's talk in terms of its effect as I have known it, not in terms of the ways it may or may not represent traditional or typical Pomo discourse, whatever that may be. What I wrote, finally, was what I knew from Mabel, the best way I knew how.

NOTE

1. The present selection is taken from chapter 2 of Greg Sarris's book, *Keeping Slug Woman Alive: A Holistic Approach to American Indian Texts*. In that edition of the story, the transcribed text of "The Woman Who Loved a Snake" is broken up, its parts presented out of narrative sequence and embedded in a larger (and fascinating) exegesis of the context and story's meaning. For this collection, what Sarris and I have done is to extract the text of Mabel's narration from its critical matrix and restore it to the chronological order of its original telling. Greg has added a few sentences of transition here and there to compensate for the reordering of the text.

Sarris's experimentation with the framework of contemporary fiction to present this story strikes me as an ingenious way of contextualizing the narrative, of incorporating both expressive and interpretive information—"atmosphere" and explanation—directly into the presentation itself, rather than handling it through the medium of footnotes and introductory essays. As a method for presenting traditional narrative (one that Jaime de Angulo experimented with as well, though from a very different perspective), it holds great promise, at least for those editors and translators who have a "first-person" recollection of the original performance.

Though it is not reflected in the title of the piece, the reader will discover that Mabel McKay actually tells *two* stories here, not just one. The second story, about the first-Contact arrival of Europeans in Kashaya territory, is technically unrelated to the main story about the woman and the snake. What I find fascinating is how the two stories, separate until Mabel called them up on this occasion, seem to adapt *toward* each other in their new surroundings. It's as if all her stories were really one, part of an endless, multivocal braid. Once Mabel has brought the two stories into one light, they remain forever intertwined.—HWL

FURTHER READING

Greg Sarris has written a number of books, including *Keeping Slug Woman Alive: A Holistic Approach to American Indian Texts* (a collection of literary essays) and *Mabel McKay: Weaving the Dream* (a collaborative account of Mabel's remarkable life, the "book" referred to in this selection). He also has a collection of short stories, *Grand Avenue,* and wrote the screenplay for the HBO miniseries of the same name.

THE WOMAN WHO LOVED A SNAKE

One day I took a colleague of mine from Stanford University to the Rumsey Wintun Reservation to meet Mabel McKay. "I want to meet this famous Pomo medicine woman," my friend said. "I've heard her talk and I've seen her baskets in the Smithsonian." My friend, Jenny, had heard me talk about Mabel also. I had been recording Mabel's stories for a book about her life. As always, Mabel proved a gracious host. She served us hot buttered toast and coffee and, for lunch, tuna fish sandwiches with pickles and lettuce. As Jenny and I ate, Mabel told about the woman who loved a snake.

"See, her husband, he would work at night. 'Lock the door,' he'd tell her. 'Don't let nobody in.' Every night he'd go off saying that: 'Lock the door, keep everything locked up.' She would fix his dinner, then his lunch." Mabel chuckled to herself. "By lunch I mean what he takes to work. That's what I call lunch when I was working nighttime in the cannery.

"Anyway, this woman, she says 'OK.' And sometimes, after he would leave, she'd stay up for a while. She'd clean up around, maybe do the dishes, get things ready for the morning, for the breakfast. I don't know.

"Then ONE TIME she hears a knock on the back door. 'What is that?' she's thinking. First she thought maybe it was her husband; maybe he was coming home early; maybe he got sick or something. 'But then why doesn't he just come in?' she was saying. Well, then she thought maybe she was hearing things. She just kept working then.

"But it kept on, this knocking. Then she got scared. See in those days no phones up there. And this was far out, up on some white man's place there, where her husband worked. She could not yell, nothing. Nobody to hear her. Maybe she's thinking this to herself. I don't know.

"'Who is this?' she is saying. Then I don't know what he said. I forgot. Something, anyway. And she opens the door. Just a little bit. He comes in and she stands there looking at him. But she doesn't recognize him.

"Anyway, she fixes some coffee. I don't know. Gives him something to eat. They're talking around there. I don't know what.

"Next day, her husband comes home. 'What's this?' he is saying. He's standing there—by the bedroom—and he's looking down in some vase. Something there. It was on the table. 'What are you talking about?' she says. Then she goes and looks where he's looking. And she sees it, too: a snake, a little black snake all coiled up. 'What is this?' he says to her. Then he takes it out and puts it in the brush. He lets it out there.

"Next day, same thing happens. Then the husband, he gets suspicious of that snake. 'What is this?' he is saying. Then she gets worried; now she knows what the snake is. But she don't say nothing. 'I'm going to kill it,' he says, 'chop it to bits out in the brush.' He's testing her, but she don't say nothing. Then she got REAL worried, seeing him go out with that snake.

"But next day same thing it happens. Maybe she tried talking to that man. I don't know. 'Don't stay around here,' she might said to him. But it's there again, that snake. Now her husband, he shakes her; he knows something is going on. 'What is this?' he's saying. But he had an idea about it anyway. 'You come with me,' he says, 'and watch me kill it.' He starts pulling on her arm, shaking her, but she refuses him. She won't go. She's crying by this time.

"He takes the snake out, same way, coiled around his hand. She just sees him go. Then he comes back. She doesn't know what happened. Maybe this time he DID kill it. She's crying yet. Her husband, he comes in and says nothing. Just goes to bed.

"But he never did chop that snake up. Maybe he did. I don't know. Anyway, it went on like that . . . "

Jenny, a Ph.D. candidate in English, asked what the snake symbolized. Mabel didn't seem to understand the question. She looked at me, then turned to Jenny. "Well, it was a problem, I don't know."

"Why didn't he, I mean the husband, just kill the snake?" Jenny asked.

With an incredulous look on her face, Mabel focused on Jenny. "Well, how could he?" she asked. "This is white man days. There's laws against killing people. That man, he would go to jail, or maybe get the electric chair, if he done that."

Mabel mentioned that she knew the woman, that she often visited her when she lived in the same area north of Clear Lake. "Then one night I seen that man. He was handsome, too," she chuckled. "It was late. Lakeport grocery was closing and I seen him come out with groceries. He didn't take the road. He went the creek way, north. Then, I say to myself, 'I bet I know where he's going.'"

"Maybe he just carried the snake with him and left it in the vase each morning before he left," Jenny offered. "Like a sign."

Mabel laughed out loud. "Like a sign. That's cute. Why he want to do that?" She lit a cigarette. "See, I knew he was odd. He's moving in cold, late at night. Snakes don't do that."

"Well, was it man or snake? I mean when you were looking at it?" Jenny was desperate now.

"You got funny ideas," Mabel answered. "Aren't I sitting here?" She tapped her cigarette in the aluminum ashtray on the table. "You do crazy things like Greg. And he's Indian! He gets ideas where he wants to know this or that so he can write it all up for the people. Well, it ain't like that what I am saying."

About a month later, after my trip with Jenny, Mabel and I took a ride and parked along a road on the south side of Clear Lake, where we had a view of the lake and of Elem Rancheria, the old village site and present-day reservation of the Elem tribe of Pomo Indians. Mabel had been talking about her maternal grandmother, Sarah Taylor, and about how the Elem people initiated her into their dances and cult activities after Sarah's people, the Cache Creek Pomo, had been removed from their land and ceremonial grounds by the non-Indian invaders.

"'You will find a way, a way to go on even after this white people run over the earth like rabbits. They are going to be everywhere,' he was saying. That's Old Man, I forgot his name. He had only Indian name, Taylor's father, Grandma's grandfather. He's the one saying these things."

Mabel opened her purse, pulled out a cigarette. She lit her cigarette and exhaled a cloud of smoke. Below us, on the narrow peninsula of Elem, smoke rose from the rusted chimney tins of the small, dilapidated houses. A lone dog barked in the distance.

"Well, it was over here, below them hills," Mabel said, gesturing south over her shoulder with her chin. "This things, they come over the hill in a trail, long trail. So much that dust is flying up, like smoke wherever they go. And first to see them this people down there, where you are looking. 'What is this?' the people saying. Things with two heads and four legs, bushy tail, standing here on this hill somewhere, looking down at Elem people.

"Lots of people scared, run off, some far as our place, Cache Creek. They tell what they seen then. All Indians, Indians all over, talking about it then. 'What is it?' they is asking. Nobody knows. People is talking about it all over the place. Lot's scared. I don't know. People say different things.

"Some people somewhere seen them things come apart, like part man, then go back together. Then I guess maybe they knew it was people— white people. I don't know," Mabel said and chuckled. "They Indians dance and pray. I don't know. Then they was saying these things [was] mean, killing Indians and taking Indians."

Mabel drew on her cigarette and leisurely exhaled. "But he seen it in his Dream, Old Man. He said what was coming one day, how this would be."

"So they knew what it was coming down this hill," I ventured.

"Hmm," Mabel said, gazing across the lake. "They knew what he meant by 'white man.'"

"So why did they run? Why all the fuss?"

Mabel rubbed out her cigarette and looked at me as if she had not understood what I said. "If they knew from Old Man's prophecy that white people were coming, why didn't they know what was coming down the hill? Why all the fuss?"

Mabel started chuckling, then exploded with loud, uncontrollable laughter. She caught her breath finally and asked, "How can that be? You ever know white people with four legs and two heads? Maybe you do. You're raised around them—your mother's people, I don't know," she said, chuckling again.

She lit another cigarette, then straightened in her seat. "Sometimes takes time for Dream to show itself. Got to be tested. Now we know what he told about, Old Man. He was told . . . He said lots of things: trails, big trails covering the earth, even going into the sky. Man going to be on moon he was saying."

"But how did HE know that?"

"But sometimes Dream forgets, too. Like them snakes. Old Man come in MY dream, give me rattlesnake song. 'You going to work with this snakes; they help you,' he is saying. Then, after that, I seen them. All over my house I seen them: porch, closet, in my bathtub when it's hot, all over. Then I say to him, to that spirit, 'This is modern times, better take that song out of me . . . I don't want nothing to happen. People around here might call animal control place.'

"You know, peoples around here they don't always understand things like that."

After Mabel told the story about the people of Elem seeing non-Indian invaders coming "over the hill in a trail," we headed east, back to the Rumsey Reservation. On the way home, Mabel again told the story of "The Woman Who Loved a Snake."

"It was across there. Up in them hills where she lived. That time Charlie* [was] running stock up there. By stock I mean the cattle. Charlie always wanted to have the stock. That woman lived there. Sometimes she would come down the road the other side there and talk to me. Anyway, how it happened, she was alone at night. Her husband used to go off working, where it was I don't know. I forgot. How it happened, she hears this knocking one night, at her door . . . "

I was quieter now, listening.

"Well, you see, I know about them snakes," she said as she finished the story. "They can teach about a lot of things."

Mabel pulled her purse to her lap and began rummaging for her cig-

* Charles McKay, Mabel's husband.

arettes. I looked to the cold, damp winter hills. Too cold for snakes, I thought to myself.

"Hmm," she said. "Maybe you'll get some idea about the snakes." I looked at her and she was laughing, holding an unlit cigarette between her fingers. "I know you. You'll . . . you're school way. You'll think about it, then write something."

She was right.

19

The Dead People's Home

LAKE MIWOK
1980

JAMES KNIGHT, NARRATOR
CATHERINE CALLAGHAN, COLLECTOR AND TRANSLATOR

INTRODUCTION BY CATHERINE CALLAGHAN

This is a Lake Miwok story, told to me in the summer of 1980 by James (Jimmy) Knight, at Middletown Rancheria in Middletown, California. Lake Miwok was formerly spoken in a triangular area south of Clear Lake, about eighty miles north of San Francisco. This language is closely related to Coast Miwok, once the language of the Marin Peninsula, and more distantly related to the Eastern Miwok languages, once spoken on the western slopes of the Sierra Nevada mountains from the Fresno River north to the Cosumnes River, as well as on the floor of the Great Valley between Ione and Mount Diablo.

Aboriginally, Lake Miwok culture resembled that of its Pomo and Wappo neighbors. Hunting, gathering, and trading expeditions took Lake Miwok Indians from the top of the Coast Range to Bodega Bay. Settlements were usually located along stream courses in fertile valleys. Acorns, harvested from a variety of oak trees, comprised the starch staple, and important game animals included deer, elk, rabbits, and squirrels, as well as several species of birds whose feathers were sometimes woven into elaborate basket designs.

Contact with the whites during the nineteenth century was traumatic. Ranchers to the south often kidnapped Lake Miwok Indians for use in work forces, and there were at least two massacres of Clear Lake Indians, one in 1843 and one in 1850. As a result, the Lake Miwok population, which might never have numbered more than five hundred, dwindled to forty-one by the turn of the century, and there are now probably fewer than half a dozen that remember the language, although many more can claim Lake Miwok ancestry.

Jimmy Knight was in his middle years when I first started working with him in the summer of 1956. I had met him through Mrs. Alma Grace, my first consultant, who was living in San Francisco. He and his brother, John Knight, conferred with me in Mrs. Grace's cabin on the Middletown Rancheria. Jimmy told the stories, which his brother later translated sentence by sentence into English. After John Knight's death in 1960, I worked with Jimmy alone, usually at his home.

This story is a version of the Orpheus Myth, common worldwide but surprisingly absent from Judeo-Christian or Islamic traditions. Briefly, the hero (or sometimes, the heroine) grieves over the loss of a loved one and finds a magical route to the Land of the Dead, but after a brief encounter with the dead relative, is forced to leave because he or she is still living.

I elicited an earlier version of this same story from Jimmy during the 1950s, in which the main character is a heroic figure from Lake Miwok history. Otherwise, the principal elements are the same. A brother grieves over the death of his sister, watches at her grave until she rises on the fourth night, and follows her to the top of Mount St. Helena, where her dead relatives greet her and accompany her to the Land of the Dead in the middle of the lake (or ocean). Her brother slips past the chief into the dead people's sweat house, but is forced to go back, following a brief visit. He returns to Cottonwood Place after stopping again on Mount St. Helena, becoming a powerful person who makes a hole through a tree. Although many elements are different, this account may be related to an earlier text that Lucy Freeland elicited from Maggie Johnson (Jimmy's aunt) in 1922, featuring a man who searches for a dead brother.

In the present version, Mr. Knight personalizes the account by casting his father and aunt as the principal characters. Ironically, Maggie Johnson is the dead sister. This version also includes extensive philosophizing, a feature that characterizes the texts Jimmy Knight gave toward the end of his life.

The Orpheus Myth reinforces belief in an afterlife where one will encounter dead relatives, as well as the hope of seeing them even in this life. I once elicited a Northern Sierra Miwok version in which a girl visits her dead mother. My consultant had heard this story after the death of her beloved grandmother, who had raised her from infancy. The heroine must walk across a swinging bridge on her way to the Land of the Dead, an element in a Yokuts Orpheus Myth (see #20a, this volume, for another example) in which the hero is following the ghost of his dead wife. This resemblance suggests a Yokuts origin for the Northern Sierra Miwok account. It is also evident that the Northern Sierra Miwok storyteller had altered its content to fit my consultant's needs—soothing the grief of a young girl whose grandmother has just died.

Versions of the Orpheus Myth were common throughout South-Central California. They were always localized to the storytellers' own tribes, indicating that they had at some previous time made conscious or unconscious alterations to render the accounts more relevant. Such traditions also facilitated the spread of the Ghost Dance during the 1870s, with the belief that dancing and good conduct would bring about the return of dead relatives in the immediate future.

James Knight was a great storyteller, and he brought verve to his art, so that it was a joy to work with him. His rare sense of irony colored the dialogue of his tales, rendering other versions flat by comparison. Especially in his later years, he believed that his mission was to transmit his cultural tradition to Lake Miwok children, and he was distressed over their apparent lack of interest.

It is impossible to reproduce his oral performance on the printed page, and I now regret that I made only tape recordings and no videos. Unfortunately, he is no longer with us (Jimmy died in 1988), and the opportunity is lost.

Translation of an oral account from a non-Western culture into readable English always presents a challenge. I have not included every instance of Lake Miwok words such as *'ekaal* 'then', *'aye* 'however', and *weno* 'they say', which often function as quotation marks or indicators of new sentences, but I have tried to remain as faithful as possible to the original, sometimes at the expense of English style.

In the native-language passage that follows, I present the opening sentences of the story just as Jimmy spoke them to me in Lake Miwok. Underneath the transcription runs a word-for-word gloss of the text. Underneath that comes a more literal translation of the sentence than is found in the translation proper.

Ném	'uṭél-yomi-n		húuni	ka-líilaw	'ena.
This.is	Magician-Home-of		story	I-tell	will.

This is the Magicians' [Dead People's] Home story I'm going to tell.

Kaníi	'aye	ka-líilaw	miṭi	kaníi	'aye,
I	however	I-tell	and	I	however

When I tell it, however,

ka-áppi,	ka-'enéene,	ka-'únu,	ka-páapa,
my-father,	my-aunt,	my-mother,	my-grandfather,

my father, my aunt, my mother, my grandfather,

ka-wée'ama-kon	ṣe	má-t	ka-hóoye.
my-relative-PLURAL	also	it-into	I-put

my relatives, too—I put them [all] in.

FURTHER READING

One text can only hint at the rich oral tradition Lake Miwok–speakers once enjoyed. Interested readers will find more Lake Miwok traditional stories in English translation in C. Hart Merriam's *The Dawn of the World*. Lucy Freeland's "Western Miwok Texts with Linguistic Sketch" provides two Lake Miwok texts in the original, accompanied by word-for-word running glosses and a free translation; these texts are "The Story of the Two Shamans" and "The Stealing of Hawk's Wife." Another of James Knight's texts, "Coyote the Impostor," appears in Victor Golla and Shirley Silver's *Northern California Texts,* and yet another, "Fire, Flood, and Creation," in William Bright's *Coyote Stories,* both of which include word-for-word translations of the Lake Miwok along with freer renditions. Readers interested in the Central California culture area might consult the appropriate chapters of Malcolm Margolin's *The Way We Lived*.

THE DEAD PEOPLE'S HOME

The story I'm going to tell is about the Dead People's Home. When I tell it, I put in my father, my aunt, my mother, my grandfather, and also my relatives. This way it's easy to tell the story. If I put in someone else, I can't tell it well. That's why I'm telling the truth. It'll come out nicely in the end.

I'm trying this; that's why I'm speaking Lake Miwok. This is Lake Miwok I'm speaking. The white people will translate this and understand it, the words that I'm saying.

They claim that dead people used to rise from the grave in three or four days. They rise up from there and land on the top of Mount St. Helena. That's what they said, the old people who knew. That's how they told it.

Then my aunt died. My father was distressed. "All right, I want to see my sister. That's why I'm going to the grave, and I'm going to sit there. And I'm going to wait for her," he said. Then he sat there about four days or five days, that many days.

He sat there day and night. He said he was sitting there four or five days, and something like wind came. Lots of wind. Then he already knew. My father was a dreamer. My aunt was a dreamer, too. So he just sat there. He didn't cry, he just listened.

In the meantime, something white appeared over his sister's grave. This was a ghost. "Sister! Sister!" he said. "Brother, what are you doing here?" said his sister. (His sister's name was Maggie Johnson; her husband's name was Johnson. So her name was Johnson.) "All right," she said. "You can't go with me, Brother. I'm going to the Chief's Home now, the Dead People's Home. I can't put you there," she said.

He tells it, my father, whose name was Henry, Henry Knight. Both whites and Indians knew he was a doctor, you see. He went doctoring all over. He went to Upper Lake—wherever someone was feeling bad or sick, he went there and doctored them. That's why they knew him all over. He made a lot of life on this earth.

Henry Knight grieved for his sister and went with his sister to the mountain top. From right there, they flew to the middle of the ocean, and they came down right there to the middle, right to the middle of the Pacific Ocean. At that place, there was a great man, a chief, standing inside the sweat house.

"All right, there's one person here that shouldn't have come. And that one will have to go back from here," he said, that's what he told them. Then his sister, Maggie Johnson, spoke to her brother Henry Knight, "All right, that's you. You can't go to the Dead People's Home. So you have to go back from here. You can't go around there. I'm going to leave. So I'm not going to see you again."

This is how they told the story many years ago.

Then he came back home from there, Henry did, from the middle of the ocean. He came out of that sweat house—a beautiful one, he said— the sweat house that was over there. He left his sister there. He came back to Cottonwood Place. He came to the top of the mountain and realized where he had come. He flew from there and hit a tree at Cottonwood Place; he claimed he hit a big tree right in the middle and made a hole there. That tree used to be standing there. But now they've pulled it out and destroyed it.

The chiefs and dreamers and doctors knew him, my father, Henry

Knight. "Where have you been?" they asked. "I've been to the Dead People's Home . . . I came from the Magician's Place, but they wouldn't have me because I'm not dead. They sent me back from the middle of the ocean." That's what he told them.

On that occasion, they danced for four days. For four days they gave a big feast. They celebrated four days. Everything used to go on for four days.

And that's how he became a great man. From then on, he became a doctor, because something was watching over him. That's why his sister was great, too, and helped him. She helped him through dreams. She guarded him with songs. They protected each other by talking. They were both great.

My mother was a doctor, too. My grandfather also was a dreamer. So everything they did came out wonderful, beautiful. They ran the land. They worked for the earth. They cured people. They even made dead people well. They did everything great. Something great granted them this power.

As for me, I claim that God has given them this, because they knew. Because they thought good things. Because they made good rules. Because they had many relatives. Because they did everything the nice way. That's why they were granted many gifts.

Because that's how it was, that's how they taught me. Since they explained it to me that way, here's what I'm telling you now. Now I'm putting what they told me a long time ago onto the tape. So [the tape] is telling you this. My friends and relatives can listen and say, "Yes, this is true." As for me, I'm happy about what I'm saying and what they know about the grave.

So what I'm saying is this. Everything used to happen four times. Look, now they die on this earth. From there they drop into the water. From there, they'll go to heaven. (Not that place, they couldn't put my father in because he hadn't died.) Pretty; up there everything is pretty. Look, this is what they teach us. So we should believe it. We should learn it, become aware of it. I'm sitting here, talking this way now. Here's the way I teach my children, because I feel sorry for them.

As for me, I'm happy to be talking like this today, just like those lying in the grave. My grandfather, my aunt, my relatives are lying in Already-My-Home, resting there. Someday I'm going to see them. That's what I feel. That's what I feel all the time. They are happy for me. And me, I keep dreaming about them.

Sometimes they come to help me. "We've come to help you," that's what they say; I see them night and day. They keep asking me questions, just like a string coming out. They come at me just like a dreamer. And me, I'm glad that something is watching over me. Look how many times I've gotten sick, how many times I could have died, but I haven't gone to the grave yet. I haven't yet gone to Already-My-Home.

Somehow they sympathize with me because of the way I talk and what I'm going to teach the little ones. The plan is still there. That's the way I'm going to work. That's why something great feels sorry for me from someplace.

As for me, I attribute this to God. And so, I'm grateful for this. I always get up in the morning and sleep in the evening. Oh, I'm grateful: make me dream pleasantly and wake up fine in the morning. What causes me pain—my arm, my eyes—press and fix everything.

"I wish." That's what I say for my little ones, too. "All right, watch over them wherever they are playing—they don't understand. They're this way because they don't know." I talk like this all the time, morning and evening.

And me, I'm grateful for what He has put in my head, my feelings, and my blood.

As for me, here's the way I'm going to be from now on. Look: my relatives are all there, my older and younger brothers, my father, my uncle, my grandmother, my aunt, my mother. When I get there, they'll welcome me, that's what I feel now. That's why I'm just sitting here not scared of anything.

I'm happy about what I'm going to do. I just say, "Thank you." I'm grateful and I say, "Thank you." I laugh because I'm happy. When I'm happy, I talk. When I'm happy, I tell things. I'm grateful for whatever they show me. When I'm happy, I'm grateful for everything: trees, birds, water, food.

Before I eat anything, before they help me, I talk to them. As for me, here's the way I'm going to travel: when I go somewhere, I talk to everything— all the cars, horses, carts.

"All right," I say. I've come this far and told this much. Now when I'm telling this, I'm enjoying myself. This far. All right, that's as far as I'm telling now.

My relatives are in the graveyard over there, filling it up. So I'm glad they're lying there peacefully. Some day when I see them, I'll teach them. I'll tell them how wonderfully I live, how He takes care of me here on earth. This is the reason I know. This is the reason I'm teaching the little ones. That's why I've been here a long time.

All right, I'm happy. That's all now.

SOUTH-CENTRAL CALIFORNIA

Kingfisher, kingfisher,
      cover me with your power,
Sho ho, sho ho, na na, het na na, het,
      I am circling around.

Wikchamni song
Anna Gayton, "Yokuts
and Western Mono: Ethnography"

But Čiq'neq'š knew that the devil [*lewelew*] wanted to deceive him, and he began to sing:

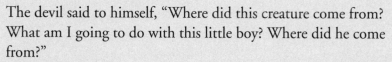

> *Now I am beginning,*
> *Beginning to make my defense.*
> *I have just put my plant in this soil.*
> *I don't know the end.*
> *I barely put my foot on land.*
> *I come from a great distance, from the clouds.*
> *I am the son of all the dead and*
> *That is why I'm hungry.*

The devil said to himself, "Where did this creature come from? What am I going to do with this little boy? Where did he come from?"

And the devil said to Čiq'neq'š: "Do you know that you are under this sun, and that you are seen by means of its light?"

And the boy started thinking, "This fellow is trying to get me all mixed up, but I'm going to make him cry."

So he said to the devil, "Do you know that we all see by the light in which we are?"

Excerpt from "The Čiq'neq'š Myth"
Ventureño Chumash, Fernando Librado
Thomas Blackburn, *December's Child*

20

Two Stories from the Central Valley

"Visit to the Land of the Dead"
and "Condor Steals Falcon's Wife"

YOKUTS

1931, 1930

JOHNNY JONES AND ROSS ELLIS, NARRATORS

STANLEY NEWMAN, COLLECTOR AND TRANSLATOR

INTRODUCTION BY GEOFFREY GAMBLE

The Yokuts people once inhabited the south-central portion of California from roughly the crest of the Tehachapi Range in the south to Stockton in the north and from the Coastal mountains in the west to the western slopes of the Sierra Nevada range in the east. This territory ranged about 350 miles from north to south and about 200 miles east to west and presented great variation in where the Yokuts people lived, from marsh lands and lakes such as Tulare and Kern Lakes to the lush banks of river canyons of the Tule, Kaweah, Kings and San Joaquin Rivers. The Yokuts people were divided into about forty small tribal groups with each tribe recognizable by its name and by its particular dialect. By and large these tribes were friendly to one another, and their dialects were similar enough that speakers from opposite ends of the territory could understand each other. Of the languages and dialects once spoken, no more than a few are spoken today, and many of those speakers live at the Yule Reservation near Visalia, California.

For most Yokuts people, disturbance by white soldiers and settlers did not come until the early 1860s. Such relatively late contact allowed the Yokuts culture and language to remain relatively intact for a much longer period of time than is seen among the coastal groups of California or in many other parts of North America. This means that the tellers of the two Yokuts stories presented here had learned them from speakers who had little or no contact with outsiders, thus considerably enhancing the fidelity of the material.[1]

Our knowledge of the Yokuts languages and dialects primarily comes from the work of Alfred L. Kroeber (1907, 1925), John P. Harrington (1914–1925), Stanley Newman (1944), and Geoffrey Gamble (1978). The Yokuts language group is included within the California Penutian stock, where it is thought to be most closely related to Costanoan and Miwokan and more distantly related to the Maiduan and Wintun families. Specific details of genetic affiliation and subgrouping are still being worked out. Yokuts is a relatively close-knit language family, and internal variation is most clearly seen among the languages and dialects of the southern-most speakers. The two stories here, "Visit to the Land of the Dead" and "Condor Steals Falcon's Wife," come from the Chawchila and Yowlumni dialects, which are fairly closely related linguistically.

The Chawchila people lived in the northern third of Yokuts territory, inhabiting both the Sierra foothills as well as the valley locations along the Fresno River. A large Chawchila village was situated near the present town of Friant where the Fresno River has now been dammed to form Millerton Lake. As with other Yokuts people, storytelling was an evening and winter activity. Good storytellers were clearly recognized by their ability to exploit the syntactic and semantic richness of the Yokuts language and to occasionally provide creative twists on the classic stories known to everyone.

"Visit to the Land of the Dead" is one of the best-known and frequently told stories among the Yokuts people and was also well-known by other tribes in the region. This version was collected by Stanley Newman in the summer of 1931 from Johnny Jones, who lived at Friant, California. A translation of the story was first published by Anna Gayton and Stanley Newman in 1940, but Newman had completed a rough translation, which forms part of his loose note sheets in the Newman collection, much earlier.

Jones's Chawchila version of the tale not only maintains all the features of this classic story, but also provides a richness that clearly indicates a skilled and talented storyteller. The main features of the story include a young couple, recently and happily married, who are punching at each other in playfulness. As the young woman cleans her ear with a small stick, her husband hits her arm and the stick pierces her ear, killing her. The distraught young man then follows his wife to the Land of the Dead, where he is challenged by the "Captain" of the dead people to identify his wife. He does so and is allowed to take his wife back to the land of the living under the condition that once they return they do not have sexual intercourse until after ten days have passed. Naturally, they do not wait the full ten days, and the young man dies. Jones's version includes the young man's confrontation with his mother about the death of his wife, a graveside vigil, a feast in the Land of the Dead, and a complex dialogue with the leader of the dead people.

The second myth, "Condor Steals Falcon's Wife," was told to Newman in the summer of 1930. Ross Ellis is the most likely storyteller, because so much of Newman's Yowlumni text material came from Ellis. This particular telling of the story, which was known not only among the Yokuts people but also by other tribes throughout the region, is unusually rich in detail and complexity. The story takes place in mythic times, when people and animal were one and the same. There is a gathering of the people to share food. While Falcon is away, Condor steals his wife. Falcon goes to the leader, Eagle, and asks for help in finding his wife. Eagle sends out a series of people to look for her (Bottlefly is the one who finally finds her), and eventually, after great daring and suspense, Falcon succeeds in rescuing his wife from the malevolent Condor.

Though the California condor today conjures up a precarious, split image of magnificence and vulnerability for those following its struggle against extinction, the Yokuts tradition as reflected in this telling appears to have focused more on the bird's enormous strength and tenacity. Here, Condor is little more than a monster, a brute who willfully kidnaps his kinsman's spouse and forces her to be his wife, keeping her in a house hidden so high among the crags that it takes magic for Falcon to reach it. Condor is so tough he can't be killed, not even cremated: though his body finally burns up, his head slips away during the night "by itself"

FIGURE 9. Ross Ellis with his son.
Courtesy of the Bancroft Library,
University of California, Berkeley.

and resumes its pursuit. Falcon, fleeing with his rescued wife, repeatedly smashes the head with a rock, but the head just keeps on coming. Taken as a latter-day ecological prophecy, this story lays down powerful odds for the condor's survival. But if the ongoing efforts at reintroduction ultimately fail, the story also leaves us a final monument: the "Echo Rock" where Condor's head finally turned to stone.

NOTE

1. The text of Newman's translations has been slightly altered in the following ways. First, as it is clearly a prominent feature of Valley Yokuts narrative style for storytellers to use what we call the "historic present" tense to highlight key moments and passages in the narrative, these sentences have been cast in italics, as a visual correlate of this special rhetorical heightening effect. Second, to conform more closely with the punctuational style of "Visit to the Land of the Dead," and also to improve readability, many cases of sentence-initial *And* in "Condor Steals Falcon's Wife" have been adjoined to the preceding sentence, either with a comma or a semicolon. For instance, in the second paragraph of that story, the sequence "And Coyote went to him. And he questioned him." becomes "And Coyote went to him, and he questioned him." Third, bracketed interpolations (some Newman's, some the editor's) have been allowed to supplant the pronominal form they clarify. For example, the sentence "But he [Condor] is already losing strength" becomes "But [Condor] is already losing strength." (This tactic has been applied to the first story as well.) Readers interested in checking Newman's original presentation of "Visit to the Land of the Dead" and "Condor Steals Falcon's Wife" may consult the versions in Gamble (1994) and Gayton and Newman (1940), respectively.—HWL

FURTHER READING

See William J. Wallace's "Southern Valley Yokuts" and "Northern Valley Yokuts" for a general overview of Valley Yokuts culture; also Anna Gayton's "Yokuts and Western Mono: Ethnography." For linguistic information, see Stanley Newman's *Yokuts Language of California,* Geoffrey Gamble's *Wikchamni Grammar,* and Alfred L. Kroeber's *Yokuts Dialect Survey.* Several important text collections have been produced: Gamble's *Yokuts Texts,* from which the story "Visit to the Land of the Dead" was taken; Gayton and Newman's "Yokuts and Western Mono Myths," from which the story "Condor Steals Falcon's Wife" was taken; Howard Berman's "Two Chukchansi Coyote Stories"; and Gamble's "How People Got Their Hands." Kroeber's "Indian Myths of South Central California" includes numerous Yokuts myths in English. In a rare stylistic study prior to 1960, Newman considers aspects of Yokuts poetics in "Yokuts Narrative Style." Stanley Newman's notes and field notebooks are housed at the Maxwell Museum of Anthropology, University of New Mexico. Before Newman, J. P. Harrington collected extensive manuscript materials on Yokuts.

VISIT TO THE LAND OF THE DEAD

CHAWCHILA YOKUTS

JOHNNY JONES

They were married six days. And they loved each other; they played with each other and punched each other in fun. And the woman got a little stick, and she twisted it around in her ear. And while she was cleaning her ear, her husband hit her with his hand; and the stick stuck there in her ear, and she died. At his wife's death, he went to tell his mother. "Mama," he said, "my wife died." And his mother said, "How did she die?" "I struck her while she was cleaning her ear." And his mother scolded him.

They mourned all night. And after mourning for two nights, they buried her. And, having buried her, the old ones went home to their houses. And they returned; and the man stayed all night at the grave, and he was taken home. And he returned to the grave and slept there on the foot of the grave. And his sister got him and took him home. And again he returned to that grave in the evening.

And he heard the dead one getting up shortly after sunset. *And she jumps up.* "Eeee," she says, jumping. And the husband saw her jumping and getting up. "I guess my wife is getting better," he says. *And his wife is standing up, shaking the dirt from her; and she goes north.*

And her husband follows. He is snatching at her in vain. And her husband puts his arms around her; he does not grasp her. When he snatched her, she melted away. He kept doing this while going along. And going far ahead, she says to her husband, "Why are you following me?" And her husband did not speak at his wife's words.

And the two of them keep going north. Already they have gone far. When daylight came, she disappeared. And at his dead wife's disappearance, he went to sleep. And toward dusk, he arose. And the dead one went north. He followed her; her husband went along behind her. He continued this while they were going. And she says to him, "Why do you keep following me? Return!" *Her husband does not hear what she is saying. And the two of them keep walking during the night.* And at daybreak he went to sleep where his wife disappeared. *And again evening comes. And the dead one gets up and walks. And they continue, her husband following her.* "Return!" she says to her husband.

And when they arrive at the bridge, [she says], "Don't get frightened. Crow will yell at us; Quail will fly; they will scare us. Don't be frightened at Quail's flying. Perhaps you will fall in the water and become a sturgeon." And her husband replies, "Yes. I don't think I shall fall in." And the woman went ahead; she crossed the bridge and arrived on the other side. And while she was looking back at her husband, he took a step on the bridge. And he shook the bridge, and he crossed over and reached his wife on the other side. And while they were going along, she advised her husband, "Don't follow me! You had better stay back there! Don't go in where the dancers are! You must stay back!" she says to the husband.

And the two of them arrived there where the dead people are. *He follows his wife in vain. He is stopped.* "That is a live man. Stop!" said the Captain to him. *He grasps [the man] with his hand.* And being spoken to, he stopped there; he stared at his wife. And when his wife reached the place where the dead people were dancing, she went in. And he stared at his wife.

And he is troubled there on his heart. "I am hungry," he says there on his heart. And the dead Captain heard his worrying there on his heart. And the Captain says to him, "Why are you troubled? You are hungry; you say you are troubled. Now I shall give you some food." And he gave him acorn mush full of acorn-heads. *And he is troubled there on his heart.* "I don't think I'll get full on this. There is too little." The Captain says to him, "Don't worry about that. You will get full soon." *And he drinks the acorn mush.* And while he was drinking it, it emptied; and again it filled up. *He keeps worrying all the time; doing this, he gets full.* "Here! I am already full doing this. Take your food away!" he says to [the Captain].

And he saw his wife dancing; he stared at his wife. And it became morning; and the dead dancers disappeared. *And her husband sits all day where he had been standing.* All the dead ones disappeared.

At sunset the messengers wake up. They call out; they are busy among themselves; they build a fire; they run around looking for wood. Some of them have already made a fire. Some [of the dead] have already emerged from the fire; they have already sat down, ready for their dance. And when the Captain saw it, he arose next to the place where the live man was. And the dead people emerged. And the messengers made a fire for the dead Captain. And the dead people danced.

And the Captain said to him, "Will you recognize your wife?" "Yes, I think I shall recognize my wife," he said to him. "If you will recognize your wife, then you will bring her [out]."

And there were five dead women, similar to one another. And they looked like recently dead women, but they had been dead a long time. The five dead women were alike beautiful. And the recently dead woman put on her dress. And the Captain said to him, "Recognize your wife!" "Yes, I shall recognize my wife," [said the husband].

At his saying this, the six women came out. *They are very similar!* In the middle, that recently dead woman was placed. And her husband saw her. And having come out, they danced around him. "Can you recognize your wife?" "Yes," he said. "Let us see. Go get your wife and bring her." And the one who was told went straight to his wife; he grasped her on the arm. "Come!" he said to his wife, looking back. "We shall go to the Captain."

And he brought his wife along to the Captain. "Yes," said the Captain. "Sit down!" And she sat by the side of her husband; and the Captain said to them, "You will go home." And they [started to] return. "Wait a little while! Listen to my words!" he said to them. And he advised them, "After arriving at your house, you must not have sexual intercourse for ten days. If you do so before ten days, you [the husband] will return here quickly. You must finish all the days as I am advising. And you will tell your people what you have seen here. You will tell your people, 'I have seen the dead.'"

And after he said that, they went to the road on which they had come; and they crossed the bridge that they had crossed before; and they went to sleep where they had slept before. And they walked all night; and they went to sleep during the day. [They continued this way until] near dusk they reached the place where she had died.

And in the morning he arose and got his people, his father. "I shall tell you what I saw where I went." And his father said, "Yes. Tell what you have seen!" And he related, "I saw many dead ones. They had a good time; they were always dancing; they had a lively time. Our life here is bad. I shall tell you everything that I saw." And his father said, "Yes, my son, tell everything that you saw there." [But] he did not tell [them], "Ten days have been counted for me." He did not relate that he was told, "Don't have sexual intercourse."

And after eight days he wanted to have sexual intercourse; and she would not permit him. [But] when there remained only one day to complete, she permitted him. After having sexual intercourse, he died.

And it became daylight. And his father said, "Tell your older brother to get up!" And being spoken to by her father, [the husband's] younger sister went. "Get up, Older Brother!" He did not wake up. "What's the matter with my older brother? I think he died." And his father came and shook him. "Wake up, my Son!" [But] he did not get up. "My son died," he said.

And they mourned, and his son was buried; he had died. And that is all.

CONDOR STEALS FALCON'S WIFE

YOWLUMNI YOKUTS

ROSS ELLIS

There they were living, above Xɔlmiu (Clover Place) at the foot of this mountain. *Their leaders are thinking about their meeting.* And Eagle said, "Tell Cougar and Big Eagle and his friend, the large Crow, and their crier, Dove, and Coyote and Falcon and Wolf." And Coyote was sent. *Now he is going to assemble the people.* "In seven days we will assemble." *Now they will be told—Wind and Thunder and Dog too.* And Coyote informed them, and Wind said, "Of course I can go anywhere. But tell Thunder. Will he go?" And, "I'm not sure that he can," he added.

And the seven days came, and already all the people were assembling there. And Thunder did not come. *The booming noise he makes is useless; he can't walk.* And Coyote went to him. And he questioned him, and Thunder said, "I can't go anywhere. Tell my friend and he will come." And Wind went to him, and there he arrived. And he said to him, "What's the matter with you! Aren't you able to walk? Haven't I been telling you, I'll see to it that you will go where they want you? Are you ready to leave now?" he says to him. "Stand up now, and you will speak," he says to him. "Ready?" Wind says to him. "Yes," then says Thunder. "Speak now," he says to him. "Will we go now?" And Thunder spoke. Just as soon as he spoke, the two of them walked off.

And they arrived there immediately, and their leader, Eagle, said to him, "Have you arrived already?" he says to him. And [Thunder] said to him, "This gathering of ours is certainly a small one. How is that?" Thunder says. "These are important people. I am thinking about our going west," says Eagle. "All the seeds are now getting ripe again." "Good," they say. "But who will go to look them over?" they say. "Antelope," they say. And Antelope said, "In the morning I will go." And he went, and there he arrived. To his surprise, there were a great many seeds. And he took a great many; he placed them in both his feet. And he arrived after sundown.

And, as before, Coyote assembled the people, and all the people assembled. A large covering was already spread over the ground. *On it he is now going to pour his load.* And he poured it, and they said, "There is certainly a lot." And, "Count these important people," they say to Dove. *Now they are going to divide it.* And each of them took his share, and the unimportant ones took what was left, and all of them were pleased. *Having taken their food, all of them will now prepare it.* And Falcon's friend, Crow, ate a lot of black seeds, and he turned black. "Well," says their leader, "in seven days we will go."

Now they are going to gather food. And the seven days arrived, and some of them asked their leader, "In how many days will we return?" "In three days." And they said, "There is food enough for our children."

And all the people went, and there they arrived; and they got many seeds. And in three days they returned.

And Falcon probably got a great many. And he said to his wife, "I'll take some of this, and I'll come right back." And his wife was working; she was getting more. And the woman heard him coming. *She looks about, but she does not see anything.* And Condor alighted close to her, and after alighting he said to her, "Are you the wife of my younger brother?" he says to her. "Is he your younger brother?" she says to him. "Yes," he says. "His name is Tsopnix." And the woman said to him, "What is your name?" she says. "Condor," he says. "So we will go now," Condor says to her. He says to her, "Take off your necklace." Her necklace was money—small beads and big dark beads and small bone beads. And she said, "No!" but it was useless. "Why should I?" she says to him. "I'm afraid he'll be angry," she says to him. "No," she says. "We will go now," [Condor said]. He took her away by force.

And then Falcon arrived after they had gone, and he couldn't find his wife. And in vain he looked for their footprints. He found nothing. And from there he returned. And he arrived at the leader's house, and the leader said to him, "Why are you alone?" "I can't find her," he says. And the leader said, "I think she has been stolen from you. Now we'll assemble the people," the leader says to him. And he sent Dove. "Assemble the people," he says. And Dove got all the people. "Falcon's wife has been stolen," he says. "Now Eagle will ask the people," he says. "Who's going to find her?" he says.

And all the people assembled, and he asked all of them, "Who can find out where she went?" And Buzzard said, "I'll try. But he must take me where she was stolen," Buzzard said. And there Falcon took him where she was stolen, and there they arrived. "For one day I will search for her," he says. And Buzzard searched all the ravines. *He looks down all the impassable places. He comes down. Where is she hidden? And in vain he goes up again. He finds nothing.*

He did not find anything. He worked for one day, and he returned. And, as before, all the people assembled, and they asked him, "What happened on your journey?" "I didn't find anything," he says. "I walked over the whole world, but it was useless," he says. "I didn't find anything."

And the leader said, "Now you," he says to Wind. "Yes," says Wind. "I think I can do something. I try to get in everywhere over the whole world," says Wind. And there Falcon took him, and they arrived there. "Is this it?" says Wind to him. "Yes," says Falcon. "Well, I'll walk now," he says. "I will arrive there after sundown," he says. And Falcon says to him, "Well, I am going now," he says. And Wind walked over the whole world. He did not find anything. He worked for one day. And he arrived late at the leader's house, and the leader asked him, "What happened on your journey?" he says to him. "I didn't find anything," he says.

"Now you," Bottlefly is told. And there Falcon took him, and they arrived there. "Did she go from here?" he says to him. And he stood right there where the woman had been sitting. And he said to Falcon, "You must not go anywhere. You must wait for me right here," he says to him. And Bottlefly says, "From here I'll find out where she went. I'll turn around here," he says. "East," and also, "North," he says, and also, "West," and also, "South." And Falcon said, "Where is she?" he says. "Not there," Bottlefly says. "She went far up," he says. "You must wait for me right here," he says.

And there he went far up, and there he remained. *He sniffs in all directions.* And he turned around, and he saw a house. It was the house of the thief. And there Bottlefly went. And on entering his house, he slipped. *He falls on his back.* His house was slippery. And it was quiet there. And he saw the woman. From there he returned. He seemed to be very quick.

He came there where Falcon remained, and he reached Falcon, and Falcon said to him, "Where?" And he said to him, "She is up there." "I have known it for a long time. I have been thinking," says Falcon. "It is best that we return, and I will go in the morning."

And they returned, and they arrived at the leader's house, and the people assembled. *Now they will listen to the one who found her.* And all the people assembled. And the leader questioned Bottlefly. "The two of us arrived there where she was stolen," he says. "We arrived there," he says. "And I couldn't find her east or north or west or south," he says. "Well! She went above," he says. "And there I arrived far up," he says. "There she was," he says, "that woman." And Coyote said, "I have known it for a long time," he says. And he named him. "That is his name," he says. "Condor," he says. "All of his body is stone, but his heart can be seen through his back," he says. And Eagle said to him, "Is he certain to fight us if he comes?" he says; and then he said, "Sparrow Hawk is Falcon's younger brother. Yayil is his name." And Falcon said, "In the morning I will get her," he says.

And in the morning Falcon went. He took his musical bow. And far off there he arrived, and there he placed it where his wife had been. And there he sat on his musical bow. And he went up. That musical bow of his took him up.

And far above he came out through a hole in the world, and after coming out he stood there. And there he saw the house. And there he went. And there he arrived at the door, and he said to her, "Come out." And she said to him, "Who are you?" And Falcon said to her, "It is I." "So it is you," she says to him. "Now I will come out," she says to him, and she came out with a string of human bones around her neck. And Falcon said to her, "Take off your necklace. Now we will go," he says to her. And from there they went to the place where he had come out, and they arrived there, and there he placed his musical bow. They sat in the middle of it. And from there they descended far below. And from there they went to their house where their leader was. There they arrived. *At their arrival, the people are happy.*

And then Condor, the fighter, arrived at his house, and there he saw their wife's necklace; she had thrown it on the door. And at that he immediately got ready to go. *Now he is going to follow his wife.* And he descended far below; and from there he went. *Now he will go toward them.* And far off there he arrived; and he asked them, "Where does Tsopnix live?" he says. And Falcon was told, "Condor is looking for you." "Has he come already?" he says. "Yes," says the speaker. And there went Falcon.

All the people are getting very frightened. "Hello," Tsopnix says to him; "It is really you." "Hello," says Condor. "So you took our wife," he says. "Therefore," Condor says to him, "therefore, we will settle it between ourselves. If you kill me, then you will take our wife. But if I kill you, then I will take her," he says. "Which one will shoot first?" he says. "I will be first," says Falcon.

And they went far off to an open plain. "Ready?" Falcon says to him. And it seems that he conjured up a fog. And "Ready?" says his opponent. And many stones fell where Falcon was standing. And Condor asked him, "Where are you?" his opponent says to him. "I'll take my turn with you. Now I come," Falcon says to him. And he conjured up a fog again. *Soon his younger brother will go in a circle around him. He has many wiregrass [cane] arrows now. He is shooting at the heart through Condor's back. There this heart of his could be seen.* "Well, get ready now," Falcon says to him. "Now I will shoot at you. Three times I will shoot at you," he says to him. "Ready," he says to him. "Get ready now. Now I will shoot at you." And he shot at him. Many stones dropped from his body when he shot. And he shot at him again; and, as before, stones dropped there. And, "Where are you?" Falcon says to him. "Here I am," he says.

"Now I will take my turn with you. I come next," Condor says to him. "Good," says Falcon. "Ready?" he says to him. "Ready," then says Falcon. *His younger brother still keeps shooting at him through his back.* And he conjured up a fog again, and many stones dropped where he was standing. And again he went far off to a different place. And he says to him, "Where are you?" "I am standing here," says Falcon.

"And now I will take my turn with you. I will come next again," Falcon says to him. *Already Condor is losing strength. Now he is going to shoot at him again.* And a lot of stones fell; they seemed to be very large ones.

"Again," Falcon says to him. And he shot at him again. "There is one more," he says to him. "Now I'll shoot at you again," he says to him. *But [Condor] is already losing strength.* And, "Again," he says to him. And finally he fell down. *Yet he does not stop talking.* And then they rested. *Now he does not get up. Now he has fallen.*

And, "What are we going to do with him?" says Coyote. "We will burn him," say all these people. And all of the people gathered wood. They piled it there where he had fallen, and it was set on fire, and the fire died out. Nothing was burning. "Hello," says Falcon to him. "Hello," then says Condor. "So! You are still alive," Falcon says to him. "There is nothing you can kill me with," [Condor] says to him. And another kind of wood was gathered; and, as before, it was again piled there where he is lying, and, as before, it was set on fire. It was not burning any longer. "Hello," Falcon says to him. "It is really you. Hello," he says to him. "I am well," he says. "So! You will not die," Falcon says to him.

And Coyote was asked, "What will we burn him with? He does not burn up," they say. And, "With grass," Coyote says; "with that he will burn," he says. And a lot of grass was brought. *Now he will be burned with it.* And it was set on fire. And all of his body was burning. *But his head still talks.* "We have probably killed him now. Leave him right there," he says.

And they stayed over night. And during the night the head, by itself, went away. His body was not there. And Falcon got the head and took it away. And the head got angry at being taken. *Now the head will try many times to harm him. And again Falcon takes it in his hands. Now he is going to keep smashing it down on these stones.* And again it kept trying to harm him.

And finally Falcon said, "We had better go to my father's sister." And Falcon and his wife went off. *Now they are going to run away.* And the two of them went. And now the head came again. It was trailing them now. And again it overtook them. Again it failed to do any harm to Falcon. And, as before, Falcon took it and kept smashing it down. He broke it in many pieces. And again the two of them went off. And again it overtook them as they were nearing his father's sister's house. And, as before, he again kept smashing it down. And with that the two of them went off again. And his father's sister shouted, "Run," she says to him. "You are coming close now," she says to him. They were getting very near. And now the head was approaching them again, and already it was overtaking them. Just as it approached, the rock closed shut. Just as it closed, the head arrived there. There the head broke. There it became Echo Rock.

And then Eagle was asked, "Where will you go?" he is asked. "Here in the mountain I am going to roam," he says then. And Cougar also was asked, "Where will you go?" he is asked. "Here in the mountain I am going to roam," he says. "I'll kill many deer," he says. Falcon also says, "I too will walk here in the mountain," he says. And Coyote was also asked, "Where will you go?" he is asked. "Here I will walk on the plains. Maybe I will steal something there," he says. And Crow also was asked. "I'll walk west," he says. "Maybe something will die, and I will eat its eyes," says Crow. That is the end.

21

The Contest between Men and Women

TÜBATULABAL
CIRCA 1932

MIKE MIRANDA, NARRATOR
ERMINIE WHEELER VOEGELIN, COLLECTOR

INTRODUCTION BY CHRIS LOETHER

The classic myth "The Contest between Men and Women" transcends the cultural milieu of its origins in the universal, timeless appeal of the issue at the heart of the story, the gender roles played out by men and women in human societies.[1] The story was told to Erminie Wheeler Voegelin, in English, by Mike Miranda during one of her summer field-trips to Tübatulabal country in Central California between 1931 and 1933. She had been collecting ethnographic information from Miranda, who offered this myth in answer to her question of whether women had ever had a role in hunting.

Mike Miranda, whose Tübatulabal name was Yukaya, was about forty-three years old at the time he worked with Erminie. Although his mother was from the neighboring Yokuts tribe, his father, Steban Miranda, was the last hereditary chief of the Tübatulabal. (After his father's death in 1955, the Tübatulabal were ruled by a Council of Elders until the early 1970s. At that time they joined with the neighboring Koso Shoshone and

Kawaiisu tribes to form the Kern Valley Indian Community, which gained tax-exempt status in 1987, though they are still fighting for federal recognition by Congress.)

The Tübatulabal consisted of three bands in aboriginal times: the Pahkanapil, the Palagewan, and the Bankalachi, which occupied three connected valleys formed by the confluence of the Kern River and the South Fork Kern River in the southern Sierra Nevada mountains. The Tübatulabal have no migration myths such as the Mojave and Navajo have; according to their traditions, they have always lived in those three valleys. Linguistic and archaeological findings confirm that they have been right where they now are for a very long time indeed. The archaeological evidence indicates that the Tübatulabal's ancestors probably occupied Kern River territory as early as 1200 B.C. They are clearly distinguished archaeologically at this early time from their Numic-speaking neighbors in terms of settlement patterns, lithic materials, rock art, and milling equipment (Moratto 1984:559). And the comparative linguistic evidence indicates that, by 1500 B.C., the Tübatulabal were already becoming distinct in language from their closest linguistic relatives, the Numic-speaking peoples of the Great Basin, such as the Shoshone, Western Mono (Monache), Owens Valley Paiute, and Kawaiisu.

The Tübatulabal first encountered the whiteman in 1776—ironically, the American year of independence—with the arrival in their territory of two different Spanish expeditions. But the people were spared the brunt of outside immigration into Native California until the 1850s, when the California Gold Rush brought hordes of newcomers into their valleys. A turning point (though not a good one) came in 1863, when some thirty-five to forty innocent Tübatulabal men were massacred by the local white population in retaliation for cattle-raids by Indians in the Owens Valley. After this time it was no longer safe to be a Tübatulabal in Tübatulabal country.

The early California anthropologist Alfred Kroeber estimated the Tübatulabal population to have been between five hundred and one thousand at time of Contact (1925:608), though this figure may be low. By the early 1990s there were approximately four hundred Tübatulabal who still lived in the three valleys, and an additional five hundred living away from the traditional homeland (Holmes-Wermuth 1994:661). As of this writing, there are less than half a dozen fluent speakers of the language.

Culturally the Tübatulabal straddle the border between two Native culture areas: California to the west and the Great Basin to the east. The Tübatulabal show influences from both culture areas. In their three valleys the Tübatulabal had access to both acorns (the main staple of California Indian people) and pine-nuts (the main staple of Great Basin Indian people). Influences from these two culture areas seem to permeate all aspects of Tübatulabal culture. Their mythology has been classified as being Great Basin in character (Gayton 1935:588, 595), but their religious rituals and material culture are clearly more similar to their California neighbors, such as the Yokuts. These dual cultural influences are reflected in "The Contest between Men and Women" where, contrary to the norm in Tübatulabal society for each politically independent band to have but one chief, there are two chiefs, Eagle and Coyote. Eagle is the character who is most often the chief in Central California mythology, and Coyote is the culture-hero par excellence of Great Basin mythology.

The Tübatulabal yearly cycle was similar to that of their Sierran neighbors. They spent the winter in permanent villages along the rivers in the three valleys and then migrated to family camps in the mountains during the summer months. Sex roles were strictly determined in Tübatulabal society, with the men hunting and the women gathering. Contact between women and men was strictly limited during certain critical periods—particularly while women were menstruating, and for a several-day period before men went hunting. There were, however, special times when everyone participated in certain food gathering activities, such as fishing in July, the pine-nut harvest in early fall, the acorn harvest in late fall, or occasional rabbit and antelope drives.

Tübatulabal cosmology and worldview were similar to that of their neighbors in that they believed in a previous world that had been inhabited by animals with supernatural powers and very human characteristics. These mythological "animal people" became the animals of this world when the current world, along with humans, was created. The story given here is set in the world of myth-time.

Let us now look at some of the cultural aspects found in the myth itself, which addresses the age-old question of why the sexes play different roles that seem in some way inherently predetermined. In this myth, it appears that men and women were created equal in the beginning, since the story hints that, were it not for Coyote's magic at the last moment, the division of labor might well have turned out differently.

As the story opens, we find the men all living by themselves. While they are out hunting all day, Coyote stays home, gathering and stacking wood for each man's camp. (Coyote here is playing the traditional role of the *berdache*, the man who stays in camp and does women's work, such as gathering and preparing food, and therefore must wear women's clothes.) What is notable is that the men know *only* how to hunt—there is no mention of any plant foods (the product of women's labor) in their camp. The women, on the other hand, who are also living by themselves, enjoy both hunted *and* gathered foods.

When the men discover the women's camp, they send Road Runner to investigate.[2] Interestingly enough, after Road Runner has arrived in the women's camp and been offered food to eat, it is the chia, a plant food, that makes him sick. Despite its thematic symbolism, though, the scene where Road Runner loses his lunch also happens to be one of the best comic moments in the story:

> Pretty soon he vomited—
> oh, vomited!—
> and everything came up;
> Lizard came up;
> he vomited Lizard and the chia too.
> Lizard,
> he chased all those women;
> they got up,
> and ran,
> and those women said,
>   "What kind of food does this man *eat?*" they said.

The women, a sensible crew overall, are clearly disgusted by this startling turn of events. On top of it all, Lizard, once on the loose again, starts running around like a sex-starved maniac when he sees all the women standing around gaping at Road Runner.

After three days, the women move to the men's camp. Now begins the big adjustment for the men (which, one can argue, is still being played out among humans today). At first they take turns with the daily tasks. First the men go hunting, while the women stay at home and prepare the acorn, pine-nuts, and other plant foods. Next the women hunt, and the men stay at home. Unlike the previous day, though, the women are all successful in their hunting; furthermore, most of the men have problems in preparing the plant foods. This leads to a lot of grumbling on the part of the men, especially Coyote, who devises the final "shooting contest" to determine who gets to go out hunting and who has to stay at home to grind seeds.[3]

The women in this myth seem to be inherently superior, in overall competence, to the men. This portrayal in turn sets up the comic necessity for Coyote to have to "cheat" in order to win the contest, thereby garnering for men the "right" to hunt and establishing for all time the division of labor between the sexes—the gender roles that characterize Tübatulabal society in their native world. The Tübatulabal have traditionally believed that they should model their behavior on that of the previous world, because the mythological animal people were so much more powerful and knowledgeable than humans are today. After all, myths (in any culture) not only explain the origins of the world as we know it, but also validate its status quo.

Just as every story has a purpose, every storyteller has a reason for telling a particular story at a particular moment to a particular audience. This time, the story wasn't told to a Native Tübatulabal audience, but was told in English to a female anthropologist, who wrote it down in a notebook in the course of collecting ethnographic information. Before the advent of recording equipment, taking down a text was a very tedious and time-consuming process, involving constant breaks in the flow of the narration. Despite these difficult conditions, Mike Miranda managed to keep his mind in his story and present a coherent text, formally structured and richly detailed, with its comic flair intact.

One is always tempted to look for the storyteller in the story itself. If Mike Miranda is "in there" at all—his cultural beliefs, his chiefly family background, his sense of the world—it is probably his gift for humor that is best revealed in "The Contest between Men and Women."

NOTES

1. The only published source for this myth is in Erminie Voegelin's ethnography of the Tübatulabal (1937:53–55). The version of the story that appears here is taken from the Charles F. and Erminie Voegelin Papers (1931–1933:26–31) in the Bancroft Library at Berkeley. The two versions are virtually the same in text; the only significant change from either involves the presentational form of the story as it appears in this volume. The ragged-line format was discerned by the

editor, Herbert Luthin, based strictly on the transparently prosodic punctuation patterns in Erminie Voegelin's prose transcription. Punctuation therefore follows prosodic-intonational contours, rather than the usage rules of formal written English. (The paragraph boundaries of the original typescript are indicated by the conjunction of a line space and a flush-left margin.) Finally, in the Bancroft typescript, Voegelin notes occasional accompanying gestures and other performance cues that she recorded at various points in the story. These gesture notes, or their likely content, are presented in the right margin of the text.

2. We have opted not to normalize Erminie's rather charming spelling of Roadrunner's name.—HWL

3. This contest seems similar in some ways to public contests that were traditionally held between shamans to show off their skills and instill respect and awe in the lay population.

FURTHER READING

For those interested in further reading concerning the Tübatulabal, Erminie Voegelin's "Tübatulabal Ethnography" is the best primary source. The most complete published collection of Tübatulabal myths and legends is found in Carl F. Voegelin's "Tübatulabal Texts," including the bilingual autobiography of the storyteller, Mike Miranda (1935:223–241). There is also a collection of largely unpublished Tübatulabal stories in Voegelin and Voegelin's "Tübatulabal Myths and Tales" at the Bancroft Library in Berkeley. Other general sources that include sections on the Tübatulabal are Alfred Kroeber's *Handbook of the Indians of California,* Charles Smith's article "Tübatulabal" in the California volume of the Smithsonian *Handbook,* and Carol Holmes-Wermuth's article "Tübatulabal" in *Native America in the Twentieth Century: An Encyclopedia.*

THE CONTEST BETWEEN MEN AND WOMEN

There were a lot of people living,
    and Eagle and Coyote were chiefs—
    and all of them were men;
    there were no women.

And they hunted rabbits;
 every day.
 Coyote stayed home every time they went;
 he never went hunting,
 he just hauled wood for them;
 he hauled wood for every camp.
 That's all Coyote did all the time.

And when they got tired of rabbits, you know,
 they went to hunt deer for a change.
 And when all of them went to hunt deer the next day they
  went farther off,
 way up in the mountains.
 And they saw smoke from there,
 way across up on another mountain.
 And they said,
  "Maybe somebody is living over there—
  people."
 And one of them said,
  "I think we should tell Coyote about it,
  when we get home tonight."
 That's what he said.

And they came home in the evening;
 every one had a deer,
 and Coyote had all the wood,
 piled up at every camp.
 And they cut a little piece of meat,
 every one,
 and gave it to Coyote for his work.
 Coyote ate that.

And pretty soon they told Coyote after supper,
  "We saw smoke from the top of the mountain,
  across on a mountain,
  far away."

And Coyote said,
  "Maybe somebody is over there;
  let's send somebody tomorrow and find out."

And they picked one man;
they said,
   "This fellow—
Road Runner.
He goes fast," they said.

And next morning Road Runner went,
   after breakfast,
   and those fellows went again,
   to hunt deer.
   And Coyote stayed home,
   and hauled wood for the camp.

And that fellow, he went;   *[gesturing]*
   he went way up on the mountain,
   and when he saw Lizard running quickly,
   close to him,
   Road Runner ran close,   *[gesturing]*
   grabbed Lizard,
   picked him up,
   and ate him.
   Lizard was his life, I think—
   Road Runner just swallowed him.

And those women—
   lots of women over there at a big pit mortar bed—   *[nodding]*
   a long one;
   and there lots of women were grinding pine-nuts.
   They were all sitting down there,
   grinding them.
   There were no men;
   all women.

And pretty soon one woman said,
     "Oh!" she said,
     "the edge of my vagina is shaking,"
   and they laughed;
   all laughed.
   And pretty soon another woman over there said,   *[pointing]*
     "Oh! Mine too.

The edge of my vagina is shaking."
Pretty soon somebody said,
    "Maybe somebody is coming;
    some man is coming."
And they said,
    "Maybe."

And then one of these women looked that way and saw one
    man coming.   *[nodding]*
She said,
    "You see.
    I told you,
    somebody is coming,
    coming over there now."

And Road Runner saw those women,
    lots of women;
    he saw those women sitting down there,
    all of them.
    And Road Runner came there;
    he said, "Hello!"

All those women said, "Hello,"
    and they asked him what he was doing way up there.
    And Road Runner said,
        "Those fellows saw smoke yesterday," he said,
        "from a long way across the mountain;
        and they told me to come and find out if somebody
            were living here.
        All of them are men over there," he said.

    "And here no men,"
        they told Road Runner;
    "all women."

And pretty soon they all of them got up,
    and they called to Road Runner,
        "Come on;
        come on down to the house,"
    and Road Runner went with them.

When they came down to the house,
    they told Road Runner,
        "Come in,"
    and they took a big basket—
    homol, you know—
    and they mixed chia in there,
    about full,
    and they gave it to that man,
    to eat;
    and a piece of meat:
    deer meat.

And Road Runner drank it all, you see,
    and when he was through eating,
    he sat down there for a while,
    and pretty soon the chia made him sick;
    he felt like vomiting,
    that man.
    Pretty soon he vomited—
    oh, vomited!—
    and everything came up;
    Lizard came up;
    he vomited Lizard and the chia too.   *[grimacing]*
    Lizard,
    he chased all those women;
    they got up,
    and ran,
    and those women said,
        "What kind of food does this man eat?" they said.
    Lizard was alive, you know.

And those women came back after the man got all right;
    the man recovered, you know;
    and those women came back.

And one woman went into the house and brought chia seeds,
    tied up in a little bag.
    She said,
        "When you get home,

give this to that Mountain Lion Man," she said.
And Road Runner said,
    "All right."

(That's a Mountain Lion Woman—
all that company of women,
were all different—
Hawk Woman,
Mountain Lion Woman,
Coyote Woman.
And it was just the same over there—   *[pointing]*
Mountain Lion Man,
Hawk Man,
and all the rest.)

And another woman—
    Hawk Woman—
came out,
and she had the same thing,
a little bag of acorns.
She gave it to that man;
    "When you get home you give this to that Hawk Man."
Road Runner said, "All right."

Well.
    All of them gave that man a little bag for those fellows.
    Road Runner said, "All right."
    And last of all came one big woman,
    a fat woman;
    she had a little bag,
    and she said,
        "You give this to Coyote."

And those women said,
        "After three days we will go over there;
        three days from now we will all go over there."
    Road Runner said, "All right,"
    and set off for home;
    he had a big load.

And Coyote, over there—   [pointing]
    Coyote looks all the time to watch for Road Runner's
        return;
    he is in a hurry,
    he wants to see.
    He goes up a hill and looks,
    every little while,
    to see when Road Runner returns.

Then he saw Road Runner coming,
    in the evening.
    Coyote went over to meet him;
    he was curious.
    Coyote said,
        "Did you find out,
        about everything over there?"
    And Road Runner said,
        "Oh," he said,
        "You'd better wait;
        you don't want to find out now;
        you'd better wait."

Coyote just came alongside of Road Runner;
    he said,
        "Hurry up—   [whispering]
        you'd better tell me!"
    Road Runner said,
        "Wait,
        until those fellows come home.
        Then you'll find out," he said.

Pretty soon those fellows came in in the evening;
    those men.
    And after supper they all gathered together;
    they are going to find out now.
    And Road Runner said,
        "They are all women over there,
        lots of them.
        And they gave me little bags," he said.

"They told me to give them to you."

(Well,
maybe that's a present—
something,
you know,
to give to the men.)

Road Runner gave all those men what the women had given
    him;
    Road Runner told those men,
        "Those women said they were going to come,
        in three days,"
    and Coyote said,
        "Good, good, good!" said Coyote.   *[laughing]*

And after three days, those women came,
    after three days.
    Every one of them had a load;
    some had acorns,
    chia,
    pine-nuts,
    all kinds;
    all different seeds.
    And all of them had bows and arrows;
    all of them had arrows,
    all those women.
    And Road Runner went to meet those women, you see;
    he was going to tell them about each man,
    where each was living, you see—
    in which house.

And Road Runner said,
        "There's that Mountain Lion Man's house over there;
        he is living over there,"
    and Mountain Lion Woman went over there.
        "And there's Hawk's house over there—
        Hawk's,"
    and Hawk Woman went over there.
    All those women,

every one,
went this way,   *[points]*
and that way,   *[points]*
and the last one—
oh!—
a big woman,
came,
and Road Runner said,
    "There's Coyote's house,
    way over there,"   *[pointing]*
and the big woman went over there.

The next day all those men went hunting, you know,
    and those women,
    all of them went to grind acorns,
    and chia, you know.
    And those men returned in the evening,
    and those women had everything ready,
    all cooked,
    and those men came home and ate.

And the next day those women told those men,
    "We are going to hunt now,
    and you men go grind some acorns";
    they told those men that, you know.

And those women returned in the evening and they had deer,
    every one of them, you know—
    those women.
    And those men,
    some of them,
    had gotten through early;
    they had returned home,
    and some of them were still over there,
    cooking acorns, you know—
    they didn't know how to very well, you know.

And came sundown;
    Coyote hadn't come home yet;
    he was still up at the pit mortar working.

Coyote was pretty mad;
at sundown he hadn't come home yet,
and his wife went over there,
to help her man.
And they got through,
and came home.

And the next day all the men went up on the hill to hunt,
and all the women went to grind acorns;
all of the men went to hunt deer,
Coyote too.
He didn't haul any more wood;
he went to hunt deer.

When they got way up in the mountains,
Coyote said,
"You fellows wait," he said.
"We are going to talk about those women," he said,
and they stopped.
And Coyote said,
"These women,
they have arrows,
and they hunt,
and they send us over there to grind acorns,"
Coyote said.
"That's not right," he said.
"I think women better handle the mortar," he said,
(you know,
where they grind pine-nuts—)
"that's just right for them;
that's woman's work," he said.
"Not man's," he said.

"And tomorrow,"
Coyote said,
"we are going to talk;
to have a big talk," he said;
"we are going to shoot at a target," he said.
"If those women win,

then they can handle the arrow," he said,
    Coyote said.
"If *we* win,
then we keep hunting and handle the arrow,
and women keep handling the mortars,
all the time."

And everybody said,
    "All right,
    we'll do that."

When they returned home in the evening,
    after supper Coyote told those men and women,
    everybody,
    to gather;
    he said,
        "We are going to have a big talk here."
    And Coyote told them all,
        "Tomorrow we are going to shoot a target;
        if you women win then you can handle the arrows and
            we can handle the mortars,
        and grind acorns," he said.
        "But this way,
        you women hunt and we handle the mortars;
        that's not right,"
            said Coyote.
        "That's woman's work," he said.

        "Tomorrow morning,"
            Coyote said,
        "I will put up a target over there;
        we will shoot," he said.
    Those women said,
        "All right."

And Coyote didn't sleep that night, you know;
    he got up,
    at midnight;
    he went way up on top of the mountain, you know,
    and built a fire way up on top.

And when he came back home he said,
    "You fellows get up now;
    the morning star is up now;
    you get up,
    hurry."

And Road Runner looked and said,
    "Oh, that's not the morning star over there;
    that's a fire you built up there on top of the mountain,
    you devil,"
        Road Runner said.
  Coyote said,
    "Hurry up!"
  but everybody went back to sleep again.

And when daylight came they all got up;
    and after breakfast Coyote went out,
    and set a target over there,
    and Coyote said,
        "Everybody line up," he said,
        "get ready."
    And one of those women,
    Mountain Lion Woman,
    was a pretty good shooter,
    pretty hard to beat with an arrow.

And every woman stood here with her husband,   *[gesturing]*
    and they were going to shoot together,
    each woman and her husband,
    at the same time.
    And Coyote and his wife stood way over there on the edge.
    And Coyote said,
        "I'm going first;
        I'm going to shoot first."   *[laughing]*
    He wanted to win, you know.   *[laughs]*

And Coyote said,
    "You ready?"
  and his wife said,
    "Yes,"

and they shot.
And they never hit the target;
Coyote missed the target,
and his wife too;
they didn't hit the target.

Coyote said,
    "Next,
        ready," he said,
and the next two shot,
and they never hit the target.
And all of them missed;
just two,
Mountain Lion and his wife,
had not yet shot.
And Coyote said,
    "You fellows next,"
and then Coyote, he came round to Mountain Lion;
he told Mountain Lion,
    "You shoot good;   *[gesturing]*
        your wife is a good one,
        but you shoot good," he said.

And when they were ready to shoot,
    one man shot—   *[pantomimes*
    that was Mountain Lion,   *drawing bow]*
    and his wife shot too.
Coyote said,
    "Break,
        you string,
        break!"
and Mountain Lion Woman's string broke,
and her arrow went to one side.
And that Mountain Lion,
Mountain Lion hit right in the center;
that man hit it.
And those women lost, you know;
the men won.
Coyote said,

"Now," he said,
"all right;
you women handle the mortars," he said,
"we will handle the arrows," he said.

"We are men,"
      said Coyote.

And those men won,
   and lived there.

That's the end.

22

The Dog Girl

INESEÑO CHUMASH
1913

MARÍA SOLARES, NARRATOR
J. P. HARRINGTON, COLLECTOR
RICHARD APPLEGATE, TRANSLATOR

INTRODUCTION BY KATHRYN KLAR

The Chumash occupied the territory of Coastal California from about
Paso Robles and San Luis Obispo in the north down to Malibu (a Ventureño name, *humaliwo* 'place where the waves make noise') in the south.
The first known recording of any California Indian language was made
by the Catalonian soldier Pedro Fages (probably in May 1772); the language for which Fages recorded some seventy vocabulary items from the
"natives of the mission of San Luís and twenty leagues round about there"
was what is now called Obispeño Chumash. Although Alfred Kroeber
asserted the relationship of the Chumash languages in the first decade
of the last century, a definitive grouping of the family had to await the
perusal of John P. Harrington's fieldnotes in the 1970s. The Chumash
family turns out to have been remarkably diverse, with three main languages (Northern, Central, and Island), each group consisting of one or
more dialects with salient distinguishing features. Northern Chumash

(two dialects) is very different from any of its cognates, and Island Chumash (one dialect) is also quite distinct from Central Chumash (four or more dialects); but regular phonological correspondences can be adduced for all the languages, and an outline of the protolanguage can be tentatively reconstructed. This pattern argues for a great time depth for the family and, by extension, a long occupation of some or all of the historical territory. The same things that still attract residents and visitors to this part of California (fine climate, beautiful scenery, and an abundance of marine and terrestrial resources) enabled the Chumash to live beyond mere subsistence. Their culture was technologically and verbally sophisticated, and the land supported a dense population organized into towns headed by chiefs, both male and female.

Chumash language and culture, broadly construed, was the field to which John P. Harrington gave his greatest and most continuous efforts; from 1912 until his death in 1961, there is no great stretch of time in which he was not engaged in some aspect of his Chumash work. Harrington's name looms so large in Chumash studies that it is sometimes hard to remember that, without the phalanx of workers who came after him and diligently deciphered his fieldnotes, almost none of the material he collected and reworked would be available or usable to Native people, scholars, or the general public. Those who work with the Chumash linguistic materials and stories Harrington collected are, perforce, a specific variety of researcher known as a philologist ("one who is fond of words or learning"). Their "field" is not the last speakers of Chumash languages or the best storytellers or the finest basketmakers; rather, the philologists work with the papers, wax cylinders, and aluminum discs on which Harrington the fieldworker recorded his consultants' information about these things. There is no way ever to add another word or sentence to the Chumash corpus, but the philological work of organization and analysis will ensure that Harrington's vast corpus can be utilized to its fullest. Any discussion of this material thus implicitly recognizes the contribution of those who have brought it to publishable form as necessary partners in the grand endeavor in which Harrington was engaged throughout most of his life.

Harrington was born in Waltham, Massachusetts, in 1884. The family—father Elliott, mother Mary Lydia, John, and younger brother Robert—moved (probably for reasons of Elliott's health) to Pasadena, California, in 1891. They then moved to Santa Barbara in 1892, where the family established a home in the city that remained Harrington's main base of operations throughout his life. Following his graduation from Stanford University in 1905, Harrington spent his *wanderjahr* studying at the Universities of Leipzig and Berlin with linguistic giants such as Eduard Sievers and Karl Brugmann. He evidently planned to return to study with Franz Nikolaus Finck in Berlin, to whom he became close during this German year; the plan was cut short by Finck's untimely death in 1910. At this point, Harrington was seriously considering extended fieldwork among the languages of the Caucasus. Finck, both personally and through his published writings, may have been instrumental in shaping the young Harrington in his characteristic way of approaching unfamiliar languages. Finck's 1899 work on an Irish Gaelic dialect, *Die araner Mundart* (The dialect of the Aran Islands), is based upon the result of a brief, intensive period of living "in the field" with the islanders in the remote western extreme of Ireland. Finck stressed the need for work with remote dialects, even of relatively well-known languages (as Gaelic was at the time), in order to carry out comprehensive comparative work on related languages. These ideas are features of Harrington's work throughout his life.

Between 1906 and 1912, Harrington cast about for a purpose in life. He never seemed to want to venture far from his boyhood home for long (his letters home from Germany are touchingly domestic), and among other things, he taught modern languages (German and Russian) at Santa Ana High School, worked on Mojave and Yuman (at Kroeber's behest), worked in several southwest fields in connection with employment at the School of American Archaeology, helped Edgar Lee Hewett prepare exhibits for the 1915 Panama-California Exposition in San Diego, and gave several series of summer lectures on anthropology and linguistics in Colorado and Washington State. He considered some academic options: further study in Germany, a graduate fellowship in anthropology at Berkeley (arranged by Kroeber, but turned down by Harrington), work on Caucasian languages, and graduate study at the University of Chicago. In 1912, however, for some reason (had he heard that Kroeber was busy in the Chumash area?) he returned home and began the work that formed a focal point for much of the rest of his life: his Chumash fieldwork. He worked on every Chumash dialect for which he could find a speaker, in a frenetic attempt to record everything. He and his new bride, Carobeth, spent their June 1916 honeymoon working on Obispeño and Purisimeño!

FIGURE 10. María Solares.
Photograph by J. P. Harrington.
Courtesy Smithsonian Institution.

Harrington did most of his Ineseño work between about 1914 and 1919. About his principal consultant, María Isabel del Refugio Solares, little is known; there is no good, extensive source of information on the fieldwork with her, only the linguistic notes themselves. She was born in 1842 at Monterey, and died in 1923, probably in Santa Inez. That she was a fluent Ineseño speaker and a master storyteller is clear from her story "The Dog Girl." She also apparently spoke some Purisimeño, though Harrington never recorded any text in that dialect from her or anyone else.

So much material has been preserved in various Chumash languages that we have an opportunity rare in California, that of getting some idea of both the range and depth of cultural experience and verbal dexterity of the people. "The Dog Girl" is the merest drop of this material; but like a drop of honey, it is very satisfying and leaves one craving more. Because the story has been left, as closely as the translator is able, in the style in which it was told, one senses the rhythm of the storyteller's art and the hearer's reception. As Leanne Hinton noted (about Yahi) in her introduction to *Ishi's Tale of Lizard,* "Some phrases are repeated a lot, and there is a rhythm in the telling that make it something like a poem. Read it out loud if you have a chance to: it sounds best that way." This applies as well to this story. It was paraphrased in Thomas Blackburn's *December's Child* (an extremely rich collection of Chumash narrative folklore), but because Blackburn worked only with Harrington's notes in translation, the full linguistic richness of the text was not realized. Blackburn's long, conjoined, written-English phrases are not characteristic of the Chumash oral storytelling style (as indeed they are not characteristic even of English oral style).

The short Chumash-language passage that follows (the nine opening lines that constitute the introductory scene of "The Dog Girl") should give readers a better sense of María's storytelling style, which can be formal, comic, and moving by turns. Here, the most striking rhetorical feature lies in the careful disposition of her phrases and the stately, almost processional rhythm that results:

Sikk'um'ewaš ahuču:	There were some very poor dogs;
šiyaqyaquyepš ašiyašɨn;	they scavenged to eat;
ma'uš'uškuyaš' šiyaqiyepš.	refuse, they scavenged.
Wahač' ač'ič'ihi':	There were lots of children:
kasilunan',	they grew,
siyoqʰo yila'.	they were all thin.
Šiyuxnišukutačiš:	They were quick to stand:
siyuqmawil;	they were suffering;
šiyaquyepš asʰese'.	they scavenged bones.

The fine, formal balance of this passage, based on increments of three, is readily apparent.

As Hinton said of Ishi's story, María's tale is something like a poem, with short narrative episodes full of concrete imagery strung together without a wasted word. Repetitions punctuate the narrative and draw attention to important actions.[1] This technique demands close attention by listeners; nothing is overtly explained, and the sequence of events must be closely observed. The tale is meant to be heard; take Hinton's advice, and your enjoyment—and understanding—will increase immeasurably.

1. Readers will find a more extended discussion of the poetics of repetition in "The Dog Girl" in the essay "Making Texts, Reading Translations" (this volume)—HWL

FURTHER READING

For a people so populous in a land so abundant with a culture so rich, surprisingly little has been published (and remained in print) on Chumash for a general audience. A series of books published (with one exception) in the 1970s, all based primarily on Harrington's notes, remain the best compilations, though one may have to look for them in libraries. Campbell Grant's *Rock Paintings of the Chumash* is an excursion into the beautiful, mystical world of Chumash art and remains accessible and readable. Thomas Blackburn's *December's Child* brings together many shorter and longer Chumash stories from throughout the Harrington corpus; the overall organization of the material is Blackburn's, however, not that of Harrington or the storytellers. *The Eye of the Flute*, edited by Travis Hudson, Blackburn, Rosario Curletti, and Janice Timbrook, gathers materials about Chumash traditional ritual from Harrington's work with Fernando Librado. *Crystals in the Sky* by Hudson and Ernest Underhay may be of particular interest to a wide audience, because it deals with Chumash archaeoastronomy; it is a good interpretive companion piece to Grant's book on rock art. *Tomol,* edited by Hudson, Timbrook, and Melissa Rempe, offers a detailed look at the building of a Chumash plank canoe according to the instructions of Fernando Librado; it includes material on the cultural complex surrounding Chumash marine culture.

Reliable Chumash language materials tend to be unpublished; the best grammar is Richard Applegate's exemplary doctoral dissertation, "Ineseño Chumash Grammar." Published dictionaries and lexicons do not exist, though several are in preparation for various dialects.

For general overviews of Harrington and his work, one can read Carobeth Laird's remarkable *Encounter with an Angry God*, with the caveat that this is the former wife's version of events, told with more than fifty years of hindsight. Carollyn James's piece in *Smithsonian Magazine*, "A Field Linguist Who Lived His Life for His Subjects," is sketchy but accurate. More recently, Leanne Hinton's "Ashes, Ashes" from *News from Native California* gives some of the seldom-heard Indians' views on Harrington and his work. Much Harrington lore remains in the realm of oral tradition; a full-scale biography is being undertaken by Kathryn Klar.

THE DOG GIRL

There were some very poor dogs:
    they scavenged to eat;
        refuse, they scavenged.
There were lots of children:
    they grew,
        they were all thin.   5
They were quick to make themselves stand:*
    they were suffering;
        they scavenged bones.

One of the children (she was already grown)
    climbed a range of hills,   10
        and she saw many people.
The men were playing the hoop game.
There she sat:
    she watched the people.
She said: "So many people,   15
    so many people!
        A town!"
They called out: "Come, come!"
She didn't go down.
She said: "Tomorrow I'll go down there."   20

When it was evening she went home.

---

* The idiomatic meaning of this line is unknown. The Chumash text reads *šiy-uxni-šukuta-čiš*. *šiy- ..-čiš* '3 PL.RFLX', *uxni-* 'quickly', *su-kuta* 'to cause to stand' (literally, then, something like 'They quickly made themselves to stand'). A wild guess as to the lost meaning of the expression might be "They were quick to beg"—but this interpretation makes some unverifiable assumptions, however plausible, about the way the Chumash interacted with their dogs.— HWL

She told her mother, she said:
   "Many people I saw;
      they were calling to me," she said.   25
         "I didn't go."
Said her mother: "Why didn't you go?
   Weren't they indulgent with you?*
      You're going to disgrace yourself.
         Go on over there."   30
"I'll go tomorrow."   *the girl said*
"Come here so I can comb you—   *her mother said*
   you will be going where there are people."
She combed her,
   she readied her by combing: 35
      the dog was beautiful.

Next day the girl got up before dawn.†
"Take heart," said her mother,
   "Don't disgrace yourself!
      You will see fine people."   40

She went,
   she came to her spot.
They saw her,
   they called out to her:
      "Quick, quick! Come, come!"   45
She went to them;
   they went to meet her.
It was good:
   the girl was beautiful,
      she was pretty.   50

---

* Harrington's notes provide a Spanish gloss for this line: *no te chiquéas!* 'Don't indulge (adorn?) yourself'. However, the Chumash text reads *'inišamuštiktikus,* which means something like 'They were not indulgent with her', making this a narrative line, not a line of dialogue. The Spanish gloss has been followed in this instance, because it appears to flow better and may have represented a revision on the narrator's part.—RA

† With respect to this and the preceding line, note that the dog girl is referred to sometimes as "the dog" and sometimes as "the girl"—perhaps depending on which aspect of the dog girl's character the narrator is emphasizing or sympathizing with at any given point in the story.—RA

"Come, come! Eat something!"
They took her to the chief's house;*
    they gave her food.†
She saw the food:
    acorn mush, islay, chia,   55
        many kinds of food;
    fish, deer meat—
        the hunters would go out to hunt,
            and bring it to the chief's house.‡
They gave her food.   60
She ate:
    there was a lot of food;
        she got full.

In the evening she said:
    "I have to go home already."   65
She was very full.
They said to her:
    "Be content,
        come back!"

Back at her house, she vomited.   70
The children ate it;
    the mother ate it, too.
She said to her: *the girl to her*
    "It's not enough,   *mother*
        not a lot of food."§   75
"My poor child,
    I made a mistake."   *said her mother*

---

* This was the old custom that a stranger was taken to the chief's house and given food, etc.—JPH

† For some reason this line was crossed out by Harrington.— RA

‡ Informant added that men were also in former times sent to the beach to bring *ʔušqoyičaš* 'shellfish'. They brought it to the captain's house, whereupon the chief paid them and women cooked it up for the people.—JPH

§ Literally, 'it's not good, lots of food', which doesn't quite make sense, though the words are simple and unambiguous. Perhaps 'This [referring to the dog-like act of regurgitation] is not good— [there was] lots of food', an interpretation that would tie in with the theme of dog behavior being "shameful"—in which case, the following line ("I made a mistake") might be interpreted as 'Sorry daughter, I was acting like a dog'.—RA

"I will go again tomorrow."   *said the girl*
"Be of good cheer;   *said her mother*
   I will comb you,   80
      come quick so I can comb you."

She went,   *in the morning*
   she sat down again at her spot.
They called: "Come, come!"
The chief's son took a fancy to the girl.   85
The chief's son no sooner saw her
   than he took a fancy to her,
      he fell in love with her.
He didn't speak to her,
   he just looked.   90
To his mother he said:
   "Mother, I like this girl."

That was the custom of the ancient people long ago.

He said to his mother:
   "I like the girl."   95
The old woman said:
   "Good,
      I will speak to her, my son."

As soon as the girl came, the old woman called her.
She said to her: 100
   "Be quick to eat,
      eat something!"
As soon as she had eaten, she said to her:
   "My child wants to marry you,
      he wants to marry.   105
         What do you say?" she said to her.
She didn't make a sound.   *the dog girl*
"Speak!" she said to her.   *to the girl*
She said: *to the chief's wife*
   "Oh!—I can't say!—   110
      Good people—
         No!—

I will tell my mother to see what she says."
Said the chief's wife: "Good."

In the evening (it was already late), she said: 115
   "I'm going already;
     I will tell my mother."
Said the old woman: "Good."
They gave her dinner,
   a good meal;   120
     she was full.
They gave her food to take to her house.

She got back home:
   she vomited;
     they ate what she had "carried."   125
Her mother said:
   "How did it go for you, my child?"
She said to her: "Good, my mother—
   the chief's son wants to marry me.
     What do you say, Mother?"   130
She said: "What am I to say?
   Good, good!" she said to her,
     "Marry him!"
"Tomorrow I will go,
   I will return."   135 *said the girl*
Said her mother: "Good."

She went;   *in the morning*
   he came out to meet her.
They were married:
   much food did the people eat at the house of the chief.   140
They were married at the chief's house;
   his wife was beautiful.

The boy had a sister;
   the sister liked her sister-in-law very much.
His mother said: 145
   "Don't let your wife go hungry."
     "Right," he said.

As for the dog girl:
   she had a bracelet,
      a bracelet of fine beads;   150
   she had a necklace,
      a pendant,
         a pendant of *apɨ* beads,
            of *apɨ* beads;
      a nose stick;   155
      a basket hat;
   she had many ornaments.
Her hair was all fixed up in a braid wrap—
   she had braid wraps—
      and her apron,   160
         her apron was of otterskin.
His wife was well dressed—
   she was adorned.

But after a while, she reverted to her old habit,
   of eating excrement.   165
And after a while, her sister-in-law saw her doing it,
   her sister-in-law saw her *šitoxčʰoš išpiliwaš.**
That's what the girl was doing:
   the girl was eating shit!
The sister stopped to look at her;   170
   she said nothing.
That's what the dog's sister-in-law saw;
   she just sat there.
The sister returned home.
"My mother," she said,   175
   "my sister-in-law has been eating excrement."
She was pounding something.†
"Don't speak of this," she told her.
   "Your poor brother!
      Stay here.‡   180
         Don't follow her where she goes."

---

* There are several words I can't figure out here—unfortunately crucial ones. The undecipherable
  words are simply retained in the original Chumash.—RA

† The chief's wife was preparing food, probably acorn meal or chia seeds.—HWL

‡ Literally, 'Sit'!—RA

As for the woman, *the dog girl*
  she stood up and went;
    she hid.
"I don't want to make my husband unhappy," she said. 185
She took nothing;
  there was nothing;
    she took nothing.

He said to his sister: *the chief's son*
  "Where did she go? 190
    Call for her!"
He looked around;
  he couldn't find her.
"I don't know where she went," she said,
  "nobody's there." 195
The man went out himself:
  he looked for his wife,
    he didn't find her.
And his mother said to him:
  "Maybe you scolded her." 200
They looked for her.
She had already gone.

She went up the hill;
  she headed back to her village;
    she wept. 205
"I did it to myself:
  there was lots of food,
    but I had to go and eat excrement.

"If only I had worn my bracelet! *[singing]*
If only I had worn my necklace! 210
If only I had worn my pendant!
If only I had worn my basket hat!
ʔiya yaya yaya!

"But I didn't.

"If only I had brought my apron, I would be happy! 215 *[singing]*
If only I had brought my bracelet, I would be happy!

If only I had brought my braid wraps, I would be happy!
If only I had brought my otterskin, I would be happy!
ʔiya yaya yaya! *

"My otterskin apron—I didn't bring it.   220
My husband would be ashamed.
    What hope have I of being kept?
      My husband would be ashamed.
Now I will turn into an animal:
    when I get back home,   225
      I will turn into an animal."

She got back home.
"How did it go for you, my child?"
"I had bad luck:
    there was no lack of food,   230
      but I wanted to eat shit.
My sister-in-law saw me.
I don't want to go back there,
    but I'll be leaving soon."

They all turned into animals;   235
    they were ashamed, all of them.
The mother and the children,
    all of them, turned into animals.
The animals, in the old days, knew shame;
    nowadays, people do not know shame.   240

---

* The second song here is reconstructed from notes in Harrington's notebook, where he transcribed the first line ('If I had brought my *smiłi*, I would be happy'), but merely alluded to the rest: "song goes on to mention *waštap̓*, *tik̓otuš*." A plausible object for the song's missing but structurally implied fourth line has been supplied.— RA

SOUTHERN CALIFORNIA

I have told you to come away from the shore,
Because the small crabs will bite you—
You [will] want to say, "Ai! Ai! Ai! Ai! Ai!"

Coyote song, San Buenaventura
(Ventureño Chumash)
Robert Heizer, "California Indian Linguistic Records"

Whatever is it,
    that stuff,
that smoke,
    when it goes—
it burns,
    and when the smoke goes,
    the person,
    the one who has come to an end and is finally gone
        goes into the sky as smoke,
he goes like this and like this,
    he is the one,
and they go back and describe it again:
    that one is cloudy,
    and it's windy,
    and it stays in the sky like this;

it's cloudy, like this;

it's windy, and it stays in the sky;

and as for the moon,
the moon is giving instructions,
that's the one,
it goes back like this,
it goes that far in time and it rains,
it goes that far in time and it's cold,
it goes that far in time and it's hot,
it goes that far in time and it's cloudy and shady,
and so,
    it goes along;

that's the tradition,
that's what it must be, they say,
    that's the tradition,
and it comes back like this.

Excerpt from an account of "The Soul"
Quechan, Tom Kelly, 1978
Abraham Halpern, *Kar'úk*

23

The Creation

SERRANO

1963

SARAH MARTIN, NARRATOR

KENNETH C. HILL, COLLECTOR AND TRANSLATOR

INTRODUCTION BY KENNETH C. HILL

Serrano is a Uto-Aztecan language formerly spoken around the San Bernardino Mountains in Southern California. With the advent of the missions, some speakers of this language retreated into the mountains, whence their name, Spanish for "mountaineer." Aboriginally, Serrano may have had around 1,500 speakers (A. Kroeber 1925:617), but at the time of my fieldwork in 1963 and 1964, on the Morongo Indian Reservation at Banning, California, there were only about half a dozen known speakers.

Mrs. Sarah Morongo Martin told me this story when I was working on the Serrano language with her in the summer of 1963. Mrs. Martin had learned this story from her mother, Rosa Morongo, who also told it to Ruth Benedict. Benedict published a version of this story in her "Serrano Tales" (1926).[1] Mrs. Martin had a copy of Benedict's publication, which she used to jog her memory before retelling it to me in Serrano.[2] (It was only many years later that I learned that the reason she felt she had to use the written copy to get her started on a story was probably a cultural constraint: I was working with her in the summer, and stories of this sort are normally supposed to be told only during the winter.)

She begins the story by citing her mother as her source. In this way it is overtly acknowledged that the narrator is not responsible for the content of the story. But then, neither is the person she learned the story from directly responsible: almost every story sentence is marked by a "quotative" modal particle (*kwun* 'it is said'), indicating that the content of the sentence comes not from personal experience, but rather from what someone has said. Except in the narrator's coda, I have represented the quotative force of each sentence either by the use of the English narrative tense (the simple past tense) or by "they say." Sentences that don't use *kwun* are rendered either as English present tenses or as appropriately modalized forms.

At one point in the narrative, the quotative marker is omitted for a couple of sentences. This seems to create a sense of immediacy:

Taaqtam *kwun*u poahu'k.
   Ama' puu-na' ovia uk hoonav.
   Ovia mumu'.
   Ovia-m maahoa'n.
Ama' *kwun* wahi'—
       ya'i.

The people were in a circle, it is said.
   Their father is already lying in the middle.
   He is already dead.
   They are already cremating him.
The coyote, it is said,—
       ran.

In the translation, such lines are set in italics, as a way of conveying this highlighting effect visually.

Mrs. Martin didn't like to translate sentence-by-sentence, but rather one word at a time, and she left it to me to understand the sentence structure. The translation offered here is my own, therefore, and is quite literal, though I have omitted the occasional false start. The division into lines is based on what the narration sounds like on the recording tape, and the indentation pattern is based on my understanding of the meaning of the text.

So that the reader may obtain some notion of the distance that separates an original oral text from its translation, I present the opening lines of the story here, as transcribed directly from the tape of Mrs. Martin telling the story.[3] The translation offered here is somewhat more literal than is the case in the finished translation. False starts are given in italics and do not appear in the finished translation.

Ni-yukchoi'v   a-päävchan   ivi'.
My late mother | her story | this
This [is] my late mother's story.

Hiita'u —/
Something-or-other

Oviht   moto'   *vum/*
Long ago | still | *(?)*

— ivi'   taamiat   kwu'/
this | sun | (?)

ivi'   tiüvaṭ
this | earth

— moto'   namaa'i   ñiaaw;
still | soft | being

kwunumu'   qaṭ   wöh.
QUOT-they-PAST | sit/dwell | two
there were two.

Puu-tuwan —
Their name(s) [were]

Paqöoktach   ami'   Kokiitach.
Paqöoktach | and | Kokiitach.

Kwunu poyo— tom hiiti icho'kin iip tiüvav—
QUOT-they | all | INT | something | make | here | on earth
It is said [that] they made everything here on earth.

Mia tamu' hiiñim— päähavim—
May | they-PAST | something-or-other | supernaturally powerful beings
They must have been powerful beings.

Kwunu icho'kin— poyo tom hiiti.
QUOT-they | make | everything
It is said [that] they made everything.

Wii'wunai-kwunu —
Want-QUOT-they
They wanted, it is said,

Haokp —
[I mean that] one [of them]

ama' Kokiitach kwun wii'wun —
the | Kokiitach | QUOT | want
Kokiitach, it is said, wanted

taaqtam püü-qöi'va',
[that] people | upon their death

puvaipa' ta qöi'v ami' ta— *mii'l*— *ami' tam/*—
if | they | will die | and | they | *(?)* | and | they*(?)*
should they die, when they

qöi'v
will die
might die,

ami(') ta möch mana'qtoi'v,
and | they | will return
they should return again

iingkwa' iingkwa',
to here | to here
this way this way,

ivi' tiüvaika'.
this | to earth
to this earth.

As a final note on the translation, the characters in this story are rendered as "the frog" and "the coyote" rather than as "Frog" and "Coyote" because that is how Mrs. Martin spoke of them in English. Names are rarely used in Serrano stories. Even when individual names are known, characters tend to be referred to as "her older sister," "the boy," "that old woman," and so on.

NOTES

1. Benedict says of the stories she published: "These stories are recorded as told by old Rosa Morongo, who learned them from her father-in-law, chief of the Marina (Morongo) ['Maarunga'—KCH] local group, who died thirty-five years ago" (1926:1).

2. For comparison, here is Benedict's published version of Rosa Morongo's story (1926:1), the version that Sarah Martin referred to to jog her memory before she retold it to me:

THE CREATION

In the beginning was darkness. Then there were two: Pakrokítatc and Kúkitatc. They made the animals. They quarreled, and Pakrokítatc departed, and Kúkitatc lived with his people. Kúkitatc said: "When people die, they shall come back." But the people said, "If they come back, the world will fill up, and there will be no room. We will get rid of Kúkitatc."

They employed a powerful shaman to bewitch Kúkitatc. He watched and saw that Kúkitatc came out every night to defecate in the ocean. Therefore he sent Frog to bite his excrement. Kúkitatc heard that the excrement did not splash as it fell into the water, and he knew that Frog was below. Now he knew he was going to die. He told his people to send Coyote far away to the north for wood to burn his body, and he said, "Immediately, as soon as I am dead, burn my body." He died, and his people lighted the funeral pyre. Coyote had not yet gone far, when he saw the pyre burning, and he knew that Kúkitatc was dead.

The people were standing close together all around the funeral fire, so close nothing could get through, for they were prepared lest Coyote should come back before the body was burned. Coyote ran round and round the circle and could not get in. But at last he saw his chance. Badger was standing bow-legged (as always) and Coyote slipped in between his legs and snatched Kúkitatc's heart before it was burned. He ran away with it and ate it.

(All prayers in the old time were addressed to Kúkitatc.)

3. The letter *u* is used for the high back (or central) unrounded vowel, the "barred i" of most Uto-Aztecan studies; *o* represents the mid-to-high back rounded vowel; the apostrophe is the glottal stop; *ä, ö, ü* are retroflexed ("r-colored") vowels; *ţ* is a *t*- or *ts*-like sound made with the tip of the tongue. Word stress is on the first syllable. The following abbreviations appear in the gloss lines: QUOT, "quotative"; INT, "intensifier."

FURTHER READING

For general information on the Serrano, see Lowell Bean and Charles Smith's entry "Serrano" in the California volume of the Smithsonian *Handbook*. J. P. Harrington collected fieldnotes on the Serrano, which are among his papers in the Smithsonian. Ruth Benedict published some "Serrano Tales" in English translation, as well as "A Brief Sketch of Serrano Culture." Kenneth Hill has written "A Grammar of the Serrano Language" and edited a couple of Serrano tales ("The Coyote and the Flood" and "The Seven Sisters").

THE CREATION

This is my late mother's story . . .

Long ago
   when this earth
  was still soft,
    there were two.   5
Their names
   [were] Paqöoktach and Kokiitach.
They made everything
   here on earth.

They must have been powerful beings. 10
They made everything.

They wanted,
   I mean that one of them, Kokiitach, wanted
      that people, upon their death,
         should they die, 15
         when they might die,
      they should return again
         this way this way,
         to this earth.

"No," said his older brother, 20
   "because if they could return again,
      then you could be crowded here,"
         he said.

Well, they quarreled then,
   and that one went away. 25
That Paqöoktach went away,
   he went away somewhere.

And then his younger brother stayed with his relatives,
      with them,
         with the people. 30
      He stayed there.

He went on creating everything then.
   Then the people got tired of him.
      They didn't like him.
      They were unhappy.* 35

And then they said, "We ought to kill this one."
Then, "Yes,"
      they said.

And then they must have sent the shaman to bewitch him.
   He became ill. 40
   Once he didn't even go to the edge of the water.

* This line is not intonationally separated from the next section.

He went there to relieve himself,
    always.

And so they said, "It looks like we can't do anything with him."
    "Yes, but we can tell the frog.   45
    Maybe he can swallow his excrement,"
        he said then.
    "Yes,"
        he said.

And then, he did go there to relieve himself.   50
And then that frog was there.
And then he swallowed his excrement.

He already knew.
    Kokiitach said, "Now indeed I'm going to die,"
        he said.   55
    "He has already eaten my excrement,"
        he said.
      He went away.
      He lay down at home.
      "I'm already dying,"   60
        he said.

And then he called the people.
And then he told them,
    "I am already dying,
    and you should send that coyote   65
      away to the edge of the earth.
    Over there is a dry stick.
    He [the coyote] should get it.
    You should cremate me with that,"
        he said.   70
    "Because he might do something,"
        he said.

And then they sent the coyote off.
      He went away.
      He ran off.   75
    But he knew.

"Something must have happened,"
   he said.
"My father must have died,"
   he said.   80
      (For that person was their father).
   Then he went.
      He went up on the mountain.

And then he looked back.
      He looked back as he went.   85
      He didn't see anything.

Suddenly he saw smoke.
   "My father has already died,"
      he said.
   He ran, grabbed the stick.   90

And then with it he returned.
   He arrived.
      The people were in a circle.
         Their father is already lying in the middle.
         He is already dead.   95
         They are already cremating him.
      The coyote—
            ran.

And then he said,
   "Let your hands go,   100
      so I can go in!"
         he said.
   "Move aside,
      move aside,
      so I can go in!"   105
         he said.
   Nobody moved.

He was running.
   He kept going around the circle.

The badger was standing there.   110
   His legs were spread far apart.

And then the coyote dived through there.
   He dives through.
   Now his father's heart was still not burning.
   He grabbed it and swallowed it.   115
      With it,
      with it he ran away.

Out of the circle and away he ran.
Up the mountain he climbed.

There this earth being still soft,   120
where he climbed, they say his footprints still show.
      The blood all spilled out from it.
      But he swallowed his father's heart.

Today they say he lives far off,
   far away.   125

"To the Pines" [Big Bear] we say now.
That is where, long ago, they stood in the circle.
      They stood in the circle.
   They say those pines were the people,
      who were standing crying,   130
      who were crying for their father,
         for their father.
   Now they are in our songs, the pine trees, far away at "To the
      Pines."

Long ago, it was different from the way it is now,
   because long ago they changed it.   135
It isn't there any more.
Long ago they cleared it all off.

This is the end.

24

A Harvest of Songs
from Villiana Calac Hyde

LUISEÑO
1988–1992

VILLIANA CALAC HYDE, SINGER AND TRANSLATOR
ERIC ELLIOTT, COLLECTOR

INTRODUCTION BY ERIC ELLIOTT

The following song texts were selected from *Yumáyk Yumáyk* (Hyde and Elliott 1994), a compilation of personal memoirs and historical texts narrated in Luiseño by Villiana Hyde.[1] Luiseño is a member of the Cupan branch of the Takic subfamily of the Uto-Aztecan family of languages. The Uto-Aztecan family includes languages spoken from the American Northwest to Central America. The Cupan languages were all spoken within the boundaries of modern California. Within the Cupan languages, Luiseño is most closely related to the now-extinct Cupeño language.

Born Villiana Calac, Mrs. Villiana Hyde was a native speaker of Luiseño and a proud member of the Luiseño community at the Rincón Reservation of San Diego County. In Luiseño orthography the name "Calac" is spelled "Qáálaq" and literally means '(the earth) caves in'. In complete contrast to the literal meaning of the family name, the Calac family has a long history of never "caving in," but rather of standing tall and providing the community and the world beyond with prominent leaders.

True to the Calac family tradition of serving the community, Mrs. Hyde found her niche early on as historian and linguist. Forbidden to speak Luiseño at Sherman Indian School in Riverside, California, Mrs. Hyde became painfully aware at a young age that her language and culture were in peril. As a young woman she gained an acute understanding of what it means for a language and culture to die. Mrs. Hyde's own mother-in-law was a native speaker of Cupeño, Luiseño's closest geographic and linguistic neighbor. The Cupeño people, including Mrs. Hyde's mother-in-law, had been forcibly evicted from their home at Warner Springs. Mrs. Hyde watched as her mother-in-law, now living among Diegueño and Luiseño speakers, saw her language and culture fade into extinction as the few remaining Cupeño speakers passed away around her.

Mrs. Hyde thus had a clear understanding of the ominous task of preserving her language and culture for future generations. Her formal career as a linguist began in the 1960s, when she first collaborated with Professors Margaret Langdon and Ronald Langacker of the Department of Linguistics at the University of California, San Diego (UCSD). This work eventually culminated in the publication of Mrs. Hyde's first book, *An Introduction to the Luiseño Language* (1971). Among those who collaborated with Mrs. Hyde on the *Introduction* were Langacker and the linguists Pamela Munro and Susan Steele, all of whom have continued their linguistic research on Luiseño language to the present day.

As an undergraduate student at the University of California, Irvine, I had the good fortune to stumble onto Mrs. Hyde's *Introduction to the Luiseño Language.* Long fascinated by the indigenous languages of California, I also happened to sign up for a class on Amerindian languages offered by Professor Mary Key, a linguist who had spent decades working on various American Indian languages of Mexico and South America. Professor Key encouraged my interest in Native American languages, opening up her office and personal linguistic library to me. When I showed up with Mrs. Hyde's *Introduction,* Professor Key further encouraged me to contact Mrs. Hyde and Professor Margaret Langdon of the Department of Linguistics at UCSD.

At the time, Mrs. Hyde's telephone number was listed in the directory. I simply called up directory assistance, got her number, telephoned Mrs. Hyde, and asked her whether she would teach me more about her language. Mrs. Hyde graciously agreed. Armed only with the *Introduction*, my tape recorder, and William Bright's *Luiseño Dictionary*, I drove to Mrs. Hyde's house. Our technique was simple. I would ask Mrs. Hyde about a particular subject of interest. She would tell me details on tape in Luiseño. I would take the tape home, transcribe the Luiseño, analyze it morphologically, translate it into English as best I could, and bring the work back to Mrs. Hyde for editing. At first, the work was painstakingly slow. Mrs. Hyde, who opened up her home to me most Saturdays, thought nothing of working from nine o'clock in the morning until as late as five o'clock at night.

Mrs. Hyde and I ended up collaborating for more than eight years. Our work has thus far yielded *Yumáyk Yumáyk* ('long, long ago'), and we also have a dictionary and grammar in the making. Mrs. Hyde passed away in 1994, several weeks before *Yumáyk Yumáyk* was published. Mrs. Hyde was a good friend to me. She was also an ideal linguistic consultant. With her passing I lost a friend and also the possibility of further data collection or further clarification of material already gathered. The following excerpts from *Yumáyk Yumáyk* are therefore presented raw, as they appeared in the original—that is, with no further interpretation or explanation on my part. Mrs. Hyde provided explanations where she felt them necessary in *Yumáyk Yumáyk*. As with any culture's history, or as with any individual's own life story, there will always be facets of that history that are more readily comprehensible to outsiders, and other aspects that are less transparent. In order to fully understand the culture of a given community or individual, one has to be a member of that culture. I am not a member of the Luiseño-speaking culture presented in *Yumáyk Yumáyk,* a culture where speaking Luiseño and having one's gallstones removed by a shaman (Hyde and Elliott 1994:175–84) were as natural to Mrs. Hyde as speaking English and going to the dentist for a filling is to me. Yet, the more one reads of Mrs. Hyde's life and times, the better picture one forms of her culture, which really did exist not so long ago. It is my hope that these selections will provide readers with a glimpse of the grace and beauty of the language and culture that Mrs. Hyde worked so hard to document.

NOTE

1. Song numbers here refer to text numbers in Hyde and Elliott's *Yumáyk Yumáyk* (1994). For the sake of reference, they have not been renumbered for this volume. The titles of songs given in Luiseño, in the absence of an explanatory phrase at the beginning, may be translated with reference to the first line of the song itself.—HWL

FURTHER READING

For a general orientation to Luiseño culture and history, see Lowell Bean and Florence Shipek's article "Luiseño" in the California volume of the Smithsonian *Handbook*. William Bright has written *A Luiseño Dictionary*. Helen Roberts's *Form in Primitive Music* contains numerous Luiseño songs collected in the 1930s. Villiana Hyde produced *An Introduction to the Luiseño Language*. Lastly, Hyde and Elliott's *Yumáyk Yumáyk (Long Ago)* contains hundreds of Villiana Hyde's stories, songs, and reminiscences, in interlinear text format.

A HARVEST OF SONGS FROM VILLIANA CALAC HYDE

BADGER SONG (#138)

These are the ones who looked down
These are the ones who peered down

The badger and the vulture, long ago
These ones [are] the vulture . . .

Look at his stained hand with a ring around it
Look at his speckled hand

These are the ones who looked down
These are the ones who peered down

I speak of my [own] spirit
I try to speak of my heart

I try to speak of my spirit
I try to speak of my heart

"They too looked down. And that's why they look that way. That badger saw, he looked down." *

KÁÁMALA SONG (#145)

Child, *ʔáskat's* song:
The ones inside her rolled and moved
The ones in her chest,
   the ones in her chest rolled and moved
The ones inside her,
   their beloved sons, rolled and moved

TEMÉÉNGANISH SONG (#149)

THE DAWN SONG†

I speak of the East
I speak of the East
I tell my story, of how I was dying
In the first little month called *Táwsanmaytal*

The *chuyúkmal* star, the *kayá'mal* star
Made growling sounds
They opened their mouths when I was dying
In the first little month called *Táwsanmaytal*

The bullfrog and the angleworm . . .

I speak of the Antares star of the East

---

* These explanations were provided by Mrs. Hyde and are not part of the song itself. The remaining lines of the song are apparently lost.

† "They would sing this song toward dawn," Mrs. Hyde explained. (The star names *chuyúkmal* and *kayá'mal* may refer to animals. The Vulture Star is Arcturus.)

I speak of the Vulture star of the East
I tell my story of the East
I tell my story of the East

LULLABY IN IMITATION OF A CRICKET CHIRPING (#153)

THE CRICKET'S SONG

The oak trees are standing there
The oak trees are standing there
In the house, in the house, in the house

PÍ'MUKVOL SONG (#162)

DEATH SONG*

1

The *mááxwala* hawk, the *wasíímal* hawk
They left speaking of their spirits, of their hearts
They left singing of their spirits, of their hearts

2

The *qáwqaw* bird, the kingbird and the *wasíímal* hawk
They left speaking of their spirits, of their hearts

PA'LÁÁKWISH SONG (#165)

THE PA'LÁÁKWISH BIRD'S SONG

My nephew, get your arrow
To shoot and kill someone

CHALÁÁWAAT SONG (#167)

THE CHALÁÁWAAT ("STANDING UP") DANCE

I suppose I've survived the first little month
I suppose I've survived the first big month

* The song has two parts, as numbered.

Oh, I am surviving through the days
I am surviving through the days

PIWÍÍSH SONG (#170)

THE MILKY WAY SONG (SECOND PART)*

It keeps waking me up
It keeps waking me up
It makes me spark
My rattle, my turtleshell rattle
My rattle keeps me awake

QAXÁÁL QAXÁÁWUT SONG (#171)

The valley quail and the mountain quail singed their hair†
They cut off their hair, with tears and lamentations
They singed their hair
The mountain quail singed off his hair
The mountain quail singed off his hair
They cut off their hair, with tears and lamentations

The flicker bird and the roadrunner
They cut off their hair, with tears and lamentations
They singed their hair
The flicker bird singed off his hair
The roadrunner singed off his hair
They cut off their hair, with tears and lamentations

PÍ' TÓÓWISH HULÚYKA SONG (#174)

And the spirit landed
And the little dove landed

---

* The phrase *makes me spark* is a poetic idiom meaning "keeps me awake." The word *rattle* at the
   beginning of lines 3 and 4 translates literally as "my little fire."
† This is not the whole of the "Qaxáál Qaxááwut" song. The two stanzas presented here represent
   two separate parts of the song. Neither part begins the complete song, but they are not necessarily sequential either.

And it stopped to warn
And so it wandered around to warn

And the coyote landed
And it stopped to warn
And so it wandered around to warn

The owl landed
And the fox landed
And it stopped to warn
And so it wandered around to warn

The screech owl landed
And the *péépimal* bird landed
And it stopped to warn
And so it wandered around to warn

The *páátapi* duck landed
And the *nóóchaqi* duck landed
And it stopped to warn
And so it wandered around to warn

The *pááwnat* bird landed
And the killdeer bird landed
And it stopped to warn
And so it wandered around to warn

TÓÓWISH MIXÉÉL SONG (#178)

The spirit, the dove
This spirit [cried] over me
This dove [cried] over me
And so it cried over our future death
Over my future death
Over my future disappearance
Over my future disappearance
The fox [cried] over me . . .

WUNÁL PÍ' TUMÁMKAWISH SONG (#181)

There was an earthquake in the north
Our future death rumbled
My storehouse was shaken up
Our hearts rumbled
Our future death rumbled
My darkness was shaken
My darkness was shaken
Our future death rumbled

There was an earthquake in the north
Our future death rumbled
My storehouse was shaken up
Our hearts rumbled
Our future death rumbled
My darkness was shaken
My darkness was shaken
Our future death rumbled

[*Singer begins dancing*]

Our future death rumbled
My storehouse was shaken up
Our house rumbled
My darkness was shaken
My darkness was shaken
Our house rumbled

SECOND KÁÁMALA SONG (#182)

THE CHILD SONG

The dust from the area around Pááyaxchi
Billowed up from their feet as they walked along
And erred along the way

CHALÁWYAX MILA MÓÓTA SONG (#190)

The gopher danced the *chaláwyax**
The meadow mouse danced
They danced the *chaláwyax* and the *yúngish*
After their father
They danced when their father died
They danced all night
They danced, *héé, héé,* amen . . .

---

* The *chaláwyax* and *yúngish* are dances. The gopher and meadow mouse's father is Móyla Wuyóót (the Moon). The vocables *héé héé* at the end of the song work in much the same way that the word *amen* does—by "sending the song to heaven."

25

From "The Life of Hawk Feather"
The Bear Episodes

CUPEÑO
1962, 1920

ROSCINDA NOLASQUEZ AND SALVADORA VALENZUELA,
NARRATORS
JANE HILL AND PAUL-LOUIS FAYE, COLLECTORS
JANE HILL, TRANSLATOR

INTRODUCTION BY JANE HILL

The "Bear Episode" is one part of a longer account of the life of Hawk
Feather, the greatest hero in Cupeño history. Roscinda Nolasquez told
me two parts of the "Bear Episode" when she was teaching me the Cupeño language during the summer of 1962. In 1920 Paul-Louis Faye collected several events from this episode in a single text. The teller was probably Salvadora Valenzuela, because, among the texts where Faye bothers
to note his consultants' names, she is consistently listed as the teller of the
longer and more elaborate stories. Salvadora Valenzuela comes from a lineage of storytellers and authorities on Cupeño culture; her mother, Mrs.
Manuela Griffith, was a principal consultant for William Duncan Strong.
Miss Nolasquez had known Mrs. Valenzuela and considered her to be a
particularly skilled narrator of Cupeño history. The 1920 text has some

elements that Miss Nolasquez's two later tellings lack, but hers includes some details that are absent in the text that Faye recorded. This publication gives us an opportunity to put the two parts of the Bear Episode together. In addition to bringing together versions by two narrators, we have inserted into the story the texts of the songs that a teller would have sung in a formal winter recitation. Faye apparently recorded the song texts separately from the story (and left us no musical notation for them), but on the story text itself, in Faye's fieldnotes, there are instructions about where the songs should be. I have placed them there, writing them in italics.

The story of Hawk Feather is in the genre that Cupeños refer to with the verb root *a'alxi* 'telling history'. Histories tell us how the world has come to be the way that it is today. The story of Hawk Feather is only one part of a longer history that begins in the creation of the world and continues into the present day. An important new history in the *a'alxi* genre includes stories about the removal of the Cupeño in 1902 from their ancestral communities at Pal Atingve 'Hot Springs' (which included the villages of Kupa 'Fire Place' and Wilakalpa 'Buckwheat Place'), known to non-Indians as Warner's Hot Springs.

Hawk Feather is born into chaos, as enemy warriors (Strong [1929] says that they were Diegueños) attack and burn the village of Kupa. His mother flees with her baby to live with relatives at Soboba, called Yuykat. The boy grows into a great hunter. But, perhaps because they are jealous of his accomplishments, people do not like him, and he hunts alone. It is in the Bear Episode that his special powers are first manifested, when he blows up the skin of the dead bear and brings it to life. In Salvadora Valenzuela's telling of how he did this, she says,

> He carried the hide to the brush.
> He gathered the softest grass that he could find.
> He stuffed the hide.
> He sewed up the hide into the shape of a body.
> And then he blew it up.
> And then it breathed.
> And he tied it with cords,
>   for it was trying to run away.

Miss Nolasquez's segment of the narrative ends in the touching moment when Hawk Feather begs his mother not to be afraid of him. At this point in the story, we switch narrators, turning to Salvadora Valenzuela's telling from 1920. We pick up her story when the hero and his mother set forth with the bear to kill their enemies, traveling across a countryside punctuated with place-names that record the moments in their quest. But when they reach Kupa, the bear is killed by the terrified people. They manage to take away from him the magic stone that was his "heart" (according to Paul-Louis Faye's notes), and the women come and "cut his beads" from the carcass. The 1920 text (as well as the present version) ends there.

In her second set of episodes from the life of Hawk Feather, Miss Nolasquez narrates Hawk Feather's maturity—events in his life that occurred after the death of the magic bear. He takes two wives. They bear three sons, who are the founders of the three Cupeño lineages. Hawk Feather continues to exhibit magical powers: his dances control whether oak trees will bear the acorns that were the staple of the Cupeño diet.

One of the most delightful moments in Miss Nolasquez's part of the Bear Episode shows her special gift for sparkling narrative. This is the section where the hero tries to figure out who might be stealing his caches of meat. Miss Nolasquez seizes the opportunity to poke fun at Coyote, through the voice of the hero's mother. (Roscinda Nolasquez knew innumerable Coyote stories and took great pleasure in the humor in these texts.) Thus lines 48–54 of her story go like this in Cupeño:

> Muku'ut aye peye peyik peyaqal,
>   "Ishmi'ishep ne'ey ni'ituqa,"
>   peyaqal ku'ut.
>   "Ivi'aw ham iyaxwe,"
>   peyaqal ku'ut.
> Pi'isniqal pexuchi.
>   "ISILYshepe"
>   peyaqal ku'ut peye.
>   "Isilyem pe' EYet!
>   Meshepe isilya i'ITU'qa!"
>   peyaqal ku'ut.

> And then they say he said to his mother,
>   "Something must be stealing from me,"
>   they say he said.
>   "Here is how it looks,"

    they say he said.
He draws the outline of a footprint.
    "It MUST be a COYOTE!"
        they say his mother said.
    "Coyote is SUCH a THIEF!
    It must be Coyote who is STEALING from you!"
        they say she said.

One interesting feature of Cupeño historical texts that we can see in this passage is that all narrative sentences (excepting those in quoted speech) contain the quotative particle *ku'ut* 'they say'. Here, I have translated all the quotatives, so that their frequency is obvious. In the main translation, only a few of these remain, but in Cupeño every sentence in a history is marked with this particle, reiterating again and again and again the authoritative force of the story and the teller's humility before tradition.

Another striking feature of Roscinda Nolasquez's storytelling style in part 1 is the exaggerated emphasis, with loud, drawn-out syllables (marked in the text in capital letters) that she gives to the speech of the mother as she diagnoses the footprint: *ISILYshepe* 'COYOTE must be him!', *pe'EYet* 'He is SUCH a THIEF!', *i'iTU'qa* 'He is STEALING from you!' This way of telling the story must have made audiences laugh out loud, thinking of all the times Coyote has foolishly stolen something that turned out to do him no good. The solemnity of history, thus punctuated with a good joke, is rendered delightful, and the serious privileges of humor are equally revealed.

There are any number of interesting problems in interpreting this story. One of them is why Miss Nolasquez finished her telling at the moment when Hawk Feather reassures his mother that she need not be afraid of him. Some are internal to the story; others are external to it, pointing to the interpersonal context of the recording session itself. Miss Nolasquez's story really centers around Hawk Feather's relationship with his mother. Miss Nolasquez herself had a very close relationship with her son and with her grandchildren. Indeed, Miss Nolasquez was known to everyone at Pala as "Grandma" Nolasquez. Furthermore, there was every reason for her to think about motherhood when she worked with me, because in August 1962 I was seven months pregnant with my first child. (The next summer, Eric went with me in his portable crib as a not-so-silent listener to Miss Nolasquez's teaching.) Finally, because I hardly knew any Cupeño, most of the stories Miss Nolasquez helped me with that summer were simple stories appropriate to children. The part of the Hawk Feather episode that she told is, in fact, excellent entertainment, with magic and humor. No enemies are killed in it—instead, Hawk Feather tricks them into using up all their arrows, which he adds to his own arsenal. However, the story grows darker when Hawk Feather, his mother, and the pet bear set out toward Kupa, slaughtering their enemies along the way. The death of the pet bear at the hands of the enemies who remained in Kupa is an especially sad moment in the history. This part of the episode might be frightening and confusing to little children, or inappropriate to an atmosphere of grandmotherly nurturing, as opposed to the solemn world-renewing ritual context of the winter tellings. Thus Miss Nolasquez's version of the Bear Episode suggests how she could use the story as a flexible resource, drawing from it for entertainment and for moral contemplation as a part of everyday life.

Another problem involves Hawk Feather's name. Miss Nolasquez used the name Kisily Pewik 'Hawk His-Wing/Plume' for this hero. Paul-Louis Faye's 1920 version calls him Kisily Pewish 'Hawk His-Down', and this is also the name recorded by Strong. The problem is, Miss Nolasquez had the latter word only in the meaning 'feces'. Apparently in her speech two ancient Uto-Aztecan words had merged in pronunciation. The first, listed by Wick Miller (1967) as Proto-Uto-Aztecan, is **pi 'feather' (probably it was **pi'wi:, with Cupeño retaining only the second syllable). The second word is listed as **kwita 'to defecate'; its etymological reflexes often mean 'feces' (in Cupeño, the sound **kw appears as /w/, and **t as /sh/, yielding wish). This ambiguity gave Roscinda Nolasquez's son, Robert Lovato, the opportunity to tease me with a naughty bilingual pun—that the hero's name was really Kisily Pewish, or "Hawk His-Number Two"! For this translation, I have decided in favor of Kisily Pewik—that is, Hawk Feather rather than Hawk Down (or worse).

The monolingual format of this volume requires a final note or two on the translation. I wish that the text did not have to be translated at all; I wish that it were being told, every winter, in community gatherings, and being quoted with pleasure, and that its songs were being hummed, by speakers of the language. I hate having to put it in English, so my translation is in a way an act of resistance to my own language; it is as literal as possible, consistent with the joy and dignity of the original. I have left in as many quotatives as I could get away with, because I think that their drumbeat rhythm is part of the power of this history.

And about the lines. The division of the text into lines partly reflects the way that Roscinda Nolasquez divided her recitation into what linguists call "breath groups" or "intonation units"; that is, it reflects her pattern of slowing down, and speeding up, and pausing. For the 1920 text, I have simply guessed about this, based on my experience with Miss Nolasquez's speech. The line divisions also serve to open the text up and make it more readable—they represent the flow and phrasings of ordinary speech. However, they do not reflect the sort of rhythmic performance—Hymes's "measured verse"—that is found in some Native American languages, especially in the Pacific Northwest. This is, in my opinion, prose, not verse, and the narrative sentences are very different from those in songs.

FURTHER READING

Versions of the story of Hawk Feather are also found in William Strong's *Aboriginal Society in Southern California* (1929:270) and in Edward Gifford's "Clans and Moieties in Southern California" (1918:199). Alfred Kroeber briefly notes the story in *The Handbook of the Indians of California* (1925:692). Both Roscinda Nolasquez's two tellings and the 1920 version collected by Faye appear in Jane Hill and Nolasquez's *Mulu'wetam*, which also includes a brief grammatical sketch and vocabulary of Cupeño.

FROM "THE LIFE OF HAWK FEATHER": THE BEAR EPISODE, PART 1

ROSCINDA NOLASQUEZ, 1962

One young man, it is said, lived there,
    and he was always hunting.

He would go to the mountains,
and he would always kill deer,
and he would bring the carcass to his mother. 5
His mother never wanted to eat,
for of course it was not proper for a woman to eat such deer.
    "Take it to the chief in the Big House,"
        she would say;
    "To the chief's house." 10
And he would take it there,
to the chief's house,
for the people to eat the deer.
And he would gather his relatives together,
and they would all eat that deer. 15
But not his mother.
For if a person kills a deer, then he should not eat it.
And his mother never wanted to eat,
since her son was the one who had killed it.
And he would go off again. 20

He would go off, it is said, to a certain place,
    going looking here and there,
    and he would always kill something, a rat, or a rabbit,
    and he would take it off to his mother.
But she did not eat. 25
    "To the other place, to the Big House,"
        she would say;
    "They will eat it there."
And it is said that the people really did dine there,
    they ate what he had killed. 30
And then he would go out again.

He used to go hunting, it is said, at a certain place,
    and he would kill a deer,
    and he would leave it there.
And ALways, when he returned again in the morning, 35
his cache would be gone,
for something was always stealing it.
And the man said,

"I wonder who is stealing from me?"
    he would say.   40
And he would go off again.

It is said he would kill some rats somewhere,
  and bring them from there to his mother.
  But when he came around,
    "To the Big House," she would say.   45
  And he would take it there,
    even if it was only one thing.
  But he said to his mother,
    "Something must be stealing from me," he said.
    "Here is how it looks," he said.   50
  He draws the outline of a footprint.
    "It MUST be a COYOTE!" said his mother.
    "Coyote is such a THIEF.
    It must be Coyote who is STEALING from you," she said.
  And he went off again.   55

And it is said then he arrived again at that same place,
  and again he saw a footprint there.
  That footprint was huge!
  And he said to his mother,
    "Something is obviously coming around.   60
    I saw the track there," he said.
    "You'll catch it," she said,
    "in a trap," she said.
    "Here is how wide the foot is," he said.
  And his mother said,   65
    "It must be a BEAR!" she said.
  And he went off again.

Now, his mother, it is said, always stayed behind when he went
  hunting.
  And he killed that bear,
  and then he carried it back.   70
  It was a really big bear.
  But he carried it back from there,
  and he brought it to his mother.

And his mother said,
    "To the chief's house," she said,   75
    "I cannot eat this, for this is a human being," she said.

And then, it is said, he skinned it, the man skinned the bear.
    He took it ALL out,
        all of that flesh,
    and he prepared the hide.   80
    And he BLEW it up,
    he BLEW it up,
    until he made it really ENORMOUS.
    And his mother was there,
    and she was watching   85
        while he made the body of the bear.
    And then he played with it there.
    It was just like a dog;
    it was playing,
    it was jumping around.   90

And it is said his mother went off to tell the other people.
    On the way she crossed a stream,
    and she scratched up her feet,
    with all the sticks, so many,
    where she crossed several times from this side to that.   95
    So her feet were completely scratched up.
    And still she kept going;
    she was looking back.
    She got home, and she said,
        "He is definitely over there," she said,   100
        "the Bear.
        He is just like a dog.
        The two of them are playing," she said.
    And so many people set off.

It is said they readied their bows and arrows.   105
    And they went off.
    And there he was, under a shelter.
    And from under there, a paw REACHED out.

And then it disappeared again.
And it came out—   110
it was the body of the bear.
And then it disappeared again.
And then the people shot at him,
their arrows flew everywhere.
Underneath the shelter he would duck,   115
he would turn into something different,
he would come out again,
and again they shot.
Back under the shelter he goes!
Then their arrows were used up,   120
    from all their shooting.
And then they went away.
And they said,
    "It is impossible for us to kill him," they said.
And then he came out.   125
He gathered up ALL those arrows.
And he piled them up.

Arrows in piles
You went looking around
You went crawling around   130
You went touching the ground
You were weak
That is all

And then, it is said, his mother came.
    And he said,
        "Where did you go?" said the son.   135
    And his mother said,
        "I went over there to the foot of the mountain."
        "You must have washed your feet.
        You got your feet all scratched up," he said.   140
        "My feet did get wet there," she said.
    And then she kept standing there,
        she kept standing there.
    His mother was afraid of that bear.
    And her son said,   145

"Don't be afraid," he said to his mother.
"It was only me," they say he said.

FROM "THE LIFE OF HAWK FEATHER": THE BEAR EPISODE, PART 2

SALVADORA VALENZUELA, 1920

And then, it is said, when the sun rose,
   all of those many warriors came again.
   Again they called him, and he came out as an old man.
   In the same way now they shot at him,
   but they could not hit him,   5
   since he would duck back under the shelter.
      "Mother," he said,
      "Now I am going to come out in the shape of a baby,
      and they're going to see me, and they're going to shoot
         at me,
      and all of them are going to grab at me.   10
      And I will come back in here,
      and you and my pet bear will come out.
      They have no arrows left.
      They are going to go away,
      they are going to say that they will come again tomorrow.   15
      And now I will say that I will show them my pet."
And then they said,
      "You won't show us your pet bear."
      "Now you will see it,
      and now you will kill me as I come out to you."   20
      "No," they said,
      "we will do it tomorrow."
And they say that he said to his mother,
      "Now we are going to chase them."
And he gave her his club.   25
And he said to his mother,
      "This pet of mine will come out of the bushes at them,

and I will shoot them from atop a level place,
    and you will hit them about the ears, breaking their jaws."

And then, it is said, they chased them, he and his mother,   30
    they caught up with them,
    he shot them,
    he killed them.
    When they tried to escape into the bushes,
    the bear then came out at them,   35
    reaching out his arms to them.
    The bear killed them,
    while the man came along shooting them
    while his mother came along clubbing them about the ears.

Halayla! Hahahalayla!   40
The bear, his paws!
Halayla! Hahalayla!
The bear, his paws!

One enemy would run to the south,
    another, in the same way, to the west,   45
    but it was no use,
    they could not pass.
    Now two of them appeared,
    and the man chased those two.
    He caught up with them,   50
    he grabbed them,
    and he dashed them repeatedly against a White Oak.
    And they say that he said,
        "You will all go and tell one another,
        so the name of this place will be   55
            'Where He Dashed Them against the White Oak,'
        and you will tell about me, how I finished them off."
    And they went away to tell.

And then, it is said, he and his mother returned to their victims,
    in order to scalp their heads.   60
    And they packed the scalps into their carrying net,
    to take them to their shelter,

to take them there.
And he said,
    "Mother, tomorrow I think that we will go home
        to Kupa." 65
In the morning they left, he and his mother,
carrying their burdens on tumplines.
And at a certain place he adjusted his burden.
And they say that he said,
    "This place will be called 'Where He Adjusted His
        Burden'; 70
    its name will be thus."
And they went on.
And then at a certain place he was climbing,
and he caught his breath.
    "This place will be called, 'Where He Caught His Breath.'" 75
And they went on.
And at a certain place he stopped to eat.
And they say that he said,
    "'Meal Place' is its name."
And then they went on from there. 80
And then they came to Mekwashma,
and because of him its name is 'Flea Place.'

And then, it is said, while they rested there at Mekwashma,
    he turned his pet bear loose.
    And the bear killed women, and men, and children, 85
    those who remained of his enemies.
    And at Kelelva, the bear would come out in the morning,
    to graze in the meadow grass.
    And there also he killed those who remained.
    And so the old women went to the chief of the Teshvekinga
        Clan. 90
    They said to him,
        "You men must do something for us,
        you should kill that bear for us,
        for he has almost finished us off.
        When the sun rises, that is when he appears." 95

And it is said that there is a place where there are rocks on each
   side.
   And the men set off.
   One sat on this side, on top of one of the rocks.
   And another did the same on the other.
   And then the bear appeared.   100
   And they tried to shoot him.
   And he caught their arrows,
      he broke them in half.
   And then the bear shook his head.
   And a stone fell from the back of his neck.   105
   And he swallowed it.
   And then those men went away, for their arrows were
      exhausted.
      "Tomorrow, we will come again."

It is said that again, in the morning, they came.
   The ones on the rocks kept watch.   110
   And one of them said to the other,
      "Now I will tell you what he is carrying on the back of his
         neck.
      And you will shoot at it first; you are to shoot.
      And I will jump down from here,
      and I will knock that thing far away,   115
      so that he cannot swallow it,
      and when he tries to grab it,
      we will shoot him from both sides."

And then, it is said, the bear appeared.
   The man did as he was told,   120
   he shot him.
   The bear shook himself as before.
   And the man on top of the rocks jumped down,
   and knocked the stone away.
   They shot at the bear,   125
   they killed him.
   And they skinned him,
   and the place is named 'Bear-skinning Place.'
   And when the bear lay dead,

those old women came.   130
And the bear was cut,
they cut loose the bear's beads.
    "He was going to eat us, he was going to catch us."

The bear's beads
They were cut   135
They were cut loose
"He is going to eat us"
"He is going to take us"

26

In the Desert with Hipahipa

MOJAVE
1902

INYO-KUTAVÊRE, NARRATOR

JACK JONES, INTERPRETER

A. L. KROEBER, COLLECTOR

INTRODUCTION BY A. L. KROEBER

[The text that follows is an excerpt from a much, much longer (yet still incomplete) Mojave migration epic collected by A. L. Kroeber in 1902. The portion reproduced here, "In the Desert with Hipahipa," is the ninth of eighteen sections distinguished by Kroeber.[1] The introduction is taken, with a few emendations and reductions, from Kroeber's own general introduction to the study as a whole. The orthographic conventions used for writing Mojave words and names have changed since Kroeber's time (as indeed has the spelling of "Mohave" itself, Mojave being the preferred form today). However, I have chosen not to modernize Kroeber's spelling system in the present selection, not only because they are appropriate to the era of collection (1902), but to avoid confusion for readers who may consult the remainder of this fascinating epic. Readers—particularly those who take the trouble to consult the original publication—may find that some of Kroeber's comments and evaluations of the text as a work of oral history seem unnecessarily dismissive. We must keep in mind, though, that he has come to his conclusions on the basis of quite exhaustive investigations into the substantive historical content of this and other versions of the narrative. Even so, I think that scholars today would be far less likely to dismiss the oral-historical basis of documents such as this one, seeking instead to understand better the nature of the interaction between dreaming and traditional knowledge.—HWL]

Circumstances and Nature of the Tale

The story of the recording of this tale is this.

In a previous visit to the Mohave I had learned of their male-lineage clans or *simulye,* known each by the name which all the women born in the clan shared, these names in turn having totemic reference or connotation, though in most of the names no etymologic denotation of the totemic animal or object was apparent. There is no evidence that these clans functioned other than as regards coresidence and exogamy: they had no ritual associations. Settlements normally consisted of kinsmen in the male line, and thereby of men of the same clan; but there were said to be usually several places thus "belonging" to each clan, especially if it was large. I found it difficult to engage Mohave interest in reciting to me a list of such clan localizations: the *simulye* were now "all mixed up," they said, compared with old times. When I said it was the old times that I wanted to know about, the answer was, that how it was with the clans in the old days, how they came to be, was known only to certain old men who had dreamed about that and about the traveling and fighting of the Mohave. *Itš-kanavk* 'great-telling' was the name of that kind of story; people who had not dreamed that—that is, did not specialize in it— would know nothing of moment about it.

Several old men were mentioned as informants; but a train of ill luck accompanied my endeavors to secure from any one of them the full version of what he knew. The well-informed on the subject, or at any rate those generally reputed well-informed, were evidently all of an advanced age that made their mortality high in the first decade of this century. As this clan or migration legend also was not associated with a cycle which would be sung at festivals or funerals, the series of men inclined to "dream" it—to hear, learn, and refantasy it—would be pretty thoroughly and suddenly cut off when the remodeling of Mohave life by American contacts had reached a certain point. To men who had worked, however intermittently, on railway maintenance of way, in the locomotive roundhouse or in the ice plant, a legend about ancient migrations of bands that lived off the land must have seemed irrelevant and fairly pointless, and even more so to the prospective all-night audiences whose interest would provide much of the stimulus for dreaming up the tale. By contrast, singing has an appeal in itself, reinforced for the Mohave by the emotional associations of their custom of singing their cycles as a gift at impending deaths of kinsmen. Around 1903, accordingly, song-cycle myths were still being learned and dreamed by individual Mohaves; but I now suspect that no one had then learned and reelaborated a version of the migration legend in several decades. If this is a fact, it was the very last of the crop of aged migration dreamers that I encountered at Needles about 1900 to 1905.

However, in March 1902, my customary guide and interpreter, Jack Jones, took me across the river from Needles and some two or three miles inland, more or less to the settlement Ah'a-kwinyevai, . . . [on the] eastern side of Mohave Valley. I was purchasing ethnographical specimens on the way. At Ah'a-kwinyevai, in a sand-covered Mohave house, we found the old man whom we had come to see, Inyo-kutavêre 'Vanished-pursue', who was reputed to know about the origin of clans. He admitted that he did, and would tell me the story. It would take a day, he said when I asked the length. As that day was partly gone, I arranged to come back in the morning.

Of course he did not realize that it would take Jack about as long to English to me his telling in Mohave as that took him, and I overlooked the fact, or had long since learned not to be too concerned about inaccuracy of time estimates by natives. However, he went on for six days, each of three to four hours' total narration by him and as many of translation by Jack and writing by me.[2] Each evening he believed, I think honestly, that one more day would bring him to the end. He freely admitted, when I asked him, that he had never told the story through from beginning to end. He had a number of times told parts of it at night to Mohave audiences, until the last of them dropped off to sleep. When our sixth day ended, he still, or again, said that a day would see us through. But by then I was overdue at Berkeley; and as the prospective day might once more have stretched into several, I reluctantly broke off, promising him, and myself, that I would return to Needles when I could, not later than next winter, to conclude recording the tale.

By next winter Inyo-kutavêre had died, and his tale thus remains unfinished, though its central theme, the final conquest of Mohave Valley and the taking of lands by the clan leaders, is completed. I made efforts to find other old men who might continue where Inyo-kutavêre had left off. I came to realize soon afterward that no Mohave could "continue" the narration of another.[3] The versions differ too much through being after all individually refantasied, as I would construe the core to be of

FIGURE 11. Jack Jones.
Courtesy Phoebe Apperson Hearst Museum of Anthropology
and the Regents of the University of California.

what the Mohave mean by "dreaming." With a different informant it
would have been necessary to get a new version of the entire tale; only
in that sense could Inyo-kutavêre's tale have been "finished" by another.
However, I was given the names of two surviving old men who might
furnish a completion; and in the spring of 1903, and again of 1904, I re-

turned to Needles to look them up: only to find that one of them was speechless from a paralytic stroke. The other, I wrote on April 15, 1904, to my chief, F. W. Putnam, I had as yet been unable to go to see because he lived too far from the telegraph office at Needles, to which I was then tied by an expected message. I do not recall now why I was unable to connect with him later; and before long he too died.

In 1908 I was again at Needles. The Mohave seemed to think that their recognized dreamers of the clan migration were all gone. But meeting an old man called Kunalye, I asked him whether he knew anything of Hipahipa, the greatest hero in Inyo-kutavêre's version. He affirmed that Hipahipa was the name of a Kutkilye clan band living in Mohave Valley in ancient times, and proceeded to tell me their story on March 1. I returned to him on March 3 for another installment, in which as yet the warfare that was to be the central theme of the plot was only being threatened. The old man then became ill. I had to discontinue, and so another attempt remained fragmentary. . . . For the time spent in its recording, its text is proportionally briefer than Inyo-kutavêre's telling, owing probably in part to my having as interpreter Leslie Wilbur, younger and less accustomed to me and the work than Jack Jones was.

To return to Inyo-kutavêre. He was stone blind. He was below the average of Mohave tallness, slight in figure, spare, almost frail with age. His gray hair was long and unkempt, his features were sharp, delicate, [and] sensitive. . . . He sat indoors, on the loose sand floor of his house, for the whole of the six days I was with him, in the frequent posture of Mohave men, his feet beneath him or behind him to the side, not with legs crossed. He sat still whether reciting or awaiting his turn, but drank in all the Sweet Caporal cigarettes I provided. His housemates sat about and listened, or went and came as they had things to do.

The tale is discussed in detail in parts 4, 5, and 6 [of Kroeber 1951]. A few of its more salient qualities are mentioned here now by way of preliminary orientation.

Like almost all elder Mohave, the narrator asserted he had dreamed his narrative, had seen it. . . .

The story is wholly without songs.

It has "historical" appearance in that it might have actually happened almost as told. There is no magic or supernatural ingredient in the tale, beyond such occasional deeds as the Mohave believed living members of their tribe were able to perform or experience: sorcery, charming, omens. The strength or size of a leader is sometimes exaggerated, but almost never with any great extravagance. The story is therefore factually sober. As regards its content and form, it might well be history.

At the same time there is nothing to show that any of the events told of did happen, or that any of the numerous personages named ever existed. The type of events is largely drawn from Mohave pre-Caucasian actual tribal experience; but I doubt whether any of the specific incidents were really handed down by tradition. In short, the story is a pseudo-history. It is a product of imagination, not of recollection, and therefore [is] an effort at literature. In that circumstance lies perhaps its greatest interest. It can in effect be characterized as a prose epic, or at least an effort at one. It is also a secular epic: it contains neither mythology nor ritual elements, just as it is without trace of metrical or other formally stylized language, except to a very slight degree in the names of personages.[4]

In my opinion, the one item of possible historical fact in the tale is that it may reflect a time when the Mohave were not yet permanent residents of Mohave Valley but were in the process of occupying it. Beyond that, the enumeration and localization of totemic bands or subclans after the conquest of Mohave Valley, as given in paragraphs 174–176 [of Kroeber 1951], probably rests on fact. But this list is static: it reflects the landholdings as they were more or less remembered to have existed synchronously a few generations ago—probably within a century before the telling. All the people and events of the long story I consider to be a fantasy, produced as an end in itself by the dreamer-narrator—and, with analogous but largely independent content, by a few other like-minded individuals.

The successful attainment of an appearance of historicity in a fantasy creation within an unlettered tribe, especially one wholly lacking mnemonic devices, is significant as a cultural event because of its unexpectedness and near-uniqueness. The historic-mindedness of the story is further evidenced by the consistent "nativeness" of the culture depicted: wheat, chickens, red cloth, white men are never even hinted at, though they have crept both into origin myths and ritual song-cycle tales of the Mohave. No purist ethnographer reconstructing the old culture could have been any stricter than Inyo-kutavêre.

In our recording, Jack Jones allowed the old man to proceed—for perhaps five to ten minutes—until the interpreter had as much as he could remember, then Englished it to me. With omission of repetitions, condensation of verbiage, and some abbreviating of words, I nearly kept up writing in longhand. If Jack got too far ahead, I signaled him to wait. On the other hand, if names of new places or persons came too thickly, Jack would stop translating and ask Inyo-kutavêre to repeat the names slowly, directly to me.

NOTES

1. At the end of his introduction, Kroeber makes the following comments, which are important to understanding the format of the text as presented here:

> To give a narrative of the prolixity of this one some organization, I have divided it into 197 paragraphs, according to sense, and then grouped these into 18 sections designated A to R [of which the present excerpt is section I]. For orientation I have also prefixed to each paragraph a summary side-head of my own manufacture, as well as title headings to the 18 sections. These heads are arbitrary: but I am sure they will help the reader. The need of organization was greater in this narrative than for most Mohave myths, which come punctuated by songs so that the narrator, as he concludes each incident or topic, naturally says "so many songs" and comes to a pause.

The translation is heavily annotated in the original publication (A. Kroeber 1951); the section presented here, for example, contains 147 endnotes. Only the most literarily germane of these notes have been included here, as footnotes. In addition, to open up the page for the reader and help make section-internal rhetorical organizations more transparent, I have "sub-paragraphed" the text within the numbered sections of Kroeber's original presentation.—HWL

2. They were not continuous. I took about two days off to wander about and pick up specimens, believing that even so Inyo-kutavêre would finish by the date on which I ought to return to the university.

3. Unless possibly, in some degree, a young man who was still learning from a father or other kinsman.

4. Unfortunately, because Kroeber did not record the Mojave and greatly reduced the amount of repetition and "excess verbiage" (see remarks in the final paragraph of this introduction), there is no way today to verify or contradict his assertion here.—HWL

Besides Kroeber's *A Mohave Historical Epic,* from which this selection was taken, the reader might wish to look at Kroeber's *Seven Mohave Myths* and *More Mohave Myths,* Herman Grey's *Tales from the Mohaves,* George Devereux's "Mohave Coyote Tales," or the bilingual selection of Mojave texts in Leanne Hinton and Lucille Watahomigie's *Spirit Mountain.* Leslie Spier's *Mohave Culture Items* provides some ethnographical information, and Pamela Munro's *Mojave Syntax* provides information on aspects of Mojave grammar.

IN THE DESERT WITH HIPAHIPA

I. IN THE DESERT WITH HIPAHIPA

92. EMPTY HOUSES AND FOOTPRINTS

Maθkwem-tšutšām-kwilyêhe said: "We will not go east. We will follow this valley northward. I know these mountains ahead: I know their name. But we do not want to go there: we do not want to go east. We will go north." Then they went north, following the valley.

In the afternoon they turned eastward. Then they were in the center of the valley.* In the middle of the valley was a little gulch, but there was no water in it. There they found twenty houses. There were ten houses on the west side of the dry ravine and ten on the east side. Wells had been dug: ten of them. There were no paths about, but they saw tracks of boys and girls and women and men all about. They looked inside the houses but saw nobody. It was one man who lived there: he made his foot large and small—like a man's, like a woman's, like a child's. He owned these twenty houses and lived in them, but he was not there now: he had been gone five days.

His name was Hipahipa.† He used to hunt. He did not hunt deer

---

* They are in "Basin and Range" country.
† Our introduction to one of the great heroes of the tale. Hipa is the girls' name of the Coyote clan.

or rabbits, but rattlesnakes. The rattlesnakes did not bite him. He picked them up with his hands and hung them by their heads under his belt, with their tails hanging down and rattling.* In this way he took ten of them home. There he cooked them in the sand. Thus he lived.

93. A RATTLESNAKE DIET

There were two men. Cut-blood-knee and Ha-yeθa-yêθwa, who lived at Avī-ny-ūlka and Aha-kwa-hêl on rats and rabbits and jackrabbits. [Now, shortly before,] they had been hunting and had cooked their meat [near Hipahipa's home] when Hipahipa came to them.† They gave him meat and said: "Eat what we eat!" He put a piece into his mouth. He said: "I do not like to eat that: it is not good. What I eat are rattlesnakes: see, I have some with me." The two men took up their meat, made it into a bundle, put it on their backs again [and went home].

Then Hipahipa cooked his rattlesnakes and ate them. But he thought: "That was good food which Cut-blood-knee and Ha-yeθa-yêθwa gave me. Why did I not eat it? What I eat is not good; it is rattlesnakes.‡ I will go to their houses and see what they eat." Then he went to Avī-ny-ūlka and Ahe-kwa-hêl, arriving at sunset. Then they gave him their meat, he ate it, and liked it. He lived with them five days.

Then he said: "Today I want to go back. I have twenty houses and twenty wells and live alone. I do not live like you. You have women and children and many people. When I am at home you know what I eat. At night I bring home rattlesnakes: in the morning I eat them: that is how I live. Now I want to go back. But I want all of you to know this before I go." Then they all said: "It is well. You can go back."§ Hipahipa said: "I am ready." His houses were to the northwest, and he went northwestward.

---

* This is quite a picture—the lonely man wearing a rattling snake skirt, living in twenty empty houses, with footprints about as a whole village. He has gone wild; but why so, the story does not tell.

† This is going back to the time before the arrival of the traveling band, and is to explain why Hipahipa was away from his twenty houses when they arrived.

‡ He had refused their food childishly or, like a hermit, gone queer; now he begins to regret it.

§ Assent, not permission.

Then he saw people living in his houses: he saw smoke.* He thought: "I wonder who is living there? I was alone, but I see smoke. Well, I must go, for they are my houses." He came nearer and heard the noise of the people. He said: "I see women and boys and girls all living in my houses." Then he went near and saw children playing about.

They saw him and went and told Maθkwem-tšutšām-kwilyêhe: "We have seen someone." "You have seen someone?" "Yes. Over there." Then he sent a man to see Hipahipa. He saw him and returned. Maθkwem-tšutšām-kwilyêhe asked him: "Did you see him?" and he said: "Yes." "What did he look like?" "He looks good: he is as large as we are." Then the four leaders said, "We had better go to see him." Hipahipa shouted loudly twice, and the children said: "Do you hear him?" The men said: "Yes. He shouts like a man. We shout like that."†

Hipahipa was standing behind a bush. He did not want the people to come nearer to him. As they approached he drew back. Maθkwem-tšutšām-kwilyêhe said: "Why do you go back? Why do you not meet me so that we can talk?" Hipahipa continued to retreat.‡ Maθkwem-tšutšām-kwilyêhe said again: "Why do you go back? Meet me and we will talk." Then Hipahipa came out and they all stood together. Hipahipa said: "All those are my houses." Maθkwem-tšutšām-kwilyêhe said: "Well, if they are your houses, let us go inside."

Then the people were outside cooking. The sun went down. It became dark and all went indoors. Hipahipa said: "I think none of you know me. Do you not know me? You have seen me before. I was at Kohôye [near Barstow] with you. I was a young man then, and a bad man. I kicked and ran and fought. I dreamed that way: that is why I did it. I could not help it. I was young then. My name was Noise-unruly-night. Now I am called Hipahipa. I have come here from Kohôye. Kunyôr-'ikorāvtši and his people went away from there and I went with them, going east. When we came to Kepetšiqô and Selye'aye-metši we crossed the [Colorado] river to this [eastern] side. We came to Amatya'āma and Ahaly-kuīrve. Then we came to Hatai-kwa'ī and Ahmo-ku-tšeθ'īlye. There we slept. Then we came to Avi-nye-hamokyê and Aqwawa-have. When

---

* Now he encounters the migrants.
† I.e., he is not a ghost.
‡ He has turned wild and shy in his isolation.

we came there it was nearly sunset and we camped. In the morning the rest went on, but I stayed there. I did not go on. I thought: 'Why do I go with them? I do not want to go with them. I will go another way.' Then I started alone and went east. I found this place. I thought: 'I will stay here and make a house and dig a well and live here. I will call my place Halyerave-kutšakyāpve. I will call it also Hanye-kwêva.'" Thus Hipahipa told it all to Maθkwem-tšutšām-kwilyêhe.

Then Maθkwem-tšutšām-kwilyêhe said: "Now we know you. We used to see you at Kohôye: you are the man." Hipahipa said: "Yes. I am the one." Maθkwem-tšutšām-kwilyêhe said: "Then you were a young man. Now you are large, as large as we. If you had not told us, we would not have known you; but I know you now. You were called Noise-unruly-night then. Now you have changed your name and are called Hipahipa.* That is why we did not know you. Well, we have come to your houses." Hipahipa said: "Very well. You say: 'Whatever you say we will follow it.'" Maθkwem-tšutšām-kwilyêhe said: "Yes, that is what I said." Hipahipa said: "Well, I do not eat what you eat. You eat melons and pumpkins and seeds. I am not eating those: I eat rattlesnakes. But I saw men living in that direction [pointing]. I will take you there. I want you to go with me. When I take your people there, perhaps those there will give them something to eat, and you will live there. In the morning we will go."

95. UNDESIRED VISITORS

In the morning Hipahipa said: "I will not go with you. I will go ahead to show the way." He had a crooked *tukoro* stick. He said: "I will go ahead and draw a line for you with this and you can follow it. There is a place [called] Hatšuvāvek-aha with a spring; when you reach it, drink. From there, tell your people to carry water. I will continue from there marking a line, and you follow it. As you go on farther, you will come to a valley and will see smoke there. That will be Aha-ku-hêl and Avī-ny-ūlka, where I want you to go." Thus he told them how to go.

Starting that morning, they came to the spring Hatšuvāvek-aha. Maθ—kwem-tšutšām-kwilyêhe said: "This is the spring he told of. Here we will drink and take water to carry." They went on a short distance and saw

---

* Mohave style: reaffirming what is known or has just been said.

smoke. "Those are the places Aha-ku-hêl and Avī-ny-ūlka." Then all knew those places. Hipahipa had gone ahead: he had begun to cut brush in order to make a house. "I want Maθkwem-tšutšãm-kwilyêhe to live here," he thought. Then he went east and brought a load of wood. He went again and again and brought five loads. All about were men playing with [hoop and] poles, but Hipahipa did not speak to them. Some of them thought: "I wonder why he clears that place and why he is getting five loads of wood?" But they did not ask him; therefore he did not say a word. This was in midafternoon.

When Maθkwem-tšutšãm-kwilyêhe approached from the northwest, those who were playing with poles looked up. They said: "Is it wind and dust? I think someone is coming." One of them told Ha-yeθa-yêθwa and Cut-blood-knee: "I think people are coming. There is dust over there." The two leaders said: "All come here to this house! All stand here! Yes, people are coming." Hipahipa said nothing. The two leaders said: "Those who are approaching come for war, I think. All you women and children climb the mountain! All you men stay here! Do not run off!"

Then all the women and girls and old men and children climbed up the mountain. Cut-blood-knee and Ha-yeθa-yêθwa said: "We will stay here and meet them and fight." These two leaders went to meet Maθkwem-tšutšãm-kwilyêhe's people. Hipahipa saw them close together; they had nearly met: then he ran toward them. He ran in front of Maθkwem-tšutšãm-kwilyêhe: then he turned and went toward Cut-blood-knee and Ha-yeθa-yêθwa; Maθkwem-tšutšãm-kwilyêhe followed him. Then Cut-blood-knee and Ha-yeθa-yêθwa said: "I do not think that they want to fight: Hipahipa has brought them here." They called the women and children to come down from the mountain; and they came. Hipahipa led Maθkwem-tšutšãm-kwilyêhe's people to the place which he had cleared off. Cut-blood-knee and Ha-yeθa-yêθwa said: "These people are travelers. They have come to my house: give them to eat." Then their people gave them rabbits and other meat and mescal. Now the newcomers had enough to eat.

96. WILL THERE BE FOOD ENOUGH?

Cut-blood-knee and Ha-yeθa-yêθwa thought: "I want to see the strangers," and went into Maθkwem-tšutšãm-kwilyêhe's camp. He said to them:

"I wonder where you have come from. You know that we all started from one place.* Then you scattered over the mountains. And we have traveled, looking for you: now we have found you." Then one of the two said: "We are scattered over the country: we have taken all the springs: there is no place for you to stay.† Everywhere our tribes have made monuments of trees or brush to claim the land. There is no room for you."

Maθkwem-tšutšām-kwilyêhe said: "We are not looking for that. We are not looking for a place to live in [here]. You have heard of the fighting and how one party was beaten. We are on the way to take back our country. We want to fight with the people there: that is why we have come." Cut-blood-knee and Ha-yeθa-yêθwa said: "We do not wish war. We live well here: we support ourselves: our women and children like living here. We do not want to take them away: they might die in the desert." Hipahipa said: "Maθkwem-tšutšām-kwilyêhe, listen to what I tell you. I want you to build a house for your people. If it rains, all that is outdoors will be wet, but if you make a house and it rains you can go inside and make a fire and it will be well." Then they built houses and lived like the other people there.

97. ANTELOPE MAGIC

Cut-blood-knee and Ha-yeθa-yêθwa had a friend called Put-it-into-eagle-down. This man had no bow and arrows: he just went in any direction— north or east or south—and brought back rabbits and jackrabbits. He caught them with his hands, seizing them by the neck, without shooting: that is how he lived. Hipahipa told Maθkwem-tšutšām-kwilyêhe: "They [Cut-blood-knee and his partner] give you meat, but they do not give you enough. I am like that man: I hunt, but without a bow. I can catch anything I want with my hands. Let us go to Ahtatš-ku-ðauve and Aha-ku-pāka. We will all go to that mountain. Take this man with you who has no bow but can kill antelope,‡ and I will go with you. The antelope have tracks like this."

* This may mean Avikwame, when they were still with Mastamho, but more likely it refers to the time before the emigration from Mohave Valley.

† The springs would be crucial for occupation of this southeast desert tract.

‡ Now we rise from rabbits to antelope. The charming of the swift antelope which live in open plains is a Basin Shoshonean specialty, found also among the Yokuts. But mountain sheep (*ammo*), big horns, would be more appropriate to a mountain range than are antelope (*umul*).

When they came to the place, Hipahipa said to Put-it-into-eagle-down: "Sit here! You, Maθkwem-tšutšam-kwilyêhe, take your men and go around the mountain and drive the antelope this way. Then I will kill them. And this man sitting here will kill them too. Then we shall have antelope meat." So they started to go around the mountain to drive them.

Hipahipa thought about Put-it-into-eagle-down: "I do not think he is wise. I do not think he is a doctor. I think I can beat him." Thereupon Put-it-into-eagle-down could not get up. He was weak and sweaty: Hipahipa made him be thus. The antelope came by but he could not see them: they all went past him. Others came to Hipahipa and he seized their necks, broke their legs, and killed many. He killed them all and piled up the meat. Then all the people came back there. "What is the matter with this man?" they said. Put-it-into-eagle-down said: "I do not know: I am sick: I cannot work with my hands." Then they divided the meat, and all ate. Put-it-into-eagle-down returned, and at night he said to Cut-blood-knee and Ha-yeθa-yêθwa: "I have killed antelope for you, but I cannot kill them any more. I am sick. Tomorrow morning I am going back to my place at Avī-kwe-hunāke."

In the morning he ate mescal, took his crooked *tukoro,* and went off, walking like a sick man, slowly.

98. SKIN CLOTHING

The people of Cut-blood-knee and Ha-yeθa-yêθwa shot deer and rabbits: Hipahipa killed antelope as before. He did it a third time. Now the antelope hides lay piled up high. Then he said: "All you women and girls are poor. I see you wearing willow bark [as skirts]. You have worn it two years: It is worn thin. Today I will kill more antelopes: today we shall all stay home. I want to make buckskin." Then they put water into large dishes and baskets and laid the hides in to soak. Then they worked on them. It did not take them long to cure the skins: in one day they had prepared them all.

The next day they made women's dresses and moccasins: "So that you can go out away and get firewood," said Hipahipa. "All these people here have moccasins." Before this they had been afraid to go out far into the cactuses because they were barefooted. When they had made all the dresses, Hipahipa said: "Pick each the one that will fit you." Then all picked dresses that fitted them. Now all the women had dresses and moccasins, and all the men had moccasins and leggings and shirts, and they were all dressed.

99. HUNGER AND JEALOUSY

Now it was about two years [later]. In the night they gathered,* and Ha-yeθa-yêθwa said: "*Kwaθepilye* seeds and *maselye'aye* seeds, and deer and antelope, and mescal, and rabbits and rats: those are what we live on. When Hipahipa came here I told him what we ate: he knew it. Then the man Maθkwem-tšutšām-kwilyêhe came here. Now when Hipahipa kills antelope, why does he not give me meat? Why does he not treat me well? That man only wandered in here, but Hipahipa gives him much food."

Now these people [the old residents] were shooting their game with bows and arrows. Thus it happened that sometimes they did not have enough to eat, because sometimes they missed when they shot; whereas Hipahipa merely seized the animals, and so Maθkwem-tšutšām-kwilyêhe's people always had enough. Then Hipahipa said [to the newcomers]: "We have taken all the antelope that are here: there are none left. Let us go south to Avī-ka-hāyihāyi and Aha-talame: there we shall find more antelope. Another man lives there: he also hunts them, but only with bows and arrows."

That night the people [originally] living there came back angry because they did not have enough to eat, while Maθkwem-tšutšām-kwilyêhe's people had abundance.

100. DOCTOR'S SORCERY

The next day in the morning they went hunting again; the women and children stayed home. Now Red-sky was a doctor of Cut-blood-knee and Ha-yeθa-yêθwa. The children were playing about the houses. The boys took ground *maselye'aye* and *kwaθepilye* seed, threw it up into the air, and

---

* Cut-blood-knee and the old residents of the region. In spite of saying that they were on their way to war, the wanderers have by now stayed another two years.

caught it in their mouths. Maθkwem-kwapāive's boy was with them.* Then Red-sky killed him:† the boy died right there. Then a boy went and told the old men and women who had stayed at home: "Maθkwem-kwapāive's boy is dead." The old people went to see. "Well, he is dead indeed," they said. They stood by the body and cried. They said to Tūkyet-nyi-hayi: "Follow the men and say: 'Maθkwem-kwapāive, your boy is dead.' Tell them that." The men had come to Avīl-he-talame and were drinking when Tūkyet-nyi-hayi arrived and told them: "Maθkwem-kwapāive, your boy is dead."

Thereupon they did not hunt but all came back; by midafternoon they returned to the houses. The boy was lying where he had fallen on the ground. All stood around him and cried. Hipahipa took a rope, went eastward, and gathered wood. He broke it with his hands or with stones and, making a bundle, brought it back to the house. Then they burned the boy. Hipahipa said: "If this boy had been sick, he would have died after two or three days. But he was not sick. I know who did this: it was the doctor. I know his name; it was Red-sky. Tonight I will kill him." But Maθkwem-kwapāive said: "No, do not kill him. When we traveled here, my daughter got married; it was the same as if we had lost her. We knew that before. Now my boy is dead, and it is as if I had lost my son and my daughter. So we will cry; that is all. Do not kill Red-sky." Then they cried.

101. NOTIFICATION OF A DAUGHTER

In the morning Maθkwem-kwapāive said: "I told you to cry, and we have cried all night. I am tired. Tonight we will cry again. In two days in the morning I will go to tell my daughter. It will take me two days to go there. The sun will be nearly down or it will be down when I arrive: I do not know when I shall arrive there. I will stay there two nights. Then

---

* Up to now [Maθkwem-kwapāive was] a sort of second-in-command to Maθkwem-tšutšām-kwilyêhe; Maθkwem-kwapāive from here on replaces him in the tale. He had previously let his daughter go in marriage; now he loses his boy, then collects gifts from his people for funeral destruction, and, when the entry into Mohaveland finally takes place, he is Hipahipa's companion and dies in battle by him when Hipahipa is driven out. [In contrast], Maθkwem-tšutšām-kwilyêhe, though the first leader of all to be mentioned in the tale, is a singularly pallid personality throughout: he leads almost abstractly; nothing ever happens to him as an individual.

† By magic or mana.

I will come back. It will take me two days to come back again. That will be six days." All said: "Good. You say you will be away six days."

Then Maθkwem-kwapāive started. He slept at Hihô-kusave. The next night he slept at Kapotak-ivauve. The third day he followed the river. When he had nearly come to where his daughter lived, the people there saw him coming. The players came to the house and said:* "Maθkwem-kwapāive is coming; I think it is he." But some said: "No, that is not the man. Maθkwem-kwapāive has long hair."† Then he arrived and all saw that it was he. They said: "Maθkwem-kwapāive, is that you?" He said: "Yes, it is I. I have come to tell my daughter that my son died." Then the woman cried. White-dream, her husband, the head man of the place, cried, and all his people cried. All gave Maθkwem-kwapāive beads or other things to burn.‡

They gave him a large pile, and he burned it all. He said: "Tonight I will sleep here. Tomorrow morning it will be one night. Tomorrow I will stay, and sleep here again. That will be two nights. In the morning I will go back." The second morning he went back. He slept again at Ota-ke-vāuve and then at Hihô-kusave, and after two days [on the way] he returned when it was nearly sunset to where he lived. Then he said to his people: "I told you I would be gone six days. Now it is six days."

102. TO KŪTPĀMA

It was night. Hipahipa said: "We have lived here four years. Your son died here. You have burned your clothes and cut your hair. I do not feel good. I want to move from this place. I do not want to stay here. We will move to Kūtpāma and Ikwe-nye-va. We will go and live there and eat tule roots and beaver and *av'a* seeds."§ Maθkwem-kwapāive said: "As you say. If you say that we should move, we will move, because you have done good to us. When you want to go, we will go." Hipahipa said: "We will start in two days."

---

* As almost always in this tale, somebody is outdoors playing hoop and poles, and the settlement is referred to as if it consisted of one house.

† It is taken for granted that he had cut it shorter in mourning, but of course they did not yet know of the mourning.

‡ To express sympathy, and honor to the dead. The destruction of property at a funeral is called *tšupilyk*.

§ Tule is cattail rush, *Scirpus acutus.* Meal from the roots is a low-grade food.

After two days, in the morning they all started and came northwest. When it was nearly noon they came to Ovālyeha and drank there and rested. That night they slept at Ahtatš-ku-ðauve. That next night they slept at Ah'ā-kuva'ê: that was two nights. The next morning they started and came to Kūtpāma and Ikwe-nye-va. There is a stream there, a little river which empties into this [Colorado] river. Now they had come to this stream: that is where they were wanting to live. Then some boys would go fishing, the women went to gather *av'a* seeds; some men went to hunt deer, others to get rats, beaver, or tules.

103. EATEN OUT

Then Hipahipa said: "We have [now] lived on these things here for four years and there are not many of them left. I think we will move again. We cannot stay here without food: we cannot live without it. There are two places. Hatūi-meðau and Mastamho-tesauve. I think we will go there. We will go downstream to those places, and we will eat there the same things that we eat here." Then they went to those places. They stayed there two years. They ate the same things as at Kūtpāma: fish and beaver, and tules and *av'a*. Then Hipahipa said: "I think we have eaten it all out." He sent four or five men to go back to Kūtpāma: "Go and look around where we lived before." They found many fish and beaver and tules and *av'a* again.*

104. MEETING A STRANGER

Then the wife of Maθkwem-kwapāive went upstream to Kūtpāma to gather *av'a*.† When she came there she met a man, Put-mark-around-neck. He was sitting under the shade of a cottonwood tree and had four jackrabbits. He asked her if she wanted some. She said: "Yes," and he

---

* The subsistence margin is shown to have been both close and resilient, in these nonfarming areas, by the way in which a band could eat out a tract and it would then recuperate in some years. Psychologically, it is remarkable how interested and informed the farming Mohave were about these desert conditions. There is a parallel in the fact that in the [Mastamho and Origins] myths, more space is given to the institution of wild desert foods than agricultural ones. It may be that the Mohave interest rests on famine experiences at home, when groups of them temporarily lunged into the desert for subsistence.

† She is the third member of his family to whom something happens.

cooked some in hot sand. Then he took her into the shade [of the tree] and cohabited with her.* When the meat was cooked, he gave her of it and she ate. She said: "It is good. I like to eat this." Put-mark-around-neck asked her: "What will you do now?" She said: "I am going back." When she returned home, she brought no seeds with her.

105. A PASSION IN THE DESERT

In the morning the woman went out to gather seeds and she went to the same place. She had agreed to meet Put-mark-around-neck there. So she met him. [This time] he had six jackrabbits. Then he undressed [her] completely, and the same thing happened. He gave her the meat, and she said: "I am going home."

Now this woman had a little boy. All day he cried. Maθkwem-kwa-pāive carried him on his arm all day trying to quiet him; Hipahipa helped him. While the woman was returning she thought: "My husband might know. But in this way he will not know: I will leave my basket and take up a stick, and walk slowly like a sick woman. Then he will not know." So she arrived at the house and said to Maθkwem-kwapāive: "I do not know how it is: I am sick; I can hardly walk. I am very sick."

106. ELOPEMENT

In the morning all got up and the women went out to gather again. This woman went too. She said: "I am [still] sick, but I think I shall be able to gather seeds for mush to eat; I will not stay home." So she went off with the other women, but hid, and ran off from them, and went back to the same place as before. There she met Put-mark-around-neck the third time; he had four [jack]rabbits with him; and they did the same way. Then he said: "What will you do now?" She said: "I want to go back." But he said: "No, no. I am your husband now. Did you not take off your clothes, and I saw you, privates and all? When a man does that to a woman, she is married to him.† And you know that I am a man: I

---

* The term "cohabit" was a common euphemism for "copulate" at the time this text was taken down.—HWL.

† Intimacy implies marriage, escapades are furtive: such seems to be the sentiment.

am not a bird.* I will take you to my house. I want you to come with me." It was midafternoon; then he took her with him. They went south-eastward past Amaṭ-akano to Opui-ku-tšumāka and Humθe-vinye-hali-āva where he lived.

107. HIPAHIPA RECOVERS THE ERRANT WIFE

Now the woman was gone all night: she had not come back. Hipahipa said: "What is the matter with her? I thought she would come back at night. Now it is morning and she has not returned. Maθkwem-kwapāive, your wife has been gone all night. You and I will go to see." They ate and started off. They came to Kūtpāma and saw tracks. Then Maθkwem-kwapāive said: "I knew it. I knew that someone took my wife; but I was ashamed to say it.† That is why she went away." The woman had left her basket, and they found it. They tracked her and Put-mark-around-neck. Then they came near his house. Hipahipa said: "Stand here now. He would see you; but he will not see me. I will make all who live there blind so that they cannot see me. I will cause them to know nothing." Maθkwem-kwapāive said: "Good. I will stand here."

Now those people used seeds, and the woman was grinding them. She stood in front of the house at the east corner. Hipahipa came around the house, stood behind her, grasped her around [the middle], and ran off with her to where his friend stood. [Only] when he had gone some dis-tance did the people there see him. The woman was unwilling and scratched Hipahipa's face. "I do not want to go with you," she cried. She tore out his nose ornament and threw it away. Then Hipahipa was an-gry: he tore off all her clothes,‡ till she had nothing on; still she strug-gled. Hipahipa said: "Do not struggle: let us go." Then they came to where Maθkwem-kwapāive was waiting and started back. They made her walk in front of them. They came to Kūtpāma and took willow leaves to make a dress for her. Then they returned to their house: it was afternoon.

* "He meant that he had a house to live in," the interpreter explained.
† A natural enough sentiment; but he gets and takes her back. There seems to be more public shame than personal resentment.
‡ Evidently in resentment, to humiliate her by her nakedness. [Or perhaps to negate the claim of "possession-by-exposure" advanced by Put-mark-around-neck.—HWL]

108. TO KŪTPĀMA AGAIN

Then they lived as before and ate the same food for a year.* Then Hipahipa said: "Let us go [back] where we were." So they all moved back to Kūtpāma. They made houses there and lived as they had before.

109. HIPAHIPA INCITES THEM TO RETURN

They were there at Kūtpāma two years. Then Hipahipa said: "We have eaten up all the food [about here]. The women have gone far and taken all the seeds. We have killed all the rabbits and rats and fish and other animals." Boys and girls were playing outside. They picked up handfuls of yellow gravel and said: "This is red beans. This is black beans. This is white beans." Hipahipa said: "There is no maize. I see no red beans or white or blue or yellow beans. I think these boys and girls say wisely. They have dreamed well. Soon we shall have that. In the place from which we came there are those things." The children playing said: "This is yucca. This is melon. This is watermelon." Hipahipa said: "They have dreamed well. After a time we shall have all those."

It was night. Hipahipa said: "There is another thing that I always think of. You know what made us angry. Let us be going against those people to fight. What do you say to what I say, Maθkwem-tšutšām-kwilyêhe and Maθkwem-kwapāive? You do not want your people to die somewhere out in the desert."† Maθkwem-tšutšām-kwilyêhe and Maθkwem-kwa-pāive said: "Good. As you say." Two, four, five times Hipahipa spoke thus.‡ He said: "Well. I am going to say the same thing. Let us go to fight them. They are rich. They have enough to live on. They laugh at us all. They say of us: 'Those in the mountains, they have died some-where. But we live well: we live better than they.' And they do have plenty. That is what makes me angry. [Though] when we go there we shall [perhaps] die before daylight."

---

* A year between talking of the move and making it! The chronology is in round numbers.
† "If you do not fight for better land, you are likely to starve here."
‡ Characteristic expression. The Mohaves are not afraid of numbers, either exact or approximative; and, according to situation, the numbers may be either formally "round" (ritual) or "odd" and specific. It is now Hipahipa, the converted and escapist hermit, who is urging invasion and war on the leaders who set out so full of purpose of reconquest.

Then Maθkwem-tšutšäm-kwilyêhe and Maθkwem-kwapäive said: "It is well: we will go with you. We will follow you. You say that when you arrive there you shall not live until the next day, but that you shall die. Well, we shall die before another day. We are not afraid." Hipahipa said: "I want all of you women and girls and old men and all to come along. If all the strong men go and are killed there, the old people will not be able to live here: they are too old. If we die, perhaps they will die too; so we will all go. Perhaps they will kill all of us; perhaps half of us. But if they do that, it will be well." Then Maθkwem-tšutšäm-kwilyêhe and Maθkwem-kwapäive told their people: "All of you [prepare to] go! No one stay here!" And Hipahipa said: "There is another thing that I want to tell you. I want to go east to Avī-ka-ha'sāle, to Kunyôre and Oskīive-tekyêre. I will see those who live there. I want to tell them that we are going, tell them before we start. Many live there. Then all will hear of it. After that we will go."

110. VISIT TO AN ALLY

Then Hipahipa started for Avī-ka-ha'sāle in the morning. He arrived there at nearly sunset. At night he told them why he had come; he spoke to Dusty-sunrise and Shadow-sun, who were the leaders there. "I am going to make war. I will take my people north. I wanted to inform you before I went to war. That is why I came here. When we arrive there, perhaps we shall die. If we die there, you will not have seen me for two or three years, when you will think of me, and remember how I looked." Before daylight, when the morning star was up, Dusty-sunrise stood and said [to his own people]:* "You know what Hipahipa says. He says: 'I am going to war. It is the last time you will see me.' You all hear what he says. He says that in the morning he is returning. I will tell you what to do. Give him something!"† Then all said: "It is good. We will give him something."

In the morning Hipahipa ate. When he had eaten, the women gave him small baskets and large baskets. They were piled as high as that. The men gave him woven blankets and woven sashes and cloth shirts. They

---

* "Standing up" means that he is orating formally, "preaching."
† Merely as an honored guest? Or in anticipation of his death in war?

piled these things as high as that. Hipahipa said: "Well. I do not know how to roll them into a bundle. Do it for me!" They said: "We will do it for you." Then they made two bundles and tied the baskets to the bundles by strings. Hipahipa took the bundles on his back. "Well, this is the last time you see me, I say."

III. GIFTS DISTRIBUTED

Then he returned to Kūtpāma where he lived, nearly at sunset. He left the bundles lying, without untying them. He said: "Tomorrow morning all of you come. All the women and girls take a basket. Let everyone take one that she likes, a large one or a small one. The men do the same. Some of you like feathers, some of you buckskin shirts and leggings, some woven blankets or coats or shirts. I will not give the things to you: take them yourselves; but not tonight: tomorrow morning take them."

In the morning the girls came and took small baskets, the women large ones. The men took blankets and clothes and feathers. Hipahipa said: "If this which I have brought is not enough [to go around], I will go again. But I will not go to the same place; and I will not go today. This is not enough perhaps. Have all something?" They said: "No, not all. Half have nothing." Hipahipa said: "I will go tomorrow. It will be two days. I will go to Huvalilyeskuva and Pakat-hôave. There are people there. To them I will go."

112. ANOTHER ALLY VISITED

After two days he went in the morning. He came again to Avī-kwa-ha'sāle nearly at sunset. Then they gave him to eat, and at night he went into the house, but he said nothing.* In the morning he started again. He came to Aspa-nye-va-ke-holêve and went past it. He came to Iðo-ke'āpe and again went past it, not resting. Then he saw smoke in the south. "That is the place to which I want to go." When it was nearly sunset he reached there. There were five leaders there: Earth-guts, Sky-guts, Hold-inside-mouth,

* Made no speech.

Hold-in-hands, and Lying-on-dust.* Hipahipa spoke to Lying-on-dust: "I know that you live here. I saw your people about the place. I have not come to stay here: I have come to tell you what I have to say. I have told my people: 'I want to go to war.' All those at the places from which I have come answered: 'Good.' That is what I wanted to come to tell you."

Lying-on-dust said to his people: "You hear what Hipahipa says. He says: 'I am going to war. This is the last time you will see me. I shall die somewhere in that country. Tomorrow I am returning.' That is what he says. In the morning I want you to give him something—baskets and small baskets and feathers and other things." Lying-on-dust gave him a bow and arrows and a quiver. "I give you this," he said. He also gave him a large bunch of long red feathers, saying: "Take this with you: you may die there." Hipahipa stayed there all day. The second day in the morning, after eating, he said: "Roll all the things for me! Make two bundles!" Then he took them on his back. "Now is the last time you see me," he said.

113. GIFTS TO GO AROUND

In the afternoon he came to Tenyi-ku-tanākwe and drank at the spring there. He stood and thought: "I will go by another way. The way I came is around; this way is straight." Then he went on. Near sunset he came to Ah'ā-kuvate. He made a fire, lay by it, and slept.

Early in the morning he started, going westward. When it was nearly noon he came to Ahtatš-kītše, where there is a spring, and he drank and rested. He went past Yamasāve-katakalālve to Aha-nye-viðūtše; there he also went by. From there he followed the gulch to Kwil-ke-holêve. He also went by that place and came to Kuya-ny-itáêrqe. There he stood a while.

Starting again, he reached Kūtpāma at sunset as all were coming home for the day. Then he said: "Tomorrow morning all of you come. All the women and girls take a basket. Let everyone take one that she likes, large or small. Let the men do the same. Some of you like feathers, some like deerskin shirts and leggings, some woven blankets or coats or shirts. I will not give the things to you. Take them yourselves, but not tonight. Tomorrow morning take them!"

---

* We have already encountered these five in E 50 [cf. the full text in Kroeber 1951] at the same place. They are tobacco clan, and apparently Mohave, since one of them participates in the reconquest.

In the morning the people came and took the things. Now all had something.

114. THE UNDERTAKING URGED AGAIN

Then Hipahipa said: "I do not want you to wear what I gave you. Do not wear the things out in this country. I am thinking of another country. When we come there, make friends with those people. If they do not follow what we say, if they wish something else, then we will make war on them. I know that they are many there, but they are not as brave as I am. I am a brave man. In two days we will go north."

27

An Account of Origins

QUECHAN (YUMA)
1908

TSUYUKWERÁU (JOE HOMER), NARRATOR

J. P. HARRINGTON, COLLECTOR AND TRANSLATOR

INTRODUCTION BY J. P. HARRINGTON

[*What follows is an excerpt from the introduction that accompanied Harrington's original publication in the* Journal of American Folklore *in 1908.[1] Some of Harrington's comments here on the Quechan reflect the times he lived in. Anthropologists today no longer believe in the old-fashioned distinction between so-called primitive and modern cultures, once a staple of anthropological discourse. All contemporary human cultures by definition are modern cultures, regardless of level of technology or social organization. In any case, what Harrington appears to mean here is more along the lines of "uncontaminated" (by European influences), rather than "primitive" per se, with all its negative connotations.*—HWL]

The Yuma occupy a central position in the Central Group.[2] They held both banks of the Colorado from fifteen miles south to sixty miles north of the Gila confluence. They are now nearly all settled on the Yuma Indian Reservation, California, where they number in 1908 about 960, including over sixty persons belonging to other tribes.

The Yuma are still primitive in religion, and largely so in life. The Christian influence has been slight. Two missions were established among them in 1780 by the military commander of Sonora, but were destroyed by the Yuma the following summer. They were then free from missionaries for over a hundred years. The present Catholic Church is attended by few Indians. The Protestants have as yet no mission building. The medicine-men, who have much influence over the people, talk openly against the missionaries and regard their traditions as a perverted form of the Yuma traditions.

The religion of the Yuma, like that of the other tribes of the Central Group, is based on revelations received in dreams. Dreaming is declared to be more real than waking. Every individual "can dream vivid dreams"; and whatever is dreamed is believed either to have once happened or to be about to happen. Only a few men, however, dream proficiently and professionally. These are known as "dreamers" (*sumátc*). They have power to reach in their dreams the ceremonial house on the summit of Avikwaamé, a gigantic flat-topped mountain thirty miles north of Needles, California, called "Ghost Mountain" by the whites. There the dreamer finds everything as it was in the mythic past. There he receives instruction from Kumastamxo, the younger of the two great gods of the Yuma. All singing and dancing ceremonies are taught by Kumastamxo and his assistants on the top of that mountain, and the dreamer of such a ceremony is bidden to teach the others who are to participate. The various practices for curing the sick may be learned there, and there only. Thus "doctor" (*kwasidhé*) and "dreamer" (*sumátc*) are synonymous. When a man dreams myths, he usually dreams his way first to the top of that mountain, and there perceives with his senses everything which is narrated in the myth.

The "best dreamer" among the Yuma is Tsuyukweráu, a man of the Xavtsáts "nation," whose English name is Joe Homer. He is about forty-five years old, and the syphilis has already affected his eyes so that he is almost totally blind. Besides the Yuma account of origins published herewith, which it takes him four days to tell, he knows a score of animal stories, some very long tales of adventure, and sixty-four ceremonial songs.[3] This material was collected by me at my own expense. It has been carefully revised by the narrator himself.

Joe Homer made to me at various times the following statements concerning his powers and training as a dreamer:

Before I was born I would sometimes steal out of my mother's womb while she was sleeping, but it was dark and I did not go far. . . . Every good doctor begins to understand before he is born, so that when he is big he knows it all. . . . When a little boy, I took a trip up to Avikwaamé Mountain and slept at its base. I felt of my body with my two hands, but found it was not there. It took me four days and nights to go up there. Later I became able to approach even the top of the mountain. At last I reached the willow-roof in front of the dark-house there. Kumastamxo was within. It was so dark that I could hardly see him. He was naked and very large. Only a few great doctors were in there with him, but a crowd of men stood under the willow-roof before the house. I tried to enter, but could not. The lightnings were playing all about. They hurt my eyes. Since then I have grown blind. . . . When I was a boy, I used to eat jimsonweed leaves (*smal'kaapít*[a]) plucked from the west side of the plant, in order to make me dream well. . . . I now have power to go to Kumastamxo anytime, tonight if I want to. I lie down and try hard, and soon I am up there again with the crowd. He tells me everything I want to know, and it takes only a little while to go there. . . . He teaches me to cure by spitting and sucking. . . . He tells me when I "speech" or sing wrong. . . . One night Kumastamxo spit up blood. He told me, "Come here, little boy, and suck my chest." I placed my hands on his ribs and sucked his sickness (*hiráv*[a]) out. Then he said, "You are a consumption dreamer.[4] When anybody has the consumption, lay your hands on him and suck the pain out continually, and in four months he will be well." When I returned home, I went to my nephew, whose lungs were all rotten. He spit all the time. I took him to my house for four months. I sucked his chest till I sucked the sickness out. Now he is well and is going to school. . . . It takes four days to tell all about Kwikumat and Kumastamxo. I am the only man who can tell it right. I was present from the very beginning, and saw and heard all. I dreamed a little of it at a time. I would then tell it to my friends. The old men would say, "That is right! I was there and heard it myself." Or they would say, "You have dreamed poorly. That is not right." And they would tell me right. So at last I learned the whole of it right.

This approval and disapproval by the old men, it would seem, tends to unify versions of the same myth originating in the dreams of various dreamers, rendering the Yuma myths less variable than those of some peoples who do not claim to dream their mythology.

Since the writer hopes to publish in a subsequent number of this journal shorter creation myths of the Cocopa, Mohave, and Wallapai, a discussion of Joe Homer's Yuma account will be reserved till then.[5] Let him here, therefore, merely hint at Christian influence, and point out how this myth differs from similar myths found among the Mohave.[6] The myth differs from any similar account which has been found among the Mohave in the prominence and creative activity of Kwikumat (in Mohave, Matavíl[ya]), who in Mohave mythology merely leads the people to Axavol[y]pó, builds a house there, and dies; in the mention of Blind-Old-Man; in the doctrine of four destructions of the people; in the prominence of Marxokuvek, "the first Yuma Indian"; in the instruction of the people by Kumastamxo (in Mohave, Mastamxó) at Axavol[y]pó as well as at Avikwaamé; and in the vivid description in the story of Rattlesnake and the account of the cremation of Kwikumat.

NOTES

1. I have done little to emend or modernize Harrington's 1908 text. Readers should note, therefore, that Harrington's spelling of Quechan words—as also his spelling of certain tribal designations, like "Mohave" and "Wallapai"—is no longer consistent with contemporary practice. (For a layperson's guide to modern Quechan orthography, see Hinton and Watahomigie 1984:296–97.)

In only three areas have I felt the need for editorial "tinkering." First, both introduction and translation are heavily footnoted in Harrington's original, mostly with etymological information; I have retained only those notes that are germane to the story itself. Second, for convenience of reference in such a long and complex myth, I have added numbering to Harrington's original paragraphs and, on occasion, seen fit to break some of the longer paragraphs into (unnumbered) "subparagraphs." Third, I have inserted section titles in brackets at three points in the narrative; these titles correspond to apparent divisions at the highest level of thematic organization and are intended as "guideposts" for the reader.

Finally, a word about the Latin passages encountered in the translation. In deference to the more delicate sensibilities of his time, Harrington translated the "dirty bits" of this myth into Latin, as was then customary in publications of this nature. Since few readers today are likely to be conversant in Latin, I have had these passages translated into English. Instead of silently replacing the Latin text with English, though, I have gathered the translated passages in a section of their own at the end of the myth—not out of some outmoded sense of decorum, but simply because I find the Latin passages of the original version pleasantly quaint. Harrington's translation—like all translations, whether we are aware of it or not—is very much a product of his literary time and fashion. To replace the Latin, I felt, would have damaged this translation's patina of age.—HWL

2. The "Central Group" that Harrington mentions here refers to an earlier classification (now no longer considered to be a single branch of Yuman) that included—in addition to Quechan (a.k.a. "Yuma") itself—Mojave, Maricopa, Diegueño, and Cocopa.—HWL

3. Only a few of these songs were recorded by me. They, as well as the songs which occur in the myths and animal stories, abound in archaic, mutilated, and repeated wordforms. Compare the song "*wat^c amár umár, wak^y ak^y ér uk^y ér*" ('the house will burn, the house will crackle') with Yuma prose, "*avat^c hamárk, hak^y érk.*"

4. A Yuma doctor usually treats only one class of diseases. He is a "specialist."

5. Harrington refers here to the *Journal of American Folklore,* where this myth originally appeared.—HWL

6. The Indians compare Kwikumat with the God, Blind-Old-Man with the Devil, and Kumastamxo with the Jesus of the Christians.

FURTHER READING

C. Darryl Forde's *Ethnography of the Yuma Indians,* besides being a primary source of Quechan (Yuma) cultural information, is full of songs and ethnographic texts. Joe Homer, the narrator of this myth, was the principal consultant for Edward Gifford's "Yuma Dreams and Omens," which contains extensive dream narratives and related commentary. Leanne Hinton and Lucille Watahomigie's bilingual anthology, *Spirit Mountain,* contains a selection of Quechan oral literature, including songs and reminiscences. Frances Densmore's *Yuman and Yacqui Music* is a classic study of California and Southwestern song traditions. Abraham Halpern published a much shorter version of part of the Quechan creation cycle, "Kukumat Became Sick—a Yuma Text," in Margaret Langdon's *Yuman Texts.*

AN ACCOUNT OF ORIGINS

[THE AGE OF KWIKUMAT]

1. There was water everywhere. There was no land. Kwikumat and another man who at that time had no name kept moving at the bottom

of the water. Suddenly with a rumbling sound Kwikumat emerged and stood on top of the water. The other man wished also to come to the surface. He asked Kwikumat, "How did you emerge from the water?" Kwikumat said, "I opened my eyes." He had really held them closed. When the other man opened his eyes, the waters fell into them and blinded him. As he emerged, Kwikumat gave him his name: Kweraák Kutár ('Blind-Old-Man').

2. All was dark. There were neither sun, nor moon, nor stars. Kwikumat was not pleased. He took four steps north, and four back. He then stepped in like manner west, south, and east. This made the water subside. He stirred the water with his forefinger as he sang four times—

I am stirring it around, I am stirring it around.
It will be dry land, it will be dry land.

The place about which he stirred became an island.

3. "Aqa," said Blind-Old-Man, "it is too small. There will not be room enough for the people."—"Be patient, you old fool!" said Kwikumat. Blind-Old-Man seated himself on the ground and took up some mud. He shaped out of it clay dolls (*hantapáp*) such as boys now make. He made them after his own fashion, asking Kwikumat for no instruction. He stood them in a row. Kwikumat stood behind Blind-Old-Man. "What are you trying to make?" asked he. "People," said Blind-Old-Man. "You must first watch how I make them," said Kwikumat. Blind-Old-Man said nothing. He was angry.

4. Kwikumat said, "I will make the moon first." He faced the east. He placed spittle on the forefinger of his right hand and rubbed it like paint on the eastern sky until he made a round, shiny place. Said Blind-Old-Man, "Something is coming."—"I call it the moon (*hal^yá*)," said Kwikumat. He made just one star at the same time. Kwikumat said, "This moon shall not stand still. It shall move toward the west." Blind-Old-Man said, "But it will go into the water, and how will it get out again?"—"I shall turn the sky, so that the moon will move along the northern horizon and thus reach the east again."

5. "I do not believe that," said Blind-Old-Man, as he continued working on his mud people. Kwikumat sat down also and took up some mud.

He feared that Blind-Old-Man might anticipate him in creating people, and that Blind-Old-Man's people might be wrongly made. First he made a Yuma man, then a Diegueño man, then a Yuma woman and a Diegueño woman. Next he made a Cocopa man and a Maricopa man, a Cocopa woman and a Maricopa woman. They lay there on the ground.

6. Blind-Old-Man showed Kwikumat some of the people he had made. They had feet but not toes, hands but no fingers. "They are not right," said Kwikumat, "the fingers are webbed. How can your man use his hands? Like you, I made hands, but I also made fingers and finger-nails; like you, I made feet, but I also made toes and toenails." Blind-Old-Man felt grieved at this. "But my man is better, because, if he wishes to pick up anything, he can pick up plenty of it."—"No," said Kwiku-mat, "your man is not right. I made ten fingers. If my man injures some of them, he has still some left, and can use his hands; but when your man hurts his hand, it will become sore all over."

Saying this, he sprang toward Blind-Old-Man and kicked the figures which he had made into the water. Blind-Old-Man, raging with anger, sank into the water after them, making a great whirlpool which emitted all kinds of sicknesses. Kwikumat promptly placed his foot upon the whirlpool. But some foul wind still escaped. If none had escaped, there would be no sickness in the world. Blind-Old-Man remained beneath the water, emitting sickness. Kwikumat stood long on the shore, watching and listening.

7. When Kwikumat returned to the people he had formed, he picked up the Yuma man. Lifting him by the armpits, he swung him far north and back, west and back, south and back, east and back. Previously this man had been as long as a human hand. Now he was as long as we are. This man had all his senses, but he could not talk. Kwikumat commanded him to keep his eyes closed. Then Kwikumat animated the other people in the same way. He swung the Cocopa man south first, then east, west, but did not swing him north, for he was to dwell in the south. He swung the Maricopa man east, north, south, but did not swing him west, for he was to dwell in the east.

8. Kwikumat next gave the people speech. He took the Yuma man aside and thrice commanded him to speak. He understood, but could not speak. At the fourth command he spoke a few words. Then Kwiku-

mat gave him his name, Kwitcʸánª. In like manner Kwikumat made each of the other men talk. He named the Diegueño Kamyá, the Cocopa Kwikapá, the Maricopa Xatpá. Kwikumat did not teach the women to talk. They learned from the men.

9. The Yuma man looked into the face of the Diegueño, and the two became friends. The Cocopa man stood close to the Maricopa, and the two became friends.

10. The Yuma woman meditated, "Why did Kwikumat make women different from men? How shall children be born?" A man overheard her and said, "I will ask Kwikumat." But Kwikumat said to the woman, "I know already the thoughts which you are hiding in your heart. Why be bashful? Women alone cannot conceive children. You must marry that Yuma man." Hearing this, the woman felt happy. But she meditated again, "I want a good-looking husband. I do not want that Yuma man. The Cocopa man is handsomer." She wished to marry the Cocopa man. She looked very sweetly at him. Kwikumat said, "Do not marry the Cocopa man, for you and he are destined to dwell in different places."

The woman did not believe Kwikumat. She went aside and sulked. Blind-Old-Man arose out of the water and found her here. He said, "Do not believe what Kwikumat tells you. He can do nothing for you. But if you believe in me, you will have many possessions and eat six meals each day." Kwikumat had become aware of Blind-Old-Man's presence, although he did not see him. As he sprang toward the woman, Blind-Old-Man disappeared in the ground. Kwikumat said to the woman, "You did not believe what I told you. Therefore I shall destroy you and all the other people."

Kwikumat then faced the north and talked rapidly four times. Then it rained for four days. Water covered the earth. The people were still swimming about when the rain ceased. Kwikumat picked them up, and said, "I will make you into wild beasts." He made from the Cocopa the mockingbird (*sukwilʸlá*); from the Diegueño the deer (*akwák*); from the Maricopa the buzzard (*asé*). The Yuma man only he retained in human form, and named him Marxókuvék.* "I cannot accomplish much thus alone in the world," said Marxókuvék. Kwikumat said, "I will teach you

* Ancestor and especial friend of the Yuma Indians. In Yuma and Mohave, *marxó* means 'ground-squirrel'.

how to make other people, and how to help me fix up the world. I made earth, sky, moon, and star, and even the darkness of night, and I shall make other things also." Kwikumat was standing on the water. He sang four times—

This water is not deep. I could drink all this water.
This water is good. I could drink it.

He told Marxókuvék to close his eyes. As he did so, the water went down until they stood on the ground.

11. "I made eight people," said Kwikumat, "and they had no faith in me. This time I shall make twenty-four. And I shall make them right." He kept wandering about. He went west, then east. At last he said, "Here is the center of this world. Here I shall build my dark-house."* He picked four head-lice (*nʸiílʸ*) off himself and threw them on the mud. They became little black-abdomened ant (*xurú*), little red piss-ant (*xanapúk*), big red ant (*tcʸamadhúlʸ*), and big black ant that lives on the mesa (*tcʸamadhulʸavi*). They dug holes. They drained the mud dry. "How will you build your house?" asked Marxókuvék. He did not have a stick or a pole or a cottonwood trunk. He created these by thought. Four posts were born in the darkness, then other material. Then he built his dark-house. "I call this place Cottonwood Post (*Axavolʸpó*)," he said.

12. Marxókuvék made a man out of mud. He asked for no instruction. His man looked good to ride on, so he jumped on his back. Kwikumat cried, "Now that you have ridden on him, he will never walk on his hind legs only. I call him the burro (*alavúr*)."

13. Kwikumat created a woman and a man. The man asked the woman, "Has Kwikumat told you any secrets?"—"None," said the woman, "but I am going to ask him." The woman went to the dark-house, and Marxókuvék called Kwikumat thither. "I want you to marry the Yuma man whom I have just made," said Kwikumat. "But I want to bear a child," said the woman, "and he does not know what to do." Kwikumat said, "I will show you, but do not tell anybody." He told Marxókuvék to prevent the Yuma man from coming about. The woman was frightened.

---

* In Yuma, *avakutinyám*—a house without openings, used, according to this myth, like any other Yuma house, both as a dwelling and for religious purposes.

She thought that she would conceive by merely standing there in the dark-house. *Ut virgo bene intellegeret, ipse ei quid facturum esset demonstravit. Cum ea enim humi concubuit et quater copulavit. Femina, multum sudans, sibi sudorem quater manibus abstersit.* [See p. 488, A.]

Kwikumat then named the woman Xavasumkul^yí, and the man Xavasumkuwá. In four days the woman became sick. She wanted a doctor. There was none to be had. But the baby within her was already a wise doctor. He told her, "Lie down!" Then he made himself very small, so that he would not cause the woman pain. In a few days he could walk and talk. Kwikumat named him Kumastamxó, and told him that he was his son and assistant in fixing up the world.

14. "Is it to be dark always?" asked Kumastamxo. "The moon and the star shine dimly." Kumastamxo spit on his fingers and sprinkled the spittle over all the sky. Thus he made the stars. Then he rubbed his fingers until they shone, and, drawing the sky down to himself, he painted a great face upon it, rubbing till it shone brightly. "What are you going to call that?" asked Kwikumat. "This is the sun (*in^yá*). The moon goes west and returns, it dies and in two days it is born again. But I have made the sun at a different time, and it shall move differently." Kumastamxo allowed Marxókuvék to make daylight and darkness. "Both eternal darkness and eternal daylight would strain our eyes. Therefore one half of the time it shall be night (*tin^yám*), and one half day (*in^yám^ʿk*). Some creatures will sleep by day, some by night."

15. Kwikumat made another Yuma man and a Diegueño man and instructed them in the dark-house. Then he made a Cocopa man, a Maricopa, an Apache, a Wallapai, a Havasupai, a Chemehuevi, and a Kawia, and a wife for each. Marxokuvek said, "These are enough. If you make more people, this earth will be too small for them." Kwikumat told him that the earth was growing bigger all the time.

16. Kumastamxo stamped until he shook earth and sky. Everything was frightened. Kwikumat was in the dark-house. He knew that Kumastamxo was trying to make cracks in the earth, so that plants and trees might grow up. The arrow-weed (*isáv*) was the first plant to grow up through the cracks in the mud.

17. Kumastamxo talked north four times. He said, "It will hail." But the sky-kernels (*amain^yetadhítc*) which fell were not hail-stones, but grains

of corn. The people began to eat them. "Do not eat them all," cried Kumastamxo. "Plant some."—"How shall we plant them? With our hands?" He sent the people north to get sticks. Each one found a sharp stick. "This is corn (*tadhíitc*)," said Kumastamxo. "Take it, plant it."

18. Kumastamxo then made seeds of the gourd (*axmá*) and melon (*tsemetó*). He made them out of spittle. He gave them to the Cocopa. He gave seeds of the prickly pear (*aá*) to the Maricopa. The people planted the seeds in the wet ground.

19. Nobody knew how to make it rain. "To the Maricopa man alone I give power to produce and to stop rain," said Kumastamxo. "When the people thirst, let them remember me, for I have power to cover up the face of the sun with a rain-cloud and to send a rain-wind every day. When a man plants upon dry ground, let him remember me. If he calls my name and sees me, it will rain four or five days, and he can plant his seed."

20. Kwikumat said, "I am tired. I think I shall take a rest. It is about time to have some darkness." Kumastamxo said, "I will give you all the darkness you want." He fastened the sky so that the sun could never rise again. But Kwikumat stamped four times. This jarred the sky free, and the sun came up. Kumastamxo was in the dark-house. He said, "I see the daylight coming. Who did that?"—"I did," said Kwikumat.

21. Marxókuvék tried to make some people. He made the coyote (*xataly̓wí*). Coyote began at once to look for something to eat. He would not stand still. Marxókuvék also made the raven (*akák*), the mountain-lion (*numéta*), and the cougar (*axatakúly̓*). Kwikumat appointed Coyote as head man (*piipá xeʟtanák*) over these three. Marxókuvék next created a girl and a boy. He was about to name them when Coyote said that he wished to. Coyote named the girl Sakily̓kily̓namá,* and the boy Ax'aly̓esmetny̓itcy̓ót.

22. Kwikumat noticed that none of these people were behaving properly. Mountain-lion tried to catch Sakily̓kily̓namá. Kwikumat told him to stop. After that he prowled about, trying to catch Marxókuvék and Kumastamxo, and even Kwikumat himself. "I must get rid of these animals," said Kwikumat. He assembled all the good people in the dark-house. He talked rapidly at each of the four corners, invoking a flood.

* Joe Homer tells a very long myth about Sakily̓kily̓namá, who weds Madhemkwisám.

First came a blinding dust storm. Then it rained thirty days. No water entered the dark-house. In vain the wicked besought Kwikumat to let them in. Most of them were drowned. Burro has, since then, great white spots on his belly.

23. Raven flew up to heaven. He hung by his beak at the very top of the sky. The water rose until it wet his tail. One can see where the water touched it. Then Kumastamxo caused the water to subside, for he did not want to drown this bird, for he was so pretty. Raven was black at first, and was then called *akák;* but Kumastamxo gave him many-colored feathers, and then named him *kukó.** Kumastamxo built him a cage, and in this he floated on the subsiding waters. Kumastamxo built the cage out of nothing, because he loved Kuko so much. When the cage rested on the earth, Kuko wished for freedom. In return for his freedom, he promised to be a faithful servant of Kumastamxo. He accompanied Kumastamxo everywhere he went. He would ascend high in the air and, descending, report to him what he saw. He could hear the tread of an enemy a day's journey distant.†

24. When the water had subsided and the earth began to grow dusty again, Kwikumat told the people that they might go outside the dark-house. Far in the west the storm was disappearing over the ocean.

25. The water sank so low that little was left in the ocean. Blind-Old-Man feared it would dry up. He crawled out upon the northern shore. He found Xavasumkul^yí and Xavasumkuwá in the dark-house. He promised them many things if they would renounce Kwikumat. He told them, "Kwikumat is going to kill you by and by." Xavasumkuwá believed him. But Xavasumkul^yí showed that she did not believe him, and feared him. Blind-Old-Man tried to seize her. She ran. He caught her. He promised her six meals a day. "Bring them here, then," she said. "I would like to," he said, "but I fear Kwikumat." Kwikumat approached, and Blind-Old-Man sank into the earth. "He had a tail, and claws on his fingers," said Xavasumkul^yí. "He wishes to take you down under the earth," said Kwikumat. "How could you catch anything to eat down there?"

* In Wallapai, *kukwóka* means 'woodpecker'.
† In Joe Homer's version of the Kwiyu myth, Kuko guides Kumastamxo to the dwelling of Axalykutatc.

26. Xavasumkul^yí walked over to where the people were standing, and told them how to produce children. They did not believe her. *Nec invitus unus ex viris conatus est ea agere quae ipsa dixisset. Penem autem in anum et non in vaginam inseruit. "Mox pariam aliquid," dixit femina. Exspectavit parere infantem paene eodem temporis momento. Cum id non accederit ea femina et ceterae ira commotae sunt. "Cur in me incensae estis?" inquit Xavasumkul^yí. Atque iterum explicavit, "Vaginae penem insere!" At ille vir in vaginam quidem non penem sed testes inseruit.*

Turn rediens ea marito dixit illas mulieres numquam concepturas esse. Kwikumat eam incusavit quod dixisset ceteris ea quae ipse eam occultim docuerat. "Nec metuo ne intellegant," Xavasumkul^yí inquit. Kwikumat jussit: "Duc has mulieres gradus quattuor ad septentriones, ad occidentem, ad meridiem, ad orientem et ego, item, viros ducam." Hac saltatione facta imperavit omnibus ut humi jacerent et copularent. [See p. 488, B.]

27. Because Kwikumat had wearied in his work and had stamped the sun loose again, Kumastamxo felt anger against him and boasted that he was the greater of the two. Kwikumat said, "You are only my little boy, too young to do better." Kumastamxo went into the dark-house and dreamed Kwikumat and Marxókuvék sick.

28. Kwikumat became crazy. He tried to turn the sky north instead of west. Then he walked from the dark-house out into the desert. He walked east, then west. Since he had turned the sky the wrong way, it got stuck, and would not turn at all. "Can I assist you?" asked Kumastamxo.

29. Kwikumat seated himself on a mountain and thought that he would make some more people. So he picked up a little stick, and, taking mud on his forefinger, he plastered it upon one end. Then he threw the stick away. This made it angry. It became the rattlesnake (*avē'*). The mud became the rattle. Rattlesnake feared the people, and they feared him. But the people discovered him and surrounded him. He tried to catch a woman. But the Apache Indian seized him and tied him around his waist. Kwikumat gave him power to do this, and he in turn gave power to his friends. Rattlesnake bit several persons. Among those bitten was Marxókuvék. Everybody said, "Kill that snake." But Marxókuvék was unwilling to kill it, for he knew that this would displease the Apache. "I suppose that I am going to die," said Marxóku-

vék. "No, you will not die," said Kwikumat, who then bade the people catch Rattlesnake and pull off his rattle, so that if Rattlesnake should thereafter bite anybody, the bite would not poison. Kwikumat then threw Rattlesnake far to the north. There he made a roaring sound, trying to make his rattle grow again. A man said that Rattlesnake had other rattles in his mouth. Kwikumat caught him again and opened his mouth. He found no rattles, no teeth, no poison. He then hurled Rattlesnake so far to the north that he fell into the ocean. He swam swiftly through the water, but soon went to the bottom, where he dwelt and grew fat.

30. The people asked Kumastamxo, "If we fall sick, who will cure us?"—"Men who have been instructed," said Kumastamxo. "We do not believe that," said the people, "for when you get sick, you cannot even cure yourself." Kumastamxo called all the Yuma men into the dark-house. "You are my favorite people," said he, "and I will tell you all secrets." He then made a dust storm arise in the east. It covered up the sun. It became like night. "Now sleep," said Kumastamxo. Dreams came. One man noticed that Kumastamxo's eyes were sore. He rubbed spittle on them and cured them. Another man saw that Kumastamxo had rheumatism. He found the pain and pressed it out. To another man Kumastamxo appeared to have the diarrhea. Kumastamxo sang, and this man sang with him, till it became cured. When a man talked wrongly, Kumastamxo stopped him, and asked another man to talk. "Most of you fellows talk right," he said, "and will be great doctors. If a man gets sick, let him call a Yuma doctor."

31. Marxókuvék had died from the snakebite. Kwikumat said, "Come here, you doctors, and cure this man. It is a difficult case. He is already dead. Well, I will show you how." He grasped Marxókuvék's hands. He then made himself imagine that Marxókuvék was breathing. "This man is not dead, but sleeps. I shall awaken him." He then took a stride in each of the four directions, reaching the ocean which surrounds the earth each time. Then a whirlwind came and breathed upon Marxókuvék. He stood up with closed eyes. Kwikumat then called the thunder from the west. All the places about grew bright. Marxókuvék opened his eyes. "You were sleeping too long," said Kwikumat, "so I awakened you."—"The snake bit me, and I felt drowsy," said Marxókuvék. "You died," said Kwikumat, "but the whirlwind came and cured you." When the people

learned that medicine-men had such power, they were afraid that they might kill as well as cure.

32. All the women asked one another, "What is coming within me?" They asked Xavasumkulʸí what was to happen, but she would not tell. All the children were born on the same day. The women were disappointed in them. "Why so small?" they said. "We wished to bear big men and women. These have not even hair on their heads, and cannot stand erect on their hind legs." They did not know that babies have to grow up. Kwikumat told them, "You will bear no more children unless you cohabit again."

33. Kwikumat created four more men—the Wallapai, Mohave, White, and Mexican. Some of these held themselves aloof from the other people. Kwikumat stamped four times in anger, and fire sprang up all over the earth. Kumastamxo saved the good people by covering them up with snow. The Mexican and the White escaped by flight. "This will not do," said Kumastamxo. "You make people and then destroy them, only because you yourself did not make them right." Kwikumat felt ashamed, and quenched the fires by rain.

34. Kwikumat took two whitish sticks. One he threw east, where it became a horse. The other he threw into the water, where it became a boat. He gave boat and horse to the whites.

35. Kumastamxo told the whites that if they would enter the dark-house, he would instruct them. But they distrusted him. They were rich and stingy. Kumastamxo told the Indians to drive them away. When the latter hesitated to do this, Kumastamxo invoked a hot windstorm, and the whites fled far to the west in a boat.

36. The people heard a great noise in the water. It seems that the figures made by Blind-Old-Man which Kwikumat had kicked into the water had come to life. The people were the duck (*xanamó*), the beaver (*apén*), the turtle (*kupéta*), and the wild goose (*yelák*). Their fingers and toes were webbed. "I fear they will kill us," said Kwikumat.

37. Kumastamxo made bow and arrows and gave them to the people. He then threw a handful of mud north, where it became a bird. "Shoot that," he said. The Cocopa man shot at it. But the arrow broke, for the bird was hard as stone. The man felt sad. He had no more arrows. Kumastamxo pulled up an arrow-weed and showed how to make arrows.

He then went west and turned himself into a deer. He asked the Yuma man to shoot the deer. He refused, for he knew it was Kumastamxo. The Apache, however, shot into the hindquarters of the deer, which fell to the ground. When he tried to skin it, Kumastamxo said, "Foolish man! That deer is of stone." This explains why the Apache kill deer. Kumastamxo was angry because the Apache shot at him and gave bow and arrows to the Yuma man alone, and forbade the others to use them. A big stone was coming out of the ground. That was the bow.

38. Kwikumat made another flood. The waves made the mountains and the high places as they now are. Before then the earth was flat. Kumastamxo lifted one man and one woman of each kind of people upon his shoulders. *Nonnulli refugium petierunt in ejus anum ascendentes.* [See p. 488, C.] Others stood on the top of Avihaatác Mountain. When these entreated Kumastamxo to save them, he turned them into rocks. It rained forty days. Kumastamxo spread his arms four times. The waters went down.

39. When the earth was dry again, Kwikumat created just one person more, Akoikwitcʸán ('Yuma-Old-Woman'). She belonged to the Xavtsats nation.

[THE DEATH OF KWIKUMAT]

40. Kwikumat had no wife, but he had a daughter, Xavasúmkulapláp ('Blue-Green-Bottom-of-her-Foot'). People now call her the Frog (Xanʸé). She was born in the water, like Kwikumat himself. They lived in the darkhouse. Kwikumat lay at the north wall of the house. Frog lay naked by the door. Kwikumat felt sick. He staggered outside to defecate. As he passed Frog, he touched her private parts with his hand. He went south and defecated. Frog straightway turned over and burrowed under the earth. Coming up under Kwikumat, she opened wide her mouth, into which fell four pieces of excrement. She then burrowed back to the hut and lay down as before. Kwikumat came back into the house dizzy and groaning. All his strength had left him. Frog said, "Father, what ails you?"

"I am sick, I am sick.
What made me sick? What made me sick?

Did rain-cloud make me sick?
Did foul-wind make me sick?
My head is sick, my belly is sick,
My limbs are sick, my heart is sick."

Kwikumat lay with his head turned successively in all four directions. The people squatted around. All the doctors together could not cure him.

41. The Badger (Maxwá) fetched cool sand and placed it on his breast. Although Badger was not a doctor and did not know the reason for his own action, Kwikumat said, "I think I am getting better." Then he grew sicker. He said, "I do not think I shall live long, I am going to die. But I shall feel all right again sometime, somewhere." The people did not understand what he meant by "die." His was the first death. Kwikumat sweated. His sweat is white pigment. They get it north of Yuma. Beaver threw some clothes over him, for he felt cold. That is why people wear clothes. Kwikumat called to Kumastamxo, "Little boy, come here!" The fourth time Kumastamxo heard him. Kwikumat told him, "I am going far away. I leave everything in your care. Complete my works! I have taught you long. Do everything right." Frog said, "He is nearly dead. I will flee from here." She burrowed under the earth.

42. When the dawn came, Kwikumat died. He lay in the dark-house. His head was toward the west. All the people were silent. They thought he was asleep. Wren (Xanavtcíp) said, "He is dead. He is a shadow. He is a wind. You will never know him more."

43. Kwikumat, when dying, told Coyote, "Since I placed you as chief over three, you must behave yourself and set a good example." Kwikumat knew that Coyote intended to steal his heart, and all the others knew it also. Wren said to Coyote, "You take my heart as a substitute" (*'Inʸép iwá madháuk matsinʸóxa'*).* And the people understood that Coyote would take Wren's heart instead of Kwikumat's.

44. Wren deliberated silently how he might thwart Coyote in his purpose. He asked himself, "Shall we hide the body? Shall we throw it into the water? Shall we burn it up?" Wren said to the people, "We must burn him up." Wren then told Beaver, "Fetch cottonwood-logs from the north,

---

* Often said at cremations in a figurative sense.

where you will find them standing dry, ready to burn." Beaver felled them with his teeth. He brought them back with his teeth. Wren told the ant-lion (*manisaár*), "Dig a hole here quickly; dig it as long, broad, and deep as a man." When the hole was finished, Wren commanded Beaver to fill it with dry arrow-weed, and then to lay three logs lengthwise across the hole, and two more on each side of these. Beaver had brought only four. He had to fetch three more. On these logs Beaver and others piled dry logs and arrow-weed.

45. There was no door nor opening in the dark-house. "Which side shall we tear open in order to take the body out?" asked Kumastamxo and Marxókuvék. They decided to bear it south. Wren said, "Because some of us are born in the north, bear it north." Wren said, "Lift him up!" They seized the body with their hands. They took one step north. Then they laid it down. They were still inside the house. Kumastamxo broke open the north wall without touching it. Then they took another step north and laid it down again. Thus with four steps they laid it, head south and face down, on the pyre, and piled wood and arrow-weed over it.

46. All was ready. But they had no fire. Wren sent Coyote east to get fire. He told him to run to the place where Kumastamxo had rubbed his spittle on the sky. He did not wish to have Coyote about. Coyote reached the dawn with four bounds. He rubbed his tail in the white fire. Mean-while Wren directed two women to make fire. They were the House-Fly (Xalesmó) and Big-Blue-Fly (Kwixvacó). They took turns at twirling a dry arrow-weed stalk on a piece of willow-wood. They fed the sparks with willow-bark. Kumastamxo said that all people would make fire thus. Lizard (Kwaatul[y]) lighted a wisp of arrow-weed. He lighted the south-east corner of the pyre first, and last of all the southwest corner.

Coyote came bounding back, his tail all light. He leaped straight for the burning pyre. He was angry. The light on his tail went out. That is why it is black on the end. "Stand close together!" all the people cried, "for he is going to jump." They crowded thickly about the fire. Badger and Squirrel (Xomir) were the shortest men. Coyote sprang over these, seized Kwikumat's heart in his teeth, and then, springing back again, ran swiftly southwest. Chicken-Hawk (Its'ór[a]) was the best runner in the crowd. They sent him after Coyote. But Coyote left Chicken-Hawk far behind. Still he did not stop. Only when he had reached the Maricopa country did he lay the heart down and eat it. The heart became a mountain. It is called Greasy Mountain (Avikwaxós). It is greasy from the fat of the heart. It is always shady about this mountain.

47. After Coyote ate that heart, his mouth was black and his tongue blood-red. They were burnt by the heart. Kumastamxo said, "Coyote is not worthy of being called a man. He shall be wild. He shall have neither a friend nor a home. He shall sneak about the mountains and sleep with the jack-rabbits. I call him Xuksaraviyŏu."

Coyote was crazy. He tried to marry his own daughter. One day he noticed a girl among the bushes *cui erat vagina ulcerosa et putrida, quam omnes fugerent. Cum ad eam lupus decurreret, exterrita in manus genuaque descendit. Tum lupus cum ea copulavit.* [See p. 489, D.] He could not disengage himself. The girl carried him with her up to the sky. Coyote may still be recognized as the dark spot on the moon.

48. All sat in silent grief about the burning pyre. The old people felt saddest, for they knew they must soon share Kwikumat's fate. But none knew about crying. It was the Yuma man who cried first. His name was Xanavá. He is now a kind of red bug which cries, "Tci-tci!" He was sitting on a mesquite-tree, looking at the ground. He raised his little voice, and cried, "Tci-tci-tci-tci!" Then Tinʸamxworxwár joined in. He cried, "Xwurrxwurr!" He was sitting on a willow-tree. He is now a green bug. All the people began to cry, everything cried. The wind cried. The sky cried. Kumastamxo shouted, "Because we have lost our father, all people will lose their fathers. Our father dies. Everybody dies. People are born and must die. Otherwise there would be too many people. They would have to sleep on top of one another. Maybe somebody would defecate all over you." As he said these words, all the people trimmed their hair (or feathers) and threw it into the fire. Deer (Akwák), Jack-Rabbit (Akúlʸ), Cotton-Tail (Xalʸáw), and Bear (Maxwát) cut their tails off and threw them in. They found it hard to make their tails grow again. Roadrunner (Talʸpó) was the only man who kept his tail long. He needed it.

49. A whirlwind now blew all about. The people thought that Kwikumat was about to appear again. "No," said Kumastamxo, "that is the holy spirit-wind. Sometimes it will come very near you. But you will see nobody, only dust-laden wind." He sang four times—

The wind is wandering, is wandering.
The wind is wandering, is wandering.

Then all the people cried anew.

50. Kumastamxo said, "Wren was a poor manager. Henceforth I will attend to everything myself."

51. Frog kept burrowing beneath the earth with guilt and fear in her heart. She felt that she must emerge in order to open her mouth and cool it, for it was burning hot from the excrement which she had eaten. But hearing the wailing of all things, she burrowed under again, lest the people discover and kill her. She emerged four times—(1) at Amatkoxwítc, a round pit near Mellen, Arizona; (2) at Samkótcave,* a hole in the ground near Bill Williams Fork, three miles above its confluence with the Colorado; (3) at Avixᵃá, Cottonwood Mountain, a mile east of Yuma, Arizona; (4) at Avixanʸé, Frog Mountain, near Tucson, Arizona. Frog was transformed into this mountain.

[THE AGE OF KUMASTAMXO]

52. Rattlesnake remained in the ocean. He feared to come on shore, lest the people take vengeance upon him for having bitten Marxókuvék. He grew to such enormous size that he could encircle the earth with his body. The people feared that if Kumaiavĕta were allowed to grow much larger, he might come on land and kill them all. Kumaiavắta was a powerful doctor. Kumastamxo feared that he might send forth pestilence from under the water, or that he might eat somebody's excrement, as Frog had done. Therefore Kumastamxo resolved to destroy Kumaiavĕta. "We will summon him to Axavolʸpo," said Kumastamxo, "and I will manage the rest." Kumastamxo sent Spider (Xalʸtót) to request Kumaiavĕta to come to Axavolʸpo in order to cure a sick man there. Spider darted down and back. "Kumaiavĕta says that he does not wish to come."—"Tell Kumaiavĕta that the man will die if he does not hasten hither," said Kumastamxo to Spider.

When Spider delivered this message, Kumaiavĕta said, "It is my duty as doctor to go, although I know exactly what you fellows are trying to do. I have, however, one request. Grind corn and place some of it at four places on my way, that I may not famish on the long journey." When Kumaiavĕta reached the first stopping-place, he found more corn there

---

* In this hole the Yavapai are said to have married.

than he could eat. He thought, "I know now that they wish to kill me, since they have placed a lunch for me here. But it is my duty to go ahead." Spider said, "You had better hasten, lest the man die." At that Kumaiavĕta grew angry. He shook his tail, making a noise like thunder. Enveloped in storm-dust and lightning, he reached Axavolʸpo. The people all fled from the dark-house when they saw that Kumaiavĕta had four heads. Only Kumastamxo remained within. Kumaiavĕta smelled of the house. "Nobody is in there," said the people. "Yes, a sick man is there," said Kumaiavĕta. "That is true," said the people, "but we thought you would prefer not to have us about when you cure him, so we came outside."

Kumastamxo stood inside the house, west of the door. In his hand he held a great stone knife. There was no sick man there. He had merely thrown up earth in the center of the floor, so as to resemble a sick man. Kumaiavĕta tried in vain to wedge his heads through the door. Kumastamxo made the door wider. Kumaiavĕta then caught scent of Kumastamxo. He pushed his four heads inside the house. With a single blow Kumastamxo severed all four heads from the neck. Then he sprang outside, leaving the heads in the room. He brandished his knife before the people. "When you want to kill somebody, use this." This is why people have knives. He tossed it up and caught it. Kumastamxo said, "Because Kumaiavĕta has been killed, other bad doctors will be killed." There is blood and spittle in the mountains all along where Kumaiavĕta's body lay. The whites call the red "gold" and the white "silver." Kumastamxo took the four heads, cut them apart, and pounded up each one separately west of Axavolʸpo. They are now gravel-beds.

Kumastamxo said, "I know you all fear that there will be another flood. There have been four floods. There will never be another; for I shall take this great body and place it along the shore about the whole world, and above it the water shall not rise. But if you kill my bird Kuko, I will make the water rise and drown you all." When Kumaiavĕta was killed, he urinated freely. The ocean is his urine. That is why it is salty, has foam on [it], [and] is not good to drink.

53. Kumastamxo said, "This place is unclean. I shall burn the house." Marxókuvék said, "No, leave it there; for I will call the birds and wild animals, and they will dwell about there when we have already journeyed forth." [Song, repeated four times:—]

The house will burn, will burn.
The house will be crackling, will be crackling.
It will blaze.
We are going to [dance?].
It is going to be lighted.
It is going to be lighted.
It will blaze.
We are going to [dance?].
Something bird-like is coming.
Bird-like tracks will be about the place. *
We are going to light this unclean house.
It will blaze, blaze.

Kumastamxo took four steps, lighting the house at the four corners. Then they all danced. When they ceased, Kumastamxo called Night-Hawk (Wiú). He taught Night-Hawk to sing when the dawn is coming, so as to awaken the people. Kumastamxo promised him great wisdom if he would do this regularly. "Let me sleep a little longer," said Night-Hawk. After a while Night-Hawk called out, "Qrr′ rr′ rr′ rr′!" When he calls thus, the people know it is time to wake up.

54. Kumastamxo said, "Let us leave this place!" He took four great strides to the north. The people moved with him. He had a wooden spear. He made it out of nothing. He pressed the sharp end into the ground and moved the other end toward and from himself four times. Then he pulled it out toward the north. Water gushed forth and started to flow north. He stopped it without touching it. A second time he drew the spear out toward the west. He stopped the water. Then toward the east. He stopped the water. Then he threw it out toward the south. He let the water flow freely. He took four strides south. At each stride he made a great scratch with his spear in order to guide the water to the ocean. Where he held the spear-blade flat, the river is broad. Where he held it sidewise, the river-channel is narrow, and most of the water flows on one side. At Yuma he cut the mountains asunder to let the river through. Taking four more steps, he returned to the source. [Song, repeated four times:—]

---

* When a man dies, and his house is burned, seeds are thrown into the fire. Birds come later and pick them up.

This is my water, my water.
This is my river, my river.
We love its water.
We love its driftwood [foamwood].
It shall flow forever.
It shall flow forever.
When the weather grows hot,
It shall rise and overflow its banks.
It shall flow forever.

55. Kumastamxo made a raft of cottonwood-logs out of nothing. On it he placed four medicine-men—a Maricopa, Yuma, Diegueño, and Cocopa. On a second raft he placed four more medicine-men. One of these was a Mohave. The other people walked down.

56. They stopped first at a whirlpool near Kwiyuhitáp, north of Mellen, Arizona.* A great snake (Xikwír) was traveling southward "behind the river." He wanted to bite somebody. Kumastamxo caught him. That he might always stay in the water, and never become a man, Kumastamxo pulled the snake's teeth out.†

57. At Avikarutát, south of Parker, they stopped a second time. Kumastamxo told the Yavapai to live there on the Arizona side. He forbade them to cross the river. They did not know how to swim. At last they crossed on a tule-raft. Kumastamxo made a bright light shine forth from Avikarutát Mountain. But the California side was dark.

58. Kumastamxo said to the people, "Because you are good people, I want you to find a good place to stay. We are going to move up to the top of a high mountain, and I shall teach you everything up there. From there we can see far over the earth." He moved north with four steps. The people moved with him. "This is my homeland," said he, "this is High Mountain (Avikwaamé)."

59. "Here is the place for the dark-house," said he. He sent Beaver to bring four cottonwood-posts. Ant-Lion (Manisaár) dug four holes.

---

* Mohave, Kwayuhitápmave ('place [ave] where Kwayu was killed [hitap]'). Kwayu was a gigantic cannibal.
† My informant explains that his body is a red stratum on the California bank. Nearby is a cave. If one enters, Xikwír will not bite, but will make one sick. He stabs in the abdomen, and blood flows forth. All about lie Xikwír's teeth. They are shiny and as large as fingers.

Lizard (Kwaatúl^y) brought willow-poles. Big Red Ant (Tcamadhúl^y) brought sand and placed it on the roof.

60. Kumastamxo stationed the learners in the northeast corner, the good doctors in the southwest corner. Dead people stayed in the southeast corner, for they go in that direction when they die. The door was in the northern side. Kumastamxo made the bad "speechers" sit down. He did not allow them to bewitch one another. Kumastamxo alone bewitched, and gave only those sicknesses which others had power to cure.

61. Kumastamxo said, "I should like to keep all of you in here all the time. But it is so crowded that you cannot learn well. So I ask you to go outside." He sent them out. Only Ampot^axasarkwitin^yám remained within. Kumastamxo produced a great star and showed it to him there in the dark. "You are a good 'speecher.' With this find the road, with this find your own house in the darkest night. This is the great star (*xamasé vatái*).* Take this out when you cannot see well." Kumastamxo called in each of the great doctors separately. He taught some of them how to kill a man in four days.

62. Kumastamxo called all the people into the dark-house again. He made everything dark. All fell asleep. He ascended into the sky. The people could not find him. He entered the dark-house again, and they discovered him there. Then the sun, moon, and stars disappeared. There was consternation among the dreamers. Even Marxókuvék did not know how to make a light. But after a while a certain man pulled out the morning star. It shed light all about. Then Kumastamxo took the very sky away with him. They found him with it in the dark-house. He taught by alarming the people and then assisting them.

63. Kumastamxo made a cottonwood-tree grow up in the dark-house. He cut the roots with his mind. It fell toward the west. "Who wishes to have this tree?"—"We," said the Yuma. "We will tie feathers along the sides of it and make the sacred sticks (*xaukwíl^y*) used in Yuma fiestas."

64. Kumastamxo bade the people go outside. He taught them how to fix up and fight. He gave them bows and arrows and war-clubs as they went out.

---

* That is, the morning star.

65. He kept the people outside. He allowed only one Yuma man and one Diegueño man to enter. He taught them how to make fiesta houses (*avakarúk*).* That Yuma Indian was Pamavíitc, ancestor of all the women who bear the name Mavé. They had no cottonwood nor willow trees. They built it out of nothing. They made a shade-roof. Meanwhile all the other people were standing in a line east of the house, and facing east. Kumastamxo announced that all was finished. When the people turned about, they beheld not one but two fiesta houses, one for the Yuma, and one for the Diegueño. Kumastamxo led one half of the Cocopa under the Diegueño house and taught them how to make one for themselves. These told the other Cocopa people. Kumastamxo said, "When you lose a big man, you will have a fiesta some months after he is dead."

66. It became dark. Kumastamxo detailed Ampot^axasarkwitin^yám to take charge of the speeches. Kumastamxo gave him many songs. Then Kumastamxo changed the darkness into daylight. He knew what each Yuma man could do. He called each man to him separately. He was in the dark-house. He said to each man, "You know to what tribe you belong. Kwikumat told you not to forget. For if you forget, you will not be swung into the right place [?]."

67. To the first man thus called into the dark-house Kumastamxo said, "Since Frog was eldest-born, I call you 'Xavtsáts'; but since Frog fled, I call her 'Xan^yé'. Call your daughters 'Xavtsáts'."†

Then he called in Paxipátc and gave him his nation, too. He said, "Call your daughters 'Hipá'. But I now call Coyote 'Xatalwí'."

To Pagel^yótc [?] he gave the nation-name 'ʟ^aots', which is connected with rain-cloud. Rain-clouds are now known as *akwí*.

To Pamavíitc he gave the name 'Rattlesnake' (Maavĕ). Rattlesnake is now called 'Avĕ'.

To the next man he gave 'Red-Ant' (Ciq^upás). Red-Ant is now called 'Ikwís'.

---

* Shade-roofs built of cottonwood-poles and willow-branches for ceremonial use during the various "fiestas."
† The informant at first stated, and later denied, that [the first man] was Ampot^axasarkwitin^yám. Each Yuma man has one or more names of descriptive or fanciful meaning. Each woman, however, bears an inherited name, which is the same as that of her full sisters, father's sisters, and father's father's sisters. The Indians, when talking English, call such names of women "nations." A woman . . . is always known by the name of her nation, although this may be coupled with one or two other names which serve to distinguish her from other women of the same nation.

To the next man he gave 'Roadrunner' (Met'á). Roadrunner is now called 'Tal'pó'. Kumastamxo named him after he ran.

To the next man he gave 'Mesquite-Beans' (Al'mō´s).*

To the next man he gave 'Deer-Hide' (Sin'kwáʟ).

To the next man he gave 'a kind of Brown Bug' (Èstamadhún), not an ant-lion.

When the next man came in, Kumastamxo had to stop and think. All the good names had been given. He gave him 'a bunch of shreds of willow-bark which had been soaked at least ten days in water' (Kwickú).

When the next man came, Kumastamxo said, "'Xal'pŏ´t', call your girl thus." Xal'pŏ´t means "already done."

One lone man came running up. "Am I too late?"—"No, I call your nation 'Hard-Ground' (Xakcí)."

68. Kumastamxo then called out the stones and trees, and gave each its nation.

69. Kumastamxo gave each man a gourd rattle and taught him to "throw the gourd." Then they all danced. They stood east of the house, grouped in tribes. Inside the house the Yuma stood north, the Diegueño west, the Cocopa south, the Maricopa east. Kumastamxo told the Wallapai and the Havasupai to go northeast, and he told the Chimehuevi to go northwest, and the Kawia to go west. Then he said to the others, "I send you four kinds of people south. Because I send you, you must remember me wherever you stay, for I am going to turn into something." The Mohave alone stayed there with Kumastamxo. They were little children, too young to march.

70. Marxókuvék led the Yuma and Diegueño people away first. The Cocopa and Maricopa followed. They marched west across the desert, crossing many mountains. When the Yuma and Diegueño reached Aviivéra, east of Riverside, they found the eastern slope wooded, and they held a fiesta there. There the Cocopa overtook them. Kumastamxo did not want them to fight. But soon they began to shoot at the Yuma and Diegueño. The Maricopa Indians stood close to the Cocopa and sided with them.

71. Kumastamxo tried to produce a thunderstorm. Only a few drops of rain fell. Then he said, "I must return to Avikwaamé." He took Marx-

---

* An old woman of this nation bears the additional name 'Akoiitchámál' ('Old-Woman-Something-White'), because the mesquite beans referred to by Kumastamxo were ripe and white.

ókuvék with him. When they neared Avikwaamé, Marxókuvék sickened. The people carried him down the Colorado river-valley, for they liked him. At Yuma the river was so swift that they could not carry him across. Kumastamxo knew their difficulty, and made the river shallow. Then they carried Marxókuvék across. At Avixolʸpó,* Marxókuvék said, "This is my homeland. Here we shall live. Burn my body by yonder mountain." Then he died, with his head to the south.

They burned him at the base of Mokwintaórv Mountain, at a place called Aauxʼrakyámp.† The rocks are still red from the fire. The people cried loudly, "He is dead, he is dead!" referring to Kwikumat and Kumastamxo, as well as to Marxókuvék. They burned Marxókuvék on top of that mountain. The Yuma go to that place,‡ and Marxókuvék shows them how to do wonderful things. He tells us everything. Men also climb this mountain. It takes four days to climb it. On its summit they fall into visions at midnight. Marxókuvék asks them what they want and satisfies them. But great doctors go up to Avikwaamé and see Kumastamxo. It takes four days to go up there. No songs are taught at Mokwintaórv.

72. Kumastamxo said, "Havíirk," meaning, "It is finished." He stood there. He thought, "I will sink into the ground." He sang four times—

Into the earth I go down, go down.
Nothing but earth will I be seeing, will I be seeing.
I sink down into the old riverbed,
Down into the interior.

The first time he sang thus, his feet sank into the earth; the second time, his thighs sank into the earth; the third time, his neck sank into the earth; the fourth time, he sank out of sight, and remained there in the interior of the earth four days.

73. Then he came up again. He stood there. He said, "I am going to ascend." He extended his arms horizontally toward either side. Then he sang four times—

I am springing, springing.
Wing-feathers!

* Now Castle Dome, on the Arizona side, near Laguna.
† Meaning 'fire all around'.
‡ In their dreams.

Body-feathers!
On my hands, wing-feathers.
On my body [?], body-feathers.

He flew awkwardly into the air as he sang this the fourth time. He flapped his wings four times. He said, "I shall be called 'the black eagle' (*aspakwaanʸílʸ*) in the west,* 'the high eagle' (*aspakwaamaí*) in the east,† 'fish eagle' (*aspaatsikwítc*) in the south,‡ 'white eagle' (*aspahamál*) in the north."

LATIN PASSAGES

A. So that the virgin might fully understand, he himself demonstrated to her what should be done. Indeed, he lay down on the ground and copulated four times. The woman, sweating profusely, four times wiped away the sweat from her body with her hands.

B. Not unwillingly, one of the men tried to do those things which [Xavasumkilʸi] herself had described. However, he inserted his penis into [his woman's] anus, not into her vagina. "Soon I will bear something," said the woman. She expected to bear a child at any moment. When it did not happen, she and the other women became greatly agitated. "Why are you all inflamed against me?" asked Xavasumkulʸi. And so she explained again, "Insert the penis into the vagina." This time, though, the man inserted not his penis but his testicles into her vagina.

Returning, [Xavasumkilʸi] told her husband that the women would never conceive. Kwikumat scolded her because she had told to the others those things that he himself had taught her in secret. "I am not afraid that they should learn," said Xavasumkulʸi. [Then] Kwikumat ordered: "Lead these women four steps toward the north, toward the west, toward the south, toward the east, and I will lead the men likewise." When this dance was done, he ordered everybody to lie down on the ground and copulate.

C. Some sought refuge by rising up into his anus.

---

* This eagle protects the whites. That is why they have it on their money.
† High eagle lives in the Maricopa country. It is seen by medicine-men only.
‡ About the gulf.

D. One day he noticed a girl among the bushes whose vagina was ulcerous and putrid, from which everything fled. When Coyote ran toward her, she fell down on her hands and knees, terrified. Then Coyote copulated with her.

II

ESSAYS ON NATIVE CALIFORNIA LANGUAGES AND ORAL LITERATURES

The acorns come down from heaven.
I plant the short acorns in the valley,
I plant the long acorns in the valley,
I sprout:
   I, the black-oak acorn, sprout—
    I sprout.

        Ceremonial acorn song, Maidu
      Stephen Powers, *Tribes of California*

WHEN I HAVE DONNED
MY CREST OF STARS

The deeds of the people,
   the way they were,
     the people who spoke those things are heard no longer.

This will surely be the end of all that.
   Those things that were said are no longer heard.
     None have lasted beyond.

Those who continue beyond into the future
   will surely say the same about me,
     when I have gone off wearing my crest of stars.

Nevertheless,
   what I've said and the way I have been
     will remain in this land.

Kiliwa, Rufino Ochurte, 1969
Mauricio Mixco, *Kiliwa Texts*

A Brief History of Collection

SALVAGE

In October of 1914, James Alden Mason, an anthropologist at the University of California at Berkeley, made a brief fieldtrip down to the Santa Cruz area in an effort to locate speakers of Costanoan, a group of closely related languages spoken, at the time of European contact, roughly from the San Francisco Bay down to Big Sur along the coast and coastal foothills. He was hoping to find fluent speakers who still used the language in everyday life and who could provide him with wordlists and grammatical information and texts—information that could help him answer questions about the structure of the language and the nature of its relationship to neighboring languages and develop a better picture of Costanoan mythology and culture. It wasn't much of an expedition— more of an overnight trip, really—but its outcome speaks volumes about the critical condition of California's native languages, both then and now, and provides insight into the imperatives of the collecting endeavor itself. When Mason returned from his trip, he filed the following report with his department head, A. L. Kroeber.[1]

REPORT

Reached San Juan in early evening. In morning had a talk with priest of mission and several other oldest inhabitants of the place. All agreed that there were no Indians remaining in San Juan, that the few remaining ones had sold their lands and moved to Gilroy where land seemed to be a little cheaper. Consequently decided to go to Gilroy. Reached there about 2.00 and hunted up Acension Solorsan, an elderly Indian woman.[2] She claimed to know absolutely nothing but referred me to a very old woman, Josefa Velasquez in Watsonville. As prospects seemed a little better there, went to Watsonville and arrived there in early evening.

Wednesday morning went out to see Dona Josefa. She lives out East Lake St. about a half hour's walk out on the road to Morgan Hill, at the first horse trough. Is an old woman born at Santa Cruz in 1833 but reared in the ranches around Watsonville. A stay of several days with her might reveal many important points of interest but she remembers very little and very slowly. Spoke the San Juan dialect originally but has had no one to talk to for many years so forgets most of it. Verified many of de la Cuesta's words which are surprisingly accurate and got a few sentences and other words but very little. Also got a myth herewith included. After several hours of work she professed to know many myths, songs, dances, etc. Returned in the afternoon and, while she continued to insist that she knew many myths, etc., she was unable to recall one all afternoon. I got a few more words, phrases and two Yokuts gambling songs from María Gomez who lives with her. I am inclined to think that with a few days['] experience the old woman could be induced to tell many myths and songs, possibly in text, but they came so slowly at the beginning I decided it was not worth while trying again.

She insisted that Acension in Gilroy knew more than she, but claimed, like all others, that these two [herself and Acension] were the only living persons who remembered anything of the language and customs. Refugio Castello spoke it well, and so did Barbara Solarsan, the mother of Acension, but these two died no more than three years ago. I could learn of no other old or middle-aged Indian in the whole country.

So Thursday morning I returned to Gilroy to see Acension again. She was born in San Juan in 1855 and her mother, who died only a few years ago[,] spoke the language well. But she [Acension] never knew it well and has not spoken it for years. With difficulty I got from her a few phrases and sentences, words[,] and corroboration of many of de la Cuesta's words[,] but as she remembered very little, I decided the result was not worth the while and took the afternoon train home. With practice she might be taught to give texts but she undoubtedly remembers very little. She knows much less than Josefa, though her memory is a little better. Jacinta Gonzales died a few years ago.

Attached to this sad report were approximately two pages of elicitation labeled "San Juan words and phrases." The wordlist was followed by two

Yokuts gambling songs and a page of desultory ethnological notes—precious little return for the hours spent in gleaning them.

Mason's dejected, disappointed tone is impossible to mistake. Yet what modern reader will not be dismayed that he did not stay with Doña Josefa for as long as it took to rekindle her memory and revive her former fluency? She was one of the last speakers of her language. Whatever myths and legends she might have been helped to recall, whatever songs she might have resurrected, whatever poetry she might have spun from reminiscences long locked away in her rusty native tongue, they are gone now, completely. "Later" is not a reliable option when your best consultant is eighty-one years of age. Surely he gave up too easily.

But when the house is afire, to use J. P. Harrington's famous metaphor, you have to rescue what can best be saved.[3] Mason judged that his limited time and energies were best spent elsewhere, working with other languages, other consultants, where the knowledge lay closer to the surface. In 1914 in California, a mere sixty-some years—a single life-span, in fact—after the ethnic catastrophe of the Gold Rush, fieldwork was too often an exercise in linguistic and cultural triage.[4] It is no less true today, and will be again tomorrow: the last, best generation of elders is always just passing through their children's hands.

So Mason returned to San Francisco disappointed in his slim pickings and no doubt depressed at finding yet another age-old California culture in such dire straits. In the midst of his notes, though, lies a scrap of text recorded in the form of a mock letter, unremarked at the time but for an oblique reference to "a few sentences" in the second paragraph of his report. I present the text just as it appears in Mason's report, surrounded by a portion of the wordlist it was embedded in.

kanša´wi	I sing
wa´tį ka	I am going
aru·´ta kawa´tį	tomorrow I will go
wakišaš	coyote
u´mų	wolf
wa´tį ka u´ršį kaniš e´kwe ni´pa	I am going because you will not teach me
e´kwe kahi´nšu	I don't know
hī´nue e´kwe kahi´nšu	when I don't know
hi´nua kamšit haiwe´	when will I see you?
e´kwe kamišie´te oišu hai´we	I will not see you again

mi´šmin   nošo´   mišho´ke   hose´fa   kọ´   men.e´kwe
Dear   heart, thee sends Josefa.   Says thou not

pe´šio   hose´fa   še   katawa·´k   haiṭu´hiš
remember   Josefa   of   as she   every day.

hi´nuakše   wakiaṭ´a´kan   miš   hai´weni
Some day   she will come,   thee to see

kutceke´kwe   se´mon   a´ram   mišminsire´   mensi´tnumak
if not   dies.   Give   thy regards   thy children.

hu´miṭ tapu´r	give me wood!
šu´nesteka	I am hungry
a´mai^x	come!
šu´niešteka	I am filled
hiu´sẹŋ kame´š	Ah! how I love thee
hi´nuame ṭa´kan	when will you come?
e´kwe ka meš hole nipa	I cannot teach you
ni ekwe semon mumuri	here the flies won't die
xutceknis	dog
ekwe ka pe´sio kanri·´tca	I don't remember my language

A free translation of Doña Josefa's long-lost message runs as follows:[5]

> Dear heart,
> Josefa sends this to you!
> She says you don't remember her, Josefa,
> as she is every day.
> When will she come to see you—
> before she dies?
> Give me good wishes,
> you and your children!

What prompted Josefa Velasquez to compose this "letter" we'll never know. Probably Mason, in a desperate attempt to jump-start her dormant fluency, had asked Doña Josefa what she would say to family and friends if he were to carry back the message in Costanoan.[6] Whatever he was hoping for, he got a brief, emotional burst from the heart, straight from the ragbag of an old woman's worries and cares. It wasn't much, as texts go, and I'm sure Mason would have regarded his attempt as a failure. But today this little text has acquired such a force of eloquence, of poignancy, over the long years it has lain forgotten in the archives, that it fairly cracked open my brain like a nut when I stumbled across it—a voice from the past, leaping out from the detritus of a musty wordlist's bits and shards. *Because it's all there was,* and because it rings true, a kind of greatness is thrust upon it, the unintended plainsong of an old woman's words.

California has a rich and spectacular oral-literary heritage, as this book attests. But sometimes literature is simply where you find it, or when. Indeed, in the absence of any form of text at all, the wordlists themselves—*mother, father, acorn, sun*—take on an importance, a luminosity, well beyond their original mundane intention: they are the atoms of lost poetics.

WORKERS IN THE VINEYARD

Men and women, J. A. Mason among them, have been collecting and analyzing California myth, song, and ceremony for nearly two centuries in an effort to preserve the traditions before they are gone forever.[7] Yet I don't mean to give the wrong impression in stating this fact. Though commonplace in the discourse of Native American studies, such pronouncements throw the spotlight always onto the role of the fieldworker, the local historian, the interested amateur collector—an "outsider" role typically played by whites of European descent. Such statements tend to ignore the role of the performers themselves, who gave them the songs and stories in the first place. The performers, too, have dedicated their lives to preserving their traditions—but *their* efforts go back, ultimately, more than ten millennia in California: a hundred centuries of listening, learning, practicing, performing—and yes, refining, forgetting, adapting, and composing anew—the traditions that have passed from one generation to the next across the long reaches of time.

It is a mistake, and a bad one, to think that the act of recording in any way marks the culmination or fulfillment, much less the validation, of any given song or story. The arrival of a folklorist with microphone or notebook is not the "moment it's been waiting for"—as if, once it is written down, the people whose culture it portrays can breathe a sigh of relief and turn their attentions to something else. Writing a story down merely makes a record of its passing, like a single line of footprints tracked in the sand along a shore.[8] We all know just how much and how little that track can teach us. Nevertheless, without the collectors and their passion for writing things down, students of language and oral literature the world over—Native Californians included—would have less to marvel at, take pleasure in, draw wisdom from, and find beauty in.

Prior to the establishment of the University of California's Museum and Department of Anthropology at Berkeley in 1901, there was no systematic program of ethnographic research or collection in California— only a handful of men over the years who, driven by their interests, tried to record the folklore and verbal art of California narrators, and to do so faithfully (at least within the dictates of their era and training) rather than interpretively. Among the most important of these early works are Father Geronimo Boscana's record of Juaneño myth and religious ceremony, *Chinigchinich* (1933 [1846]); Alexander Taylor's enthusiastic but somewhat erratic series of articles on "Indianology" between 1860 and 1863 in *The California Farmer and Journal of Useful Arts* (an early California periodical conveniently owned by his father-in-law); Stephen Powers's important, indefatigable early work in Northern California during the 1870s, which culminated in his now badly dated *Tribes of California* (1877); and Jeremiah Curtin's large collection of Wintu and Yana myths in English (1898). Aside from these few mostly amateur collectors, prior to 1900 we have little but the passing anecdotal reports of travelers, settlers, and journalists, the occasional words and place-names recorded by early explorers (nautical expeditions by Cabrillo in 1542–1543 and Drake in 1579; overland explorations by Portolá in 1769, Frémont in 1846, and others), and the vocabularies and grammars compiled by Franciscan missionaries (for instance, de la Cuesta's early Salinan vocabulary [1825], or the later Costanoan materials [1861–1862] mentioned above in Mason's report).

With the dawn of the twentieth century, we enter a new stage in the documentation of California's native oral literature. Kroeber's Department of Anthropology was founded in 1901 with the specific goal of focusing and accelerating research on California cultures and languages— a goal that matured rapidly and with resounding success.[9] The next few decades saw a great explosion of scholars, students, and independent field-workers who contributed significantly to the corpus of California oral literature. In addition to Kroeber himself, these included such now-legendary collectors as Pliny Earl Goddard, Roland B. Dixon, Samuel Barrett, C. Hart Merriam, John Peabody Harrington, Carobeth Laird, Edward Sapir, Constance Du Bois, Edward W. Gifford, T. T. Waterman, Paul Radin, James A. Mason, Helen R. Roberts, Jaime de Angulo, L. S. Freeland, Susan Brandenstein Park, Dorothy Demetracopoulou, Anna Gayton, Stanley Newman, Gladys Reichard, Hans Jørgen Uldall, C. F. Voegelin, and Erminie Wheeler-Voegelin. A search through the published (and unpublished) work of any one of these researchers will lead the reader directly to important primary sources of California myth, song, and storytelling.

What distinguishes the work of these collectors from those who came before, and from the sundry amateur collectors who have tried their hand at presenting Indian stories in memoirs and magazines, is their attention to the actual words, not merely the gist, of the performances they recorded. All aspired to rigorous Boasian principles of textual documentation, and most had the phonetic training to take down texts in the original language, word-for-word as the narrator pronounced them. As a result of this care, this teneted belief in the primacy of the spoken word, the texts they later published from their fieldnotes are accurate records of actual narrative performances, not ex post facto re-creations of remembered events.[10] When it comes to the translations, of course, these are subject, like all translations the world over, to the whims of personal and period style—compare, say, Edward Sapir's translations from the Yana, made in 1910, with Jaime de Angulo's translations of Eastern Pomo (#16), made just twenty-five years later. But the texts themselves, the true legacy, stand always in testament to, or judgment of, their translators.[11]

Most of this early authoritative work was done by hand, laboriously, by taking manual dictation, a process that has stylistic consequences for the performance thus recorded. (See table 2 in the "General Introduction" for a list of the selections in this volume that were recorded by this and other methods.) A few researchers, notably J. P. Harrington, experimented with the early sound-recording technology, such as wax or wire cylinders and aluminum phonograph discs. Because of the awkwardness of the devices themselves—they were expensive, heavy, finicky, fragile, limited in capacity, and low in fidelity—machine recording was the exception rather than the rule. Kroeber and his colleagues at Berkeley made a great many recordings at the university, but the early machines were seldom practicable for use in the field (though Jack Marr, one of Harrington's intrepid young assistants, tells some hair-raising tales of trying to backpack phonographs and heavy cartons of aluminum discs across swaying rope bridges in the mountains of Northern California, on assignment from Harrington to reach important narrators).

The side effects of manual dictation on style are easy to predict: the pen, being slower by far than the voice, forces delivery to a crawl; at this slower pace, it is easy for narrators to lose the thread of their composition; longer, more complex sentence patterns may not be ventured, being rejected in favor of shorter, more direct phrasings that better suit the dribs-and-drabs progress of the dictation; and because it takes so long, there is a strong tendency toward truncation, so that the elaborate rhetorical patterns of episodic and incremental repetition that often characterize oral poetics are suppressed in the interests of economy. (The approach of evening after a grueling day of dictation must have hastened many a grand tale to a premature conclusion.) Time and again, though, in the earlier decades of this century, California's tribal narrators, answering the call of posterity, somehow managed to adjust to the limitations and artificiality of the work, minimizing its deleterious effects, and to deliver performances that transcended the special circumstances of their recording. In this volume, Jo Bender's "Loon Woman" (#12), William Benson's "Creation" (#16), and Johnny LaMarr's "Naponoha" (#9) all illustrate narrators who rose magnificently above the limitations of the collection methods of the time (though it remains true: we can still never know what performances they might have delivered had they been working with a tape recorder instead of dictation).

Later, when portable recording equipment became widely available, the dictation problem was effectively eliminated. But comparison of dictated and tape-recorded texts reveals that there is still an enormous range and diversity of style and helps validate the essential (if not the particular) stylistic integrity of the older texts. For instance, Minnie Reeves's crisply told "The Boy Who Grew Up at Ta'k'imiłding" (#6a) and James Knight's wonderfully loose, rambling version of "The Dead People's Home" (#19) are both from tape-recorded texts. Similarly, Margaret Harrie's blunt "Coyote and Old Woman Bullhead" (#4) and Joe Homer's

FIGURE 12. *From left:* Sam Batwi, Alfred L. Kroeber, and Ishi.
Courtesy Phoebe Apperson Hearst Museum of Anthropology
and the Regents of the University of California.

densely detailed "An Account of Origins" (#27) are both from dictated texts.

Nevertheless, the advent of tape recording ushered in a new era in the collection of California oral literature. Under Mary Haas's direction of Berkeley's new Department of Linguistics, inaugurated in 1953, a new generation of researchers, trained in anthropological linguistics, began working the field. The tape recording of texts became the rule rather than the exception. (Nowadays, of course, videotaping is gradually becoming the new standard of documentation.) In 1951 Haas and Murray Emeneau founded the Survey of California and Other Indian Languages (initially as "The Survey of California Indian Languages"), which has sponsored research and archived tapes, fieldnotes, and other linguistic materials through the present day.[12] Inspired directly or indirectly by Haas and her colleagues and successors, dozens of students and scholars have made a vocation of California languages—among them Richard Applegate, Thomas Blackburn, William Bright, Sylvia Broadbent, Catherine Callaghan, James Crawford, Jon Dayley, Geoff Gamble, Victor Golla, Abe Halpern, Jane Hill, Ken Hill, Leanne Hinton, William Jacobsen, Richard Keeling, Martha Kendall, Kathryn Klar, Sidney Lamb, Margaret Langdon, Sally McLendon, Wick Miller, Mauricio Mixco, Julius Moshinsky, Pamela Munro, Mike Nichols, Mark Okrand, Robert Oswalt, Harvey Pitkin, R. H. Robins, Alice Shepherd, Hans Jacob Seiler, William Shipley, Shirley Silver, Len Talmy, Karl Teeter, Russell Ultan, and Ken Whistler.[13] Most of these scholars, in trying to honor Haas's demanding documentational goal of "grammar, texts, and dictionary," have made it a point to collect and publish oral-literary texts.

In the end, this storehouse of work recalls for us the hundreds of California singers and storytellers (without whom, nothing) who have dedicated their time and services—their personal repertoires, their cultural insight, their performing skills, and (perhaps above all) their patience—to the program of documentation over the last hundred years and more. Some were undoubtedly attracted to the idea initially by the pay, since it is customary for fieldworkers to compensate their consultants with a modest hourly wage. But truth be known, most would have carried on the work regardless. All too many elders have looked around to find themselves increasingly alone in language, among the last native speakers of their tribes, and they become as anxious as their linguists to help document its richness and repertoire before they themselves pass on.

Most language consultants, young or old, have a keen sense of posterity when it comes to the work they do. As James Knight observed, speaking "through" the tape in an aside while telling "The Dead People's Home" (#19), he had a compelling reason for recording his stories:

Because that's how it was,
    that's how they taught me.
Since they explained it to me that way,
    here's what I'm telling you now.
Now I'm putting what they told me a long time ago onto the tape.
    So it [the tape] is telling you this.
My friends and relatives can listen and say,
    "Yes, this is true."

Besides, singers and storytellers *like* to sing and tell stories. And the work they do with their field researchers often gives them the opportunity to focus on their art in a new way. Many also enjoy the intellectual pursuit of glossing and explicating their texts once they are recorded, and excel at this kind of linguistic work; others find the "drudge" work of analysis a burden to be avoided if possible. Of course, the sense of posterity "looking over your shoulder" that comes with making a permanent record of a song or story puts a special pressure on the performers. Jean Perry, in her introduction to "The Young Man from Serper" (#3), details the way Florence Shaughnessy would fret about getting her stories just right, reviewing her own work with a critical ear, knowing that the versions she taped were "for the record." She was not alone in feeling this way.

Unfortunately, we don't always know the identity of the singers and narrators of California's recorded literature. It wasn't always considered important information, owing to an early and flawed theory of folklore that viewed individual singers and narrators as passive and faceless "passers-on" of their traditions rather than as active and potentially idiosyncratic "shapers" of the traditional materials in their personal repertoires. Even so, fieldworkers always had a keen sense of their consultants as individuals, as personalities. Often the information is there, buried in the archived fieldnotes or correspondence of the linguist or anthropologist who collected the materials for publication. We know the names of many, many of the men and women who took the time to dictate or record their best work for the generations to come—names that we should hold in honor. The list is an amazingly long one—and open-ended, because the work is still going on—but a few among those who have contributed substantial bodies of their own art to the canon of California oral literature are Sam Batwi (Yana), Jo Bender (Wintu), William Ralganal Benson (Eastern Pomo), Annie Burke (Southern Pomo), Ted

Couro (Iipay Diegueño), Hanc'ibyjim (Maidu), Joe Homer (Quechan), Villiana Calac Hyde (Luiseño), Ishi (Yahi), Killeli (Yosemite Miwok), James Knight (Lake Miwok), George Laird (Chemehuevi), Fernando Librado (Ventureño Chumash), Harry and Sadie Marsh (Wintu), Mabel McKay (Pomo), Grace McKibbin (Wintu), Mike Miranda (Tübatulabal), Rufino Ochurte (PaiPai/Kiliwa), Lela Rhoades (Achumawi), Florence Shaughnessy (Yurok), María Solares (Ineseño Chumash), Robert Spott (Yurok), Tom Stone (Owens Valley Paiute), Lucy Thompson (Yurok), Lame Billy of Weitspus (Yurok), and Mary Yee (Barbareño Chumash).

Individually, each of the people named here, scholars and Indians alike, and so many unnamed others besides, have made significant contributions to the field of California oral literature. Collectively, the combined impact of their labors is enormous, and the value of their legacy, beyond measure.

NOTES

1. From papers in the ethnographic collection of the Bancroft Library, University of California at Berkeley (Valory Index, #23). The manuscript report is reproduced here in its entirety.

2. According to Catherine Callaghan, Ascensión Solarsano de Cervantes was J. P. Harrington's principal Mutsun (San Juan Bautista Costanoan) consultant. She was dying of cancer in the late 1920s but was still able to recall almost everything.—HWL

3. The phrase comes from a letter Harrington wrote in 1941 to his young neighbor and assistant, Jack Marr (who was just a teenager at the time). In full, and retaining Harrington's urgent underscores (now in italic), the passage reads:

> You've been a good friend if ever I had one, you just rushed at the work. You know how I look at this work, you and I are nothing, we'll both of us soon be dust. If you can grab these dying languages before the old timers completely die off, you will be doing one of the *few* things valuable to the people of the *remote* future. You know that. The time will come and *soon* when there won't be an Indian language left in California, all the languages developed for thousands of years will be *ashes,* the house is *afire,* it is *burning.* That's why I said to go through the blinding rain, roads or no roads, that's why I thanked God when you tried to cross the Mattole River, haven't I gone back even two weeks later to find them *dead* and the language *forever dead?*

4. The Gold Rush, which affected primarily the northern half of the state, followed upon a previous sixty-five years of Indian exposure to the Spanish mission system, whose main influence extended over the southern half of the state.

5. I am grateful to Catherine Callaghan for her help in making this translation. In return for her assistance, she has prevailed upon me to make the following corrections to the Costanoan language data reproduced here verbatim from Mason's unedited fieldnotes. (As she says, there may never *be* another opportunity to set this particular record straight.)

Corrected (and converted to modern orthography, where ʔ represents a glottal stop and doubled characters represent length), these forms should read:

OPENING WORDLIST

/kan šaawe/	'I am singing'.
/watti ka/	'I am going'.
/ʔaruuta ka watti/	'Tomorrow I will go'.
/wakšiš/	'coyote'
/ʔummuh/	'wolf'
/watti ka ʔussi kannis ʔekwe niipa/	'I am going because you will not teach me'.
/ʔekwe ka hinsu/	'I don't know'.
/hinwa ʔekwe ka hinsu/	'when I don't know'
/hinwa ka mes yete haywe/	'When will I see you'? [rapid speech]
/ʔekwe ka mes yete ʔoyšo haywe/	'I will not see you again'.

WORDS FROM TEXT

/mišmin/	'good one'
/nossow/	'soul, spirit; heart'
/mes/	'thee'
/hokke/	'to send away'
/hoseefa/	'Josefa'
/koo/	'to say'
/men/	'thou, thy'
/ekwe/	'not'
/pesyo/	'to think, remember'
/hoseefa-se/	'Josefa-OBJECTIVE CASE'
/kata/	'like, as'
/waak/	'he, she'

/hayi/	'all'
/ṭuuhis/	'day(s)'
/hinwa-kše/	'when-INDEFINITE(?)'
/wak/	'he, she'
/ya/	'also'
/ṭaakan/	'to come'
/mes/	'thee'
/hayweni/	'to come-see'
/koč/	'if, when'
/ʔekekwe/	'not' [intensified]
/semmon/	'to die'
/haram/	'you [PLURAL] give me'
/mišmin/	'good'
/sire/	'wishes' [*literally* "liver" (seat of emotions)]
/men/	'thy'
/sitnunmak/	'children'

CLOSING WORDLIST

/hummit tappur/	'Give me wood'!
/šunneste ka/	'I am hungry'.
/ʔammay/	'Eat'!
/sunyište ka/	'I am full'.
/hiwse ka mes/	'I love thee'.
/hinwa me ṭaakanʔ/	'When will you come'?
/ʔekwe ka mes holle niipa/	'I cannot teach you'.
/ni ekwe seemon muumuri/	'Here the flies won't die'.
/hučeknis/	'dog'
/ekwe ka pesyo ka riiča/	'I don't remember my language'.

6. Unfortunately, it is not entirely clear just who Doña Josefa is addressing in this text.

7. The whole concept of preserving a culture—or a literary tradition or a language—on paper is a vexed one. What does it mean to "preserve" a tradition? To what extent is the page merely the literary and cultural scholar's equivalent of formaldehyde? There has long been a tendency—a pernicious weakness, in truth—among American and European scholars steeped in the hyperliteracy

of the Western academic tradition to "confuse the map with the territory," as the saying goes. Would that scholars of American Indian cultures had always been as active in helping to preserve their people as their languages and traditions.

8. There's a fundamental difference, it seems, between the way a scholar thinks of preservation and the way a Native performer does: for the former, the goal is *documentation,* a record of what went on or what was said; for the latter, the goal is *continuation*—a preservation of the continuity of tradition and, most important of all, the people themselves, who bear that tradition into the future. This difference comes about not because the scholar is by nature indifferent, but simply from a difference in the underlying interests of scholars as opposed to Native peoples. It's no secret that a great deal of frustration and resentment has grown up in the chasm of this divide during the last few decades of interaction between these two parties, each of whom tends to view the other in a kind of client or worker relationship—researchers and "their" consultants, Indians and "their" researchers—and is surprised to feel underappreciated or exploited as a result.

9. A concise summary of the history and influence of this research program may be found in Robert Heizer's essay "History of Research" in the California volume of the Smithsonian's *Handbook of North American Indians* (1978), which he edited.

10. Absence of this rigor results in the myriad well-intentioned but bogus collections of Native American oral literature, such as Bertha Smith's *Yosemite Legends* (1904), which Stephen Medley, annotating a bibliography at the back of the recent and lovely *Legends of the Yosemite Miwok* (La Pena et al. 1993), describes as follows: "This is an attractively designed and presented selection of six Yosemite legends of suspect origin. Using Hutchings (1860) as a primary source, the author demonstrated her skill at the art of turning a short, concise legend into a longwinded and romantic epic. The writing is stylized and reflects a Europeanized concept of Native American thought" (94).

11. It must be said that when anthropologists and linguists took down texts *in English* before the advent of recording devices, they were not always so faithful to the word of their texts, feeling free—in ways they did not with native-language texts—to silently edit or recompose the words of their narrators. One is far less sure with English-language narratives (often signaled by the use of the words *myth* or *tale* in the title, as opposed to *text*) that they have not passed through the grammatical and stylistic filter of their collectors. Such filtering is always for the worse, never the better, as far as authenticity is concerned.

12. Though the *University of California Publications in Linguistics* series, which took over the burgeoning publication of linguistics monographs from the older *University of California Publications in Archaeology and Ethnology*

(1903–1969) in 1943, long ago widened its horizons to encompass the globe, it still publishes important monographs on California languages (see "Selected Resources for Further Study" for examples).

13. This list was compiled primarily from Victor Golla's obituary for Mary Haas in the *SSILA Newsletter* 15.2 (July 1996).

WOMEN'S BRUSH DANCE SONG

The owl cries out to me,
the hawk cries out to me as death approaches.

The killdeer, the mountain bird,
cry out to me as death approaches.

The black rattler, the red rattler,
cry out to me as death approaches.

The red racer, the gartersnake,
cry out to me as death approaches.

A large frog, a little frog,
cry out to me as death approaches.

An eagle, a condor,
cry out to me as death approaches.

Ceremonial song, Luiseño
Helen H. Roberts, *Form in Primitive Music*
(version by Brian Swann, *Song of the Sky*)

Notes on Native California Oral Literatures

INTRODUCTION

No detailed, comprehensive survey of California's oral literature has ever been done. Accessible recent overviews include William Wallace's "Comparative Literature" (1978c) and William Bright's "Oral Literature of California and the Intermountain Region" (1994b), which the reader is urged to consult, along with Robert Heizer's "Mythology: Regional Patterns and History of Research" (1978b). Edward Gifford and Gwendoline Block's lengthy introduction to their *California Indian Nights Entertainments* (1930) still makes, even after seventy years, a reliable layperson's entry into California culture patterns, oral-literary genres, and storytelling customs.[1]

Most California cultures had no restrictions on who could perform verbal art. Men and women alike sang songs, recited myths, and told stories. (Though I'm aware of very few instances of speeches recorded from female orators, that doesn't mean—particularly when the record is so spotty and incomplete—that women never made speeches.) There does seem to have been an overall tendency for men to be the performers on the more public and formal occasions—to recount the stories of creation in the roundhouse at night when everyone is gathered, to conduct the ceremonies and dances, to make the public announcements, and so forth (Gifford and Block 1930:43). But in many cultures, women were involved in ceremonies as well, and curing rituals, and storytelling sessions. The pages of California's many text collections (this one included) attest to the great significance of women as bearers of their oral traditions and to their skill as narrators.

Songs by and large are closely tied to their occasions—that is, you wouldn't normally sing a hunting song except in the proper context of hunting, or a ceremonial song apart from its attendant ceremony—but there are so many different kinds of songs and song contexts, that few aspects of life are devoid of the opportunity for singing them. Myths, in contrast, at least the more serious ones, were typically restricted to the winter cold-rainy season, when they helped to pass the time during the long nights and spells of bad weather. (In a great many California cultures, telling a myth out of season, in summertime, tempted fate by aggravating Rattlesnake.)

Like songs, stories are performed in a great variety of settings and contexts, both public and private, from the most weighty and formal of ceremonies to the most lighthearted of entertainments. They are told in connection with dances and ceremonies, religious initiations, rainy days, moral instruction, and funeral rites, as well as parties, family gatherings, and children's bedtimes. They are told to affirm the deepest cultural verities, to conserve knowledge, to explain the world, to interpret human and animal behavior, to illustrate points in public or private debate—or just to pass the time, to get a laugh or make people think, to sound a warning or sugarcoat friendly advice. In short, they perform all the functions that stories, from Bible stories to fairy tales to personal narratives to traveling salesman jokes, perform in Western cultures—and every other culture, for that matter.

In terms of genre, it is customary to recognize at least three broad categories or oral-literary *phyla*—narrative, song, and oratory, each of which is eager for further subdivision. In the remainder of this essay, I take up each of these genres in turn, hoping to give the reader a general "lay of the land" for each broad category.

NARRATIVE

Narrative itself might be further subdivided into myths, tales, legends, and personal reminiscences, along with various minor genres. Scholars tend to draw more distinctions than do ordinary people—the "folk" themselves. Still, most cultures draw at least a loose distinction between myth and tale, myths being stories that relate the actions of the First People in the world before human beings came into existence, and tales being stories dealing with human beings and their doings. (Note that this is not a distinction between supernatural and realistic stories, because tales are often just as fantastical as their mythic counterparts.) Often, too, the distinction between the two is a blurry one.

Beginning with Alfred Kroeber's "Indian Myths of South Central California" (1907b), later refined and expanded by Anna Gayton's "Areal Affiliations of California Folktales" (1935), California's oral literatures have typically been classified loosely according to the pattern of their creation myths. These rough "mythological zones" correspond by and large to the main culture areas agreed on by anthropologists: that is, allowing for exceptions, we find a Northwestern California creation pattern, a Southern California creation pattern, and a Central California creation pattern (itself often divided into North-Central and South-Central subareas).

Briefly, in Central California we tend to find a variation of the "Earth-diver" motif, where the Creator, assisted by a handful of other original beings (Coyote among them, as a rule), manages to procure a little bit of mud or sand brought up by a helper from the bottom of the primordial ocean they find themselves in, and stretches it out to make the earth. One of the most powerful yet lyrical examples of this type in the California canon was narrated in 1902 or 1903 by a brilliant Maidu storyteller named Hánc'ibyjim. In William Shipley's fine translation (1991:19–20), this portion of the creation myth runs as follows:

And then, they say, Earthmaker sang.
"Where are you, my great mountain ranges?
O, mountains of my world, where are you?"

Coyote tried. He kept on singing.
"If, indeed, we two shall see nothing at all,
traveling about the world,
then, perhaps,
there may be no misty mountain ranges there!"

Earthmaker said:
"If I could but see a little bit of land
I might do something very good with it."

Floating along, then,
they saw something like a bird's nest.
Earthmaker said:
"It really is small.
It would be good if it were a little bigger,
but it really is small.
I wonder if I might stretch it apart a little.
What would be good to do?
In what way can I make it a little bigger?"

As he talked, he transformed it.

He stretched it out to where the day breaks;
he stretched it out to the south;
he stretched it out to the place where the sun goes down;
he stretched it out to the North Country;
he stretched it out to the rim of the world;
he stretched it out!

When Earthmaker had stretched it out,
he said, "Good!
You who saw of old this earth, this mud,
and made this nest, sing!
Telling old tales, humans will say of you:
'In ancient times, the being who was Meadowlark,
making the land and sticking it together in just that way,
built the nest from which the world was made.'"

Then Meadowlark sang—
sang a beautiful song about Earthmaker's creation.

In Hánc'ibyjim's version, there is no diving, and a floating scrap of bird's-nest takes the place of mud, but the basic design of the myth is the same. In this collection, Darryl Wilson's Atsugewi creation myth, "Kwaw Labors to Form a World" (#1), lies closest to this pattern, drawing on this notion of stretching or "kneading" out the earth from a small dollop of initial substance (in Wilson's case, mist). Similarly, in William Benson's Eastern Pomo "Creation" (#16), two brothers—the creator Kuksu and his brother-helper Marumda (one of Coyote's many mythical names)— create the world from a ball of "armpit wax" (whatever that might be) and hair, by singing and dreaming it into being.[2]

In the South-Central literatures, the role played by a nonhuman, nonanimal creator or "Earthmaker" figure in the northern myths is often filled by Eagle. Sometimes, even, Coyote himself is in charge of the creation, as in certain Pomo, Patwin, and Miwok traditions (A. Kroeber 1907b:195; Gayton 1935:584). Usually, though, Coyote is just a helper— and a bumbling, contrary one at that, who is more apt to tamper with the Creator's efforts, spoiling them, than to follow directions.

In contrast, the Northwestern literary complex is characterized by its technical absence of creation myths (A. Kroeber 1925). Instead, the world is seen as having always been in existence (though humans were not among the race of First People). The annual World Renewal ceremonies of the Yurok, Karuk, Hupa, Tolowa, and others were, and still are, conducted to ensure the proper continuance of this eternal world.[3] The following passage comes from Francis Davis's account of the Karuk version of the ceremony performed in 1938:[4]

Between Yusarnimanimas and the mouth of Clear Creek I take a swim
    in the Klamath River.
When I get into the water so it runs over my head, I pray.
I think the prayer,
I do not say it aloud.
When I sink my head into the water,
the world will recognize me and awaken everyone to a realization that
    it is the beginning of *irahiv.*
When I pray, I pray for all to have luck.

When I get out of the water,
I put my shorts on again and go down the west bank of the river
    to a bedrock flat.
As I walk along,
I pray that all people who believe will walk as easily as I walk along this
    rough place.
The *ixkareya animas* walked over this in mythical times.
As I walk over it, I tramp it down,
I make room for everyone to live well and for there to be no sickness in
    the world.

Near Yusarnimanimas the people have placed a stone,
which has lain there for long years.
With my hands I rotate it slightly to make it sit more solidly,
so that the world will be solid too.

Everyone,
when I move it around,
will have the same power that *ixkareya animas* has.
Then I sit on the stone.

While I sit on the stone,
people come to see me.
All who come to see me will be lucky.
Besides[,] I pray for everyone else.
Then the *ipnipavan* paints me while I sit on the stone.

In Northwestern California, in place of creation myths per se, what we find is a body of "institution myths" (so-called by Kroeber), which relate the story of how various customs and ceremonies were first established for humankind by the Spirit People. Minnie Reeves's account of the "The Boy Who Grew Up at Ta'k'imiłding" (#6a) is an example of this type of myth from the Hupa.

In Southern California, too, a very different creation pattern is found. In some traditions (summarizing Gayton 1935), an Earth Mother figure and her brother-lover, together with their dying son, create the sun and moon and other features of the physical universe, including people, to whom they give customs and cultural institutions, instructing them in the conduct of proper human lives. In other traditions, two brothers take the place of the divine brother and sister and emerge, quarreling, from a primordial ocean to complete the work of creation. In the process, one of the brothers dies, thereby introducing death to the world. Either way, the story of this "dying god," of his death and burial, serves as a focus of cathartic grief for the people of the cultures that worship him.

The collector Paul Faye took down a small set of creation and burial songs in 1920 from a Cupeño singer named Salvadora Valenzuela (coincidentally the narrator of one of the two "Hawk Feather" episodes translated by Jane Hill in selection #25), songs that dwell on the themes and characters of this creation. Two of these songs may be found on page 57, where they serve to open part 1 of this book. The remaining songs in this set are presented below.[5] (The reference to "hell" in the second song should not be taken as a reference to the Hell of Christian theology, although there may be a degree of cultural overlay involved, but to the traditional Cupeño underworld or land of the dead.)

DEATH SONG
OF MUKAT

Far away they died,
Mukat, Tamayowet,
Mukat, Tamayowet.

Their hair they cut,
Their hair they banged,
Red-Bird, Roadrunner.

BURIAL SONG

My heart gives out, gives out,
My heart turns over, turns over.

My heart goes down to hell,
My heart goes down to hell.

My heart goes to the ocean,
My heart goes to the ocean.

More recently, Villiana Calac Hyde, the late, lamented Luiseño tradition-bearer and educator, saw fit to record a great many of her own store of songs before she died, including several long and profoundly moving funerary songs. (These songs have since been published in Hyde and Elliott 1994.) Taken as a whole, the creation and burial songs point to the key intermingling of two griefs that is so characteristic of the Southern California culture area: a religious grief felt for the death of the god in the story and a personal grief for one's own mortality and the very real death of family and friends. In the lines of the Luiseño mourning song that follows (Hyde and Elliott 1994:#175), we can see this intermingling made explicit:[6]

POPÍ'MUKVOY NÓÓNKWA
PÍ'MUKQA SONG

I am dying his death
I am dying his death
I am dying his death
I am dying his death
His death is my death

The death of the Moon
It became foggy at the time of his death
It was foggy when he expired
I am dying his death
I am dying his death
His death, hóó, hóó, hóó, amen . . .

Some of Mrs. Hyde's less culturally sensitive songs are presented in "A Harvest of Songs" (#24), this volume.

There are two Southern California creation myths included in this volume: Joe Homer's "An Account of Origins" (#27) and the Serrano "Creation" told by Sarah Martin (#23). The stylistic contrast in the two narrators' handling of the same basic myth-type is profound: where Homer is formal and detached, Martin is emotional and immediate; where Homer is profuse of detail, Martin is sparing, even stark at times; where Homer is complex, Martin is simplicity itself.[7] Yet both are expressions of the same essential pattern.

But creation myths are not the be-all and end-all of a literary tradition. Besides creation myths specifically, there is a whole constellation of stories set in this myth-time of creation, before the race of human beings came to dwell upon the earth—stories like "Theft of Fire," "Origin of Death" (blame Coyote), "Theft of the Sun," and the many versions of the "Pleiades" myth.

Perhaps the most significant and extensive genre or body of traditional stories in California centers on the mythic persona of Coyote. Actually, it's probably wrong to label the Coyote story as a narrative genre in its own right, because Coyote stories run the gamut from core cosmological myths and creation elegies, through just-so stories and picaresque adventure yarns, all the way to tall tales and the cultural equivalent of the raunchy joke. You name it, and Coyote has poked his nose into it somewhere. In any case, there's no question that Coyote is a favorite subject of Native California's narrators and audiences alike. As readers will come to see as they explore the contents of this volume alone (see table 1 in the "General Introduction"), Coyote is a complex and multivarious personality: now hero, now fool, now trickster, now lech, now spoiler, now all of these things rolled up in one.[8]

Myths are often distinguished from legends and other narrative genres by literary and linguistic features. The Karuk story "Coyote and Old

Woman Bullhead" (#4) is a myth not just because it happens to be set in the time of the Ikxaréeyav, the 'Spirit People', but because its special opening and closing formulas—"*Uknîii*" and "*Kupánakanakana*"—declare it to be a myth. Myths are also very often marked as such by the presence of a special grammatical element, usually referred to as a remote-past "quotative." In Yana, a Hokan language of Northern California, this element takes the form of a verbal suffix, *-n't^h(i)*, and indicates that the actions being related took place long ago, outside the direct experience of the narrator.[9] The use of this quotative (highlighted in boldface) is demonstrated in the following excerpt taken from a Northern Yana myth, "Coyote, Heron, and Lizard," narrated by Betty Brown in 1907 (Sapir 1910). In this passage, Coyote is seeking revenge on Heron Woman and all her companions for cuckolding him at a dance and for not sharing food with him.[10]

Sáadipsitdi**n't^h**,
They were all sleeping now, they say—

  ayji 'iwílsapc'i,
  [all] across one another,

    sáadipsiyaw,
    all sleeping,

      petgáa'ayaw.
      all snoring.

Púllay'atdi**n't^h** ay míc'i,
Now Coyote smeared pitch on it, they say,

  aygi wátguru^w.
  on the sweat house.

Púllayjiba**n't^h** ayk^h lalúu^wki,
He smeared pitch all over their feet, they say,

  púulay**n't^h** aygic^h yàa.
  He smeared pitch on the people, they say.

"Kúuyawgummagat^h bátdiduwálsa'a'!"
"May you not run out and save yourselves!"

Wáyr^u,
Now then,

híiram**n'tʰ** ay míc'ⁱ.
Coyote ran out of the house, they say.

Yámʰjatdi**n'tʰ** aycʰ yàa,
Now the people all burned up, they say,

    wátguruʷ.
    the sweat house [too].

"Túuma'ninj ayje asinj míik'áy'ⁱ.
"I have always done like this when I was angry.

"Wáyrᵘ,
"Now then,

    ditbílpaw' ayji c'áxaa'ays.
    cook for your loved one!

"K'un c'úps,
"So it's good,

    ayji túuyawna,"
    this doing of mine,"

      tíi**n'tʰ**.
      they say he said.

The passage shows how this suffix (translated as 'they say' or 'it is said') is typically attached only to the verbs in narrative clauses—that is, those statements the narrator is personally responsible for, which negotiate the temporal distance that separates myth-time from the present world—and not to the verbs in dialogue, which are made by the characters and are seen as statements belonging *to* that time.[11] In contrast, personal reminiscences, which relate events that the narrators themselves have been witness to, will not involve the use of a quotative, except perhaps incidentally. Many California traditions observe loose genre distinctions where the classification correlates with the appearance of a quotative element.

There are a great many narrative subgenres, both localized and widespread. Many Southern California repertoires reveal a great interest in legends of "witches" or sorcerers. Among the Northwest cultures, stories about the antics of Indian "devils," like "The Devil Who Died Laughing" (#5) and "It Was Scratching" (#6d), are a favorite genre. In

Central California, the Pomo stand out—even against a broader cultural background where birds like Falcon, Condor, Loon, Eagle, and Meadowlark are frequent and important characters in the mythic dramatis personae—as having an especial fondness for songs and stories featuring birds; Annie Burke's "The Trials of Young Hawk" (#17) is an example from Southern Pomo.

In contrast, so-called monster stories may be found pretty much everywhere; tales like "Mad Bat" (#15) and "Condor Steals Falcon's Wife" (#20b) are instances in this volume.[12] In the same way, most tribes tell stories about a culture hero—differently conceived for each group, it seems—who personifies the moral and physical ideals of his society. The Central Yana tale of "Flint Boy" (Sapir 1910) makes as good a template as any: a common outline might include the birth or arrival of a baby (often under supernatural circumstances, such as springing up from the ground like a plant, or from a clot of blood or spittle on the floor) who grows to maturity in a matter of days or weeks and sets off to right outstanding wrongs or kill monsters (marauding Grizzly Bear women in Flint Boy's case) or fight wars, rescuing his people by virtue of his physical prowess, cunning, and moral single-mindedness. Jane Hill's translation of episodes "From 'The Life of Hawk Feather'" (#25) provides an example of this genre here.

The distribution of tale-types can also make for interesting study. Some stories, like the "Grizzly Bear and Deer" myth, are known in the northern half of the state but not in the southern half, while others, like the "Visit to the Land of the Dead" myth (#20a), have the reverse distribution. Both stories are widespread favorites in their respective areas of California, yet are well-known outside the state as well. The "Loon Woman" myth (#12), in contrast, is unique to the North-Central region of California. Readers interested in such regional patterns should consult Gayton's "Areal Affiliations of California Folktales" (1935).

A final type of narrative, common in the primary literature but not represented formally in this collection, is the ethnographic text. It is an artificial genre, because these texts have been elicited in response to a direct question from the collector, usually an anthropologist or linguist seeking information about some aspect of culture: "What was an Indian funeral like?"—"How did people used to make acorn mush?"—"Describe a typical puberty ceremony"—and so on. Such narratives don't conform to any traditional genre; they would have no natural context in the Native culture, in which the answers are simply part of the fabric of life,

and by and large they would never have been produced but for the in-
quisitiveness of the collector (though it's easy to imagine children asking their grandparents questions like "What games did kids play when
you were growing up?" and getting what amounts to an ethnographically rich personal reminiscence in response).

Sometimes these ethnographic texts amount to little more than verbal descriptions of traditional activities, such as basketmaking or acorn
preparation—activities that are better documented visually, language being rather a poor medium for this sort of task. (Try explaining how to
tie a shoe over the phone.) Typically, such descriptions have been collected, in the untimely absence of a camera, purely for the sake of documentation, but often linguists will elicit them for reasons that have little to do with the nominal subject matter itself. Asking a consultant to
describe *in words* some such procedure as arrow-making is a little like
administering a stress test to the language itself: the unusual demands
placed on the syntax and lexicon often reap unsuspected grammatical
constructions and vocabulary items that might otherwise never have been
observed in hours of conventional narrative or conversation. But even
in scenarios like this, narrators will occasionally produce texts that manage to transcend their utilitarian origins. In the following passage, linguist Judith Crawford has asked Robert Martin, a Mojave, to describe
the making of a cradleboard:[13]

CRADLEBOARD

I'm going to make a baby cradle now.
I go, I go, I look for mesquite root, mesquite root, mesquite root.
I dig anywhere up in the valley and I'll stay until I get one—if I'm
    lucky, if the tree "gives it to you."
If it is straight lying in the ground, then I take it. I bring it home, I
    bend it, I lay it down until it is dry, and in one week or so, I'll put
    the crosspieces on.
I'll go after some arrowweeds and put the crosspieces on, and I do it
    and then I finish.
Then I finish, then, I'm going again, after the [things for tying] on the
    cradle. I peel mesquite bark and I bring it home. That's all.
I tie it up and finish. Then that's all.
Then I finish the baby cradle. I finish in one week or so. That is a baby
    cradle, and that's the way I make them, and that's all.

Martin's account may not give much in the way of detail regarding the actual techniques of manufacture—no one could make a cradleboard on the strength of his description alone—but it does convey a nice sense of the speaker's state of mind as he goes about his imagined way, gathering his materials and working them. There's a personality here that shines through, despite the unlikely context and subject matter.

Artificial or not, these texts can often be quite interesting from a literary standpoint, as well, even apart from the cultural information they contain. The linguist Robert Oswalt recorded the following ethnographic "textlet" from Essie Parrish in 1959, one of many he collected in the course of his extensive work with Kashaya Pomo speakers. Mrs. Parrish would have offered it in response to queries from Oswalt regarding food preparation techniques (it is one of several such texts she contributed to *Kashaya Texts*).[14]

PRESERVING SHELLFISH

In the old days we could keep food without it rotting.

When winter came and the sea ran high, the Indians could not go to gather food along the coast for long periods. Before the water had already become rough, the leader would command, "Store away your food." Having had him say when [to go], they went up to the gravel beach, pried off mussels, gathered turban snails, packed them up the coastal cliffs, dug holes, poured the shellfish in there, packed up gravel, poured it on top, and poured ocean water over all that.

Then even when it rained, the mussels were still good and unspoiled for several days or even one week—turban snails they kept the same way. Because they did that, the old time people did not die off from starvation.

That is all there is of that.

Though this account may seem to be off-hand, the information conveyed is in fact quite carefully organized. It opens with a formulaic reference to "the old days," thereby situating the text in the realm of memory (paragraph 1), then moves into that time-frame for a sparse but detailed description of the season, social context, harvested species, physical setting, and steps involved in preserving shellfish (paragraph 2). She then closes the window she has opened into the past, returns us to the present with her reference once again to the "old time" people, and—storyteller that she is—finishes up with a "moral" about survival and the importance of diligence and know-how (paragraph 3), before terminating the topic at hand (paragraph 4). The sense of literary form and closure, even in so short a discourse, is unmistakable.

Indeed, sometimes narrators can deliver goods that far exceed the relatively narrow, prosaic expectations of the genre. Betty Brown, the Northern Yana consultant Edward Sapir worked with in 1907, dictated a series of ethnographic texts—ethnographic *vignettes* might be a better description—that soar far above most other texts of their kind. In this excerpt, from a much longer text Sapir called "Indian Medicine-Men," a frantic husband has just called in a powerful shaman to try to save his dying wife.[15]

> NARRATOR: [The medicine-man] has arrived.
>
> DOCTOR: "Put some water down on the ground!"
>
> NARRATOR: He offered him round white shell beads as payment,
> he offered him dentalia.
>
> HUSBAND, TO HIMSELF: "He will be glad because of these,
> when he sees them."
>
> DOCTOR: "I don't like these trinkets here—
> I like *p'aléhsi* shell beads."
>
> HUSBAND: "So you will doctor her!
> Doctor her during the night—
> perhaps she will recover."
>
> DOCTOR: "Oh, I am not afraid of doctoring the one who is sick.
> Why should I be afraid?
> I am a medicine-man!
> She will not cry.
> She will yet eat her own food."
>
> HUSBAND: "Go forth from the house!
> Shout!
> Call upon your dream-spirit!
> That's what a medicine-man always does."
>
> DOCTOR: "She will recover—I dreamed it.
> *Pray speak to the spring of water,*
> my dream tells me.

Pray do not eat!
Go ahead and eat tomorrow when the sun is overhead.
You shall go to the spring to bathe.

[Thus] I dreamt.

Pray pass the night on the mountain!

Now then,
I shall return in the night.
Wake up the people.
They will help to sing.
I am a great medicine-man.

Pray ask the rocks!
Ask the trees!
Ask the logs!
Go about twice, and the owl will talk,
and the yellowhammer [too],
and pray roll tobacco between your hands and smoke it!
Eat nothing!
Pick up the round luck-stones!

Thus did I dream.
She will recover."

Rather than responding to Sapir's requests with the critically detached descriptions of the practiced cultural interpreter, she throws herself into the scene, re-creating not so much the details but the life and spirit of the occasion.[16] Her re-creation is so vivid and emotional, so immediate, that it essentially takes the form of a drama. Describe an Indian burial? Describe a curing ceremony? Betty Brown did that and more.

SONG

Songs were an integral part of life in Native California, and still are today. There were curing songs, love songs, dance songs, power songs, gambling songs, hunting songs, mourning songs, ritual songs, luck songs, dream songs, work songs, and traveling songs, to name just a few. Songs were sung publicly, to accompany dances, ceremonies, and games, or in smaller settings, to be shared with friends and family. The girls' puberty songs of the Wintu (#11), for instance, were public songs, sung by visiting parties as they entered the village where a puberty celebration was being held. Their dream songs, in contrast, typically would have been sung first for a more intimate audience—though once debuted, they could then be sung to accompany dances. Of course, songs were also sung privately, to help the singer think, pray, or focus an emotion. The Wintu cry song that Grace McKibbin sings—"*Which trail should I take to go over the hill? I guess I'll take the south trail over the hill*" (#13)—is an example of a song that originated as a private song, composed by her grandfather while traveling, and later was passed down through the singer's family as part of its oral tradition.

Songs are frequently incorporated into stories and myths. Four of the selections in this volume demonstrate this characteristic: William Benson's "Creation" (#16) from Eastern Pomo (sadly, the songs accompanying this myth were not preserved); the Chumash story of "The Dog Girl" (#22), told by María Solares; the older of the two Cupeño "Hawk Feather" episodes (#25b), dictated by Salvadora Valenzuela; and Joe Homer's "An Account of Origins" (#27). As this sampling suggests, myths and other sacred narratives are perhaps more likely than other genres to have a significant component of song, just as hymns and liturgical music form an integral part of Western (and other) religious ceremonial traditions. But the example of "The Dog Girl," a secular tale if there ever was one, shows that song may be associated with other genres as well.[17]

Leanne Hinton has observed, for Yuman storytelling traditions, that the songs often create key interludes of emotionality, which are set off like jewels against an essentially neutral or reportorial narrative background. Where the narrative portions of Yuman stories are invariably told from a third-person, remote-past quotative point of view, the songs tend to be first-person expressions of what the protagonist is feeling at that point in the story, giving the audience a view directly from the story's heart, its emotional core. Though Hinton's observations were originally made for Havasupai, they clearly have a wider application: for instance, it is easy to see exactly this same stylistic pattern—of inner versus outer experience, the subjective emotionality of song against the objective reportage of narration—at work in the Chumash story of "The Dog Girl."

Songs can vary greatly in terms of content, as well. A lot of California songs are actually wordless—that is, they consist entirely of nonsense syllables or vocables,[18] much like the Irish lilting tradition, or the burdens of so many English and Celtic folk songs (*hey-nonny-nonny, fol la diddle dido, down-a-down hey down-a-down,* and the like). For instance, one of the many Miwok gambling songs consists of the vocable phrases *Wa ni ni ni, wa ah ha, yo wa ha* sung in litany, over and over, until the singer's gambling turn is over (Angulo 1976a:85). It is not accurate, however, to call these vocable songs "meaningless." Although they may not have explicit lexical content, they carry an emotional weight and often tap into their true meaning by association with a particular ritual or story.

At the other extreme are the long, verbally complex song cycles of many Southern California tribes. For the most part these songs are connected with religious ceremonies. The following example, taken from the Quechan "Lightning Song" as sung by William Wilson (Halpern 1984), presents a sampling of eight song texts drawn almost at random from within the longer cycle. Each song, probably interwoven by strings of vocables, would be sung a specified number of times—or simply over and over until its particular segment of the ceremony was concluded. It took all night to sing the complete cycle.

He stands and looks from afar
He looks from afar and sees
He looks from afar and describes

He sees the quivering foggy cloud
He describes the quivering foggy cloud
He sees the cloud passing
He describes the cloud passing
He is looking at the clouds as they turn this way and that
He describes the clouds turning this way and that

He sees lightning
Lightning flashes in the darkness
He describes lightning

He sees its impossibility
He describes its impossibility

He clumps it together
He takes darkness and clumps it together
He describes taking darkness and clumping it together

You have mistaken it
He sees you mistake it

Coyote is there describing dawn
He describes you mistaking it

Stars pass overhead
Stars wandering overhead
Stars pass overhead
Stars trail across the sky
Stars trail across the sky
He describes stars sitting in the sky

He sees sunrise
He describes sunrise

The Luiseño songs of Villiana Calac Hyde, some of which are presented in this volume (#24), likewise illustrate this more elaborate lyric tradition. In Northern California, the Karuk "Evening Star" songs, too, can be quite involved, verging on a quasi-narrative form.[19]

The vast majority of known California songs are considerably less complex, at least as far as their explicit verbal content is concerned. They tend to consist of a few lines—often just one or two—of verse sung in alternation with lines of vocables. Grace McKibbin's songs (#13) are good examples of this most typical California pattern and have the advantage of representing complete performances, including repetitions and vocables, rather than just the abstract of the words alone. Hinton's presentation gives us the full text of one particular performance—a bit different each time the song is sung—as words and vocables intertwine.

Usually, though, the verbal abstract is all that is presented of a song; the vocables are ignored, and the organic cycle of repetitions eliminated.[20] What we see of a song then is merely the distillation of its verbal essence. It doesn't mean that the song's text is not authentic—just a bit diminished, removed still further from its spontaneous musical and performance context. Here are some examples, striking nonetheless, drawn from a variety of sources and singing traditions:[21]

Who is like me!
My plumes are flying—
They will come to rest in an unknown region
Above where the banners are flying.

Chumash song, from a story

Listen to what I am about to sing.
Listen to my breathing on high.
Listen to my stamping, I tear the ground up.
Listen to my groaning.
I am done.
I-ha-ya-a-ha-hu-ha!
I-ya-ka-mi-ha-mi!

Bear Dance song (Santa Rosa Island)

Jumping echoes of the rock;
Squirrels turning somersaults;
Green leaves, dancing in the air;
Fishes, white as money-shells,
Running in the water: green, deep, and still.
Hi-ho, hi-ho, hi-hay!
Hi-ho, hi-ho, hi-hay!

Modoc puberty song

I am traveling—me, me, me!
I go around the world—me, me!
I cause the mist—me, me!
When I climb the mountaintops
I cause [the] clouds,
I cause the rain.
Long live Coyote!
He will always be.

Coyote's song while traveling
(Chumash)

Going along singing,
Following the deer trail,
Hunting deer,
Going along singing,
Going along singing.

Yahi mouth-bow song

In this more common, stripped-down mode of presentation, California songs tend to resemble Japanese haiku more than anything—indeed, it's an obvious and striking connection to make. Consider these examples, again drawn from a variety of sources and singing traditions:[22]

> The dawn is dawning,
> a shadow—
> I come home, I come home.
>> Achumawi waking song

> Where we used to make love,
> the grass is grown up high now.
>> Hupa brush dance song

> I am the only one, the only one left—
> An old man, I carry the gambling board,
> An old man, I sing the gambling song.
>> Costanoan gambling song

> Come! Come!
> I mean you
> With the brown hat . . .
>> Costanoan love song
>> (post-Contact)

> Dancing on the brink of the world . . .
>> Costanoan dance song

> Jump, salmon, jump!
> So you may see your uncle dance!
>> Coyote's song to catch salmon (Chumash)

In truth, many of the songs *do* resemble haiku in terms of their imagery, as well as in their perceptual and emotional immediacy, the "here and now" of their subject matter. But, when we recall that these songs are typically sung over and over again, the words being repeated many times over, we see that they share some of the characteristics of the mantra, as well.

Because of their essential textual brevity, songs tend to be highly elliptical and allusive. It is often impossible to draw the true meaning of a song merely from its words alone. The impression of understanding that someone outside the tradition gets can well be a mistaken one: we only *think* we get it, because we are able to respond to the surface of the words as we do to any poetic image.[23] But songs presented this way are isolated from their context, and their context is often the primary place where their deepest meaning resides. Take this Tachi Yokuts song, "Dawis Sapagay's Song," recorded from Leon Manuel by James Hatch in 1957:

> Where will I go in?
> I will go in
> where green scum is on the pool.

Even knowing that Dawis Sapagay was a well-known Tachi shaman and that this was his personal power song does not take us very far along the path to understanding. Still, we form an impression, and after a while, feel that we have established some sort of connection with the song. What we don't know is that the song refers to a story, the story of how Sapagay received his doctor's power to cure sickness. Manuel told Sapagay's story this way:

> Looking for a doctor who would teach him curing power, Sapagay went to the edge of Wood Lake to find the underwater entrance to the place where the doctor lived. He dove in (at the place where the green scum is), and came up in a cave in which he met the guardians of the doctor. There was a man-sized spider with voracious jaws, and, afterward, a rattlesnake coiled ready to strike. Last, there was a puma and a bear who tore men to pieces. Sapagay used a kingsnake charm against the spider and the rattlesnake (kingsnakes eat spiders and rattlesnakes), while against the puma and the bear he used a weasel charm which made him small and agile. He thus passed them by.

At length he came to the end of the cave. It was a new and strange land which he had not seen before. After looking around, he came upon the doctor sitting steadfast as a stone and looking straight at him. After a time the doctor looked up and asked Sapagay, "What are you doing here? How did you get in? You must have some sort of power to get past my guardians." Sapagay told him of the charms he had used and the doctor approved of them. They were the right charms for the man who wanted doctor power.

Sapagay looked about and saw that there was no one around. He said, "This must be a very lonely place; there are no other people here." The doctor replied, "You don't seem to like it here; why did you come?" And he continued, "I will show you the people who live here." So he called, and a long line of deer came out of the black mountain to the west. Sapagay thought to himself, "These aren't real people, but just deer from the woods." But the deer came and formed a circle about him and lost their horns and hooves, and turned into beautiful girls dressed in string aprons, beads, and clamshell ornaments. The doctor then addressed the girls, "Now give him your songs, that he may have doctor power among his people." And the girls taught Sapagay their songs so that he could use their secret power.

When Sapagay learned all that he could, he asked the doctor how he could get back to his people. The doctor told him that the guardians would be asleep when he returned through the tunnel. And then Sapagay returned to his people and became a famous doctor who was called to all parts of California to cure the sick.

Without knowing the story, we can only aspire to the most superficial appreciation for the song—its words, perhaps, but not its meaning. Once we do know the story, we see just how far off-base our understanding really was. So much is implied here, that the song itself is merely an allusion. To be sure, there is a clear image captured in these words, the image of algae floating on the surface of a pond. But this image is actually a bit like the green scum in the song itself—its true meaning lies beneath it: the pool itself, and what was down there.

Examples like the Sapagay song serve as cautionary tales, warning us not to be too confident that we can ever fully understand the meaning of a song—even if it seems laid out before us in crystalline form. The words of a song are the looking-glass through which we, as readers, enter the world of the song—but they themselves are not that world, just its signifiers. When seen in this light, it is clear that a song composed mostly or even entirely of vocables will be as rich in meaning as a song composed with many verses of words.

ORATORY

This category, which variously includes prayers, eulogies, sermons, morning speeches (in some cultures given daily by the chief from atop the assembly house), public announcements, and instructional lectures, among other genres, is little documented in California and can only be touched on here. The print literature provides us with very few reliable examples (too often the content of the speeches has merely been paraphrased or summarized), and discussions of the topic therefore tend to draw from the same few published sources: Edward Gifford's "Central Miwok Ceremonies" (1955), Philip Sparkman's "Culture of the Luiseño Indians" (1908), C. Darryl Forde's "Ethnography of the Yuma Indians" (1931), Samuel Barrett's "Wintun Hesi Ceremony" (1919), and perhaps a few others. Further examples will yet turn up in private and archival collections of unpublished fieldnotes, as these are box-by-box uncovered. As if in proof of this belief, a careful examination of Richard Keeling's *Guide to Early Field Recordings (1900–1949) at the Lowie Museum of Anthropology* (1991) suggests that a considerable store of potentially retrievable oratory on wax cylinder and aluminum disc may lie waiting in the vaults.

Most of the oratory that has been published consists of either prayers or public speeches. Here and there may be found examples of other genres, though. The following passage forms the conclusion of the lengthy lecture or "counsel" given to initiates at the *Yuninish,* the girls' puberty ceremony of the Luiseño (Sparkman 1908:226):

> See,
> these old men and women,
> these are those who paid attention to this counsel,
> which is of the grown-up people,
> and they have already reached old age.
>
> Do not forget this that I am telling you,
> pay heed to this speech,

and when you are old like these old people,
you will counsel your sons and daughters in like manner,
and you will die old.

And your spirit will rise northwards to the sky,
like the stars, moon, and sun.

Perhaps they will speak of you
and will blow three times
and thereby cause to rise your spirit and soul to the sky.

The dynamics of setting can contribute nearly as much to the structure of an oration as its content does. Numerous observers have commented on the peculiar vocal and rhythmic characteristics of public speaking as delivered by California orators. In Northern California, the Yana, like most people, even had a specific word, *gaac'an'i* 'to talk like a chief', to refer to this speaking style. Forde, describing the special effects of a Quechan funeral speech, noted that "normal word order is changed. Words are omitted and others repeated to produce the rhythm of the speech. They are sometimes abbreviated, sometimes expanded by the addition of consonants to increase the staccato of the speech" (1931:212). This example, from a Patwin Hesi oration, was described as being "delivered in very high voice and jerky phrases" (A. Kroeber 1925:389), and illustrates some of the features of this type of address:[24]

Be like this!
Be like this!
Be good!
Be good, good!
Be glad of it!
Rejoice in it!
Rejoice in this speech!
Rejoice in this!
Rejoice in these roses!
Rejoice in these healthy roses [you're wearing]!
Say yes!
Say yes!
We come approving!
We come approving!
We shall do it like that!

We shall approve!
We shall be glad!
Father will be glad!
Mother's brother will be glad!
Older brother will be glad!
When we gather like this!
When we gather like this!
We shall rejoice, therefore!
Our speech!
Our speech!
Be glad, therefore!
I was glad, was glad!
I rejoiced!
Rejoice and approve!
Rejoice and be glad!
Approve of it!
Rejoice in it!

It is easy to see how the economics of breath constrains the form of this oration. As everyone who has ever hollered at a friend or called a child to supper knows, the louder you shout, the less you can say on your lungful of air. The need to be heard, to broadcast the voice across the widest area, often to a dispersed audience, has certain predictable consequences for the shape of the message. We should *expect* to find short, jerky phrases and repetitions (for the sake of both emphasis and of euphony), distorted vocal qualities, and a powerful rhythmic drive. Most of the recorded examples of California public oratory exhibit these or similar signs. Indeed, when these features are less in evidence, it often turns out that the speech has been re-created "in the studio," as it were. Then again, it may simply represent a less bombastic genre appropriate to a smaller or more intimate or indoor audience— for instance, the girls' puberty lecture quoted earlier. Add to these physical constraints the purely stylistic tropes and quirks, embellishments and deviations, that accumulate in an art form with the most ancient of roots, and it's no wonder these examples command our attention.

What has survived of California oratory presents a tantalizing picture. But I look forward to a time when more examples of these marvelous verbal art forms have been found and brought to light, and we can begin at last to appreciate their multiplexity and discern something of their poetics. Still more, I look forward to the minting of *new* examples, to hearing how the living generations of California Indians have carried these traditions into modern life.

Indeed, that should make a fine "best hope" for the future of California's oral-literary heritage at large—the whole constellation of its indigenous verbal arts, of myth and song, chant and celebration—as this new century gets under way. In the meantime, let us "rejoice in these roses" that have come down, by some of the hardest paths imaginable, into the hands of posterity.

NOTES

1. Theodora Kroeber has a nice essay, "Some Qualities of Indian Stories," in *The Inland Whale* (1959), her book of literary "retellings" of five California stories.

2. Benson's version, though, contains ideas that are unusual in the Central California traditions: *cycles* of creation and destruction—by flood, fire, whirlwind, and the like—brought on by the Creator's dissatisfaction with the results of his labors. Versions by neighboring Pomo and Lake Miwok narrators (for example, Callaghan 1978) conform to the Earthdiver type. Such ideas are more common in Yuman literatures such as the Mojave and Halchidhoma, though they are not unheard of elsewhere. Alfred Kroeber (1925:206) speculates that this subordinate "cycles" pattern in Central California may be associated with the Kuksu religion.

3. Sources regarding the World Renewal ceremonies include A. Kroeber and Gifford (1949).

4. From A. Kroeber and Gifford (1949:14). This does not appear to be a verbatim record of Mr. Davis's account, because it shows clear signs of paraphrasing, probably introduced during the dictation process. The Karuk term *Írahiv* refers to the World Renewal Ceremony; *Ixkareyev Animas* is the name of one of the Spirit People from the prehuman myth-time.

5. The texts reproduced here and on page 57 come from a fair-hand copy found among Faye's notes in the Bancroft Library. Readers familiar with the literature will notice some variation from a version of these songs first published in Joughlin and Valenzuela (1953) and subsequently reprinted in a variety of sources.

6. Out of respect for the feelings of contemporary Luiseño singers who consider the funeral songs both sacred and private, I present only the first stanza of

this beautiful and powerful song—just enough to illustrate the point I make here. Readers interested in studying this and other such songs in their entirety may consult *Yumáyk Yumáyk (Long Ago)*, Mrs. Hyde's extraordinary collection of narratives and songs (Hyde and Elliott 1994).

7. There are other reasons besides stylistic choice why these two versions are so different—the foremost being the age of the narrations and the narrators themselves. Joe Homer told his myth in 1912, and Sarah Martin told hers in 1960. Many details, and indeed the practice of extended narration itself, would have "evaporated"—been lost from tradition during the generations that separated the two performances.

8. Coyote stories, of course, are not confined to California. Far from it: Coyote is an important mythic character throughout much of the American and Canadian West. William Bright's book, *A Coyote Reader* (1993), is a fascinating and very readable celebration of mythology's most notorious multiple-personality disorder; it will point the reader toward all kinds of interesting Coyote sources. Gary Snyder's essay, "The Incredible Survival of Coyote" (1975), is well-known but still rewarding. Most any collection of myths or stories you might pick up, especially from California, will contain at least a few stories featuring Coyote; it's actually hard to avoid him once you start looking. Indeed, because there are so many collections out there that focus on Coyote stories, I haven't gone out of my way to include examples in this volume—so if anything, the importance of Coyote to the oral-literary canon of California is underrepresented by the selections in this volume.

9. Actually, this element is a complex unit combining a remote-past tense suffix *-n'(i)* with the actual quotative *-tʰ(i)*, each of which has an independent function. The former may be used for remembered events of long ago, whereas the latter may be used for reporting direct discourse or information acquired through hearsay. Together, though, they have this special narrative function in myth.

10. This Northern Yana passage is cast in an informal practical orthography designed to balance linguistic needs with the need for phonetic transparency. Doubled characters represent length, stress is indicated with an acute accent over the vowel, and superscript letters are voiceless. Certain phonetic processes involved with prosody (final aspiration, devoicing, secondary and emphatic primary stress) are preserved in the transcription. For a more detailed description of linguistic writing systems, see the "Pronunciation Guide" at the beginning of the book.

11. Often there is a poetics involved with the use of this element. Ken Hill, in his introduction to Sarah Martin's Serrano "Creation" (#23), points out that its occasional suppression seems to have a heightening or intensifying effect. And

sometimes narrators will deploy the quotative element in their stories tactically, controlling that element's placement so as to section the story into passages, rather like paragraphing in written prose.

12. Perhaps unwisely, I collapse two related but rather different types of story into this ad hoc designation. First are stories like "Grizzly Bear and Deer" (Whistler 1977a) and "Condor Steals Falcon's Wife" (#20b), where the "monster" is simply bad by disposition. For example, it is in Bear's nature to be violent—she's almost always the villain in her own stories and usually suffers the deadly revenge meted out for her actions; likewise, Condor appears to be "bad by nature." Second is a class of stories like "Rolling Skull" (Luthin 1994) and "Mad Bat" (#15), where an otherwise "normal" character begins behaving in a psychotic manner. In the Yana "Rolling Skull" story, Wildcat has a bad dream, which deranges him, sending him off on a terroristic rampage until someone (Coyote, in this instance) steps in to "end his career" and restore harmony. In Mad Bat's case, we don't know the cause of his deranged behavior, but eventually he, too, is stopped, and pays with his life for his actions.

13. In Langdon (1976:34), I have slightly altered Crawford's free translation, as indicated by brackets.

14. This text, in both Kashaya and English, may be found in Oswalt (1964:300–301).

15. The translation is my own, based on Sapir's 1910 free translation and the original Yana.

16. Sapir began eliciting ethnographic texts from Betty Brown because he was doubtful of her skill as a teller of traditional myths and stories. As it turned out, he was also less than satisfied with her ethnographic work. In a footnote to the present text, he comments on this matter: "In this and the following texts an attempt was made to secure from Betty Brown an account in her own language of some phases of Yana religious and social life. Owing to her tendency to use conversational narrative instead of general description, these texts are rather illustrative by means of real or imaginary incidents in the life of the Yana than ethnologically satisfying statements" (1910:178).

17. Some traditions seem to exploit this characteristic more than others. Mojave stories, for instance, are often densely interspersed with songs—so much so that their complete absence from the archaic migration epic (#26) strikes contemporary Mojaves as distinctly peculiar and un-Mojave-like. The Chumash, Chemehuevi (Laird 1984), and other Southern California cultures also seem to have a preference for this style of storytelling.

18. For a more detailed look at vocable elements in California song, see Hinton 1994d.

19. See William Bright's translation of one such song ("Myth, Music, and Magic: Nettie Reuben's Karuk Love Medicine") in Swann 1994.

20. This approach is typical of earlier ethnolinguistic collections, made before the field's relatively recent advances in ethnopoetics and performance theory.

21. Chumash song (Blackburn 1975); Santa Rosa Island Bear Dance song (Heizer 1955); Modoc puberty song (Powers 1877); Chumash Coyote song (Blackburn 1975); Yahi mouth-bow song (T. Kroeber 1964).

22. Achumawi waking song (Angulo 1990); Hupa brush dance song (Keeling 1985); Costanoan gambling song (A. Kroeber 1925); Costanoan love song (A. Kroeber 1925); Costanoan dance song (A. Kroeber 1925); Chumash Coyote song (Blackburn 1975).

23. This can be nearly as true for members of other California tribes—or even other family traditions *within* a tribe—as it is for people with no experience of Native culture at all.

24. I have taken the text as reported in A. Kroeber (1925) and "smoothed it up" a bit for use in this discussion. Though my alterations stick very close to the original English glosses, this still should not be considered an "authoritative" rendering of the Patwin original, for which the reader should consult the original text. For those who were wondering, the Hesi is a dance ceremony.

Oh, people!
Our hearts are good and strong!
We can work all day!
This sickness does go away, I know it!

I go off by myself.
Alone in the house, I lie down on the bed
And forget everything.
All this fades away.

All the people!
All our sick hearts will change!
This day is passing away,
Passing [away] from here.
We are all together.
Now will we think well,
Now will we think in this place,
Now that we are all together.

I tell you, when we lose a strong man,
Our hearts cannot be good—but now,
We must not think about it.

I will end right now,
I will end [it] well.

We [must] think now, about being here all together now.

People!
It will be good when this day has passed,
[That's what] we are thinking here.
I will find our strength, I will find our good.
It used to be that my body [felt bad],

When I lay down alone.
On that I rely:
We trust our sick hearts will change.
I rely on that!

I will finish.
Rightly we are thinking good things.

Quechan funeral speech
C. Darryl Forde, *Ethnography
of the Yuma Indians*

Notes on Native California Languages

LANGUAGE FAMILIES

Kelp-beds, redwoods, desert scrub, oak savannah: from the coastal waters of the Pacific to the crest of the high Sierras, from the Sacramento Delta to the dry sands of the Baja Peninsula, California has always been a land of abundance. Most of us are aware of the extremes of habitat, the tremendous biological and geographic diversity that California embraces. Not so many are aware that this exuberance extends to its Native cultures and languages as well. Yet aboriginal California was one of the most linguistically diverse places on earth, and its great abundance helped support the single highest population density in North America (A. Kroeber 1939:153)—that is, until the Spanish, and later the new "Americans," came and began to change the lives of its people forever, constraining their ways, restricting their freedoms, and dispossessing them of their lands. California was home to at least eighty to one hundred distinct languages—and probably more—at the time of European contact. (Each language reflects a cultural division, too; see map 2, p. 574.) As always, though, language is an early casualty in the forced assimilation of other cultures. It is a tribute to the tenacity of California Indians that some fifty of these languages are still spoken today.[1] The majority of these languages are severely endangered, however, and drastic measures need to be taken to ensure their survival into the next century.

Most of California's many languages were in turn spoken in different dialects as well, just as the English "accents" of Brooklyn, Atlanta, Dublin, Nairobi, Bombay, and Perth are different today. Our world

Englishes, though, have only been developing for a few hundred years, whereas California's languages have been rooted and changing, many of them, for thousands of years—and thus the dialect differences within a language can be quite profound. The three attested dialects of Yana, for instance—Northern, Central, and Yahi—vary from each other about as much as do the Romance languages, say Spanish, Portuguese, and Italian, which are themselves really just the modern descendants of medieval Latin dialects. (In truth, the Yanan dialects are not excessively differentiated. There are much greater differences to be found among the various Shastan and Chumashan "dialects," which are more properly classified as distinct languages than as dialects.) It is easy to see that the distinction between language and dialect is not always a straightforward one: sometimes it's just a matter of convention or historical accident or politics whether two related forms of speech are labeled as dialects or as separate languages.

So when linguists cite a figure like the conservative "eighty to one hundred distinct languages" figure for pre-Contact California, astonishing though it may be, the reality was even more complex: there are layers of diversity *within* that overall diversity that the general figure doesn't even hint at. Finally, as if this complexity were not enough in itself, the stability and relatively small size of most California tribal territories (and the close contact with neighboring groups through trading and intermarriage that this implies) means that bilingualism and even trilingualism must have been a commonplace. California truly was a linguistic land of plenty—a proud trait that modern California, thanks to its surviving native languages and the multilingual constellations of its major cities, preserves to this day.[2]

Given their tremendous diversity, it's unsurprising that California's languages bear genetic resemblances among themselves. (By *genetic resemblance* we mean that the languages in question trace back to a common ancestor language, just as Spanish, French, and Italian have evolved or descended from Latin.) There are approximately twenty language families in California (see table 5).[3] Some, like Pomoan or Utian, are relatively large families of languages, having many sibling members (fifteen in the case of Utian); others, like Karuk or Washoe, are "only children" within their respective families.

In turn, these twenty or so California language families may ultimately descend from five superfamilies, or stocks. (In the same way, the

Table 5. Language Families:
California Languages and Genetic Affiliations

YUKIAN

Yukian Family
  Yuki (Yuki/Coast Yuki/Huchnom)
  Wappo

CHUMASHAN

Chumashan Family
  Obispeño
  Purisimeño
  Ineseño
  Barbareño
  Ventureño
  Island Chumash

HOKAN STOCK (PROPOSED)
  Karuk
  Chimariko
  Yana (N. Yana/C. Yana/Yahi)
  Washoe
Shastan Family
  Shasta
  Konomihu
  New River Shasta
  Okwanuchu
Palaihnihan Family
  Achumawi
  Atsugewi
Pomoan Family
  Northern Pomo
  Central Pomo
  Northeastern Pomo
  Eastern Pomo
  Southeastern Pomo
  Southern Pomo
  Kashaya (Southwestern Pomo)
Salinan Family
  Antoniaño
  Migueleño

HOKAN STOCK (*continued*)

Yuman Family
  Ipai (Northern Diegueño)
  Tipai (Mexican Diegueño)
  Kumeyaay (Southern Diegueño)
  Mojave
  Halchidhoma (Maricopa)
  Quechan (Yuma)

ESSELEN
  Esselen

PENUTIAN STOCK (PROPOSED)
Wintuan Family
  Wintu (Wintu/Nomlaki)
  Patwin (Hill Patwin/River Patwin/
    Southern Patwin)
Maiduan Family
  Maidu
  Konkow
  Nisenan
Miwokan Family (Utian)
  Coast Miwok (Bodega/Marin)
  Lake Miwok
  Saclan (Bay Miwok)
  Plains Miwok
  Northern Sierra Miwok
  Central Sierra Miwok
  Southern Sierra Miwok
Costanoan Family (Utian)
  Karkin
  Chochenyo
  Ramaytush
  Tamyen
  Awaswas
  Chalon
  Rumsen
  Mutsun

Continued

Table 5—*Continued*

PENUTIAN STOCK *continued*
Yokutsan Family
  Valley Yokuts
    Far Northern (Yachikumne
          [Chulamni]/Lower San
          Joaquin/Lakisamni-
          Tawalimni)
    Northern Valley (Nopchinchi/
          Chawchila/
          Chukchansi/Merced/
          Kechayi-Dumna)
    Southern Valley (Wechihit/Nutunutu-
          Tachi/Chunut/Wo'lasi-
          Choynok/Koyeti-
          Yowlumni)
  Buena Vista (Tulamni/Hometwoli)
  Gashowu
  Kings River (Chukaymina/
          Michahay/Ayticha/
          Choynimni)
  Tule-Kaweah (Wikchamni/Yawdanchi)
  Palewyami
Plateau Penutian Family
  Modoc

UTO-AZTECAN STOCK
  Tübatulabal
Takic Family
  Kitanemuk
  Tongva (Gabrielino/Fernandeño)

UTO-AZTECAN STOCK *continued*
  Serrano
  Luiseño (Luiseño/Ajachmem
          [Juaneño])
  Cupeño
  Cahuilla
  Tataviam
Numic Family
  Northern Paiute
  Mono (Monache/Owens Valley
          Paiute)
  Panamint (California Shoshone)
  Kawaiisu
  Chemehuevi (dialect of Ute)

ALGIC STOCK
Ritwan Family
  Yurok
  Wiyot

NA-DENE STOCK
Athapaskan Family
  Tolowa (Tolowa/Chetco)
  Hupa (Hupa/Chilula-Whilkut)
  Mattole (Mattole/Bear River)
  Eel River (Nongatl/Lassik/
          Sinkyone/Wailaki)
  Cahto

SOURCE: Goddard (1996).

Germanic family—which includes English, Dutch, German, and the Scandinavian languages—is itself a member of the Indo-European superfamily of languages, a stock that incorporates such seemingly disparate languages as French, Armenian, Greek, Croatian, and Hindi under its umbrella.) Two of the five stocks, Penutian and Hokan, are closely or quintessentially associated with California and are so ancient that the resemblances among their constituent language families are barely discernible. Indeed, the resemblances are so hard to pin down, and the time-depth involved is so profound, that many linguists believe them to be chimerical. We may catch a glimmer here and there, as in the various words for 'two', but their interrelationships are deeply buried in time.[4] The other three stocks—Algic, Na-Dené, and Uto-Aztecan—are well accepted and have their primary distributions outside the California region.[5] In addition, there is one "family isolate" that can't be plausibly linked up with any of the other stocks: Yukian, which includes the Yuki, Coast Yuki, and Huchnom dialects of Yuki proper, together with the remotely related Wappo.[6] (Isolates are languages, like Basque in Europe, that have no known genetic affiliation to any other language groups.) Like the Hokan language families, Yukian represents an ancient presence in California. Map 3, page 575, shows the geographic distribution of these stocks and families.

The prehistory of the California languages makes for a challenging study. Of Penutian, Michael Silverstein has written, "There is, first, tremendous linguistic diversity, *equalling perhaps that of the entire continent,* encompassed within the proposed 'superstock'" (1979; italics mine). So much time has passed that the modern descendants of that original language—if we can even be sure there *was* but one such language—have metamorphosed dramatically. Yet, although Penutian is a venerable family in its own right (there are ten-thousand-year-old sites in southern Oregon, the presumed Penutian homeland, distributed along the shores of ancient lakes, that were probably Penutian sites), as a family presence in California proper it is not terribly old: on the order of forty-five hundred years or more, dating from the first incursions of Proto-Utians into the Sacramento Valley. Hokan, in contrast—or anyway, the distinct language families that traditionally comprise this grouping—is much, much older in California, going back beyond our ability to calculate with any certainty. Its ancestral speakers are, along with ancestral Yukian speakers, if not the first, certainly among the oldest inhabitants of California. We must presume they were already here—long in residence, families of an old and already divergent stock—when the earliest Period II archaeological sites begin to enter the record, some eight thousand years ago.[7] If demonstrable as a language family or superstock, Hokan would be much older than Indo-European, perhaps even older than Penutian itself. A rough general consensus puts its time-depth at twelve thousand years old.[8]

The presence of the other three groups (though ancient in and of themselves) in California is much more recent. Indeed, by taking a closer look at the family-and-stock map (map 3) of California, we can get a glimpse of its linguistic past. Like the residue of waves fossilized in the rippled sediments of an ancient shoreline, the contemporary language map of California (map 5, p. 573) reveals a tracery of ages-old patterns of migration. But first we have to learn to see that map as if in motion.

We can start by imagining a time, some five thousand years ago—consistent with the linguistic evidence—when long-resident, already divergent Hokan-affiliated peoples were spread pretty much across the coast and heartland of the Central California culture area, sharing parts of this territory with early Chumashan and Yukian peoples (and no doubt other groups as well, who have passed from the record without trace). Then, beginning around forty-five hundred years ago, Proto-Utian peoples—the Penutian ancestors of the Miwok and Costanoan families—began moving into California from the northeast along the great river-and-valley systems—first along the Klamath, then over to the Sacramento, following it all the way down into the Bay region and up its tributaries into the Sierra Nevada and south along the coast to Monterey—the very territories that they occupy today. As they went, they would have displaced some of the already-settled "Old California" peoples from these regions. The Utians were followed in time by ancestral Yokutsan peoples, who began their long move down into the Central Valley and southern Sierra foothills about thirty-five hundred years ago. Both these expansions into California would have taken place over the course of centuries, involving generations of geographic adaptation to new lands and the give-and-take of cultural accommodation with new neighbors.

Later, beginning around two thousand years ago, ancestors of the Wintuan peoples, probably pushed by Athabascan groups still farther to the north, made *their* move into California, following the by-now well-worn Penutian migration routes down into the upper Sacramento Valley, spreading slowly south over the course of the next thousand years (Whistler 1977b). At about the same time the Wintuan groups were beginning their descent, around two thousand years ago, ancestral Maiduan people, who had been living in the Tahoe region from about 4000 B.P., began expanding into their present territories, at the expense of the Washoe and Yana. All these waves of Penutian migrations have greatly enriched the linguistic tapestry of California.[9]

Looking again at the modern distribution of Hokan and other Old

California families (see map 4, p. 576), you will see them displaced in clumps and islands along the periphery of cartographic California, pressed outward in a great, broken ring around the central region of the state, beginning with Karuk, Chimariko, and Shasta in the northwest, over to Achumawi, Atsugewi, and Yana, and skipping down to Washoe in the east. Then comes a big gap in that ring, where Uto-Aztecan tribes from the interior much later flowed out of the Great Basin or southeastern Sierra into southern California, eventually reaching all the way to the Pacific. The pieces of the ring pick up again, hundreds of miles further on, with the Yuman tribes far to the south: Mojave, Halchidhoma, Quechan, Cocopa, and Tipai-Ipai.[10] Fragments of the great ring can be seen scattered northward along the coast, as well: beyond the Chumash we find Salinan and Esselen, and finally, north of the Penutian expansions into the San Francisco and Monterey Bay areas, the Pomoan languages and languages of the Yukian stock.

On the map, the Uto-Aztecan territory looks like nothing so much as a vast cultural and linguistic lava flow that has displaced or simply covered over the traces of whatever groups may have lain in its path. The Takic ancestors of modern-day California Uto-Aztecan peoples (the Serrano, Luiseño, Cupeño, Gabrielino, and others) began expanding westward into California from the southern Sierra Nevada about three thousand years ago, reaching the coast as early as 2500 B.P.[11] As they came, they would have pushed the resident Yuman groups out and away to the south and east, where they are found today. Behind them, and later, came Numic groups from further out in the Great Basin.

Following the many and staggered Penutian and Uto-Aztecan migrations, around one thousand years ago according to available evidence, the ancestors of the two Ritwan languages, Wiyot and Yurok, arrived (separately, it appears) to claim territory in the northwest—though how they came to be here, so far from their distant Algic relatives in the Algonquian family, is a mystery that may never be solved. Later still, as late as A.D. 900, the California Athabascan groups—the Tolowa, the Hupa/Chilula-Whilkut group, the Mattole, the Eel River cluster (Nongatl-Sinkyone-Lassik-Wailaki), and the Cahto—drifted down from Oregon, further displacing the descendant speakers of those original California language families.

Not many places on earth could sustain the diversity such repeated incursions have engendered in California.[12] In a different landscape—a land of more limited resources, of harsher climate, of less rugged and varied terrain—there would have been insufficient room, ecologically speaking, for new populations. In a more pitched competition for resources, the newcomers would have been repulsed, or the incumbents vanquished, else both groups would have risked starvation. In hostile environments—say, the Arctic or Great Basin regions of North America—human populations must be highly nomadic, requiring large territories to provide more than the meagerest sustenance of life. True to expectation, the linguistic and cultural diversity in both those regions is relatively minimal. From Alaska to Greenland, we find but a single language, Inupiaq, spoken in a long chain of dialects across the entire circumpolar region. A similar dialect continuum of closely related Numic languages (Northern Paiute, Mono, Shoshoni, Comanche, Southern Paiute, Chemehuevi, and Kawaiisu) spreads through the Great Basin from Wyoming and Montana in the north down through Utah and Nevada, all the way to Mexico.[13] But California's geography and rich ecology have afforded it an extraordinary carrying capacity for human cultures and the languages they bear with them.

CALIFORNIA LANGUAGES
IN THE POST-CONTACT PERIOD

So what has become of this great diversity of tongues? Sadly, California's languages have been fighting for survival since the day the first Spanish mission was established in 1769 at what is now San Diego. Against all odds, some fifty ethnic groups still have active speakers of their native language (Hinton 1994a). Yet this situation, always a precarious one, is changing ever faster, as last speakers one by one pass on, taking their words and the music of their voices with them. (Map 5, based on a study reported in Leanne Hinton's *Flutes of Fire,* shows the areal distribution of these remaining speakers, by language.) Some of the losses have been recent indeed: for instance, when Laura Somersal, the last fluent speaker of Wappo, died in 1990, the Wappo language died with her. Of the fifty or so still-active languages, many are being taught to schoolchildren and young adults in the classroom, but not one is currently being passed on to the youngest generation of speakers, to be learned by children as their mother tongue, the language of home and family. How could this have happened? How could so many languages have fallen silent? In the end, the history of languages is inseparable from the history of the people who speak them.

The story of California's holocaust has been told many times, though still the truth of it is not yet common knowledge.[14] Estimates of the pre-Contact Native population of California range from a conservative 310,000 to nearly a million. By the end of the nineteenth century, that population had fallen to 20,000 or even less (Cook 1978). Even at the most conservative estimate, this represents a loss of more than 90 percent. (It takes a great deal of restraint to print a figure like this without an exclamation mark.) This catastrophic decline encompasses two main cycles or epicenters of destruction: one in the south from 1769 to about 1834, spreading inland and north along the coast with the expansion of the iniquitous Spanish mission system; the other in the north from 1848 (when gold was discovered at Sutter's Mill) to roughly 1865—the madness of the Gold Rush, which quickly spread throughout the mountainous regions of the state. The brief period between these cycles was no haven of recuperation. In addition to increased European-American encroachment on Indian lands amid the upheavals of the Mexican War, epidemics of malaria and smallpox decimated already stressed populations reeling from the onslaught of sustained contact begun a mere sixty years before. Cook (1978:92) mentions eyewitness reports of "entire villages of several hundred people being exterminated, of masses of skeletons found for years after."

It would be comforting to all of us—not just for those who must come to terms with the dark underside of their forebears' history of conquest, but also for those whose peoples have paid the price of that conquest— if we could believe that this waste and devastation was largely unintended, the sad but inevitable by-product of worlds in collision: microbial tragedies played out in the blood, ecological tragedies brought on by inexperience in a new environment, cultural tragedies kicked off by the discrepancy in medical and technological skills—all of which opened the way to a gradual abandonment of traditional ceremonies and crafts. Unfortunately, the reality of what happened between Indians and whites in California was not always so innocent. Genocide is a hard word but the only right one for what took place.

I don't mean to dwell on the issue here. This book is intended as a celebration, not a court-martial, still less a requiem. But certain facts must be faced squarely in order to understand the odds against *any* of the cultures represented here surviving into the twentieth century, let alone the twenty-first, with some semblance of their languages and traditions intact. Rather than attempt to cover this history discursively, I will take a testimonial approach, using the particulars of three short narratives to suggest the type and existence of more general conditions.

The Mission period, whatever the intentions of the Franciscan padres, was not a benign one for the Native cultures scorched by their influence. Forced labor, starvation, disease, rape, slavery, incarceration, torture, execution—these were commonplaces of Mission life. The brutality of the padres and soldiery is well-documented, through both eyewitness reports and archaeological findings (see Jackson and Castillo 1995). Needless to say, Native memory of the Mission era runs deep. Quite a few autobiographical and oral-historical accounts have been collected over the years, some published, most probably not. Even today, many Indian families have stories, passed down through the generations to the present, that date back to this period.

The text that follows was narrated by Rufino Ochurte, and describes the slow but inexorable process of Spanish enculturation among the Kiliwa down in the Baja Peninsula.[15]

THE FRIARS AT KILIWA

There were "pagan" Indians in this land. They were in these mountains. There was a friar, [but] no one came near him. When they least expected it he would seize one or two people. That's how he used to do it.

All of the people he had done that to went in, and when they had become acquainted they didn't flee anymore. "Well, it's very good, I tell you," they would report. In that manner one or two more would come in, and so it went until there were many people at the Mission.

The friars would make the people work. When they were disobedient, they whipped them. They gave them corn mush to drink so that they could work. They built houses. But they didn't earn anything. As for food, those with families they paid a sackful of corn. The others ate at the Mission. That's what they used to do. The disobedient ones were seized and beaten and dunked in water.

They used to baptize people. The friar would say, "What I am doing is a good thing. I'm going to do that to the others, also." The Indians would say, "I don't know about that." No one came near. It continued that way. Slowly the friar began to get more people. Everyone knew the friar. Then they were all pacified. They came to the Mission—not many, [just] a few. In that way, people kept arriving.

They saw what the friar did and spoke about it. Slowly, more people approached. So many came closer—[but still] not a large number. They would say, "This is queer." "It's evil," they said. "You never know," they said. The people remained at a distance, spread out; the friar pacified them.

Some understood a little Spanish. They translated [for those who didn't]: "He says 'such-and-such'." They told the others [about] what the friars did and what they said to those who did not understand. They began understanding one or two words.

The friars would sponsor the unbaptized as godparents. They gathered the non-Christians together.

It seems to me that they should have taught them something. If they had, these people would now be educated. They didn't do that; they just baptized everyone. They deceived these people. They didn't do anything good for them at all.

As this and numerous similar narratives show, even the most dispassionate and even-handed recollections of Spanish encroachment and coercion reveal the essential blindness and insensitivity at the heart of the Mission enterprise, even where large-scale atrocities did not occur.

Of course, California Indians did not take the Spanish assaults on their societies and sovereignty lying down. There must have been active resistance movements and renegade bands all up and down the California coast during the Mission period. Indians did lash back at their oppressors from time to time, though their efforts to control the Spanish were futile in the end. Native accounts of retaliation, like Mary Yee's Barbareño Chumash story of the 1824 Santa Barbara uprising or Lorenzo Asisara's account of the death, in 1812, of Father Quintana at Mission Santa Cruz, are relatively rare.[16] Yet these narratives paint a chilling picture of the prevailing mood of suspicion, threat, and violence that the warped Mission societies induced for everyone involved, Spaniard and Indian alike. Fear, stymied anger, paranoia—and something almost like a continuing disbelief that the Spanish could really commit the kinds of atrocities they did in fact, again and again, commit—these kept the Indians in check just as surely as the Spanish militias did with their muskets, swords, and cannon.

Less than a hundred years after the mission system began spreading in the south came the Gold Rush. If the devastation of the missions swept through the Southern and South-Central California cultures like a fire, the Gold Rush hit the Northern cultures like an atom bomb. Some of the most shameful passages in United States history took place in California during the decades immediately following the Gold Rush of 1849. Basic human rights, as far as Indians were concerned, were nonexistent. De facto slavery was institutionalized by the California legislature under the auspices of a variety of labor and indenture laws, such as an 1850 vagrancy law that allowed any white man, without burden of proof, to declare any Indian a "vagrant." Once so declared, Indians could be incarcerated, and the rights to their labor—up to four months without pay (Castillo 1978:108)—auctioned off to the highest bidder. The kidnapping of children and young girls for purposes of domestic and sexual servitude was also legally sanctioned and widely practiced (Cook 1943).

As if these offenses to civil liberties and human rights weren't bad enough, the legislature also allocated huge sums of money to fund military and paramilitary campaigns against Indian communities. The newspapers of the time are full of reports, both pro and con, of the so-called Indian wars. But the term *war* is misleading: the carnage of these vigilante campaigns was truly bestial in nature, shocking sometimes even to the citizenry they hypocritically claimed to "defend." Though often decried by reporters, scholars, federal agents, and a few righteous voices among the white community, the state nevertheless saw fit to sponsor them. According to Castillo (1978:108), "Almost any White man could raise a volunteer company, outfit it with guns, ammunition, horses, and supplies, and be reasonably sure that the state government would honor its vouchers." One of the most infamous of these many actions took place at Clear Lake in 1850 and became known as the Stone and Kelsey Massacre.

Most accounts of hostilities, even when sympathetic to the Indian plight, come from the reports of whites; rarely do we glimpse how the same events looked from an Indian point of view. The Stone and Kelsey Massacre is a notable exception. William Ralganal Benson, an Eastern Pomo man and narrator of the myth of "Creation" (#16) presented earlier in this volume, was born in 1862, some thirteen years after the killings that sparked the massacre, but he knew men who had taken part in the killings, suffered through the retaliation, and survived to tell the tale. To bear their witness, he wrote a detailed account based on their firsthand descriptions of what had transpired. Benson's account, originally published in 1932 in the *California Historical Society Quarterly,* begins: "The Facts Of Stone and Kelsey Massacre. in Lake County California. As it was stated to me by the five indians who went to stone and kelseys house purpose to kill the two white men. after debateing all night." (Benson, an extraordinary individual and something of a renaissance man, did not learn English until he was a young man and, without benefit of schooling, taught himself to read and write.) The first, and longer, portion of his account documents the brutal conditions on the Stone-Kelsey ranch—the starvation, whippings, torture, and executions—that motivated the killings; gives an account of the all-night debate that ultimately authorized the attack; and graphically details the killing itself. The remainder of his account describes what happened next: the inevitable retaliation, when government troops and vigilante militias "avenged" the killing of Stone and Kelsey. The following excerpt is taken from this latter section and is presented verbatim, without editorial change, in Benson's own words:[17]

one day the lake watchers saw a boat come around the point, som news coming they said to each others. two of the men went to the landing. to see what the news were. they were told that the white warriors had came to kill all the indians around the lake. so hide the best you can. the whites are making boats and with that they are coming up the lake. so they had two men go up on top of uncle sam mountain. the north peak. from there they watch the lower lake. for three days they watch the lake. one morning they saw a long boat came up the lake with pole on the bow with red cloth. and several of them came. every one of the boats had ten to fifteen men. the smoke signal was given by the two watchmen. every indian around the lake knew the soldiers were coming up the lake. and how many of them. and those who were watching the trail saw the infantrys coming over the hill from the lower lake. these two men were watching from ash hill. they went to stones and kelseys house. from there the horsemen went down torge the lake and the soldiers went across the valley torge lakeport. they went on to scotts valley. shoot a few shoots with their big gun and went on to upper lake and camped on Emmerson hill. from there they saw the indian camp on the island. the next morning the white warriors went across in their long dugouts. the indians said they would meet them in peace. so when the whites landed the indians went to wellcome them. but the white man was determined to kill them. Ge-We-Lih said he threw up his hands and said no harm me good man. but the white man fired and shoot him in the arm and another shoot came and hit a man staning along side of him and was killed. so they had to run and fight back; as they ran back in the tules and hed under the water; four or five of them gave alittle battle and another man was shoot in the shoulder. some of them jumped in the water and hed in the tuleys. many women and children were killed on around this island. one old lady a (indian) told about what she saw while hiding under abank, in under aover hanging tuleys. she said she saw two white man coming with their guns up in the air and on their guns hung a little girl. they brought it to the creek and threw it in the water. and alittle while later, two more men came in the same manner. this time they had alittle boy on the end of their guns and also threw it in the water. alittle ways from her she, said layed awoman shoot through the shoulder. she held her little baby in her arms. two white men came running torge the woman and baby, they stabed the woman and the baby and, and threw both of them over the bank in to the water. she said she heared the woman say, O my baby; she said when they gathered the dead, they found all the little ones were killed by being stabed, and many of the women were also killed stabing. she said it took them four or five days to gather up the dead. and the dead were all burnt on the east side the creek. they called it the siland creek. (Ba-Don-Bi-Da-Meh). this old lady also told about the whites hung aman on Emerson siland this indian was met by the soldiers while marching from scotts valley to upper lake. the indian was hung and alarge fire built under the hanging indian. and another indian was caught near Emerson hill. this one was tied to atree and burnt to death.

the next morning the solders started for mendocino county. and there killed many indians. the camp was on the ranch now known as Ed Howell ranch. the solders made camp a little ways below, bout one half mile from the indian camp. the indians wanted to surrender, but the solders did not give them time, the solders went in the camp and shoot them down as tho they were dogs. som of them escaped by going down a little creek leading to the river. and som of them hed in the brush. and those who hed in the brush most of them were killed. and those who hed in the water was over looked. they killed mostly women and children.

More than 135 Indians (60 at the island, another 75 along the Russian River) were indiscriminately killed in this campaign, according to the army's own report (Castillo 1978:108). Tribe after tribe during these bad California years came to know what it was like to be hunted down, and suffered crippling population losses to large- and small-scale "military" actions, as well as to disease and starvation.

By the 1880s this kind of direct physical assault, this war on Indian peoples and territories, had become more sporadic. In its place came more insidious modes of assault, directed at the languages and cultures themselves. We may think that the recent hysteria over "family values" is a new phenomenon in our public and political discourse. But the American people (that is to say, their legislators, policymakers, educators, and social critics, on their behalf) have long understood the importance of the family in the continuity of culture and preservation of ethnic identity. Unfortunately, this insight has all too often been used for ill as well as good: to *disadvantage* families—through politically motivated withholding of funds for key social programs in endangered communities, for instance—as well as to help them. The strategy is not new. One of the most devastating (and, sadly, effective) social policies this country has ever known was aimed at the heart of the Indian family—devised and implemented expressly to ensure its destruction.[18] I refer to the establishment of the federal Indian boarding school system in 1887, the year of the Dawes Act, which mandated the educational model pioneered by Richard Pratt at the Carlisle Industrial Training School in Pennsylvania.[19]

Carlisle-style boarding schools came to California in 1881 with the opening of a school on the Tule River Reservation in Tulare County. Numerous other schools followed over the course of the next twenty years. Given the high value Americans have always placed on education, at least until recently, it may be difficult to see the establishment of an Indian educational system as a destructive act. But when you consider that Indian children, by decree of state and federal law, were taken from their families (sometimes forcibly) and sent off to distant boarding schools where they were forbidden to speak their languages under penalty of physical punishment, where local white households could buy their labor as domestic servants for a pittance (Pratt 1964), and where the integrity of their Native culture was systematically demeaned—well, it's not so hard to see the destructive potential of such a program. Imagine, too, what it felt like for helpless parents to see their children taken from them, as if into custody, though they'd done no wrong; or what it felt like for the children themselves, frightened and homesick, stolen from their families and put down in a barracks with strange bunkmates far from home, to be whip-taught an alien standard by teachers who too often considered them barbarians. For that's what the boarding school system was, at its worst; and at its best, it was not much better—just less brutal. The federal Indian boarding school system was, and still is, a textbook illustration of how you break the spine of another culture. It's simple: remove its children from their families and home communities and keep them away long enough that they come back (if they do come back) something like strangers to their own people and traditions, to their own pasts, and to their own new futures. Fortunately, more liberal and humane heads prevailed, and critics eventually called a halt to the system before Native American cultures and communities were entirely flat-lined. But the reprieve came too late for all too many cultures. The damage done has proved immeasurable. And hardest hit were the languages—which is why the schools have garnered so much attention here.

What the boarding schools were most effective at killing was not the spirit of Native peoples—though the toll was heavy, the spirit survived—but their languages. As with a flame, as with a species, all it takes to extinguish a language forever is an interruption, however brief—just one broken link in the chain of transmission. And so it was that the generation "attending" the boarding schools during the first decades of the twentieth century turned out to be the last generation of speakers for hundreds of native languages across the United States. What may come as a surprise, though, is the conscious role this generation of parents took in the demise. The following personal reminiscence shows how the school-instilled psychology of persecution and humiliation could have brought this about. Few recollections could spell out the connection between language extinction and the boarding school experience as clearly as this one does. Elsie Allen, the narrator and a renowned Central Pomo basketmaker, was born in 1899 and got sent to Covelo Indian School in 1911. Her account, taken from an interview published in *News from Native California* in 1989, demonstrates just how successful the boarding schools were at alienating Indian children from their own cultures, especially their languages.[20]

BOARDING SCHOOL

When I went to school at that time [to the boarding school at Covelo,] there were three girls there from Hopland. I already knew some of their language, it's a different dialect from mine. I couldn't talk the English language in the school at Covelo, so I hollered at them when we lined up. Then one of the girls that was in my line reported me. They took me and strapped the heck out of me with a big leather strap. I didn't know what I got strapped for. Three days later those girls told me it was for talking the Indian language on the grounds, which I'm not supposed to do.

I was eleven years old [when I went to Covelo], and every night I cried and then I'd lay awake and think and think and think. I'd think to myself, "If I ever get married and have children I'll *never* teach my children the language or all the Indian things that I know. I'll *never* teach them that, I don't want my children to be treated like they treated me." That's the way I raised my children. Everybody couldn't understand that, they always asked me about it in later years. My husband has a different language. He can't understand me, but I learned his language much faster. I can talk it too, but I never taught my children. That's why they don't know. [My daughter] can understand it, but she can't speak the language.

In later years I found lots of ways they could have taught me in school but they didn't. They just put me in a corner and gave me a card with a lot of holes in it and a needle and yarn. They didn't say, "This is a needle." I would if I was teaching, if the child didn't know. Nobody said that. Well, I guess they just thought I was dumb or deaf or something. They treated me just like I was deaf and dumb. I was eleven years old, I wasn't a little kid, a baby. It should be easy to teach a person like that, but they didn't.

How I got to school in Covelo was every year the agent of the government school came around in the fall of the year and gathered the children to take them to the school. My mother signed a paper for me to go up there. In the morning [after a two-day trip to Covelo by wagon, flatbed railroad car, stage coach, and gravel wagon with six other children from the Hopland/Ukiah area], I just kind of stood around and watched the other girls, what they were doing and where to go. I didn't know what to say. I think I only knew two words of English, "yes" and "no." I never got to ask my mother why she sent me like that when I didn't know the English language.

I was scared, I had no one to talk to [because no one spoke my dialect]. That was sure hard. I felt that if I said something or fought against how we were treated, they might kill me. I cried every night. I couldn't talk to anybody or ask anybody anything because I didn't know how to. I was so dumb, that's the way I felt. They knew that I couldn't understand, so nobody talked to me. I was the only one that had my language.

California, because of its great diversity of languages, was perhaps especially affected by the federal program, as Elsie Allen's story suggests. Her experience—of doing time in communicative solitary confinement, not knowing anyone who shared her mother tongue—must have been a common one in California's gagged but polyglot boarding schools.[21]

In the end, though, governments and would-be conquistadores always underestimate the capacity of the human spirit to endure. Despite these two centuries and more of persecution and cultural devastation, California Indians have survived, their cultures strained and changed, but with the heart intact.

REVIVAL: A CALIFORNIA RENAISSANCE

Today in California, Native people and their cultures are experiencing a revival, a renaissance. Language is often at the center of the new interest, seen in some ways as the "book" in which the deep patterns of a culture, the life and heart's blood, are written. In language lies continuity with the past. It holds the keys to religion, ritual and ceremony, philosophy, art, song and story, healing, traditional crafts, and, through place-names, a centuries-deep sense of place. After all the decades of scorn and disparagement—and in the boarding schools, of active suppression—by white civilization, Indians are once again looking to their languages with pride. The turn has come not a moment too soon (and indeed, too late for real recovery in all too many cases). In the remainder of this essay, I will try as much as possible to allow those most closely involved in this revival to speak for themselves.

At a conference on Pomoan languages held in 1994, Edna Guerrero, a Northern Pomo elder, tells of her frustration and her commitment to the cause of language preservation:[22]

> My language is the thing that has always meant a lot to me. I became interested in it more and more because I resented the remarks made by (what we say) the white man. They say we grunted and nothing else; there were no words. And I thought to myself, "How can you [the white man] say that these people grunt, when there's an *entire conversation* being carried on in words that *they* [the Indians] understand!"

But now people are running around trying to find the languages . . . [S]o much of it is gone and will never be recovered . . . It's tragic. I think the young people are just beginning to realize what a tragedy it is. A well-known philosopher once said that when people lose their language, they lose their identity. You're nobody. And this is very true because the majority do not speak their language . . . What can be done about it? Where are you going to find the people that speak the language? There's no one left anymore. . . .

It's all that's interested me and I've done my best to preserve my share of it, and I hope that someone will benefit from it . . . I hope they continue . . . I don't know . . . That's all I can say. I've done the best I can; it's up to the rest.

Edna Guerrero speaks for many California elders, past and present, who have felt the same sense of loss and mystified resentment and have dedicated their energies to doing what they can to preserve their languages. More and more younger people have been taking up her challenge, following in these elders' footsteps. Nancy Richardson, in a 1992 essay, "The State of Our Languages," describes the dire situation this current generation of revivalists face, now that the torch is being passed:[23]

Since the first contact between the indigenous people of California and the western world, the original language and culture of this land have been endangered. Language has declined in a rapid, downward spiral from the very onset of that first contact. In my own experience, I have watched this painful loss of language in my tribe, the Karuk. In the early '70s, I began an optimistic journey of language work, recognizing and valuing the beauty and uniqueness found within my language. Twenty years ago, I kept hearing the language must be saved for the future. With 150 strong, fluent, tenacious Karuk elders in the background in those days, the urgency was not so apparent.

As I paid my last respects to my elders, one after another, as they crossed over to the next world, I began to directly feel the impact and the loss. I remember in 1981, how angry I was when Daisy Jacobs, 111, passed away. I thought, "How dare she die at one hundred and eleven. My work is not finished! I have so much still to learn from her." Then a few years later, when my teacher and the medicine man of the tribe, Shan Davis, passed away at a relatively early age, I was forced to come to terms with the reality of the situation. The details of this reality were simple, in that the death of each elder, each fluent speaker, was the death of my language.

The death of our language was inevitable and terminal . . . without new birth.

[The] Karuk language is considered by linguists and anthropologists as one of the oldest languages in California, spoken for many thousands of years, belonging to one particular place and one particular people. It is at the brink of extinction in the very immediate future, if drastic measures are not taken to reverse this trend. Currently there are 12 elderly fluent speakers of the Karuk language and approximately 40 more semi-fluent speakers at varying levels of speech competency. The Karuk language has reached a critical state. All of the languages in California have reached a similar state of language loss or passed beyond it.

Without immediate and proactive intervention, the majority of California's surviving native languages are doomed to extinction within the next twenty years. Richardson, along with dozens of other language activists, is keenly aware of this threat, but has taken it as a challenge, not a fait accompli. Her essay concludes with her hopes for the future:

In California, the children that are being born today are the seventh generation since first European contact. From out of this seventh generation will come the next fluent speakers of the indigenous languages of California. The number may be great or small; one alone is invaluable. But this effort will not be easy—it will involve a lot of work, commitment as well as courage and faith. It is a grim situation, that we as the indigenous people of California must face head on, yet I have no sadness, only faith. I look forward optimistically to the innovative challenges and the unknown possibilities.

One of the most promising of recent efforts to turn things around is California's own Master/Apprentice Language Learning Program. (The MALLP is conducted and administered by the Advocates for Indigenous California Language Survival [AICLS], which is an affiliate of the Seventh Generation Fund, an important umbrella organization for a number of Native American activist groups.) Nancy Richardson was one of the program's founding forces, along with people like Ray Baldy (Hupa), Mark Macarro (Luiseño), L. Frank Manriquez (Tongva/ Acagchme), Parris Butler (Mojave), Darlene Franco (Wukchumni), Leanne Hinton, and others. Since its first season in 1993, the Master/ Apprentice program has initiated training sessions for more than seventy master/apprentice pairs, involving (at the time of writing) twenty-five languages—most of them down to their last handful of fluent speakers—with more being added every year. Its success and the enthusiasm it generates have made it a model for similar programs around the country and abroad.

The AICLS, part of a larger revival that includes the California Indian Basketweavers Association and the California Indian Storytelling Association,[24] has initiated a number of other projects as well. One of these is the "Breath of Life" Native California Language Restoration Workshop, first held in 1996 at Berkeley and targeted at languages that now exist only in "fieldnote form."[25] The workshop answers a problem that the Master/Apprentice program, which presumes the existence of elders who still speak the language, cannot address. The problem is that not all tribal communities are lucky enough to have any native speakers left, and those who seek their languages must rely on the fieldnotes, recordings, and publications of the linguists who worked with the last generation of fluent elders. There are thirty or so such languages in California, languages that are sometimes described as "merely sleeping" (Hinton 1996). With this kind of proactive involvement, intelligence, and determination driving the California language revival movement, there is once again hope for the future of California's Native tongues.

There is still a long, long way to go, however, and California's remaining indigenous languages are not out of danger, by any stretch of the imagination. In truth, many of these flickering flames will yet be extinguished, despite the best efforts of Native communities and scholars combined. But the all-important start has been made, and at this point, it is only the road that matters. The people, programs, and communities fighting for their linguistic and cultural survival need all the help, understanding, and encouragement they can get. Which languages will survive and which pass into memory? No one knows. With the struggle for revival just enjoined, it is too soon to write the final chapter on California native languages. And with cooperation, faith, and hard work, that chapter will never need to be written. Here, in California at the beginning of the twenty-first century, in the seventh generation since European contact, we can find a new and thankful—if unintended—meaning in Villiana Calac Hyde's lovely translation of the Luiseño "Chaláawaat Song":

Tásmomaytal nevétiqankwa,
tááṣutal chulúpiqankwa.
'áá, temét nóó nevétqankwa,
temét nóó chulúpiqankwa.

I suppose I've survived the first little month,
I suppose I've survived the first big month.
Oh, I am surviving through the days,
I am surviving through the days.

NOTES

1. For a summary of the most recent data on language survival, see Hinton's "Living California Indian Languages" in her book *Flutes of Fire* (1994a); map 5 generalizes some of the information in this article.

2. Unfortunately, language diversity is not celebrated in all quarters. Beginning with Senator S. I. Hayakawa, California has seen more than its share of "English-Only" referendums in recent years. See Hinton's "The Native American Languages Act" in *Flutes of Fire* (Hinton 1994a). For a wider discussion of such matters, see James Crawford's book *Language Loyalties* (1992) or visit his website (http://ourworld.compuserve.com/homepages/JWCRAWFORD/). The University of Northern Arizona maintains a web-page on "Teaching Indigenous Languages" (http://jan.ucc.nau.edu/~jar/TIL.html) that contains a variety of links and resources related to this topic as well.

3. William Shipley's essay, "Native Languages of California" (Shipley 1978), in the California volume of the Smithsonian's *Handbook of North American Indians*—an indispensable reference found in most libraries—is probably the most accessible and concise scholarly introduction to the language families of California. For those with some linguistic training, there are detailed chapters on California language families in Lyle Campbell and Marianne Mithun's *The Languages of Native America* (1979) and the Smithsonian's *Handbook of North American Indians* (volume 17: *Languages*, ed. by Ives Goddard, 1996). I merely provide a general orientation here.

4. The names for these superstocks are separately based on similarities for the number 'two' within the languages of the individual families. For instance, the Atsugewi word *hoqi* (compare Achumawi *hak'*, Shasta *xokwa*, Chimariko *xok'u*, Diegueño *xawok*, and Salinan *hakic*, all meaning 'two') gives rise to the term *Hokan*. (The phonetic letter [x] represents a velar fricative—the hard, *h*-

like sound in the German pronunciation of *Bach* or the Scottish *loch*.) The term *Penutian* is actually a compound of the Proto-Maiduan and Proto-Costanoan forms for 'two'—*pé'ne* and *uṭxi,* respectively (Shipley 1978).

5. Uto-Aztecan languages are found throughout the Great Basin and American Southwest (languages like Paiute, Shoshone, and Hopi) and in Mexico (Yaqui, Nahuatl, Huichol, and Pipil, to name a few). The main branch of Algic is Algonquian—a very large and widespread family of languages concentrated in the East (Delaware, Micmac, Abenaki, Passamaquoddy), the Midwest (Shawnee, Kickapoo, Fox, Potawatomi), and fanning west across Canada (Ojibwa and the great Cree continuum); the Ritwan languages, Wiyot and Yurok, are the two California representatives of this superstock. The large Athabascan family, part of the Na-Dené superstock (Haida, Tanaina, Koyukon, Carrier, Chilcotin, Dogrib, Chipewyan, and Umpqua, to name a few), is primarily concentrated in the Pacific Northwest, Alaska, and the Canadian North. Navajo and Apache are southwestern "walkabouts" of this same family.

6. And probably Chumashan as well, if Chumash proves to be unrelatable to other so-called Hokan languages. Yukian has long been chalked up as an isolate family, but Chumash, until recently, was presumed to be a member of the Hokan superstock. Current research, encouraged by a large-scale examination of Harrington's vast Chumash corpora now under way at the University of California, Santa Barbara, suggests that this long-standing assumption (going at least back to Sapir 1925) is becoming increasingly difficult to maintain (Foster 1996:86). Indeed, recent classifications (Ives Goddard 1996) do not include either Chumashan or Esselen within the proposed Hokan grouping. However, the dust has yet to settle on this reevaluation.

7. Foster's (1996) *Handbook* discussion of California linguistic prehistory, in "Language and the Culture History of North America," is an extremely valuable overview of the field, and I have relied heavily on his synthesis of past and present scholarship in the account that follows. (See especially his sections on Yukian, Hokan, Penutian, and Uto-Aztecan, pp. 83–95.) Other useful resources include Shipley (1978), Wallace (1978a), Whistler (1977b), and Moratto (1984).

8. Should conclusive linguistic evidence for the Hokan grouping remain beyond the reach of our methodological grasp, the term *Hokan* may yet survive as a kind of shorthand for referring to some of these "Old California" languages and language families. Indeed, informed speculation (for example, Moratto 1984) associates ancestral Yukian and "Hokan" peoples with the ancient Western Fluted Point tradition, which dates to 9,000–10,000 B.P.

9. This model of Penutian southern expansion echoes what has come to be called the "Multiple Entry Hypothesis." A great deal of new work has come out in the past couple of decades (see Foster 1996 for summary and orientation),

work which has largely dismantled the prevailing older notion that there was ever a genetically unified "California Penutian" subgroup from which the contemporary California Penutian families evolved. Rather, the Penutian incursions into California seem to have come in distinct and chronologically separate waves, as outlined here.

Furthermore, if Mike Nichols (1981) is correct, and the long and complex Pre-Uto-Aztecan dispersal can in fact be traced out of the Basin and Southwest, back through the Central Valley and Southern Sierra and north toward Oregon, then it may have been Pre-Uto-Aztecan peoples who actually pioneered the ancient Penutian route south out of Oregon, down through the river systems of northern California, and into the Central Valley and foothills of the Sierra, long before the ancestral Yokutsan, Utian, and Wintuan peoples, who by turns followed in their footsteps.

10. The southern distribution of Hokan, in the form of Yuman-family languages, continues down into the Baja peninsula with PaiPai and Kiliwa, and back into the Southwest with the other Yuman tribes (Havasupai, Walapai, Yavapai, and Maricopa). There are also distant "Hokan" languages in Mexico: for instance, Seri and Chontal-Oaxaca.

11. California Uto-Aztecan groups include Tataviam; Tübatulabal in the mountain foothills; the Takic group (Luiseño, Gabrielino, and Juaneño along the coast; Serrano, Kitanemuk, Cupeño, and Cahuilla inland); and the Numic group (Mono, Owens Valley Paiute, Panamint, Kawaiisu, Southern Paiute, and Chemehuevi) out in the Basin proper, beyond the boundaries of the California culture area per se. For discussions of California Uto-Aztecan prehistory, see Bean and Smith (1978), Nichols (1981), Moratto (1984), and Foster (1996).

12. The discussion here owes much to Johanna Nichol's pioneering work on the geographical aspects of linguistic diversity, *Linguistic Diversity in Space and Time* (1992).

13. In effect, this tendency holds true even within California itself. The linguistically least diverse area of California—the desert territories of its closely related Uto-Aztecan tribes—is also the most inhospitable.

14. I would urge the interested reader to look for Robert Heizer's *The Destruction of California Indians* (1993), Robert H. Jackson and Edward Castillo's *Indians, Franciscans, and Spanish Colonization: The Impact of the Mission System on California Indians* (1995), Rupert and Jeannette Henry Costo's *The Missions of California: A Legacy of Genocide* (1987), and Albert Hurtado's *Indian Survival on the California Frontier* (1988), among other works on this subject.

15. This account is taken from Mauricio Mixco's "Kiliwa Texts." The only editorial liberties I have taken—as this is not a technical publication—is to remove the brackets and clause numbers from Mixco's free translation and supply occasional punctuation marks where they seemed appropriate. The brack-

etted words and phrases in the text here are my own insertions, provided for clarity.

16. Yee's narrative, which was brought to my attention by linguist Suzanne Wash, was collected in the 1930s by J. P. Harrington; it is unpublished, but may be found among Harrington's voluminous Barbareño fieldnotes at the Santa Barbara Museum of Natural History. Asisara's account, collected in 1877 but dating to 1818, is reprinted in Malcolm Margolin's *The Way We Lived*.

17. Margolin reprints Benson's account in its entirety in *The Way We Lived: California Indian Stories, Songs, and Reminiscences* (1993).

18. True, many of the most disastrous Indian policies and programs were conceived with "the best of intentions." It's just hard to understand, today, how a program that intentionally dismembers families can be seen in a humanitarian light. We are left with a historical view of a society so blinded by its own presuppositions and prejudices that up is seen as down, and a sow's ear is taken for a purse of gold. Let our forebears be a lesson to us today, where such reactionary and mean-spirited public policies as immigrant health-care bans or English Only movements are concerned, and examine our ethnic legislations with a true humanitarian eye.

19. See Hamley 1994 for a comprehensive treatment of the history and cultural effects of the federal boarding school system.

20. *News from Native California* 4.1 (1989):40–41. The interview was conducted by Vic Bedoian and Roberta Llewellyn, and transcribed by Vera Mae Fredrickson.

21. Margolin, in a postscript to this interview as excerpted in *The Way We Lived,* writes: "Elsie Allen did have children, and true to her resolve she, like so many of her generation, did not teach them her Pomo language. She did, however, become a masterful weaver of baskets, and until her death in 1990 she was tremendously important in passing along traditional skills and knowledge to her children and to many others" (1993:183).

22. From an article published in *News from Native California* 8.4 (1994): 40.

23. This essay appeared in *The Advocate* (the newsletter of the Advocates for Indigenous California Language Survival), published as an inset to *News from Native California* 7.1 (winter 1992–1993): 40–41.

24. See Lauren Teixeira's "California Indian Stories and the Spirit" in *News from Native California* 9.4 (1996).

25. See Leanne Hinton's "Breath of Life/Silent No More: The Native California Language Restoration Workshop" in *News from Native California* 10.1 (1996). Sixteen languages were represented: Rumsien, Mutsun, Awaswas, Coast Miwok, Patwin, Nomlaki, Nisenan, Central Pomo, Northern Pomo, Chimariko, Salinan, Ventureño Chumash, Tongva (Gabrielino), Ajachmem (Juaneño), Wiyot, and Mattole.

MAPS

Do you come from the north?
Do you come from the east?
Do you come from the west?
Do you come from the south?
Do you come from above?
Do you come from below?

> Hai´-kut-wo-to-peh's song
> Ceremonial acorn song, Maidu

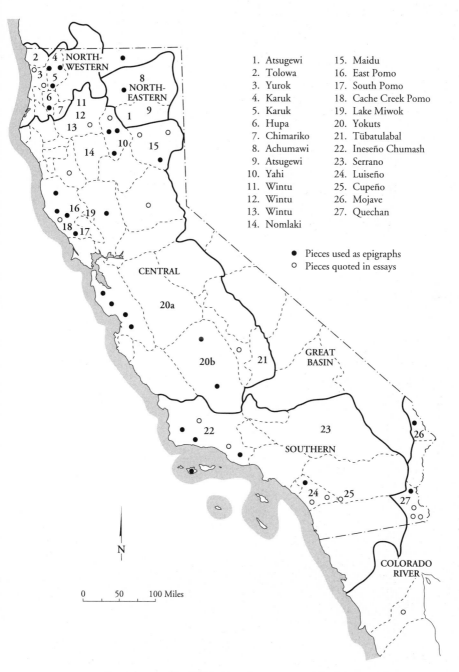

1. Atsugewi
2. Tolowa
3. Yurok
4. Karuk
5. Karuk
6. Hupa
7. Chimariko
8. Achumawi
9. Atsugewi
10. Yahi
11. Wintu
12. Wintu
13. Wintu
14. Nomlaki

15. Maidu
16. East Pomo
17. South Pomo
18. Cache Creek Pomo
19. Lake Miwok
20. Yokuts
21. Tübatulabal
22. Ineseño Chumash
23. Serrano
24. Luiseño
25. Cupeño
26. Mojave
27. Quechan

● Pieces used as epigraphs
○ Pieces quoted in essays

NORTH-WESTERN

NORTH-EASTERN

CENTRAL

20a

20b

GREAT BASIN

SOUTHERN

COLORADO RIVER

N

0   50   100 Miles

MAP I. Locator map. The California culture areas are Northwestern, Northeastern, Central, and Southern. Parts of the Great Basin and Colorado culture areas are also shown. The numbers correspond to the selections in the text. Divisions based on Kroeber (1936), in Heizer and Elsasser (1980).

MAP 2. California linguistic diversity.

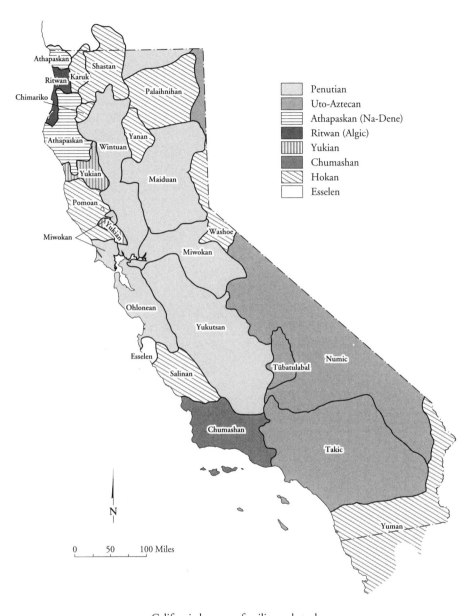

Athapaskan
Ritwan
Chimariko
Athapaskan
Yukian
Pomoan
Miwokan

Shastan
Karuk
Palaihnihan
Yanan
Wintuan
Maiduan
Yukian
Washoe
Miwokan

Ohlonean
Esselen
Salinan
Yukutsan
Tübatulabal
Numic
Chumashan
Takic
Yuman

Penutian
Uto-Aztecan
Athapaskan (Na-Dene)
Ritwan (Algic)
Yukian
Chumashan
Hokan
Esselen

N

0   50   100 Miles

MAP 3. California language families and stocks.

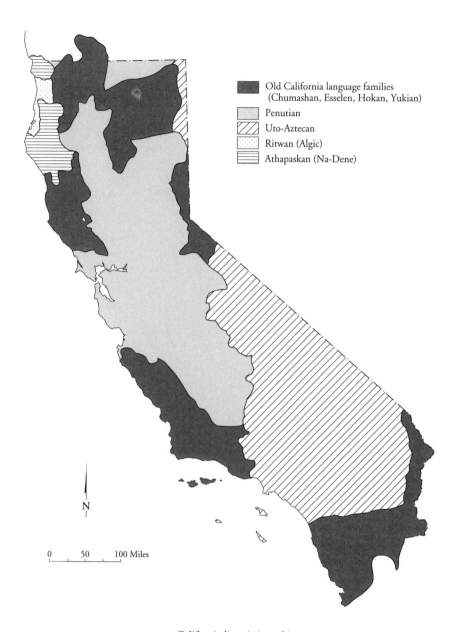

N

0   50   100 Miles

MAP 4. California linguistic prehistory.

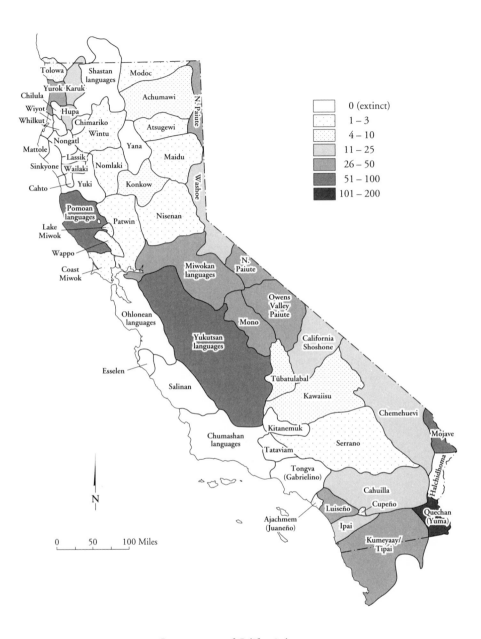

MAP 5. Current status of California languages.

BIBLIOGRAPHY

There is an entire world of information on California Native cultures, languages, and oral literatures for interested readers to explore. Some of it is in books, some in magazines and journals, some in archives, some on websites. Some of it is geared more toward a general audience, as this book is, and some of it is technical or scholarly in nature. But all of it will help to illuminate, in one way or another, the selections of California oral literature contained in these pages. All items mentioned here are listed in full in the "References" section.

A. General-Interest Books

Malcolm Margolin's *The Ohlone Way* is perhaps the best possible popular introduction to the unique Native California patterns of life and worldview—beautifully written and evocative rather than academic in nature. (Margolin is also the publisher of *News from Native California,* a quarterly magazine providing "an inside view of the California Indian world," and Heyday Books, which has a fine line of general-audience books celebrating Native Californian peoples and cultures.) Leanne Hinton's *Flutes of Fire,* a collection of articles originally written for her regular "Language" column in *News for Native California,* provides an accessible and engaging introduction to the world of California languages through a miscellany of essays on place-names, songs, language legislation, basketry terms, language families, writing systems, and many other topics, including a variety of fascinating grammatical features of California languages. If you only read two popular books on California Indians, these would be the two I recommend.

There are several biographies of real interest to the general reader: Theodora Kroeber's *Ishi: In Two Worlds,* which documents the life of California's so-called last wild Indian and provides a good bit of Yahi ethnography and contact history in the process; Carobeth Laird's *Encounter with an Angry God,* an extended reminiscence of her not-so-happy life as J. P. Harrington's wife; Gui de Angulo's *The Old Coyote of Big Sur,* a biography of her famous linguist father, Jaime de Angulo; Lucy Thompson's *To the American Indian: Reminiscences of a Yurok Woman,* an early Indian autobiography; *The Autobiography of Delfina Cuero,* a Kumeyaay woman, as told to Florence Shipek; Darryl Babe Wilson's *The Morning the Sun Went Down;* Victor Golla's edition of *The Sapir-Kroeber Correspondence,* which gives a fascinating inside view of the early days of anthropology and linguistics in California, including quite a few letters concerning Ishi; and Greg Sarris's *Mabel McKay: Weaving the Dream,* a captivating blend of biography and oral autobiography telling the life story of his remarkable and provocative aunt, a basketmaker and one of the last Pomo doctors.

Other general-interest books include Greg Sarris's *The Sound of Rattles and Clappers,* an anthology of contemporary poetry and fiction by Native California writers; Jaime de Angulo's classic *Indians in Overalls,* an account of the author's first season of fieldwork among the Pit River Achumawi; Thomas Mayfield and Malcolm Margolin's *Indian Summer: Traditional Life among the Choinumne Indians of California's San Joaquin Valley;* Brian Bibby's *The Fine Art of California Indian Basketry;* and Jeannine Gendar's *Grass Games and Moon Races: California Indian Games and Toys.*

Regarding the post-Contact history of California Indian peoples, there are a number of important and useful works, including Robert Heizer's *The Destruction of California Indians,* Robert Jackson and Edward Castillo's *Indians, Franciscans, and Spanish Colonization: The Impact of the Mission System on California Indians,* Albert Hurtado's *Indian Survival on the California Frontier,* and Rupert Costo and Jeannette Costo's *The Missions of California: A Legacy of Genocide.*

B. Collections of Story and Song in Translation

There is a surprising amount of California oral literature in English translation. Malcolm Margolin's *The Way We Lived: California Indian Stories, Songs, and Reminiscences* is a fine and wide-ranging newer collection, drawn from authentic sources, with enlightening commentary on each selection. Earlier anthologies include Frank Latta's *California Indian Folklore* and Edward Gifford and Gwendoline Block's *California Indian Nights.* Theodora Kroeber's *The Inland Whale* contains literary reworkings of authentic traditional stories. One of the oldest sources is Jeremiah Curtin's *Creation Myths of Primitive America,* originally published in 1898 and containing a large body of Yana and Wintu myths. Beyond these, there are quite a number of collections focused on particular tribes and languages: Thomas Blackburn's *December's Child: A Book of*

Chumash Oral Narratives; Alfred Kroeber's *Yurok Myths, A Mohave Historical Epic, Seven Mohave Myths,* and *More Mohave Myths;* Alfred Kroeber and Edward Gifford's *Karok Myths;* Robert Spott and Alfred Kroeber's *Yurok Narratives;* Istet Woiche's *Annikadel: The History of the Universe as Told by the Achumawi Indians of California;* Julian Lang's *Ararapíkva: Creation Stories of the People;* Jaime de Angulo's *How the World Was Made, Shabegok,* and *Indian Tales* (fictionalized settings of mostly retold Achumawi, Miwok, and Pomo tales); William Shipley's wonderful translations of *The Maidu Indian Myths and Stories of Hánc'ibyjim;* Leanne Hinton and Susan Roth's children's-book version of *Ishi's Tale of Lizard;* and Carobeth Laird's *Mirror and Pattern,* a collection of Chemehuevi stories (with commentary) told by her second husband, George Laird.

Two publications stand out for their pure loveliness as books to have and hold: *Mourning Dove, a Yurok/English Tale* (a chapbook put out by Heyday Books); and the Yosemite Association's *Legends of the Yosemite Miwok,* edited by Frank LaPena, Craig D. Bates, and Steven Medley.

Finally, though they do not focus exclusively on California traditions, the following works incorporate significant California materials: Brian Swann's *Song of the Sky* and *Wearing the Morning Star,* which contain the poet's versions of several classic and beautiful California songs; Leanne Hinton and Lucille Watahomigie's *Spirit Mountain,* which presents bilingual (and occasionally trilingual) versions of Yuman oral literature, including Mojave, Diegueño, Quechan, and Kiliwa; William Bright's *A Coyote Reader,* which contains translations of Coyote tales from a number of different California traditions; and Brian Swann's mammoth anthology *Coming to Light: Contemporary Translations of the Native Literatures of North America,* which includes selections from Yana, Karuk, Atsugewi, and Maidu.

C. Studies of Native California Oral Literature

There are a few studies that focus specifically or largely on California traditions: Greg Sarris's collection of literary essays, *Keeping Slug Woman Alive: A Holistic Approach to American Indian Texts;* Richard Applegate's "Chumash Narrative Folklore as Sociolinguistic Data"; Carobeth Laird's *Mirror and Pattern;* and Thomas Blackburn's *December's Child: A Book of Chumash Oral Narratives,* an extended folkloristic analysis. Anna Gayton's "Areal Affiliations of California Folktales" and Alfred Kroeber's "Indian Myths of South Central California" are both useful attempts at areal classification. Dorothy Demetracopoulou and Cora du Bois's "A Study of Wintu Mythology" is an important early work of stylistic analysis, as is Anna Gayton and Stanley Newman's "Yokuts and Western Mono Myths." Studies of Native California song include Richard Keeling's

Cry for Luck, which focuses on Northwestern California singing styles; George Herzog's "The Yuman Musical Style"; Bruno Nettl's "The Songs of Ishi: Musical Styles of the Yahi Indians"; R. H. Robins and Norma McLeod's "Five Yurok Songs: A Musical and Textual Analysis"; and Helen Roberts's *Form in Primitive Music: An Analytical and Comparative Study of the Melodic Form of Some Ancient Southern Californian Indian Songs.*

For readers wishing to broaden the scope of their exploration, there are many useful and important studies of Native American oral literature. Seminal works include Melville Jacobs's *The Content and Style of an Oral Literature: Clackamas Chinook Myths and Tales;* Dell Hymes's *'In vain I tried to tell you': Essays in Native American Ethnopoetics;* and Dennis Tedlock's *The Spoken Word and the Work of Interpretation.* Other important studies from the linguistic or ethnopoetic side are Karl Kroeber's recently reissued *Traditional American Indian Literatures: Texts and Interpretations;* Brian Swann and Arnold Krupat's *Recovering the Word: Essays on Native American Literature;* Leanne Hinton's *Havasupai Songs: A Linguistic Perspective;* Brian Swann's *Smoothing the Ground: Essays in Native American Oral Literature* and *On the Translation of Native American Literatures;* and Joel Sherzer and Anthony Woodbury's *Native American Discourse: Poetics and Rhetoric.*

On the more literary side of the equation are Arnold Krupat's *Ethnocriticism: Ethnography, History, Literature* and *New Voices in Native American Literary Criticism,* an anthology of critical essays; David Brumble's *American Indian Autobiography;* and Gerald Vizenor's *Narrative Chance: Postmodern Discourse on Native American Indian Literatures.*

D. Linguistic Text Collections

Linguistic editions of texts collected in the field are the foundation, the documentary base on which the study of Native American oral literature is built. As far as California cultures are concerned, most of these primary text collections are published as volumes in serial publications like the *University of California Publications in American Archaeology and Ethnology (UCPAAE),* which in 1943 shifted its specifically linguistic monographs over to the *University of California Publications in Linguistics* (UCPL).

Major book-length collections are Samuel A. Barrett's *Pomo Myths;* James Crawford's *Cocopa Texts;* Grace Dangberg's *Washo Texts;* Roland Dixon's *Maidu Texts;* L. S. Freeland's *Freeland's Central Sierra Miwok Myths* (edited by Howard Berman); Pliny Earl Goddard's "Hupa Texts," "Kato Texts," and "Chilula Texts"; Jane Hill and Roscinda Nolasquez's *Mulu'wetam (The First People): Cupeño Oral History and Language;* Wick Miller's *Newe Natekwinappeh: Shoshoni Stories and Dictionary;* Robert Oswalt's *Kashaya Texts;* Paul Radin's *Wappo Texts: First Se-*

ries; Gladys Reichard's *Wiyot Grammar and Texts;* Edward Sapir's *Yana Texts;* Hansjakob Seiler's *Cahuilla Texts;* William Shipley's *Maidu Texts and Dictionary;* and Stuart Uldall and William Shipley's *Nisenan Texts and Dictionary.* (Many of these scholars have also produced grammars and dictionaries for their respective languages, and most grammars also contain a few texts as well.) Certain volumes in the *Native American Texts Series* (both the new series and the old) also feature texts from a variety of California literary traditions: William Bright's *Coyote Stories;* Geoffrey Gamble's *Yokuts Texts;* Margaret Langdon's *Yuman Texts;* Victor Golla and Shirley Silver's *Northern California Texts;* and Martha Kendall's *Coyote Stories II.*

Many important linguistic texts and short collections also appear in journal format, among them Jaime de Angulo's "Pomo Creation Myth"; Jaime de Angulo and L. S. Freeland's "Karok Texts"; Madison Beeler's "Barbareño Chumash Text and Lexicon"; L. S. Freeland's "Western Miwok Texts with Linguistic Sketch"; Pliny Earl Goddard's "Wailaki Texts"; John Peabody Harrington's "Karok Texts" and "Karok Indian Myths"; Robert Lowie's "Washo Texts"; William Seaburg's "A Wailaki (Athapaskan) Text with Comparative Notes"; and Carl Voegelin's "Tübatulabal Texts."

E. Handbooks, Bibliographies, and Archives

The single most useful reference work—your bible for beginning research or simply seeking information on California Indians—is the California volume of the Smithsonian's *Handbook of North American Indians* (volume 8, edited by Robert Heizer). Next come Alfred Kroeber's *Handbook of the Indians of California,* Robert Heizer and M. A. Whipple's *The California Indians: A Source Book,* and Lowell Bean and Thomas Blackburn's *Native Californians: A Theoretical Retrospective.* Stephen Powers's *Tribes of California,* important and even groundbreaking in its day (1877) and still a valuable source of information and firsthand observation, has not aged well. (It is entirely too easy to stumble across sentences like the following, which introduces the text of a Konkow song: "The reader will understand, if he knows anything about Indian habits, that there was a great deal introduced into this performance which no man can describe or imitate—unutterable groans, hissings, mutterings, and repetitions, with which the savage so delights to envelop his sacred exercises" [307].)

William Bright's annotated *Bibliography of the Languages of Native California* is an invaluable reference tool, though it runs out at its date of publication, 1982, and much new work has been produced since then; an updated version is available on the web (see section I here). Robert Heizer, Karen Nissen, and Edward Castillo's *California Indian History: A Classified and Annotated Guide to*

Source Materials is likewise an useful tool, as is Richard Keeling's *Guide to Early Field Recordings (1900–1949) at the Lowie Museum of Anthropology.* One of the most comprehensive bibliographic sources is on-line at the California Indian Libraries Collection website (see section I here). This site provides fairly comprehensive bibliographies organized by tribe and draws on historical, anthropological, and linguistic sources; unfortunately, the project has not yet been expanded to cover Southern California cultures.

For those interested in archival materials, the Bancroft Library at Berkeley has a vast collection of California ethnographic and linguistic holdings, including the A. L. Kroeber Papers and the Frank J. Essene collection. (Researchers should ask for Dale Valory's "Guide to Ethnological Documents" [CU-23.1]—the "Valory Guide," for short.) The Phoebe Appleton Hearst Museum of Anthropology (formerly the Lowie) at Berkeley has a collection of sound recordings and an extensive photographic collection now in the process of being catalogued electronically. The archives of the Survey of California and Other Indian Languages, also at Berkeley, is administered by the Department of Linguistics; the Language Lab with its tape archives is conveniently located in the same building. Other important archival sites for California materials include the American Philosophical Library in Philadelphia, the Huntington Library in San Marino (especially the Wieland collection), the Santa Barbara Museum of Natural History, the Southwest Museum in Los Angeles, and the Malki Museum at the Morongo Indian Reservation.

Finally, researchers should be aware of the huge Harrington collection archived at the National Anthropological Archives at the Smithsonian Institution in Washington, D.C. There is a complete microfilm edition of the Harrington papers (running to 283 reels) distributed by Kraus International. Many university libraries own at least selections from this microfilm collection; larger universities and institutions, such as U.C. Berkeley and the University of Pittsburgh, are likely to possess the entire set.

F. Magazines and Newsletters

For more than a decade, the quarterly magazine *News from Native California* has been an important forum for news and views of California's Native communities and a major force in encouraging the current renaissance of contemporary California languages and cultures. Another lively and informative periodical, *The Masterkey,* put out by the Southwest Museum, is sadly now defunct. Two newsletters provide useful and engaging sources of information on California languages: the *SSILA Newsletter* (where SSILA stands for the Society for the Study of the Indigenous Languages of the Americas), which occasionally mentions topics germane to California, including conference schedules; and the occasional *Newsletter of the J. P. Harrington Conference,* which serves as a clearing-house of information for scholars working with the Harrington materials.

There are several California-oriented conferences that convene annually: the California Indian Conference, an "interdenominational" gathering of people—specialist and nonspecialist, Native and non-Native—to read papers and give talks on topics and issues of interest to Native California studies; the Hokan/Penutian Workshop, a gathering of linguists specializing in Hokan and Penutian languages (watch for announcements in the *SSILA Newsletter*); and the California Indian Storytelling Festival, which was inaugurated in 1995 (check their website for information).

G. Tribal Booklets and Instructional Materials

Many tribes, sometimes working in cooperation with linguists, sometimes working on their own, produce documentary and pedagogical materials for their languages, in the form of text collections, teaching grammars, vocabularies and dictionaries, videos, and so forth. These materials tend to be geared more toward the classroom and the community—practical applications—than to the specialist audience of professional linguists and language consultants. Sometimes these materials are readily available, but often they are distributed only locally and can be very difficult to obtain. Accessible or not, they do exist, and it seems worthwhile to list them here.

Some examples I've run across include Lucy Arvidson's *Alaawich (Our Language): First Book of Words in the Tübatulabal Language of Southern California;* James Bauman, Ruby Miles, and Ike Leaf's *Pit River Teaching Dictionary;* Ruth Bennett's *Hupa Spelling Book;* Catherine Callaghan and Brian Bibby's *Northern Sierra Miwok Language Handbook* and *Let's Learn Northern Sierra Miwok;* Ted Couro and Christina Hutcheson's *Dictionary of Mesa Grande Diegueño;* Ted Couro and Margaret Langdon's *Let's Talk 'Iipay Aa: An Introduction to the Mesa Grande Diegueño Language;* Victor Golla's *Hupa Stories, Anecdotes, and Conversations;* Villiana Hyde's *An Introduction to the Luiseño Language;* Roscinda Nolasquez and Anne Galloway's *I'i Muluwit: First Book of Words in the Cupeño Indian Language of Southern California;* Jesús Ángel Ochoa Zazueta's *Ya'abú ti'nñar jaspuy'pai (Esta es la Escritura Pai'pai);* Thomas Parsons's *The Yurok Language, Literature, and Culture;* and Katherine Saubel and Pamela Munro's *Chem'ivillu': Let's Speak Cahuilla.*

H. Films and Documentaries

Several recent movies and documentaries have focused on California Indian cultures. Two of them concern Ishi: the Ishi Documentation Project's excellent documentary *Ishi, the Last Yahi,* and the considerably more popularized HBO production *Ishi, Last of His Tribe,* starring Graham Green as Ishi and Jon Voight as A. L. Kroeber. Ken Burns's PBS series *The West* contains a good bit of California coverage, including (for once) some Indian perspective on the Spanish Mission period and the Gold Rush. Finally, Greg Sarris's miniseries *Grand Avenue,* which follows the lives of contemporary Indians in Northern California (and is based on his short-story collection of the same name), aired on HBO in 1996.

I. Internet Sites and Discussion Groups

The Survey of California and Other Indian Languages maintains a website with a searchable database indexing its holdings, along with pointers to other relevant addresses. The California Indian Library Collections site mentioned in section E provides maps, pictures, and basketry information, in addition to the tribal bibliographies. The UC Berkeley linguistics department has a homepage that includes information about conferences and California language courses, sometimes even including data gathered from ongoing classes in linguistic field methods. The California Indian Storytelling Festival also has a website, with information on upcoming festivals and other issues. Addresses for these and other relevant sites, as of time of publication, are as follows:

The California Indian Storytelling Festival:
http://www.ucsc.edu/costano/story1.html

California Indian Library Collections:
http://www.mip.berkeley.edu/cilc/brochure/brochure.html

Survey of California and Other Indian Languages:
http://www.linguistics.berkeley.edu/lingdept/research/Survey/SCOIL.html

The Cahto (Kato) Language Page:
http://www.geocities.com/Athens/Parthenon/6010/

Costanoan-Ohlone Indian Canyon Resource:
http://www.ucsc.edu/costano/

UC Berkeley Department of Linguistics:
http://www.linguistics.berkeley.edu/lingdept/

Society for the Study of the Indigenous Languages of the Americas:
http://www.trc2.ucdavis.edu/ssila

REFERENCES

This bibliography contains the full citations for all works referred to in this volume, including the "Further Reading" sections found with each individual introduction.

Abbreviations

CAL-HB *California,* ed. Robert F. Heizer. Vol. 8 of the Smithsonian *Handbook of North American Indians,* ed. William C. Sturtevant (1978). Washington, D.C.: Smithsonian Institution.

IJAL *International Journal of American Linguistics.* Chicago: University of Chicago Press.

IJAL-NATS *International Journal of Linguistics,* Native American Texts Series. Chicago: University of Chicago Press.

JAF *Journal of American Folklore.* Boston and New York: Houghton, Mifflin and Co. for the American Folklore Society.

NNC *News from Native California: An Inside View of the California Indian World.* Berkeley: Heyday Books.

RSCOIL *Reports from the Survey of California and Other Indian Languages.* Berkeley: Survey of California and Other Indian Languages, University of California.

UCAR *University of California Anthropological Records.* Berkeley: University of California Press.

UCPAAE *University of California Publications in Archaeology and Ethnology.* Berkeley: University of California Press.

UCPL *University of California Publications in Linguistics.* Berkeley: University of California Press.

Allen, Elsie. 1972. *Pomo Basketmaking: A Supreme Art for the Weaver.* Healdsburg, Calif.: Naturegraph Publishers.

———. 1989. "Boarding School." *NNC* 4.1.

Angulo, Gui de. 1995. *The Old Coyote of Big Sur: The Life and Times of Jaime de Angulo.* Berkeley: Stonegarden Press.

Angulo, Jaime de. 1935. "Pomo Creation Myth." *JAF* 48.189: 203–262.

———. 1953. *Indian Tales.* New York: A. A. Wyn.

———. 1976a. *Shabegok.* Old Time Stories 1. Berkeley: Turtle Island Foundation.

———. 1976b. *How the World Was Made.* Old Time Stories 2. Berkeley: Turtle Island Foundation.

————. 1990. *Indians in Overalls.* San Francisco: City Lights Books.

Angulo, Jaime de, and L. S. Freeland. 1930. "The Achumawi Language." *IJAL* 7: 77–120.

————. 1931a. "Karok Texts." *IJAL* 6.3–4: 194–226.

————. 1931b. "Two Achumawi Tales." *JAF* 44.172: 125–136.

Apodaca, Paul. 1997. "Completing the Circle." Review of *My Dear Miss Nicholson . . . Letters and Myths,* by William R. Benson. *NNC* 11.1 (fall): 32–34.

Applegate, Richard. 1972. "Ineseño Chumash Grammar." Ph.D. diss., University of California at Berkeley.

————. 1975. "Chumash Narrative Folklore as Sociolinguistic Data." *Journal of California and Great Basin Anthropology* 2: 188–197.

Arvidson, Lucy. 1976. *Alaawich (Our Language): First Book of Words in the Tübatulabal Language of Southern California.* Banning, Calif.: Malki Museum Press.

Barrett, Samuel A. 1919. "The Wintun Hesi Ceremony." *UCPAAE* 14.1: 437–448.

————. 1933. *Pomo Myths.* Bulletin of the Public Museum of the City of Milwaukee 15. Milwaukee.

Bass, Howard, and Green Rayna, prods. 1995. *Heartbeat: Voices of First Nations Women.* Washington: Smithsonian/Folkways Records (CD SF 40415).

Bauman, James. 1980. "Chimariko Placenames and the Boundaries of Chimariko Territory." In *American Indian and Indo-European Studies: Papers in Honor of Madison S. Beeler,* ed. Kathryn Klar, Margaret Langdon, and Shirley Silver, 11–29. The Hague: Mouton Publishers.

Bauman, James, with Ruby Miles and Ike Leaf. 1979. *Pit River Teaching Dictionary.* National Bilingual Materials Development Center, Rural Education, University of Alaska.

Baumhoff, Martin A., and David L. Olmsted. 1964. "Notes on Palaihnihan Culture History: Glottochronology and Archaeology." In *Studies in Californian Linguistics,* ed. W. Bright. UCPL 34: 1–12.

Beals, Ralph. 1933. "Ethnography of the Nisenan." *UCPAAE* 31.6: 335–414.

Bean, Lowell John, and Thomas Blackburn. 1976. *Native Californians: A Theoretical Retrospective.* Socorro, N.Mex.: Ballena Press.

Bean, Lowell John, and Florence C. Shipek. 1978. "Luiseño." CAL-HB: 550–563.

Bean, Lowell John, and Charles R. Smith. 1978. "Serrano." CAL-HB: 570–574.

Bean, Lowell John, and Sylvia Brakke Smith. 1978. "Gabrielino." CAL-HB: 538–549.

Bean, Lowell John, and Sylvia Brakke Vane. 1978. "Cults and Their Transformations." CAL-HB: 662–672.

Bedoian, Vic, and Roberta Llewellyn. 1995. "Interview with Edna Guerrero." *NNC* 8.4 (spring): 40.

Beeler, Madison. 1979. "Barbareño Chumash Text and Lexicon." In *Festschrift for Archibald A. Hill,* vol. 2, ed. M. A. Jazayery et al., 171–193. The Hague: Mouton.

Benedict, Ruth. 1924. "A Brief Sketch of Serrano Culture." *American Anthropologist* n.s.26:366–394.

———. 1926. "Serrano Tales." *JAF* 39.151: 1–17.

Bennett, Ruth S. 1981. *Hupa Spelling Book.* Arcata, Calif.: Center for Community Development, Humboldt State University.

Benson, William Ralganal. 1932. "The Stone and Kelsey Massacre on the Shores of Clear Lake in 1849." *Quarterly of the California Historical Society* 11.3: 266–273.

———. 1997. *"My Dear Miss Benson . . .": Letters and Myths.* Ed. Maria del Carmen Gasser. Pasadena, Calif.: Bickley Printing Company.

Berman, Howard. 1980. "Two Chukchansi Coyote Stories." In *Coyote Stories II,* ed. Martha B. Kendall. *IJAL*-NATS, Monograph 6: 56–70.

Bevis, William. 1974. "American Indian Verse Translations." *College English* 35: 693–703.

Bibby, Brian. 1992. "The Grindstone Roundhouse." *NNC* 6.3 (summer): 12–13.

———. 1996. *The Fine Art of California Indian Basketry.* Sacramento: Crocker Art Museum in association with Heyday Books.

———, ed. 1992. *Living Traditions: A Museum Guide for Native American People of California.* Vol. 2: *North-Central California.* Sacramento: California Native American Heritage Commission.

Blackburn, Thomas. 1975. *December's Child: A Book of Chumash Oral Narratives.* Berkeley: University of California Press.

Blackburn, Thomas, and Kat Anderson, eds. 1993. *Before the Wilderness: Environmental Management by Native Californians.* Ballena Press Anthropological Papers 40. Menlo Park, Calif.: Ballena Press.

Bommelyn, Loren, and Berneice Humphrey. 1985. *Booklet of Tolowa Stories.* 2d ed. Crescent City, Calif.: Tolowa Language Committee and the Del Norte County Title IV-A American Indian Education Program.

———. 1987. *Xus We-Yo': Tolowa Language.* 2d ed.. Crescent City, Calif.: Tolowa Language Committee.

———. 1995. *Now You're Speaking Tolowa.* Happy Camp, Calif.: Naturegraph Publishers.

Boscana, Geronimo. 1933 [1846]. *Chinigchinich: A Revised and Annotated Version of Alfred Robinson's Translation of Father Geronimo Boscana's Historical Account of the Belief, Usages, Customs, and Extravagencies[!] of the Indians of This Mission of San Juan Capistrano Called the* Acagchemem *Tribe.* Ed. P. T. Hanna. Santa Ana, Calif.: Fine Arts Press.

Bright, William. 1957. *The Karok Language.* UCPL 13.

———. 1968. *A Luiseño Dictionary.* UCPL 51.

———. 1977. "Coyote Steals Fire (Karok)." In *Northern California Texts,* ed. Victor Golla and Shirley Silver. *IJAL*-NATS 2.2: 3–9.

———. 1978a. *Coyote Stories. IJAL*-NATS, Monograph 1.

———. 1978b. "Karok." CAL-HB: 180–189.

———. 1979. "A Karuk Myth in 'Measured Verse': The Translation of a Performance." *Journal of California and Great Basin Anthropology* 1: 117–123.

———. 1980a. "Coyote Gives Salmon and Acorns to Humans (Karok)." In *Coyote Stories 2,* ed. Martha Kendall. *IJAL*-NATS, Monograph 6: 46–52.

———. 1980b. "Coyote's Journey." *American Indian Culture and Research Journal* 4.1–2: 21–48.

———. 1982a. *Bibliography of the Languages of Native California.* Native American Bibliography Series 3. Metuchen, N.J.: The Scarecrow Press.

———. 1982b. "Poetic Structure in Oral Narrative." In *Spoken and Written Language,* ed. Deborah Tannen, 171–184. Norwood, N.J.: Ablex Publishing.

———. 1984. *American Indian Linguistics and Literature.* Berlin: Mouton de Gruyter.

———. 1993. *A Coyote Reader.* Berkeley: University of California Press.

———. 1994a. "Myth, Music, and Magic: Nettie Reuben's Karuk Love Medicine." In *Coming to Light,* ed. Brian Swann, 764–771. New York: Random House.

———. 1994b. "Oral Literature of California and the Intermountain Region." In *Dictionary of Native American Literature,* ed. Andrew Wiget, 47–52. New York: Garland Press.

Brumble, H. David. 1988. *American Indian Autobiography.* Berkeley: University of California Press.

Burns, Ken. 1996. *The West.* Dir. Steven Ives. Alexandria, Va.: PBS Video.

Callaghan, Catherine A. 1977. "Coyote the Impostor." In *Northern California Texts,* ed. Victor Golla and Shirley Silver. *IJAL*-NATS 2.2: 10–16.

———. 1978. "Fire, Flood, and Creation." In *Coyote Stories,* ed. William Bright. *IJAL*-NATS 1: 62–86.

Campbell, Lyle, and Marianne Mithun. 1979. *The Languages of Native America: History and Comparative Assessment.* Austin: University of Texas Press.

Castillo, Edward. 1978. "The Impact of Euro-American Exploration and Settlement." CAL-HB: 99–127.

Chafe, Wallace. 1980. *The Pear Stories: Cognitive, Cultural, and Linguistic Aspects of Narrative Production.* Norwood, N.J.: Ablex Publishing.

———. 1994. *Discourse, Consciousness, and Time: The Flow and Displacement of Consciousness in Speaking and Writing.* Norwood, N.J.: Ablex Publishing.

Chase-Dunn, Christopher, and Mahua Sarkar. 1993. "Place Names and Intersocietal Interaction: Wintu Expansion into Hokan Territory in Late Prehistoric Northern California." Paper presented at the Thirteenth Annual Meeting of the Society for Economic Anthropology, Durham, N.H., April 23, 1993.

Chase-Dunn, Christopher, S. Edward Clewett, and Elaine Sundahl. 1992. "A Very Small World-System in Northern California: The Wintu and Their Neighbors." Paper presented at the Fifty-Seventh Annual Meeting of the Society for American Archaeology, Pittsburgh, Pa., April 8–12.

Cook, Sherburne F. 1943. "The Conflict between the California Indian and White Civilization, 1: The Indian versus the Spanish Mission." *Ibero-Americana* 21. Berkeley.

———. 1978. "Historical Demography." CAL-HB: 91–98.

Costo, Rupert, and Jeannette Henry Costo. 1987. *The Missions of California: A Legacy of Genocide.* San Francisco: Indian Historical Press for the American Indian Historical Society.

Couro, Ted, and Christina Hutcheson. 1973. *Dictionary of Mesa Grande Diegueño: 'Iipay Aa–English / English–'Iipay Aa.* Banning, Calif.: Malki Museum Press.

Couro, Ted, and Margaret Langdon. 1975. *Let's Talk 'Iipay Aa: An Introduction to the Mesa Grande Diegueño Language.* Ramona, Calif.: Ballena Press.

Crawford, James. 1983. *Cocopa Texts.* UCPL 100.

———. 1992. *Language Loyalties: A Source Book on the Official English Controversy.* Chicago: University of Chicago Press.

Crawford, Judith. 1976. "Seven Mohave Myths." In *Yuman Texts,* ed. Margaret Langdon. *IJAL*-NATS 1.3: 31–42.

Crozier-Hogle, Lois, and Darryl Babe Wilson. 1997. *Surviving in Two Worlds: Contemporary Native American Voices.* Austin: University of Texas Press.

Cuero, Delfina. 1970. *The Autobiography of Delfina Cuero, a Diegueño Indian.* As told to Florence C. Shipek. Banning, Calif.: Malki Museum Press and the Morongo Indian Reservation.

Curtin, Jeremiah. 1898. *Creation Myths of Primitive America, in Relation to the Religious History and Development of Mankind.* Boston: Little, Brown. (Reprint, New York: Benjamin Blom, 1967.)

Dangberg, Grace. 1927. "Washo Texts." *UCPAAE* 22.3: 391–443.

Demetracopoulou, Dorothy. 1933. "The Loon Woman Myth: A Study in Synthesis." *JAF* 46: 101–128.

———. 1935. "Wintu Songs." *Anthropos* 30: 483–494.

Demetracopoulou, Dorothy, and Cora Du Bois. 1932. "A Study of Wintu Mythology." *JAF* 45.178: 375–500.

Densmore, Frances. 1932. *Yuman and Yacqui Music.* Bureau of American Ethnology Bulletin 110. Washington, D.C.: Government Printing Office.

Devereux, George. 1948. "Mohave Coyote Tales." *JAF* 61: 233–255.

Dixon, Roland. 1902. "Maidu Myths." *Bulletin of the American Museum of Natural History* 17.2: 33–118. New York: The Knickerbocker Press.

———. 1905. "The Northern Maidu." *Bulletin of the American Museum of Natural History* 17.3: 119–346. New York: The Knickerbocker Press.

———. 1910. "The Chimariko Indians and Language." *UCPAAE* 5.5: 293–380.

———. 1912. *Maidu Texts.* Publications of the American Ethnological Society 4: 1–241. Leyden: E. J. Brill.

Dozier, Deborah. 1997. *The Heart Is Fire: The World of the Cahuilla Indians of Southern California.* Berkeley: Heyday Books.

Drucker, Philip. 1937. "The Tolowa and Their Southwest Oregon Kin." *UCPAAE* 36: 221–300.

Du Bois, Cora. 1935. "Wintu Ethnography." *UCPAAE* 36.1: 1–148.

———. 1939. "The 1870 Ghost Dance." *UCAR* 3.1: 1–151.

Du Bois, Cora, and Dorothy Demetracopoulou. 1931. "Wintu Myths." *UCPAAE* 28.5: 279–403.

Eargle, Dolan H. 1986. *The Earth Is Our Mother: A Guide to the Indians of California, Their Locales, and Historic Sites.* San Francisco: Trees Company Press.

———. 1992. *California Indian Country: The Land and the People.* San Francisco: Trees Company Press.

Finck, Franz Nikolaus. 1899. *Die Araner Mundart: Ein Betrag zur Erforschung des Westirischen.* Marburg: N. G. Elwert'sche Verlagsbuchhandlung.

Forde, C. Darryl. 1931. "Ethnography of the Yuma Indians." *UCPAAE* 28.4: 83–278.

Foster, Michael K. 1996. "Language and the Culture History of North America." In *Languages,* ed. Ives Goddard. Vol. 17 of the Smithsonian *Handbook of North American Indians,* ed. William Sturtevant. Washington, D.C.: Smithsonian Institution.

Freeland, Lucy S. 1947. "Western Miwok Texts with Linguistic Sketch." *IJAL* 13.1: 31–46.

———. 1982. *Freeland's Central Sierra Miwok Myths,* ed. Howard Berman. RSCOIL 3.

Gamble, Geoffrey. 1978. *Wikchamni Grammar.* UCPL 89.

———. 1980. "How People Got Their Hands." In *Coyote Stories II,* ed. Martha B. Kendall. *IJAL*-NATS, Monograph 6: 53–55.

———, ed. 1994. *Yokuts Texts.* Native American Texts Series [n.s.] 1. Berlin: Mouton de Gruyter.

Garth, Thomas R. 1953. "Atsugewi Ethnography." *UCAR* 14.2: 129–212.

———. 1978. "Atsugewi." CAL-HB: 236–243.

Gayton, Anna. 1935. "Areal Affiliations of California Folktales." *American Anthropologist* 37.4: 582–599.

———. 1948. "Yokuts and Western Mono: Ethnography." *UCAR* 10.1–2: 1–302.

Gayton, Anna, and Stanley Newman. 1940. "Yokuts and Western Mono Myths." *UCAR* 5.1: 1–110.

Gendar, Jeannine. 1995. *Grass Games and Moon Races: California Indian Games and Toys.* Berkeley: Heyday Books.

Gifford, Edward Winslow. 1918. "Clans and Moieties in Southern California." *UCPAAE* 18: 1–285.

———. 1926. "Yuma Dreams and Omens." *JAF* 39.151: 58–69.

———. 1955. "Central Miwok Ceremonies." *UCAR* 14.4: 261–318.

Gifford, Edward W., and Gwendoline Block. 1930. *California Indian Nights Entertainments: Stories of the Creation of the World, of Man, of Fire, of the Sun, of Thunder, etc.; of Coyote, the Land of the Dead, the Sky Monsters, Animal People, etc.* Glendale, Calif.: Arthur H. Clark. (Reprint, Lincoln: University of Nebraska Press, Bison Books, 1990.)

Goddard, Ives. 1996. "Introduction." In *Languages,* ed. Ives Goddard. Vol. 17 of *The Handbook of North American Indians.* Washington, D.C.: Smithsonian Institution Press.

———, ed. 1996. *Languages.* Vol. 17 of the Smithsonian *Handbook of North American Indians,* ed. William Sturtevant. Washington, D.C.: Smithsonian Institution.

Goddard, Pliny Earle. 1903–1904. "Life and Culture of the Hupa." *UCPAAE* 1.1: 1–88.

———. 1904. "Hupa Texts." *UCPAAE* 1.2: 89–368.

———. 1909. "Kato Texts." *UCPAAE* 5.3: 65–238.

———. 1914. "Chilula Texts." *UCPAAE* 10.7: 289–379.

———. 1921–1923. "Wailaki Texts." *IJAL* 2.3/4: 77–135.

Goldschmidt, Walter. 1951. "Nomlaki Ethnography." *UCPAAE* 42.4: 303–443.

———. 1978. "Nomlaki." CAL-HB: 341–349.

Golla, Victor. 1984a. *Hupa Stories, Anecdotes, and Conversations.* Told by Louisa Jackson, Ned Jackson, and Minnie Reeves. Recorded, transcribed, and translated by Victor Golla. Arcata, Calif.: The Hoopa Valley Tribe.

———. 1996. "Mary Haas." [Obituary.] *SSILA Newsletter* 15.2 (July). Arcata, Calif.: Society for the Study of the Indigenous Languages of the Americas.

———. 1996. "Review of *The Old Coyote of Big Sur.*" *SSILA Newsletter* 15.1: 7–8. Arcata, Calif.: Society for the Study of the Indigenous Languages of the Americas.

———, ed. 1984b. *The Sapir-Kroeber Correspondence: Letters between Edward Sapir and A. L. Kroeber, 1905–1925.* RSCOIL 6.

Golla, Victor, and Shirley Silver, eds. 1977. *Northern California Texts.* IJAL-NATS 2.2.

Gould, Richard A. 1978. "Tolowa." CAL-HB: 128–136.

Grant, Campbell. 1965. *The Rock Paintings of the Chumash: A Study of California Indian Culture.* Berkeley: University of California Press.

Grey, Herman. 1970. *Tales from the Mohaves.* Norman: University of Oklahoma Press.

Halpern, Abraham M. 1976. "Kukumat Became Sick—a Yuma Text." In *Yuman Texts,* ed. Margaret Langdon. *IJAL*-NATS 1.3: 5–25.

———. 1984. "Quechan Literature." In *Spirit Mountain: An Anthology of Yuman Story and Song,* ed. Leanne Hinton and Lucille Watahomigie. SunTracks 10. Tucson: Sun Tracks and University of Arizona Press.

———. 1988. "Southeastern Pomo Ceremonials: The Kuksu Cult and its Successors." *UCAR* 29.

———. 1997. *Kar'úk: Native Accounts of the Quechan Mourning Ceremony.* Ed. Amy Miller and Margaret Langdon. UCPL 128.

Hamley, Jeffrey Louis. 1994. "Cultural Genocide in the Classroom: A History of the Federal Boarding School Movement in American Indian Education, 1875–1920." Ph.D. dissertation, Harvard University.

Harrington, John Peabody. 1907–1957. The Papers of John Peabody Harrington in the Smithsonian Institution, 1907–1957. National Anthropological Archives, Washington, D.C. (Microfilm edition, Millwood, N.Y.: Krauss International, 1984.)

———. 1908. "A Yuma Account of Origins." *JAF* 21: 324–348.

———. 1921–1922 and 1928. Chimariko Field Notes. The Papers of John Peabody Harrington in the Smithsonian Institution, 1907–1957. National Anthropological Archives, Smithsonian Institution, Washington, D.C. (Microfilm edition: Vol. 2, Northern and Central California, Chimariko/Hupa, Reels 20–24, 31, and 35. Millwood, N.Y.: Krauss International, 1984.)

———. 1930. "Karok Texts." *IJAL* 6.2: 121–161.

———. 1932. "Karok Indian Myths." Bureau of American Ethnology Bulletin 107. Washington, D.C.: Government Printing Office.

Hatch, James. 1958. "Tachi Yokuts Music." *Kroeber Anthropological Society Papers* 19: 47–66. Berkeley.

Heizer, Robert F. 1978a. "History of Research." CAL-HB: 6–15.

———. 1978b. "Mythology: Regional Patterns and History of Research." CAL-HB: 654–657.

———. 1993. *The Destruction of California Indians: A Collection of Documents from the Period 1847 to 1865 in Which are Described Some of the Things That Happened to Some of the Indians of California.* Lincoln: University of Nebraska Press.

———, ed. 1955. "California Indian Linguistic Records: The Mission Indian Vocabularies of H. W. Henshaw." *UCAR* 15.2: 85–202.

———, ed. 1978. *California.* Vol. 8 of the Smithsonian *Handbook of North*

American Indians, ed. William Sturtevant. Washington, D.C.: Smithsonian Institution.

Heizer, Robert F., and Alan J. Almquist. 1971. *The Other Californians: Prejudice and Discrimination under Spain, Mexico, and the United States to 1920.* Berkeley: University of California Press.

Heizer, Robert F., and M. A. Whipple, eds. 1951. *The California Indians: A Source Book.* Berkeley: University of California Press.

Heizer, Robert F., Karen N. Nissen, and Edward Castillo. 1975. *California Indian History: A Classified and Annotated Guide to Source Materials.* Ballena Press Publications in Archaeology, Ethnology and History 4. Ramona, Calif.: Ballena Press.

Herzog, George. 1928. "The Yuman Musical Style." *JAF* 41.160: 183–231.

Heth, Charlotte. 1992. *Songs of Love, Luck, Animals, and Magic: Music of the Yurok and Tolowa Indians.* Recorded Anthology of American Music. New York: New World Records (NW 297).

Hill, Jane H., and Roscinda Nolasquez. 1973. *Mulu'wetam (The First People): Cupeño Oral History and Language.* Banning, Calif.: Malki Museum Press.

Hill, Kenneth C. 1967. "A Grammar of the Serrano Language." Ph.D. diss., University of California at Los Angeles.

———. 1978. "The Coyote and the Flood." In *Coyote Stories,* ed. William Bright. *IJAL*-NATS, Monograph 1: 112–116.

———. 1980. "The Seven Sisters." In *Coyote Stories 2*, ed. Martha Kendall. *IJAL*- NATS, Monograph 6: 97–103.

Hinton, Leanne. 1984. *Havasupai Songs: A Linguistic Perspective.* Tübingen: G. Narr.

———. 1994a. *Flutes of Fire: Essays on California Indian Languages.* Berkeley: Heyday Books.

———. 1994b. "Ashes, Ashes: John Peabody Harrington—Then and Now." In *Flutes of Fire: Essays on California Indian Languages,* 195–210. Berkeley: Heyday Books.

———. 1994c. "Song: Overcoming the Language Barrier." In *Flutes of Fire: Essays on California Indian Languages,* 39–44. Berkeley: Heyday Books.

———. 1994d. "Songs without Words." In *Flutes of Fire: Essays on California Indian Languages,* 145–151. Berkeley: Heyday Books.

———. 1996. "Breath of Life/Silent No More: The Native California Language Restoration Workshop." *NNC* 10.1 (fall): 13–16.

Hinton, Leanne, and Susan L. Roth. 1992. *Ishi's Tale of Lizard.* New York: Farrar, Straus and Giroux.

Hinton, Leanne, and Lucille Watahomigie, eds. 1984. *Spirit Mountain: An Anthology of Yuman Story and Song.* SunTracks 10. Tucson: Sun Tracks and University of Arizona Press.

Holmes-Wermuth, Carol. 1994. "Tübatulabal." In *Native America in the Twentieth Century: An Encyclopedia*, ed. Mary B. Davis, 660–661. New York: Garland Publishing.

Hook, Harry, dir. 1992. *The Last of His Tribe*. A River City Production.

Hudson, Travis, and Ernest Underhay. 1978. *Crystals in the Sky: An Intellectual Odyssey Involving Chumash Astronomy, Cosmology, and Rock Art*. Socorro, N.Mex.: Ballena Press.

Hudson, Travis, Thomas Blackburn, Rosario Curletti, and Janice Timbrook, eds. 1977. *The Eye of the Flute: Chumash Traditional History and Ritual*. As told by Fernando Librado Kitspawit to John P. Harrington. Santa Barbara: Santa Barbara Museum of Natural History.

Hudson, Travis, Janice Timbrook, and Melissa Rempe, eds. 1978. *Tomol: Chumash Watercraft as Described in the Ethnographic Notes of J. P. Harrington*. Socorro, N.Mex.: Ballena Press.

Hurtado, Albert L. 1988. *Indian Survival on the California Frontier*. New Haven: Yale University Press.

Hyde, Villiana Calac. 1971. *An Introduction to the Luiseño Language*. Ed. Ronald Langacker et al. Banning, Calif.: Malki Museum Press.

Hyde, Villiana Calac, and Eric Elliott. 1994. *Yumáyk Yumáyk (Long Ago)*. UCPL 125.

Hymes, Dell. 1976. "Louis Simpson's 'The Deserted Boy.'" *Poetics* 5.2: 119–155.

———. 1977. "Discovering Oral Performance and Measured Verse in American Indian Narrative." *New Literary History* 8: 431–457.

———. 1980. "Particle, Pause, and Pattern in American Indian Narrative Verse." *American Indian Culture and Research Journal* 4.4: 7–51.

———. 1981. *'In vain I tried to tell you': Essays on Native American Ethnopoetics*. Philadelphia: University of Pennsylvania Press.

———. 1983. "'Gitskux and His Older Brother': A Clackamas Chinook Myth." In *Smoothing the Ground: Essays on Native American Oral Literature*, ed. Brian Swann, 129–170. Berkeley: University of California Press.

———. 1992. "Use All There Is to Use." In *On the Translation of Native American Literatures*, ed. Brian Swann, 83–124. Washington, D.C.: Smithsonian Institution.

———. 1994a. "Helen Sekaquaptewa's 'Coyote and the Birds': Rhetorical Analysis of a Hopi Coyote Story." *Anthropological Linguistics* 34: 45–72.

———. 1994b. "Ethnopoetics, Oral Formulaic Theory, and Editing Texts." *Oral Tradition* 9.2: 330–370.

———. 1995. "Reading Takelma Texts: Frances Johnson's 'Coyote and Frog.'" In *Fields of Folklore: Essays in Honor of Kenneth Goldstein*, ed. Roger D. Abrahams, 90–159. Bloomington, Ind.: Trickster Press.

Jackson, Robert H., and Edward Castillo. 1995. *Indians, Franciscans, and Span-*

ish Colonization: The Impact of the Mission System on California Indians. Albuquerque: University of New Mexico Press.

Jacobs, Melville. 1959. *The Content and Style of an Oral Literature: Clackamas Chinook Myths and Tales.* Chicago: University of Chicago Press.

James, Carollyn. 1989. "A Field Linguist Who Lived His Life for His Subjects." *Smithsonian Magazine* 15.1 (April): 153–174.

Jeffers, Robinson. 1983. *Cawdor.* California Writers of the Land 1. Covello, Calif.: Yolla Bolly Press.

Joughlin, Roberta, and Salvadora Valenzuela. 1953. "Cupeño Genesis." *El Museo* [n.s.] 1.4: 16–23.

Keeling, Richard. 1985. "Contrast of Song Performance Style as a Function of Sex Role Polarity in the Hupa Brush Dance." *Ethnomusicology* 29.2: 185–212.

———. 1991. *Guide to Early Field Recordings (1900–1949) at the Lowie Museum of Anthropology.* Berkeley: University of California Press.

———. 1992. *Cry for Luck: Sacred Song and Speech among the Yurok, Hupa, and Karuk Indians of Northwest California.* Berkeley: University of California Press.

Kendall, Martha. 1980. *Coyote Stories 2.* IJAL-NATS, Monograph 6.

Kinkade, M. Dale. 1987. "Bluejay and His Sister." In *Recovering the Word: Essays on Native American Literature,* ed. Brian Swann and Arnold Krupat, 255–296. Berkeley: University of California Press.

Kroeber, Alfred L. 1907a. "Shoshonean Dialects of California." *UCPAAE* 4.3: 65–166.

———. 1907b. "Indian Myths of South Central California." *UCPAAE* 4.4: 167–250.

———. 1917. "California Kinship Systems." *UCPAAE* 12.9: 339–396.

———. 1925. *Handbook of the Indians of California.* Berkeley: California Book Company.

———. 1932. "Yuki Myths." *Anthropos* 27.5–6: 905–939.

———. 1939. "Culture and Natural Areas of Native North America." *UCPAAE* 38: 1–242.

———. 1951. "A Mohave Historical Epic." *UCAR* 11.2.

———. 1953. "Seven Mohave Myths." *UCAR* 11.1.

———. 1963. "Yokuts Dialect Survey." *UCAR* 11.3: 177–251.

———. 1972. "More Mohave Myths." *UCAR* 27.

———. 1976. *Yurok Myths.* Berkeley: University of California Press.

Kroeber, Alfred L., and Edward Gifford. 1949. "World Renewal: A Cult System of Native Northwest California." *UCAR* 13.1: 1–156.

———. 1980. *Karok Myths.* Ed. Grace Buzaljko. Berkeley: University of California Press.

Kroeber, Karl. 1981. *Traditional American Indian Literatures: Texts and Interpretations.* Lincoln: University of Nebraska Press.

Kroeber, Theodora. 1959. *The Inland Whale.* Bloomington: Indiana University Press.

———. 1963. *Ishi in Two Worlds: A Biography of the Last Wild Indian in North America.* Berkeley: University of California Press.

———. 1964. *Ishi, Last of His Tribe.* Berkeley: Parnassus Press.

Krupat, Arnold. 1992. *Ethnocriticism: Ethnography, History, Literature.* Berkeley: University of California Press.

———. 1993. *New Voices in Native American Literary Criticism.* Washington, D.C.: Smithsonian Institution Press.

Laird, Carobeth. 1975. *Encounter with an Angry God: Recollections of My Life with John Peabody Harrington.* Banning, Calif.: Malki Museum Press.

———. 1984. *Mirror and Pattern: George Laird's World of Chemehuevi Myth.* Banning, Calif.: Malki Museum Press.

Lang, Julian. 1993. "The Dances and Regalia." *NNC* 7.3 (fall–winter): 34–41.

———. 1994. *Ararapíkva: Creation Stories of the People.* Berkeley: Heyday Books.

Langdon, Margaret. 1976. *Yuman Texts. IJAL*-NATS 1.3.

LaPena, Frank R. 1978. "Wintu." CAL-HB: 324–340.

LaPena, Frank, Craig D. Bates, and Steven Medley, eds. 1993. *Legends of the Yosemite Miwok.* Yosemite National Park, Calif.: The Yosemite Association.

Latta, Frank. 1936. *California Indian Folklore, as told to F. F. Latta by Wah-nom-kot, Wah-hum-chah, Lee-mee [and others].* Shafter, Calif.: Shafter Press.

Lee, Dorothy [Demetracopoulou]. 1940. "A Wintu Girl's Puberty Ceremony." *New Mexico Anthropologist* 4.4: 57–60.

———. 1944. "Linguistic Reflection of Wintu Thought." *IJAL* 10.4: 181–187.

———. 1959. *Freedom and Culture.* Englewood Cliffs, N.J.: Prentice-Hall.

Lévi-Strauss, Claude. 1981. *The Naked Man.* Introduction to a Science of Mythology 4. New York: Harper and Row. (Translation of *L'Homme Nu* [Paris: Plon, 1971].)

Loeb, Edwin. 1926. "Pomo Folkways." *UCPAAE* 19.2: 149–405.

Lord, Alfred. 1960. *The Singer of Tales.* Harvard Studies in Comparative Literature 24. Cambridge: Harvard University Press.

Lowie, Robert H. 1963. "Washo Texts." *Anthropological Linguistics* 5.7: 1–30. Bloomington: Indiana University Press.

Luthin, Herbert W. 1991. "Restoring the Voice in Yanan Traditional Narrative: Prosody, Performance, and Presentational Form." Ph.D. diss., University of California at Berkeley.

———. 1994. "Two Stories from the Yana: 'The Drowning of Young Buzzard's Wife' and 'A Story of Wildcat, Rolling Skull.'" In *Coming to Light,* ed. Brian Swann, 717–736. New York: Random House.

Manriquez, L. Frank. 1998. *Acorn Soup*. Berkeley: Heyday Books.

Margolin, Malcolm. 1978. *The Ohlone Way*. Berkeley: Heyday Books.

———. 1993. *The Way We Lived: California Indian Stories, Songs, and Reminiscences*. Berkeley: Heyday Books.

Margolin, Malcolm, and Yolanda Montijo, eds. 1995. *Native Ways: California Indian Stories and Memories*. Berkeley: Heyday Books.

Matthiessen, Peter. 1979. "Stop the GO Road." *Audubon Magazine* 81.1 (January): 49–84.

Mayfield, Thomas Jefferson, and Malcolm Margolin. 1993. *Indian Summer: Traditional Life among the Choinumne Indians of California's San Joaquin Valley*. Berkeley: Heyday Books and The California Historical Society.

McKibbin, Grace, and Alice Shepherd. 1997. *In My Own Words: Stories, Songs, and Memories of Grace McKibbin, Wintu*. Berkeley: Heyday Books.

McLendon, Sally. 1975. *A Grammar of Eastern Pomo*. UCPL 71.

———. 1982. "Meaning, Rhetorical Structure, and Discourse Organization in Myth." In *Analyzing Discourse: Text and Talk*, ed. Deborah Tannen, 284–305. Washington, D.C.: Georgetown University Press.

———. 1990. "Pomo Baskets: The Legacy of William and Mary Benson." *Native Peoples* 4.1: 26–33.

McLendon, Sally, and Michael J. Lowy. 1978. "Eastern Pomo and Southeastern Pomo." CAL-HB: 306–323.

McLendon, Sally, and Robert L. Oswalt. 1978. "Pomo: Introduction." CAL-HB: 274–288.

Merriam, C. Hart. 1910. *The Dawn of the World: Myths and Weird Tales Told by the Mewan Indians of California*. Cleveland: Arthur H. Clark.

———. 1930. "The New River Indians Tol-hom-tah-hoi." *American Anthropologist* 32: 280–293.

Miller, Wick. 1967. *Uto-Aztecan Cognate Sets*. UCPL 48.

———. 1972. *Newe Natekwinappeh: Shoshoni Stories and Dictionary*. Anthropological Papers 94. Salt Lake City: University of Utah Press.

Mithun, Marianne. 1993. "Frances Jack, 1912–1993." [Obituary.] *NNC* 7.3 (summer): 11–13.

Mixco, Mauricio. 1983. *Kiliwa Texts: 'When I have donned my crest of stars.'* Anthropological Papers 107. Salt Lake City: University of Utah Press.

Moratto, Michael J. 1984. *California Archaeology*. Orlando, Fla.: Academic Press.

Mourning Dove, a Yurok/English Tale. 1993. Berkeley: Heyday Books.

Munro, Pamela. 1976. *Mojave Syntax*. New York: Garland.

Nettl, Bruno. 1965. "The Songs of Ishi: Musical Styles of the Yahi Indians." *Musical Quarterly* 51.3: 460–477.

Nevin, Bruce E. 1991. "Obsolescence in Achumawi: Why Uldall Too?" In *Papers from the American Indian Languages Conferences, Held at the University of California, Santa Cruz, July and August 1991.* Occasional Papers on Linguistics 16: 97–127. Carbondale: Department of Linguistics, Southern Illinois University.

———. 1998. "Aspects of Pit River Phonology." Ph.D. diss., University of Pennsylvania.

Newman, Stanley A. 1940. "Linguistic Aspects of Yokuts Narrative Style." *UCAR* 5.1: 4–8.

———. 1944. *Yokuts Language of California.* Viking Fund Publications on Anthropology 2. New York: Viking Fund.

Nichols, Johanna. 1992. *Linguistic Diversity in Time and Space.* Chicago: University of Chicago Press.

Nichols, Michael P. 1981. "Old California Uto-Aztecan." RSCOIL 1: 5–41. Berkeley: Survey of California and Other Indian Languages, University of California.

Nolasquez, Roscinda, and Anne Galloway. 1979. *I'i Muluwit: First Book of Words in the Cupeño Indian Language of Southern California.* Pala, Calif.: Alderbooks.

Norton, Jack. 1979. *Genocide in Northwestern California: When Our Worlds Cried.* San Francisco: Indian Historian Press.

Ochoa Zazueta, Jesús Ángel. 1976. *Ya'abú ti'nñar jaspuy'pai (Esta es la Escritura Pai'pai).* Cuadernos de Trabajo 2. Mexicali: Colección Paisano, Universidad Autónoma de Baja California.

Olmsted, David L. 1966. *Achumawi Dictionary.* UCPL 45.

———. 1984. *A Lexicon of Atsugewi.* RSCOIL 5.

Oswalt, Robert. 1961. "A Kashaya Grammar." Ph.D. diss., University of California at Berkeley.

———. 1964. *Kashaya Texts.* UCPL 36.

———. 1975. *K'ahšáya cahno kalikakh [Kashaya Word Book].* Rohnert Park: Kashaya Pomo Languages in Culture Project, Department of Anthropology, California State University at Sonoma.

———. 1977. "Retribution for Mate-Stealing." In *Northern California Texts,* ed. Victor Golla and Shirley Silver. IJAL-NATS 2.2: 71–81.

Parsons, Thomas, ed. 1971. *The Yurok Language, Literature, and Culture.* Textbook, 2d ed. (mimeo). Arcata, Calif.: Center for Community Development, Humboldt State College.

Pilling, Arnold R. 1978. "Yurok." CAL-HB: 137–154.

Pitkin, Harvey. 1977. "Coyote and Bullhead." In *Northern California Texts,* ed. Victor Golla and Shirley Silver. IJAL-NATS 2.2: 82–104.

———. 1984. *Wintu Grammar.* UCPL 94.

———. 1985. *Wintu Dictionary.* UCPL 95.

Pope, Saxton T. 1918. "Yahi Archery." *UCPAAE* 13.3.

Powers, Stephen. 1877. *Tribes of California.* Contributions to North American Ethnology 3. Washington, D.C.: U.S. Geographical and Geological Survey of the Rocky Mountain Region.

Pratt, Richard H. 1964. *Battlefield and Classroom: Four Decades with the American Indian, 1867–1904.* New Haven: Yale University Press.

Propp, Vladímir. 1968. *Morphology of the Folktale.* Austin: University of Texas Press.

Radin, Paul. 1924. "Wappo Texts: First Series." *UCPAAE* 19.1: 1–147.

Rawls, James J. 1984. *Indians of California: The Changing Image.* Norman: University of Oklahoma Press.

Reichard, Gladys. 1925. "Wiyot Grammar and Texts." *UCPAAE* 22.1: 1–215.

Richardson, Nancy. 1992. "The State of Our Languages." *NNC* 7.1 (winter): 40–41.

———. 1994. "Indian Language Is Happening in California." *NNC* 8.3 (winter): 47–49.

Riffe, Jeff, and Pamela Roberts, prods. and dirs. 1994. *Ishi, the Last Yahi.* Written by Ann Makepeace. Newton, N.J.: Shanachie Entertainment Corp.

Roberts, Helen H. 1933. *Form in Primitive Music: An Analytical and Comparative Study of the Melodic Form of Some Ancient Southern California Indian Songs.* New York: W. W. Norton.

Robins, R. H. 1958. *The Yurok Language: Grammar, Texts, Lexicon.* UCPL 15.

Robins, R. H., and Norma McLeod. 1956. "Five Yurok Songs: A Musical and Textual Analysis." *Bulletin of the School of Oriental and African Studies* 18: 592–609. University of London.

Sackheim, Daniel, dir. 1996. *Grand Avenue.* Santa Monica, Calif.: Wildwood Enterprises and Elsboy Entertainment.

Sapir, Edward. 1910. "Yana Texts (together with Yana Myths, collected by Roland B. Dixon)." *UCPAAE* 9.1.

———. 1925. "The Hokan Affinity of Subtiaba in Nicaragua." *American Anthropologist* 27.3: 402–435 and 27.4: 491–527.

———. Forthcoming. "Unpublished Yahi Texts (1915)." In *The Collected Works of Edward Sapir,* vol. 9, ed. Victor Golla, Leanne Hinton, Herbert W. Luthin, and Jean Perry. Berlin: Mouton de Gruyter.

Sapir, Edward, and Victor Golla. Forthcoming. "Hupa Texts, with Notes and Lexicon." In *The Collected Works of Edward Sapir,* vol. 14, ed. Victor Golla and Sean O'Neill. Berlin: Mouton de Gruyter.

Sapir, Edward, and Leslie Spier. 1943. "Notes on the Culture of the Yana." *UCAR* 3.3.

Sarris, Greg. 1993. *Keeping Slug Woman Alive: A Holistic Approach to American Indian Texts.* Berkeley: University of California Press.

———. 1994a. *Grand Avenue.* New York: Hyperion Press.

————. 1994b. *Mabel McKay: Weaving the Dream.* Berkeley: University of California Press.

————, ed. 1994c. *The Sound of Rattles and Clappers: A Collection of New California Indian Writing.* Tucson: University of Arizona Press.

Saubel, Katherine Siva, and Pamela Munro. 1981. *Chem'ivillu': Let's Speak Cahuilla.* Los Angeles: American Indian Studies Center, University of California.

Schlicter, Alice. 1981. *Wintu Dictionary.* RSCOIL 2.

————. 1986. "The Origins and Deictic Nature of Wintu Evidentials." In *Evidentiality: The Linguistic Coding of Epistemology,* ed. Wallace Chafe and Johanna Nichols, 46–59. Norwood, N.J.: Ablex Publishing.

Seaburg, William. 1977. "A Wailaki (Athapaskan) Text with Comparative Notes." *IJAL* 43: 327–332.

Seiler, Hansjakob. 1970. *Cahuilla Texts, with an Introduction.* Indiana University Language Science Monographs 6. Bloomington: Indiana University Press.

Shepherd, Alice [Schlicter]. 1989. *Wintu Texts.* UCPL 117.

Sherzer, Joel. 1987. "Poetic Structuring of Kuna Discourse: The Line." In *Native American Discourse: Poetics and Rhetoric,* ed. Joel Sherzer and Anthony C. Woodbury, 103–139. Cambridge: Cambridge University Press.

Sherzer, Joel, and Anthony C. Woodbury. 1987. *Native American Discourse: Poetics and Rhetoric.* Cambridge Studies in Oral and Written Culture. Cambridge: Cambridge University Press.

Shipley, William. 1963. *Maidu Texts and Dictionary.* UCPL 33.

————. 1964. *Maidu Grammar.* UCPL 41.

————. 1978. "Native Languages of California." CAL-HB: 80–90.

————. 1991. *The Maidu Indian Myths and Stories of Hánc'ibyjim.* Berkeley: Heyday Books.

Shipley, William, and Richard Alan Smith. 1979. "The Roles of Cognation and Diffusion in a Theory of Maidun Prehistory." *Journal of California and Great Basin Anthropology—Papers in Linguistics* 1: 65–74.

Silver, Shirley. 1978. "Chimariko." CAL-HB: 205–210.

Silverstein, Michael. 1979. "Penutian: An Assessment." In *The Languages of Native America,* ed. Lyle Campbell and Marianne Mithun, 650–691. Austin: University of Texas Press.

Slagle, Allogan. 1987. "The Native American Tradition and Legal Status: Tolowa Tales and Tolowa Places." *Cultural Critique* 7: 103–118.

Smith, Bertha. 1904. *Yosemite Legends.* San Francisco: Paul Elder and Co.

Smith, Charles R. 1978. "Tübatulabal." CAL-HB: 437–445.

Snyder, Gary. 1975. "The Incredible Survival of Coyote." *Western American Literature* 9: 255–272.

Sparkman, Philip Stedman. 1908. "Culture of the Luiseño Indians." *UCPAAE* 8.

Spier, Leslie. 1955. "Mohave Culture Items." *Museum of Northern Arizona Bulletin* 28. Flagstaff, Ariz.: Northern Arizona Society of Science and Art.

Spott, Robert, and Alfred L. Kroeber. 1942. "Yurok Narratives." *UCPAAE* 35.9: 143–256.

Strong, William Duncan. 1929. *Aboriginal Society in Southern California.* (Reprint, with an introduction by Lowell John Bean, Banning, Calif.: Malki Museum Press, 1972.)

Swann, Brian. 1993. *Song of the Sky: Versions of Native American Song-Poems.* Amherst: University of Massachusetts Press.

———. 1996. *Wearing the Morning Star: Native American Song-Poems.* New York: Random House.

———, ed. 1983. *Smoothing the Ground: Essays in Native American Oral Literature.* Berkeley: University of California Press.

———, ed. 1992. *On the Translation of Native American Literatures.* Washington, D.C.: Smithsonian Institution Press.

———, ed. 1994. *Coming to Light: Contemporary Translations of the Native Literatures of North America.* New York: Random House.

Swann, Brian, and Arnold Krupat, eds. 1987. *Recovering the Word: Essays on Native American Literature.* Berkeley: University of California Press.

Taylor, Alexander. 1860–1863. "Indianology of California." Column in *The California Farmer and Journal of Useful Arts,* vols. 13–20, February 22, 1860, to October 30, 1863.

Tedlock, Dennis. 1983. *The Spoken Word and the Work of Interpretation.* Philadelphia: University of Pennsylvania Press.

Teixeira, Rachel. 1996a. "California Indian Stories and the Spirit." *NNC* 9.4.

———. 1996b. "Like Air We Breathe." *NNC* 9.4.

Thompson, Lucy. 1991 [1916]. *To the American Indian: Reminiscences of a Yurok Woman.* Berkeley: Heyday Books.

Uldall, Stuart, and William Shipley. 1966. *Nisenan Texts and Dictionary.* UCPL 46.

Valory, Dale, comp. 1971. "Guide to Ethnographic Documents (1–203) of the Department and Museum of Anthropology." University of California Archives, Bancroft Library, Berkeley.

Vizenor, Gerald. 1989. *Narrative Chance: Postmodern Discourse on Native American Indian Literatures.* Albuquerque: University of New Mexico Press.

Voegelin, [Carl] Charles F. 1935. "Tübatulabal Texts." *UCPAAE* 34.3: 191–246.

Voegelin, Carl F., and Erminie Wheeler Voegelin. 1931–1933. "Tübatulabal Myths and Tales." [Unpublished Manuscript #73.] Ethnological Documents of the Department and Museum of Anthropology. University of California Archives, Bancroft Library, Berkeley.

Voegelin, Erminie [Wheeler]. 1937. "Tübatulabal Ethnography." *UCAR* 2.1: 1–90.

Wallace, William J. 1978a. "Post-Pleistocene Archaeology, 9000 to 2000 B.C." CAL-HB: 25–36.

———. 1978b. "Hupa, Chilula and Whilkut." CAL-HB: 164–179.

———. 1978c. "Southern Valley Yokuts." In CAL-HB: 448–461.

———. 1978d. "Northern Valley Yokuts." In CAL-HB: 462–470.

———. 1978e. "Comparative Literature." CAL-HB: 658–661.

Wallace, William J., and J. S. Taylor. 1950. "Hupa Sorcery." *Southwestern Journal of Anthropology* 6: 188–196.

Walters, Diane. 1977. "Coyote and Moon Woman (Apwarukeyi)." In *Northern California Texts,* ed. Victor Golla and Shirley Silver. *IJAL*-NATS 2.2: 147–157.

Waterman, T. T. 1910. "The Religious Practices of the Diegueño Indians." *UCPAAE* 8.6: 271–358.

Whistler, Kenneth W. 1977a. "Deer and Bear Children." In *Northern California Texts,* ed. Victor Golla and Shirley Silver. *IJAL*-NATS 2.2: 158–184.

———. 1977b. "Wintun Prehistory: An Interpretation Based on Linguistic Reconstruction of Plant and Animal Nomenclature." *Proceedings of the Annual Meeting of the Berkeley Linguistics Society* 3: 157–174.

Whittemore, Kathrine. 1997. "To Converse with Creation: Saving California Indian Languages." *Native Americas,* 1 14.3 (fall 1997): 46–53.

Wilson, Darryl Babe. 1998. *The Morning the Sun Went Down.* Berkeley: Heyday Books.

———. Forthcoming. *Yo-Kenaswi Usji (Necklace of Hearts).* Tucson: Sun Tracks and the University of Arizona Press.

Woiche, Istet. 1992 [1928]. *Annikadel: The History of the Universe as Told by the Achumawi Indians of California.* Recorded and ed. C. Hart Merriam. Tucson: University of Arizona Press.

Woodbury, Anthony C. 1987. "Rhetorical Structure in a Central Alaskan Yupik Eskimo Traditional Narrative." In *Native American Discourse: Poetics and Rhetoric,* ed. Joel Sherzer and Anthony C. Woodbury, 176–239. Cambridge: Cambridge University Press.

Yamane, Linda. 1995. *When the World Ended—How Hummingbird Got Fire—How People Were Made: Rumsien Ohlone Stories.* Told and illustrated by Linda Yamane. Berkeley: Oyate Press.

ACKNOWLEDGMENTS
OF PERMISSIONS

Grateful acknowledgments are made to the following for permission to reprint or excerpt copyrighted or archival materials:

Gui de Angulo, for permission to reprint the song "The dawn is dawning" from *Indians in Overalls* by Jaime de Angulo (City Lights, 1990).

Anthropos, for permission to reprint selections from "Wintu Songs" by Dorothy Demetracopoulou (*Anthropos* 30, 1935).

The Bancroft Library, for permission to use or translate "Mason's Report," Paul Faye's Cupeño "Creation Songs," "A Story of Lizard," and "How I Became a Dreamer."

The California Historical Society, for permission to reprint sections of "The Stone and Kelsey Massacre on the Shores of Clear Lake in 1849" by William Ralganal Benson (*Quarterly of the California Historical Society* 11.3, 1932).

Larry Evers, Leanne Hinton, and Lucille Watahomigie, for permission to reprint excerpts from "Lightning Song" by Abraham Halpern, in *Spirit Mountain: An Anthology of Yuman Story and Song,* edited by Leanne Hinton and Lucille Watahomigie (Sun Tracks and University of Arizona Press, 1984).

Heyday Books, for permission to reprint an excerpt from "In the Beginning" in *The Maidu Indian Myths and Stories of Hánc'ibyjim* by William Shipley (Heyday, 1991)—as well as excerpts from the following articles in *News from Native California:* "Boarding School" by Elsie Allen (*NNC* 4.1, 1989); "The State of Our Languages" by Nancy Richardson (*NNC* 7.1, 1992); "Frances Jack, 1912–1993" by Marianne Mithun (*NNC* 7.3, 1993); "Interview with Edna Guerrero" by Vic Bedoian and Roberta Llewellyn (*NNC* 8.4, spring 1995); and the Linda Yamane commentary from "Like Air We Breathe" by Rachel Teixeira (*NNC* 9.4, 1996).

Houghton Mifflin, for permission to reprint "Yahi mouth-bow song" from *Ishi, Last of His Tribe* by Theodora Kroeber (Parnassus Press, 1964).

The Journal of American Folklore, for permission to reprint "A Yuma Account of Origins" by J. P. Harrington (*JAF* 21, 1908); "Creation" from "Serrano Tales" by Ruth Benedict (*JAF* 39.151, 1926); "Winter mosquitos go" from "A Study of Wintu Mythology" by Dorothy Demetracopoulou and Cora Du Bois (*JAF* 45.178, 1932); and "Pomo Creation Myth" by Jaime de Angulo (*JAF* 48.189, 1935). These four items are not for further reproduction.

Mouton de Gruyter, for permission to reprint "Journey to the Land of the Dead" from *Yokuts Texts* by Geoffrey Gamble (Native American Texts Series 1, Mouton de Gruyter, 1994).

Oxford University Press, for permission to reprint the Yurok doctor dance song "Why is the water rough" from "Five Yurok Songs: A Musical and Textual Analysis" by R. H. Robins and Norma McLeod (*Bulletin of the School of Oriental and African Studies* 18, 1956).

Jean Perry, for permission to quote Florence Shaughnessy's recitation of "You come upon a place you've never seen before," which appeared in "Stop the GO Road" by Peter Matthiessen (*Audubon Magazine* 81.1 January 1979).

The Smithsonian Institution, for permission to use the "House Is Afire" excerpt (letter from J. P. Harrington to Jack Marr, 1941), as well as to retranslate the following materials from "The Papers of John Peabody Harrington in the Smithsonian Institution, 1907–1957" (National Anthropological Archives, Smithsonian Institution, Washington, D.C.): "The Bear Girl" (Chimariko fieldnotes, 1921–1922); "The Dog Girl" (Ineseño fieldnotes, 1919).

The University of California Press, for permission to reprint "The acorns come down from heaven" and "Do you come from the north?" both from *Tribes of California* by Stephen Powers (reprinted 1976); "Chalááwaat Song" from *Yumáyk Yumáyk* by Villiana Calac Hyde and Eric Elliott (text #167, 1994); excerpt from "The Čiq'neq's Myth," in *December's Child* by Thomas Blackburn (1975); "I have told you to come away from the shore," from "California Indian Linguistic Records: The Mission Indian Vocabularies of H. W. Henshaw" by Robert Heizer (*UCAR* 15.2, 1955); "Kingfisher, kingfisher," from "Yokuts and Western Mono Ethnography: I" by Anna Gayton (*UCAR* 10.1, 1948); Quechan funeral speech from "Ethnography of the Yuma Indians" by C. Darryl Forde (*UCPAAE* 28.4, 1931); excerpt from an account of "The Soul" in *Kar'uk: Native Accounts of the Quechan Mourning Ceremony* by Abraham Halpern, edited by Amy Miller and Margaret Langdon (*UCPL* 128, 1997); "Spell said by a girl desirous of getting a husband" from *Yana Texts* by Edward Sapir (*UCPAAE* 9.1, 1910); Nisenan prayer from "Ethnography of the Nisenan" by Ralph Beals (*UCPAAE* 31.6, 1933).

The University of Chicago Press, for permission to reprint "Cradleboard" by Judith Crawford, song from the myth "Kukumat Became Sick" ("My heart, you might pierce it") by Abraham Halpern, and "The Coming of the Friars" by Mauricio Mixco, all from *Yuman Texts,* edited by Margaret Langdon (*International Journal of American Linguistics—Native American Texts Series* 1.3, 1976).

University of Illinois Press, for permission to reprint the song "Where we used to make love" from "Contrast in Song Performance Style as a Function of Sex Role Polarity in the Hupa Brush Dance" by Richard Keeling (*Ethnomusicology* 29.2, 1985).

The University of Massachusetts Press, for permission to reprint "Women's Brush Dance Song" from *Song of the Sky: Versions of Native American Song-Poems* by Brian Swann (1993).

The University of Utah Press, for permission to reprint "When I Have Donned My Crest of Stars" from *Kiliwa Texts* by Mauricio Mixco (*University of Utah Anthropological Papers* 107, 1983).

INDEX

A'alxi genre of stories ("telling histories"), 422

"An Account of Origins" (Quechan), 20n6, 461–89; alterations of Harrington's original text, 464n1; collection and translation of, 15(table 1), 22, 503; as example of Southern California creation pattern, 520, 539n7; Latin passages in, 489–90

Achumawi: geographical territory, 127; "How My Father Found the Deer," 127–38; waking song, 532

Achumawi language: Jaime de Angulo's work on, 264; sample passage, 130–31, 132n3

Acorns: ceremonial acorn song (Maidu), 491; as food, 90, 104, 204, 251, 334, 365, 390; gathering, 102, 113, 246; leaching and cooking, 227–28, 290, 291, 303, 376; shell transformed into Marumda's boat (Eastern Pomo), 279, 304

Advocates for Indigenous California Language Survival (AICLS), 564–65

Aisisara, Lorenzo, 555

Algic stock, 548, 549, 567n5

Algonquian language family, 551, 567n5

Allen, Elsie (Central Pomo), 313, 560–62, 569n21

Animals: anthropomorphism of, 38–40; as both characters and part of nature,

39, 49; creation of, in Eastern Pomo origin myth, 277; creation of, in Quechan origin myth, 468, 471, 473; creator's instructions to (Eastern Pomo), 307–9; as food for Lake Miwok, 334–35; made by Kwaw (Atsugewi), 60–61; named by Kumastamxo (Quechan), 485–86; people growing up to be (Chimariko), 118; people turned into (Chumash), 395; tails cut in mourning (Quechan), 479; trapped in pits (Achumawi), 127. *See also specific animals*

Antelope, killed without bow for food (Mojave), 448–49

Anthropomorphism, 38–40

Applegate, Richard, 504; "The Dog Girl" (translator), 382–95

"Areal Affiliations of California Folktales" (Gayton), 515, 523

Arrow-making, in "A Story of Lizard" (Yahi), 155, 156, 161n3, 163–64, 166–68, 171–72, 173–76. *See also* Bow and arrow

Arrowweeds: cradleboard made of (Mojave), 524; as first plant (Quechan [Yuma]), 470

Arroyo de la Cuesta, Father Felipe, 500

Athabascan language family, 548, 551, 567n5; bascan on, 551

Atsugewi, 129, 132n2; geographical territory, 140; "Kwaw Labors to Form a World," 14, 59–61; "Naponoha (Cocoon Man)," 14, 139–51; song given by Lela Rhoades, 142

Av'a seeds, as food for Mojave, 452, 453

Avikwaamé (Ghost Mountain), 462, 463

Badgers: "The Creation" (Serrano), 406n2, 409–10; "The Death of Kwikumat" (Quechan [Yuma]), 477

Baldy, Ray (Hupa), 7, 564

Barnes, Nellie, 46

Barrett, Samuel, 501; "Wintun Hesi Ceremony," 535

Baskets: Eastern Pomo's uses for, 290–91; feathers in (Lake Miwok), 335; for fetching water (Hupa), 109; magic Jump Dance, 112; Marumda teaches making and use of (Eastern Pomo), 289–91; Southern Pomo, 312, 313, 318, 319; talking, 61; woven by Annie Burke, 313; woven by Elsie Allen, 313, 569n21; woven by Mabel McKay, 324–25; woven by William Benson and wife, 261–63

Bat, "Mad Bat" (Maidu), 248–59

Bathing, baby-bath basket for (Southern Pomo), 318, 319

Batwi, Sam (Yana), 503(fig. 12), 505

Beads, clamshell and magnesite (Pomo), 312

"The Bear Girl" (Chimariko), 115–22; anthropomorphism in, 39; parallelism in, 44–45

Bears: "The Bear Girl" (Chimariko), 39, 115–22; "Grizzly Bear and Deer" (Yana), 25–26, 28–29, 30; "The Life of Hawk Feather: The Bear Episodes" (Cupeño), 426–35; "A Story of Lizard" (Yahi), 155, 156–57, 164–66; white grizzly (Hupa), 111

Beauty, 63

Beavers: "The Death of Kwikumat" (Quechan [Yuma]), 478; as food for Mojave, 452, 453; "The Trials of Young Hawk" (Southern Pomo), 318–19

Belts, feather (Nomlaki), 235–36

Bender, Jo (Wintu), 505; "Loon Woman" (narrator), 43, 192–218, 200n2

Benedict, Ruth, version of Serrano creation story, 401, 405n2

Benner, Lena (Maidu), 248

Benson, Addison, 261

Benson, William Ralganal (Eastern Pomo), 262(fig. 7), 505; biography of, 261–63, 272n2; "Creation" (narrator), 13, 260–310; Stone and Kelsey Massacre account by, 556–58

Bevis, Bill, 54n23

Bibby, Brian, 235–41, 564

Birds: as both character and part of nature, 49; inventory of, in Eastern Pomo myth, 308–9; in Pomo narratives, 523; wounded, in "Loon Woman," 197, 201n6, 214–18. See also *specific birds*

Blackburn, Thomas, 504; *December's Child,* 386

Blake, Ramsey Bone, 61

"Blind Bill and the Owl" (Yurok), 78–79, 81–82

Block, Gwendoline, *California Indian Nights Entertainments,* 513

Boarding-school system, 559–62; impact on languages, 560–62; underlying philosophy of, 559, 569n18

Bommelyn, Loren, 51n2; "Test-ch'as (The Tidal Wave)" (author and translator), 47–48, 67–76

Bone, Lee, 140

Boone, Yanta (Pomo), 324

Boscana, Geronimo, *Chinigchinich,* 500

Bottlefly, "Condor Steals Falcon's Wife" (Yowlumni Yokuts), 358–59

Bow and arrow, Marumda teaches people to make (Eastern Pomo), 288–89, 301. See also Arrow-making

"The Boy Who Grew Up at Ta'k'imił-ding" (Hupa), 35, 104–110; collected by tape recording, 16(table 2), 502; as ethnographic text, 35; as "institution myth," 518

Brandenstein, Susan, "Naponoha (Cocoon Man)" (collector), 14, 139–51

Bright, William, 78, 504; *A Coyote*

Chumash languages, 382–83; sample passage (Ineseño), 386

"TheČiq'neq's Myth" (excerpt), 345

Clear Lake, Stone and Kelsey Massacre at, 556–58

Clothing: belts (Nomlaki), 235–36; jewelry (Chumash), 393; men's (Karuk), 95; skin (Mojave), 449–50; willow bark for women's skirts (Mojave), 449

The Collected Works of Edward Sapir (Sapir), 105

Collectors: preservation of traditions by, 499–500, 508n7, 509n8; at University of California at Berkeley Department of Anthropology, 500–501; at University of California at Berkeley Department of Linguistics, 503–4; unpublished material of, 7–8. *See also names of specific collectors and scholars*

Comanche, George, 313

Coming to Light (Swann), 11

"Comparative Literature" (Wallace), 513

Condors, 349–51

"Condor Steals Falcon's Wife" (Yowlumni Yokuts), 349–51, 356–62, 523, 540n12

"The Contest between Men and Women" (Tübatulabal), 35, 363–81

Cook, Sherburne F., 553

Corn, as food for Quechan (Yuma), 471

Costanoan language: dance song, 532; fieldtrip to record, 495–99, 506n2, 507nn5,6; gambling song, 532; love song, 532; wordlist and text, 497–98, 507n5

Cottonwood: for funeral pyre (Quechan [Yuma]), 477–78; sacred sticks for Yuma fiestas made from, 484; shade-roofs constructed of (Quechan [Yuma]), 485

Couro, Ted (Iipay Diegueño), 505–6

Covelo, Indian boarding school at, 560–61

Coyote: in Central California creation myths, 515, 516, 517; Coyote songs (Chumash), 397, 531, 532; Coyote stories, 15(table 1), 520–22, 539n8;

creator's relationship to (Eastern Pomo), 267, 272n4; personality of, 39, 92; Trickster cycle (Maidu), 249

Coyote, selections and excerpts involving, 15(table 1); "Condor Steals Falcon's Wife" (Yowlumni Yokuts), 356–57, 359, 361; "The Contest between Men and Women" (Tübatulabal), 365–67, 368–69, 373–81; "Coyote, Heron, and Lizard" (Yana; excerpt), 521–22; "Coyote and Old Woman Bullhead" (Karuk), 92, 94–97; "Coyote Steals Fire" (Karuk; excerpt), 32–33; "The Creation" (Serrano), 405, 405n2, 408, 409–10; "The Death of Kwikumat" (Quechan), 477–79; "The Life of Hawk Feather: The Bear Episodes" (Cupeño), 423–24, 428; "In the Beginning" (Maidu; excerpt), 515; "Kwaw Labors to Form a World" (Atsugewi), 59–61; "Loon Woman" (Wintu), 195, 196, 207, 208–9; "Mad Bat" (Maidu), 250, 258; "Naponoha (Cocoon Man)" (Atsugewi), 143, 146–47; "The Young Man from Serper" (Yurok), 80, 86–89

"Coyote and Old Woman Bullhead" (Karuk), 90–97, 502–3, 520–21

"Coyote, Heron, and Lizard" (Yana), 521–22, 539n10

A Coyote Reader (Bright), 539n8

"Coyote Steals Fire" (Karuk), ethnopoetic presentation of, 31–33

"Cradleboard" (Mojave), 524–25

Crawford, James, 504

Crawford, Judith, "Cradleboard" (collector), 524–25

Creation: of animals, 277, 468, 471, 472; of humans, 279–81, 466–68, 469, 470; of plants, 278, 470

"Creation" (Eastern Pomo), 13, 260–310, 502; episodic repetition in, 41; as example of Central California creation pattern, 516, 538n2; published versions of, 265–68; songs in, 270–71; thematic structure of, 271

"The Creation" (Serrano), 35, 401–10;

alternate version of, 401, 405n2; as example of Southern California creation pattern, 520, 539n7

Creation myth patterns: Central California, 515–17; Northwestern California, 517–18; Southern California, 518–20. *See also* Destruction of the world

Creation myths. *See* Origin myths

Creation Myths of Primitive America (Curtin), 22

Creation songs (Cupeño), 57, 538n5

Crescent City, "Ragged Ass Hill" near, 79, 82–85

Crow, "Condor Steals Falcon's Wife" (Yowlumni Yokuts), 356, 357, 362

Crum, Beverly (Shoshone), 12

Cry songs (Wintu), 219, 223, 225, 230–34, 528

"Culture of the Luiseño Indians" (Sparkman), 535

Cultures, Native California: dominant pattern numbers of, 41, 53n15; geographic distribution of, 6, 573(map 1); language as embodying, 10, 563; oral literature's link to, 47–50; preservation of, 508n7; variation in documentation of, 7

Cupan languages, 411

Cupeño: burial songs, 518–19, 538n5; creation songs, 57, 538n5; "The Life of Hawk Feather: The Bear Episodes," 421–35

Cupeño language: extinction of, 411, 412; quotatives in, 424; sample passage, 423–24

Curl, Jennie, "A Selection of Wintu Songs" (singer), 178–81, 190–91

Curtin, Jeremiah, 500; *Creation Myths of Primitive America,* 22

Dances: Ball (Nomlaki), 243, 243n, 244–45; Brush (Hupa), 112; Bullhead (Nomlaki), 243n; Dream (Wintu), 179–80, 181nn2,3, 182n; Hesi (Nomlaki), 236, 238, 245, 245n, 246–47; *hisi* (Wintu), 221, 222; Jump (Hupa), 106, 110, 112; Marumda's (Eastern Pomo

Creator) instruction on, 283–84, 302–3, 305–7; Night (Yahi), 155–56, 157–58, 168–71; White Deerskin (Hupa), 106, 110. *See also* Ceremonies

Dance songs: Bear Dance song (Santa Rosa Island), 531; brush dance song (Hupa), 532; brush dance song (Luiseño), 511; Chaláawaat Song (Luiseño), vii, 416–17, 565–66; Costanoan, 532; Yahi, 170; Yurok doctor dance song, 65

Davis, Francis, account of Karuk World Renewal ceremony, 517–18

Davis, Shan (Karuk), 563

"Dawis Sapagay's Song" (Tachi Yokuts), 533–34

Dayley, Jon, 504

"The Dead People's Home" (Lake Miwok), 13, 35, 334–42, 502

De Angulo, Jaime, 501; advice to readers, 50; biography of, 263–65; "Creation" (collector and translator), 13, 260–310; fictionalized publications of, 264; *How the World Was Made,* 264, 265–66, 269–70; Karuk creation stories transcribed by, 92–93

Death song (Luiseño), 416

December's Child (Blackburn), 386

Deer: antlers as quiver (Yahi), 171; cooking (Wintu), 222–23, 227–28; "Grizzly Bear and Deer" (Yana), 25–26, 28–29, 30; hunting (Maidu), 255; hunting and skinning (Eastern Pomo), 289; killed by magic (Hupa), 112; necessity of sharing meat (Achumawi), 132–38; not eaten by one who kills deer (Cupeño), 427; shot by Apache, 476; tracks of, as sign of male power (Wintu), 197, 211; white, as sacred (Yurok), 80, 85, 87–88

Deities, in Native California religions: Aboni-ka-ha (Atsugewi), 142; anthropomorphic Creator figures (North-Central California), 268–69; Blind Old Man (Quechan), 464, 465n6; Coyote, 267, 272n4, 515, 516, 517; "dying god" (Southern California), 518–20; Eagle (Southern California), 517; Earthmaker (Maidu), 515–17;

Deities *(continued)*
Earth Mother (Southern California), 518; God (Christian), 340, 341; Kumastamxo (Quechan), 465n6, 480–88; Kuksu (North-Central California), 268–70, 516; K'wan'-lee-shvm (Tolowa), 70; Kwaw (Atsugewi), 59–61; Kwikumat (Quechan), 464, 465n6, 465–80; Marumda (Pomo), 267–70, 272n4, 516; Mukat and Tamayowet (Cupeño), 57, 519; Paqöoktach and Kokiitach (Serrano), 405–10. *See also* Coyote

Demetracopoulou, Dorothy, 501; "Loon Woman" (collector), 192–218; "A Selection of Wintu Songs" (collector and translator), 178–91, 180n1; Wintu Dream songs, 20n9, 181–84

Destruction of the world: by fire, 284–87; by flood, 281–83, 468, 471–72, 476, 481; by whirlwind, 296–300; by snow and ice, 291–93

Devils: "The Devil Who Died Laughing" (Karuk), 98–103, 522; excerpt from "The Čiq'neq's Myth" (Ventureño Chumash), 345; "It Was Scratching" (Hupa), 107, 113–14, 522; as sorcerers, 99, 522; stories about, 99, 522

"The Devil Who Died Laughing" (Karuk), 35, 98–103, 522; ethnopoetic structure of, 99–102

Dictation, phonetic/verbatim, 23, 51n1; limitations of, 502; lines in texts derived from, 53n12; selections collected by, 16(table 2), 502–3

Diegueño Eagle Ceremony songs, 20n9

Dixie Valley, 140; people, conflict with Klamath people, 142–51

Dixon, Roland B., 501; "Mad Bat" (collector), 248–59

Doctors (shamans): "Dawis Sapagay's Song" (Tachi Yokuts), 36, 533–34; death by gunshot wounds (hupa), 110–11; dream doctor (Nomlaki), 238; dreamers as (Quechan [Yuma]), 462–63, 465n4, 474–75; "Indian Medicine-Men" (Yana; excerpt), 526–27; Lake Miwok, 339–40; Mabel

McKay as "sucking doctor," 324–25; relationships healed by (Achumawi), 129, 132–38. *See also* Dreamers

"The Dog Girl" (Ineseño Chumash), 35, 382–95; parallelism in, 45–46; repetition in, 46, 386; songs in, 394–95, 528

Dogs: "The Dog Girl" (Ineseño Chumash), 35, 382–95; talking (Tolowa), 69–70, 71

Dollar, Elizabeth (Southern Pomo), 313

Dove, "Condor Steals Falcon's Wife" (Yowlumni Yokuts), 356, 357

Drake, Sir Francis, 500

Dream Dance cult, 179

Dreamers: Lake Miwok, 338, 339, 340, 341; Mojave, 437, 438, 439, 440; Nomlaki, 235–47; Quechan, 462–63, 465n4, 474–75. *See also* Doctors (shamans)

Dreams: "How I Became a Dreamer" (Nomlaki), 235–47; "Indian Medicine-Men" (Yana), 526–27; of Mabel McKay (Cache Creek Pomo), 324–26; Marumda (Eastern Pomo Creator) sees state of people on earth, 281, 291–92, 293, 296; role of, in Quechan religion, 462; as source of authority for narration (Mojave), 437, 440; of white people coming (Cache Creek Pomo), 331–32; Yana spell for girl wanting husband, 125

Dream songs (Wintu), 20n9, 179–80, 181–84, 181nn2,3

Du Bel, Dum (Wintu), 183

Du Bois, Constance, 501

Du Bois, Cora, 179, 180, 192–93

Ducks: dream about (Nomlaki), 244; mallard, feather in feather belts, 236

Eagle: "Condor Steals Falcon's Wife" (Yowlumni Yokuts), 349, 356, 357, 359, 362; "The Contest between Men and Women" (Tübatulabal), 365, 368; in South-Central creation myths, 517

Eagle Ceremony songs, Diegueño, 20n9

Earthdiver motif, 515–16

Earthmaker, 515–17

Earthquake, as causing tidal wave, 71–72

Elders: contribution of, to oral literature documentation, 504–5; as diminishing resource for languages, 497, 506n3; necessity of sharing food with (Achumawi), 130–31, 132–38

Elem Rancheria, 330

Elliott, Eric, 51n2; "A Harvest of Songs from Villiana Calac Hyde" (collector), 411–20; on Villiana Calac Hyde (Luiseño), 411–13

Ellis, Ross (Yowlumni Yokuts), 350 (fig. 9); "Condor Steals Falcon's Wife" (narrator), 349–51, 356–62

Emeneau, Murray, 504

Enmai (Mount Emily), 70n1, 71, 73–74

Episodic repetition, 40–43, 46–47, 53n17; in "Creation" (Eastern Pomo), 41; pattern numbers as element of, 41, 43, 53nn15,18; in "A Story of Lizard" (Yahi), 41, 155–58; in "The Trials of Young Hawk" (Southern Pomo), 41. See also Repetition

Esselen language, 7, 547, 567n6

Essene, Frank J., 239

Ethnographic texts, examples of: "Cradleboard" (Mojave), 524; "Four Songs from Grace McKibbin" (Wintu), 224–34; "Indian Medicine Men" (Yana; excerpt), 526–27; "Preserving Shellfish" (Kashaya Pomo), 525; "The Soul" narrative (Quechan; excerpt), 399–400; World Renewal narrative (Karuk; excerpt), 517–18; "You come upon a place" (Yurok), 63. See also Narrative

"Ethnography of the Yuma Indians" (Forde), 535

Ethnolinguistic translations, 25–27, 51nn4,5; example of, 25–27, 51n3; selections exemplifying, 35; of songs, 530, 541n20

Ethnopoetic translations, 27–35, 52nn6,7; example of, 28–31, 52nn8,9; integrated approach to, 31–33, 35; lines in, 33–34, 52n11, 53n12; prosodic approach to, 31, 35, 52n10; selections exemplifying, 35; structural approach to, 31, 35

Europeans: Atsugewi restricted by, 61;

creation of (Quechan), 475; folk stories of, 36; foreknowledge of (Cache Creek Pomo), 331–32; Hupa grandfather wounded by, 111; Karuk culture disrupted by, 91; Lake Miwok contact with, 335; Native California cultures destroyed by contact with, 7; Tolowa life changed by, 68; Tübatulabal encounters with, 364; Yokuts contact with, 348. See also Gold Rush; Mission system

"Evening Star" songs (Karuk), 530

Facing page formats, 51n4

Fages, Pedro, 382

Falcon, "Condor Steals Falcon's Wife" (Yowlumni Yokuts), 349, 351, 357–62

Fall River: Achumawi, 127; Atsugewi, 143, 150

Fauna, inventory of (Eastern Pomo), 307–9

Faye, Paul-Louis, 518; Cupeño creation and burial songs (collector), 57, 518–19, 538n5; "The Life of Hawk Feather: The Bear Episodes" (collector), 421–35

Feathers: in basket designs (Lake Miwok), 335; belts made of (Nomlaki), 235–36; flicker, as nose ornament (Tolowa), 73

Federal boarding schools. See Boardingschool system

Fender, Jim (Wintu), 200n2

Fieldmice, "The Trials of Young Hawk" (Southern Pomo), 320–21

Field notes: Harrington's, 7, 19n3, 383; unpublished, 7–8, 19n3

Field trip, Mason's Costanoan, 495–99, 506n2, 507n5

Fieldwork, accounts of: Achumawi (Nevin), 129; Central Pomo (Mithun), 24–25; Cupeño (J. Hill), 424–25; Karuk (Bright), 98; Luiseño (Elliott), 413; Maidu (Shipley), 248–49; Mojave (A. Kroeber), 438–40; Southern Pomo (Oswalt), 313; Yurok (Robins), 77–78

Fieldwork, relationship between people involved in, 24–25. See also Collectors

Finck, Franz Nikolaus, 384

Fish: Marumda (Eastern Pomo Creator) teaches how to catch, 290–91; "Preserving Shellfish" (Kashaya Pomo), 525–26

Fishing nets (Eastern Pomo), 294–95, 302

Fishing practices (Tolowa), 68–69

"Five Yurok Songs: A Musical and Textual Analysis" (Robins and McCloud), 65

Flicker feathers, used as nose ornament (Tolowa), 73

"Flint Boy" (Yana), 523

Flood, caused by tidal wave (Tolowa), 71–76

Food: Achumawi, 128; Chimariko, 119, 120; Chumash, 390; Eastern Pomo, 276, 279, 280, 281, 289–91, 294, 295, 296; Hupa, 104, 113; Karuk, 90, 94, 102; Lake Miwok, 334–35; Maidu, 251, 253; Mojave, 444, 449, 450, 452, 453, 456; Quechan (Yuma), 471; shared with elders (Achumawi), 132–38; shared with strangers (Chumash, Eastern Pomo), 304, 390; theft of (Karuk), 94–95; Tolowa, 67, 68, 74; Tübatulabal, 365, 370, 372, 373, 375, 376; Wintu, 204, 227–28; Yurok, 77. *See also specific plants and animals*

Forde, C. Darryl: "Ethnography of the Yuma Indians," 535; Quechan funeral speech, 536, 543–44

Formulaic repetition, 43–44

Formulas, story opening and closing: in Karuk, 93–94, 520–21; in Wintu, 123, 196, 201, 218

"Four Songs from Grace McKibbin" (Wintu), 12, 35, 219–34, 528, 530

Fox, "Kwaw Labors to Form a World" (Atsugewi), 59–61

Franco, Darlene (Wukchumni), 564

Freeland, Lucy S., 335, 501

Freeland, Nancy, 260, 261, 263, 264

Frémont, John Charles, 500

"The Friars at Kiliwa," 554–55, 568–69n15

Frog: "The Creation" (Serrano), 405, 405n2, 408; as daughter of Kwikumat (Quechan [Yuma]), 476, 477, 480;

"Naponoha (Cocoon Man)" (Atsugewi), 143, 147

Gallagher, Maym Benner (Maidu), 248–49

Gamble, Geoffrey, 504; on Yokuts, 347–51; Yokuts language work by, 348

Gambling: Maidu, 251, 257; Nomlaki, 243–44, 243n; Yurok, 83

Gambling songs: Costanoan, 532; Miwok, 529; Yokuts, 496

Games: hoop game (Chumash), 388; hoop and poles (Mojave), 447, 452; tag (Eastern Pomo children's), 283

Gayton, Anna, 348, 501; "Areal Affiliations of California Folktales," 515, 523

Geese, "Flying North with the Geese" (Wintu), 223, 228–30

Gender roles: baskets made by both men and women (Pomo), 261–62; "The Contest between Men and Women" (Tübatulabal), 363, 365–81; Marumda's (Eastern Pomo Creator) teachings on, 289–91; for performing verbal art, 513–14

Generosity, consequences of not sharing deer meat (Achumawi), 132–38

Genocide: in California, 553–54, 556–59; of Tolowa, 68

Genre, oral-literary, 514; of selections, 15(table 1). *See also* Narrative; Oratory; Songs; *specific genres*

Genres, native: *a'alxi* (Cupeño; "telling histories"), 422; cry songs (Wintu), 219, 223; "devil" stories, 107, 522; dream songs (Wintu), 179; girls' puberty songs (Wintu), 105n1; *itš-kanavk* (Mojave; "great-telling"), 437; *nini* (Wintu; "love songs"), 187n2, 219, 222

Gepigul (Eastern Pomo), 261

Ghost Dance, 336

Gifford, Edward W., 501; *California Indian Nights Entertainments,* 513; "Central Miwok Ceremonies," 535; Mamie Offield's work with, 98

Global form/content parallelism, 53n18

Goddard, Pliny Earle, 105, 501

Gold Rush: impact on Native California cultures, 91, 497, 556; geographic area impacted by, 507n4, 553

Golla, Victor, 504; "The Boy Who Grew Up at Ta'k'imiłding" (collector and translator), 104–110; "Grandfather's Ordeal" (collector and translator), 107, 110–11; "It Was Scratching" (collector and translator), 107, 113–14; "The Stolen Woman" (collector and translator), 107, 112–13; Yahi Translation Project, 161n1

Gomez, María, 496

Gophers, "The Trials of Young Hawk" (Southern Pomo), 319–20

Gourds, grown by Quechan (Yuma), 471

Grace, Alma, 335

"Grandfather's Ordeal" (Hupa), 107, 110–11

Grant, Samson, 129, 130, 131

Gregory, Dick (Wintu), 184

Grief. *See* Mourning

Griffith, Manuela, 421

Grindstone Creek Reservation, 235, 239, 246

"Grizzly Bear and Deer" (Yana), 540n12; ethnolinguistic presentation of, 25–27, 51n3; ethnopoetic presentation of, 28–31, 52nn8,9; geographic distribution of, 523

Ground-Squirrel, "Creation" (Eastern Pomo), 299

Guerrero, Edna (Northern Pomo), 562–63

Guide to Early Field Recordings (1900–1949) at the Lowie Museum of Anthropology (Keeling), 535

Haas, Mary R., University of California at Berkeley Department of Linguistics work of, 6, 503–4

Halpern, Abraham M., 504; studies of Quechan (Yuma) language, 313; "The Trials of Young Hawk" (collector), 311–23

Hánc'ibyjim (Tom Young; Maidu), 506; "Mad Bat" (narrator), 248–59; Maidu creation myth (excerpt), 515–16

Hansen, Daisy (Pomo), 324

Harrie, Benonie (Karuk), 92

Harrie, Margaret (Karuk), "Coyote and Old Woman Bullhead" (narrator), 90–97

Harrington, John Peabody, 501; "An Account of Origins" (collector and translator), 20n6, 22, 461–89; "The Bear Girl" (collector), 115–22; biography of, 116, 383–84; Chumash work by, 382, 383, 384–85; "The Dog Girl" (collector), 382–95; early sound recordings by, 501–2; Ohlone culture fieldnotes of, 48–49; unpublished fieldnotes of, 7, 19n3; on urgency of Indian language fieldwork, 497, 506n3; Yokuts language work by, 348

"A Harvest of Songs from Villiana Calac Hyde" (Luiseño), 51n2, 411–20, 530

Hat Creek, Atsugewi, 129, 140

Hat Creek people. *See* Atsugewi

Hawk, sharp-shinned, "The Trials of Young Hawk" (Southern Pomo), 317–23

Hazelnuts, as food (Chimariko), 120

Heizer, Robert, "Mythology: Regional Patterns and History of Research," 513

Hesi: dance ceremony (Nomlaki), 236–37, 234n1; oration (Patwin), 536

Hewett, Edgar Lee, 384

Hill, Dan, 105

Hill, Jane, 504; "The Life of Hawk Feather: The Bear Episodes" (collector and translator), 421–35

Hill, Kenneth C., 504; "The Creation" (collector and translator), 401–10

Hill, Tom, 105

Hinton, Leanne, 12, 385–86, 504, 564; "Four Songs from Grace McKibbin" (analysis and transcription), 219–34, 530; on songs in Yuman stories, 528; "A Story of Lizard" (translator), 152–77; Yahi Translation Project, 161n1

Historical epic, selection classified as, 15(table 1)

Hokan languages, 90; Chimariko as, 115; speakers of, geographical retreat of, 128

Language diversity, 566n2, 574(map 2); California's ecology as enabling, 552, 568n13; extent of, 6, 545; geographical history of, 549–51; within superstocks, 549

Language families, 546–52, 547–48(table 5); geographic distribution of, 575(map 3). *See also* Language stocks

Language revival, 6–7, 412, 562–65

Languages: bilingual format for collection of oral literature, 19n5; boarding schools' impact on, 560–62; current status of, 545, 552, 577(map 5); dialects in, 545–46; elders as diminishing resource for, 497, 506n3; as embodying culture, 10, 563; geographic distribution of, 573(map 1); multiple, in "Creation" (Eastern Pomo) myth, 297, 300, 302; of narration of selections, 18–19(table 4); prehistory of, 549–52, 576(map 4); pronunciation guide for, xix–xxi; renaissance of, 562–66. *See also specific languages*

Language samples: Achumawi, 130–31; Cupeño, 423–24; Hupa, 107–8; Ineseño Chumash, 386; Karuk, 93–94; Lake Miwok, 337; Maidu, 251; Northern Yana, 521–22; Serrano, 402, 403–5; Southern Pomo, 315–16; Wintu, 199–200; Yahi, 159

Language stocks, 546–49, 566–67n4; geographic distribution of, 575(map 3); history and geographical expansion of, 549–52. *See also* Language families

Lark, "Naponoha (Cocoon Man)" (Atsugewi), 146, 147, 148

Lassen, Mount: Táyyamanim (West Mountain), 250, 258; Ye:dí:jana, 130

Legal system, Tolowa, 67–68

Legends, as genre of narrative, 514

Lévi-Strauss, Claude, 40; "Loon Woman" analysis by, 198, 201n6

Librado, Fernando (Ventureño Chumash), 506

"Life and Culture of the Hupa" (Goddard), 105

"The Life of Hawk Feather: The Bear Episodes" (Cupeño), 35, 421–35, 523;

problems in interpreting, 424–26; songs in, 430, 432, 435, 528

"Lightning song" (Quechan [Yuma]; excerpt), 529–30

Line breaks in ethnopoetic presentations, criteria for, 34, 52n11, 53n12; "The Bear Girl," 118; "The Contest between Men and Women," 367–68n1; "Coyote Steals Fire," 31–33; "Creation" (Serrano), 402–3; "Four Songs from Grace McKibben," 220–21; "From 'The Life of Hawk Feather,'" 426; "Mad Bat," 252; "A Story of Lizard," 161n5. *See also* Typographical conventions

Lizards: "The Contest between Men and Women" (Tübatulabal), 366, 370, 372; Long-Tailed, 155–77; "A Story of Lizard" (Yahi), 162–77

Loeb, Edwin, 263

Loether, Chris, on Tübatulabal, 363–68

Loon: "Loon Woman" (Wintu), 192–218; personality of, 39

"Loon Woman" (Wintu), 192–218, 502; geographic distribution of, 523; interpretations of, 196–99; numerical patterns in, 43, 194–95; repetition in, 41–43, 44, 53n17

Lord, Alfred, 46

Love songs: Costanoan, 532; Wintu, 187–90, 187n, 219, 221–23, 224–30

Lowie, Robert, 139

Lucas, Bun (Kashaya), 7

Luiseño: "Chaláwaat Song," vii, 416–17, 565–66; "A Harvest of Songs from Villiana Calac Hyde," 411–20; lecture at girls' puberty ceremony, 535–36; mourning song, 519–20, 538n6; "Women's Brush Dance Song," 511

Luiseño Dictionary (Bright), 413

Luiseño language, 411–13

Luthin, Herbert W.: on "Creation" (Eastern Pomo), 260–72; "A Story of Lizard" (translator), 152–77; Yahi Translation Project, 161n1

Macarro, Mark, (Luiseño), 564

"Mad Bat" (Maidu), 35, 39, 248–59, 523, 540n12

to the Land of the Dead" (collector and translator), 348–49, 351n1, 352–55; Yokuts language work by, 348

News from Native California, 141

Nichols, Mike, 504

Nisenan prayer, 55

Noble, Sally, 117(fig. 2); "The Bear Girl" (narrator), 115–22

Nolasquez, Roscinda, "The Life of Hawk Feather: The Bear Episodes" (narrator), 421–35

Nome Lackee Reservation, 238–39

Nomlaki: birds of, 197, 201n7; "How I Became a Dreamer," 235–47

Northwestern California: creation myth pattern, 517–18; linguistic prehistory of, 351

Noweedehe, 236, 242, 243

Numerical patterning. *See* Pattern numbers

Numic languages, 552

Ochurte, Rufino (PaiPai/Kiliwa), 506; "The Friars at Kiliwa" (narrator), 554–55, 568–69n15; "When I Have Donned My Crest of Stars," 493

Offield, Mamie, "The Devil Who Died Laughing" (narrator), 98–103

Ohlone culture, 48–49

Okrand, Mark, 504

"Old California" language families, 550–51

Oral literature, Native California: anthropomorphism in, 38–40; categories of, 514; confusion when first reading, 35–37, 50, 53n14; continuing growth of, 8–10, 48; creation myth classification of, 515–20; culture's link to, 47–50, 54n23; difficulties in producing collections of, 6–10; Europeanized collections of, 509n10; gender of performers of, 513–14; history of documentation of, 499–506, 509nn9–11, 509–10n12; overviews of, 513; parallelism in, 44–46; pattern numbers in, 41, 43, 53nn15,18; pronunciation guide for, xix–xxi; repetition in, 40–44, 46–47, 53n17. *See also* Narrative; Oratory; Songs

"Oral Literature of California and the Intermountain Region" (Bright), 513

Oratory, 12, 535–38; sources of, 535; vocal and rhythmic characteristics of, 536–37. *See also* Speeches

Oratory, examples of, by genre: interviews, 63, 562–63; prayers, 55; speeches, 535–36, 536–37, 543–44; spells, 125

Oregos (rock at mouth of Klamath River), 80, 86

Origin myths: selections classified as, 15(table 1); Atsugewi, 59–61; Eastern Pomo, 273–310; Hupa, 109–10; Maidu (excerpt), 515–16; Quechan, 465–89; Serrano, 405–6, 406–10; Tolowa, 71–76. *See also* Creation

Orpheus myth, 13, 335; Chawchila Yokuts version, 13, 336, 348–49, 351n1, 352–55; Northern Sierra Miwok version, 336. *See also* "The Dead People's Home" (Lake Miwok)

Oswalt, Robert L., 504; "Preserving Shellfish" (collector), 525–26; "The Trials of Young Hawk" (translator), 311–23

Ouzel, "Mad Bat" (Maidu), 39, 250, 259

Owl: in doctor's dream (Northern Yana), 527; as messenger of death (Yurok), 79, 81–82; screech, hired to track deer (Achumawi), 136, 138

Paqöoktach (Serrano deity), 406, 407

Pal Atingve 'Hot Springs' (Warner's Hot Springs), 422

Parallelism, 44–47; global form/content parallelism, 53n18

Park, Susan Brandenstein, 501

Parrish, Essie (Kashaya Pomo), "Preserving Shellfish" (narrator), 525–26

Pattern numbers, 41, 43, 53nn15,18; in "Grizzly Bear and Deer" (Northern Yana), 29–31; identified by Dell Hymes, 31, 52nn8,9; Lake Miwok, 340; in "Loon Woman" (Wintu), 194–95; Pomo, 314

Patwin, Hesi oration, 536

Penutian stock, 547–48; geographic expansion of, 550, 567–68n9; similarities among language families of, 548–49; speakers of, contact with Hokan speakers, 128

Performances: date of, of selections, 17(table 3); "live" vs. "in studio," 20n8; personal and period style's effect on recording of, 501, 509n11; selections based on, 11; transformed into printed word, 21–25

Performers: contribution of, 504; gender of, 513–14; preservation of traditions by, 499, 509n8

Perry, Jean: "Blind Bill and the Owl" (collector), 78–79, 81–82; "Ragged Ass Hill" (collector), 79, 82–85; Yahi Translation Project, 161n1; "The Young Man from Serper" (collector of alternate version), 78, 79–80, 85–89, 505

Personal reminiscences: absence of quotatives in, 522; as genre of narrative, 514; selections classified as, 15(table 1)

Philologists, 383

Phonetic dictation. *See* Dictation, phonetic/verbatim

Pikva (Karuk creation stories), 91–93

Pine-nuts: Tübatulabal, 365, 370, 375; Yahi, 155, 156, 162, 172–73, 176–77

Pine trees, Serrano, 410

Pitkin, Harvey, 193, 504

Pit River: Achumawi, 127, 128; Wintu, 178

Pit River people. *See* Achumawi

Plants, created by Marumda (Eastern Pomo Creator), 276, 277, 278. *See also specific plants*

Poetic repetition, 44

Pomo: baskets woven by, 261–63, 312, 313, 324–25, 569n21; birds in narratives of, 523; Central Pomo, relationship developed doing linguistic fieldwork among, 24–25; quotatives in, 316; geographical territory, 311; historical overview of, 311–12; Marumda (deity) of, 266–67, 272nn3,4; Northeastern Pomo, scant documentation of, 7; pre-Contact population, 311–12

Pomo, selections and excerpts: Cache Creek Pomo, "The Woman Who Loved a Snake," 324–33; Eastern Pomo, "Creation," 13, 260–310; Kashaya Pomo, "Preserving Shellfish," 525–26; Southern Pomo, "The Trials of Young Hawk," 311–23

Pomoan languages, 546; 311, 312; Hokan affiliation of, 311; quotatives in, 316; preservation of, 562–63; Southern Pomo, 312, 313, 314–16

Popejoy, Bill, 182n

Portolá, Gaspar de, 500

Potatoes, as food for Eastern Pomo, 279, 281

Powers, Stephen, *Tribes of California,* 500

Prayer, Nisenan, 55

Prehistory, linguistic, 549–52, 576(map 4)

Preservation: of languages, 6–7, 412, 562–65; of traditions, 499–500, 508n7, 509n8

Prickly pear, as food for Quechan (Yuma), 471

Puberty songs: Modoc, 531; Wintu, 185–87, 185nn, 186n, 527–28

Purity, 63

Putnam, F. W., 440

Quechan (Yuma): "An Account of Origins," 20n6, 461–89; Central Group relationship to, 461, 465n2; dreamers (doctors), 461–62, 465n4; funeral speech, 536, 543–44; geographical territory, 461; Halpern's studies of, 313; "Kwikumat Became Sick," 3; "Lightning Song" (excerpt), 529–30; religion of, 461–62, 465n6; songs, 3, 462, 465n3; "The Soul" (excerpt), 399–400; surviving population, 461

Quotatives: absence or suppression of, 522, 539n11; in Cupeño, 424; in Pomo, 316; in Serrano, 402; in Yana, 26, 51n3, 521–22, 539nn9,10

Radin, Paul, 263, 501

"Ragged Ass Hill" (Yurok), 79, 82–85

Rancherias. *See* Reservations

Rattlesnakes: "An Account of Origins"

(Maidu), 491; "Chalááwaat Song" (Luiseño), xviii; creation songs (Cupeño), 57; doctor dance song (Yurok), 65; "I warned you" (Chumash), 397; "Kingfisher, Kingfisher" (Wikchamni), 343; "My heart, you might pierce it and take it" (Quechan), 3; song from "The Čiq'neqš Myth" (Chumash), 345; women's brush dance song (Luiseño), 511

"The Soul" (Quechan; excerpt), 399–400

Southern California creation pattern, 518–20

Southern Pomo language: kinship terms, 314–15; proper names in stories, 314; sample passage, 315–16; sentence connectors, 315–16; surviving dialects, 312, 313

Southland Dance cult, 180, 181n2

Spanish mission system. *See* Mission system

Sparkman, Philip, "Culture of the Luiseño Indians," 535

Speakers, last: Chimariko, 115; Wappo, 552; Yahi, 152–53

Speakers, native: of California languages generally, 552–53, 577(map 5); of Karuk, 563–64; of Lake Miwok, 335; of Serrano, 401; of Southern Pomo, 312; of Tübatulabal, 364; of Yokuts, 348; of Yurok, 80

Speeches: by Dusty-sunrise (Mojave), 457; by Eastern Pomo chief on Marumda (Creator), 291; by Hipahipa (Mojave), 457, 458–59, 460; by Kuksu in Eastern Pomo creation myth, 274, 275, 276; lecture at girls' puberty ceremony (Luiseño), 535–36; Lying-on-dust (Mojave), 459; by Marumda in Eastern Pomo creation myth, 276, 277–79, 283, 284, 288, 289, 290, 294, 296, 304, 306, 307–9; Patwin Hesi oration, 536–37, 541n24; Quechan funeral speech, 536, 543–44. *See also* Oratory

"Spell Said by a Girl Desirous of Getting a Husband" (Yana), 125

Spider: "Creation" (Eastern Pomo), 282–83, 286–87; "An Account of Origins" (Quechan), 480–81

Spott, Robert (Yurok), 506

Starritt, Julia (Karuk), "Coyote Steals Fire" (narrator), 31–33

State Emergency Relief Administration Project, salvage ethnography work by, 239–40, 240n1

"The State of Our Languages" (Richardson), 563–64

St. Helena, Mount, 335, 338

Stinginess, consequences of (Achumawi), 132–38

"The Stolen Woman" (Hupa), 107, 112–13

Stone, Tom (Owens Valley Paiute), 506

Stone and Kelsey Massacre, 556–58

Stories: about culture heroes, 523; about devils, 522; about monsters, 523, 540n12. *See also* Narrative

Storytelling: California Indian Storytelling Festival, 565; Native American vs. European, 36–37; true oral, 36–37, 53n14; as wintertime activity, 93, 193, 402, 514

Strong, William Duncan, 421

Sucker fish, as food (Karuk), 102–3

Supahan, Sarah (Karuk), 19n2

Supahan, Terry (Karuk), 19n2

Survey of California and Other Indian Languages, 504; phonetic transcriptions of Karuk creation stories, 93; work on Yurok language, 77–78

Swann, Brian, 5; *Coming to Light*, 11

Sweat house: Atsugewi, 60, 61, 145, 146, 150; Lake Miwok, 339

Tachi Yokuts. *See* Yokuts

Ta'k'imiłding (Hoopa Valley village), 106, 109–10

Tales: as genre of narrative, 514; geographic distribution of types of, 523; vs. myths, 515; selections classified as, 15(table 1)

Tale types, 523. *See also* Orpheus myth

Talmy, Len, 504

Tape recording: as collection method, 24–25, 51nn1,2; early, 501–2, 503–4; "live" vs. "in studio," 20n8; selections collected by, 16(table 2), 502; of Yurok stories, 78

Tataviam language, scant documentation of, 7

Taylor, Alexander, *The California Farmer and Journal of Useful Arts* articles on "Indianology," 500

Taylor, Sarah (Cache Creek Pomo), 324, 330

Tedlock, Dennis: ethnopoetics pioneered by, 27, 31; lines as defined by, 52n11

Teeter, Karl, 504

"Test-ch'as (The Tidal Wave)" (Tolowa), 67–76; cultural understanding behind, 47–48

"They say." *See* Quotatives

Thomas, Edo, "A Selection of Wintu Songs" (singer), 178–81, 184

Thomas, Jim (Wintu), 182–83, 182n

Thompson, Lucy (Yurok), 6, 506

Thrasher, "Creation" (Eastern Pomo), 293

Thunder: "Condor Steals Falcon's Wife" (Yowlumni Yokuts), 356; "The Trials of Young Hawk" (Southern Pomo), 322–23

Tobacco smoking: by Marumda during Creation (Eastern Pomo), 277, 279, 284, 292, 300; in meeting of deities (Eastern Pomo), 274–75, 276, 282, 285, 292, 297; by Naponoha (Atsugewi), 150; as sealing contractual agreement (Achumawi), 131, 134, 136

Tolowa: geographical territory, 67; history and culture, 67–70; surviving population, 70; "Test-ch'as (The Tidal Wave)," 67–76

To the American Indian (Thompson), 6

Traditions, preservation of, 499–500, 508n7, 509n8

Transformations: of acorn shell into Marumda's boat (Eastern Pomo), 304; of girl into bear (Chimariko), 118–22; of girl into white fawn (Yurok), 87–88; of handsome man into snake and back into handsome man (Cache Creek Pomo), 329–30; of Immortals into elements of natural world (Karuk), 91–92; of Kumastamxo into eagles (Quechan), 487–88; of Mad Bat into ordinary bat (Maidu), 250, 259; of Naponoha into Night-Flying Butterfly (Atsugewi), 141–42; of old woman into Bullhead (Karuk), 92, 96–97; of people into animals (Ineseño Chumash), 395

Translations: based on unpublished texts, 20n7; interpreter, 16(table 2), 22–23; methods of making, 21–25, 51nn1,2; modes of presenting, 25–35; personal and period styles' effects on, 501, 509n11; replicability of, 11; verifiability of, 11. *See also* Ethnolinguistic translations; Ethnopoetic translations

"The Trials of Young Hawk" (Southern Pomo), 35, 311–23, 523; anthropomorphism in, 38; episodic repetition in, 41

Tribes of California (Powers), 500

Trinity River, 104, 105, 115

Trout, caught by boy (Karuk), 94–95

Tsuyukweráu (Joe Homer; Quechan), 506; "An Account of Origins" (narrator), 20n6, 22, 461–89, 520, 539n7; biography of, 462–63

Tübatulabal: "The Contest between Men and Women," 363–81; cultural influences, 365; geographical territory, 364; surviving population, 364

Tule, as food for Mojave, 452, 453

Turner, Katherine, "The Bear Girl" (translator), 115–22

Turtle, "Naponoha (Cocoon Man)" (Atsugewi), 143, 150

Tututni division of Tolowa, 68

Typographical conventions, 28–29, 33; Bright's early, 31–32, 33; in "The Contest between Men and Women," 367–68n1; in "The Creation" (Serrano), 402–3; in "Four Songs from Grace McKibbin," 220–21; in "From 'The Life of Hawk Feather,'" 424, 426; in "Loon Woman," 200–201n5; in "A Story of Lizard," 160; in "Two Stories from the Central Valley," 351n1.

Designer:	Sandy Drooker
Cartographer:	Bill Nelson
Indexer	Jean Mann
Compositor:	Integrated Composition Systems
Text:	11/14 Adobe Garamond
Display:	Lithos
Printer and binder:	Edwards Brothers, Inc.